P9-EDJ-984

Yale Historical Publications, Miscellany, 111

THE YOUNG CZECH PARTY
1874-1901
AND THE
EMERGENCE OF
A MULTI-PARTY SYSTEM

Bruce M. Garver

New Haven and London
Yale University Press

1978

Published under the direction
of the Department of History of Yale University
with assistance from the income of the
Frederick John Kingsbury Memorial Fund.

Copyright © 1978 by Yale University.
All rights reserved. This book may not be
reproduced, in whole or in part, in any form
(beyond that copying permitted by Sections 107
and 108 of the U.S. Copyright Law and except by
reviewers for the public press), without written
permission from the publishers.

Printed in the United States of America by
The Murray Printing Co., Westford, Massachusetts.

Published in Great Britain, Europe, Africa, and
Asia (except Japan) by Yale University Press,
Ltd., London. Distributed in Australia and
New Zealand by Book & Film Services, Artarmon,
N.S.W., Australia; and in Japan by Harper & Row,
Publishers, Tokyo Office.

Library of Congress Cataloguing in Publication Data

Garver, Bruce M
    The Young Czech party, 1874-1901, and
the emergence of a multi-party system.

    (Yale historical publications : Miscellany ; 111)
    Bibliography: p.
    Includes index.
    1. Political parties—Czechoslovakia—Bohemia—
History. 2. Bohemia—Politics and government.
I. Title. II. Series.
JN2210.G37   329.9'437'1   78-8584
ISBN 0-300-01781-2

27,963

CAMROSE LUTHERAN COLLEGE
LIBRARY

Contents

Contents

T. G. Masaryk and the Progressive Party
The Democratization of Czech Politics

Tables in Appendix

Acknowledgments

This book grew out of a dissertation approved by the Graduate School of Yale University in March 1971. Support for the research and writing of that dissertation came primarily from an NDEA Title IV fellowship for six semesters of study at Yale and an NDEA-related Fulbright-Hays fellowship for eleven months of study in Europe during 1967. I am grateful to the former Inter-University Committee on Travel Grants for having at that time arranged my participation for nine months in Czechoslovakia on the official exchange of students between that country and the United States. The Concilium on International and Area Studies at Yale funded a short research trip to Prague in August 1971. During 1973, a stay of five months in Czechoslovakia and two months in Western Europe enabled me to complete all research for this book as well as to begin work on its sequel, a study of Czech and Slovak politics from 1901 to 1914. For making that research possible, I thank Yale University for awarding me a Morse fellowship to pay for a leave of absence of one year and the International Research and Exchanges Board (IREX) for providing travel funds and arranging for my stipend and housing as an exchange scholar in Czechoslovakia. A grant from the Faculty Senate Research Committee of the University of Nebraska at Omaha helped pay for the typing of the final book manuscript. I thank that committee and my colleagues in the Department of History for their support.

I am much indebted to the inspiration and example of the late Professor S. Harrison Thomson who at the University of Colorado first aroused my interest in East European history and encouraged me to make its study my life's work. Plans for the dissertation from which this book developed took shape at Yale in 1966 with the help of Professors Karl Deutsch, Firuz Kazemzadeh, and Hajo Holborn. Professor Piotr Wandycz, my advisor after September 1966, helped guide the dissertation to completion. For criticism while writing that dissertation, I also thank Professors Hans Gatzke and Wolfgang Leonhard of Yale University and Professor Stanley B. Winters of the New Jersey Institute of Technology. For teaching me Czech at Yale, I am much obliged to Mrs. Peter Demetz, Mrs. Leopold Pospisil, and the late Dean George P. Springer.

This book owes much to the publications and to the advice of Czechoslovak scholars and archivists. During my nine months in Czechoslovakia in 1967, Dr. Zdeněk Šolle at the Historical Institute of the Czechoslovak Academy of Sciences gave generously of his time and knowledge in serving as my academic sponsor. Dr.

Pavla Horská of the same institute advised me on the use of French
diplomatic reports, on questions concerning industrial development,
and criticized the first drafts of two chapters. Other Czechoslovak scholars who in 1967 helped me with research included Dr.
Jan Havránek of Charles University, Dr. Jurij Křízek of the Historical Institute, and Drs. Václav Žácek and Jaroslav Valenta of the
Institute for the Study of the European Socialist Countries. Dr.
Miloslav Kaňák of the Hus Theological Faculty and the late Dr.
Josef Lukl Hromadka of the Komenský Theological Faculty talked to
me about religion and Czech politics during the later nineteenth
century. The late František Hlaváček and the late Dr. Jaroslav
Werstadt, both eyewitnesses to some of the events that this book
discusses, shared with me their clear memories and perspicacious
analyses of Czech politics from 1894 to 1914.

The directors and staff of the various Czechoslovak archives
and libraries at which I worked in 1967, 1971, and 1973 were
unfailingly courteous and helpful. I would especially like to
thank Dr. Vojtěch Sýkora, Dr. Zdeněk Šamberger and Ms. Květa
Kulírová of the State Archival Administration for helping make
all administrative arrangements for archival research. Dr. Pavel
Křivský at the Literary Archive of the Memorial of National Literature and Dr. Aleš Chalupa of the Literary Archive of the National
Museum pointed out to me many items of interest, including some
uncatalogued materials. At the National Museum, Dr. Karel Švehla
made arrangements for me to read pertinent newspapers and periodicals. The following persons also gave generously of their time
and advice: Dr. Miloslav Kost'al and Mrs. Helena Smísková of the
Děčín branch of the State Archive at Litoměřice, Dr. Jiří Kyncil,
director of the Klášterec nad Ohří branch of the State Archive at
Pilsen, Dr. Josef Křivka, director of the Žitenice and Libochovice
branches of the Litoměřice State Archive, Mr. J. Hezl, director of
the State Archive in Třeboň, Mr. František Marchal and the staff
of the Archive of the Institute for the History of the Communist
Party of Czechoslovakia, and Dr. Miloslav Bělohlávek of the Muni-
cipal Archive in Pilsen. Elsewhere abroad, the staff of the Haus-,
Hof- und Staatsarchiv and the Allgemeines Verwaltungsarchiv in
Vienna and the staff of the Diplomatic Archives of the French
Ministry of Foreign Affairs extended every courtesy and assistance.

Through several years, the staff of Sterling Library at Yale
University helped me obtain needed publications and microfilms.
I especially thank Mr. W. S. Debenham, formerly director of acquisitions, Mr. Joseph Danko, head cataloguer of Slavic language materials, and Mr. and Mrs. Aleksis Rannit, curator and assistant
curator of the Slavic and East European collections. I thank too
the staff members at the Bibliothèque Nationale in Paris, the New
York Public Library, Widener Library at Harvard University, and
the libraries of the University of Nebraska, the Ohio State University, and the University of California at Los Angeles (UCLA).

I am most of all indebted to the following colleagues for criticizing the manuscript for this book in one or several of its

drafts: Professors Piotr Wandycz, Frederick Barghoorn, Peter
Demetz, and William Foltz of Yale University; Professor Josef
Anderle of the University of North Carolina; Professor Emeritus
Eugene N. Anderson of UCLA; Dr. Roland Hoffmann of the University
at Tübingen; Dr. Jiří Kořalka of the Institute of Czechoslovak
and World History of the Czechoslovak Academy of Sciences; Dr.
Otto Urban of Charles University; Dr. Miroslav Tejchman of the
Czechoslovak-Soviet Institute; Dr. Valentin Urfus of the Institute of the State and Law of the Czechoslovak Academy of Sciences;
Dr. Karen Johnson Freeze of the Russian Research Institute at
Harvard University; and the late Professor Otakar Odložilík of
the University of Pennsylvania. That each draft of this book was
an improvement over the one before is due in large part to the
advice and criticism of these readers. I assume, of course, all
responsibility for any errors or shortcomings that may remain.
    At the Yale University Press, Ms. Joanne Ainsworth, Chief
Manuscript Editor, and Ms. Beverly Cayford, copy editor, helped
me prepare the book for publication. I also thank Mr. Edward
Tripp, Editor-in-Chief of the Press, for advice and assistance.
    I owe a great debt to my wife, Dr. Karen K. Garver, who gave
helpful editorial advice as well as typing most of the manuscript
in three different drafts. I also thank her and my parents, Mr.
and Mrs. Lee W. Garver, for their continuing encouragement of my
work.

Omaha, Nebraska   BRUCE M. GARVER
October, 1977

Abbreviations

AHY	-- Austrian History Yearbook
ČČH	-- Český časopis historický
ČsČH	-- Československý časopis historický
HHSA	-- Haus-, Hof-, und Staatsarchiv, Vienna
IB	-- Informations Bureau, Ministerium des Aussern
JCEA	-- Journal of Central European Affairs
LANM	-- Literární archiv Národního musea, Prague
MI	-- Ministerium des Innern (Ministry of the Interior)
MMP	-- Moravské místodržitelství Presidium
NS	-- Nouvelle série
PM	-- Presidium místodržitelství (Bohemia)
PMT	-- Presidium místodržitelství tajné (Bohemia)
PMV/R	-- Presidium ministerstva vnitra/R
PNP	-- Památník národního písemnictví na Strahově, Prague
PŘ	-- Policejní ředitelství
Rozpravy	-- Rozpravy Československé Akademie věd, Řada společenských věd
SA	-- Státní archiv
SEER	-- Slavonic and East European Review
SPHA	-- Stenographische Protokolle über die Sitzungen des Hauses der Abgeordneten des österreichischen Reichsrathes
SR	-- Slavic Review
SÚA	-- Státní ústřední archiv, Prague
SZSČ	-- Stenografické zprávy sněmu českého (Stenographische Berichte des böhmischen Landtages)
ÚDKSČ	-- Ústav dějin Komunistické strany Československa, Prague
VA	-- Allgemeines Verwaltungsarchiv, Vienna
Zákonník řísský	-- Zákonník řísský pro království a země v radě řísské zastoupené

Introduction

The National Liberal, or Young Czech, party (Národní strana svobodomyslná or Mladočeská strana) predominated in Czech politics
for sixteen of the forty years from its founding in 1874 until
the First World War. Initially identified with the Young Germany,
Young Italy, and Young Poland movements, it gradually came to re-
semble the liberal parties of Central and Western Europe. The
Young Czech party helped perpetuate the bonds between anticlericalism, liberalism, and Czech nationalism forged in 1848; and it
introduced to politics during the nineties many of the men who in
1918 would establish an independent Czechoslovakia. After 1918,
Young Czechs called themselves National Democrats; their successor
parties after 1900 included the National Socialists, the State
Rights Radicals, and the Agrarians.

The Young Czech party and the National, or Old Czech, party,
from which it seceded in 1874, maintained a keen rivalry through
nearly four decades while still remaining complementary parts of
a broadly-based Czech national movement under predominantly
middle-class leadership. Both parties grew out of the Czech National Revival, the revolutions of 1848, and that subsequent
transformation of society wrought by peasant emancipation, accelerated industrialization, and the introduction of limited
constitutional rule. Both sought to promote the material and
cultural welfare of their nation and to achieve legislative and
administrative autonomy for the three Czech lands of Bohemia, Moravia, and Silesia as a reconstituted kingdom of Bohemia within
the Habsburg Monarchy. These specifically national goals took
precedence over efforts to encourage mutual aid and understanding
among the various Slavic nations, but both parties recognized
that the continued progress of the Czech nation depended upon the
freedom and prosperity of the Slavs in the Dual Monarchy and the
Balkans. Members of both Old and Young Czech parties held Russophile and Francophile views but expected little and received no
official aid from France or Russia. Each party claimed to represent the entire Czech nation despite its leaders having been
elected to public office on the basis of a highly restrictive
suffrage based on curias and property qualifications. Both parties derived their limited political authority primarily from the
institutions of provincial and district self-government and in
organization resembled the early elite parties of France, Italy,
Prussia, and Great Britain.[1]

A more strident nationalism and anticlericalism as well as a
more forceful advocacy of extended manhood suffrage and civil

1

liberties differentiated Young Czechs from Old Czechs. Though
both parties competed for the votes of prosperous property owners,
the Old Czechs derived their greatest support from the urban upper middle class, estate owners, and the Prague intelligentsia,
while the Young Czechs, who were more accommodating to popular
pressure, relied primarily upon businessmen, farmers, and school-
teachers. The parties did not represent different generations,
for their leaders differed little in age, most having reached
maturity between the 1840s and the late 1870s.

A conflict over tactics led most directly to the split between
Old Czechs and Young Czechs in 1874 and reflected existing ideological and class differences between the two parties. After
that date the Young Czechs always pursued an "active" policy of
working for reform through all institutions of government, however inadequate, and of advocating a multi-party system that they
believed would better serve the nation than the one-party system
heretofore favored by the Old Czechs. Until 1897, the Young
Czechs allied less often and more reluctantly with the Bohemian
nobility than did the Old Czechs, who had maintained an unbroken
alliance since 1861.

The Young Czech party in failure as well as success adhered
to liberal principles and tried to work through established political institutions. During the seventies, the newly independent
party under the Grégr brothers and Karel Sladkovský actively opposed the authoritarian and centralizing policies of the imperial
government, in contrast to the Old Czechs, who endorsed passive
resistance. As factions within the parent National party during
the sixties and as parliamentary allies during the eighties,
Young and Old Czechs sought to achieve a common national and liberal program until Old Czech endorsement of certain reactionary
policies of the Taaffe government led to a renewed split in 1887.
After defeating the Old Czechs in the Reichsrat elections of
March 1891 in Bohemia, the Young Czechs tried with limited success to represent the interests of all Czech citizens and maintained themselves as the leading Czech political party until
surpassed by their offspring and rivals, the Agrarians and National Socialists, in the 1901 Reichsrat elections. At the same
time, the Young Czechs subsidized their Moravian counterpart and
ally, the People's party (Lidová strana), founded in February
1891 by Adolf Stranský, as this, the first avowedly anticlerical
and liberal party in Moravia, began to challenge Old Czech hegemony in that province. The fall of the Badeni and Thun governments in 1897 and 1899 discredited the moderate Young Czech party, which had supported them, and accelerated its fragmentation
and decline. The introduction of universal manhood suffrage to
the lower house of the Reichsrat in 1907 confirmed the preeminence of mass parties in Czech politics, including Czech Social
Democrats as well as Agrarians and National Socialists. In the
decade before 1914, the Young Czech party, led by Karel Kramář,
Bedřich Pacák, and Václav Škarda, increasingly became the

spokesman of Czech banking and industrial interests. Works on
the Habsburg Monarchy in Western languages have usually caricatured the Young Czechs as radical troublemakers wanting in moderation and understanding. Though several party members like Jan
Vašatý and Václav Březnovský fit this stereotype, it is more
correct to describe the Young Czechs during their heyday as pragmatic lawyers, journalists, doctors, and farmers who tried to
achieve their goals within the limits defined by law.

The Young Czechs are of interest not only for their preeminence in later nineteenth-century Czech and Cisleithanian politics, but also as the party of transition between the revolutions
of 1848 and 1918 and between the parties of notables organized
after 1860 and the mass political parties that came to dominate
Czech politics after 1900. Founders of the Young Czech party included several radical democrats and revolutionaries of 1848 who
had turned to liberalism and moderation in the sixties. Many
politicians who in 1918 would help establish the Czechoslovak
Republic entered politics during the nineties as moderate Young
Czechs, including President-Liberator T. G. Masaryk, Václav J.
Klofáč, Karel Kramář, Alois Rašín, and František Udržal. Although the Young Czech party never became a mass political party,
from its ranks emerged two of the four Czech mass parties, the
National Socialists and the Agrarians. And, by its opposition,
it helped condition the growth of the other two, Social Democracy
and Christian Socialism.

No comprehensive and interpretive study of the Young Czech
party has appeared in any language. The most complete accounts
may be found in the detailed general surveys of later nineteenth-
century Czech political history by Adolf Srb and Zdeněk Tobolka.[2]
No scholarly monographs appeared on the party in the years before
the First World War, but eight essays by five party members and
three by former party member T. G. Masaryk dealt with the party
and its policies in an unusually informed and analytical manner.[3]

Why has no history of the Young Czech party appeared in Czech,
given the great wealth of archival and printed sources? During
the First Czechoslovak Republic, Czech historians, besides working on the popular themes of the Hussite, Reformation, and National Revival periods, took the greatest interest in those parties and forces which had helped to establish an independent
Czechoslovakia. Apart from the former Young Czech Zdeněk Tobolka, few wrote extensively about the Young Czechs, who had so
often cooperated with imperial authorities and so long opposed
T. G. Masaryk. Nonetheless, a number of excellent articles and
monographic studies appeared on topics related to the Young
Czechs, including voluminous literature on Masaryk.[4]

Between 1948 and the mid-1960s, Czechoslovak Marxist historians dealt primarily with long-term social and economic developments, with crises reflecting class conflict, and with the history of the Czech workers' movement.[5] Although these themes had by
no means been neglected by earlier historians, they received more

exhaustive treatment and different interpretations reflecting
new evidence, new historiographical methods, and changing political circumstances.[6] The Marxists' works provide an indispensable background for any study of later nineteenth-century Czech
and Slovak political development. From the early 1960s through
1969, Czech and Slovak historians returned to political themes,
problems, and personalities neglected during the previous two
decades. Foremost among these were the struggle for national
independence in 1918, the influence of statesmen like T. G. Masaryk, Milan Rastislav Štefaník, and Edvard Beneš, and problems in
the relationships of Czechoslovakia with other East European
countries in the inter-war period.

In Western languages, few monographs have appeared on topics
related to later nineteenth-century Czech history apart from studies on T. G. Masaryk, the Habsburg Monarchy, and Czech-German
relations. The relative neglect of the Young Czechs in general
surveys of Czechoslovak history may be attributed primarily to
the fact that no Young Czech ever became an uncontested national
leader as did František Palacký or Masaryk.[7] General surveys of
the Habsburg Monarchy have only cursorily discussed the Slavic
peoples and their political parties in relation to imperial problems, aspirations, and policies.[8] The three principal surveys
of Czech-German relations deal only indirectly with the growth of
political parties in general or with any Czech party in particular.[9] A number of articles have treated various aspects of later
nineteenth-century Czech politics, some of which pertain to the
Young Czech party.[10]

This book aims to provide the first comprehensive study of the
Young Czech party in any language and the first general survey of
later nineteenth-century Czech social and political development
in a non-Slavic language. These two complementary goals cannot
be understood apart from each other. A survey in Czech could
largely dispense with the second theme because it could be assumed that Czech readers would already be acquainted with the
pertinent historical literature. That this work cannot make such
assumptions explains its unusual length. To treat in English
only one or two aspects of nineteenth-century Czech politics
would be to risk superficiality if not unintelligibility.[11]

This work is based primarily upon the abundant archival and
printed primary sources pertaining to the Young Czech party and
to later nineteenth-century Czech politics which have long been
known to Czech historians but which have heretofore been sparing-
ly used by scholars in the West.[12] It is designed to complement
as it builds upon the many fine Czech scholarly works on later
nineteenth-century Czech and Habsburg history and to acquaint
Western scholars with their scope and content. As a contribution
to the large historical literature on the Habsburg Monarchy, this
dissertation serves to correct superficial interpretations of
Czech and Slavonic politics, which have most often arisen from
exclusive reliance on German sources or from excessive

preoccupation with problems of the crown, the Foreign Office, and the bureaucracy.

The history of the Young Czech party pertains to scholarly inquiry in fields apart from Central and Eastern European history. The disintegration of the Young Czech party after 1897 forms a part of the general crisis of European liberalism, most apparent in the decline of liberal parties in Great Britain, Italy, and Germany after the turn of the century. Besides contributing to an understanding of that crisis, this work adds to the growing number of scholarly studies on nineteenth-century European political parties which seek to understand political development in relation to social change as well as to ideas and institutions.[13] This work also aims to contribute to the growing literature on the role of political parties in political development and on the growth of political parties in developing nations.[14] It seeks to complement the general surveys on nationalism and Pan-Slavism which have often concentrated on ideas at the expense of men, institutions, and society.[15] This book observes the customary distinctions between nationalism and patriotism and between nation and state and treats nationality as a largely cultural and subjectively determined phenomenon, conditioned by experience and by linguistic, ethnic, religious, and family ties.[16]

Since this book on the development of Czech political parties from 1874 to 1901 cannot thoroughly treat all aspects of party history, it will concentrate on the decade of the nineties, in which the Young Czechs were the predominant Czech party and in which the peoples of the Dual Monarchy experienced the greatest social, intellectual, and political upheaval between the constitutional crises of the sixties and the First World War. In order to survey the growth of the Young Czech and other Czech political parties through twenty-seven years with a minimum of repetition, the book is organized primarily in a topical manner. Only the four chapters on the 1890s are primarily chronological in organization to facilitate discussing the predominant party's reaction to important crises as they arose.

A new and separate work recently commenced by the author of this book will study the development of Czech political parties from 1901 to 1914 and delineate the relationship between this development and the origins of the First World War.

Social Foundations of Later Nineteenth-Century Czech Politics

The development of Czech political parties in the second half of
the nineteenth century is best understood when considered in relation to the great social, economic, and cultural changes under
way since the beginning of the century. Czechs first organized
political parties during the 1848 revolution, only to have them
destroyed by the reaction. After the introduction of limited
constitutional rule in 1860, Czechs reestablished parties and
developed them along with other new institutions like trade
unions, corporations, producers' and consumers' cooperatives,
and mutual insurance and savings associations. The Habsburgs,
like the Hohenzollerns, regarded political parties as an undesirable but unavoidable part of constitutional government and
subjected them to prevailing restrictions on freedom of speech
and assembly.
     The three interrelated events that most conditioned the nature
of later nineteenth-century Czech politics were the Czech National Revival, the 1848 revolution, and the industrial revolution.
These events and their manifold effects will be discussed briefly
before delineating the principal social classes in the Czech
lands whose aspirations and interests greatly influenced the development of political parties.

The National Revival

     The Czech National Renaissance, or Revival, broadly conceived,
encompassed the nineteenth-century transformation of the Czechs
from a predominantly peasant people subject to servile dues to
one of the most educated, prosperous, and industrialized nations
of Europe.[1] Not surprisingly, many Czechs have considered this
revival to have been an event of almost uniquely heroic propor-
tions and have viewed the establishment of an independent Czechoslovakia in 1918 as its crowning achievement. Others more accurately have recognized it as one of many revivals among European
small nations that occurred along with the transformation of European society through industrialization, urbanization, and the
expansion of communications. The leaders of every such revival
sought in various ways to advance individual freedom, national
self-determination, and material prosperity as well as to develop
a richer and more distinctively national culture.
     Most Czechs of the later nineteenth century, including the
Young Czechs, regarded their National Revival as part of a larger
European development and derived great confidence from the fact

that their efforts to establish national autonomy and civil liberties represented the wave of the future. From this perspective, they viewed the Habsburg Monarchy as an anachronism that
could not long endure without accommodating itself to popular
desires for national and individual freedom. The Young Czechs,
like most of their contemporaries in politics, believed that
their work both continued and complemented the cultural achievements of the National Revival.[2] Some politicians, notably T. G.
Masaryk and Josef Kaizl, critically studied the Revival in order
better to understand the sense as well as the tasks of the Czech
national movement. In 1901, F. X. Šalda, one of the greatest
Czech literary critics, accurately summed up the continuing influence of the National Revival in all aspects of Czech society:

> The most important question for every small nation is that of
> securing and justifying its right to an independent spiritual
> life. This question has been continuously formulated and
> clarified in literary and critical discussions, approximately
> as it was first affirmed by our National Revival. How can we
> overcome physical smallness? How can we as a small nation
> give a good account of ourselves in comparison with large na-
> tions? How can we elevate our national individuality to a
> universally human quality and provide through it a typical
> solution that is universal and popular in content? The his-
> tory of our literary and artistic development is contained in
> these questions and in the answers to them.[3]

The intensity of the modern Czech nationalism which grew out
of the National Revival can better be appreciated if the Czech
experience in medieval and early modern times is taken into consideration. Like almost all smaller peoples in Eastern and Central Europe, the Czechs can look back on a long history of great
cultural achievements as well as much suffering and many political defeats.[4] Beginning with the National Revival, Czech understanding of this experience colored all national aspirations,
although contemporary social, political, and economic issues
greatly outweighed past grievances, real or imagined, in the determination of policy. Czech politicians and intellectuals
since the National Revival have so often stated that great
events and ideas of the past should serve as guides to present
conduct that this belief must be taken seriously. Nineteenth-
century peasant and working-class leaders were among those who
especially admired the achievements of Hussite Tábor and extolled them as precedents for their own libertarian and egalitarian goals.[5]
The small band of intellectuals who led the National Revival
built in part upon a living popular culture and found the Czech
people willing to reaffirm and cultivate a distinctively national culture as one means of asserting their individuality and
freedom. Through centuries of alien rule after 1620, the Czech

peasantry had preserved the national language, which only awaited codification and purification to reemerge as a literary vehicle, and had maintained a distinctive folk art, literature, and
music which would inspire future generations. If the Czech intellectuals overestimated their role in bringing about the National Revival, their achievements, from the first scholarly history of the Czech people to pioneering work in Slavic ethnography
and linguistics, compel admiration. At the same time, the creation of patriotic and cultural societies complemented individual
achievements in awakening Czech national consciousness and in advancing Czech culture. These included the Royal Bohemian Society
of Sciences (Královská česká společnost nauk), organized in 1771,
the National Museum (Národní museum), founded as the Patriotic
Museum Association (Společnost vlastenského musea) in 1818, and
the Czech Foundation (Matice česká), established in 1831 to publish books and set up lending libraries.[6]

Besides establishing a solid literary and institutional basis
for a rich and distinctively national Czech culture, the Czech
National Revival conditioned the nature of Czech politics in a
number of ways. In struggling against great odds, the Awakeners
set a heroic example that future generations would seek to emulate and that would inspire Czechs in trying times. Moreover,
by placing literature and the arts at the service of the National
Revival, they set a precedent for the continuing involvement of
the Czech intelligentsia in the struggle for civil liberties and
national autonomy. For Czechs, the cultural work of the National
Revival provided a substitute for political activity during the
Vormärz, when only nobles and higher governmental officials could
exercise political influence. And, in organizing political parties in 1848 and again in 1860, the Czechs benefited from the
leadership and experience acquired through the various cultural
and economic institutions of the National Revival. These parties
in turn acknowledged their intellectual debt to the Revival and
their obligation to continue its work. The more democratic parties naturally acclaimed the popular nature and aspirations of
the Revival, while the more conservative parties emphasized its
having largely been the work of an intellectual elite enjoying
the patronage of the Bohemian nobility.

The National Revival, despite its emphasis upon positive
goals, inevitably came into conflict with the German minorities
in Bohemia and Moravia. The first leaders of the Revival did not
dislike the Germans, often wrote in German, and fully acknowledged their great debt to German culture.[7] In turn, many German
writers and philosophers, including Herder, Goethe, Grillparzer,
and Jacob Grimm, encouraged the work of the National Revival.
So did the Bohemian German writers Moritz Hartmann, Alfred Meissner, and Karl Egon Ebert, who composed dramas and epic poems on
great personages or events in the Czech past. But as soon as
the Czechs began to seek equal rights and political as well as
cultural autonomy, they came into conflict with the German

minority, numbering a third of the population in the Czech lands, which refused to relinquish the special privileges and political preponderance it had enjoyed for eight generations. Therefore, the Czech National Revival took on a certain anti-German charac- ter as soon as it turned to primarily political goals. Gener- ally Czechs succeeded in keeping the negative or anti-German as- pects of the Revival from supplanting the positive efforts toward cultural progress and political reform. But as Czechs appeared increasingly likely to achieve political preponderance in the Czech lands, most Germans took fright and made little effort to distinguish the predominantly positive goals of the Revival from its incidental anti-German overtones.

The close ties between the cultural and political phases of the Czech National Revival are best illustrated by the career of František Palacký, a leading Awakener and after 1860 chairman of the National, or Old Czech, party until his death in 1876. Lead- ers of all Czech parties acquired their understanding of the past primarily from his monumental *History of the Czech Nation*, which depicted the "contact and conflict" between Czechs and Germans as the principal theme of Czech history and the Hussite movement as its most glorious achievement. Thanks to his intellectual preeminence, practical moderation, and generally prudent conduct, Palacký remained the foremost Czech political leader from the 1848 revolution through the early seventies.[8]

During the seventies and eighties, the Czech intelligentsia continued to broaden and refine the cultural achievements of the National Revival and thus insured that poetry became "the guard- ian angel of politics" as Jan Neruda had wished.[9] Like Neruda, all leading intellectuals considered themselves to be good patri- ots and showed at least some degree of interest in adopting new or attractive foreign practices in the arts and letters. Two ri- val groups, organized in the seventies around the journals *Lumír* and *Ruch*, came to represent respectively the cosmopolitan and patriotic schools in Czech literature. The former group, whose principal spokesmen were J. V. Sládek, Jaroslav Vrchlický, and Julius Zeyer, grew out of the journal *Lumír* established in 1873 and helped open Czech culture to international influences by translating the best in foreign literature and producing works on universal and Parnassian themes. Meanwhile, the *Ruch* group and the literary monthly *Osvěta* under editor Václav Vlček gave greater emphasis to folk culture and those patriotic topics that had long preoccupied many Czech writers.[10] Among the most widely read works in this genre were the epic poems of Svatopluk Čech and the historical novels of Alois Jirásek which were written in the manner of Walter Scott to glorify and popularize the Czech past.

The great nineteenth-century Czech composers Bedřich Smetana and Antonín Dvořák contributed more than any of their fellow countrymen to winning international recognition of the Czechs as a distinct and cultured nation. Both believed that love of country should not preclude openness to foreign influences and composed accordingly. The chorus from Smetana's *Brandenburgers in Bohemia*, traditionally the opera of Czech national liberation, summed up as well as any statement the essence of the nineteenth-century Czech struggle for national freedom and social justice: "We are not rabble, we are people."[11]

Two events of the early eighties, the dedication of the National Theater and formation of an autonomous Czech university in Prague, symbolized to Czechs their having become a cultured nation in every respect.[12] Opening the National Theater in 1883 culminated fifteen years of organized effort to build a truly national cultural institution largely by popular subscription. The division of Charles-Ferdinand University in Prague in 1882 into separate Czech and German institutions gave the Czechs a university of their own to complete a recently established system of excellent schools at the primary and secondary levels. Publication of the twenty-eight-volume Otto encyclopedia (*Ottův slovník naučný*) between 1888 and 1909 gave the small nation a reference work comparable in scope and quality to that of any country. The Prague Technical Institute, established in 1869 as the first exclusively Czech institution of higher learning, earned an enviable reputation for excellence. Its graduates contributed greatly to the success of Czech endeavors in the machine tool, metallurgical, and automotive industries. The institute became a stronghold of Young Czech liberalism during the 1880s, with professors Gabriel Blažek and František Tilšer serving the party respectively as chairman of the board of trustees and chairman of the clubs of delegates.

The 1869 imperial school law for Cisleithania provided the institutional and legal groundwork for the Czech educational system at the elementary and secondary levels. It established secular and state-supported schools and required every citizen to complete eight years of education. The Cisleithanian Ministry of Worship and Public Instruction set general guidelines for school organization and curriculum but delegated executive powers to the provincial diets. In each of the Czech lands the Provincial Executive Council, empowered by the diet, in turn established a Provincial School Board to administer schools through local boards. A majority of local board members, all those except governmental and church appointees, were elected, thereby providing considerable scope for local initiative. Given this initiative, the Czechs, traditionally a learned people, created an extensive system of fine schools which promoted Czech patriotism along with the standard curriculum. All classes of Czech society took an interest in education; witness the rapid growth of agricultural and technical schools and of peasant or working-class associations devoted to improving both adult and child education.[13]

Within one generation, Czech public schools all but eliminated illiteracy and acted as a powerful stimulus to Czech

nationalism. According to the 1890 census, Bohemia and Moravia
ranked third and fifth respectively among the seventeen Cisleithanian provinces in lowest percentage of illiteracy.[14] By
1891 in Bohemia, a total of 2,767 Czech primary schools served
564,421 students in the sixty Czech school districts.[15] And in
Moravia by 1900, Czechs had established twenty-six secondary
schools where none had existed in 1866.[16] In 1899, Young Czech
efforts finally won imperial permission to establish a technical
institute in Brno but could not overcome German opposition to
the establishment of a Czech university in Moravia, where Czechs
comprised over 70 percent of the population.[17] Czech political
parties in Bohemia, Moravia, and Silesia continued mutual endeavors to improve public education and to build Czech schools for
the Czech minorities in predominantly German districts, where
Czech children numbered less than the forty with five years' residence required by law for a state-supported school. Meanwhile,
the schools contributed to the making of an increasingly literate
and articulate electorate that demanded more democratic and more
sophisticated party policies.

Slavism

The "Slavic reciprocity" (*Slovanska vzajemnost*) advocated by
the leading scholars or poets of the National Revival, sometimes
seen as a precursor of Pan-Slavism, became a permanent feature
of Czech cultural and political life.[18] It originally applied to
literary and cultural endeavors but soon took on marked political
overtones without ever becoming the principal basis of any Czech
or international political movement. The smaller Slavic peoples
naturally looked to each other and to Russia for support as a
means of overcoming their individual weaknesses. Efforts to
achieve Slavic reciprocity also arose from the mutual intelligi-
bility of the Slavic languages and from a common interest in opposing foreign rule. Prague became an intellectual center for
the national revivals among the Slovaks and Southern Slavs, while
the Slovaks Kollár and Šafařík played leading roles in the Czech
National Revival. The Czechs continued to cultivate cordial relations with the Slovaks and never ceased to emphasize the importance of the Slovaks as a "bridge" to Russia without which they
would be isolated "in a German and Hungarian sea."[19] But only
in the nineties would many Czechs begin to appreciate for its
own sake the distinctively national Slovak culture.[20]
Besides seeking one another's support, the smaller Slavic
peoples also looked for inspiration and guidance to Russia and
Poland, the two large Slavic nations with rich and long-established cultures. Russophilism and to a lesser degree Polono-
philism therefore became features common to all Slavic national
revivals.[21] Imperial Russia took a lively interest in the
Ukrainians of the Habsburg Monarchy and in the Orthodox Balkan
Slavs, but it never reciprocated the strong Czech Russophile

sympathies or tried to meddle in the conflict between Czechs and Germans.

Advocates of Slavic reciprocity emphasized the individuality of the Slavic nations as well as the need for their cooperation and viewed nationality primarily as a humanistic and cultural phenomenon conditioned by language and experience but largely determined by personal choice. They knew that Slavic reciprocity could not overcome the many profound social, religious, and political differences between the various Slavic peoples, but they still hoped to promote the welfare and individuality of each nation by encouraging cooperative work toward mutually acceptable goals.

Slavism assumed at least four distinct forms besides the Slavic reciprocity advocated by the leaders of the National Revival and the Neo-Slavism of the twentieth century: Slavophilism, Russo-Slavism or Russophile Pan-Slavism, Pan-Russism, and Austro-Slavism.[22] Like Slavic reciprocity, each was primarily an intellectual movement. All leading Slavophiles believed Orthodoxy to be the highest form of Christianity and Russia's historical mission to be the regeneration of mankind. Some, like Constantine Aksakov, Alexis Khomiakov, and the Kireevsky brothers, also rejected Western ideas and institutions.[23] Such opinions held a limited appeal for Orthodox Southern Slavs but little or none for Czechs. The political successor to Slavophilism was the Russo-Slavism or Russophile Pan-Slavism proposed in 1869 by the Russian writer Nicholas Danilevsky, which envisioned the subordination of all Slavic nations to Russia in a great Pan-Slavic empire. This program received no official backing from the Russian government, though it enjoyed support among highly placed officials. Danilevsky's views aroused some interest but little support among Czechs, although he postulated the inclusion of Czechs and Slovaks in a common state.[24] Another form of Slavism called Pan-Russism implied either Russification or voluntary adoption of the Russian nationality by all Slavs. It enjoyed official sanction under Emperor Alexander III but found almost no support among non-Russians.[25]

Slavism never became a political movement among the Czechs but did constitute a genuinely popular sentiment for friendship and cooperation with other Slavic peoples and in this form influenced political attitudes and behavior. Its popularity attested to the refusal of Slavs to accept second-class citizenship under the Habsburgs but did not necessarily imply any desire to destroy the monarchy. Czech appeals to Slavic solidarity usually were of a sentimental nature or were intended to remind the Germans that no small Slavic people stood alone. In no case did such appeals constitute Pan-Slavist conspiracies of the sort conjured up by poorly informed German publicists and police officials.[26] Efforts to achieve a common Slavistic political program foundered in the political arena when advocates of such a program could not overcome serious and long-standing differences

between the various Slavic nations. The Prague Slavic Congresses
of 1848 and 1868, the 1867 Moscow Congress, and the two congresses of Neo-Slavism in 1908 and 1910 could not overcome in
particular the antipathy between Poles and Russians.   *

Austro-Slavism, first proposed by Josef Dobrovský, became the
subject of lively discussion among the Slavs of Austria, beginning in the early forties and culminating in the Slavic Congress
in Prague in 1848.[27] Its advocates envisioned cooperation among
the different Slavic nations within a federalized Habsburg Monarchy in which the Slavs, numbering almost half of the population,
would someday exercise influence in proportion to their numbers.
Efforts to implement Austro-Slavism failed largely because of
conflicting national interests and their exploitation through the
Habsburgs' policy of "divide and rule." The German minority in
the monarchy continued to regard all attempts at Slavic cooperation as a danger to German hegemony in Central Europe and to the
survival of the monarchy itself. By an uninformed and vigorous
reaction against any form of Slavic reciprocity, the Germans
eventually helped transform these nightmares into reality.

The Legacy of 1848

The revolution of 1848 constitutes one of the important water-
sheds in Czech as well as general European political development
in the nineteenth century. It led to the establishment of the
first Czech political movements, national liberalism and radical
democracy, and appeared to contemporaries as the political continuation of the National Revival. The events of the revolution
are well enough known to need no summary here, but the legacy of
1848 to Czech politics of the later nineteenth century should be
delineated.[28]

Czechs always looked back on the revolution of 1848 as a positive achievement. It clearly demonstrated the vitality of the
Czech national cause, evident in the demands of the peasantry
for schools and courts to be conducted in the Czech language, in
the enthusiastic popular reception of Czech newspapers and patriotic literature, and in the large popular demonstrations
during the several months in which the authorities permitted
freedom of assembly. At the same time the Czechs acquired their
first experience in self-government as municipal officials, as
civilian jurors, and as organizers of political parties.

While Czechs continued to look back with pride upon their
struggle for rights and justice from 1848 to 1851, they had also
come to recognize that without a strong material and institutional basis the Czech national movement could not ultimately
prevail. The revolution had revealed Czech political weakness
and dependence on the great landowning nobility for political
guidance and support. Palacký and his son-in-law F. L. Rieger,
recognizing this situation and hoping for imperial recognition
of Czech autonomy, had urged the people to act and speak with

moderation.[29] They had also worked to uphold the Habsburg Monarchy while advocating its reform primarily out of fear that its
collapse would lead to the absorption of the Czechs by a greater
Germany. On April 11, 1848, Palacký had refused a German request
that Czech delegates attend the Vorparlament in Frankfurt because he did not want to appear to sanction the inclusion of Bohemia and Moravia in any future German national state. His letter of reply also contended that a reformed Austria could provide a proper home for the Czechs and other smaller Slavic nations: "Surely, if the Austrian state had not existed for centuries, we would be compelled in the interests of Europe and indeed of humanity to try promptly to create it."[30] Palacký, of
course, spoke of Austria as he thought it ought to be, a federation of nations with equal rights, not as it was, an authoritarian state that upheld privileges for certain nations and classes.

Imperial abolition of the robota, compulsory labor by peasants
upon their lord's estate, on September 7, 1848, completed the
emancipation of the peasantry begun by Joseph II in 1781.[31]
This and the replacement of manorial by civil administration of
law and justice proved to be the two achievements of 1848 which
the Habsburgs never dared revoke. Though these reforms blunted
the revolutionary enthusiasm of the peasantry, they and the 1852
law authorizing the formation of corporate organizations re-
leased the human energies required to realize unprecedented economic development and a great transformation of Czech society.[32]

Czechs of subsequent generations generally agreed in honoring
the memory of 1848; but certain signal events of the revolution,
notably the tentative alliance with the great landowners and the
June 12 uprising in Prague, remained issues for political debate
well into the twentieth century.[33] Debate on the Prague uprising
of June 12, 1848, centered on two issues: whether or not the
riots had been a tactical mistake, and the larger issue of whether or not violence had a place in politics under certain circumstances. No Czech party or politician ever glorified violence
for its own sake or advocated unremittingly violent resistance
to the Habsburgs. Those who would accept violence under certain
circumstances regarded it as no more than a means to an end. In
keeping with František Palacký's strong condemnation of the uprising by the Czech radical democrats in June 1848, the National,
or Old Czech, party categorically condemned violence and believed
abstention from parliamentary politics to be an effective form of
passive resistance. The Young Czechs, some of whom had endured
imprisonment or exile for their revolutionary actions in 1848 and
1849, did not so readily condemn the June 12 uprising but did
reject violence as unproductive and stressed the need for peaceful struggle for reform within the existing institutions of
society.

Two assemblies of 1848, the Slavic Congress (Slovanský sjezd)
of June 1848 in Prague and the Imperial Constituent Assembly of

July 1848 to March 1849, defined issues that influenced future
Czech politics.[34]   The Slavic Congress had made little progress
toward promoting Slavic reciprocity and formulating a Slavic program for Austria before it was dispersed by imperial troops.   It
nonetheless helped inspire all future Czech efforts to promote
understanding and cooperation among the Slavic peoples.   The Imperial Constituent Assembly produced the first comprehensively
delineated program of federalism for Austria to which all Czech
national liberals and some radical democrats could subscribe.
The assembly long debated whether the criterion for dividing
Austria into federal units should be historical provinces or nationality groups before opting for the former.   From 1860 to
1914, Czech political parties continued this debate as they argued the relative merits of historical as opposed to natural Bohemian state rights.[35]   Hopes that the Habsburgs would ever sanction federalism or Austro-Slavism as principles of state organization proved to be illusory; nonetheless, up to 1914, Czech
middle-class parties continued to espouse both principles in one
form or another.

   Josef Hybeš, the leading Czech Social Democrat from Brno, concisely summed up the legacy of 1848 to later nineteenth-century
parties of the left:

   We were born and raised and formed in all our opinions under
   the influence of our parents' tales of 1848.   Revolution was
   the sole logic of those who suffered.   Only by comprehending
   the development of history could we work out our own new and
   appropriate ways of looking toward the future.[36]

Economic and Demographic Development

   The economic and demographic transformation of the Czech
lands through industrialization accelerated after 1848 and continued to condition the development of society and politics, including the Young Czech party and the institutions that most influenced its growth.   Between 1848 and 1880, the steady migration of Czech peasants to Bohemian and Moravian cities gave both
numerical and political preponderance to the Czechs in almost
all urban and industrial areas except those in predominantly German districts along the provincial frontiers.   Thanks in large
part to improved educational facilities, working-class and lower
middle-class Czechs as well as Czech peasants acquired a greater
sense of national identity and of participation as "foot soldiers" in the National Revival.   Growth in agricultural and industrial productivity and the concomitant increase in personal
income helped provide adequate resources for the rapid development of arts and letters and of political parties aiming to advance civil liberties and national autonomy.   That such steady
economic and cultural progress occurred despite a series of

severe political setbacks contributed greatly to the confidence
and perseverance of all patriotic and popular Czech political
parties.[37]

Any correlation between economic and social development on
the one hand and that of political parties on the other must account for differing rates of development within each of the
three Czech lands. By 1900, 68 percent of all Czechs lived in
Bohemia, the largest and richest of these lands and the center
of Czech political, economic, and cultural life.[38] But the over-
all development of Czech politics cannot be understood by studying events and problems in Bohemia alone, given the importance
of Czech political parties in Moravia and the many ways in which
Czech politics generally may be much better understood by comparing developments in Bohemia with those in Moravia.[39] For example, one may better explain why the more radically national
and liberal parties, like the Young Czechs, the State Rights Radicals, and the National Socialists, won substantial support
only in Bohemia.

A slower rate of economic growth and proportionately greater
Roman Catholic influence in Moravia accounted in part for the
fact that Moravian cultural and political development lagged fifteen to twenty years behind that of Bohemia. The cultural phase
of the National Revival culminated in most parts of Moravia only
after 1848, at a time when it had already been complemented by
political revival in Bohemia. This occurred despite the fact
that Palacký and other early leaders of the Revival had come to
Prague from Moravia. The Moravian Foundation (Matice moravská),
for example, developed out of the 1848 revolution, whereas the
Matice česká, founded in 1831, had long preceded it.[40] Industrialization and the attendant acceleration of social change
also appeared later in Moravia, with the result that upper
middle-class Germans continued to dominate politics in most
large urban centers as late as the seventies or early eighties,
nearly two decades after they had relinquished city government
to the Czechs in most parts of Bohemia. Beginning in the sixties, therefore, the Czech national political movement in Moravia grew in large part out of rural self-governmental bodies and
acted much more pragmatically and cautiously than did its counterpart in Bohemia. Moreover, because the Catholic Church
wielded proportionately much greater influence in Moravia than
in Bohemia, it was able to retard the advance of reform-minded
Moravian political parties long after its political supporters
had succumbed to progressive and anticlerical opponents in Bohemia. The first strongly liberal Czech political party in Moravia, the People's party, did not form until February 15, 1891,
more than seventeen years after the inaugural Young Czech party
congress in Prague.[41]

The Czechs of Silesia exercised little influence on the development of Czech political parties apart from Social Democracy.[42]
Of the nearly six million Czechs residing in the Czech lands in

1900, only 147,000, or 2.5 percent, lived in Silesia, where they
comprised 22 percent of the total population of 650,000.[43]
There, in contrast to Bohemia and Moravia, local and provincial
government remained almost exclusively in the hands of the Germans, the most numerous of the three nationalities. The Poles
and Czechs, together numbering 55 percent of the population in
1900, could compete equally with Germans for parliamentary seats
only after the introduction of universal manhood suffrage in
1907. The struggle of the Czech minority in Silesia to preserve
its national identity and raise its low standard of living won
support from Czech patriotic organizations and political parties
in Bohemia and Moravia, notably in the long and ultimately successful struggle against German opposition to establish a Czech
secondary school in the capital city of Opava (Troppau).[44] That
the majority of Czechs employed in Silesia by 1900 were miners
or industrial workers accounts for Social Democracy having won
over 65 percent of the Silesian Czech votes in the two parliamentary elections held under universal male suffrage.[45]

The Czech lands constituted the premier industrial area of
the Austro-Hungarian Monarchy, in fact its only region comparable
to the Ruhr, Prussian Upper Silesia, or the English Midlands.
By 1900, the Czech lands ranked first among all lands of the
Habsburg Empire in railway mileage and in the production of iron
and steel, hard and soft coal, armaments, transportation equipment, machine tools, glass, ceramics, paper, textiles, electrical
goods, and chemicals. In agriculture, they accounted for the
bulk of Austro-Hungarian beet sugar, beer, and dairy products
and ranked second only to Hungary in the total value of agricultural produce.[46] These developments assured a higher per-capita
income for the Czech lands than for any other area of Austria-
Hungary except lower Austria, and a proportionately greater number
of industrial workers and clerical employees in the labor force.[47]

The enterprise in which Czech entrepreneurial talent, technical ingenuity, and peasant resourcefulness most completely coincided was the production of beet sugar, the largest and most
profitable of all Czech food processing industries and popularly
known as the Czech "national industry." This industry above all
others helped insure the success of the Young Czech party, whose
main centers of electoral and fiscal support from its founding
in 1874 until 1894 were the sugar beet producing districts of
north central Bohemia in and around Podřipsko.[48]

The Czech lands continued to lead all other Austrian crown
lands in the third phase of the industrial revolution, characterized by technological innovation and the opening of new industries for the manufacture of precision machine tools and
electrical equipment, including turbines, trolley cars, power
transmission equipment, and electric locomotives, by such firms
as Škoda in Pilsen and the Daněk, Kolben, and Czech-Moravian
(Českomoravská) works in the Prague metropolitan area.[49] During
this phase, Czech labor, management, and capital, as opposed to

German, continued to capture an ever-increasing share of industrial production. After 1900, Bohemian Germans dominated only
the textile, glassware, paper, and ceramics industries, while
private Viennese capital controlled most iron and steel compa-
nies. Czech entrepreneurs and engineers, backed by Czech capital accumulated primarily in the sugar industry and food processing, took the lead in the manufacture of machine tools,
transportation equipment, and leather goods and competed equally
with Germans in the production of chemicals and electrical apparatus. Not only did the first three firms in the Dual Monarchy
to manufacture internal combustion vehicles arise in the Czech
lands, but two of the three were established by Czechs: Laurin
and Klement at Mladá Boleslav in 1896, and the Prague Automotive
Works in 1906.[50] Meanwhile, other Czech firms had taken the
lead in providing machinery for the mechanization of the brewing,
sugar refining, and other food processing industries. And in
1905, Tomáš Bat'a, who had studied and worked at shoemaking in
Massachusetts, founded what soon became the largest shoe factory
in Europe at the small Moravian town of Zlín, now Gottwaldov.
All of these Czech advances in industry along with simultaneous
cultural achievements powerfully stimulated Czech aspirations
for political autonomy within a federated Austria.[51] At the
same time, the intensive economic development of the Czech lands
made their retention by the Dual Monarchy even more indispensable
to its survival as a great power.

The third phase of the Czech industrial revolution was also
characterized by the increasing concentration of capital and by
the formation of larger units of corporate organization. The
rapid expansion of Viennese cartels after 1873 led the Czechs to
form similar organizations, notably Škoda of Pilsen, and the
Czech-Moravian, Kolben, and Daněk works in Prague, and to seek
legislation to curb the larger Viennese firms.[52] After 1899,
cartels and banking interests gradually became the dominant ele-
ment in determining the policies of the Young Czech party and
became a stronger force generally in Czech political life.

The growing Czech share in the agricultural and industrial
wealth of the Czech lands facilitated the establishment of an
autonomous and diversified Czech banking system. The independent Czech banks, notably the Tradesman's Bank for Bohemia and
Moravia (Živnostenská banka pro Čechy a Moravu, or simply Živnobanka) organized in 1865 and chartered in 1868, played a vital
role in providing the economic independence from Viennese and
German capital necessary to an autonomous Czech political and
social development.[53] The Živnobanka provided a clearinghouse
for a Czech banking system that by 1880 extended throughout Bohemia, Moravia, and Silesia and included industrial banks, savings banks, and mortgage banks with branches in all principal
cities, and a smaller network of credit unions and savings and
loan associations.[54] These banks provided the capital resources
necessary for the expansion and modernization of Czech industry

and agriculture and were protected in turn during financial crises by the reserves of the Živnobanka. The Živnobanka also provided the economic muscle which after the turn of the century
helped the Prague Chamber of Commerce finance the profitable and
patriotically expedient expansion of Czech industry and investments in northern Hungary and the Balkans.[55] By 1914, the Czech
banking network controlled 23.75 percent of all corporate banking stock in Cisleithania, a share that equalled the percentage
of Czechs in the Cisleithanian population.[56]

Industrial, agricultural, and population growth in the later
nineteenth-century Czech lands varied markedly from region to
region and therefore did not uniformly condition Czech politics.
To understand better the variety of political responses to social change it is therefore helpful to review the four distinct
areas of economic and demographic development discerned by Czech
demographers: (1) depressed agricultural areas, (2) intensive
agricultural areas, (3) older industrial areas based on textile
manufacturing, and (4) new industrial areas based on the iron
and steel industry. The official census figures for these areas
between 1857 and 1910 shown in table 1 reflect the growing importance of heavy industry and intensive agriculture in determining population growth.[57]

The older depressed areas, which encompassed most of south
Bohemia and parts of Moravia around Šternberk, Rýmařov, Tišnov,
and Jihlava, were dominated by the great latifundia and characterized by low crop yields, reforestation, subsistence agriculture, and a high rate of emigration to newly industrialized
areas and to the United States. In south Bohemia, the area included many once powerful and prosperous cities, including Tábor
and Domažlice of Hussite fame and the old royal cities of Klatovy and Sušice. Here too lay most of the great landed estates
of the Schwarzenbergs, Buquoys, Lobkowiczes, and other leading
families of the Bohemian nobility. Despite attempts to introduce mechanization and modern agricultural techniques to the estates, their productivity was falling behind the middle-sized
farms and large estates of the Czech peasantry in the intensive
agricultural areas of central and eastern Bohemia. Also predominant in south Bohemia were Czech peasant smallholders and dwarfholders owning less than five and less than two hectares respectively, who increasingly could not meet domestic and foreign
competition and had to move to the cities or emigrate abroad.[58]

In depressed rural areas, Czech political parties developed
tardily and then primarily through associations of peasant smallholders like those that supported Alfons Šťastný's founding of
the Peasant Union (Selská jednota) of Bohemia in February 1889.
These smallholders, especially in southern Bohemia, differed politically with the great landowners, whom they blamed for helping perpetuate rural poverty by withholding land from cultivation and by not being obliged to pay a fair share of taxes to
local government.[59]

The intensive agricultural areas included the fertile Labe valley of eastern and north central Bohemia and the Haná region of central Moravia around Olomouc, Přerov, and Prostějov. The cities in this area grew steadily, spurred by the development of light industry and mechanized food processing.[60] Here emigration remained low, and an independent peasantry prospered despite tax exemptions and government subsidies granted to the great landowners. Strong Old Czech and Young Czech party cadres arose through district and communal self-governmental boards as growing prosperity stimulated political activity by enabling more and more Czechs to meet the property qualifications required of voters in local, provincial, and parliamentary elections.

The older industrial areas, based on textile manufacture, covered the tier of northern Bohemian districts beginning at Aš in the west and extending through Varnsdorf and Liberec (Reichenberg) to Trutnov. Textiles, which had accounted for 51 percent of Bohemian industrial production in 1857, accounted for only 42 percent in 1880.[61] That the relative decline in the fortunes of the predominantly German textile industry coincided with the successful Czech development of new industries in food processing, leather goods, and machine tools further weakened the German economic and political position vis-à-vis the Czechs.

The new industrial areas registered a rate of population growth of 126 percent from 1857 to 1910, compared to 24 percent for the older industrial areas.[62] Here arose the coal and steel industries and the related manufacture of railway equipment, industrial machinery, and chemicals. These areas included the almost exclusively Czech districts around Pilsen, Kladno, Prague, and Brno and the northern Moravian and southern Silesian industrial complex around greater Ostrava in which Czechs, Poles, and Germans resided in almost equal numbers. The north Bohemian coal mining and steel producing belt that stretched eastward from Chomutov through Most, Teplice, and Duchcov to Ústí nad Labem was predominantly German prior to the 1860s. Thereafter it acquired new chemical and metallurgical industries and began to take on a more Czech character as tens of thousands of Czechs, many from depressed southern Bohemia, moved north in search of employment.[63] According to census data based on *Umgangssprache*, the number of Czechs in this area increased more than 300 percent between 1880 and 1900, as opposed to a 60 percent increase in the German population. Statistics on the growth of particular towns during the same decades more clearly reveal the rapidly changing balance between Czechs and Germans.[64] So swiftly did that balance shift that conflict between nationalities and between classes was severely exacerbated. German workers complained that Czechs would often work for lower wages and take jobs away from them. As newly arrived Czechs promptly established their own schools, businesses, and patriotic societies, middle-class Germans expressed alarm that the prevailing "German

character" of the region would soon be lost.[65] At the same time
these Czechs received fiscal and moral support from Czech political parties and national organizations elsewhere in Bohemia.

Social Classes

   Rapid industrialization, urbanization, and improvements in agriculture transformed traditional Czech society and led to growing popular demand for political and institutional reform.
Therefore, a survey of the principal social classes and their
interrelationship should precede that of the various political
and institutional responses to social change.
   Middle-class Czechs, like their counterparts throughout most
of Europe, worked to modernize and rationalize business and society and to abolish the last remnants of aristocratic privilege.
By 1910, they had surpassed the Bohemian German middle class in
wealth as well as numbers, principally by virtue of their domination of the newly established machine tool, metallurgical, and
automotive industries, their investments in coal, chemicals,
electrical goods, and fertilizers, and their ownership, usually
in partnership with Czech farmers, of the principal food processing industries, notably beet sugar refining, flour milling,
brewing, distilling, and starch manufacturing. Middle-class
Czechs owed their political preeminence in Czech society to domination of representative governmental institutions at the
communal level through three-class voting and at the district
and provincial levels through curial voting. A franchise restricted to those male citizens paying at least four gulden in
direct annual taxes further insured that material wealth and political power would reinforce one another.[66] Besides these privileges, the German middle class also enjoyed electoral gerrymandering in its favor and a preponderance in higher bureaucratic
and judicial offices. Despite similar economic interests and a
mutual fear of social revolution, middle-class Czechs and Germans
remained political and commercial rivals and could find no common
ground on questions related to language and nationality.
   Along with a prosperous Czech middle class emerged a large
and impoverished urban proletariat numbering 30.8 percent of all
gainfully employed Czechs in the Czech lands by 1900.[67] Low
wages, long hours, poor working conditions, and higher-than-
average rates of infant and adult mortality remained the lot of
Czech workers well into the twentieth century.[68] As elsewhere
in Europe, an unprecedented demand for food, housing, and sani-
tary facilities created severe social problems in the many industrial towns. Government inspection and regulation of working
conditions in the factories of Cisleithania came only with imperial law 117 of June 17, 1883, and then at a time when the
Taaffe government was attempting to eradicate socialism by means
of emergency antisocialist legislation.[69] The growth of the
Prague suburbs of Vinohrady, predominantly middle-class, and

Žižkov, predominantly working-class, in the later nineteenth
century revealed not only residential segregation according to
class but also substantially higher infant and adult mortality
and a greater incidence of tuberculosis and pneumonia among proletarian families.[70]

Czech middle-class citizens and workers were united by a common language and by pride in Czech national culture but lived
apart and viewed politics from different perspectives. The welfare of both classes was to a large degree dependent upon the
continued expansion of industry and commerce. That this mutual
dependence did not lead to cordial relations between management
and labor was evidenced by the increasing number of strikes in
the Czech lands between the 1860s and 1900 and by the rapid
growth of the Czechoslavonic Social Democratic party from its
founding in 1878 to its winning more votes than any other Czech
party in 1907.[71]

The transformation of Czech society through industrialization
and urbanization strengthened the Czech national movement while
creating a greater differentiation of classes within Czech society. This became particularly evident after 1900 as the new
mass Czech parties, organized on a class basis, continued to advocate greater Czech national autonomy. German socialists like
Otto Bauer and Friedrich Stampfer as well as Young Czech and
Czech Socialist leaders recognized that the Czech national movement owed much of its popularity to the fact that to a large degree it constituted a movement for social emancipation.[72] The
Habsburgs, great landowners, and German middle classes opposed
socialism and Slavic national political movements primarily on
the same grounds: all threatened the privileged old order by
advocating universal suffrage and popular sovereignty. This
helps explain why the Habsburgs could satisfactorily come to
terms only with the Bohemian great landowners, with the German
upper middle class, and with the Polish and the Hungarian nobility.[73]

Both the Czech middle class and working class were at most
only one or two generations removed from a peasantry for which
they usually retained some degree of affection. Between 1890
and 1900, this Czech peasantry declined very slightly in absolute numbers but greatly as a percentage of the total Czech
population, as it dropped from 46.86 percent to 41.26 percent of
the work force and furnished new recruits to the middle class
and the urban proletariat.[74] At the same time, many peasants
profoundly altered their way of life by adopting scientific
farming methods and organizing either corporations or cooperatives to purchase supplies and to process and market their produce. The law of April 9, 1873, that authorized the formation of
producers' and consumers' cooperatives proved a great boon to
Czech peasants, who by 1912 had established 938 such institutions. Peasants complemented these organizations by establishing mutual insurance funds and savings and loan associations

(*kampeličky* or *Raiffeisenkassen*), and after the turn of the century an Agrarian bank, thus keeping as much money as possible
within the rural community and growing wealthy by lending one
another money.[75] By 1912, 3,588 peasant savings and loan associations numbering 58,333 shareholders had guaranteed loans to
the value of 362.2 million crowns.[76]

Bohemia, Moravia, and Galicia were the leading agricultural
lands in Cisleithania; and in Bohemia and Moravia small and middling landholders predominated.[77] Modern techniques of agricultural production and food processing in Bohemia and Moravia more
than compensated for the greater acreage in Galicia. The advanced state of agriculture in Bohemia and Moravia and the economic and political independence of most small- and middlehol-
ders from the great landowners account in large part for the
development of powerful agrarian movements in these provinces
and for the relative wealth and stability of Czech society.

Rural society in the Czech lands comprised essentially six
groups: (1) the great landowners, identified by their voting
privileges in the first curia, dependent on having entailed estates or on paying taxes in excess of 200 crowns on estates inscribed in the feudal land records (*zemské desky* or *Landtafeln*);
(2) estate owners or large landholders holding estates in excess
of 100 hectares not inscribed on the land records; (3) large
farmers owning 20 to 100 hectares, including owners of estates
of 50 to 100 hectares; (4) middling farmers holding 5 to 20 hectares; (5) smallholders, with the two- to five-hectare minimum
required for adequate family subsistence; and (6) peasant dwarfholders with less than two hectares, who usually had to work
part-time on neighboring estates.[78] Most landless rural workers,
numbering over a third of all Czechs engaged in agriculture,
generally held steady jobs at low wages on larger estates; but
almost a third worked as day laborers on a seasonal basis.[79]

Farming by independent peasant proprietors organized in producers' and consumers' cooperatives proved to be more productive
than farming on the great landed estates (latifundia, *velkostat-
ky, Grossgrundbesitz*). This was evident from the higher rate of
emigration from areas in which latifundia predominated, from the
much higher percentage of estate land in forests and meadows,
from the growth of mechanized food processing industries in
those areas most completely dominated by middling peasant proprietors, and from the gradual increase in the percentage as
well as in the amount of land held by peasants as opposed to
that held by nobles. Table 3 indicates the extent to which in
one century the amount of arable land held by noblemen in Bohemia declined absolutely as well as relatively.[80] Peasants made
greater gains by opening new areas to cultivation than by buying
formerly noble land; and from 1880 to 1910, peasants or farmers
with 3- to 20- and 20- to 50-hectare holdings grew at the expense of smallholders and dwarfholders as well as at the expense
of the great landowners.[81]

The independent peasant landholder's increasing productivity
and share of all arable land contradicted the long-cherished
assumption of both great landowners and doctrinaire Marxists
that large estates constituted the most effective unit of agricultural production. Statistical evidence from Germany, Denmark,
and the Netherlands as well as from the Czech lands indicated
that the middling peasant landholder continued to gain ground at
the expense of estate owners, thanks in large part to scientific
farming and the widespread application of farm machinery.[82]

The Czech peasantry generally remained political opponents of
their former masters, the great landowners, despite the fact
that the two had common interests in such matters as high prices
for agricultural produce, low transportation fees, and the adoption of farm machinery.[83] The peasants believed correctly that
the great landowners did not make the most effective use of their
land, which often lay fallow or remained in forests for recrea-
tion and hunting. They wanted to buy and exploit this land themselves and resented the laws of entail, the tax exemptions, and
the government subsidies that helped the great landowners to continue profitable operations. Moreover, the peasants nourished a
certain class hatred for the nobles, who were well remembered as
collectors of the robota and as the arbitrary manorial judges of
the Vormärz. In many respects, the struggle of the Czech peasants against the great landowners thus resembled that of the
Irish peasantry against the "Protestant ascendancy" and the
Ukrainian peasantry against the Polish szlachta. In all cases,
national and class conflicts accentuated economic conflict and
outweighed any common material interests.

Given the strong and lasting influence of the noble great
landowners (velkostatkāři or Grossgrundbesitzer) on Czech peasant and middle-class politics of the later nineteenth century,
it is important to examine their status, prerogatives, and interests. In Bohemia, great landowners holding estates in excess
of 2,000 hectares in size and numbering 151, or 0.02 percent of
the population, held 28.31 percent of the land. Comparable figures for Moravia, where Czech smallholders were even more predominant, are 73, or 0.01 percent, and 25.6 percent.[84] One-
fifth of the arable land in Bohemia lay on 38 estates, of which
those belonging to the Schwarzenberg, Colloredo-Mansfeld, and
Valdstein families were the largest.[85] The great landowners remained especially powerful in southern Bohemia, an area of depressed agricultural production, poverty, and high rates of
emigration.

Most great landowning families owed their fortunes in land to
their having taken over estates confiscated from the rebellious
Czech nobility during the Thirty Years War.[86] Given their predominantly foreign origin and their strong loyalty to the Habsburg dynasty, the great landowners did not identify strongly
with either the Czech or the German national movements. Most
spoke and wrote exclusively in German, and very few took the

trouble to learn Czech. During the Vormärz, they had subjected
Czech and German peasants alike to the robota and to manorial
justice and opposed any extension of the limited franchise by
which they dominated the provincial diets. At the same time
they helped promote the economic development of the country, recognizing that this would increase their material prosperity.
In keeping with their own provincial patriotism (*Landespatriotismus*) and the Romantic spirit, they had also encouraged the Czech
National Revival and patronized scholarship, arts, and letters.
Some great landowners participated in the revolution of 1848 in
hopes of moderating its course, notably Count Albert Rudolph
Deym, publisher of the patriotic *Národní noviny* (National news),
and Count Joseph Matthias Thun-Salm, who like Palacký refused to
attend the Frankfurt Vorparlament and helped organize the 1848
Slavic Congress. Most great landowners supported the proposals
of the Imperial Constituent Assembly and after its dissolution
accepted Bach's reactionary rule as more desirable than continued revolution or popular sovereignty.

After the establishment of constitutional rule in Austria in
1860, the great landowners maintained their privileged status
primarily by two means: entailed estates and special political
privileges. The entailing of an estate meant that it could not
be subdivided or be alienated from the family that owned it. In
1901, forty families controlling 124 entailed estates held 11.15
percent of all land in Bohemia. Entailed estates occupied 7.99
percent of the land in Moravia and 3.45 percent in Silesia.[87]
The reservation of certain first curia diet seats to entailed
estates, 16 of 70 in Bohemia and 10 of 20 in Moravia after 1905,
insured disproportionately large political representation for
the same families.[88] Table 16 in the appendix, showing representation to the diets in the Czech lands, reveals the privileged status of the great landowners, who through control of the
first electoral curia held 28.9 percent of the seats in Bohemia,
30 percent in Moravia, and 29 percent in Silesia.[89] They likewise dominated the upper house of the Reichsrat through hereditary representation until 1918 and enjoyed disproportionately
large representation through control of the first curia of the
lower house of the Reichsrat until the introduction of universal
manhood suffrage in 1907.[90] Even if representation in the diets
or the Reichsrat had been proportional to direct taxes paid, the
great landowners still would have received far more than their
fair share of seats.[91]

The great landowners after 1860 divided into two political
parties reflecting disagreement on the issues of autonomy for
the Czech lands and alliance with the Czech National party. The
conservative great landowners, including more than three-quarters
of the leading noble families, were led by Count Henry Jaroslav
Clam-Martinic and advocated association with the National party
and the federalization of Austria in accordance with the October
Diploma of 1860 as the surest way to preserve their privileged

economic and political status while moderating the social changes
wrought by industrialization. The smaller Constitutional (Ver-
fassungstreue) party generally allied with the German Liberals
and believed the centralized government established by the February Patent of 1861 to be the most suitable for Austria. Noble
families in the Czech lands who supported this party included the
Aehrenthals, Auerspergs, Clam-Gallases, and Thun-Salms.[92]

The Germans too enjoyed a privileged position in the Habsburg
Monarchy until its disintegration in October 1918. They constituted the largest single nationality in Cisleithania, a vast majority in the Alpine lands and Austria proper, and a minority of
one-third in the Czech lands. This led naturally to German becoming the principal language of communication and by law the
internal service language of the bureaucracy. Czechs never objected to this natural preeminence of German, and almost all educated Czechs used it as their second language. They objected
only to attempts to impose German as the official language of
state, which would relegate other native languages to an inferior
status under law.[93] Czechs and other Slavs also objected to the
privileged status enjoyed by Germans through "electoral geometry"
in curial voting to the diets and the Reichsrat. In 1897, Germans, numbering 37 percent of the population in Bohemia, held 44
percent of the Reichsrat seats in the third or urban curia. After the introduction of universal manhood suffrage to the lower
house in 1907, the Germans still retained an enormous advantage:
comprising 36 percent of the population of Cisleithania, they
elected 45 percent of the delegates.[94]

A franchise based on property qualifications and curial voting
appeared to insure German preponderance in provincial and municipal government in Bohemia and Moravia when introduced in the sixties. But it did not anticipate rapid Czech advances in industry
and agriculture, which soon brought the Czechs up to a level of
economic parity with the Germans and increased their political
representation accordingly. The expulsion of Austria from Germany following the Seven Weeks War of 1866 and the creation of
Imperial Germany at Versailles in 1871 further disoriented the
Cisleithanian Germans, who had heretofore considered themselves
citizens of the larger Germanic Confederation. They then turned
their attention to the difficult tasks of trying to maintain
their political preeminence in the Habsburg Empire, where they
constituted only 36 percent of the population, and of trying to
maintain the closest possible ties between the Habsburg Monarchy
and Imperial Germany. Contributing to their unease and sense of
isolation was their being unable to look for leadership to the
great landowners as the Prussian middle class had looked to the
junkers.

The rapid political, cultural, and economic advances made by
the Czechs after 1860 caught the Germans by surprise and made
them cling more desperately to their customary political privileges and pretensions to cultural superiority.[95] The rapid

increase in the number of Czechs in business and in the professions previously dominated by Germans accentuated the German
sense of being overwhelmed. While the ratio of Czechs to Germans in the population of the Czech lands had remained relatively
constant during the nineteenth century, urbanization and industrialization brought hundreds of thousands of Czechs from the
countryside to the cities, reducing the Germans to small minorities in all cities except those along the frontiers of Bohemia
and Moravia. German predominance in the Czech lands during the
Vormärz had been based upon German and German-Jewish majorities
in the principal cities, including Prague, Brno, and Pilsen. By
the end of the sixties, Prague and Pilsen had Czech governments
and were almost exclusively Czech in character, while Brno had a
growing and politically active Czech minority. After 1860, the
movement of many Czechs into the northern Bohemian industrial
cities in search of jobs also gave rise to unfounded German
charges that the Czechs were bent on "Czechizing" the German
population in the three crown lands. Czechs indeed aspired to
predominance within an autonomous kingdom of Bohemia but recognized that great German strength in Cisleithania and the proximity
of Imperial Germany would require them to be on their best behavior toward the Bohemian Germans.

Among many middle class Germans prevailed an unexamined belief
in German cultural superiority and an ignorance of Czech cultural
achievements past and present. Ironically, some of these Germans
greatly lauded Goethe, whose dictum that German culture owed much
to German receptiveness to foreign influences and whose patronage
of the National Revival were generally overlooked. Many Czechs,
on the other hand, continued to learn German as a second language,
while leaders, like Young Czech chairman Emanuel Engel and parliamentary tribune Edvard Grégr, often acknowledged the German contributions to Czech culture and society.[96] But most Germans took
Czech appreciation as their due and generally did not reciprocate
it.

Popular later nineteenth-century slogans that distorted Darwin's theories of "natural selection" and "survival of the fit-
test" reinforced the German sense of superiority and enmity toward Czechs, Jews, and other non-German peoples.[97] By refusing
to accept the Czechs as equals, the Germans of Cisleithania foreclosed any possibility of political cooperation based on liberal
or democratic principles; and the many who also succumbed to
anti-Semitism cut themselves off from the best in contemporary
Austrian-German culture.

Whereas the Czechs could confidently proceed in the knowledge
that the principal forces of the nineteenth century--industriali-
zation, liberalism, and the coming of democracy--worked to their
advantage, the Germans watched the same forces undermine their
privileged position. This fact, far more than any German political immaturity or supposedly authoritarian character, determined
the decidedly antimodern, antidemocratic, and anti-Semitic nature

of right-wing political parties among Germans in the Czech lands.

Perhaps the greatest tragedy of Central and Eastern Europe in modern times has been the inability of nations large and small to reconcile peacefully their conflicting aims and interests. Every nation has at times behaved badly toward its neighbors or its national minorities. But the small nations cannot be blamed for having resisted domination by larger nations and having sought to achieve national autonomy and civil liberties comparable to those enjoyed by most nations of Western and Northern Europe. The Germans, who made little effort to treat their smaller East European neighbors tactfully, acted all too often like powerful nations or privileged classes in other times and places by intransigently defending their interests and what they deemed to be prerogatives well deserved. Furthermore, the Habsburg Monarchy, while giving some protection and economic advantages to its subjects, exacerbated tensions between them by denying them the civil liberties and political responsibility that might have encouraged their cooperation and responsible behavior. Apologists for the old order have often claimed that the imperial bureaucracy actually as well as ostensibly ruled in the best interests of all subjects because of its expertise and ability to stand above class or nationality conflicts. In fact, the Habsburgs and their officials maintained the supranational and authoritarian state by catering to privileged classes and nationalities and by granting as few concessions as possible to reform-minded political movements whether national, agrarian, or Social Democratic.

By the turn of the century, the Czech lands approached the level of Western Europe in economic and social development and outpaced all parts of Austria-Hungary except Lower Austria. If prosperity and economic growth had been the principal criteria for political stability, the Czechs and Germans in the Czech lands should have been among the most contented peoples in the monarchy. They were not. Economic growth and concomitant social change continued to foster discontent so long as all citizens did not enjoy equal rights and have some hope of attaining civil liberties comparable to those enjoyed by most nations in Western and Northern Europe.

The Czechs and the Habsburg Monarchy

The first Czech political parties cannot be understood apart
from the authoritarian supranational state in which they developed, just as they cannot be understood apart from the social
and economic changes that facilitated their growth. The seven
years of constitutional crisis culminating in the Austro-
Hungarian Compromise and the December Constitution of 1867 not
only were the formative period for both the Old and Young Czech
parties but, by establishing the laws and institutions that
would endure largely unchanged until 1918, they profoundly conditioned the development of all political parties up to that time.

The Czechs and the Establishment of Dualism

During the 1860s, the Habsburgs sought without jeopardizing
their own authority to come to terms in a limited way with the
persistent demands for civil liberty and national autonomy first
raised by their subjects in the revolutions of 1848. Defeats
abroad helped accelerate the pace of political reform at home.
Only after defeat by France and Piedmont at Solferino in 1859
did the Habsburgs grant limited constitutional rule to their
subjects, and only after losing to Prussia at Sadowa in 1866 did
they begin to come to terms with Hungary by negotiating the establishment of a dual monarchy. The first defeat initiated and
the second prolonged a severe constitutional crisis and persuaded the Habsburgs that if they wished to restore internal order
and maintain the monarchy as a great power they would have to
make citizens of their subjects and compromise with the strongest domestic forces, the Hungarian magnates and gentry, the German upper middle class, and great landowners regardless of nationality. Moreover, these two defeats, by completing the expulsion of the Habsburgs from Italy and Germany, forced them to
consolidate their territories in and around the Danube basin and
to look upon the Balkans as their only area for territorial
expansion.[1]

On August 22, 1859, less than two months after Solferino, Emperor Franz Joseph replaced the Bach government by one under the
Polish Count Agenor Gołuchowski which was to prepare a constitution that would maintain imperial authority while granting a
modicum of civil rights to all subjects and greater autonomy to
nationalities and special interest groups. During the sixties,
the Gołuchowski ministry and its successors faced the classic
dilemma of all authoritarian governments that seek to retain

power while implementing a limited number of long-overdue reforms. To what extent could they undertake reform and arouse
popular expectations without losing control over events? Franz
Joseph aimed above all to preserve Austria as a great power
while maintaining royal authority. Since pursuit of these aims
precluded his ever satisfying all nationalities and interest
groups, he relied primarily on those most willing to accept authoritarian rule. In cases where such reliance proved inadequate, he offered minimal concessions to the strongest groups.
That the most conservative forces during the sixties were usually
the strongest facilitated his efforts to inaugurate a constitutional rule compatible with dynastic interests beginning with
the October Diploma of 1860 and the February Patent of 1861.[2]

Imperial promulgation of the October Diploma reestablished
limited constitutional government in Austria for the first time
since Franz Joseph had on December 31, 1851, abrogated the constitution that he had granted after dismissing the Imperial Constituent Assembly in March of 1849.[3] The Diploma was approved
by the Goluchowski ministry and the "Enlarged Reichsrat" (ver-
stärkter Reichsrat, rozmnožená říšská rada), essentially an expanded crown council whose members had been appointed by the emperor in March 1860 from the various crown lands.[4] The Diploma
confirmed the emperor's exclusive control over foreign and military affairs and granted considerable autonomy to the revived
diets of the crown lands, now regarded officially as "historical-
political entities." The diets, elected by a highly restrictive
curial franchise favoring the great landowners and the urban upper middle class, were to elect the members of the central parliament, or Reichsrat, which could legislate on matters pertaining to the whole empire. Supplementary legislation rescinded
some restrictions on civil liberties and for the first time
granted full citizenship to Protestants and Jews.

The pace and scope of popular political activity in the Habsburg Monarchy increased rapidly after the introduction of constitutional rule and limited civil rights in 1860. Newly formed
political parties, patriotic associations, and newspapers among
peoples of every nationality contributed to the growing public
discussion of long-standing political, social, and economic problems. The nobility in the various crown lands regained a measure
of political power; and the non-Germanic peoples of the monarchy
began to work openly for the first time since 1851 to extend civil liberties and national autonomy within the framework of a
federated and constitutional Austria.[5]

The October Diploma gave the Czechs, like every other nationality, a second chance to participate in public political life
and led to the immediate establishment of the predominantly
upper middle-class Czech National party, led by František Palacký and his son-in-law, F. L. Rieger, which aimed primarily at
achieving a large measure of political and cultural autonomy for

the Czech people within a federated Austria. The *Národní listy*
(National news), the first Czech political daily since the advent of the Bach era, began publication on New Year's Day in
1861 under the editorship of Julius Grégr, a young lawyer of liberal views. Czechs formed new patriotic and cultural societies
besides resurrecting others that had gone underground during the
fifties. Among the former, the Sokol (Falcon), a gymnastics society founded in February 1862 by Jindřich Fügner, Miroslav Tyrš,
and the Grégr brothers, made the greatest contribution to reviving Czech patriotism and self-confidence.

The Czech National party, mindful of Czech isolation and defeat from 1848 to 1851 and of the enormous political influence
wielded by the conservative majority among the great landowners
of Bohemia, allied with them on January 6, 1861, thereby establishing a majority coalition in the Bohemian Diet and an agreement to advance Bohemian state rights. This alliance was to endure until 1914 despite some modification and occasional inter-
ruptions. The conservative great landowners, most of whom professed a Bohemian territorial patriotism (*Landespatriotismus*) as
opposed to a Czech or German national identity, had every expectation that through this alliance they might better preserve political influence and privileges while tempering Czech advocacy
of social and political reform. Self-interest as well as a
sense of noblesse oblige therefore prompted such noblemen as
Clam-Martinic, Lobkowicz, and Thun to champion once again autonomy for the lands of the Bohemian crown. In western Galicia and
in central Hungary, where citizens from every walk of life professed the same nationality, great landowners and prosperous upper middle-class leaders much more readily concluded similar
alliances.

Popular advocacy of national autonomy and civil liberties as
well as efforts by most provincial diets to increase their authority at the expense of the crown frightened German notables
and bureaucrats as well as the emperor, the latter worrying lest
events get out of hand and the former groups fearing that German
predominance in the empire might soon be lost. These developments
as well as Hungarian refusal to accept anything less than internal
independence for Hungary prompted the emperor to dismiss Gołuchowski on December 14, 1860, and appoint in his stead a primarily German and ostensibly liberal government headed by Anton
Ritter von Schmerling, a judicial official and long-time advocate
of an authoritarian and centralized constitutional monarchy.[6]

Within two months, Schmerling issued the February Patent of
1861, officially an amendment to the October Diploma, which
transformed the reinforced Reichsrat from an enlarged crown council into a bicameral central parliament and effectively superimposed a centralized state apparatus over all institutions of
local and provincial self-government including the diets, whose
legislative powers it circumscribed. The emperor chose members
for the lower house of this new Reichsrat from lists prepared by

the diets and could appoint life members to the upper house to
join those who already sat there by right of title or birth,
that is, all male members of the royal family, noble scions and
heirs to the larger landed estates, and princes of the Church.
One provision unwittingly helped accelerate the advent of dualism
by permitting a "narrower" Reichsrat to meet in the absence of
Hungarian delegates to discuss any matters not pertaining to
Hungary.

Schmerling replied to Polish, Czech, and Hungarian opposition
to the Patent by declaring martial law in Galicia and Hungary
and by confiscating Czech newspapers and fining or imprisoning
many editors. Despite boasts that he would outlast any discontent, he had to resign on July 27, 1865, after resistance by the
non-German nationalities did not abate. The crown thereby tacit-
ly recognized that the reintroduction of centralized bureaucratic
rule throughout the empire was no longer practicable.

As Franz Joseph had replaced Bach by Gołuchowski, he now replaced Schmerling by Count Richard Belcredi, who intended to seek
a federal solution to the constitutional crisis more responsive
to the interests of the great landowners and the non-German nationalities. The Belcredis, of Lombard origin, had become one of
the most distinguished and wealthy great landowning families of
Moravia after having received large estates at Líšeň and Jimramov
from Maria Theresa for service in the Seven Years War. An able
and prudent administrator, Belcredi had spent seventeen years as
an imperial official, including six years as regional captain in
Znojmo (Znaim), Moravia, and fourteen months as governor of Bohemia beginning in May 1864. The Czech National party and the
conservative great landowners, including Belcredi's brother Egbert who led that party in Moravia, expected him to try to increase the state rights autonomy of the Czech lands, the latter
party because he would uphold the interests of noblemen and the
former because he sought equal rights for all nationalities.
When Belcredi left Prague in August 1865 to become Imperial Minister-President, the city government made him an honorary citizen
and named in his honor the main thoroughfare north of the Vltava.[7]

Belcredi's principal task was to establish a constitutional
arrangement acceptable to the Poles, Czechs, and Hungarians as
well as to the emperor and the Germans. Toward this end, he
named Gołuchowski governor of Galicia, martial law having been
lifted there during May, abolished the Transylvanian Diet to facilitate the incorporation of Transylvania into Hungary, and set
up a Bohemian court chancellery to prepare for the eventual coronation of Franz Joseph as king of Bohemia. He "suspended" the
February Patent until a satisfactory agreement with Hungary could
be obtained, thereby reviving provincial autonomy under diets dominated by the great landowners, and convened the "narrower
Reichsrat" to carry on legislative matters for all parts of the
monarchy except Hungary.

The Prussian defeat of the Austrian armies at Sadowa on July 3,

1866, marked the beginning of the end of the Belcredi government.
Franz Joseph, recognizing that he could no longer wear down Hungarian resistance, decided to accept Ferenc Deák's moderate terms
as the basis for negotiating an agreement and, to fulfill this
task, brought in a new government on February 7, 1867, headed by
Count Friedrich Beust. The resultant Compromise (Ausgleich) between the emperor and the Hungarians granted internal independence to Hungary and was consummated by Franz Joseph's coronation
as king of Hungary in Budapest on June 8, 1867. Beust also issued the December Constitution to the Cisleithanian half of the
monarchy, whose first ministry, dominated by the German Liberals
and led by Prince Carlos Auersperg, took office on December 30,
1867.

The Compromise of 1867 established two autonomous states under
a common crown, foreign office, army, and exchequer--the kingdom
of Hungary, sometimes called Transleithania, and "the Kingdoms
and Lands represented in the Reichsrat," generally known as Cisleithania, the official title being too cumbersome for ordinary
use. The Germans alone preferred to call the western half of
the monarchy "Austria," a name correctly referring only to two
of the fifteen crown lands. The Germans tried repeatedly to make
"Austria" the official name for Cisleithania but were always defeated in Parliament by Slavic and Italian votes.

The Compromise required that agreements concerning tariffs,
taxation, coinage, and military conscription be renegotiated at
ten-year intervals with the approval of both parliaments. Given
the many differences of opinion between Hungary and Cisleithania
on these matters, the monarchy faced a serious political crisis
every ten years as parties seeking to modify certain terms of
earlier agreements invariably called into question the Compromise
itself. Ruling on other matters of concern to both Hungary and
Cisleithania became the responsibility of the Delegations (Dele-
gationen), which met annually and comprised sixty delegates, each
parliament having chosen half from among its own members. In
case of a tie vote, the emperor cast the deciding ballot.[8]

The Compromise ratified the customs agreement of 1850 between
Hungary and the rest of the monarchy but by providing for a decennial renegotiation of the agreement recognized in theory a
Hungarian right to customs autonomy. The free trade area established in principle by the Compromise could not be maintained in
practice, so different were the needs of regional economies and
so fervent the economic rivalries between nationalities. Every
nationality sought to promote a degree of national economic self-
sufficiency and frequently resorted to boycotts of nonnational
products, as did the Czechs in their "each to his own" (svůj
k svému) movement and the Hungarians in their "Tulip" campaign.[9]
Several provinces in Cisleithania, notably the Tyrol, followed
the Hungarian lead in raising de facto customs barriers against
goods from other provinces by means of special fees, surtaxes,
circuitous routing, or rigid inspection procedures. By 1910,

each half of the monarchy exchanged a greater value of goods
with foreign countries than with the other half.

The Compromise unofficially elevated the Germans, numbering
37 percent of the population in Cisleithania, and the Magyars,
numbering slightly under 50 percent in Hungary, to the status of
"ruling" nationalities.[10] Each nationality could by virtue of
its preponderance in numbers, wealth, and political privileges
dominate politics, commerce, and society in one half of the monarchy. Restrictions continued to limit the use of languages
other than German or Hungarian in some areas of public life; and
the German and Hungarian ruling classes enjoyed proportionately
much greater political representation than other national elites,
thanks to gerrymandering as well as to suffrage based primarily
on wealth or social status. Of course, all other nationalities
resented this Compromise which had been negotiated without their
advice and approved without their consent and which relegated
them to the status of second-class citizens. But, because these
nationalities were more numerous and enjoyed greater civil liberties, cultural autonomy, and material prosperity in Cisleithania
than in Hungary, Germans enjoyed less preponderance in the former
than did Hungarians in the latter.

The Compromise of 1867 constituted an accommodation of the imperial authorities to the strongest social, political, and economic forces of that time, forces which were also those most opposed to extending representative government or equal rights to
all citizens regardless of wealth or nationality. The Compromise
thus reflected imperial deference in Hungary to the Hungarian
magnates and gentry and in Cisleithania primarily to the great
landowning nobility, the predominantly German higher officials,
and the German and German-Jewish upper middle classes.

After 1867, both the October Diploma and the February Patent
remained fundamental parts of the Cisleithanian constitution, despite their modification by subsequent legislation. The former
often served as the point of departure for proposals to reform
the monarchy along federalist lines, while the latter provided a
model for those who sought greater centralization in Cisleithania
if not reconstitution of the monarchy as a unitary state.[11] Belcredi and Hohenwart followed Gołuchowski as advocates of further
federalization, while the ministries of the brothers Auersperg,
Carlos and Adolf, sought to perpetuate insofar as possible the
Schmerling tradition. From 1879 to 1893, Minister-President
Eduard Taaffe advanced alternately federalism and centralism before trying to strike a balance between them. He preserved the
liberal and centralizing statutes of the Auersperg ministries
while granting fewer concessions than did Belcredi to advocates
of greater provincial and national autonomy. The language ordinances issued by the Badeni and Thun ministries in 1897 and 1899
respectively proved to be an unsuccessful but more thoroughgoing
attempt to realize the aims of Belcredi and Hohenwart. And

ministries after the turn of the century increasingly followed
policies reminiscent of Schmerling. Imperial suspension of provincial self-government in Bohemia by the St. Ann's Patent of
May 1913 began a vigorous reassertion of centralized authoritarian rule that was fully realized once the First World War began.

Despite the continuing importance of the October Diploma and
February Patent in determining the form of political debate in
Austria-Hungary, it would be an oversimplification to view the
constitutional struggles of the Dual Monarchy after 1867 as
solely or even predominantly variations on the theme of federalism versus centralism. Informed politicians in the monarchy
never viewed these political principles as ends in themselves
but rather as means by which individual, class, or national aspirations might be expressed. Moreover, given the serious nature
of social and political problems in Austria, no constitutional
adjustment could provide more than transitory relief.[12]

The proponents of greater federalism, including most nobles
and most Slavic-speaking citizens, sought to uphold and extend
the powers of provincial diets and local self-governmental bodies. National political movements had in large part grown out
of these institutions and found it expedient to ally with the
nobility so long as highly restricted curial suffrage and dynastic favor gave this class a disproportionately influential voice
in affairs of state. But such an alliance seldom worked smoothly
because the nobles would not support many reforms advocated by
national movements, such as extended civil liberties, universal
manhood suffrage, and more direct and equitable taxation.

Centralism as well as federalism served as the vehicle for
powerful interest groups. Those institutions which most strongly
advocated a unitary state were themselves highly centralized organizations with interests in every part of the empire. Viennese
banks and corporations, the Roman Catholic Church, and the imperial bureaucracy all stood to lose power and status in a federalized and democratic state. Moreover, most Germans, whether liberal or radical, had believed since the days of Bach and Schmerling that only a state both highly centralized and undemocratic
could guarantee continued German preponderance.

However much noblemen and middle-class Germans might debate
the desirability of federalism as opposed to centralism, most
believed that the authoritarian supranational state should serve
the interests of wealth and political privilege and that universal manhood suffrage or anything likely to foster popular sovereignty should be opposed. Most also contended that the common
man should remain disfranchised because he had so little understanding of his own interests as well as those of the state.
Their acceptance if not encouragement of repeated imperial suppression of popular national and socialist movements attested to
their willingness to use force, if necessary, to keep the common
people, especially those of Slavic nationalities, in their place.

Maintaining insofar as possible the old order in Central and
Eastern Europe remained their principal interest in common with
the dynasty from 1867 to 1918.

In the long run, imperial accommodation to the strongest forces within the empire could only succeed in a static society.[13]
This accommodation could not maintain the political status quo
in a society increasingly transformed by industrialization, economic growth, and popular recognition of class and nationality
interests. Discontent arose among workers and peasants increasingly well organized and striving to advance their particular
interests. Dissatisfaction likewise continued to grow among
non-German middle-class citizens denied civil liberties and political responsibilities commensurate with their increasing wealth
and education. In response, the privileged classes and nationalities at best made small concessions, usually too little and
too late. So truly did the Compromise of 1867 and the Cisleithanian constitution reflect the interests of the Habsburgs and
the privileged classes and so little did these arrangements provide for an orderly political response to social and economic
change that the ruling classes ultimately chose to risk self-
destruction in war rather than allow any fundamental domestic
reform.

The "Two-Tracked" System of Government

Cisleithania acquired a "two-tracked" system of government by
virtue of the October Diploma, the February Patent, and subsequent legislation including imperial laws no. 18 of March 5, 1862,
and no. 44 of May 19, 1868.[14] This system divided governmental
responsibilities at the provincial, district, and communal levels
between imperial officials on the one hand and self-governmental
bodies elected by highly restrictive curial or class suffrage on
the other. Though the Habsburgs gave precedence to the former
track, they recognized the practical need to make some concessions to classes traditionally privileged and to grant some cultural and political autonomy to every nationality. Also, the
two-tracked system in many respects perpetuated while updating
the two original institutional bases of the monarchy, the dynastic *Obrigkeitsstaat* superimposed upon a traditional *Standesstaat*.
In sum, in establishing the system, the Habsburgs practically
and simultaneously applied centralism and federalism in ways primarily designed to serve the interests of privileged classes and
the dynasty.

In the long run, the most serious defect of the two-tracked
system, aside from its unrepresentative character, was the lack
of any clear distinction between the authority of imperial officials and that of self-governmental bodies, despite the fact
that the former were often expected to supervise the latter.
Thus any jurisdictional dispute between locally elected officers
and district captains could readily become a constitutional

issue. The Habsburgs, wishing themselves to remain the court of
last appeal, never permitted the establishment of an independent
judiciary which might have been able to resolve the inevitable
disputes. The dynasty could therefore prevail in any dispute,
given its power to appoint and influence judges as well as to
monopolize executive power and exercise emergency legislative
power.

The communal and district governing boards and the provincial
diets and executive committees that comprised the self-governmental "track" will be thoroughly discussed in chapter 4. Suffice
it here to note that these institutions constituted the principal basis of political power for the more privileged social
classes within each nationality. In Galicia, for example, the
Polish gentry largely controlled self-government, while in the
Czech lands, upper middle-class Czechs and Germans did so.

On the bureaucratic "track" in every province, a governor
(místodržitel, Statthalter), appointed by the emperor, took
charge of internal security, taxation, military affairs, the
census, judicial administration, and surveillance of self-
governmental bodies.[15] Each governor in turn appointed and delegated supervisory authority over district and communal self-
government in each district to a district captain (okresní hejtman, Bezirkshauptmann). Law no. 44 of May 19, 1868, which established district captaincies in that form in which they endured till 1918, made each captain accountable to his provincial
governor for supervising all aspects of "political administration" (politické správy), including most affairs handled by the
four Cisleithanian ministries of Interior, Agriculture, Defense,
and Worship and Public Instruction as well as some affairs for
which other ministries were responsible.[16]

Besides broad executive authority derived solely from the emperor, the higher officials of the bureaucratic track also possessed limited legislative and judicial powers. Within the borders of their districts and within limits set by law, district
captains could issue binding ordinances and commands and could
indict and punish by fines or short prison terms persons who had
disturbed the peace, offended public morality, committed minor
violations of health or commercial codes, or showed deliberate
disrespect for officials or governmental institutions. These
extensive powers together with their concentration almost exclusively in the hands of one man, the district captain, accountable
only to higher appointed imperial officials, most sharply differentiated the Cisleithanian civil service from its counterparts
in North America, Great Britain, and parts of Western and Northern Europe.

The district captain was also empowered to remove local self-
governmental officials from office and order a new election if
they failed to fulfill their duties or exceeded their circumscribed powers. Moreover, he could veto any decision of communal
or district self-governmental bodies which he deemed to be

contrary to law. Despite this enormous political authority, the
district captain had neither time nor personnel enough to over-
see carefully all self-governmental bodies. Preoccupation with
matters affecting the stability and security of the empire also
prevented him and his subordinates from attending too closely to
local politics. Therefore, imperial authority decreased in fact
if not in theory at each successively lower level of government.

The entire police apparatus remained firmly under control of
the imperial bureaucracy and could not be held accountable to
elected representatives. Citizens seeking redress against certain actions of the police could do so through administrative
courts or, that failing, try to persuade some political party to
present their case in the Reichsrat, where police injustice
could be exposed but not corrected. Even if a citizen wronged
by capricious bureaucratic action were denied redress of grievances, he held an unassailably superior moral position. And tens
of thousands of protests by such citizens gradually helped undermine the credibility of the imperial government at home and
abroad.

Responsibility for the police in each land or province rested
with the governor, who was in turn responsible to the emperor
through the minister-president in Vienna; and in all districts
the police, like other officials on the bureaucratic track, were
responsible to the governor through the district captain. In
addition to enforcing the laws, the police reported on political
activity to the governor, who would in turn forward pertinent information to the Ministry of Interior or to the Foreign Office
in Vienna.[17] In the seven large cities of Prague, Brno, Vienna,
Graz, Trieste, Lvóv, and Czernowitz, a separate municipal Police
Administrative Board (*c.k. policejní ředitelství, k.k. Polizei-
direktion*) responsible directly to the governor looked after all
aspects of public security. The secret police served as the
governor's main intelligence arm. Among their manifold duties
was spying, usually by means of paid informers, on closed meetings of political parties, trade unions, and patriotic associations. That no party or group remained above suspicion is evidenced by secret police reports on such pillars of the monarchy
as the conservative great landowners and the German Liberals.
To spy on Czech parties after 1859, the secret police for thirteen years employed Karel Sabina, novelist, 1848 revolutionary,
and author of librettoes for Smetana operas. Among later police
hirelings was Karel Šviha, chairman of the parliamentary club of
delegates for the Czech National Socialist party from 1911 to
1914. Sabina fled abroad after being exposed in 1872, and Šviha's exposure in 1914 led to a political controversy terminated
only by the outbreak of war.[18]

Through their police and civil bureaucracy the Habsburgs hindered the development of political parties that sought to circumscribe imperial authority and bring citizens into a more direct, mutual, and moral relationship with the government. To

such a relationship the Habsburgs preferred a governmental authority that would be carefully defined by law but that would in no way rest upon the consent of the governed. In fact, an authoritarian state that oversaw every aspect of public life constituted the logical form of government for the Habsburgs, given their fear and distrust of the common people. On the other hand, public inexperience in politics helped perpetuate a paternalistic attitude on the part of the authorities. Centuries of dynastic rule had sapped individual initiative and civic courage and had fostered public deference to officialdom as well as arrogance and rude behavior on the part of many officials. Most observers pointed out that habits so ingrained did not vanish immediately upon the introduction of constitutional rule in 1860.[19] Most also attested to the general honesty and competence if not to the efficiency or intelligence of imperial bureaucrats. Perceptive critics like Viktor Adler, Oscar Jászi, and Wickham Steed further noted that the easygoing disposition and sloppy work of the typical imperial official mitigated the worst features of authoritarian rule and made public life in Cisleithania somewhat more tolerable than in Prussia. In this regard, Adler very aptly characterized the Habsburg state as "an absolutism tempered by slovenliness."[20]

The Slavic peoples of Cisleithania never ceased trying to increase the powers of local and provincial self-government at the expense of the bureaucracy at least to the extent promised by the October Diploma.[21] Middle-class Germans on the other hand often relied upon the bureaucratic track, in whose higher offices they predominated, to uphold their privileged status and advance their interests.[22] The German Liberals even seemed satisfied that their liberalism would not be compromised by their support of a bureaucracy in no way responsible to Parliament and in many ways discriminatory in its treatment of Slavs and social democrats.

The Slavic peoples of Cisleithania also recognized that in spite of their efforts to strengthen the self-governmental track its authority would continue to be exceeded by that of the bureaucratic track. They therefore sought to minimize discriminatory bureaucratic policies and practices by the two most practicable means: trying to place more persons of their nationality in bureaucratic positions, and trying to insure that in any encounter with officialdom a citizen's native language would be employed in all conversations and written records.

Given the importance of the language question in Cisleithanian politics, especially in efforts by Czechs and other Slavs to make the bureaucracy more accountable to public opinion, one should review the extent to which the civil service transacted its business in languages other than German. German always remained the sole language of command and internal administration in the army and foreign ministry and in the railway, postal, and telegraphic services. In all other branches of the bureaucracy in

Cisleithania, German alone was designated as an official language in both "internal" and "external" business, excepting Galicia where the ordinance of June 5, 1869, gave the same privilege to Polish. The "official language in external service"
*(Amtssprache im äusseren Dienstverkehre, úřední jazyk ve vnějším
úřadování)* was that in which officials conducted all business
with the public; and with few exceptions they had to employ in
addition to German the language or languages customarily in use
in a particular district. The "official language for internal
service" *(Amtssprache für den inneren Dienstverkehr, úřední
jazyk ve vnitřním úřadování)* applied to all business carried on
within each branch of the civil service and included an "internal official language" *(innere Amtssprache, vnitřní úřední jazyk)*
for all internal correspondence and testimony related to cases
involving the public and an "internal service language" *(innere
Dienstsprache, vnitřní služební jazyk)* for purely internal administrative business. Citizens of every nationality recognized
that the unity and efficiency of the civil bureaucracy in Cisleithania required that German remain the sole "innermost service language" *(innerste Dienstsprache, nejvnitřnější služební
jazyk)*, that is to say the language in which all business would be
conducted between one branch of the civil service and another or
between the sections of any single branch and its headquarters
in Vienna.[23]

During Belcredi's tenure as governor of Bohemia, Czech along
with German became an internal as well as external official language of the civil service in that province. After Beust repealed this measure, the Czechs never ceased trying to reinstate
it. The Stremayr language ordinances of April 1880 restored
Czech as an external official language in Bohemia and Moravia,
but all subsequent attempts to make Czech an internal official
language in those provinces met unyielding German and imperial
opposition. The Germans feared that any increase in the use of
Czech or in the number of Czech civil servants in Bohemia and
Moravia would ultimately lead to Czech political preponderance
in those provinces. The Germans especially opposed making Czech
an internal official language because this would require most if
not all governmental officials in the Czech lands to be bilin-
gual. Whereas all educated Czechs knew German, all but a hand-
ful of German officials would have to learn Czech, a task too
difficult for many and too "demeaning" for most.

Young Czech efforts to make Czech an internal official language and to place more Czechs in imperial administrative positions, always cardinal tenets of party policy, have sometimes
been ascribed primarily to exaggerated national pride and a desire to gain secure and easy employment. Far more important was
a desire to increase Czech influence in the bureaucratic track
and thereby increase the likelihood of its treating Czech citizens fairly.

In establishing two-tracked government in Cisleithania, the

Habsburgs gave centralism the upper hand over federalism without
entirely opting for the former. They thereby granted the still
dissatisfied non-Germanic peoples a circumscribed national autonomy, limited personal liberty, and some hope for diminishing
arbitrary rule. Moreover, so long as the Habsburgs conducted
foreign policy independently of Imperial Germany, they could
with some justification claim to be protecting the smaller Slavic nations from foreign domination. But, in managing the affairs of state, the Habsburgs consistently refused to be accountable to anyone but themselves. Therefore, until the disintegration of their empire in October 1918, they and the privileged
classes that supported them remained the principal obstacles to
the advancement of civil liberties, national autonomy, and social
reform.

The Constitution of Cisleithania and
the Question of Civil Liberties

A series of imperial laws that followed the 1867 Compromise
amended the October Diploma and February Patent to make a more
liberal, secular, and centralized constitutional government in
Cisleithania. This series comprised the "five fundamental laws"
or "December Constitution" of 1867, law no. 44 and the three
"May laws" of 1868, and laws no. 60 and no. 63 of May 1869.
Like the constitution of Imperial Germany, that of Cisleithania
left great authority in the hands of the emperor, established
parliamentary institutions of very limited power, and often
masked authoritarian practices by liberal rhetoric. But by recognizing a measure of civil liberty in principle if not always
in fact, the constitution gave some leverage to any person or
group seeking to enlarge civil rights and promote social justice.
    The Cisleithanian Constitution provided the institutional and
legal framework for the development of political parties and organizations.[24] In the case of the Young Czechs, it also intensified their anticlerical and liberal outlook by giving them a
stake in defending its liberal provisions against renewed conservative and clerical attack. And, much though the Young Czech
party might subsequently disagree with the German Liberals on
questions concerning national autonomy, it always gave them credit for having enacted liberal laws at a time when no Young
Czechs were represented in the Reichsrat.[25]
    The three "May laws" of 1868 and the Imperial School Law of
May 14, 1869, powerfully stimulated the growth of secular and
national educational and charitable institutions among both
Czechs and Germans. The "May laws" revoked the Concordat of
1855, provided for state regulation of the Roman Catholic Church,
instituted civil marriage, and provided for separation of church
and state in all areas of public life including education. On
this basis, law no. 63 of May 14, 1869, established state-
supported primary and secondary schools throughout Cisleithania

and provided for their administration by the provinces in accordance with general guidelines issued by the Ministry of Education.

The ostensibly liberal "five fundamental laws," numbers 141 through 145 of December 21, 1867, sometimes called the December Constitution, established in principle parliamentary government and civil rights, which were greatly restricted by existing or subsequent legislation including law no. 44 of May 19, 1868, and law no. 60 of May 5, 1869.

Imperial law no. 141 established a bicameral parliament of limited power with an upper house of hereditary members and imperial appointees and a lower house of representatives chosen by the various provincial diets. It resembled the "narrower" parliament established by the February Patent and retained its name of "Reichsrat," which literally means "Imperial Council." Imperial laws no. 40 and no. 41 of April 2, 1873, amended law no. 141 by introducing direct elections to the lower house in three curiae and indirect elections in a fourth and by increasing the number of delegates from 203 to 353; only property holders paying an annual tax of at least ten gulden could vote. These amendments maintained the privileged and unrepresentative character of the Reichsrat while making it independent of the provincial diets. The lower house became slightly more representative after an amendment of October 1882 lowered the tax requirement for voting to five gulden and after an amendment of June 1896 added a fifth curia based on universal manhood suffrage. Table 18 in the appendix reveals the increase in representation to that house after each amendment as well as the disproportionately large influence still wielded by men of wealth and privilege. The great landowners and chamber of commerce members voting in the first two curiae numbered less than six thousand but chose almost one-third of all lower-house delegates; and the third or urban curia elected almost three times as many delegates per eligible voter as did the fourth or rural curia. The lower house remained highly unrepresentative until the introduction of universal manhood suffrage and the abolition of curiae in January 1907. Even after that date, the authorities continued to draw electoral districts to give greater weight to the votes of wealthier or German-speaking citizens.[26]

The lower house of the Reichsrat increasingly became an important forum for public opinion as the electoral franchise gradually widened from 1873 to 1907. But, given the Reichsrat's limited authority and its inability to hold imperial ministers accountable, it could not develop into a parliament of the West European type and was discouraged from acting responsibly and in the public interest. The requirement that all legislation be approved by both houses and signed by the emperor gave veto power over measures passed by the lower house to a very conservative and unrepresentative upper house as well as to the crown. Besides, no majority coalition in the lower house could expect to accomplish much of anything unless it worked in harmony with ministers appointed by and responsible solely to the emperor, while parties opposed to ministerial programs could do little more than offer criticism, suggest alternatives, or resort to parliamentary obstruction.

According to the notorious article 14 of law no. 141, a minister-president could rule by decree in the absence of Parliament and was prohibited only from arbitrarily seizing private and public property and from drastically increasing the public debt. Theoretically any decrees based on article 14 would become invalid if not presented to the Reichsrat within four weeks after it came into session or if not after that time authorized by both houses.[27] But in no instance did the Reichsrat ever refuse to endorse actions taken by the government under article 14. The upper house, very conservative in outlook, as a rule made no protest at all. Given the diversity and conflicting interests of the groups represented in the lower house, some of whom had no objection to a dictatorial executive, the government could easily prevent formation of a hostile majority by threatening to dissolve Parliament, by playing one group off against another, or, all else failing, by buying off enough opposition votes through agreements to sign other legislation or to approve measures like tax relief and the funding of railway and canal construction. Since the emperor could at his discretion dismiss or call Parliament, he could readily create the circumstances in which article 14 might be applied. He always preferred persuasion to force in politics but, persuasion failing, did not hesitate to resort to dictatorial measures.[28]

Minor restrictions of the emperor's authority by law no. 141 did not impair his control over military and foreign affairs. In military matters, the Reichsrat was empowered only to determine the number of conscripts and to approve all defense budgets. But the emperor could use article 14 to get funds for the army if a parliamentary majority was not immediately forthcoming. With regard to foreign affairs, the emperor's actions required the approval of the Reichsrat only for those commercial treaties which would entail financial obligations by private citizens or individual crown lands.

Fundamental law no. 145, which defined "the exercise of administrative and executive power," declared the emperor to be "sacred, inviolable, and responsible to no one" and reaffirmed his almost absolute authority over foreign and military affairs.[29] He appointed all imperial ministers, and they remained solely responsible to him. The law declared a minister "responsible" to Parliament only for insuring the legality of any measure it passed. Parliament could indict a minister only if evidence indicated he had violated the constitution, but the trial had to take place in an imperial court, where the minister would be judged by fellow officials. The possibility of indictment as well as limitations on the exercise of article 14 or the declaration of "emergency" powers helped persuade public officials to act with some discretion but offered no guarantees of responsible behavior toward a parliamentary majority, since all officials derived their authority solely from the emperor. Until 1900, the emperor usually appointed "parliamentary" cabinets representative of but not accountable to a majority of parties in Parliament. After that date, he more frequently employed article 14 and relied almost exclusively on ministerial appointees from the ranks of the bureaucracy and upon "professional" cabinets "above the parties."[30]

Law no. 144 on judicial power reaffirmed in theory the division between judicial and executive powers. In fact, the courts could not rule on the constitutionality of imperial executive acts or on the constitutionality of existing laws. Judicial officials *(richterlichen Beamten)*, appointed to life tenure, could not be removed administratively but owed their appointments and promotions to the executive and could exercise only limited authority. For example, military justice or complaints concerning the imposition of martial law were excluded from the competence of the Imperial Court. Civil trials were to be held publicly, require oral testimony, and allow interlocutory procedures. Juries were supposed to try "serious" or "political" cases; but only the courts could determine whether or not a case was "serious" or "political." No citizen could by right demand trial by jury.[31]

Law no. 143 instituted an Imperial Court *(Reichsgerichte)* with limited authority and members appointed for life by the emperor. It was to judge disputes arising between administrators and judicial officials as to whether a case should be handled administratively or in the courts and to rule in administrative conflicts of authority between the provincial administrations and the governor's office. The Imperial Court could not arbitrate or judge disputes between the self-governmental and bureaucratic tracks of government unless asked to do so by the Highest Court of Administrative Justice *(Verwaltungsgerichteshof)*. The law thus prevented the Imperial Court from assuming most powers customarily accorded to an independent judiciary. All other jurisdictional disputes between the Imperial Court and the Higher Court of Administrative Justice would be decided by a panel of eight judges, half chosen from each court. The Imperial Court was further empowered to rule in cases involving jurisdictional disputes between any one crown land and the whole as presented in the Reichsrat and to rule on any complaint by a citizen who claimed his rights had been violated by imperial officials, providing his case had been referred to it by the courts of administrative justice. It was therefore impossible for any citizen to appeal outside of an administrative chain of command in which higher officials reviewed the behavior of subordinates. This procedure gave the citizen some assurance of successfully challenging discriminatory actions by lower-echelon officials, but it gave him no assurance of protection against capricious or unlawful actions initiated by the state itself.

Law no. 142 on "the general rights of citizens" listed the rights to be enjoyed by citizens but did not in theory or in fact guarantee their enforcement. In practice, the government upheld freedom of movement, the inviolability of private property, and freedom of conscience and public worship for recognized religions. Freedom to teach and to study were infringed upon by the close state supervision of secondary schools and universities.[32] Article 19 affirmed language rights in principle:

> All peoples of the State enjoy equal rights and every people has an inalienable right to the maintenance and cultivation of its nationality and language.
> The equality of rights of all languages in use locally will be recognized by the State in schools, administration, and public life.
> In Lands inhabited by several peoples, the public educational systems are to be so organized that each of those peoples receives the necessary facilities for education in its own language without being compelled to learn a second language.[33]

This article constituted no more than a statement of intent, admirable in its fairness and felicity of expression, which the government could enforce at its discretion. Any citizen whose language rights had been violated could enhance his moral position by citing article 19 but could hold no governmental authority legally responsible for failing to enforce it. Moreover, it was the government's prerogative to determine the language or languages "in use locally" and therefore "recognized" by law.[34]

Articles 8 through 13 of law no. 142 recognized in theory fundamental civil rights to be enjoyed by every citizen, including inviolability of the person, the home, and the mails (8, 9, and 10), the right to petition (11), freedom of assembly and association (12), and the freedoms of speech and of the press(13). Though the government in practice seldom upheld these rights, law no. 142 nonetheless marked an advance over laws of the Vormärz and Bach eras in which civil rights had not even been recognized in principle. No subsequent legislation guaranteed the enforcement of law no. 142, nor could any citizen take legal action against the state should any of his "rights" be abridged. Under the terms of article 11, a citizen could petition for redress of grievances, but he could not sue the state for nonenforcement of civil rights because the state had never promised to enforce them. He could take legal action against the state only to contest the ruling of an official or court against him. And if the case had been decided by a court of administrative justice or by a military court, he could not appeal beyond the highest court

in either system. The authorities could thus easily quash any
citizen's petition or appeal and were bound only not to prosecute him for having complained.

Imperial law no. 60 of May 5, 1869, further abridged civil
liberties by allowing imperial authorities in case of war, domestic unrest, or actions deemed treasonable or inimical to public
safety to declare a state of emergency and suspend in whole or
in part articles 8, 9, 10, 12, and 13 of fundamental law no. 142.
The law required only that every state of emergency be sanctioned
by the emperor and his cabinet ministers and be widely publicized
in all areas in which it was to apply. Approval of both houses
of the Reichsrat when in session had to be obtained within thirty
days.[35] But, as in the case of article 14, the emperor could
eventually get his way.

Imperial officials did not hesitate to use the extensive powers granted by law no. 60 if they believed imperial authority or
public security to be threatened or if they had, in accordance
with existing laws, failed to moderate the behavior of opposition parties and newspapers. They invoked this law to crack
down on liberal and radical Czech parties from 1869 to 1873,
from 1889 to 1891, from 1893 to 1895, and again in 1897 and 1899,
and to break up the Austrian Social Democratic party during the
eighties.[36]

Conflict between the Czechs and imperial authorities in Parliament, the diets, and the courts occurred most often with regard to imperial abridgement of freedom of speech and of the
press. Article 13 of law no. 142 read as follows:

> Everyone has the right within the limits of the law to
> express freely his opinion in speech, writing, print, or
> pictorial representation. The press may not be restricted by
> censorship or by a system of concessions. Suppression of the
> mails by administrative fiat may not be used against domestic
> publications.[37]

Article 13, like articles 8 through 12, constituted little more
than a liberal statement of good intentions. The oppressive
Schmerling law on publications of December 17, 1862, remained in
force to define "the limits of the law." Article 13 did not
abolish censorship and concessions defined by the Schmerling law;
it merely stated that they could not be used to restrict the
press. What constituted "restriction" would of course be decided
by imperial courts. Moreover, the authorities employed "suppression of the mails" with telling effect against foreign publications deemed to be subversive, especially those concerning socialism.[38]

The Press Law of December 17, 1862, placed many restrictions
on the content and circulation of printed matter but nevertheless
represented an improvement over the de facto preventive censorship of the fifties.[39] Even after amendments had lessened its

severity, the law appeared primitive when contrasted to later
nineteenth-century American and Western European press laws; but
it still compared favorably with those of Imperial Germany and
was more liberal than those of Czarist Russia.[40] Imperial authorities retained some control over the printing and distribution of publications by granting official concessions only to
those publishers, booksellers, and reading room managers who met
its criteria for honesty and character. No newsboys appeared on
the streets because sale of papers by solicitation was prohibited. More importantly, the law required that a copy of every
newspaper be submitted upon publication to local police officials
and to the office of the state attorney. Books and periodicals
had to be submitted at least three days before publication, except for those containing five pages or less, which would be accepted on twenty-four-hour notice. The authorities could then
prevent the circulation of undesirable news or opinion by seizing
newspapers before distribution or by deleting passages from books
and periodicals before publication.[41] They usually tried to examine each newspaper edition as it came off the presses in order
to have time to intercept all copies should the edition prove to
be offensive. After April 1872, the authorities often posted
policemen by 4:30 A.M. at the printing plants of the *Národní
listy* and other leading Czech papers with instructions to stand
by to seize any edition upon command.[42]

Editors and publishers customarily left blank spaces where
censored passages would normally have appeared in order to publicize the censorship and to obviate the necessity of resetting
type. Until amended in June 1894, the December 1862 press law
required every editor to deposit "caution money" which he would
have to forfeit if convicted of printing anything deemed disrespectful of the emperor or potentially dangerous to the state.
The 1894 amendment still allowed the authorities to take an offending editor to court to try to impose fines or imprisonment.
If a convicted editor did not pay his fine within eight days,
the state could seize his paper until payment was received. Except for lese majesty, the law never clearly defined the grounds
for confiscation of printed matter, thereby facilitating the
harassment of journalists by police officials. The authorities
had merely to argue that something "was written in a provocative
tone" in order to initiate confiscation and prosecution.[43]
Thereafter they could usually count on the support of imperial
courts.

Besides trying to regulate the content of newspapers, the authorities sought to hinder their circulation by requiring that
every copy bear a tax stamp (*kolek, k.u.k. Zeitungsstempel*),
which in many cases doubled its price. Until its repeal in December 1899, this measure had the desired effect of retarding
the growth of newspapers that appealed to the poor and disfranchised.[44] To supplement all restrictions on the press and to
sway public opinion, the government published official papers

like the *Prager Zeitung-Pražské noviny* and granted special subsidies to independent papers which would support the imperial
line. Subsidies rarely succeeded in altering Czech political
views, witness the Young Czech electoral eclipse of the Old
Czechs in 1891 despite funding of the latter party's daily *Hlas*
Národa (Voice of the nation) by the Bohemian governor's office.[45]

The application of the press law of December 17, 1862, showed
continuing Habsburg hostility toward a free press. Czech editors
imprisoned or fined under provisions of this law included Jakub
Arbes (fourteen months and 1,420 gulden "caution money"), Edvard
Grégr (four months and 810 gulden), Karel Tůma (twenty-six
months and 6,400 gulden), Vilém Erben (nine months), Karel Krous-
ky (thirteen months and 820 gulden), and J. V. Kout (three years
and 4,550 gulden). Josef Anýž, editor-in-chief of the *Národní*
listy after 1881, calculated that from 1861 to 1886 the paper
paid fines and caution money to the government totaling 38,061
gulden, 74 kreutzer.[46] Within a period of eighteen months in
1868 and 1869, Czech editors received prison sentences totaling
seventy-three years and paid a total of 48,965 gulden in fines.[47]
Prosecution and confiscation of the Czech press continued apace
during the seventies. Under the German Liberal government of
Count Adolf Auersperg, court cases involving press offenses rose
from 474 in 1877 to 626 in 1878, declining to 499 in 1879.[48]
The decade of the eighties saw the Taaffe government, which allegedly ruled against the Germans, make 330 confiscations of the
Národní listy, an average of one every twelve days. By comparison, the governments before Taaffe had seized the paper only 152
times in eighteen and one-half years.[49] Repeated Czech appeals
to Parliament from 1891 to 1912 to safeguard freedom of the
press obtained few satisfactory results apart from helping to
abolish "caution money" and tax stamps.[50]

An incident from 1895 illustrates the two-faced imperial attitude toward civil rights and lends credence to charges that imperial administrators often acted with stupidity and guile. On
June 17 of that year, at a time when Governor Thun had for more
than twenty months maintained a "state of emergency" in metropolitan Prague, Imperial Minister of Justice Schönborn decreed
that "henceforth printed matter may only be prohibited or confiscated by authorization of imperial courts" and required a
jury trial for any defendant whose publication had been seized
on "subjective" grounds. Three days later the *Neue Freie Presse*
hailed the decree as another great step toward realization of
freedom of the press. Young Czech delegate Gustav Eim reminded
the Reichsrat on October 20 that Thun's "state of emergency,"
including arbitrary censorship, had entered its twenty-sixth
month and denounced Schönborn's decree for what it was, a none-
too-cleverly contrived effort to disguise authoritarian practices and a measure that would do little to advance a free press.
Since state courts alone could determine the difference between
"subjective" and "objective" prosecution, the government could

continue to avoid jury trials by prosecuting on "objective" grounds.[51]

The Czech press grew rapidly in circulation and influence from 1861 to 1914 despite every imperial effort to restrict it.[52] Nonetheless, given harsh restrictions, newsmen as a rule avoided outspokenly critical statements about the emperor, the army, or foreign affairs and frequently employed irony and understatement in discussing domestic problems. They also sharpened their wits in an unending war of nerves with the imperial authorities. Anyone successful in politics or journalism had to be able to recite imperial laws chapter and verse and to anticipate the ever-shifting limits of the law which it would be hazardous to transgress. Young Czechs generally spoke more candidly about politics in their private correspondence or at closed party meetings than they did in published speeches or editorials. Evidence suggests that this lack of candor arose as much from fear of official reprisal as from any desire to avoid publicizing information that might aid political opponents or antagonize potential allies. The prevalence of police informers in all party circles insured that little could long be hidden from the government, and imperial disrespect for civil rights insured that most politicians and publishers would act discreetly.

Young Czechs were numbered among the most forceful opponents of arbitrary bureaucratic rule, and many leading party spokesmen paid for their opposition with heavy fines and imprisonment. The Young Czech radicalism so often decried by imperial authorities or by Viennese publicists was usually no more than a very vocal refusal to settle for less than the rights of free speech and a free press enjoyed by the peoples of Western Europe and an effort to reassert civil courage and responsible political activity as the proper bases of public life. The campaign for civil rights undertaken by the Young Czechs and more liberal-minded parties asked that public life in Cisleithania be transformed peacefully to allow universal manhood suffrage and the unfettered expression of political opinion.[53]

Bohemian State Rights

As the constitutional crises of the sixties began, leaders of the Czech National party formulated its program in terms of historic Bohemian state rights *(České státní právo, böhmisches Staatsrecht)* instead of citing the natural rights of man as they had done in 1848 and 1849. Nonetheless, despite this change in terminology, the aims of most middle-class Czechs had remained constant: to achieve greater political autonomy and civil liberties for the Czech people within a federated Austria.[54]

After 1860, all factions in the National party, including the future Young Czechs, supported a program of Bohemian state rights and all agreed in defining these rights as the historical continuity and political autonomy of a kingdom of Bohemia embracing

the provinces of Bohemia and Moravia and the crown land of Silesia, the territorial integrity and indivisibility of that kingdom,
the full equality within its borders of the Czech and German
languages in all areas of public life, and the right of its diets
to elect its king should the Habsburg dynasty ever die out. All
factions also agreed that imperial recognition of these state
rights required the coronation of Franz Joseph as king of Bohemia. But beyond these points, party factions disagreed on how
best to justify, interpret, and implement a state rights program.
The conservative great landowners and most upper middle-class
Czechs had traditionally justified state rights primarily on historical grounds and sought to realize an updated version of the
old Bohemian *Ständestaat* by persuading the emperor to revive the
constitution his predecessors had violated in the seventeenth
and eighteenth centuries. The more liberal and progressive-
minded National party members, including most future Young Czechs,
justified state rights primarily on the natural right of any
people to an autonomous political and cultural development and
sought to make any state rights program include an extension of
manhood suffrage and civil liberties and a requirement that in
each province the governor be made responsible to the diet. The
few radical party members, like later Czech social democrats and
progressives, upheld the goal of greater political autonomy for
the Czech nation but had little use for a state rights program
based on historical precedent which promised nothing in the way
of legislation for social welfare and land reform or which sought
to increase the authority of provincial diets and local self-
governmental bodies without opening these institutions to popular
political control through universal manhood suffrage.

The emperor never looked kindly on any program aimed at limiting his prerogatives, even one like Bohemian state rights in
which demands were respectfully couched in the most traditional
and legalistic phraseology. According to Count Franz Thun, any
mention of Bohemian state rights in Franz Joseph's presence was
like "waving a red flag in front of a bull."[55] Nonetheless,
despite his repeated refusal to grant such rights, the emperor
kept his options open by never categorically refusing to do so.
Throughout his reign he thereby nourished false hopes among many
great landowners and National party members.

German political parties in Cisleithania rejected Czech arguments for national autonomy on the basis of state rights as they
had earlier rejected those based on the "natural rights of man."
Most Germans thought that power and the interests of the state
primarily determined the relationship of Czechs to Germans as
well as of all peoples to the monarchy. According to this notion, the Habsburgs, after defeating the Czechs in 1620 at the
White Mountain, had justifiably, in accordance with dynastic interests, curtailed Bohemian autonomy and attempted to extirpate
Protestantism and sever all links between the Czechs and their
Hussite past. Moreover, most German scholars also contended

that the Bohemian Estates, by rebelling against the Habsburgs in 1618, had forfeited all claim to any historic "rights." Beginning in the 1860s, the Czech National and the German Liberal parties could never make common cause on the basis of a mutual interest in enacting certain liberal measures primarily because of irreconcilable views on the desirability of Bohemian state rights. Even the very liberal Young Czechs remained at loggerheads with the German Liberals on this and other proposals favored by the former, including universal manhood suffrage and the complete abolition of censorship.[56]

Bohemian state rights, first proclaimed by the conservative great landowners of Bohemia during the Vormärz era, became the basis of all Czech National party programs only after January 6, 1861, when František Palacký and F. L. Rieger forged the alliance with Count Jindřich Jaroslav Clam-Martinic that would for two generations profoundly influence the course of Czech politics.[57] So well did the three party leaders work together that wits began to call Palacký "God the Father," Reiger "God the Son," and Clam-Martinic "God the Holy Spirit."[58]

Why did Palacký and Rieger, both lifelong advocates of liberalism and national autonomy, retreat from their liberal program of 1848, based primarily on the natural rights of man, to embrace a program originally designed to advance the interests of privileged nobles who were the economic competitors and former overlords of the Czech peasantry? At the same time, why did they also ally with a party of conservative landowners who acted primarily out of self-interest and resisted the advance of liberalism as well as the democratization of society so much desired by the Czech common people?

First and foremost, Palacký and Rieger, cognizant of Czech political weakness and isolation after 1848 and of the consequent need for powerful political allies, recognized that the only such potential allies in any way favorably disposed toward Bohemian autonomy were the conservative great landowners, who wielded great influence at court and constituted the strongest single party in the reinforced Reichsrat and in the diets of Bohemia and Moravia. The National party would have to ally with these noblemen if it expected to obtain the majority of votes in each diet necessary to pass any legislation at all favorable to Czech interests, because four-curial voting restricted Czech representation in each body to little more than one-third. Only a program of Bohemian state rights could legitimize both Czech aspirations for national autonomy and the political prerogatives of the nobility.

Second, the emperor appeared to have endorsed provincial autonomy in principle by his promulgation of the October Diploma of 1860, which revived the provincial diets and authorized the establishment of elected local self-governmental bodies in each province. National party leaders could therefore regard historic Bohemian state rights as the most logical basis on which to obtain imperial approval for the autonomy of the lands of the Bohemian crown.[59]

Third, Palacký and Rieger thought that the Czechs might profit from modeling their movement for national autonomy upon that of the Hungarians, by far the most powerful within the monarchy in 1860 as in 1848 and a movement that in seeking to realize historic state rights enjoyed the leadership and support of powerful landed aristocrats. At the same time, Palacký and Rieger took little note of the fact that the Hungarians owed much of their success to having had greater numbers and resources than did the Czechs and, more importantly, to having long exercised through the *Comitas* system many of those historic political rights for which they sought imperial sanction. Unlike the Czechs, they could therefore count on a powerful native aristocracy and claim an unbroken tradition of political autonomy in fact as well as in theory.

Fourth, Palacký and Rieger and their allies among the conservative great landowners believed that trying to justify national autonomy on the basis of natural rights or popular sovereignty might jeopardize the realization of that autonomy by frightening or antagonizing the emperor and higher governmental officials. Therefore they chose to present a conservative program for federalization and reform based on historical precedent and on existing laws. Such a state rights program appealed to the good will of the dynasty in the language of loyal subjects petitioning the crown for restoration of lost "rights" and redress of legitimate grievances.[60]

Fifth, Palacký, the foremost Czech historian and politician of his generation, had been so deeply moved by events of the past that he believed the Czech nation could fully develop its strength and confidence only by reviving its Hussite and Protestant traditions. Bohemian state rights, besides providing historical precedent and legal argument for the restoration of an autonomous Bohemian kingdom, would help bind Czechs to this rich heritage.[61]

Finally, the National party hastened to conclude the January 6, 1861, alliance with the conservative great landowners in order that it might more effectively resist the impending German effort, signaled by Schmerling's replacement of Gołuchowski in December, to establish a more centralized Austrian state. Schmerling's appointment also helped persuade Clam-Martinic and other conservative great landowners to conclude this alliance already deemed desirable for ending their political isolation and helping them henceforth to preserve their political privileges and exercise a moderating influence on the Czech national government.[62]

The events of the early sixties that led the National party to endorse Bohemian state rights and ally with the conservative great landowners also dictated diminishing National party adherence to the ideas of Austro-Slavism and Slavic reciprocity, which had since the early years of the National Revival been

integral parts of any program seeking to realize national political autonomy. The introduction of dualism decisively set back
any Czech hopes for basing a political program on Austro—Slavism
by making impossible any direct political cooperation between
the Slavic peoples of Cisleithania and those of Hungary. Since
Slavic reciprocity lacked an explicit political dimension it had
never been of much use in politics. And, after 1860, many conservative Czechs thought any advocacy of Slavic reciprocity to
be counterproductive if it so frightened imperial officials and
German politicians that they became even more opposed to Czech
national aspirations.

Palacký and Rieger regarded neither alliance with the nobility
nor the program of Bohemian state rights as an end in itself but
only as the most effective means at a particular time of acquiring greater political autonomy and civil liberties for the Czech
people. Nonetheless, this alliance and program adopted out of
necessity soon became cardinal features of National party policy.
Their long retention may be explained in small part by the emperor's refusing to opt entirely for either centralism or federalism. More importantly, the self-governmental institutions established at the local and provincial levels during the sixties
so well served the mutual interests of conservative great landowners and Old and Young Czechs that these institutions helped
perpetuate an alliance based on state rights long after it ceased
to serve the interests of a majority of Czech citizens.[63] Czech
dependence on the great landowners was further reinforced after
June 1869, when the Polish gentry won more autonomy for Galicia
than that ever enjoyed by the Czech lands and therefore showed
much less interest in making common cause with the Czechs to
achieve greater national autonomy. Moreover, as the years
passed, Rieger and many younger Old Czech leaders, including
Karel Mattuš and Antonín Otakar Zeithammer, became increasingly
enamored of and dependent upon able and high-ranking noblemen
like the Belcredis, Clam-Martinic, Lobkowicz, and the Schwarzenbergs. Much as they honestly professed to cherish and serve the
interests of all Czechs, they did not consider the common people
competent to share responsibility for determining national political objectives. In their view, exemplary representatives of
the Czech upper middle class and intelligentsia like themselves
could best determine these objectives, even if this meant doing
so in consultation with the very gentlemen who until 1848 had
exacted feudal dues from the Czech peasantry.[64]

As the Czech national movement after the sixties gradually
assumed a more popular character, the National party alliance of
convenience with the conservative great landowners and with it
National party hegemony in Czech politics became increasingly
difficult to maintain. Even a common state rights rhetoric
could not obscure the fundamental disparity between the long-
range political goals of the Czech people and those of the great
landowning nobility. Whereas the Czechs sought primarily to

achieve greater national autonomy, personal freedom, and social
reform, the nobility first of all wished to preserve its privileged political status and voice in determining affairs of state.
Nonetheless, no strong public challenge to the traditional state
rights program and alliance with the nobility occurred until after 1871, when it began to appear ever less likely that the emperor would accept coronation as king of an autonomous Bohemia.

The National party committed itself ever more firmly to advocacy of Bohemian state rights while supporting Count Richard Belcredi, governor of Bohemia after May 27, 1864, and imperial
minister-president after July 27, 1865. Achievement of state
rights appeared possible as Belcredi attempted to realize a federalized Austria in accordance with the October Diploma and as a
coalition of Czechs and conservative great landowners won a majority of seats in the Bohemian Diet in 1864 and again in 1867.[65]
The diet, empowered to legislate after Belcredi's "suspension"
of the February Patent, passed bills to fund Czech public schools
and to insure freedom of association for all patriotic societies
and enacted a law, denounced by the Germans as the "compulsory
language law" (Sprachenzwanggesetz), which required instruction
in both Czech and German for all pupils in Bohemian secondary
schools.[66] These measures and the simultaneous Czech takeover
of most district and communal self-governmental bodies in central
and eastern Bohemia appeared to Czechs and Germans alike as the
first steps toward the realization of political autonomy for the
Czech lands.

Prussian victory in the Seven Weeks War of 1866 prompted the
Czechs to accelerate their efforts to achieve political autonomy
within a federalized Austria of autonomous crown lands. By weakening imperial authority, this victory renewed Czech as well as
Polish and Hungarian hopes of persuading the emperor to meet
their terms. And, by renewing Czech fears of absorption into a
greater Germany, it strengthened the resolve of the National party to work with the conservative great landowners and the Belcredi government toward the greater federalization of Austria.[67]
Even Belcredi's replacement by Beust on February 7, 1867, which
revealed imperial intentions to seek a rapprochement with Hungary, did not dampen Czech hopes or efforts, especially since
the January and February elections to the Bohemian Diet gave the
Czechs and conservative great landowners a majority of 156 seats
to 76 for the Germans.[68] Privately and publicly, Czech politicians speculated that an imperial compromise with a resurrected
kingdom of Bohemia would be forthcoming.[69] Similar expectations
led many conservative great landowners in the diet to begin
speaking almost exclusively in Czech, much as two decades earlier
Hungarian aristocrats had substituted Magyar for Latin in
speeches to the Hungarian Diet. Imperial officials and Bohemian
Germans alike took fright at the appearance of a Czech-speaking
majority in the diet, believing this to signal the impending transformation of the Czech lands into an autonomous Bohemian state.[70]

Contrary to the expectations of the Czechs and conservative great landowners, imperial recognition of an autonomous kingdom of Bohemia did not come to pass. The 1867 Compromise with Hungary indicated that the emperor would grant autonomy to no more than one nationality at a time. Beginning in the spring of 1868, throughout the Czech lands, Czechs made manifest their desire for imperial recognition of Bohemian state rights by holding mass public demonstrations, called *tábory* after the Hussite encampments of old. In the summer, delegates of the National party and the conservative great landowners announced their decision to oppose the government of Prince Carlos Auersperg, which had taken office in December, and to withdraw from participation in the Bohemian and Moravian diets until they obtained a Compromise comparable to that granted to Hungary. On August 22, the eighty-one Czech delegates to the Bohemian Diet withdrew from that body and issued the "Declaration of 1868," essentially a plea for Bohemian state rights revised to conform with the terms of the 1867 Compromise. The Declaration asked for the creation of a Tripartite Monarchy in place of a Dual Monarchy and until that occurred pledged its signatories to remain loyal to the dynasty and to oppose dualism through a "passive resistance" of boycotting the provincial diets as well as the Reichsrat. The Czechs and great landowners from Moravia ratified the same document and issued an analogous declaration of their own in withdrawing from the Moravian Diet on August 25.[71] By contrast, the Poles did not resort to such "passive resistance" and made more modest demands for autonomy in their "Galician Resolution of 1868," thereby, unlike the Czechs, indicating a readiness to come to terms with dualism. Moreover, never did the Czechs receive from the emperor a concession so great as the Imperial Ordinance of June 5, 1869, which made Polish the language of the internal and external bureaucratic service in Galicia.[72]

The repeated frustration of the Czech national movement from 1867 to 1871 also led National party leaders both to revive demonstrations of Slavic solidarity and to appeal to potentially friendly foreign opinion. In May 1867, Palacký, Rieger, Brauner, and the Grégr brothers led a "pilgrimage" of twenty-seven prominent Czechs and Slovaks to Moscow to attend a Slavic ethnographic exhibition.[73] Twelve months later, fifty delegates from various Slavic nations reaffirmed Slavic reciprocity by attending a great patriotic festival in Prague to celebrate laying the cornerstone of the National Theater, that crowning achievement of the Czech National Revival. Imperial authorities also looked with disfavor on the several attempts by Palacký and Rieger between 1867 and 1870 to show French journalists and governmental officials to what extent the tripartite Austria advocated by Czechs would serve French interests by becoming an effective barrier to Prussian expansion. These attempts included an 1867 visit to Paris, the 1868 reception of Prince Jerome Bonaparte in Prague, interviews in July 1869 with Napoleon III in Paris, correspondence

between Rieger and the French ambassador in Vienna during the
spring of 1870, and the December 1870 declaration of Czech sympathy for France and opposition to German annexation of Alsace-
Lorraine.[74] Palacký and Rieger did not help the Czech cause in
Vienna by going to Moscow or by appealing to the French and at
the same time inadvertently reinforced the already-exaggerated
German fears of Pan-Slavism. Nonetheless, they had strengthened
Czech morale and served notice on the Habsburgs that Czech loyalty would henceforth have to be cultivated rather than taken for
granted and that in desperation Czech politicians might seek to
make the Czech question an international rather than a domestic
issue. Their appeals to foreign public opinion in times of domestic crisis set a precedent in Czech politics that would be
followed more timidly by Karel Kramář after 1899 and more forcefully by T. G. Masaryk and the Czech National Socialists and
State Rights Progressives after 1908.[75]

The program of Bohemian state rights gained another lease on
life during the Franco-Prussian War, as the National party and
the conservative great landowners in August 1870 opened secret
and informal negotiations with representatives of the Potocki
government aimed at obtaining a tripartite empire in which a revived kingdom of Bohemia would take its place alongside Hungary
on the one hand and the remaining crown lands on the other.[76]
In the expectation that these negotiations would eventually succeed, National party delegates to the Bohemian Diet voted almost
unanimously on August 30 to take their seats in that body and
for the time being to cease "passive resistance" in provincial
politics. Count Karl Hohenwart, who succeeded Potocki as
minister-president on April 5, 1871, continued these negotiations.
In this as in all policies, he relied heavily on the advice of
his ablest theoretician and minister, Freiherr Albert Schäffle,
likewise an advocate of a federated Austria in which all nationalities would enjoy equal rights. Hohenwart staked the success
of his government on bringing the National party and the conservative great landowners back into the Reichsrat and, as a first
step toward this end, appointed to his cabinet two conservative
Czech scholars and civil servants, Karel Habietinek as Minister
of Justice and Josef Jireček as Minister of Education.[77] As the
second and more important step, he and Schäffle persuaded the
emperor to issue an imperial rescript to the Bohemian Diet on
September 12, 1871, recognizing the historical privileges of the
Czech lands and promising to accept coronation as king of Bohemia
in Prague on an unspecified date:

> Mindful of the constitutional position of the Czech crown and
> being aware of the glory and might which that crown has
> brought to Us and Our predecessors and, furthermore, remem-
> bering the extraordinary faithfulness with which the people
> of that kingdom have always supported Our throne, We take
> pleasure in recognizing the privileges of that kingdom and

declare ourselves ready to renew that recognition by a coronation oath.[78]

All German delegates withdrew from the Bohemian Diet to protest the rescript, leaving the field to the majority coalition of Czechs and great landowners which had been returned by the elections of September 14. In both the Bohemian and Moravian diets this coalition drew up and ratified on October 10, 1871, eighteen "Fundamental Articles," which requested autonomy for the lands of the Czech crown in accordance with that achieved by the Hungarians in the 1867 Compromise.[79] A delegation led by Rieger and Clam-Martinic took the Articles to Vienna in hopes of receiving imperial approval. Contrary to Rieger's expectations, the imperial Russian government took little interest in the Czech struggle for autonomy and did not intervene diplomatically on the Czechs' behalf.[80] At the same time, Imperial Germany threw its support unequivocally behind Hohenwart's principal opponents, the German Liberals and the Hungarians.

Given the decisive defeat of France by Germany and the intransigence of German Liberal and Hungarian opposition to Hohenwart, Franz Joseph had little choice but to accept dualism once and for all as the price for coming to terms with this opposition at home and with the newly established German Empire abroad. On October 26, 1871, he dismissed the Hohenwart ministry and, after four weeks of a caretaker government, appointed a German Liberal ministry headed by Prince Adolf Auersperg. All Czechs were angered and disheartened by Franz Joseph's having for the second time broken a solemn promise to recognize Czech autonomy and be crowned king of Bohemia in Prague.[81] To crush the inevitable public protests throughout the Czech lands, the imperial authorities again followed the time-honored practice of suspending civil liberties and intimidating Czech newspapers and patriotic organizations. General Kollar, Auersperg's appointee as governor of Bohemia, did the job in an especially thorough and brutal fashion. By way of protest, National party delegates withdrew in December 1872 for a second time from participation in the Bohemian and Moravian diets. And in years to come, other Czech politicians and journalists joined them in frequently quoting Palacký's warning of May 1865 to the Habsburgs: "We [Slavs] were here before Austria, and we shall be here after she is gone."[82]

Advocacy of Bohemian state rights further estranged the Czechs from the Slovaks, with whom they had enjoyed unbroken intellectual ties since the early days of the National Revival. The Slovaks could under no circumstances accept any federalization of Austria on the basis of historic territorial entities because it would deny autonomy to them and the other non-Magyar peoples of Hungary. The plans of Rieger and Clam-Martinic to win Czech political autonomy on this basis would clearly sacrifice the Slovaks to Magyar control in the interests of gaining Magyar

acceptance of an autonomous kingdom of Bohemia. In contrast to
the enthusiastic Czech reception of Belcredi's policies, the
Pestbudinske vedemosti of September 7, 1865, proclaimed, "The
Slovak nation cannot under any circumstances accept the program
of Federalists in its present form," and argued for a federation
of provinces.[83]

Few Poles could ever consider Galicia to be a "historical political entity" like the three Czech crown lands constituting
the kingdom of Bohemia. They sought to obtain the greatest possible political autonomy for Galicia while continuing to believe
that for Poles the only valid historical political entity could
be an independent Poland.[84] Differences of opinion on states
rights did not alone impede good relations between Czechs and
Poles after the sixties. The Czechs generally sympathized with
and gave limited encouragement to the Ukrainians in Galicia,
whose domination by the Poles received imperial approbation in
return for Polish support in Vienna. Czech Russophilism and to
a lesser extent Czech anticlericalism also remained stumbling
blocks to cordial cooperation between the two nations, the Polish
nation having traditionally been identified with the Polish nobility whereas the Czechs, like the Slovaks and Slovenes, had no
native aristocracy. During the eighties, the Old Czechs in alliance with the great landowners proved to be much more congenial
allies for the Polish Kraków Conservatives than did the radical
and anticlerical Young Czechs. On the other hand, the latter
had much in common with the Galician Democrats, whose leader
Franciszek Smolka, a veteran of Young Poland, would in the nineties join the Young Czechs in supporting the ministries of Badeni
and Thun.

The nationalities and social classes consigned to second-class
status by the constitutional arrangements of the sixties could do
no more than work for reform within the framework of the Dual
Monarchy while awaiting another crisis in foreign affairs that
would either compel the Habsburgs to liberalize the constitution
or lead to a war which would destroy the empire. Economic backwardness and reactionary authoritarian government characterized
Hungary, where the authorities resisted social change and political reform and exacerbated nationality conflicts by attempting
to Magyarize the subject nationalities.[85] In Cisleithania, where
citizens possessed relatively greater personal liberty and could
hope to achieve small gains through lawful politics, political
parties of various persuasions grew apace among all classes and
nationalities.

During the later nineteenth century, national movements among
the smaller Central and Eastern European peoples generally became
popular in outlook and aimed at curbing the power of the three
authoritarian supranational states--imperial Russia, the Ottoman
Empire, and Austria-Hungary. This situation contrasted markedly
to that in Germany and Western Europe, where nationalism often

CAMROSE LUTHERAN COLLEGE
LIBRARY

reinforced state imperialism, the very force that most East European national movements opposed.[86]

The constitutional crises of the sixties forged the institutions and the political programs which largely defined the relationship of the Czechs to the Habsburg Monarchy until 1914. Each side continued to pursue goals which ultimately proved irreconcilable and impossible of peaceful resolution. Czechs sought to realize greater civil liberties, national equality, and independence in cultural life within the framework of the monarchy and recognized that the large Cisleithanian trading area helped advance their economic interests.[87] The Habsburgs desired to maintain Austria-Hungary as a great power and their own unimpeded control over its foreign, military, and fiscal affairs; they could make very few concessions to popular sovereignty and social change which did not endanger these goals. Czech efforts to achieve national autonomy and equal rights within the monarchy therefore entailed a never-ending struggle against the authoritarian state. Short of revolution, which in peacetime would surely be suppressed, lawful resistance to authoritarianism and patient work for reform offered the only prudent course. In this sense Richard Charmatz and Karl Renner correctly contended that the nationalities at the turn of the century still sought to control the state rather than to destroy it. Ultimately, the Habsburg attack on Serbia in 1914 led the disaffected Slavic nationalities to give precedence to destroying the Dual Monarchy, which through two generations had made little progress toward political and social reform and which then sought by violence to crush the internal and external forces of change to which it could not adjust.

The Founding of the Young Czech Party

The Young Czechs did not establish themselves as an independent
political party until December 1874, more than eleven years
after their rivalry with the Old Czechs had begun. Clearly defined Young Czech and Old Czech factions within the National
party first emerged in 1863 not only because of a more pronounced
Young Czech advocacy of civil liberties and anticlericalism but
because of disagreement on four other issues: the extent to
which the party should cooperate with the conservative great
landowners; how best to define and advance Bohemian state rights;
whether or not "passively to resist" centralization of the monarchy by refusing to participate in the Reichsrat; and what opinion to express on the Polish insurrection in Russian Poland.

Divisions within the National Party during the Sixties

Throughout the 1860s, the more liberal members of the National
party, most of whom later became Young Czechs, reluctantly accepted that party's alliance of January 1861 with the conservative great landowners as one means of achieving Bohemian state
rights. At the same time, they regarded that alliance as inimical to the political aspirations and material interests of the
largely disfranchised Czech peasants and tradesmen. In March
1863 and again in April 1864, the more liberal Czech delegates
to the Bohemian Diet refused to vote with the National party majority for legislation to increase special privileges already
enjoyed by that party's aristocratic allies. On March 10, 1863,
Karel Sladkovský and Alois Pravoslav Trojan, both veterans of
1848, and other liberal delegates advocated extension of the
electoral franchise and reduction of the disproportionately large
representation awarded to the great landowners by four-curial
voting. Ten days later, they helped defeat a bill endorsed by
Palacký and Rieger, which would have allowed any great landowner
to make his estate a self-governing unit apart from communal
self-government.[1] Over one year later, on April 17, 1864, Rieger
and Clam-Martinic introduced a second and watered-down bill which
allowed great landowners to be independent of communal self-
government in matters relating to building permits, field inspection, gamekeeping, welfare funds, and highway maintenance. This
bill in effect gave great landowners considerable administrative
autonomy and exemption from most taxes which supported public
services. The diet passed it by a vote of 127 to 70 despite opposition from liberal members of the National party.[2]

The Young Czech faction consistently supported the state rights program as drawn up by Palacký and Rieger but did not favor party efforts to win these rights as a grant from the crown. Instead, as 1863 editorials in the *Národní listy* indicate, that faction wished to realize Czech autonomy on the basis of the historical and natural rights of a people to determine its own destiny and sought to make universal manhood suffrage and extended civil liberties an integral part of any state rights program.[3]

The most serious conflict within the National party after 1863 and that which most directly led to the founding of an independent Young Czech party in December 1874 concerned whether or not to pursue a policy of passive resistance in opposition to efforts by the Schmerling and Auersperg ministries to centralize governmental authority in the empire. The first intra-party clash on this issue occurred in April 1861 as left-wing National party delegates voted with a majority in the Bohemian Diet against F. L. Rieger's proposal that the diet defy the recently issued February Patent by refusing to send representatives to the Reichsrat thereby established.[4] Nearly two years later, on March 21, 1863, Rieger proposed that the Bohemian Diet vote not to send delegates to fill seven vacant seats in the Reichsrat. In support of this proposal, he read a declaration signed by the sixty-three Czech deputies to the diet contending that to send additional delegates to a "narrower" Reichsrat in which no Hungarians participated would hasten the advent of dualism and diminish chances for imperial recognition of Bohemian state rights.[5] Undeterred by the diet's rejection of this proposal by a vote of 138 to 63, Rieger next asked that Czech delegates to the Reichsrat refuse on the same grounds to participate in future sessions. In effect, he proposed that the Czechs thereby pursue a policy of passive resistance similar to that employed since 1861 by the Hungarians, despite the fact that the Czechs lacked comparable resources, influence, and experience. On June 4, 1863, this proposal barely passed the twenty-one-member National party governing board, with only eight of fourteen members present voting to endorse it.[6] Thirteen days later, on June 17, the eleven party delegates to the Reichsrat published a memorandum announcing and justifying their decision not to take their seats at the opening of the forthcoming summer session.[7] When they did not comply with Minister-President Schmerling's ultimatum to attend or face expulsion, his government on July 17, 1863, declared their mandates invalid and ordered new elections for the following year.[8] Palacký, at that time the only National party representative in the upper house of the Reichsrat, had taken leave on September 30, 1861, and never returned.

Rieger's policy of passive resistance, which widened the rift between Young Czechs and Old Czechs in the National party, stipulated that party members and the conservative great landowners withdraw from participation in the Reichsrat until the emperor

suspended the February Patent and began to implement Bohemian
state rights. At the same time, Czechs would continue to serve
on communal and district self-governmental bodies and in the provincial diets. Rieger and the Old Czech majority in the National
party twice extended "passive resistance" to include a boycott
of the Bohemian Diet. They did so for the first time on August 22, 1868, in issuing the "Declaration of 1868" to protest
continuing imperial infringement of civil rights in the Czech
lands.[9] Not only did six Young Czech delegates, including Edvard Grégr and Karel Sladkovský, oppose that decision, but all
Young Czechs two years later made up the majority of National
party delegates which on August 30, 1870, voted to return to the
diet after having received assurances from the governor that imperial recognition of Bohemian state rights would be forthcoming.
Before both party decisions, Young Czechs had argued against passive opposition on the grounds that participation in the diet
should be regarded primarily as a means of overseeing all levels
of self-government and not as involvement in the body that chose
delegates to a higher central parliament.[10] On December 3, 1872,
National party delegates voted for the second time to withdraw
from participation in the Bohemian Diet in order to protest the
emperor's unwillingness to honor his promise of September 1870
to be crowned king of Bohemia and take the first steps toward
making a compromise with the Czechs comparable to that made with
the Hungarians in 1867.[11] Although the Young Czech minority had
initially opposed and then reluctantly upheld a passive opposition which entailed no more than boycotting the Reichsrat, they
did not long abide by the second National party withdrawal from
the Bohemian Diet. Their return to that body in November 1873
heralded their decision in December 1874 to establish an independent Young Czech party. Until that break occurred, they proposed to replace passive resistance by an "active" policy, believing that Czechs could best serve national interests and extend civil liberties by participating in all institutions of government, however inadequate or unrepresentative those might be.
Moreover, this participation would insure that the German Liberals and constitutional great landowners could not increase their
political influence by monopolizing Bohemian representation in
the Bohemian Diet. The active politics that would characterize
the Young Czechs from 1874 to 1914 was called "politics step by
step" in the seventies and eighties, "responsible and active political work" during the later nineties, and "positive politics"
after 1900.[12] Beginning in the seventies, all Czech delegates
to the Moravian Diet, led by the lawyers Alois Pražák and Antonín Mezník, held identical views and by their example encouraged
active Young Czech politics.[13]
    The Polish insurrection of 1863 in Russian Poland widened the
rift between radical and moderate factions in the National party,
as the *Národní listy* in June denounced Palacký's and Rieger's
partiality toward Russia. Editor Julius Grégr thereafter refused

to give the two party leaders space to reply and declared the paper independent of party control.[14] The party responded by bringing out in December a new daily called *Národ* (The Nation), which under editor František Šimáček pledged itself to promote the unity and interests of "the entire nation."[15] All National party members remained to some degree Russophiles, but the more liberal among them, including the Grégr brothers and Václav Březnovský, sympathized with the Polish uprising primarily because the Poles were politically more liberal than the Russians and like the Czechs were seeking to emancipate themselves from authoritarian foreign rule.[16] At the same time and on similar grounds, the liberals evinced little appreciation for Slovak demonstrations against Magyar domination: "We sympathize with the Poles but not with the Slovaks who heretofore have not embraced liberal politics."[17]

The Young Czech name was first applied to the left wing of the National party in July 1863 by the Prague *Morgenpost* (Morning Post) and *Bohemia*, which referred to the emergence of a "Young Czech" party in describing the dispute between Rieger and the *Národní listy* on the Polish question. The German press continued to identify as "Young Czechs" those radicals who supported Josef Barák's candidacy against the more conservative Vojta Náprstek, despite claims by the *Národní listy* that Barák had chosen to run independently and that its having endorsed him constituted no act of disloyalty to the National party. After briefly rejecting the Young Czech name, the radicals came to adopt it as an accurate reflection of their radical liberalism and identification with the earlier movements of Young Germany, Young Italy, and Young Poland.[18] Their becoming "Young Czechs" also meant that the National party majority could not avoid being identified by the much less attractive "Old Czech" label.

Old Czechs and Young Czechs did not as their names implied represent different generations. In fact, the average age of members in both factions differed very little. The old war horse of the Young Czechs, Alois Pravoslav Trojan, was three years older than F. L. Rieger; and Rieger's chief lieutenants, A. O. Zeithammer and Karel Mattuš, were several years younger than the Grégr brothers, František Tilšer, and Karel Sladkovský.[19]

Who were the principal Old Czech leaders against whose authority the Young Czechs rebelled? Foremost stood František Palacký, party patriarch and the historian and "father of the nation," whose seventieth birthday in June 1868 occasioned an enormous outpouring of public affection. He remained a sacrosanct figure to Young as well as Old Czechs, obliging the former to vent their anger against F. L. Rieger, his chief political associate since 1848 and son-in-law since 1853. Rieger, who became titular head of the party upon Palacký's death in May 1876, had not only negotiated the party's 1860 alliance with Clam-Martinic but would become the principal architect of its participation in the parliamentary "Iron Ring of the Right" during the eighties.

His long association with Palacký, his unquestionable patriotism
and honesty, and his great forensic and organizational skills
won widespread respect among Czechs of every political persuasion. His political career spanned more than half a century,
and he gave to Czech national politics one of its most enduring
slogans: "Nejdeme se"--"We shall never give in!" But Rieger
never believed the common people to be capable of determining
their own best interests, and as he grew older he became hyper-
sensitive to criticism and insisted on party obedience to his
will.[20] The fact that he seldom modified his moderately liberal
views to reflect the enormous changes occurring in Czech politics
and society made these views increasingly anachronistic and unpopular with each passing decade. Many Czechs would recognize
that his funeral in March 1903 not only commemorated the passing
of a great man but marked the end of an era in which men of
wealth and education had tried to take exclusive responsibility
for the direction of Czech national politics.

    Almost all Old Czech leaders, whether lawyers, scholars, busi-
nessmen, or landowners, came from the upper strata of Czech society. Antonín Otakar Zeithammer, a secondary-school teacher
turned politician in 1863, served not only as Rieger's personal
secretary and right-hand man but as an important party administrator and public spokesman. Zeithammer moved with ease in aristocratic and upper middle-class circles and acquired a reputation
for both sartorial and rhetorical elegance. An equally prominent
party theoretician and speechmaker was Karel Mattuš, long-time
chairman of the Mladá Boleslav district board and a leading representative of banking and business interests.[21] Jan Stanislav
Skrejšovský and František Šimáček won recognition as the ablest
Old Czech newspaper editors of the sixties and seventies, but
neither they nor their less talented successors ever equaled the
Grégr brothers in popular esteem and influence.[22] August Zátka,
the principal representative of wealthy Czech landed and commercial interests in south Bohemia, often worked hand in hand with
the conservative great landowners Charles Buquoy and Charles of
Schwarzenberg and during the nineties maintained České Budějovice
as an Old Czech bastion while almost all other municipal governments fell to the Young Czechs.[23] Prominent professors at
Charles-Ferdinand University also numbered among the most influential Old Czechs and included the historians Jaroslav Goll and
W. W. Tomek, the classical philologist Jan Kvíčala, the jurists
Antonín Randa, Jiři Pražák, and Bohuslav Rieger, and the political economist Albín Bráf. The latter two scholars were respectively F. L. Rieger's son and son-in-law.

    All Old Czechs believed that the rights and interests of the
Czech people could best be advanced with the assistance of the
Bohemian nobility and within the framework of the Habsburg Monarchy. Whether Catholic or not, all appreciated the conservative
and stabilizing influence of the Roman Catholic Church. They
considered themselves to be good patriots while regarding the

lower classes of society, the vast majority of the Czech nation,
as social and intellectual inferiors in need of benevolent and
informed guidance. These prosperous Old Czech scholars, lawyers,
and businessmen showed less concern with material interests in
politics or with making ends meet than did Young Czech farmers,
teachers, lawyers, artisans, or newspapermen. Because of this
and their generally better education, Old Czechs could pride
themselves on being able to take a more detached and informed
view of public issues than could their more radical and "opportunistic" political opponents.[24]

Conflicts within the National party during the sixties arose
primarily from long-standing disagreements on political issues
or tactics. For example, the conflict between party radicals
and moderates dated in part from differences of opinion on the
Polish insurrection of 1863 and in part from the Prague uprising
of June 12, 1848, which radical democrats including Sladkovský
and Vávra had helped carry out against the advice of Palacký and
Rieger. These conflicts intensified personal rivalry between
the leaders of each faction without in most cases leading to
personal antipathy or irreconcilable quarrels. As a rule, intra-
party disputes reflected class and occupational differences. Rieger and the predominantly upper middle-class Old Czech leaders
showed little appreciation for rough-hewn Young Czech editors
like Julius Grégr, Josef Barák, or Karel Tůma or for the many
small-town businessmen and farmers who predominated among the
Young Czech rank and file, especially when such fellows refused
to defer to the prerogatives and opinions of their better-educated
social superiors. Conflict between Young and Old Czech factions
intensified during the later sixties as Young Czechs more often
ran afoul of imperial laws restricting the press and public assembly. Young Czechs never let the national electorate forget
the fact that during the state of emergency enforced by Governor
Koller in central Bohemia from October 11, 1868, to April 28,
1869, their leaders had frequently endured fines and imprisonment
for advocating national autonomy and civil liberties while only a
few Old Czechs like Skrejšovský and Rieger had risked displeasing
the imperial authorities.[25]

Differences of opinion between Old Czechs and Young Czechs
corresponded in many respects to those between the two principal
Czech literary groups of the sixties and seventies: *Ruch* and
Lumír. The *Ruch* movement, established in the early sixties, gave
priority to patriotic themes in literature and published its
first *Almanach* in 1868. An editor of this publication, the young
poet and medical student Emanuel Engel, would serve as Young
Czech party chairman during the nineties; and the leading *Ruch*
figures of the seventies and eighties, like Svatopluk Čech, Alois
Jirásek, and Eliška Krásnohorská, remained sympathetic to the
more strident Young Czech nationalism. By contrast, the *Lumír*
group gave precedence to aesthetic criteria and to cosmopolitan
themes and won its greatest following among the wealthier members

of the intelligentsia and upper middle classes, who generally
supported Old Czech policies.[26]

The relationship between Old Czechs and Young Czechs during
the sixties and early seventies was affected by two other factions in the National party. The Catholic conservatives pulled
the Old Czechs toward the right while the radical democrats
tried to draw the Young Czechs farther to the left. The conservatives sought to retard the advance of liberalism and seculari-
zation and to restore to the Catholic Church a measure of its
former influence in public affairs. In these aims as in their
devout Catholicism, they differed markedly from Palacký, a Protestant, and from the majority of Old Czech leaders who, like
almost all Young Czechs, were at best nominal Catholics if not
free-thinkers. The Catholic conservative faction published its
own newspaper, Čech (The Czech), as a weekly beginning in 1869
and as a daily after 1871. Given the strongly anticlerical and
liberal character of politics in Bohemia, the Catholic conservatives recognized that if they constituted themselves as an independent party they would stand much less chance of advancing
conservative and Church interests than they would as the loyal
right wing of an influential National party associated with the
conservative great landowners. Therefore, they remained in that
party throughout the three decades in which it dominated Czech
political life.[27]

Scholars and middling-to-higher-ranking clergymen and imperial
officials predominated among the comparatively few adherents of
the Catholic conservative faction. Its leader for nearly forty
years was Wáclav Wladivoj Tomek, a prolific and respected historian and author of the monumental twelve-volume History of the
City of Prague. Also among its more forceful spokesmen were
Jakub Malý, a publicist and amateur historian, and Josef Jireček,
an educator and literary historian who in 1875 became chairman
of the Royal Bohemian Society of Sciences. A critic of every
manifestation of liberalism in the Czech national movement from
Havlíček in the early fifties to the Young Czechs and certain Old
Czechs of the sixties and seventies, Jireček had served for twelve
years as a secretary in the Ministry of Worship and Public Instruction before becoming minister during the short-lived Hohenwart
government of 1871. Hohenwart's Minister of Justice, the Czech
lawyer and legal scholar Karel Habietinek, not only opposed liberalism in politics, but, unlike Tomek, Jireček, and Malý, did
not wish to advance Czech national autonomy or Slavic reciprocity. He did not participate in partisan politics after his
appointment in 1879 to the upper house of the Reichsrat and two
years later to a series of posts on higher imperial courts.
Such very conservative Czech notables enjoyed very little political popularity or influence in Bohemia and by contrast made the
vast majority of Old Czechs appear to be staunchly patriotic and
liberal. Conservatism, Catholicism, and political deference to
the emperor as well as administrative and intellectual competence

helped insure the rapid rise of several conservative Czech Catholics to high offices in the imperial civil service where they
helped lend credence to the notion that this service stood
"above politics" and "above nationality."[28]

The radical democrats in the National party stood to the left
of the Young Czechs on most issues but shared their anticlericalism and advocacy of active participation in all representative
institutions. They wished to extend civil liberties primarily as
a first step toward resolving the social question and, despite
their fervent patriotism, had since the early sixties maintained
generally good relations with the nascent Czech workers' organizations that helped establish the first all-Austrian Social Democratic party in April 1874. The radical democrats also sought
with limited success to persuade the Young Czechs to take a more
sympathetic view of socialism and to try to represent working-
class as well as peasant and middle-class interests. After the
formation of an independent Young Czech party in December 1874,
the radical democrats constituted themselves as its left wing.

Four of the most popular radical democratic Young Czech leaders simultaneously pursued careers in journalism and in literature, and a fifth was a colorful renegade nobleman. The 1848
revolutionary Josef Václav Frič wrote propaganda for the Prussians to use against Austria in 1866 and later as an exile in
Berlin edited all ten issues of the short-lived radical democratic and antidynastic weekly *Blaník*, beginning in November 1868.[29]
Josef Barák, a popular publicist and sometime poet, and Jan
Neruda, one of the greatest figures in modern Czech literature,
served on the editorial board of the *Národní listy* after having
published their own radical daily, *Hlas* (The voice), between 1862
and 1868. In 1872, they founded the *Dělnické listy* (The workers'
news), a socialist fortnightly journal with a nationalist rather
than an internationalist outlook.[30] Jakub Arbes also wrote for
the *Národní listy* and *Hlas* during the sixties but thereafter concentrated on writing romantic social novels which exposed many
inequities in Czech society and on chronicling in multivolume
studies the repeated imperial abridgements of Czech civil liberties.[31] A fifth pioneer among radical democrats was the renegade
nobleman and lawyer, Prince Rudolf of Thurn-Taxis, who had since
1860 worked with radical Czech nationalists and had during the
Seven Weeks War endorsed Frič's anti-Habsburg agitation. In 1861
and 1862, he had also helped establish and later helped manage
the patriotic Czech singing society, Hlahol ("The Resounding
Peal"), which took as its motto "through song to the heart and
through the heart to the homeland." That Thurn-Taxis and subsequently Count Václav Kounic supported radical Young Czech policies inimical to the interests of both conservative and constitutional great landowners further demonstrated the fact that the
nobility in the Czech lands did not form a solid political bloc.[32]

Throughout the sixties and early seventies, the Young Czechs
did not leave the National party, despite many disputes with its

leadership and one abortive attempt to set up an independent
party on January 8, 1864.[33] A recognition of common interests
in advancing state rights and cultural and economic development
and a reluctance to divide the National party in trying times
kept the Young Czechs in the fold as partners as well as critics.
Imperial refusal to grant terms to the Czechs comparable to the
1867 Compromise with Hungary disappointed Young and Old Czechs
alike. At that time, Edvard Grégr confessed in his diary that
he could no longer believe in the eventual realization of an
"Austrian idea" acceptable to all nationalities.[34] Together
with other prominent National party members under Palacký's leadership, he took part in the May 1867 Czech "pilgrimage" to the
Moscow Slavic Congress in order to reassert Slavic solidarity
and protest the expected advent of dualism.[35] Also by way of
protest, the National party endorsed Rieger's having in 1869
brought Czech political aims directly to the attention of French
journalists and governmental officials and having tried to persuade Napoleon III that Austro-Hungarian dualism would in the
long run serve Prussian interests to the detriment of those of
France and of the Slavic and Roumanian citizens of the monarchy.[36]
But no Young Czechs, in contrast to many Old Czechs, ever thought
that appeals to Slavic solidarity or to friendly foreign governments, however useful in advertising Czech grievances or in
boosting national self-confidence, could satisfactorily advance
national interests unless Czechs also participated actively at
all levels of Cisleithanian political life.

In accordance with Rieger's policy of passive resistance, National party delegates did not participate in the Reichsrat from
1863 to 1879 or in the Bohemian Diet from 1872 to 1878. Such
steadfast adherence to passive resistance reflected not only a
refusal to compromise a state rights program by serving in institutions authorized by the February Patent and by the 1867 Compromise but also an expectation that the Habsburgs might suffer
another serious setback in foreign affairs and therefore have to
grant to the kingdom of Bohemia an autonomy similar to that enjoyed by the kingdom of Hungary.[37] At the time of his appeals
to France, Rieger expected the Habsburgs to intervene in any war
between France and Prussia and, after avenging their defeat by
Prussia at Sadowa, to improve the status of their Slavic subjects. When this did not come to pass during the swift German
victory over France in 1870 and 1871, Rieger pinned his hopes on
continued instability in the Balkans, where Russian support of
efforts by the Southern Slavs to liberate themselves from Ottoman
rule could be expected indirectly to advance the cause of Slavic
citizens in Cisleithania and in Hungary. These illusions vanished only after the 1878 Congress of Berlin checked Russian expansion and forced the newly independent Balkan states to relinquish part of their recent territorial gains at Turkish expense.
Only after this development, which appeared to increase the likelihood of stability in both Austro-Hungarian foreign policy and

domestic politics, did Rieger and the National party finally
abandon their boycott of the Bohemian Diet. In the following
year, 1879, both Old Czech and Young Czech delegates returned to
the Reichsrat to join the newly formed majority of the Iron Ring
of the Right, which appeared willing to make substantial cultural
and educational concessions to its supporters among the non-
German nationalities.

After 1874, the Young Czechs claimed increasingly to be the
heirs and continuators of the courageous journalist and patriotic
martyr, Karel Havlíček, the principal "political awakener" of
his countrymen who urged utilization of the press and representative institutions to advance liberalism and national autonomy.
Highly critical of authoritarian government in Russia as well as
in Austria, he advocated Slavic reciprocity as opposed to any
Russophile Pan-Slavism. Czech readers well understood that his
frequent exposure of shortcomings in Russian autocracy or British
rule in Ireland served simultaneously as veiled criticism of Austrian laws and institutions which would not arouse the wrath of
imperial censors. As editor from 1846 to 1848 of the government
newspapers in Czech, *Pražské noviny* (Prague news) and *Česká
včela* (The Czech bee), and as editor from 1848 to 1851 of the
liberal and patriotic journals *Národní noviny* (National news)
and *Slovan* (The Slav), Havlíček set an example of courageous
and objective journalism which future generations of Czech intellectuals and newspapermen would seek to emulate. For his outspoken criticism after 1849 of the reactionary policies of the
Bach and Schwarzenberg government, the imperial authorities sentenced him to confinement in exile at Brixen in the southern
Tyrol, where, isolated, ill, and impoverished, he remained three
and one-half years. His death from tuberculosis in July 1856,
attributed to this long confinement, made him the foremost Czech
martyr to Habsburg oppression and occasioned demonstrations of
patriotic solidarity and national mourning.[38]

Havlíček's legacy in word and deed served the newly founded
Young Czech party in at least three distinct ways. First, Czechs
from all walks of life so highly esteemed Havlíček both as a
politician and as a man of letters that the Young Czechs, by
identifying themselves as his heirs, could claim to have a predecessor comparable in stature to the Old Czech mentor, František
Palacký. To be sure, few National party members in eagerly
claiming one man or the other for their respective factions took
cognizance of the fact that both Palacký and Havlíček transcended
the faction that claimed them and so well interpreted respectively the history and the political problems of their nation that
Czechs of all political persuasions have, with the exception of
certain clerical leaders, expressed their intellectual indebtedness to them. Second, to Young Czech journalists who constantly
worked under governmental surveillance and threats of prosecution, Havlíček embodied that honest and fearless journalism to
which they aspired. Third, Havlíček, a man of extraordinarily

critical and wide-ranging intelligence and a great master of
Czech prose style, had also first formulated and clearly justified many of what became cardinal Young Czech policies. Among
his contemporaries, he had been the most articulate advocate of
universal manhood suffrage, civil liberties, and separation of
church and state, the three issues on which Young Czechs came to
differ most markedly from the Old Czechs. At the same time, he
had also been an early proponent of organizing Czech politics
from the ground up and building a sense of community through
"self-help" and public participation in politics from the lowest
level of government to the highest. To be sure, Young Czech
hagiographers of Havlíček, notably *Národní listy* editorialist
Karel Tůma, chose to emphasize if not exaggerate his radicalism
on certain issues and to play down his advocacy of peaceful and
responsible political behavior. On both counts, courageous advocacy and prudent conduct, Havlíček nonetheless provided the
nascent Young Czech party with a ready-made philosophical discussion of its programs and policies. Edvard Grégr in his inimitable and florid style best expressed the Young Czech idealiza-
tion of Havlíček in his May 1870 speech dedicating a memorial
plaque at the house in Prague where the great patriot died:

> Like an angel of the Lord calling past generations to a new
> life, Karel Havlíček with his great voice summoned our nation
> to a new life and to a struggle for freedom and justice and
> for its language, homeland, and glory. Not by the bloody
> sword or brute force of arms did he lead his holy struggle,
> but by his shining spirit, barbed wit, and clear intellect he
> vanquished the enemies of freedom and of our rights.[39]

Consonant with Havlíček's legacy, the Young Czechs always advocated a more "active" and more "democratic" state rights program than did the Old Czechs and opposed all efforts by the Old
Czechs and conservative great landowners to boycott the Bohemian
and Moravian diets, believing that all forums of public opinion
should be used to advance Czech aims, especially the diets and
their executive councils, which served as the guarantors of the
entire self-governmental track. They also repeatedly pointed out
that if carried to its logical conclusion this Old Czech policy
of passive resistance would also entail withdrawal of Czech representation from local and district self-governmental bodies, thereby allowing the German parties and imperial authorities to rule
by default.[40]
The most direct and forceful Young Czech opposition to passive
resistance during the sixties occurred at the March 31, 1867,
meeting of the National party trustees, as the Grégr brothers,
Karel Sladkovský, František Brauner, and Jakub Škarda constituted
the minority who voted against Rieger's proposal to withdraw
Czech delegates from the Bohemian Diet in order to protest the
special first-curial elections of February in which the great

landowners had, under imperial pressure, chosen for the first time a majority of centralist delegates who would insure that the Reichsrat endorsed the forthcoming Compromise with Hungary. However, the Young Czechs' desire to pursue more active and more liberal parliamentary policies independently of the conservative great landowners had not yet led them to disregard party discipline or refuse to support a state rights program broadly conceived. All National party delegates walked out of the diet on April 13, 1867, after signing a statement of protest; and all later endorsed the State Rights Declaration of August 22, 1868, and a boycott of the diet which lasted till August 30, 1870.[41]

In an effort both to persuade the imperial authorities to recognize Bohemian state rights and to arouse popular support for a state rights program, Young Czechs helped take the lead in organizing peaceful open-air demonstrations called *tábory* in Bohemia, Moravia, and Silesia. The name *tábor*, which literally means encampment, identified these mass patriotic assemblies with Hussite Tábor of old, whose ideas and heroic deeds continued to inspire Czech political leaders.[42] From May 1868 until the fall of the Hohenwart ministry in October 1871, almost a million and a half Czechs participated in the various tábory throughout the Czech lands, usually in defiance of police bans, to sing patriotic songs, to hear speeches by popular leaders like Edvard Grégr, Josef Barák, and Sokol chairman Miroslav Tyrš, and to demonstrate their support for Czech "freedom and independence." To set the proper patriotic mood, tábory generally assembled on sites hallowed in Czech history or legend, like Žižkov, the hill in suburban Prague where the Hussites under Jan Žižka had routed the armies of empire and papacy on July 14, 1420, or like Blaník, a mountain in south central Bohemia where the knights of Saint Wenceslas supposedly sleep awaiting a call to help save the Czech nation in perilous times.

On May 10, 1868, nearly 40,000 Czechs gathered atop Říp to hold the first tábor which would set the pattern for 142 others during the next three years. Říp, a dome-shaped hill arising from the middle Labe plain twenty-five miles north of Prague, was the place from which the legendary Father Czech had surveyed central Bohemia before instructing the first Czech tribes to settle there. Young Czech leaders from Podřipsko, the region surrounding Říp, who organized this tábor included Václav Janda, Václav Kratochvíl, Ervín Špindler, and G. Švagrovský.[43] The assembly on Říp, composed of large delegations from Prague and all principal cities of the Labe Valley, adopted a resolution calling for universal manhood suffrage to the diets and "the renewal of our historical rights which means nothing less than the freedom, independence, and separateness of the glorious Czech kingdom" based on terms like those obtained by Hungary in the Compromise of 1867.[44]

Imperial authorities, from the emperor down to district captains, took fright at the tábory which so effectively mobilized

Czech patriotism and enthusiasm for state rights and universal manhood suffrage.[45] Minister-President Taaffe therefore authorized the governor to declare a state of emergency in any district and to suppress Czech patriotic societies and newspapers along with the tábor meetings. The ensuing repression, comparable to that earlier unleashed by Schmerling, put hundreds of Czech reformers and patriots, including several dozen Young Czechs, behind bars for six months to five years. The authorities sentenced Young Czechs Janda and Kratochvíl to six months at hard labor for organizing the first tábor and gave even longer sentences to other organizers, like Karel Tůma, Jan Matous Černý, Josef Barák, and the young law student Bedřich Pacák. As Young Czechs, they later became prominent national political figures, Pacák as chairman of the party club of parliamentary delegates after 1900, Tůma as lead writer and Barák as responsible editor of the *Národní listy*, and Černý as a director of the patriotic Central School Foundation (Ústřední Matice školská). These imprisoned organizers became heroes of the national movement and inspired the organization of additional tábory in defiance of the police.[46] Imperial officials also jailed political activists from many other Czech organizations, including Oul (The beehive), a consumers' cooperative for workers, Jednatelství z Blaníka (The agency from Blaník), a radical student society, and the Sokol. Among the Czechs receiving the longest sentences were Čeněk and Vilém Körber, publishers of the secret journal *Pochoden z Blaníka* (The torch from Blaník), who called for "revolution" and the establishment of a republic and who collaborated with J. V. Fric in bringing out the anti-Habsburg *Blaník* in Berlin.[47]

The tábor assemblies enormously influenced future Czech political development. From them Czech politicians learned not only how to organize and manage mass demonstrations but to appreciate more fully the extent and force of popular aspirations for national autonomy and civil liberties. And Bohemian state rights won a new lease on life by becoming identified with these aspirations.[48]

The success of the tábor demonstrations hastened the formal split between Old Czechs and Young Czechs. The large crowds that assembled at the first tábory encouraged the six Young Czech delegates to the Bohemian Diet to oppose the majority decision of the National party in August 1868 to boycott sessions of the diet along with the conservative great landowners until state rights demands were met. Popular participation in tábory throughout the Czech lands also reinforced the Young Czechs' belief that a parliamentarily active patriotic and liberal party could win the allegiance of most Czechs who would be enfranchised by any future adoption of universal manhood suffrage. Unlike the National party leadership, they did not fear that the Czech masses would betray the national cause if given the vote.[49] They also recognized that given a mass electorate no party that aimed at

preeminence in Czech politics could long afford to maintain an
alliance with the great landowners.

By returning to the Bohemian Diet on September 15, 1874, in
defiance of the boycott ordered by the National party, the seven
Young Czech delegates led by A. Pravoslav Trojan and Edvard
Grégr took the step which led directly to the formation of an
independent Young Czech political party in December. This act
was the logical result of a long-held belief that nothing constructive could come from the National party's policy of passive
resistance. According to most Young Czechs, the short-lived Hohenwart ministry of 1871 had offered the last practicable chance
of realizing Bohemian state rights through association with conservative great landowners and a right-wing ministry. The
Czechs would have to make the best of a bad situation in which
passive resistance appeared even more futile in light of the
now-established Compromise of 1867 and the foundation of a powerful and united Imperial Germany in 1871. To Old Czech charges
that they had acted rashly in returning to the diet, the Young
Czechs replied that they had steadfastly refused to participate
in the body for more than three years after the emperor's dismissal of Hohenwart had indicated that he did not intend to grant
to Czechs any political autonomy comparable to that enjoyed by
most Germans and the Hungarians. Moreover, on November 23, 1873,
the last time at which National party delegates had voted on
whether or not to take their seats in the diet, the Young Czech
faction had commanded almost half, or thirty-five, of eighty-two
votes cast; and most attributed the Old Czechs' having mustered
a majority of forty-seven to Rieger's having threatened to resign
if the vote did not once again endorse his policy of passive resistance.[50] The Young Czechs therefore believed their decision
to participate in the diet not only served the public interest
but reflected the views of a majority of electors and of National
party delegates.

That the Young Czechs' defiant return to the diet in September
1874 generated great political controversy is evidenced by the
intemperate rhetoric employed by all parties. The *Národní listy*
set the tone for the liberal press by saluting the "seven Macca-
bees" who unsheathed the sword of political activism to defend
their homeland. At the same time, loyal Old Czech papers denounced "the seven Krauts" who carried "the national cross to
Golgotha."[51] Both sides also resurrected unresolved conflicts
of the sixties over such issues as passive resistance, the status
of Russian Poland, the controversy between *Ruch* and *Lumír*, the
interpretation of Bohemian state rights, the desirability of
tábor demonstrations, and continuing National party association
with the conservative great landowners.

The series of events that exacerbated existing tensions within
the National party and helped bring about the formal division
between Young and Old Czechs included the political repression

undertaken by Bohemian Governor Koller in 1871, the 1873 introduction of direct curial elections to the lower house of the
Reichsrat, the great economic depression beginning in 1873, the
return of Czech delegates from Moravia to the Reichsrat in January 1874, and the founding two months later of the Austrian
Social Democratic and Catholic Conservative parties. The ease
with which Governor Koller had intimidated the Old Czechs and
their aristocratic allies after October 1871 had further discredited their claims to exclusive national leadership and reinforced
Young Czech views that active parliamentary politics would better
advance the national cause than would passive resistance. Frequent intervention by district captains in the affairs of local
and district self-government during that period especially persuaded the Young Czechs that these institutions could not in and
of themselves adequately serve as a basis for advancing political
autonomy and civil liberties. Furthermore, Koller's relaxation
in 1873 of the state of emergency and extraordinary restrictions
on assembly and the press unintentionally facilitated the Young
Czechs' embarking upon active politics in the following year.

The direct four-curial election of delegates to the Reichsrat
authorized by the law of April 2, 1873, gave the liberal Young
Czech minority in the National party a chance to advance their
program by appealing directly to the electorate rather than to
the Old Czech majority among National party delegates in the Bohemian Diet.[52] Obviously, if they were to attempt such an appeal they would have to establish an independent party organization and slate of candidates. Both Young and Old Czechs had in
January petitioned against the introduction of direct curial
voting on the grounds that it violated Bohemian state rights by
bypassing the Bohemian and Moravian diets. But once this voting
order became law, the Young Czechs alone promptly considered how
they might make the best of what had appeared to be an undesirable situation.

The great depression that spread throughout central Europe
after the fall of the Viennese bourse in May 1873 diminished
Czech confidence in National party leadership as the infant Czech
banking system collapsed, as prices for agricultural produce
dropped, and as iron and steel production declined by two-thirds.
Moreover, many citizens who sought aid from provincial or imperial government to offset the ill effects of the depression could
expect little assistance from a party righteously committed to a
policy of passive opposition.[53]

Alois Prazák and the Czech deputies from Moravia who took
their seats in the Reichsrat on January 21, 1874, and announced
their intention to return to the Moravian Diet encouraged by
their example the Young Czech decision to resume participation
in the Bohemian Diet in the fall. Anticipating this reaction,
the conservative but pragmatic Prazák promptly warned Rieger
that should the National party persevere in passive opposition
it would surrender all political initiative to the "leftist"

Young Czechs.[54] Both the Moravian and Young Czech deputies recognized that the diets and the Reichsrat, despite their fundamentally powerless and unrepresentative character, remained among
the few institutions through which political parties might attempt to influence governmental domestic policies.

In deciding to break with the National party, the Young Czechs
also responded to the challenge of two new political parties
founded in Cisleithania in the spring of 1874. With some apprehension they noted the establishment in March of the new Catholic
"party of the right" led by former Minister-President Hohenwart
and aiming to make the National party one of several allies.
Young Czechs feared that such an alliance would draw the National
party into even greater dependence upon conservative interests,
thereby diminishing within it their own influence as well as that
of political liberalism.[55] They observed with somewhat less apprehension the emergence of a potentially powerful political rival to the left. Ten Czechs numbered among the seventy-four
delegates from working-class organizations and journals who on
April 6, 1874, at Neudörfl, founded the Austrian Social Democratic party with a platform based on the Eisenach program of German
Social Democracy. Thereafter the Young Czechs recognized that
they dared not long delay constituting themselves as an independent and popular political party if they wished to extend or to
retain their limited support among Czechs workers and tradesmen.[56]

The Young Czech Party and Its Program

On December 27, 1874, in Prague, the Young Czech faction of
the National party constituted itself as the wholly independent
National Liberal party (Národní strana svobodomyslná), thus completing the division of the Czech national movement begun eleven
and one-half years before. The first party congress, billed as
"the greatest political gathering held to date in all of Austria,"
brought together 800 delegates, including liberal-minded journalists and elected self-governmental representatives as well as the
seven Young Czech delegates who had defiantly returned to the Bohemian Diet in September.[57]

Karel Sladkovský, a former radical democratic revolutionary of
1848, chaired this congress and became the first Young Czech party chairman. He remained one of the most popular and influential
party members until his death at age fifty-six in March 1880.[58]
For his part in leading the June 12, 1848, Prague uprising and
in planning a second uprising for May 1849, the Habsburg authorities had sentenced him to death for treason on August 20, 1850,
but later commuted the sentence to twenty years imprisonment.
On May 13, 1857, he emerged from prison after amnesty, "broken
in health but not in spirit," and resumed political activity
following issuance of the October Diploma.[59] By that time he
had come to advocate the achievement of civil liberties and national autonomy by peaceful as opposed to violent means.[60]

Consonant with his staunchly liberal views, he authored in 1875
the first concrete Young Czech proposal for universal manhood
suffrage based on proportional representation.[61] Moreover, like
most party colleagues, he refused to embrace national chauvinism
or anti-Semitism, despite the fact that he considered German
Jews as well as Germans to be enemies of the Czech national movement. Although long vilified by the German press, he proposed
in 1879 as a member of the Prague city council that the local
German-speaking minority be proportionately represented on that
body. The Old Czech majority voted down the proposal. Sladkovský and his associate, the journalist Vincenc Vávra, best represented the transformation of the revolutionary democratic radicalism of 1848 into the cautious national and liberal Young Czech
radicalism of the sixties and seventies. Like all Young Czechs,
neither became reconciled to authoritarian rule or to the second-
class status of the Czech nation within the monarchy: they only
hoped that the introduction of constitutional government in 1860
would facilitate orderly political and social reform.[62]

Leaders of the newly independent Young Czech party came from
six principal groups, united by a common liberalism, nationalism,
and anticlericalism, and by opposition to the National party's
policy of passive resistance. Sladkovský and Vávra personified
the party's ties to the patriotic revolutionaries of 1848 who had
been martyred by the Habsburgs during the fifties. The radical
newspapermen Julius Grégr, Josef Barák, and Karel Tůma ran the
Národní listy, the principal Czech daily and party asset, and had
endured fines and imprisonment for having courageously criticized
the Schmerling and Auersperg governments. A third group included
doctors and scientists whose belief in scientific progress and
whose hostility to ideologies based on class or religious affiliation reinforced the liberal and anticlerical proclivities of the
party. Their participation in politics owed much to the example
of the great Czech physiologist, Jan Evangelista Purkyně, who
actively supported many Czech patriotic and cultural organizations as well as National party policies during the sixties.[63]

Edvard Grégr, the leading voice of Young Czech radical liberalism and foremost Czech critic of authoritarian monarchy and
Church, first entered public life as a medical doctor and writer
of popular scientific articles during the 1850s. After gradu-
ating from medical school in 1854, he also served as one of Purkyně's research assistants. His work with Purkyně and reading
of Darwin soon led to his publication of studies on anthropology,
Věčný boj (The eternal struggle), and on biology, "Darwin o vzni-
kání rostlin a živočichu na naši zemi" (Darwin on the origins of
flora and fauna in our lands).[64] Through these and other works
he helped popularize Darwin's theory of evolution and view of
nature as a struggle for survival but did not apply them to politics in any way that would justify the exploitation of one nation
by another. Because the Bach government had so thoroughly

proscribed public political life, Grégr viewed science and medicine as the two means by which he might best work for a more
just and rational ordering of society. A trip to Western Europe
in the summer of 1860 confirmed his desire to become a professor
of medicine, but hopes for national emancipation aroused by the
establishment of constitutional rule in Austria led him to enter
politics and journalism instead. He joined his younger brother
Julius on the editorial board of the *Národní listy* at its inception in January 1861 and took a more active hand in management
after Julius's imprisonment in 1862 for violating the draconian
Schmerling press law. That same year, he and Julius had helped
Jindřich Fügner and Miroslav Tyrs set up the first Sokol organization. By 1874, Edvard Grégr had emerged as the leading stump
speaker and parliamentary tribune of the Young Czech party and
henceforth devoted increasingly less time to scientific work.[65]

František Tilser, a prominent mathematician, numbered among
the most important officers, parliamentarians, and pamphleteers
of the Young Czech party during the two decades after its founding. He also taught descriptive geometry for more than forty
years, including twenty-seven as a professor at the Prague Technical Institute. Beginning in 1874, he represented the Young
Czech party for twenty-one years in the Bohemian Diet and after
1879 for nearly sixteen years in the Reichsrat, where he distinguished himself by drafting legislation for railway and canal
construction as well as for educational improvement and the advancement of civil rights. He served from 1884 to 1892 as chairman of the party club of Reichsrat delegates and in the Bohemian
Diet chaired the party club of delegates from its reestablishment
in October 1887 until February 1892.[66]

Elected representatives of district self-governmental boards
made up the fourth group of Young Czechs and included Václav Kratochvíl, Antonín Nedoma, and Ervín Špindler from Podřipsko, Karel
Adámek of Hlinsko, František Schwarz of Plzeňsko, and Jakub
Hruška of Německý Brod. Responsible to articulate local constituencies, they did not wish to see public works atrophy because
National party leaders maintained a principled but futile boycott
of the diet and the Reichsrat. This outlook they shared with
leaders of the National party in Moravia like Alois Pražák, Antonín Mezník, and Josef Fanderlík.

To the fifth party group belonged leaders of patriotic agrarian organizations, including Václav Janda, the "peasant king" of
Podřipsko. These leaders all thought that active party participation in the diets and Reichsrat would help improve economic
conditions and advance popular politics in the countryside.
Their peasant constituents were proud to be Czechs but took less
interest in the immediate realization of Bohemian state rights
than in obtaining concessions on bread-and-butter issues. Moreover, the passive resistance endorsed by Rieger and the privileged Prague intelligentsia did nothing to prevent the police

from confiscating peasant newspapers, breaking up peasant assemblies, or arresting peasant leaders for exercising rights supposedly guaranteed in the December Constitution.

The sixth group included the Prague lawyers who became the power brokers of the new party. Alois Pravoslav Trojan, a moderate veteran of 1848, always took sympathetic interest in peasant problems and chaired several patriotic and cultural societies; Jakub Škarda maintained close connections with business and banking interests; and Jan Kučera, long-time chairman of the party executive committee, had won popular esteem for having been the most forthright defender of newspapermen hauled into court by the two Auersperg governments. This trio took the lead in professionalizing the party's operations and advocated active and moderate policies to achieve greater national autonomy and civil liberties.[67]

The comprehensive Young Czech program adopted by the first party congress on December 27, 1874, and supplemented by the proclamation of the third party congress on September 14, 1879, formed the basis for all subsequent party programs and electoral manifestoes.[68] Party members more thoroughly discussed certain aims and more clearly explained their grounds for leaving the National party in three other contemporary documents: the November 28, 1873, proclamation by twenty-nine liberals favoring Czech participation in the Bohemian Diet; the manifesto issued by the seven Young Czech delegates upon returning the diet on September 15, 1874; and Edvard Grégr's widely circulated pamphlet, *K objasnění našich domácích sporů* (Toward an explanation of our domestic conflicts.)[69]

The first section of the December 1874 program listed as long-range goals the education and enlightenment of the nation and the establishment of free and democratic institutions for Czech society. This entailed freedom of conscience and equal rights for all religions, *"increasing the self-governmental authority of districts and communes,* and making every effort to oppose reaction whatever its guise or origin in order that the Czech nation might not again be overwhelmed by absolutism as after 1848."

The second section summarized earlier objections to Old Czech passive resistance and envisioned closer cooperation in the future among all Slavic peoples.

The third advocated an autonomous Czech state within Austria-Hungary, as the party promised not only to try to achieve "the *recognition and realization of the independence and self-government of the Czech lands on the basis of valid and inviolate state rights,* but also to strive for the promulgation of *a just law for the defense of nationalities in these lands* in order that in the future there will be no oppression of one nationality by the other."[70] Fourth, in contrast to the Old Czechs, the party advocated holding elections to the diet on "the basis of universal suffrage."[71] The fifth point, "education and enlightenment," asked for a separate Czech university in Bohemia and

various improvements in the elementary and secondary schools,
including free instruction, higher payment for teachers, an administration free from government intervention, and the equitable
distribution of state funds to both Czech and German schools.

The sixth paragraph dealt with "the material interests of the
people." The party committed its delegates "to the improvement
of agriculture, to the revival of industry and trade, and to
[the] support of working-class needs," without presenting any
specific planks to be implemented. In section seven the party
announced its intention to encourage popular participation in
political and national affairs and to submit bills to the diet
to fulfill its program. [72]

Young Czech efforts from 1874 to 1914 to have Czech become the
equal of German as the external and the internal official language of the courts and public administration in Bohemia and Moravia derived from three sources: pride, practicality, and
power. Czechs rankled at their legally sanctioned inferior status to Germans in lands where Czechs numbered two-thirds of the
population. Young Czechs contended that making Czech the equal
of German in public life would help consummate the work of the
National Revival; and T. G. Masaryk among others believed that
Czechs "had the most keenly felt their political subjugation" in
the inability to use their own language. [73] Czech workers and
peasants, unlike the middle classes, generally did not speak
German fluently and would find it especially helpful to have
justice and public administration conducted in their own language. Finally, the equality of the Czech language with German
in certain areas of civil service would increase the numbers of
Czechs there employed at German expense. Since the bureaucracy
served a political as well as an administrative function, Czechs
would then enjoy political influence in their native provinces
more in proportion to their wealth and numbers.

Young Czechs and Old Czechs continued to adhere to Bohemian
state rights in principle but could not agree on how those rights
should be defined or implemented. After 1874, continuing Young
Czech participation in the Bohemian Diet and efforts to increase
the authority of that body led to Edvard Grégr's 1876 remark
that Bohemian state rights without the necessary institutional
means to enforce them were "not worth a pipe of tobacco." [74] In
his 1874 "Explanation," he had asserted that in contrast to Old
Czechs the Young Czechs preferred to emphasize not only "historical" state rights but also the "natural rights" which under-
lay the original state rights program drafted by Brauner in
March 1848. [75]

The new Young Czech party differed from the parent National
party more in its tactics and constituency than in its political
principles or long-range goals. Although the Young Czechs continued to place much greater emphasis on the extension of civil
rights and suffrage, their formal split with the National party
in December 1874 arose primarily from a difference of opinion on

contemporary issues and from a desire to take up active politics
instead of passive resistance. An active policy under various
names remained a cardinal tenet of Young Czech platforms until
1914, with Young Czechs debating only the extent to which such
activity required cooperation with successive imperial governments.[76]

Up to 1897, Young and Old Czechs disagreed on what should be
the proper political relationship of the national movement to
the Bohemian and Moravian nobility. By 1863, Young Czechs had
challenged the Old Czech view that the alliance with the conservative great landowners would enhance the likelihood of achieving
greater national autonomy and economic prosperity. A majority
of Young Czechs, including the Grégr brothers, Janda, and Tilšer,
continued to oppose the alliance on principle, believing that
little good could come of tying Czech political fortunes to a
class that opposed all democratic and anticlerical measures and
did not have the best interests of ordinary Czech citizens at
heart. These men opposed deference to aristocratic leadership
generally and thought the Czech nation strengthened rather than
weakened by its lack of a genuine aristocracy.[77] Škarda, Adámek,
and Trojan numbered among the Young Czech minority that wanted
to avoid dependence on the great landowning nobles but that refused to rule out any alliance with them as a matter of principle.
By 1897, this became the majority view, thanks in large part to
the precipitous decline of the National party after 1890 and the
influx of many of its members into the Young Czech ranks.

In keeping with their advocacy of active and liberal politics,
the Young Czechs differed from the Old Czechs in favoring a multi-
party system in place of the single party which had heretofore
included all factions under the leadership of Palacký and Rieger.
In his "Explanation," Edvard Grégr on behalf of the Young Czechs
argued that the future success of the Czech national movement depended upon its adopting two features of modern liberal politics:
participation in parliamentary government and a system of competing political parties which reflected the differing interests
and opinions within the nation. Parties and parliaments did not
cause dissension within society, Grégr continued; instead they
provided the surest means of articulating and resolving those
long-suppressed conflicts between classes and between nations:
"Political parties are of great benefit to every state, for only
from the struggle among different policial parties arises true
and enduring progress."[78] The Young Czech party followed the
same argument in defending itself against Old Czech charges of
"deserting the nation," contending that a multi-party system
characterized modern Western and Central European nations, and
that a system of competing parties would ensure greater "honesty"
and a truer measure of strength between the various Czech interests and opinions.[79]

The Young Czechs adopted a more strident nationalism and more
doctrinaire anticlericalism and liberalism than the Old Czechs.

In keeping with their more democratic orientation, the Young Czechs advocated universal manhood suffrage, encouraged popular participation in politics, and included larger numbers of peasants, farmers, and tradesmen in their rank and file. On economic issues, the slight differences between the parties reflected the interests of their constituencies. The successive programs of both parties upheld the inviolability of private property and advocated tariffs, taxes, and regulation of cartels which would benefit Czech business and banking interests. Young Czechs differed from Old Czechs in advocating greater aid to Czech farmers and small businessmen.

Young Czech liberalism reinforced Czech nationalism and differentiated the Young Czechs from the German Liberal party, which refused to accept universal suffrage, equal civil rights for all nationalities, or the use of Czech language as well as German in all courts and public administration. The devotion of party delegates to liberal principles as well as national interests cannot be questioned, although Edvard Grégr probably spoke for a majority in the party when he remarked in 1879 that if forced to choose between national interests and liberal ideals, he would give precedence to the former.[80]

The Young Czech party's spirited defense of national and minority interests reflected its having originated in Podřipsko and its continuing to find support in other Czech districts along the "language frontier." Six of its seven delegates to the diet elected in 1874 and two more elected in 1875 represented rural districts along that "frontier." Six other members of the original party board of trustees also came from this area.[81] Prosperous and enfranchised Czech farmers of the central and eastern Labe valley generally continued to support the Old Czech party, while their counterparts in south Bohemia largely remained under the influence of Old Czech cadres and great landowning families like the Schwarzenbergs and the Buquoys. But the Young Czechs drew much greater support than did the Old Czechs from the nascent peasant movement of predominantly disfranchised middling to poorer peasants, whose interests were best represented after 1889 by the Peasant Union of the Kingdom of Bohemia, whose founder and chairman, Alfons Šťastný, remained from 1874 to 1894 a close associate of the Young Czech party. His 1872 brochure *On the Completion of Our National Program* advocated the promotion of national and peasant interests through a popular and active politics closely resembling that adopted two years later by the Young Czechs.[82] Josef Barák, in his 1881 speech, "Sword, Book, and Ploughshare," contended, as did many of the more radical Young Czechs, that any parties aiming to advance the political and economic welfare of the Czech nation would have to further the interests of its largest social class:

> The rural Czech peoples defended and preserved for us the
> maternal language which is the basis of our national

existence. . . . Poverty for the Czech peasants means
decline for all other Czechs. The prosperity of the
countryside comes as a golden rain to the nation.[83]

Young Czechs and Old Czechs as Complementary Parts
of the Same Political Movement

That very real differences of opinion on political tactics
and issues continued to divide Young Czechs and Old Czechs after
December 1874 should not obscure the fact that both parties remained complementary parts of the same political movement. This
is evident in party statements on policy, in deeds, and in the
similarity of party organization.

The Young Czechs always contended that they established an
independent liberal party to strengthen the Czech national movement and not to weaken or destroy the parent National party.[84]
When the seven Young Czech delegates to the diet took their
seats on September 15, 1874, in defiance of Rieger's orders,
they reaffirmed their loyalty to Bohemian state rights and argued
that this program and greater civil liberties could best be
achieved by parliamentary cooperation between all Czechs and Germans of liberal views.[85] Edvard Grégr, in his 1874 pamphlet, explained that the Young Czech party did not regard itself as the
antithesis of the Old Czechs but rather as their necessary complement and likened what should be the proper relationship between the parties to a well-regulated clock:

> The mainspring which unwinds to drive the clock is the Young
> Czech party. The weight which restrains this mainspring is
> the Old Czech party. If the weight were not present, the
> mainspring would run down too quickly; and if there were no
> mainspring as the driving force, the weight would stop the
> whole machine. Only where both parts are in a properly
> balanced and weighted relationship will the clock keep time
> correctly.[86]

The Old Czechs continued to regard the independent Young
Czech party as an erring partner which could eventually be
brought back into the fold. František Palacký in his May 1875
article, "On the Divisions within the Czech Nation," expressed
this view, to which his successor F. L. Rieger also subscribed.[87]
In contrast to the Young Czechs, who thought that competing
parties would be a boon to the national cause, the Old Czechs
considered any multi-party system to be detrimental and wasteful
because it diverted to domestic quarrels energies which could
better be spent on constructive mutual endeavors. In any case,
both parties agreed that any harm or benefit from the two-party
system would accrue not to one party but to the common national
movement of which each was a part.

The National party leadership also charged that the Young

Czechs had exaggerated the differences between the two parties
and even implied that they did so to advance selfish ends. Palacký and Rieger especially resented the Young Czechs' having
appropriated the title of "liberal party" (svobodomyslná strana)
and having labeled the Old Czechs by contrast as "conservative,"
"feudal," and "clerical."[88] The two men emphatically denied
that any such arbitrary distinctions could be made between the
two parties, stating that the Old Czechs had always considered
themselves to be liberals. Though both men had good grounds for
objecting to any Young Czech exaggeration of differences between
the two parties, Palacký's contention that the Young Czechs established themselves as an independent party primarily out of
personal ambition had no basis in fact.[89]

     That both Old and Young Czechs continued to function as parts
of one national political movement is best illustrated by their
cooperation in the Bohemian Diet and in Parliament during the
Taaffe era. By abandoning passive resistance in 1878, the Old
Czechs removed the principal obstacle to such cooperation and to
the joint adoption of a state rights program. On August 8 of
that year, Old and Young Czech delegates to the Bohemian Diet
formed a "state rights club" eight weeks before the opening of
the fall session. Neither party began to participate in the
Reichsrat until October 7, 1879, when their fifty-four delegates
elected in June jointly established a "Czech club" in Vienna.
Both parties expected to obtain substantial political concessions
from the government of Minister-President Eduard Taaffe, whom the
emperor had appointed on August 13, primarily because their participation would help give him a right-of-center majority and end
nearly a decade of German Liberal hegemony. On September 18, the
two parties, together with the Polish club, the conservative
great landowners, and Hohenwart's "German party of the right,"
formed a majority parliamentary bloc, soon called the "Iron Ring
of the Right" by the German Liberal opposition. These parties
sought to advance mutual interests by supporting the Taaffe
government, in which their representatives along with high-
ranking civil servants held all ministerial posts. Alois Pražák,
the leading Old Czech in Moravia, assumed the newly created post
of Ministr krajan, or Minister without Portfolio for Czech Affairs, and later served simultaneously as acting Minister of Justice, thus becoming the third Czech to serve in an imperial cabinet and the first to remain more than seven months.[90] Given
their long devotion to liberalism and distrust of aristocrats,
the Young Czechs associated with the Iron Ring much more reluctantly than did the Old Czechs but expected that the advancement
of Czech national interests would outweigh any slowdown in the
extension of civil rights.[91]

     Taaffe, a trusted friend of the emperor since childhood,
sought to rule with parliamentary support but without jeopardizing imperial authority or becoming beholden to any one party or
majority coalition of parties, including his own Iron Ring.[92]

He managed to stay in office more than fourteen years in part by adroitly playing one party off against another. At the same time, supported by the Iron Ring, he brought a measure of domestic tranquillity to Cisleithania but at the price of suppressing social democracy for nearly five years and postponing any serious attempt to deal with pressing social, political, and nationality problems. Thanks to Young Czech as well as German Liberal opposition, his Iron Ring never mustered enough support from its own or other parties to dismantle secular education, the May Laws, or the December Constitution. Taaffe initially obtained Old and Young Czech votes for the annual budget, the decennial tariff agreement with Hungary, and an enlarged army by partially fulfilling three of several aims posited by the Czech club's memorandum to him dated November 17, 1879. First, in the spring of 1880, the government issued language ordinances prepared by Karl von Stremayr for Bohemia and Moravia, which designated Czech in addition to German as an official external language in the courts and in branches of the civil service dealing directly with the public. Czechs thus obtained for the first time the right to use their native tongue to conduct all business with certain designated courts and governmental agencies; at the same time, all records relating to any case or transaction were still to be kept in German. Second, on February 28, 1882, by the division of Charles-Ferdinand University in Prague into separate Czech and German universities, Czechs acquired their own institution of higher learning with instruction in Czech in the humanities, liberal arts, and professional curricula.[93] This institution complemented the Prague Technical Institute, a fine Czech school of engineering and applied science founded in 1869.[94] Third, Taaffe's limited extension of the electoral franchise to the Reichsrat by the law of April 10, 1882, which reduced the tax requirement for voting in the third and fourth curias from ten to five gulden, enabled the Czechs to increase their representation in those bodies both absolutely and proportionately. The 1883 revision of the voting order to the chambers of commerce enabled Czechs to win in 1885 all second-curial seats to the diet from the chambers in Prague, Pilsen, and České Budějovice.[95]

Many Young Czech lawyers and district self-governmental officials, notably Alois Pravoslav Trojan, Jakub Škarda, Karel Adámek, and František Schwarz, affirmed by their transfer of party allegiance to the Old Czechs in 1879 and back to the Young Czechs in 1890 that they regarded both parties as complementary parts of the same political movement in which Young Czechs were boldly to chart new courses to determine whether or not the rest of the movement could safely and expediently follow. In 1879, after the National party had resumed active participation in the Reichsrat and the provincial diets, Trojan, Škarda, Adámek, Schwarz, and other like-minded politicians who had since 1874 served as Young Czechs in the Bohemian Diet took what they

considered to be the logical step of again becoming Old Czechs.
The same men rejoined the Young Czechs after the National party
had by endorsing the Agreement of 1890 in their opinion flouted
Czech public opinion and endangered liberal and state rights objectives. Neither in 1879 nor in 1890 did they consider their
actions to have been unprincipled or unduly opportunistic.[96]

The complementary nature of the two parties also manifested
itself in similar forms of party organization and in dependence
upon the same private and self-governmental institutions. Both
were typical cadre parties dominated by notables *(Honoratiorensparteien)* and based upon highly restrictive suffrage. Each was
comparable on a smaller scale to the National Liberal party in
Prussia, the German Liberal party of Cisleithania, the French
Radical party, and the democratic wing of the Polish club led by
Franciszek Smolka.

At their first party congress on December 27, 1874, the
Young Czechs organized themselves as an elite or cadre party
similar to the parent National party with a twenty-one member
board of trustees *(sbor zemských důvěrníků)* and with "trusted
men" *(místní důvěrníci)* in most localities chosen by local party
members.[97] The party congress, the highest party authority, convened periodically but at least once every six years and was composed of all "important" members and "friends," including all
trustees, leading journalists, local "trusted men," elected representatives to district and communal self-governmental bodies,
and delegates to the Diet and, after 1879, to the Reichsrat.

The Young Czechs at their second congress of November 2,
1875, enlarged their board of trustees to thirty-six members,
including all party delegates to the Bohemian Diet, and established as the basic party administrative cadre in every district
a committee of five "trusted men" *(pětka důvěrnická)* elected by
local party members. In turn, each committee of five *(pětka)*
sent to the board of trustees one representative, who there as
elsewhere spoke for local party needs and interests. Every committee of five took charge of party affairs in its district, including public meetings and publicity, scheduling speeches by
party delegates or candidates, and making preparations for local,
provincial and Reichsrat elections that often required formation
of ad hoc electoral committees. Each committee of five also reported regularly to the party executive committee and clubs of
Diet and Reichsrat delegates on public opinion and any strong political opposition locally and suggested how to obtain greater
local support for party candidates and programs.[98]

As a first step toward establishing an independent party the
Young Czechs had on April 20, 1873, organized their own "National
Club" *(Národní klub)* of Diet delegates within the framework of
the National party. This club, renamed in 1875 the "Club of the
National Liberal Party" *(Klub národní strany svobodomyslné)*, performed tasks similar to those of all clubs of parliamentary or
diet delegates in the Habsburg Monarchy. Under elected officers

and standing committees, the club coordinated all activities of
the party delegation, issued all public statements for that
delegation, and interpreted and enforced all guidelines for
policy and tactics designed by the party board of trustees.
With the return of the Old Czechs to the Bohemian Diet in 1878,
Young and Old Czechs merged their clubs of delegates in a joint
"State Rights Club" but again went their separate ways in 1887
after strong disagreement on national and civil rights issues.
Upon returning together to the Reichsrat in 1879, Young and Old
Czech delegates established a joint Czech Club (Český klub) that
undertook in parliament tasks almost identical to those performed
by clubs of party delegates in the Bohemian and Moravian diets.
Increasingly conservative Old Czech policies beginning in the
mid-eighties led the Young Czechs at their fourth party congress
of April 1887 to establish their own entirely separate club of
parliamentary delegates. Thus, from 1873 to 1887, the relationship of Young to Old Czech delegates closely reflected that between the Young and Old Czech parties generally.[99]

The party board of trustees stood next to the party congress
in authority and met at least annually to review and, if necessary, modify party policies and organization. The third party
congress of September 14, 1879, after authorizing the return of
Young Czech delegates to the Reichsrat, enlarged the board of
trustees by adding these delegates to those from the Bohemian
Diet, to the trusted men representing committees of five, and to
the twenty-one board members elected by the congress itself.
Given this composition, the board thereafter grew in size as
party membership and influence increased, especially from 1889
to 1895. Every party congress delegated to the board of trustees
the responsibility for managing party affairs and determining
party policies until another congress could be convened. To insure that the party represented "the will of the Czech nation,"
the board was also obliged to approve all official party statements or policies, establish rules of discipline for all parliamentary and Diet delegates, and sanction any agreements negotiated between these delegates and the government.[100]

To handle day-to-day party administration and finances, the
board of trustees elected from its midst and funded an executive
committee (výkonný výbor) of seven members, increased to thirteen
by 1888 and to twenty-two in 1894. The board as a whole retained
the right to make changes in party policies or programs, including as it did representatives from all permanent party administrative units, including all members of the executive committee
and of the two clubs of delegates as well as one representative
from every committee of five. Having such broad representation
facilitated the board's authority to resolve any disagreements
on policy or tactics that arose among party administrators,
"trusted men," and Diet or Reichsrat delegates.[101]

Young Czech like Old Czech trustees and "trusted men" were
usually persons of property and some social standing in their

communities. In their fiscal conservatism and advocacy of private enterprise, they differed much less from Old Czechs than in
their fervent advocacy of civil rights and during the seventies
and eighties, their desire to extend suffrage at all levels of
self-government. As the Young Czech party grew to include many
diverse rural and urban interests by the early nineties, the
three successive party chairmen, Karel Sladkovský, František
Tilšer, and Emanuel Engel, encouraged lively private debate of
policy among party members before stating their own opinions to
delegates or trustees. By contrast, Palacký and Rieger ruled
the comparatively much more homogeneous Old Czech party with a
firm hand and could usually expect majority acceptance of their
recommendations.

Similarities in the organization, policies, and tactics of
the Old and Young Czech parties were in large part determined by
the unrepresentative system of self-government instituted during
the sixties. However much the Young Czechs might criticize or
disavow the Old Czech alliance with the conservative great landowners, they could not escape returning to it once they became
the majority Czech party obliged to work within the unrepresentative political institutions which that alliance had helped establish. To understand how the Young Czechs became the dominant
rather than the junior party in the Czech national movement, one
must thoroughly survey the institutional foundations of the party
that conditioned its organization and policies and its interrelationship with Czech society.

4

The Institutional Foundations of the Young Czech Party

The middle-class leadership, the cadre organization, and the nationalist and liberal policies of the Young Czech party can only in part explain the preponderance it achieved in later nineteenth-century Czech political life. In order to understand more fully how the party rose to preeminence one must examine the interplay between the party and those governmental and private institutions that conditioned its growth and through which it influenced the development of Czech politics and society. Such an examination reveals party strengths and weaknesses as well as those forces that helped define policy, including those uncompromisingly patriotic, liberal, and anticlerical platforms that enjoyed great popular support. This also helps explain why the Young Czech party remained so closely tied to the Czech middle classes and why, despite its claim to be *the* national party, it could not win the allegiance of all social classes and thus become a mass political party.

Governmental institutions to be considered in relation to the Young Czech party are those of local self-government (*samospráva* or *Selbstverwaltung*) at the provincial, district, and communal levels. Private institutions may be divided into three principal groups: commercial institutions--including banks, corporations, and cooperatives--the press, and patriotic and cultural societies. Each type of institution interacted with the party in a particular way. The institutions of local self-government provided the principal basis for the limited political autonomy enjoyed by the Czechs in Austria from Solferino to the First World War. Besides carrying out important governmental functions subject to review by imperial officials, these institutions provided the framework for Young Czech and Old Czech party cadres and helped shield Czech patriotic and cultural organizations from arbitrary police interference. It is therefore not surprising that most Young Czechs, like Karel Pippich, believed "the school of self-government" to be "the best school for politics."[1]

Among the enormous changes wrought by industrialization and urbanization on nineteenth-century Czech society was the growing influence of Czech corporations and cooperatives on party politics. And behind these institutions stood a strong Czech banking network which provided that fiscal independence from Viennese capital necessary to the success of an autonomous Czech political development. Every Czech political party relied upon the support of its own press, especially the Young Czechs, whose popularity may in large part be explained by their close association with

the largest and most influential Czech daily, the *Národní listy*.
Finally, various Czech patriotic and cultural societies provided
both a community of opinion and an institutional framework propitious to party growth.

Self-Government

The growth of political parties as well as the great constitutional crises in the Habsburg Monarchy during the nineteenth century cannot be understood apart from the development of governmental institutions and policies. Oscar Jászi aptly remarked
that anyone who seeks to understand that Monarchy must carefully
examine the relationship of peasant to local police official.
Revolution in 1848 eliminated arbitrary manorial political authority along with serfdom, only to have the Bach government then
substitute the authority of police officials for that of the
manor. The establishment of limited constitutional rule in the
sixties brought a measure of local self-government to all peoples
in Cisleithania without eliminating police supervision. Since
Czechs enjoyed the greatest political autonomy at the district or
communal levels of self-government, they usually there initiated
political as well as cultural and commercial activity. Czech
patriotic societies, cooperatives, savings and loan associations,
and political party cadres usually originated locally and only
later developed or merged into national organizations. All developed through private initiative and voluntary financing and
emphasized disciplined cooperation for the achievement of mutually desirable goals. They advanced with self-governmental support and often in the face of imperial harassment. On all these
grounds, they reflected an individualistic as well as a fraternal
and patriotic national outlook.

The policies and tactics of both the Old and Young Czechs only
become intelligible if one always keeps in mind the disparity between the substantial powers they exercised locally and their
relative impotence at the provincial and Cisleithanian levels of
government.[2] Party members could act boldly in the relatively
powerless Reichsrat, where they had little to lose and enjoyed
immunity from prosecution for their speeches. But local self-
governmental officials acted cautiously in order to avoid intervention of the district captain in matters where they already
enjoyed considerable discretion in the exercise of autonomous
powers. Debates in the Reichsrat on matters affecting local
politics may appear petty or irrational if considered only from
the imperial point of view; considered in relation to local problems, they concern the fundamental issues of public life. Control of a local school board or the appointment of judges to a
local court affected virtually every aspect of life; once aroused
to the possibilities inherent in local self-government, Czechs
would no longer be satisfied with administrative solutions imposed from above.

To assess the considerable influence of local self-government upon the development of the Young Czech party in particular and Czech society in general requires a more detailed survey of its powers and problems. It will be remembered that the most striking characteristic of Cisleithanian government was its two-tracked nature, a compromise in fact between the authoritarian imperial bureaucracy, which wished to control all governmental matters, and the newly established provincial diets, which wished to retain a large measure of authority. The law establishing this compromise also attempted to placate some of the demands for local autonomy in an empire comprising many nationalities and privileged classes.

The system of communal self-government established by imperial law no. 18 of March 5, 1862, varied in its institutional arrangements but not in its essential responsibilities and powers from province to province.[3] In Bohemia, in accordance with provincial laws no. 7 of April 16, 1864, and no. 27 of July 25, 1864, governing bodies were responsible through a locally elected District Board of Representatives (*Okresní zastupitelstvo, Bezirksvertretung*) in each district to the Provincial Executive Council (*Zemský výbor, Landausschuss*) elected by and responsible to the diet (*Zemský sněm, Landtag*).[4] Moravia and Silesia never established the district boards but followed the Bohemian pattern in other respects.[5] By 1882, the diets in the Czech lands had abolished the regional self-governmental bodies utilized by the Bach administration as intermediaries between province and district. This made the district the largest possible unit of self-government in each province and thereby encouraged a more autonomous and democratic political development by creating more elective offices of responsibility and giving voters more direct control over their own affairs. This was especially true in Moravia, where, in the absence of district boards, communes constituted the largest unit of local self-government. German attempts to revive regional government, usually in the name of "efficiency" or "reform," always aroused Czech opposition. The Germans regarded its revival as a step toward the administrative division of Bohemia into separate Czech and German areas and as a means of enabling German officials in certain regions to overrule Czech district boards. Most Czechs viewed its revival as an attempt to undermine the powers they enjoyed through district self-government and reestablish that "regional authority" they associated with the odious Bach era.[6]

The law of March 5, 1862, applied universally at the communal level throughout the Czech lands and established the commune (*obec, Gemeinde*) as the basic unit of self-government responsible for all persons, goods, and communications in its territory. Eleven cities in the Czech lands acquired special charters which exempted them from responsibility to district authorities and placed their self-governing bodies under direct supervision of the Provincial Executive Council,[7] but their governmental

structure corresponded to that of the communes in most essentials.
The law differentiated between autonomous powers *(samostatné
púsobnosti)* and delegated powers *(přenesené púsobnosti)* of local
self-government.[8] Delegated powers comprised those tasks carried
out for the imperial authorities at communal expense, the most
important being tax collection and the recruitment and quartering
of soldiers. In theory, locally elected officials remained responsible to local constituents while performing delegated powers.
The district captain *(okresní hejtman, Bezirkshauptmann)* could
hold them responsible for fulfilling these lawful duties; but
since they acted on behalf of the state and not as its agents, he
could not hold them directly responsible to himself or his office.
His having to take legal rather than administrative action against
local elected officials thus made his intervention less arbitrary.

Through exercise of autonomous powers, communes enjoyed considerable discretion in managing their own affairs. All communes
administered education, public health, public utilities, and communications facilities. Many communes and municipalities set up
profitable public utilities, food processing plants, and public
transportation systems. Larger municipalities like Pilsen also
ran their own orphanages, hospitals, swimming pools, poorhouses,
and public housing units.[9] Many municipally or communally owned
industries concentrated on the production of building materials,
which could be sold if not used by the cities for construction
and maintenance. For example, large municipal forests and lumber
yards contributed greatly to the prosperity of Písek. In municipalities and in district seats, urban planning was conducted at
an advanced level with great concern for aesthetic appearance and
preservation of historical monuments as well as for proper hygiene
and adequate transportation.[10]

Communal and district self-governmental bodies could not have
undertaken such projects without a steady source of revenue. An
expanding and prosperous economy provided an adequate tax base,
and accountability to the Provincial Executive Council for collection and expenditure of taxes generally prevented profligacy
or corruption. Thorough annual inspections turned up very few
cases of governmental abuse of public funds. One notorious exception to the rule was the communal government in Horní Bělá,
Bohemia, which for five years pilfered from the public welfare
funds by submitting false budgets to the district board in
Manětín. Within the limits set by law, officials enjoyed some
discretion in determining assessments and in raising funds for
local enterprises after necessary monies had been collected for
the provincial and imperial authorities. Local taxes or bond
issues often exceeded taxes raised for the higher authorities.[11]

Supervision of self-governmental institutions by an elected
body apart from the imperial bureaucracy increased their powers.
The Provincial Executive Council served as both the executive
body and highest court of appeal for the entire self-governmental
track.[12] Although the imperial authorities could readily and

directly intervene in the affairs of any local self-governmental
bodies, the right of petition by these bodies to the Provincial
Executive Council, itself subject to being overruled by the governor, served to discourage the district captain from taking
rash or ill-considered actions. The right of appeal to the Provincial Executive Council against elected officials either dere-
lict or overzealous in performing their duties generally assured
an honest and relatively efficient local government. This right
also helped insure that elected German officials would respect
the rights of the Czech minority in predominantly German areas.
Among the many reasons why Young Czechs opposed the Agreement of
1890 was their fear that these rights might be endangered if the
proposed separation of Czech and German self-governmental systems
were to be carried out at all levels, including the Provincial
Executive Council.[13]

Cooperation among representatives of the various Czech self-
governmental institutions occurred regularly through the diet and
the Provincial Executive Council and informally when these bodies
were not in session. Beginning in 1907, Czech officials from all
levels of self-government held an annual Congress of Czech Cities
(Sjezd českých měst) at which they discussed topics of mutual interest and made plans to coordinate such activities as legislative lobbying and the improvement of roads, sewers, and waterways.[14]

Authoritarian governmental practices and class privileges had
long characterized Austrian society; the emperor and the privileged social strata reluctantly conceded to local self-government
only those limited powers which changing circumstances made necessary. To compel even this concession, it had taken revolution in
1848, a humiliating defeat at Solferino, and unrelenting pressure
from the non-Germanic nationalities. The danger to imperial prerogatives in granting even limited powers to self-governmental
bodies appeared to be mitigated by the fact that highly restrictive three-class suffrage insured control of these bodies by local
notables and men of property. But the authorities underestimated
both the disaffection of the non-German propertied classes and
their capacity for fully exploiting the limited powers of self-
government.

The law of March 5, 1862, established three-class voting for
communal self-government, in which electors carried weight in
proportion to the amount of direct taxes they paid.[15] The small
number of wealthy citizens who paid the first third of all direct
taxes elected a third of all town council representatives. The
more numerous second class and the very numerous third class of
voters likewise each paid a third of all taxes and cast one-third
of the ballots. Those taxpayers contributing the upper one-sixth
of direct taxes automatically served on the local council. Men
of certain professions, collectively called the notables, received the right to vote whether they paid direct taxes or not.
They included court, state, and provincial officials, army

officers whether on active duty or retired, doctors with academic
degrees, higher echelons of teachers and administrators in local
and district schools, and local priests, clergymen and rabbis.[16]
Open balloting offered many opportunities for subtle persuasion
or intimidation. This electoral system excluded factory workers
and landless peasants and severely limited the participation of
small farmers and tradesmen in community affairs. A typical
example was Královo Pole, a Brno suburb, where in 1902 only 15
percent of the 10,228 inhabitants elected all representatives to
the communal self-governing board.[17]

The law of March 5, 1862, also upheld the privileged status
of the great landowners by allowing them with permission of the
diet to withdraw their great landed estates from communal or
district supervision. They lacked only the authority to exercise
police powers over residents on their estates or to call on
neighboring communes for welfare services. After stormy debate,
the diets in the Czech lands voted to allow the estates autonomous powers only on matters pertaining to highway maintenance,
building construction, and game laws.[18]

Imperial authorities erred in believing that retention of
class voting and aristocratic privileges at local levels of
government would promote political tranquillity. Slower rates
of economic development and less vehement strife between nationalities kept local government in Galicia and the Alpine regions
securely in the hands of the privileged classes. But in the
Czech lands, where the contending nationalities were more evenly
matched, local self-government provided an excellent vehicle for
the realization of national ambitions. Rapid industrialization
and growing prosperity in commerce and agriculture promoted social unrest through rising expectations. This prosperity also
enabled more Czechs to qualify as voters in the third and fourth
curias and to buy their way collectively or individually into
the first or second curia, through purchase of land or industrial stock.

The law of March 5, 1862, indirectly fostered close ties between local self-government and national political parties by
allowing self-governmental officials to voice publicly their
views on provincial and imperial as well as local affairs. Locally elected officials in Prussia, France, and Russia did not
enjoy this privilege, which encouraged mayors and town officials
in Cisleithania to serve as delegates to the diet or to the
Reichsrat while directing at a local level the affairs of national political parties.[19]

The influence of limited self-government on the growth and
policies of the Young Czech party may best be seen in the two
higher institutions of that system, the Provincial Executive
Council, elected by and responsible to the diet, and the District Board of Representatives, elected by four-curial voting in
every district. In each of the Czech lands, the Provincial Executive Council served both as the executive branch of the diet

and as the highest authority and court of appeal for the whole
system of limited self-government. In Bohemia, its chairman was
the provincial marshal and in Moravia and Silesia, the provincial captain, these posts being filled by imperial appointment
after nominations from the diets. In Bohemia and Moravia, the
Provincial Executive Council numbered eight members and in Silesia, four. Each of the first three curias of the diet elected
one-quarter of the delegates to the council, with the remaining
one-quarter elected by the diet at large. By excluding the
fourth curia, that representing the greatest number of citizens,
from electing delegates as a curia, the law insured that the
Provincial Executive Council would be even less representative
of all citizens than the diet. This also explains why the Young
Czechs could maintain a majority of Czech seats on the Bohemian
council after the Agrarians became the majority party in the
Bohemian Diet of 1908. In Bohemia and Moravia, the great landowners were assured of two seats on the council in addition to
the provincial marshal and thus held the balance of power in any
dispute between Czech and German delegates, who generally numbered three each. This composition of the council had long encouraged Old Czech cooperation with the great landowners and
would encourage the Young Czechs to do likewise once they became
the majority Czech party in the Bohemian diet.

The Provincial Executive Council served as the executive arm
of the diet, responsible to that body in all its actions. While
the diet was not in session, the council could act in the name
of the diet subject to confirmation by the diet upon its recon-
vention. In its capacity as the highest authority for the whole
self-governmental system, the council supervised provincial agriculture, trade, finance and banking, communications, public education, libraries, and public health. It delegated powers of
supervising agriculture and education respectively to the Provincial Agricultural Council *(Zemská zemědělská rada)* and the Provincial School Board, each of which in turn delegated authority to
local boards. The Provincial Executive Council worked with the
chambers of commerce in the compilation of statistics for and
regulation of trade and banking. Powers of the council were
themselves circumscribed because the council had no executive
apparatus. To enforce decisions it had to rely on the police
and armed forces responsible solely to the governor.[20] Furthermore, in any dispute between the elected officials of self-
government and the bureaucracy, it could be overruled by the
governor's office.

Since the Provincial Executive Council served as guarantor
and as supervisor of the entire self-governmental system, all
political parties and interest groups sought to influence its
composition and decisions. In its capacity as the highest executive body, the council could insure that self-governing bodies
in predominantly Czech areas could pursue legitimate business
without fear of excessive imperial intervention. It could give

a fair hearing to Czechs deprived of their legal rights by German self-governing bodies in predominantly German areas. For
example, the spread of schools privately constructed by the Central School Foundation *(Ustřední Matice školská)* and the aid to
Czech minorities rendered by the various National Unions *(Národní
jednoty)* could not have been effectively carried out without this
assurance. Young Czech opposition to the Vienna Agreement of
1890 arose in large part from recognition that Czech minorities
and Czech patriotic organizations in predominantly German areas
might suffer if the division of all administration and self-
government in Bohemia into separate Czech and German systems prevented their appealing to the Provincial Executive Council and
required them to appeal instead to the executive body of a German
Bohemia dominated almost exclusively by German interests.

Provincial law no. 27 of July 25, 1864, established a District
Board of Representatives in each of the eighty-nine districts of
Bohemia as the intermediate body responsible to the Provincial
Executive Council for the supervision of all communal self-
governmental bodies within its borders. Membership of the boards
varied from eighteen to thirty-six according to the size of the
district, and triennial election of members by four curias insured that any board would be run by the privileged classes.
Large estate owners comprised the first curia, all citizens paying a direct tax in excess of 100 gulden the second, representatives of commercial and industrial organizations the third, and
rural communes the fourth. From its membership the district
board elected an executive council *(okresní výbor)* of six members and as its presiding officer, a mayor *(starosta)*, the
latter subject to confirmation by the emperor.[21] In predominantly Czech districts, Czechs controlled all curias or all but
the first and were therefore assured of controlling the board
itself. The board's powers to set policy for and supervise all
functions of communal self-governmental bodies gave effective
control over self-government throughout Bohemia to commercial
and industrial interests and larger estate owners.

District boards provided the principal institutional basis
for both the Old and Young Czech parties. F. L. Rieger hailed
their establishment by the Bohemian Diet in July 1864 as a desirable complement to communal government and as a step toward
fulfillment of Bohemian state rights, and his words of praise
were echoed through the years by prominent figures in both parties.[22] Illustrative of the importance of district boards in
party development was the growth of strong Young Czech party organizations in Podřipsko, Hlinsko, and Plzeňsko, under the respective leadership of Ervín Špindler, Karel Adámek, and František Schwarz, and the development of Old Czech party cadres in
České Budějovice, Jičín, and Mladá Boleslav under August Zátka,
František Dolanský, and Karel Mattuš.[23] Schwarz and Adámek,
Young Czechs who rejoined the National party in 1879, brought
their district organizations back into line behind the Young

Czechs during the 1890 campaign against the Agreement of 1890.
In fact, the overwhelming defeat of the Old Czechs in the 1891
Reichsrat elections may in part be attributed to the defection
of most of their district cadres to the Young Czechs.

Since local self-governmental officials could simultaneously
hold seats in the diet and in the Reichsrat, their personal influence permeated all levels of party organization and activity.
Many likewise served as editors of regional or national party
papers and held offices in patriotic organizations. They constituted, in effect, the party itself. Of forty-five Young Czech
deputies elected to the Reichsrat in 1897, at least thirty had
entered politics through communal or district political organizations; at least twelve had served at one time on editorial
boards of local or national newspapers; and at least eighteen
simultaneously held office in one or more patriotic or cultural
societies. Comparable figures for the eighty-eight Young Czech
delegates elected to the Bohemian Diet in 1895 are fifty-one,
nineteen, and twenty-seven.[24]

The inability of the Young Czechs to establish themselves in
Moravia can be partially explained by the absence of district
boards in that province. In Moravia communal self-governmental
bodies were responsible in financial and self-governmental matters directly to the Moravian Provincial Executive Council.
Without district boards, privileged urban or industrial interests
could not directly control the poorer or more rural communal self-
governmental bodies as they did in Bohemia. This fact alone cannot account for Young Czech weakness in Moravia. A more restrictive suffrage to the Moravian Diet obtained until 1905 which
excluded the small and middling peasant landholders whose counterparts in Bohemia had supported liberal Young Czechs during
the eighties and early nineties. And in a devoutly Catholic province, liberal and anticlerical Young Czech programs had less
appeal. Cognizant of this fact and unable to rely on district
boards, the Moravian liberals, unlike the Young Czechs, advocated
extension of universal suffrage to the lower levels of self-
government and allied as equals with other anticlerical groups,
including the Agrarians and the Social Democrats.[25]

The system of local self-government in Bohemia not only provided the principal institutional basis for the Young Czech party
but also exercised manifold influence upon party development.
The retention of class or curial suffrage at every level of self-
government after universal suffrage had been introduced for
Reichsrat elections insured that notables and the propertied
upper middle class would continue to exercise a decisive voice in
the making of Young Czech policies. As popular support was captured by parties more responsive to a mass electorate, the Young
Czechs relied even more upon the support of privileged commercial and industrial interests. The party, having always relied
on local cadres and district boards to fulfill those tasks which
normally devolve upon a branch of a political party, never

developed a centralized organization and branches comparable to
those of the more popular Social Democratic, National Socialist,
and Agrarian movements. The influence of district boards on
party policy, like that of patriotic and cultural societies, was
transmitted primarily through personal rather than institutional
relationships. This in large part accounts for the great importance of personality and personal conflicts in determining Young
Czech party policies.

The close ties between the Young Czechs and the institutions
of local self-government also help explain the increasingly greater reliance by the party upon practicality and compromise in its
tactics and upon bargaining with successive imperial governments
for concessions. The party in Bohemia that controlled the institutions of district self-government could best allocate and
profit from imperial subsidies to transportation, public welfare,
industry, and agriculture. Practicality and caution became the
rule for Young Czech mayors and members of district boards who
did not want to provoke intervention by the district captain and
risk losing their vested interests. After 1891, tension built up
within the party between those members who derived their powers
from membership in district boards, most of them former Old
Czechs, and those who did not. Among the latter, newspaper editors, seeking to stir up popular support, and Reichsrat delegates,
enjoying immunity so long as parliament was in session, could afford to speak more critically of imperial policies. This intra-
party tension is perhaps best illustrated by the thirty years of
disagreement on party tactics between old friends, Julius Grégr
and Ervín Špindler, mayor of the Roudnice District Board and
leading party figure in Podřípsko.[26]

The extensive power Young Czechs enjoyed through control of
district boards based on a highly unrepresentative curial suffrage
precluded any alliance or substantial agreement on issues between
them and the leadership of the new mass parties. After the turn
of the century, Czech Socialists, Agrarians, National Socialists,
and Progressives all explicitly attacked Young Czech entrenchment
in the privileged institutions of district self-government and
campaigned for universal suffrage not just at one but rather at
all levels of government.[27]

František Schwarz's many articles on self-government and his
fictional but partly autobiographical stories about district
mayor Václav Dobrovský reveal the importance of self-government
to later nineteenth-century Czechs as an institution that allowed
them to determine their own destinies to an unprecedented degree.
Starosta Václav Dobrovský, reformátor obce Nezdarovské (Mayor
Václav Dobrovský, reformer of the Nezdarov commune) told how the
fictional commune of "Failure" came to prosper after individual
citizens cooperatively applied their energies and abilities
through communal self-government.[28] By intelligently exercising
the "autonomous powers" of that government and by founding local
cooperatives and corporations, including a sugar refinery,

Dobrovský and his associates transformed a backward village into
a thriving community. The sequel, *Působení Václava Dobrovského
jako okresního starosty* (The work of Václav Dobrovský as district
mayor), showed how the successful communal politician traveled
to the district seat, Spáňova or "Sleepy City," where he helped
make both city and district a thriving modern community.[29] Although Dobrovský, a Czech Horatio Alger, was more consistently
successful than real-life prototypes like Karel Adámek or Karel
Mattuš, he helps illustrate why Czechs of a century ago so enthusiastically embraced self-government.

The enormous influence of self-government in Czech politics
may also be appreciated if viewed in light of the long-standing
Czech tradition of regional loyalty. An intense regional as well
as national patriotism moved most Czech politicians, writers, artists, and scholars of the nineteenth century. This is illustrated by the popularity of regional museums, literature, and
historical journals and is reflected in the works of such different authors as K. H. Mácha, Petr Bezruč, Karolina Světlá, and
Viktor Dyk. Works on local history occupy an especially important place in modern Czech historiography. Among the fine multivolume classics are Dobiáš's history of Pelhřimov, Nejedlý's
study of Litomyšl, Sedláček's history of Písek, Teplý's history
of Jindřichův Hradec, Tomek's history of Prague, and Vančura's
history of Klatovy.[30] Such works indicate not only that there
was a continuing interest in local traditions but also that
Czech history from the White Mountain to the nineteenth century
was in large part that of a peasant people whose lives revolved
around their particular locality.

Commercial Institutions

By 1890, the growing power of Czech commercial institutions
permeated the whole system of limited self-government. Directly,
business interests dominated second- and third-curial elections
of delegates to district boards and to the provincial diets. Indirectly, commercial institutions provided that fiscal independence from Viennese capital necessary to an autonomous Czech political development and paid many of the direct taxes which made
possible the continual expansion and relatively efficient operation of self-governmental bodies.

The essential role of Czech economic growth in political development was recognized by the leading Czech political economists, who developed a theory of "national economy" (*národní
hospodářství*), based upon the principles of "political economy,"
which argued that primacy be afforded to economic, commercial,
and industrial development in promoting the welfare of the Czech
nation.[31] Three of the four leading Czech political economists--
František Fiedler, Josef Kaizl, and Alois Rašín--rose to important positions within the Young Czech party. The fourth was
Albín Bráf, son-in-law and successor to F. L. Rieger as chairman

of the Old Czechs. To this group might also be added the Young
Czechs Karel Adámek and Karel Kramář, who published works on
economic policy. Kramář, like Kaizl, had earned a doctorate in
jurisprudence and had studied under Adolf Wagner and Gustav
Schmoller in Germany. During the nineties, these men helped
strengthen already-existing ties between the party and the Czech
business community as they argued against the traditional radicalism of the Grégr brothers. Their influence in party circles
became paramount in the decade and a half before the First World
War.

Young Czech party correspondence for the 1890s indicates no
direct involvement by Czech banks or corporations in the making
of party policies. Instead, their influence appears to have been
exercised primarily through second- and third-curial voting and
through the district boards and chambers of commerce on which the
Young Czech party relied as the bases for its party organization.
Also, a number of leading Young Czechs served on boards of directors of various banks. Emanuel Engel, chairman of the clubs of
delegates, Václav Škarda, chairman of the executive committee,
Josef Horák, and Alois Pravoslav Trojan served as board members
for the Hypoteční banka at an annual salary of 1,200 gulden.[32]

Of all commercial institutions, the chambers of commerce exercised the most direct and easily discernable influence upon political parties. They constituted the second of four curias which
elected delegates to the provincial diets. Until 1907, nine of
twenty-nine chambers of commerce in Cisleithania with a total of
583 members in 1891 elected twenty-one deputies to the Reichsrat
as its second curia. In the 1891, 1897, and 1901 Reichsrat elections, three of the five chambers of commerce in Bohemia elected
Czech delegates, the Prague Chamber electing two and those of
Pilsen and České Budějovice (Budweis) one each. Chambers in
Liberec (Reichenberg) and Cheb (Eger) traditionally elected German delegates, two from the former and one from the latter. The
chambers of commerce could directly influence decisions of a
party's parliamentary club of delegates through instructions to
their delegates and thus indirectly influence those of the party
executive committee as well.

Commercial organizations exercised a more substantial but
also more indirect influence on the formation of party policies
through the third electoral curia, that of municipalities. Business interests prevailed in that body, which gave the urban taxpayers more than four times the representation of taxpayers in
rural areas. A comparison of the second and third curias with
others further indicates the extent of upper middle-class privileges.[33] In the 1897 Reichsrat elections, this curia, comprising less than 6 percent of the eligible voters in predominantly
Czech districts, elected 36 percent of Czech delegates for all
parties and 38 percent of the Young Czech delegates. It returned
seventeen Young Czechs and one candidate jointly sponsored by

both Old and Young Czechs in the České Budějovice district, where Czech voters constituted a bare majority. An examination of the 1897 electoral returns for all curias in predominantly Czech districts of Bohemia, attached as table 20C in the appendix, should more clearly indicate the importance of the municipal curia and the chambers of commerce in electing Young Czech candidates.

More popular commercial organizations also influenced party development. Consumers' and producers' cooperatives and savings and loan associations, first authorized in Cisleithania by imperial law no. 70 of April 9, 1873, greatly encouraged self-help, material improvement, and fiscal independence among the less privileged classes in Czech society. The publication of many manuals explaining the rights and limitations of cooperatives under this law attested to the immediate interest aroused by cooperatives. Thousands of cooperatives, especially among peasants, proliferated throughout the Czech lands despite the fact that the law clearly discriminated in favor of corporate forms of organization.[34] Under the 1852 law on corporations, a stockholder could be held liable only to the extent of his investments, whereas investors in cooperatives could be held personally liable for any debts incurred by the cooperative.[35] In forming cooperatives, social idealism went hand in hand with the desire for material betterment.

The agrarian cooperatives and credit unions accelerated the entry of Czech peasants into politics by contributing to their prosperity and their ability to manage their own capital. Publishing cooperatives assured to political parties the control of presses, paper, and newsprint necessary to any successful and independent political journal. The prosperous and independent sugar beet growers of Podřípsko, who controlled their own producers' cooperatives and savings and loan associations, predominated among those voters who elected the first Young Czech delegates to the diet and Reichsrat after 1874. Comparable organizations among the wealthier Czech landholders in the Kolín area constituted an integral part of the peasant movement organized by Jan Antonín Prokůpek under the auspices of the Old Czech party during the eighties.[36] Throughout Bohemia and Moravia, cooperatives grew hand in hand with peasant political associations like the Peasant Union (Selská jednota) for Bohemia, founded by Alfons Šťastný, and its counterpart, the Peasant Union for Moravia.

The influence of commercial institutions on the Young Czech party is reflected in the economic planks of party platforms and in regular party support for taxation and tariff measures favorable to upper middle-class interests. The party programs of 1874, 1879, 1891, 1897, 1901, and 1907 firmly upheld the principles of private property and laissez-faire economics and proposed specific measures to encourage Czech industrial and agricultural production.[37] In Reichsrat debates on the Cisleithanian budget, notably in 1897, 1899, and 1906, party delegates supported

measures which would perpetuate through reforms the privileged
status of corporations, landlords, and banking interests and
hopefully improve the material well-being of all classes of society. In 1892, the Young Czechs supported the Reichsrat bill
that led to imperial adoption of the gold standard and defla-
tionary revaluation of Austro-Hungarian currency. Kaizl and
Kramář helped prepare the bill as members of the parliamentary
finance committee. During the decennial parliamentary debates
on renewal of the customs union between Hungary and Cisleithania,
Young Czechs sought to reduce the barriers to trade between the
two halves of the monarchy in order to facilitate the export of
superior and less-costly Czech industrial and agricultural products into Hungary. Financial interests generally acted as a
brake on traditional Young Czech radicalism and nationalism,
particularly at the time of the Nymburk meeting of the board of
trustees in 1894 and after the 1897 riots between Czechs and Germans in central and northern Bohemia. Czech businessmen were
proud of their Czech heritage and identity but wished to do
nothing that might so inflame national passions that the tranquillity necessary for profitable business would be impaired.[38]

Czech banking and commercial interests did not act solely out
of self-interest in helping to formulate Czech party programs
and in providing funds for various Czech patriotic societies.
Liberal legislation, including self-government and limited freedom of association, certainly contributed to the power and prosperity of the Czech middle classes. But a desire to achieve a
national identity, autonomy, and self-respect appears to have
been another principal motive behind their undoubtedly genuine
attachment to liberal and patriotic politics. Moreover, these
businessmen responded to Young Czech appeals to their sense of
personal dignity. Most had memories going back to 1848 and had
at some time been abused or humiliated by Germans or by imperial
officials. On these as well as on patriotic or pragmatic
grounds, they advocated the extension of civil liberties and,
albeit reluctantly, the introduction of universal suffrage in
elections to the lower house of the Reichsrat. Only one or two
generations removed from the peasantry, they generally displayed
some sympathy and understanding for the problems and aspirations
of the peasant and working masses. But, like most Young Czechs,
they belonged to that middle class which by virtue of its superior wealth and education believed itself entitled to provide
leadership for the Czech nation (národ).

The influence of the commercial and industrial middle class
upon the policies of the Young Czech party grew steadily after
1891 and was exercised primarily through the party board of trustees and district boards and through second- and third-curial
election of delegates to the diets and the Reichsrat.[39] This
influence, tempered during the nineties by traditional Young
Czech radicalism and by party association with peasant organizations, lower middle-class voters, and the progressive

intelligentsia, became paramount after 1898 when these forces
largely withdrew to form their own parties.

The Press

National and regional newspapers representing every shade of
political opinion played a leading part in Czech politics during
the later nineteenth century.[40] Their circulation grew rapidly,
harsh imperial restrictions on freedom of the press notwithstanding.[41] From 1863 to 1895, the number of political Czech newspapers in Bohemia rose from 10 to 120 and the number of special-
ized periodicals from 17 to 210. During the same period the
ratio of Czech to German periodicals increased from 53:47 to
66:34.[42] In 1899, repeal of the tax stamp, long advocated by
all Czech parties except the Old Czechs, accelerated the growth
of the Agrarian and Social Democratic press more than that of
the *Národní listy* or other long-established journals.

The titles of almost all Czech newspapers evidenced advocacy
of patriotism, national solidarity, and a democratic spirit.
The names of twenty-four Czech papers published between 1863 and
1895 commenced with the possessive pronoun "Our," a word which
by contrast appeared on the masthead of no Bohemian German papers.[43] Other words appearing in the titles of Czech newspapers
in the order of their frequency were: "Slav" (*Slovan*) or "Slavic" (*slovanský*), sixteen times; "national" (*národní*), fifteen
times; "freedom" (*volnost*) or "free" (*volné*), twelve times;
"guard" (*stráž*), ten times; "truth" (*pravda*), nine times; and
"freedom" (*svoboda*), eight times.[44]

The leading Czech daily of the period 1861 to 1914 was the
Národní listy (National news), the principal spokesman after
1863 for national and liberal Young Czech policies. Czech National party leaders had established it as the national daily in
January 1861 to succeed Karel Havlíček's *Národní noviny*, of almost identical name, which Bach had suppressed in 1850. To facilitate getting imperial permission for its publication, they
chose as its editor a politically unknown but able young lawyer
of twenty-nine, Julius Grégr. The paper's initial statement of
purpose, composed by F. L. Rieger, set its tone for the next
sixty years:

This paper aims to advance the political and public education
of our nation [národ] in order that we may grow stronger in
association with the other peoples of Austria and someday
realize that constitutional independence which alone can
guarantee the preservation of our nationality and the
spiritual heritage of our past.[45]

Publication figures for Czech newspapers reflected the *Národní*
listy's preeminence among independent Czech dailies. A daily

circulation of 14,100 in 1894 placed it second only to the official government paper, *Prager Zeitung-Pražské noviny* (Prague
news) with 44,900 copies per issue, and ahead of all other papers including the Old Czech *Hlas národa* (The voice of the nation) at 6,400 per issue, the Agrarian *Selské noviny* (Peasant
news) at 1,650, the Catholic weekly *Čech* (The Czech) at 1,600,
the Social Democratic *Právo lidu* (The rights of the people) at
1,500, and the Realist *Čas* (Time) at 1,500.[46] Circulation figures reflected only a small proportion of all readers. Leading Czech papers sold subscriptions to coffee houses, saloons,
and reading rooms, and Czech political parties reached even more
readers through regional newspapers.

How can one account for the striking success of the *Národní
listy*? Under the management of Julius Grégr, the paper consistently spoke for liberal and patriotic Czech opinion and by its
defiance of authoritarian imperial policies during the sixties
won a deserved reputation for courage and radicalism. It gave
editorial support to many Czech patriotic and educational societies and campaigned to raise funds for the National Theater,
the Hus monument in Prague, and the Czech minorities in northern
and western Bohemia. These deeds alone cannot explain the
daily's extraordinary popularity; to a lesser degree other papers did likewise.

Until the Brno *Lidové noviny* (People's news) appeared in
1893, the *Národní listy* knew no peer in breadth of news reporting. It had been the first Czech journal to adopt telephonic
reporting and to send reporters to the larger European capitals.
In its successive Vienna correspondents, Gustav Eim from 1879 to
1897 and Josef Penížek until 1918, the *Národní listy* possessed
two of the very best Czech reporters of that era. As the leading Czech daily, it attracted more than its share of open letters,
which in turn enhanced its appeal. A case in point is Masaryk's
two letters of 1901 to the *Národní listy*, in which he defended
the program of his recently established People's party.[47] The
Národní listy also served as the principal Czech paper of public
record, printing verbatim the important campaign speeches of
Young Czech party members and the notable parliamentary addresses
by Czech politicians regardless of party. The *Národní listy*,
like other liberal Czech papers, won popularity by condemning
the imperial authorities for their policy of printing Reichsrat
debates exclusively in German and by itself publishing the more
important debates in Czech.

Besides its courageous editorial policy, the *Národní listy*
owed its preeminence among Czech political journals to its
having employed many of the finest Czech writers of its times
and published the work of many others. The Grégrs paid dearly
for this talent both in salaries and in freedom from editorial
control. The novelists Vitěslav Hálek and Servác Heller served
as editors, Heller in 1897 also becoming a Young Czech delegate

to the Reichsrat. Bedřich Smetana became the paper's first
music editor and used its columns to explain the revolution he
effected in Czech music.[48]

Jan Neruda, a prominent spokesman for the radical democratic
faction of the Young Czech party and one of the greatest Czech
poets and storytellers of the nineteenth century, joined the
editorial staff of the *Národní listy* in 1865 and until his death
twenty-six years later wrote many of its literary columns and
feuilletons. The latter often dealt with timely political
issues and perceptively satirized human foibles and pretensions.
Paragons of the Czech bourgeoisie, enamored of material posses-
sions and modest cultural embellishments, acquired a false sense
of security and became hardened to the plight of the poor and
down-trodden. Czechs and Germans alike placed too much stock in
official titles and took altogether too seriously political slogans that they really did not understand. The strident and ri-
diculous German claims to cultural superiority gave way to even
more far-fetched and potentially dangerous claims to primacy
based on pseudoscientific criteria of "blood" and "race."[49]
Viennese publicists who extolled the "Austrian idea" fooled themselves into believing they spoke for all nationalities. Obtuse
imperial officials took pleasure in badgering citizens or in trying to hoodwink them by procedures deemed sly but which were altogether transparent. The same officials could not enforce the
laws so rigorously or so uniformly as they followed their own
petty routines. In conclusion, Neruda usually let it be known
that human sympathy and decency, if reinforced by civil courage
and democratic ideals, would ultimately prevail. Quite logically, this man who began as a pupil of Heine and an advocate of
the 1848 revolution wrote one of his last feuilletons in praise
of the socialist May Day celebrations of 1890, which to him signaled the advent of a brighter future.[50]

The *Národní listy* owed much of its success as well as its
association with the Young Czech party to its owner Julius Grégr.
His obscurity may have dictated his having been chosen its first
editor; but once in charge, he and his brother Edvard built it
into a powerful enterprise through shrewd business sense, a crusading spirit, and a good understanding of popular psychology
and public issues. He declared the paper independent of National
party control in June 1863 and despite numerous attempts by opponents to take it over, including those by the Old Czechs in the
seventies and by the Realists in the nineties, he ran it until
becoming seriously ill in the spring of 1894.

From the day of its inception, Julius Grégr identified the
Národní listy with partisan causes; witness his praise of Garibaldi, his support of the 1863 Polish revolutionaries, and his
vigorous attacks on the Schmerling, Beust, and Auersperg ministries. For criticizing educational policies of the Schmerling
government, which he believed inimical to the interests of non-
German nationalities, he was sentenced in June 1862 to ten

months' imprisonment, a 3,000-gulden fine, and loss of his academic degrees.[51] Overnight he became a national hero and received a tumultuous welcome upon his release from prison.[52]

Long an advocate of active politics, the *Národní listy* helped establish the Young Czech party and backed Karel Sladkovský's 1875 campaign for universal and proportional manhood suffrage.[53] The paper's complete coverage of the Balkan wars of the later seventies, thanks in large part to frontline reports from Servác Heller, and its support of Southern Slavic aspirations increased its circulation enough to pay off all creditors. Its finest hour came during the successful campaign against the Vienna Agreement of 1890, as it helped establish the Young Czechs as the predominant Czech political party.

The *Národní listy* also backed losing causes with equal fervor and with almost equal benefit to its paid circulation. In 1886, Julius Grégr tried to defend the authenticity of the allegedly early medieval Green Mountain and Queen's Court manuscripts against Jan Gebauer and T. G. Masaryk, who had identified them as early nineteenth-century forgeries. In defying scholarly opinion, Grégr catered to popular patriotic emotion as well as his own propensity to regard national pride as the greatest of virtues.[54] There can be no doubt that he backed partisan and radical causes out of genuine conviction and not, as some critics have alleged, in a calculated effort to increase newspaper circulation. On serious political matters like the Agreement of 1890, he carefully considered all issues involved before committing the *Národní listy* to an opinion.[55] Moreover, his patriotic enthusiasm followed a consistent pattern from the young man's naive praise of Garibaldi to the older man's obdurate defense of bogus manuscripts.

The *Národní listy* prospered to a degree because Julius Grégr genuinely shared and ably articulated the views and prejudices of his compatriots. He dared say publicly what many thought privately. An impetuous and sometimes vindictive man, intelligent and industrious but wanting in sophistication and breadth of outlook, he epitomized the self-made middle-class Czech of his generation. The decline of his influence dated from the early nineties, when a younger, better-educated, and more sophisticated generation ceased to pay him homage and attempted to wrest the paper from his control. Radical slogans which seemed fresh and courageous to the generation of the sixties sounded hollow thirty years later. This was especially true after the antidynastic riots of 1893, when Governor Franz Thun intimidated Julius Grégr and crippled the *Národní listy* by imposing three-hour precensorship in order to silence public opinion before prosecuting the alleged *Omladina* (Youth) "conspiracy."[56] The death of Julius Grégr in 1896 coincided with the end of the radical era in Young Czech development. His successors adopted a more moderate attitude; and after Karel Kramář bought the paper in 1910, it became the spokesman of Czech financial and industrial interests.

Next to Julius Grégr, the two most influential men at the
Prague offices of the *Národní listy* were the editors and Young
Czech diet delegates Josef Anýž and Karel Tůma. Anýž, former
editor of the liberal Moravian weekly *Občan* (citizen) in Brno
and Prostějov and an active member of patriotic school associations, succeeded Josef Barák as responsible editor of the
Národní listy. For almost twenty-nine years, until his death in
June 1912, Anýž bore the brunt of imperial attacks upon the paper. Anýž, like Tůma, upheld the radical views of his mentor
Julius Grégr and long remained an influential voice on the Young
Czech party executive committee.[57] Karel Tůma joined the *Národní listy* editorial staff in 1862 and remained for fifty-five
years until his death in 1917. He wrote most lead articles for
the paper, and for his work as its editorial hatchet man he
earned the epithet of "bloody Tůma." In both capacities he
covered for Julius Grégr, who usually tried to maintain a states-
manlike posture. Tůma had been sentenced to three years' imprisonment along with Bedřich Pacák and the Young Czech from Podřipsko for his part in organizing tábory in 1868, and he never
ceased to oppose authoritarian Habsburg practices. A great partisan of French radicalism, he reminded Czechs that their national movement belonged to a larger European effort to achieve
personal freedom and national identity in his many essays and
books on American, Irish, and Belgian nationalism and on notable
liberals and revolutionaries including Mazzini, Garibaldi, Gambetta, Gladstone, Cavour, John Brown, and George Washington.[58]

Gustav Eim, Vienna correspondent for the *Národní listy* from
1879 to 1897, was incomparably the greatest Czech reporter of
his time and a model to succeeding generations.[59] He combined
attention to detail with an unusual breadth of outlook and de-
tachment from peculiarly Czech national concerns. A scintillat-
ing wit and a fondness for classical allusion further distinguished him from other Czech correspondents. At the behest of
Servác Heller, he came to the *Národní listy* in 1874 and immediately enlisted in the defense of active and liberal Young Czech
policies, a position he never abandoned. His enthusiasm for the
theater as for politics knew no bounds. He married an actress,
helped win the fight for a realistic Czech theater, and thereafter campaigned to establish a Czech theater in Vienna.[60]

Many contemporary testimonies indicate that Eim's telephonic
dispatch from Vienna was among the *Národní listy*'s most popular
features. Invariably he went directly to the heart of any matter
to discuss it in an analytical manner. When the Reichsrat was
in session, he nightly telephoned his hurriedly but superbly
written dispatches to Prague in time to be set up for the morning
edition, thus enabling the *Národní listy* to come out with informed commentary on the latest news many hours before its competitors.

Eim's fondness for extravagant living, his drinking problem,
and his friendships in Viennese society bothered many of his

Young Czech colleagues as much as his poor attendance at meetings of the parliamentary club of delegates and his outspoken citation of imperial strength as an argument for conciliatory behavior by the party.[61] He could usually fend off hostile colleagues by using wit or by cashing in old political debts. In the editorial offices of the *Národní listy*, he cut a wide swath, demanding and receiving the highest salary and achieving virtual independence in expressing his views. Whenever his editorial disagreements with Prague editor Josef Anýž came to a head, he could usually get his way by threatening to resign.

Eim's preeminence as a journalist and his strategic position in Vienna gave him an extraordinarily powerful voice in the making of party policy. Having spent most of his adult life reporting on events from the Reichsrat, he remained more impressed than many Young Czechs with the possibilities for party bargaining with imperial administrations. Moreover, he had formed close friendships with political leaders of all persuasions which kept him at all times front and center on the political stage. After the *Omladina* trials, he came to favor Young Czech collaboration with any imperial government willing to grant concessions to Czech interests. His private correspondence with party leaders during 1894 and 1895 confirms his having been the leading architect of the Young Czech compromise with Badeni.[62]

Eim's concern for social justice and his wish to see the Dual Monarchy constituted as a liberal state in which all nationalities enjoyed equal rights and opportunities led him several times to propose a working agreement between Czech and German liberals. But the German Liberals would have nothing of his liberalism, particularly extension of the franchise and the guarantee of civil rights, for they considered inimical and "anti-German" (*Deutsch-feindlich*) anything that directly or indirectly promoted Czech interests.[63]

As negotiations for the Agreement of 1890 opened in January of that year, Eim promptly telephoned reports and commentary to the *Národní listy*. After the terms became known, he was the first to denounce them as a retreat from liberal principles and a blow to the powers of self-government as well as a step inimical to the future of Bohemian state rights and to the status of Czech minorities in northern and western Bohemia.[64] His was the clarion call to resistance that most Czech politicians, regardless of party, soon heeded.

The *Národní listy* and many of its local affiliates existed before the founding of the Young Czech party and helped create the climate of opinion necessary for its success. In fact, in many respects the party grew out of the *Národní listy* and other liberal and anticlerical journals, and by 1877 it enjoyed the support of thirty-one papers.[65] All but ten of the party founders had been associated with the journal since the 1860s. Ervín Špindler, on the *Národní listy* editorial board from 1864 to 1867 and mayor of the Roudnice nad Labem district board, began his political career in Podřipsko as founder and editor of the liberal weekly *Podřipan*.[66] Many problems of the party in adjusting after 1891 to its status as the dominant Czech party could be traced to its having arisen from a crusading radical journal.[67]

In statements on policy, the *Národní listy* first anticipated and ultimately helped create the division of the Czech National party into opposing Young and Old Czech factions. In its inaugural issue in 1861, it explicitly rejected any reliance on the patronage of the great landowners: "With or without the Bohemian nobility we shall proceed resolutely to improve the spiritual and material life of our people."[68] By praising the Polish revolutionaries of 1863 and advocating universal suffrage in in 1874, the *Národní listy* further alienated the conservative Old Czechs and great landowners. When the Young Czechs formally broke with the Old Czechs in 1874, they did so confident of having a powerful journal behind them. When Young Czech delegates rejoined Old Czechs in a common Czech parliamentary association (*klub*) upon the return of the latter to the Reichsrat in 1879, the *Národní listy* kept up its criticism of Old Czech policies in an attempt to guide them in a more liberal direction.

The Young Czechs, in keeping with their liberal outlook, recognized much sooner than their Old Czech opponents the importance of the press in molding public opinion. Unable to exploit those traditional avenues of political influence in Bohemia monopolized by the Old Czechs and Bohemian nobility on the basis of curial suffrage, the Young Czechs advocated extension of the franchise and used their journals to appeal directly to the largely disfranchised Czech public. They aimed to capture the loyalty of this public before the advent of universal suffrage and tailored their programs accordingly. Up to a point, this policy succeeded, as the party became the largest Czech party in the Reichsrat from 1891 to 1907 and in the Bohemian Diet from 1890 to 1908.[69]

The *Národní listy* continued its policy of appealing directly to public opinion even after the Young Czechs became the majority Czech party in 1891. Its editors soon divided on the question of whether this policy any longer served the interests of the large party it helped create. Chief editor Josef Anýž and lead writer Karel Tůma led the larger group which sought to maintain the paper's radical posture and to emphasize peculiarly Czech interests. Reichsrat delegate and Vienna correspondent Gustav Eim led those who advocated a policy more understanding of imperial interests and the aims of other nationalities.[70] Julius Grégr generally agreed with Anýž and Tůma, but he could not afford to lose Eim's services. As a result, the paper during the nineties often presented two faces to its reading public: on any given day, Anýž's editorials and Eim's reports from Vienna might present conflicting opinions.[71]

The support of a local or regional paper usually proved essential to anyone seeking election to the diet or Reichsrat as

well as to a district board of representatives. Young Czech
victories in elections to all three bodies from the lower Labe
valley districts during the eighties had been facilitated by the
support of papers like the *Mělničan* in Mělník, the *Podřipan* in
Roudnice nad Labem, the *Pardubické listy* in Pardubice, and the
Čáslavské listy in Čáslav.[72] Emanuel Engel bought up the
Benešov weekly *Hlasy z Blaníka* (Voices from Blaník) in 1890 and
transformed it into a liberal organ to advance party policies
and his candidacies to the diet and the Reichsrat. Since the
district boards generally supported either the Old Czech or the
Young Czech party programs, many local papers in Bohemia had by
1890 affiliated with one party or the other. For example, in
Pilsen the *Plzeňské listy* supported the Old Czechs while the
Plzeňské noviny served the Young Czechs. The latter customarily
distributed important editorials from the *Národní listy* and
official party declarations to their local affiliates for repub-
lication.

The spread of Young Czech influence to Moravia occurred in
large part through two liberal and anticlerical papers, the
Selské listy (Peasant news), established in 1886 by the Peasant
Union for Moravia (Selský spolek pro Moravu), and the *Moravské
listy* (Moravian news), founded in November 1889 by Adolf Stránský and after December 1893 called the *Lidové noviny* (People's
news). The Young Czech party granted Stránský the generous subsidy of 1,000 gulden per year to get the *Moravské listy* started.[73] Once established as the organ of the Moravian People's
party, an autonomous affiliate of the Young Czechs, the *Lidové
noviny* became the leading competitor of the *Národní listy* for
recognition as the foremost liberal Czech daily.[74]

The *Národní listy* and many of the regional liberal journals
remained largely independent of Young Czech control. No formal
structure existed which would permit either party or paper to
control the other by institutional means. Their close and
usually cordial association continued to be based on mutual aims
and common leadership. Many party officials simultaneously
served as editors or reporters for the various affiliated papers.
Their disagreements on policy affected both the party and its
press as well as the relationship between them.

Patriotic and Cultural Societies

As the national revivals among the various smaller Eastern
European peoples began primarily as cultural and ended primarily
as political movements, so did patriotic and cultural societies
precede and in some respects lay the groundwork for institutions
of self-government, corporations and cooperatives, and a political press. Patriotic and cultural societies also facilitated
the development of Czech political parties. So long as serfdom
and authoritarian government prevailed in Austria, these societies had helped nurture and articulate national consciousness.

During the revolution of 1848, they helped provide nascent Czech
parties with experienced leaders and an institutional framework,
however inadequate, which could be adapted to politics. Cultural endeavor again provided a substitute for political activity,
which was proscribed during the Bach era, as new or reorganized
cultural societies provided a training ground for the political
leadership which would emerge in 1860 upon the establishment of
limited constitutional rule.

After 1860, patriotic and cultural organizations remained
among the more important private institutions that provided
ideas and an institutional framework propitious to the growth of
the Young Czech party. At no time did they play so direct and
integral a role in party affairs as did the institutions of local self-government or the chambers of commerce. Rather, they
worked hand in hand with the party to achieve common national
and liberal programs, taking care to preserve a nonpolitical
status. The party thereby acquired greater popular support,
while the patriotic and cultural societies acquired an agent and
defender in the diets and the Reichsrat.

Under Austrian law, the various patriotic and cultural societies could not engage directly in politics and could lose their
charter if imperial officials considered them to have done so.[75]
On this basis, Governor Alfred Kraus of Bohemia disbanded the
Academic Reading Association (Akademický čtenářský spolek) in
1889; the governor of Moravia dissolved the Peasant Union for
Moravia in 1890; and Governor Franz Thun dissolved all politically oriented Czech student organizations in Bohemia during
September and October of 1893. Members of patriotic and cultural organizations could participate in politics only as individuals or as members of recognized political institutions. As a
result, party leadership often corresponded closely to that of
private patriotic and cultural societies, thus facilitating the
party's ability to represent and defend nonpolitical societies.[76]

The older Bohemian cultural and scientific societies, notably
the Royal Bohemian Society of Sciences formed in 1771 and the
National Museum founded in 1818, made great and lasting contributions to the revival of national consciousness and higher culture among the Czechs.[77] Established under royal auspices and
encouraged by the Bohemian nobility, these societies soon became
predominantly but not exclusively Czech in membership. Their
generous encouragement of the arts, sciences, and history indirectly affected Czech political life by helping to train future
political leaders like Palacký and by arousing popular interest
in the past glories and present possibilities of Czech national
culture.

The Czech Foundation (Matice česká) and the Moravian Foundation (Matice moravská), founded in 1831 and 1849 respectively,
constituted a second generation of Czech patriotic and cultural
organizations, which sought to popularize as well as to build
upon the work of the Bohemian Society of Sciences and the

National Museum. At a time when the autocratic Metternich regime recognized neither freedom of speech nor freedom of association and severely restricted any activity considered political,
the Matice česká attempted to stimulate national consciousness
and pride by encouraging literary, scholarly, and artistic
achievement and avoiding any direct opposition to the reactionary
government. Toward this end, it and its Moravian counterpart
established lending libraries and scholarly journals and raised
funds for the support and publication of archeological, historical, and ethnographical research. They were patterned upon the
Serbian Foundation (Matica srpska) and served as counterparts to
the Matice among other Slavic peoples in the Habsburg Monarchy.
The various Slavic Matice primarily wished to cultivate and preserve their own respective national cultures but also sought to
promote brotherhood and mutual understanding among the different
Slavic peoples, recognizing that the culture of any one nation
would atrophy if it remained closed to foreign influences and
that the success of any one small Slavic nation depended upon
the success of others.[78]

The Czech and Moravian Foundations influenced the development
of political parties only indirectly, by reinforcing party patriotism and by encouraging party leaders to work for the improvement of schools and libraries. More importantly, they provided
an institutional framework in which Czech leaders could develop
at a time when public political life was all but proscribed. In
keeping with promises to further all work of the National Revival, many leading Young Czechs, including Chairman Emanuel Engel
and Josef Herold, served on the board of the later nineteenth-
century Matice česká.

The Czech patriotic and cultural societies which directly interacted with political parties flourished only after the introduction of limited constitutional rule in 1860. Foremost among
these were the Central School Foundation (Ústřední Matice školská), the several National Unions (Národní Jednoty), and the
Falcon (Sokol) gymnastic organization. The Czech National
Theater (Národní divadlo) incorporated features of both the
older and the newer societies. Its history illustrates how a
patriotic association devoted primarily to cultural advancement
came also to serve political ends.

The National Theater grew out of the numerous local patriotic
theater groups founded at the time of the National Revival.[79]
During the Bach era, efforts to build the theater served as a
substitute for political activity. After the introduction of
constitutional rule, construction of the theater became an
avowedly political as well as cultural enterprise. Both Young
Czechs and Old Czechs served on the building committee and each
faction sought to build a theater that would reflect its view of
politics and society. F. L. Rieger wished construction to proceed under the direction of the Bohemian Diet and to rely on the
patronage of the great landowners. Young Czechs, including the

Grégr brothers, Vitězslav Hálek, and Karel Sladkovský, revived
Havlíček's 1849 plan to build an independent and popular Czech
national theater and to encourage participation by all classes
of society in its funding and construction. Old and Young Czech
committeemen finally resolved their dispute by agreeing to carry
out the Young Czech plan under Rieger's chairmanship and to
accept patronage from the Bohemian nobility. Both parties cited
their contribution to the theater's construction in appeals to
the electorate, especially the Young Czechs, who deliberately
used the theater-building campaign as a means of arousing popular support for their liberal and democratic policies.[80]

The building of the National Theater in Prague represented to
all Czechs a truly national and democratic achievement, a belief
reflected in the motto "the nation to itself" ("národ sobě").
Although the Czech notables and intelligentsia took the lead in
establishing the building committee for the theater, all classes
of Czech society donated funds or labor toward its construction.
When the first theater burned upon completion in October 1881, a
second public subscription funded the building of the second and
present National Theater by 1883. Within three months after the
fire, contributions for reconstruction totaled 745,000 gulden,
exceeding by almost 25 percent the 600,000 raised during the
preceding thirty-six years.[81] The laying of the cornerstone for
the theater in 1868, its grand opening in 1881, and its reopen-
ing in 1883 all occasioned patriotic celebrations of a political
nature and included dignitaries from other Slavic nations. This
cornerstone was cut from Říp and bore the following inscription:

Ze Řípu Čech svůj domov vzal,   From Říp Czech took his home,
Na Bílé Hoře dokonal   On the White Mountain he
                                       expired,
V maticce Praze z mrtvých vztal.   In Mother Prague he arose
                                       from the dead.[82]

The hopes and fears men entertain for the future of their
children and their society have usually placed schools at the
center of any political controversy. This has been particularly
true during times of rapid social change and in areas of mixed
ethnic or religious groups. The Czech experience during the
later nineteenth century is a case in point. As the struggle
between Czechs and Germans became more intense, Germans attempted to prevent Czech minorities in predominantly German
districts from establishing their own schools and justified
these actions by unfounded claims that Czechs sought to "Czech-
ize" German children. Czechs, who generally found knowledge of
German to be advantageous, objected only to schools in which
Czech children would be taught exclusively in German. On particular issues involving schools, the Young Czechs opposed any
retreat from the provisions of the liberal 1869 school law, as
they sought more resolutely than the Old Czechs to preserve

Czech minority schools and to keep schools free of any clerical
influences. The Young Czechs thereby more closely followed public opinion and vigorously backed the various patriotic associations which sought to provide schools for Czechs in predominantly German districts.

Given the widespread Czech support of education for its own
sake and for developing national pride and identity, the Central
School Foundation naturally numbered among the more powerful and
aggressive Czech patriotic societies. Representatives from
Czech educational associations, newspapers, and the Old and
Young Czech parties established the foundation in December 1880
largely in response to the organization of the Austrian German
School Union (Schulverein) in the spring of that year.[83] The
Central School Foundation helped set up and fund private Czech
schools in those predominantly German school districts where
there were less than the forty Czech students of at least five
years' residence required by law for the establishment of a
state-supported Czech public school. The foundation coordinated
the activities of existing local Czech school foundations in Bohemia, in Moravia at Brno, Olomouc, Znojmo, and Prostějov, in
Vienna, and in Opava, Silesia.[84] It also worked closely with
other patriotic educational societies, including the Matice
česká, and Matice moravská, and the Association of Teachers' Unions (Spolek učitelských jednot), and with educational journals
like the *Beseda učitelská* (The teacher's literary magazine).

In 1900 the Central School Foundation numbered 30,000 members
and had in twenty years granted 4 million gulden in aid to
schools. Ten thousand Czech students were enrolled in its private schools which it subsidized.[85] It remained a force in
Czech society until the First World War and again during the
First Czechoslovak Republic.

Without direct support from Czech political parties, the Central School Foundation could not have so readily fulfilled its
tasks. In predominantly Czech areas of Bohemia, cooperation of
local self-governmental bodies and the press remained indispensable to fund-raising campaigns and protection from police intervention. In defending itself against police harassment in predominantly German areas, the foundation depended upon the editorial protests by the Czech press and the influence of Czech
delegates to the diet and Parliament.[86]

Interaction between the Central School Foundation and the
Young Czech party developed only gradually. Young Czechs numbered among the eleven members of the organizing committee of
the foundation: Josef Anýž, Josef Herold, and Jan Jestecký.
Both Old and Young Czechs held office in the foundation and
elected F. L. Rieger to be its first chairman. The foundation
never owed allegiance to any one political party but worked with
all groups that shared its objectives. It gradually drew closer
to the Young Czechs as they more unequivocally than the Old
Czechs opposed attempts to revive clerical influence in the

schools and to make German the official language of state. Collaboration between the Young Czechs and the Central School Foundation aided parliamentary defeat of the clerical Lienbacher bill of 1882, and during the campaign against the 1890 Vienna Agreement, the Central School Foundation joined the Young Czechs in rejecting all agreements except that which created separate Czech and German school boards in localities of mixed nationality. The relationship between party and foundation was of a personal rather than an institutional nature and was maintained by frequent exchange of correspondence between the respective chairmen and by the presence of so many party members on the executive committee of the foundation.[87]

Young Czechs helped direct and support the activities of other patriotic educational organizations, among them the Academic Reading Society (Akademický čtenářský spolek), which served the Czech university students of Prague until disbanded by Governor Alfred Kraus in August 1889 for having repeatedly engaged in unlawful and "provocative" political activity, and the People's Foundation (Matice lidu), an inexpensive subscription library founded at Edvard Grégr's behest in 1867 and taken over by his publishing firm in 1882. The People's Foundation popularized typically Young Czech liberal, freethinking, and anticlerical views and published an inexpensive subscription series of booklets aimed at promoting Czech patriotism and an understanding of other Slavic peoples.[88]

The Young Czech party helped promote the welfare of the Czech minorities in predominantly German districts throughout the Czech lands by cooperating with the several Czech National Unions as well as with the Central School Foundation. The very size of this minority, numbering over 750,000 of the 6.5 million Czechs in 1910, made its status and aspirations a matter of national concern. Moreover, this minority bore the brunt of any conflict between Czechs and Germans; and its presence in the outlying districts of Bohemia and Moravia encouraged Young Czechs to uphold the indivisibility of the Czech lands.[89]

The four Czech National Unions stood foremost among the many organizations established to improve the material and cultural situation of Czech families in mixed or predominantly German districts. The two largest and most powerful unions were the Šumava National Union (Národní jednota pošumavská) and the North Bohemian National Union (Národní jednota severočeská), established in 1884 and 1885 respectively. Their counterparts in Moravia were the National Union for Eastern Moravia (Národní jednota pro východní Moravu), founded in Olomouc in 1886, and the National Union for Southwestern Moravia (Národní jednota pro jihozápadní Moravu), organized in Brno in 1886.[90] In the absence of a comparable union in Silesia, the Central Business Association for the Czech Region of the Duchy of Silesia (Ústřední hospodářská společnost' pro české kraje ve vojvodství Slezském), an economic self-help society organized in 1896, served as a substitute.[91]

The National Unions assisted the Central School Foundation in matters concerning minority schools and offered legal aid for Czechs in predominantly German districts involved in litigation with self-governmental or imperial authorities. In the same districts, the unions conducted private censuses in which a person could declare his nationality. These censuses naturally counted more Czechs than did the official census, in which officials determined a person's nationality on the basis of "the language of everyday business" (*Umgangssprache*) customarily used in his locality.[92] Throughout Bohemia and Moravia the unions raised funds to help Czech minority families purchase additional land or improve existing farms or businesses. The unions maintained branches or auxiliaries in the principal cities of central Bohemia which gave fiscal and material aid to designated branches in predominantly German districts.[93] Especially effective were appeals for funds to offset aid flowing to the Germans of northern and central Bohemia from the Pan-German League and other Imperial German organizations.

The large membership and extensive organization of the National Unions enabled them to carry out manifold tasks and reflected their popular appeal. After its first quarter-century in 1910, the Šumava National Union numbered 39,050 members in twenty-three districts and 642 local branches and had expended over 1.25 million crowns in western and southern Bohemian districts. During the same period, the North Bohemian National Union grew to over 600 local units with a total of 50,000 members. It had likewise granted generous aid to Czechs in border areas, including 360,000 crowns for economic development, over 200,000 for education, and almost 70,000 for libraries alone.[94] Each union published a fortnightly journal, *Stráž severu* (Guard of the north), later *Hraničář* (The frontiersman), appearing in the north, and *Česká stráž* (The Czech guard) in the west.[95] Given the greater prosperity and industrialization in northern Bohemia, the North Bohemian National Union could devote a greater percentage of its funds to political and cultural affairs than could the Šumava National Union. The latter, because of the relative backwardness of southern Bohemia, spent proportionately more money, usually over one-third of its expenditures, on economic aid.[96]

The emergence of the Young Czechs as the principal Czech political party by 1891 may be traced in part to their long-standing association with the National Unions. The Old Czechs took little interest in the farmers and tradesmen who comprised the Czech minority to the north, though several Old Czechs personally served on union executive committees. The Young Czechs manifested great concern primarily because their constituents in Podřipsko and the upper Labe districts had long helped the Czech minorities in the adjacent and predominantly German districts to the north. In turn, all Czechs residing along the language frontier between Czechs and Germans responded readily to the patriotic and liberal Young Czech appeals.[97]

Given their long-standing support of Czech minorities, Young
Czechs naturally numbered among the founders and executives of
the two National Unions in Bohemia. Alois Pravoslav Trojan,
Prague lawyer Miroslav Krajník, and Liberec doctor Václav Šamánek
helped found and served respectively as first chairman, second
chairman, and trustee of the North Bohemian National Union.
Josef Anýž was cofounder and board member of the Šumava National
Union. Emanuel Engel, after retiring as party chairman in 1900,
continued to serve the union (jednota) for the Czech minority in
Karlsbad (Karlovy Vary). A particularly important source of
funds for the National Unions remained Vinohrady, an upper middle-
class and solidly Young Czech suburb of Prague.[98]
The two National Unions in Bohemia remained closely associated
with the Young Czech party through personal ties and common goals
but in no way became subordinate to it. Correspondence from
these Unions to Julius Grégr commending the campaign against the
Agreement of 1890 and to party chairman Emanuel Engel during
the nineties illustrates the personal nature and continuity of
the relationship. The party chairman and executive committee
seldom initiated and rarely supervised party collaboration with
these unions. Rather, the party generally responded to requests
from these unions and would often receive their commendations for
having defended minority interests in the diet or on the floor of
the Reichsrat.[99] Throughout the nineties, all four National
Unions continued to reinforce Young Czech nationalism and collaborated with the party in advancing the interests of Czech minorities. Subsequently, the two Bohemian unions also joined
forces with the more radical and the more socialist progeny of
the Young Czechs, the State Rights Radicals and the National
Socialists respectively.[100]
The interplay between Young Czechs and the four National
Unions helps demonstrate that the party's radicalism, nationalism, and defense of Czech minorities responded to popular demands. In predominantly Czech areas, the party utilized district
and communal self-governmental bodies as the basis of its
strength; among Czech minorities in the predominantly German
areas, it exerted its influence through the already-established
Central School Foundation and the National Unions.
The Sokol (Falcon), a patriotic gymnastics fraternity, likewise played an important but indirect part in the development of
Czech political parties.[101] Founded in 1862 by Jindřich Fügner,
Miroslav Tyrš, and the Grégr brothers, it soon became the largest
and best-beloved Czech patriotic organization. In keeping with
its motto, "Let us strengthen ourselves" ("Tužeme se"), and its
theme song, "Hail Falcons, manfully onward" ("Hej Sokolíci mužně
v pred), it sought to promote self-confidence and self-improvement
love of country, and a sense of social responsibility as well as
physical fitness.[102] Fügner and Tyrš patterned its organization
after that of the German Turnerverein but as guides to conduct
emphasized the French "liberty, equality, and fraternity" more

than the Germanic "morality and discipline." A desire to emulate
the athletic achievements of ancient Greece and Rome also played
its part. Tyrš, a classical scholar and art historian, admired
the arts and letters as well as the physical culture of antiquity
and sought through the Sokol to mold patriots and public servants
of sound mind and body. In its efforts to advance popular education, the Sokol also owed much to the teachings of Komenský,
Rousseau and Pestalozzi. Renowned artist Josef Manes designed a
uniform for the Sokol that resembled not only the costume of
Czech peasants but of Garibaldi's red shirts.[103]
   The presentation of the Sokol colors on June 1, 1862, occasioned a joyous national celebration. After a dark decade of
police rule, the Sokol appeared as the embodiment and reaffirmation of the national and liberal ideas of 1848.[104] The novelist
Karolina Světlá, as "mother of the colors," led a procession of
writers, politicians, and notables that constituted a veritable
Who's Who of contemporary Czech society.[105]
   After 1862, the Sokol grew rapidly in popularity and in size.
Despite police harassment, the Moravian Czechs gradually established a network of Sokol chapters, which in May 1871 held their
first parade and public demonstration in Brno. Thereafter, in
Moravia as well as in Bohemia, the Sokol grew hand in hand with
Czech national politics. In 1868 in Bohemia and in 1881 in Moravia, local Sokol chapters formed a central provincial organization. Seventy-five chapters from both provinces performed en
masse at the first national Sokol congress, which Tyrš convened
at Prague in 1882. Nine years later, the second Sokol congress
featured exercises by 300 Polish Falcons and 200 Croats and Slovenes in addition to 17,000 Czechs.[106] The provincial Sokol organizations merged in 1896 under the chairmanship of Jan Podlipný, the Young Czech mayor of Prague, and by 1913 numbered
130,000 members. In 1912 workers comprised 28 percent of the
rank and file and over half of the performing members.[107] The
popularity of the Sokol among the masses before 1912 is also indicated by the inability of the Social Democratic and Czech
Catholic parties to field gymnastics groups that could rival the
Sokol in members and prestige.
   Among all classes of society, Sokol gymastics meets provided
occasions for a vigorous display of Czech solidarity and national
aspirations. These ostensibly nonpolitical gatherings were regarded as political as well as athletic demonstrations by both
Czechs and imperial officials. Sokol exercises in Prague in
1912 and in Brno in 1914 made a particularly strong impression
on foreign observers: Czechs noted with pride and imperial officials with trepidation that this disciplined patriotic fraternity
could in time of crisis transform itself into an army.[108]
   International gymnastics meets gave Sokol members an opportunity to display Czech physical prowess and national pride to
foreign audiences. Especially important were exchanges with Polish and Southern Slavic gymnastics associations and annual

meets with the French Society of Gymnasts. Festive excursion
groups from Prague attended the meets held in France, stopping
en route at Constance to honor the memory of Jan Hus. Agents of
the ever-distrustful Austrian police generally attended and reported at length on Sokol exercises abroad.[109] Even the Imperial
German authorities, including Kaiser Wilhelm II, took alarm. The
Prague Sokol maintained close ties with the numerous Sokol
branches in America, including a regular exchange of visits and
correspondence, also subject to police surveillance. Little won-
der, for on festive occasions, speakers from Czech-American Sokols often denounced the Habsburgs while praising American liberties.[110]

So long as the Sokol in the Czech lands engaged in no overtly
political activity, the imperial police, however suspicious, had
no grounds for repressive action. A case in point is the annual
toasts by the chairman of the Prague Sokol, Jan Podlipný, in
praise of France and Franco-Czech friendship: he left no doubts
concerning his liberal and Francophile sentiments but said nothing that could be considered disrespectful of Franz Joseph or
that implied a desire to overthrow the dynasty. Only after the
outbreak of the First World War did the imperial police attempt
to disband the Sokol and then merely succeeded in driving it
underground.[111] It emerged in 1918 to help establish an independent Czechoslovak republic.

The Sokol influenced the growth of Czech political parties
primarily by stimulating Czech patriotism and self-confidence.
Although the Young Czech party and the Sokol shared many common
ideas and objectives, their archives include no exchange of correspondence directly related to political matters.[112] This may
be explained by the Sokol's having wished to avoid political action as an institution. What members of the Sokol did in politics as individuals or as members of a political organization was
another matter. The Sokol therefore most directly influenced the
growth of political parties by furthering the careers of leading
party members. This was especially true of the Young Czechs, for
leaders of the Sokol came principally from the upper middle class
while the lower middle and working classes predominated in the
rank and file. Cofounder Jindřich Fügner had become a wealthy
businessman before devoting himself to patriotic and philanthro-
pic activities and brought to the Sokol organizational talents
which had accounted for his success in business. Cofounder Miroslav Tyrš, who married Fügner's daughter Renáta in 1872, wrote
most of the Sokol promotional literature and manuals on physical
culture and served as its chief (náčelník) from 1862 till his
death in 1884. He also won renown as a critic of arts and letters and became a professor of fine arts at Charles-Ferdinand
University in 1883.[113]

Besides the Grégr brothers, the most famous Young Czechs to
come up through the Sokol ranks were Ervín Špindler, Václav
Šamánek, and Emanuel Engel, founder and vice-chairman of the

Sokol in Benešov, and the lawyers Bedřich Pacák, chairman of the
Kutná Hora Sokol, Josef Herold, founder of the Sokol in Vršovice
in 1869, Karel Pippich, chairman of the Chrudim Sokol, and Jan
Podlipný, long-time chairman of the Prague Sokol.[114] While
president of the Prague Sokol, Jan Podlipný won election to the
diet as a Young Czech in 1889, the first of his party to represent the Old Town of Prague, traditionally an Old Czech stronghold. Governor Alfred Kraus's prohibition of the twenty-fifth
anniversary parade of the Sokol in Prague and Minister-President
Taaffe's belated attempt to prevent the Sokol from exercising
with French gymnasts in Nancy contributed to Podlipný's upset
victory. In 1895, he was elected by the diet as one of three
Czechs to the Provincial Executive Committee and in the same
year was chosen to succeed Jan Kučera as chairman of the party's
executive committee. Two years later he won election as mayor
of Prague for a four-year term.[115] Unlike many of his compatriots, Podlipný never tried for a seat in the Reichsrat and took
little interest in Cisleithanian or international affairs.
Rather, he worked exclusively in the institutions of provincial
and municipal self-government, where he earned a reputation as
a colorful and forthright if somewhat narrow-minded defender of
Czech civil liberties and national autonomy. High political and
academic honors notwithstanding, his happiest moments came when
in Sokol regalia and on horseback he annually led Sokol parades
through the streets of Prague to the cheers of tens of thousands.[116] The Czechs who knew little of his manifold political
activities honored him as the popular and uncrowned "King of the
Sokol."[117]

Members of other political parties besides the Young Czechs
actively participated in local Sokol organizations. Witness Old
Czech Tomáš Černý, who as mayor of Prague and Sokol chairman in
the eighties popularized the slogan "our golden Slavic
Prague."[118] Young Czechs continued to predominate in positions
of Sokol leadership until the First World War, but by 1912 a
majority of the rank and file belonged to the Czech National
Socialist party and over a quarter to Social Democracy.[119] The
Young Czech leadership, as the French consul in Prague reported
and as the National Socialist chairman Klofáč later charged,
tried to use their association with the Sokol to compensate for
their willingness to cooperate with the imperial authorities.[120]
The working-class and lower middle-class rank and file stood by
the Sokol traditions to the end.

In large measure, the Young Czechs owed their position as the
predominant Czech political party of the nineties to their having long defended national and liberal ideals in cooperation
with the liberal press and the larger patriotic and cultural societies. Equally important to its maintaining this predominance
during the decade was its control of district and communal bodies
of limited self-government and the support it received from the
more powerful commercial organizations. Having grown out of the

Národní listy and in close association with the more popular patriotic and cultural societies, the party retained its traditionally radical liberalism and anticlericalism and its custom
of appealing to the disfranchised majority. So long had the
Národní listy spoken for the minority party that the post-1891
majority party found it difficult to speak for itself.[121]   On
the other hand, the party became increasingly tied to privileged
elements in Czech society through its dependence upon the institutions of commerce and self-government. The incorporation of
many traditionally Old Czech district boards and electoral committees into the Young Czech party cadres after 1891 further increased the influence of privileged upper middle-class interests
in party circles.

The Young Czech party therefore entered the nineties divided
in many respects against itself. The struggle which then developed between radical and moderate party elements resembled
the contest between Young and Old Czech factions within the National party of the sixties and reflected in many ways the Young
Czech party's having been the product of both the popular and
the privileged institutions of Czech society.

5

The Making of the Young Czech Majority

Intensified conflict between Old and Young Czechs within the
Czech club during the later eighties ultimately led the Young
Czechs, on January 26, 1888, to constitute themselves as the
club of independent Czech delegates in the Reichsrat (*Klub
neodvislých českých poslanců na říšské radě*). In the elections
of early July 1889, the Young Czechs increased their share of
the ninety-seven Czech seats in the Bohemian Diet from ten to
thirty-nine, including thirty of forty-nine seats in the rural
fourth curia. After broadening their base of support, they won
an overwhelming victory over the parent National party in the
Reichsrat elections of March 1891 in Bohemia, thereby supplanting
it as the dominant force in Czech politics. This electoral victory and the conflict that preceded it arose primarily from the
Old Czechs' inability to make much progress in resolving the
serious political and economic issues which confronted the Czech
people during the last years of the Taaffe era.

Issues in Czech Politics during the Taaffe Era

From 1879 to 1890, the conservative and clerical Iron Ring
government of Count Eduard Taaffe provided a higher degree of
stability in Cisleithanian politics than did any of its predecessors or successors. But it achieved this stability at the
high cost either of trying to suppress serious social and political problems or of postponing any attempt at their solution.
Taaffe maintained the support of a parliamentary majority based
on the Iron Ring of the Right, but his policy of playing one nationality off against another only exacerbated conflict between
nations and made any future reconciliation all the more unlikely.[1] Beginning in 1881 and continuing more systematically after
January 1884, he attempted to destroy the workers' movement by
an antisocialist campaign inspired by that underway in Imperial
Germany since 1878.[2] But such arbitrary and discriminatory actions only aroused greater popular discontent, despite the fact
that Taaffe, to a lesser extent than Bismarck, had complemented
antisocialist legislation by a series of laws designed to effect moderate improvements in working conditions and hours.
Four important reforms, all supported by both Young and Old
Czechs, began with law no. 117 of June 17, 1883, which established criteria and officers for factory inspection.[3] Law no.
115 of June 21, 1884, regulated labor in the mines, limiting the
working day to ten hours and prohibiting Sunday labor and

121

regular employment of children under fourteen. Among the most
vigorous proponents of this legislation was Karel Adámek, National party representative from Hlinsko, who contended that
state regulation of mining labor was compatible with liberal
economic principles and promoted the welfare of society as well
as benefiting every individual laborer.[4] Law no. 22 of March 8,
1885, which pertained to factories employing more than twenty
persons, established, among other reforms, an eleven-hour day
and further limitations on the use of child labor. Law no. 1 of
December 28, 1887, provided state-sponsored accident insurance
for workers with funds contributed by both employer and em-
ployee.[5]

By the fall of 1889, Taaffe had run out of room for maneuver.
Repression of Social Democracy was proving to be counterproductive as its more anarchistic and violence-prone elements gave
way to the disciplined mass all-Austrian Social Democratic party
founded at Hainfeld on December 30, 1888. On July 2, 1889, the
Young Czechs, his declared opponents on most political issues,
dealt a severe blow to his Old Czech allies by winning thirty of
forty-nine seats in the rural fourth-curial elections to the
Bohemian Diet.[6] Faced by a resurgence of popular unrest, including that of Czech farmers and students in league with the Young
Czechs, and possible loss of his parliamentary majority in the
next Reichsrat elections, Taaffe tried to bring the German Liberals back into the Bohemian Diet, from which they had withdrawn
in December 1886, and to crush the Young Czechs while retaining
Old Czech support. The latter agreed to support his efforts to
conciliate the German Liberal party in order to enlarge his parliamentary majority and persuade that party to stop boycotting
the Bohemian Diet, although this would require their allowing
amendment of the Stremayr ordinances in favor of the Germans and
circumscribing their program for Bohemian state rights. But
both Taaffe and the Old Czechs underestimated what it would take
to satisfy the Germans and also underestimated Young Czech popular appeal and capacity for resistance.

The Young Czech victory over the Old Czechs in the parliamentary elections of 1891, in which the party took all but one seat
from Czech districts in Bohemia, may be attributed primarily to
the Old Czech party's inability to deal successfully with the
serious social, political, and economic problems facing the
Czech nation. The Young Czechs of 1891 appealed to an electorate
dissatisfied with Old Czech handling of five principal issues:
the simmering nationality conflict between Czechs and Germans
which the Vienna Agreement of 1890, endorsed by the Old Czechs,
appeared unlikely to moderate; Taaffe's encouragement of clerical attempts to influence the public schools; a worsening crisis
in Cisleithanian agriculture; continuing governmental prosecution of Czech newspapers and patriotic and peasant organizations;
and governmental obstruction of Czech efforts to build a monument
to Jan Hus in Prague. Foremost among these issues was the

nationality conflict, which the Old Czechs appeared to exacerbate by putting up little resistance to German Liberal efforts
to return to the status quo ante 1882: Young Czechs thought
that any attempt to appease the German Liberal party by limiting
the state rights program would end all hope of Czechs ever exercising political influence in Bohemia and Moravia in proportion
to their numbers. Second, the Old Czechs had supported the Iron
Ring's Lienbacher-Conrad bill of January 1882, which aimed to
facilitate the restoration of clerical influence in the public
schools, whereas the Young Czechs had firmly opposed it.[7] Third,
the European-wide agrarian crisis of falling grain prices, caused
primarily by inexpensive imports from the newly mechanized farms
of the Americas, jeopardized the livelihood of many Czech farmers, especially those who had not yet adopted scientific methods
of agriculture or cooperative forms of organization. Fourth,
Taaffe's ultimately counterproductive attempts to intimidate the
Young Czechs and their peasant and student allies profoundly embarrassed the Old Czech party because of its close ties to his
government. Finally, celebration of the Hussite past became a
popular political issue after November 25, 1889, when the younger Prince Charles of Schwarzenberg, in arguing against placing a
memorial plaque to Jan Hus in the new National Museum, denounced
the Hussites as "a band of looters and arsonists." In the face
of Old Czech indifference to this insult, the Young Czechs not
only endorsed placing such a plaque but began a fund-raising
drive to erect an imposing monument to Hus on the Old Town
Square. Contributions rapidly poured in from districts and communes throughout the Czech lands and from Czechs abroad, making
this the largest popular subscription campaign since the one
that had financed rebuilding the burned-out National Theater.
The immediate success of this drive as well as the Provincial
Executive Council's decision of December 28, 1889, to contribute
funds for erecting the Hus memorial plaque conclusively demonstrated that Hus remained an extraordinarily revered figure and
that for having denigrated his achievements the Old Czechs and
their conservative great landowning allies would pay dearly in
the forthcoming Reichsrat elections.[8] On all five of the above
issues the Young Czechs more closely reflected public opinion
than did Rieger and his Old Czech associates, whose continuing
support of Taaffe markedly diminished their popular support.

Young Czech electoral gains also owed much to legislation of
October 4, 1882, and May 20, 1886, which extended the franchise
for electing delegates respectively to the Reichsrat and to the
Bohemian Diet. In both cases, lowering the tax requirement from
ten gulden to five for voters in the third and fourth curias
primarily enfranchised farmers and small businessmen who favored
the Young Czech ticket.[9] In the July 1889 Bohemian Diet elections, the Young Czechs increased their number of seats in the
fourth curia from six to thirty and in the third curia from four
to nine, as Old Czech delegates declined from forty-three to

nineteen and from thirty-six to thirty-one respectively. In the
Reichsrat elections of March 1891, the five-gulden vote helped
give Young Czech candidates a majority in several districts and
thus contributed to the party's landslide victory.[10] By contrast, in the July 1890 elections to the Moravian Diet, where
the ten-gulden tax limitation still obtained, the liberal and
anticlerical People's party sponsored by the Young Czechs won
only a single seat in the fourth curia, the National party retaining the remaining six as well as every Czech seat in the
third or urban curia. A slight increase in the number of voters for chamber of commerce elections, authorized on March 31,
1884, accelerated the Czech takeover of the chambers of commerce
in Prague and Pilsen and insured that August Zatka's Old Czech
cadres would continue to hold the one in České Budějovice. In
Moravia, where proportionately fewer Czechs resided in urban
areas, Czech parties captured one-third of all seats on the
chambers of commerce in both Brno and Olomouc but could not better
this position till the end of the First World War.
    The German Liberal opposition to the Taaffe government grew
steadily more vehement during the middle 1880s as party representation declined and as middle-class Germans in the Czech
lands, who witnessed the inexorable advance of Czech influence
in politics, culture, and the economy, grew more fearful that
Czechs would soon exercise political power commensurate with
their growing material wealth and numbers, thus ending the German hegemony established during the Thirty Years War.[11] These
fears found concrete expression in the Reichsrat as German Liberals presented in January 1884 the Wurmbrand bill to make German the official state language of Cisleithania, and after its
rejection, as they introduced its watered-down version in the
Scharschmid resolution of February 1886. Young and Old Czechs
helped the Iron Ring vote down both proposals, against which the
Young Czechs had more forcefully spoken.[12] Both Czechs and Germans regarded these proposals as steps toward the realization of
the August 1882 Linz program of German nationalism, by which the
middle-class German parties proposed to change the configuration
and constitution of Cisleithania to preserve it as an Austrian-
German state: Galicia, Dalmatia, and the Bukovina were to be
detached to give Germans a numerical majority in the remaining
crown lands, which would then be united to Imperial Germany by a
customs union. This implied the subordination if not the assi-
milation of the Czech nation in a greater German state. As modified slightly by the Whitsun program of May 21, 1899, which
allowed for some Czech autonomy in predominantly Czech districts, the Linz program remained the basic statement of German
national aims in the Habsburg Monarchy until 1918.[13]
    The same limited extension of the franchises to the Reichsrat
and the Bohemian Diet that had helped increase Young Czech representation also redounded to the disadvantage of the German
Liberals, as Czechs were able to capture several more districts

in Bohemia and Moravia and as clerical parties received many
votes from the newly enfranchised five-gulden electorate, primarily in Lower Austria and the Alpine lands. The Reichsrat
elections of June 1 through 5, 1885, irretrievably weakened the
German Liberals as they lost several mandates to a united slate
of Young Czech and Old Czech candidates and many more elsewhere
to the reinforced German Clericals and the recently founded
German People's party (Deutsche Volkspartei). They retained
only 87 to the 106 seats they had held going into the election.
In predominantly Czech districts of the rural fourth curia, the
united Czech slate won all mandates in Moravia and all but one
in Bohemia, with the latter going to a farmer who soon came over
to the Young Czech camp. The Germans lost their sole remaining
representative from Prague as the Malá Strana district returned
a Young Czech candidate. Total German representation in the
Reichsrat declined for the first time to less than one-half of
all delegates, despite gains by Clericals and Populists at the
expense of the Liberals, with only 175 Germans as opposed to 178
non-Germans, of whom 157 were Slavic-speaking delegates.[14]

After defeating the Scharschmid resolution, the Iron Ring
took a further step toward making the Czech language the equal
of German in the public life of Bohemia. On September 23, 1886,
acting Minister of Justice Alois Pražák issued, with Taaffe's
approval, an official instruction to the supreme provincial
courts in Prague and in Brno that henceforth all trial proceedings and final verdicts should be issued in the language of the
plaintiff and defendant involved in each case. This practical
measure, designed to insure that a citizen in court could read
and understand all testimony and records involving his case, was
supported by both Old and Young Czechs and the conservative
great landowners. It introduced the use of Czech as an internal
official language of administration in one specific instance.[15]
The German parties continued to advocate the exclusive use of
German as an internal official language and began on December 23,
1886, to boycott the Bohemian Diet in hopes of persuading the
Taaffe government to repeal the "Pražák instruction" and to form
a new majority more responsive to their interests. Before walk-
ing out, the Germans announced their aims to be the immediate
administrative and the eventual territorial division of Bohemia
according to nationality in order to insure political preponderance for Germans in all districts where they constituted a majority and to insure equal rights for them in all other districts.[16]

Growing German intransigence toward the Iron Ring was not long
in achieving results. The newly crowned German Emperor William II, while on a state visit to Vienna in early October 1888,
ostentatiously ignored Cisleithanian Minister-President Taaffe
while giving a decoration to Hungarian Minister-President Kálmán
Tisza. In this and in other more subtle ways, he and Bismarck
manifested their displeasure at Taaffe's conciliation of the

Slavic parties and at Czech "flirtation" with France.[17] Taaffe,
who had to date succeeded in striking a balance among all parties without wholly satisfying any, had always hoped to rule
with the concurrence of both the German Liberals and the Slavic
and clerical parties of the right. In the interests of maintaining domestic tranquility as well as good relations with the empire's Imperial German ally, he would have to conciliate the parties of the German left. To assure them that his government
would favorably consider their interests, Taaffe brought two
career civil servants of German Liberal proclivity, Baron Paul
von Gautsch and the Marquis de Becquehem, into his cabinet as
Minister of Worship and Public Instruction and Minister of Commerce respectively. By appointing Count Frederick Schönborn to
be Minister of Justice on October 11, 1888, to succeed Alois
Prazák, author of the unpopular instruction, Taaffe sought to
satisfy all parties by replacing a venerable Czech advocate with
a conservative great landowner who had heretofore shown no partiality for any national cause. The Old Czechs made no determined effort to reverse Taaffe's overtures to the German Liberal
party, content as they were to uphold his government from which
they had received many concessions and from which they hoped to
receive more at a later date. This prudent policy, based on the
premise that cooperation with a chastened German Liberal party
might be possible, contrasted markedly with their initial plans
to take immediate advantage of the German boycott of the diet by
trying to initiate legislation favorable to Czech interests.[18]
    Young Czech delegates in the united Czech club took exception
to Rieger's acquiescence in Prazák's dismissal and policy of accommodation toward the German Liberals generally. Both growing
German Liberal intransigence and the recent series of German
Liberal electoral defeats indirectly stimulated conflict between
the Young and Old Czech camps. On the one hand, the Young
Czechs, given their greater susceptibility to popular pressure,
sought to implement Bohemian state rights rather than accommodate to German Liberal efforts to turn back the clock. On the
other hand, after the German Liberal electoral defeats in 1885,
the Young Czechs no longer saw any pressing need to maintain
unity between Old and Young Czech delegations in Vienna and
Prague. This unity, which had facilitated obtaining substantial
concessions from Taaffe during the early eighties, also appeared
less warranted because by 1887 Taaffe had few concessions left
to give.
    In May 1887, when Young Czech delegates in the Czech club
challenged his policy of collaboration with Taaffe, Rieger replied in words which he soon came to regret: "Since we have not
succeeded in recovering all our rights at once, that is to say
by employing passive resistance, we must now demand and acquire
them by bits and pieces even if we have to forage for such
crumbs under the table."[19] On May 12, 1887, the editors of the
Národní listy published this policy statement which, they

contended, offered neither security nor hope to the Czech nation
and should therefore be repudiated. Editors Karel Tůma and Josef Anýž had read about Reiger's remarks in a personal letter
which Edvard Grégr had sent to Tilšer and which Tilšer in anger
had shown to them; they had then authorized publication without
Grégr's approval. When Rieger objected to what he termed a
breach of trust, Grégr expressed regret that publication had occurred and honestly disclaimed any complicity in having done it.
Still dissatisfied, Rieger demanded that Grégr deny ever having
heard the "crumbs" statement. When Grégr refused, Rieger expelled him and two other Young Czechs, Count Václav Kounic and
Jan Vašatý, from the Czech club. Emanuel Engel voluntarily de-
parted with them primarily because he thought that Rieger had
treated Grégr unjustly. His action caught most Old Czechs by
surprise, including Rieger, who remarked that this appeared "in-
comprehensible--he boasted of his loyalty, but aligns himself
with the immoral elements and engages in factional opposition.
Why I don't know."[20]

On January 26, 1888, Josef Herold, Jan Kučera, Bedřich Pacák,
and František Tilšer joined Engel, Grégr, Kounic, and Vašatý to
form the club of independent Czech delegates (*Klub neodvislých
poslancu českých*) to the Reichsrat under Tilšer's chairmanship,
thus ending the working agreement of the past eight years between
Old and Young Czechs.[21] Revival of the Young Czech party organization nationally and in districts occurred during the year under
the direction of Julius Grégr, Jan Kučera, chairman of the executive committee, and Gabriel Blažek, chairman of the board of
trustees. The newly reinvigorated Young Czech party had much in
its favor. It enjoyed the support of the largest and most influential Czech daily, the *Národní listy*, and stood closer to public
opinion on nationality and social issues than did the Old Czechs.
It had acquired new allies among reform-minded university youth
and leaders of the various peasant unions, now organizing for
political action in the wake of declining agricultural prices and
the deteriorating status of smaller Czech peasants.[22] And its
parliamentary delegates had long been critical of Old Czech dependence upon the conservative great landowners, a dependence
best caricatured by Edvard Grégr in his diary entry of December 20, 1879:

The whole delegation is hitched to the governmental cart;
Clam sits in the driver's seat and whips them; and they pull
like blind men--yes, like blind men because none of them knows
why--simply on Clam's assurance that all will be well. To be
sure, we believe in Clam--but we also believe in the Czech
nation.[23]

Alliance with the peasantry and strong backing from all
liberal-minded newspapers enabled the Young Czechs to sweep
thirty of forty-nine fourth-curial seats and nine of thirty in

the third curia in the July 1889 elections to the Bohemian Diet,
where they now for the first time seriously challenged the Old
Czech hegemony. These constituted gains of fourteen and five
seats respectively. During the following twenty-one months, the
Young Czech party vigorously championed state rights and political reform and grew from a small radical nucleus led by the
Grégr brothers, Tilšer, and Kučera into the predominant Czech
political party, a position it would retain throughout the following decade. This came about as that nucleus grew to encom-
pass a number of political groups including former Young Czechs
like Škarda, Schwarz, and Trojan who had become Old Czechs in
1880, several long-time Old Czechs who anticipated a Young Czech
victory, liberal Czechs from Moravia led by Adolf Stránský,
leaders of the peasant unions in Bohemia and Moravia, younger
intellectuals who called themselves Realists and advocated a
more democratic and socially responsible politics, and radical
students at Charles-Ferdinand University who were beginning to
organize themselves as a progressive movement of Czech and Slavic youth. The coalition of these groups made possible the
landslide victory of the Young Czechs over the Old in the Reichsrat elections of March 1891 in Bohemia. In order to understand
the creation and success of this coalition, one must determine
what sort of men led the newly expanded Young Czech party and
the extent to which their professional and political experience
conditioned its programs and actions.

Who Were the Young Czechs?

The Young Czechs of the nineties were primarily farmers or
professional men, at most one or two generations removed from
the peasantry. This is clearly revealed in table 15 of the Appendix, which lists party delegates and trustees by occupation.
The Young Czechs generally adhered to middle-class values and as
successful professional men of means believed it their duty and
privilege to lead the nation. In many instances they all too
readily identified the national interest with their personal interests or those of their occupation and class.
Young Czech party members at the time of the 1891 electoral
campaign may be divided according to occupation into eight principal groups. First, farmers and representatives of farming interests from the intensive-agricultural and sugar beet areas of
north central and eastern Bohemia, including the leaders of the
Podripsko canton, the traditional seat of party strength, had
from 1874 to 1891 constituted the nucleus of party leadership
and the largest party constituency. Second, the anticlerical
peasant smallholders of southern Bohemia and Moravia, hurt by
the worsening agrarian crisis, joined the Young Czechs in time
for the 1889 and 1891 electoral campaigns. Third, newspapermen,
especially the editors of the *Národní listy*, had long had an important voice in determining party policies and in maintaining

the party's reputation for radicalism. Fourth, doctors of medicine, engineers, and scholars in scientific disciplines brought
strong liberal and anticlerical views and an ethos of profes-
sionalism and public service to the party. Fifth, lawyers, the
most influential occupational group and the largest in number
after the farmers, were the first group to make politics a profession and together with the doctors and scientists held most
higher party offices. Sixth, several radical mavericks, who
defy inclusion in any social or occupational group, enlivened
internal party debate and often publicly embarrassed the party
by their outrageously radical opinions on nationality problems.
Seventh, many businessmen served on the party board of trustees,
but few chose to participate as parliamentary delegates. Eighth,
a small group of younger professors and intellectuals, calling
themselves the Realists, joined the party just before the 1891
elections in hopes of making it more responsive to popular aspirations and social problems. A ninth group which did not join
the party but which supported it in the elections of 1889 and
1891 included leaders of the reform-minded Czech university students who in the latter year emerged as the Progressive movement.
A discussion of the leading figures in each group should help
identify the principal social and ideological forces within the
party as well as portray the men who formulated party programs
and tried to put them into practice.[24]

The Podřipsko canton, as the Young Czech-controlled districts
of Roudnice and Mělník were popularly called, typified the sugar
beet producing areas along the language frontier which elected a
majority of all party parliamentary delegates from 1874 until
the 1891 victory over the Old Czechs. During those seventeen
years, the party won a majority of fourth-curial votes there
among those farmers and rural entrepreneurs prosperous enough to
meet the tax requirements of ten, later five, gulden. Throughout the nineties, farmers remained the largest occupational
group among party delegates. But aside from Václav and Heřman
Janda from Podřipsko, few farmers played leading parts in managing the party or won a great popular following comparable to
that of Edvard Grégr or Josef Herold. The most powerful party
figures even in the predominantly rural districts were usually
lawyers or men with higher education, like Karel Adámek in the
Hlinsko-Vysoké Myto district, Václav Kratochvíl and Ervín Špindler in Podřipsko, and Emanuel Engel in Benešov. Party representatives from rural areas, whether farmers or not, recognized
that unless the party upheld the interests of its strongly rural
rank and file, it could not hope to maintain its preponderance
in Czech politics after the introduction of universal suffrage.

For twenty-five years, the Podřipsko canton constituted the
principal seat of Young Czech party strength. The first tábor
on Říp of May 10, 1868, and the subsequent imprisonment of its
organizers, Václav Kratochvíl and Václav Janda, spurred the
growth of patriotism and liberalism among the common people.

The Young Czech faction of the National party frequently met in
Roudnice or Mělník, especially during Koller's state of emergency in Prague, to make plans for the eventual establishment of a
separate political party.[25] Upon release by the authorities
after serving six-month terms, Kratochvíl and Janda began building a strong political organization in the region, using as
their basis the Roudnice nad Labem and Mělník district boards.
The voluminous correspondence between Julius Grégr and Ervín
Špindler indicates that the Podřipsko canton worked closely with
the *Národní listy* throughout the seventies and eighties.[26] The
canton could insure the election of four to six Young Czech candidates in any election, and its peasant movement, headed by
Václav Janda, was expected to deliver popular support to the
party in the event suffrage was ever extended. The *Národní
listy* in turn provided editorial support for internal improvements, secular schools, and civil liberties in Podřipsko. So
thoroughly did Kratochvíl, Špindler, and Janda dominate Podřipsko for the Young Czechs that Old Czechs were virtually excluded
from district or communal government. This in turn gave rise to
charges of terrorism and conspiracy from the embattled National
party. But in fact the Young Czechs of Podřipsko did no more
than did Old Czechs in districts where they could command an
overwhelming majority. In the south Bohemian Old Czech bastion
of České Budějovice, August Žatka worked closely with the conservative great landowner Charles Buquoy to exclude Young
Czechs from self-government and administration.[27]

The great landowners who held estates near Roudnice or Mělník,
including Bohemian Grand Marshall George of Lobkowicz among the
conservatives and the Aehrenthal family among the constitutional
party, regarded with alarm the powerful Young Czech and peasant
movements in Podřipsko, which constituted a challenge to their
political and economic privileges. George of Lobkowicz, long an
ally and patron of the Old Czech party, even likened the Podřipsko canton to a den of thieves.

Who were the principal Young Czech leaders in Podřipsko?
Václav Kratochvíl, the patriarch and first mayor of the Roudnice
district board, for twenty years oversaw the building of regional economic prosperity through canals, railways, and the development of the sugar beet industry. He remained until his death
in 1893 a trusted man of the local party committee of five
(*pětka*) but took little interest in politics elsewhere.[28]

Ervín Špindler, long-time board secretary and Kratochvíl's
successor as mayor in 1884, had complemented his political activities by founding in Roudnice in 1870 the first liberal weeklies in Podřipsko, *Říp* and *Podřipan*. Unlike Kratochvíl, he took
an interest in provincial and imperial politics, repeatedly winning election to the diet and to the Reichsrat. His poetry,
short stories, and translations of Heine's *Songs* and Alfred
Meissner's *Žižka* had established by the seventies his reputation
in Czech intellectual circles. His historical tales of

considerable literary merit dealt principally with life and
legend in his native Podřipsko.[29] Špindler always declared himself to be a "writer" even after he had grown wealthy by helping
manage many of the industrial enterprises in and around Roudnice.
He dominated politics in Podřipsko as mayor of the Roudnice district from 1884 until his death in December 1918. Long experience in district self-government inclined him toward prudent conduct and emphasis on material development without compromising
his efforts to extend civil liberties. Špindler, unlike Kratochvíl, worked through the diet and the Reichsrat to bring to his
constituency public works and improved transportation facilities
like the Vltava and Labe Canal. Like most of his prosperous educated urban and rural constituents, Špindler was an archetypal
Young Czech free-thinker. Masaryk remembered having cordially
debated religion with Špindler on several occasions at which the
mayor expressed his inability to comprehend how anyone as educated as Masaryk could seriously hold religious beliefs.[30]

Václav Janda, a prosperous farmer and ultimately an estate
owner from Budohostice, earned the affectionate title of "peasant
king" as he became the undisputed leader of the agrarian movement
in the north central Bohemian districts of Podřipsko and the Ohře
valley.[31] His eldest son, Herman, born in 1860, followed his
father's steps in Young Czech politics, first winning election to
the diet in 1892 and to the Reichsrat in 1895 by a special election. The family reputation for agrarian radicalism twice held
up imperial confirmation of Herman Janda's election in 1895 to
the chairmanship of the Provincial Agricultural Council of Bohemia.[32]

Why did the Young Czech party exert a much greater electoral
appeal in Podřipsko and the lower Ohře valley than in other sugar
beet producing regions? Given the intense rivalry between Czechs
and Germans along the language frontier, which roughly paralleled
the northern borders of the Mělník, Roudnice, and Louny districts,
Czechs in those areas especially appreciated the party's strident
defense of national interests, including those of the Czech minority to the north. One of the most relentless and prolonged
later nineteenth-century struggles between Czechs and Germans
occurred in the commune of Liběchov, five miles north of Mělník.
Czechs from adjacent communes in Podřipsko, encouraged by the
Young Czech party, the Roudnice and Mělník district boards, and
the North Bohemian National Union, gradually bought up land formerly belonging to the Liběchov estate and thereby very gradually extended the language frontier several miles northward during the last quarter of the nineteenth century. Neither the great
landowners nor the Germans in the area could match the tenacity
or the funds of the Czech peasantry, who purchased the land principally as a means of livelihood and secondarily as a means of
promoting the interests of the nation. All Czechs took pride in
their ability to best their former masters and their German
neighbors in peaceful economic competition.[33]

The small and middle peasants recently enfranchised by the
new five-gulden tax requirement gave the Young Czechs their substantial margin of victory over the Old Czechs in the 1889
fourth-curial diet elections and in the Reichsrat elections of
1891.[34] The Old Czechs had long cultivated votes in rural areas
and especially enjoyed loyal support from prosperous peasants
organized and led by Jan Antonín Prokůpek in the middle Labe
valley around Kolín and Kutná Hora.[35] But the Young Czechs had
deservedly earned a reputation for being more liberal in politics and for better defending the interests of small and middling farmers and of the Czech minority in northern Bohemia.

During the later 1880s, a worsening agrarian crisis as well
as extended suffrage stimulated the formation of independent political organizations among Czech farmers and peasants.[36] These
organizations grew out of the hundreds of rural cooperatives and
credit unions founded after 1873. In Olomouc in September 1883,
representatives from Czech agrarian societies in the fertile
Hana area established the Czechomoravian Peasant Association for
Moravia (Českomoravský spolek selský pro Moravu) under the lead-
ership of Josef Vychodil, Jan Rudolf Demel, and Josef Jeronym
Tvrdík. Agrarian interests in Podřipsko, led by Young Czech
Václav Janda, and an agrarian economic association founded in
Písek in 1879 by Alfons Št'astný provided the nucleus of the
Peasant Union for the Kingdom of Bohemia (Selská Jednota pro
Království české), which formed in Prague during May 1889 under
Št'astný's chairmanship.[37] Both the Bohemian and Moravian associations aimed in rural districts to supplant the predominantly
upper middle-class Old Czech political representatives with men
of agrarian occupations and interests. Both also first entered
provincial politics in 1889 as champions of Young Czech nationalism, liberalism, and anticlericalism as well as of tax relief
and greater tariff protection for Cisleithanian agriculture.[38]
Among the many peasant politicians who entered public life
through local politics in the late eighties was Stanislav Kubr,
later a founder of the Agrarian party. He won election to the
communal governing board of the Kneževes commune in 1887 and together with his Young Czech colleague, Václav Krumbholz, was
elected to the district board for the Smíchov district in October 1891.[39]

Peasant anticlericalism, demands for pragmatism in politics,
and refusal to accept the leadership of the Prague intelligentsia found their most notable representative in Alfons Št'astný.
He and his associate Jan Rataj, chairman of the Peasant Union
for Bohemia, and their Moravian counterparts, Vychodil and
Demel, pioneered the political organization of Czech peasant
smallholders. Št'astný, who argued vigorously throughout his
life against accepting Biblical mythology or the divinity of
Jesus, looked and acted very much like the archetypal Old Testa-
ment prophet. A largely self-educated peasant from Padařov in
southern Bohemia, he had twice interrupted his medical studies

because of ill health before giving up in 1855 to take over the
family farm. In medical school he struck up what was to be a
lifelong friendship with Edvard Grégr, with whom he shared liberal and anticlerical views. Šťastný's famous 1872 pamphlet
O doplnění našeho národního programu (On the completion of our
national program) called for a more liberal and anticlerical
politics, in many respects anticipating the resolution of the
first Young Czech party congress in December 1874, and celebrated
Jan Hus as the proper guide to moral behavior in contrast to the
Catholic Church, which he saw leagued with the great landowners
and upper middle class to keep the Czech people in spiritual as
well as material bondage.[40] On political and social issues
generally, Šťastný expressed himself more forcefully and intem-
perately than all but the most radical Young Czech spokesmen.
Not only did he believe the "agrarian question" to be "the ker-
nel of the social question," he viewed the great landowners as
"a cancer on the body politic." Given such strongly egalitarian
and anticlerical views, Šťastný supported the Young Czechs during
the seventies and eighties and encouraged Czech peasants and farmers to do likewise. His insistence that rural folk be second to
none in national politics also helped insure his recognition as
prophet and leading founder of the Czech agrarian movement.[41]

The editors and correspondents of the *Národní listy* contributed mightily to the founding and development of the Young
Czech party, but of the four editors most involved in party
work, only Gustav Eim actively took part in parliamentary politics. Aside from journalism, Julius Grégr, Josef Anýž, and
Karel Tůma restricted their political activity to the Bohemian
Diet and the party executive committee in Prague.

Doctors of medicine, engineers, and professors from the
Prague Technical Institute numbered eight among the prominent
Young Czech leaders and brought to the party a strong faith in
liberalism and scientific progress and a desire and ability to
manage public affairs in a professional manner. Besides František Tilser, elder statesman, versatile party official, and professor of descriptive geometry at the Prague Technical Institute,
this group included Gabriel Blažek, professor of mathematics at
the same institute and chairman of the party board of trustees
from 1888 through the nineties, and Jan Kaftan, a renowned civil
engineer and railroad builder. The five doctors were Jan Dvořák,
Edvard Grégr, Václav Šamánek, Josef Šíl, and Emanuel Engel, Tilser's successor as chairman of the parliamentary club from 1892
to 1901 and as chairman of the party club of delegates in the
Bohemian Diet from 1892 until 1907.[42]

Young Czech doctors and engineers generally took an optimistic
view of human nature as well as of scientific and industrial progress and believed that the application of a liberal and scientific spirit in politics would help overcome class and nationality
conflicts. Tilser held the view that educating students in the
exact sciences, especially mathematics and descriptive geometry,

would create a logic and precision of mind which would see
through the foolish slogans and trappings of monarchism and extreme nationalism. Kaftan did outstanding work in designing and
building parts of the Austro-Hungarian railway system which, it
was hoped, would link the various peoples of the monarchy together in brotherhood as well as in greater prosperity. To improve transportation in Bohemia, he drew up plans to extend
canal traffic on the middle Labe from Mělník to Jaroměř and on
the Vltava from Smíchov all the way to České Budějovice. These
ambitious projects have to date been only partially completed.

Young Czech doctors and scientists found their view of politics as public service reinforced by professional experience as
well as by liberal ideals. Edvard Grégr, Tilšer, Šamánek, and
Šíl numbered among the most stalwart party radicals, while Blažek, Engel, and Kaftan, no less liberal or patriotic in conviction, generally counseled moderation in tactical questions. By
way of contrast, no doctors, scientists, or engineers played a
prominent role in Old Czech politics, where the learned professions of law and the liberal arts prevailed. In the number of
medical doctors among party leaders as well as in fervent anticlericalism, the Young Czechs resembled the contemporary French
Radical party more than did any other political party in Cisleithania. Engel and Kaftan also brought a heretofore lacking
international perspective to party politics and could be counted
upon in any party debate to oppose parochial views. Engel had
studied medicine in France as a young man and retained a lifelong
interest in French and Russian literature as well as in international medical research. Kaftan, whose work in railway and
canal construction won international recognition, frequently
traveled abroad as a consultant on foreign engineering projects.

Emanuel Engel's long and successful tenure as chairman of the
party clubs of delegates in the Reichsrat and in the diet and
his equally long service on the party executive committee and
board of trustees made him the most important Young Czech of the
1890s. Evidence in the party archives corroborates the almost
invariably complimentary testimony from contemporaries, whether
friends or rivals, which reveals him to have been the party's
"guiding spirit" (*spiritus rector*) and master manipulator and
conciliator whose consummate skill as an executive contributed
mightily to the party's preeminence in Czech politics from 1891
to 1900.[43] He skillfully managed a party composed of diverse
interest groups and of many strong and ambitious personalities.
A man of retiring nature, he did not seek publicity, despite his
lifelong interest in questions of agriculture and public health,
and never spoke as the leader of any party faction. This greatly facilitated his coordinating party activities and persuading
disgruntled factions to accept majority rule. Private correspondence reveals him to have been an honest and clear-thinking
leader who enjoyed the trust of all and whom no one regarded as
a personal rival.[44] He served as the personal physician as well

as the confidant of many party members. Even the poet J. S.
Machar, a leading critic of the Young Czechs, attested to Engel's sense of humor and his being "every inch an honest man."[45]
In a party which contained its share of schemers, Engel's honesty
and tact helped keep the party on an even keel and were no small
ingredients in his generally successful tenure as chairman.

While a medical student in Paris during the middle sixties,
he had decided to serve the public through politics as well as
medicine.[46] This he did in Prague, where he worked in hospitals,
and in Benešov, where he maintained his practice. His father
was a famous surgeon in Vienna and in Prague; and the family,
like the Palacký and Rieger families, numbered among the foremost
in Prague society. Though his social status assured him easy
entry to inner circles of the Old Czech party, Engel pronounced
in favor of the Young Czechs after 1874 out of strong patriotic
and liberal convictions acquired through association with the
tábor movement, the nationalistic *Ruch* intelligentsia, and the
Sokol in Benešov. His social standing reinforced his self-
confidence and won him access to higher society in Vienna as
well as in Prague, no small asset for a party chairman.

Few politicians in Austria-Hungary worked as diligently or
constructively for reform within the established political system as did Emanuel Engel. He was typical of Young Czechs in his
willingness to work within and help to improve that system but
extraordinary in the great energy and organizational ability he
applied to this task. Few Young Czechs could so tactfully and
clearly make a case for Czech national interests to political
opponents or imperial officials. Given Engel's reputation for
prudent conduct, some confidants were surprised to hear him in
1886 privately confess his desire to serve if necessary as the
administrator of a Czech kingdom occupied by Russian troops. He
was not alone among Czech political leaders in expressing such a
view at times when war between Russia and Austria-Hungary appeared likely. Others would privately assert similar opinions
in 1908 and again during the First World War. An intense patriotism and distrust of the Habsburgs on the one hand and a willingness to work for reform within the law on the other characterized Czech politics throughout the era of dualism.[47]

All who knew the Young Czech doctor Jan Dvořák considered him
to be an unusually industrious delegate who conscientiously
looked after the needs of his constituents. In publications and
parliamentary work, he concentrated on improving public health
and urban sanitation. His raising funds for foundling hospitals
led to many jokes about his motives for doing so. He always remained something of an innocent in politics, expecting colleagues
to agree if his arguments were clearly and logically presented.
Once, in a speech to the diet, he naively called on the Bohemian
nobility to reconcile those "divided brothers," the Young and
Old Czechs.[48]

Whereas Jan Dvořák was an industrious and very circumspect

parliamentarian on the model of Engel, doctors Josef Šíl and
Václav Šamánek numbered among the radical associates of the
Grégr brothers. Like Edvard Grégr, whom they resembled in many
respects, they had been led by concern for social and political
problems from medicine into politics. Šíl came from Hradec
Králové and Jičín and was among the most vocal advocates of
placing a Hus plaque in the National Museum. A thoroughgoing
radical, he resigned his Reichsrat mandate in 1896 rather than
enter into an alliance with the great landowners and the Badeni
government. Šamánek practiced medicine in Liberec beginning in
1873 and helped establish the Sokol there in 1881. He founded
the Liberec Foundation (Matice liberecká) and served as the
leading spokesman for the Czech minority in northeastern Bohemia
and as a trustee of the North Bohemian National Union. This
work helped him win election to the Reichsrat from Prague in
1893 and to the Bohemian Diet in 1895 from the predominantly
Czech district of Turnov near Liberec.[49]

Edvard Grégr continued throughout the eighties and nineties
to be the leading pamphleteer and parliamentary tribune of the
Young Czech party. He had ceased to practice medicine or to conduct scientific experiments after commencing a full-time political career in 1862. He and his younger brother Julius made the
Grégr name synonymous with radical Young Czech liberalism and
anticlericalism and were invariably credited with any success or
shortcoming of radical politics. Ideological agreement facilitated their division of tasks on the party's behalf. While the
Národní listy grew and prospered under Julius's management, Edvard became the principal party speechmaker on nationality issues and on relations between church and state. Colleagues like
Engel and Špindler who wanted Edvard to tone down his "theatrical radicalism" nonetheless recognized that so beloved by the
people was he that speeches which might embarrass the party in
Vienna would win many votes on the hustings. Unlike Julius, Edvard possessed a calm and reflective temperament and revealed no
personal animosity or vindictiveness. Agreement between the
brothers on political issues overshadowed a certain coolness and
perfunctoriness in their personal relations which many observers
traced to some long-buried quarrel of childhood or adolescence.
Be that as it may, Julius usually sought advice and reassurance
from his older brother in times of difficulty or doubt.[50]

Almost all associates of Edvard Grégr, even those who did not
share his doctrinaire radicalism and profound distrust of the
Habsburgs, recognized that he held no grudges, sought no enemies,
and was a man of warmth and generosity.[51] His diary shows that
his hostility toward the monarchy grew gradually, only after it
had repeatedly imprisoned and fined him and other Czech political leaders for expressing liberal and patriotic opinions. Until 1871, he had believed the monarchy capable of peacefully
adjusting to social change and even thereafter worked for its
gradual reform in hopes that the Czech nation should some day

stand second to none. There is no evidence that he bore malice
toward anyone, including the Germans. His informed public
speeches condemning German political policies or national arrogance resorted to nothing stronger than irony or occasional sar-
casm. Like almost every educated Czech of his time, he appreciated the value of German as an international language and,
given his training in science and medicine, always appreciated
the many German contributions in those fields. His call to the
Bohemian Germans to recognize Czech culture as the equal of German fell on deaf ears, as did his appeals for cooperation between Czechs and Germans based on mutually held liberal ideals.
    Edvard Grégr's speeches in Parliament dealt with specific is-
sues and aimed to persuade Czech public opinion as well as parliamentary delegates to oppose any policies of the Habsburgs or
Bohemian Germans that he and the party thought inimical to Czech
interests. The imperial authorities and the Germans, unaccus-
tomed to such strong language from Palacký or Rieger, immediately
caricatured Grégr as a firebrand, a label which more accurately
described his brother Julius or Vašatý and Břevnovský among party
radicals. Even Gustav Eim, who contended privately that the
radical speeches and histrionics of the Grégr brothers might
bring "a disaster for the nation," always maintained cordial relations with Edvard Grégr.[52]
    While the doctors of medicine and professors of mathematics
brought professional abilities to politics, it was the party
lawyers who made politics a profession. In both the organizational and parliamentary work of the party, lawyers played the
leading role from 1874 until the First World War. They numbered
twelve among the thirty-two members of the 1897 party executive
committee and eight among twenty-one party founders in 1874, including Karel Sladkovský, Julius Grégr, and Jan Kučera.[53] Lawyers traditionally held the post of chairman of the executive
committee, Karel Sladkovský holding it until 1880, Jan Kučera
until 1895, Jan Podlipný to 1897, and Václav Škarda until 1912.
By contrast, a lawyer did not become chairman of the parliamentary club of delegates until Bedřich Pacák succeeded Emanuel
Engel in 1901. All lawyers in the party generally acted as a
force for moderation, even those closest to the radical democratic tradition like Jan Kučera, Edvard Brzorád, Josef Fořt, and
Jan Slavík. Twenty-two of the many Young Czech lawyers were
among the most important party figures. Of these, eight who had
doctorates in jurisprudence dedicated themselves primarily to
activities other than the practice of law, including Julius
Grégr and Karel Sladkovský and the two Realists Josef Kaizl and
Karel Kramář. Jaromír Čelakovský, after 1886 Professor of Czech
Legal History at Charles-Ferdinand University, devoted much of
his time to chairing the Central School Foundation and to the
scientific ordering of Bohemian provincial and municipal archives. Josef Fořt served thirty years as draftsman for the
Prague Chamber of Commerce and authored several books on business

and finance. Alois Rašín, who entered politics as a progressive, very successfully pursued careers in finance, journalism, and politics and as he grew older gradually adopted more conservative political and fiscal views. In Brno, Adolf Stránský concentrated on editing the daily *Lidové noviny* (People's news) and chairing the Young Czech-affiliated People's party of Moravia, which he helped to found on June 22, 1890. This Moravian counterpart of the Grégr brothers was noted for his ready wit and eagerness to debate political issues. Born of Jewish parents, he joined the Catholic Church at the age of thirty, with Gustav Eim serving as his sponsor during the baptism. Conversion to Catholicism did not, however, moderate his liberal and anticlerical views. On account of his Jewish origins he was not well received in higher Prague society or even socially by some of his Young Czech colleagues.[54]

Fourteen leading party spokesmen regularly practiced law. Among the most influential party administrators and policy-makers were Alois Pravoslav Trojan, patriarch and elder statesman of the party; the Škardas, father Jakub and son Václav, both conservative lawmakers and fine scholars; and Jan Kučera, long-time chairman of the party executive committee. Josef Herold and Bedřich Pacák won renown as outstanding party parliamentarians and public speakers. The two party members most prominent in advancing the Sokol were Jan Podlipný, sometime mayor of Prague, and Karel Pippich, organizer of Czech cultural institutions in eastern Bohemia and chairman of the Chrudim Sokol. Jan Slavík from Jindřichův Hradec became after 1892 the foremost party crusader for universal manhood suffrage. Ladislav Pinkas, chairman of the Alliance française in Prague and the party's foremost Francophile, was born in France of a Czech father and French mother and was the grandson of Adolf M. Pinkas of 1848 fame. Edvard Brzorád served as a radical liberal spokesman and able party administrator; Josef Tuček was Stránský's right-hand man in Brno and the second Moravian to serve on the party executive committee. Prokop Podlipský became the first editor of *Česká Revue* (The Czech review), the party quarterly founded in 1897; and Emanuel Dyk from Pilsen was noted for his editorship of the 1899 party report on Bosnia-Hercegovina and for having given the longest Young Czech sppech on record, a six-and-one-half-hour filibuster on June 14, 1895, against the Windischgrätz tax bill.[55]

The party patriarch, Alois Pravoslav Trojan, in 1891 at age seventy-five looked back on a career of more than half a century in governmental administration and politics. The son of a prosperous rural miller, he was born on April 2, 1815, in Knovíz near Slaný and began work in the state administrative service in 1838. From the revolution of 1848 until his death at seventy-seven in 1893, he remained a widely revered and moderate Czech political leader. In 1874, he was one of the twenty-one founders of the Young Czech party and among its first seven delegates

elected to the Bohemian Diet. Respected by friend and foe alike
as a simple man without ostentation, hatred, or guile, he participated in politics, as he put it, "to see that the Czechs
should be inferior to no other people in their enjoyment of
rights in their own homeland."[56] According to Jan Neruda in
1882, no Czech patriot equaled Trojan in the extent or diligence
of activity in defense of "progress" and "freedom."[57] By 1890,
he remained among the few Czech politicians still alive who had
participated in the work of the National Revival, the 1848 revolution, and the reestablishment of constitutional rule during
the sixties.

Among Young Czechs of the seventies, Alois Pravoslav Trojan
and Jakub Škarda excelled as tacticians and most fervently advocated working for economic growth and political reform through
established governmental, patriotic, and commercial institutions. This largely explains their having broken company with
Rieger and Palacký in 1874 in opposition to Old Czech passive
resistance. It also helps explain their return to Old Czech
ranks after Young and Old Czechs united in a common parliamentary club in support of the Taaffe government. They broke for a
second time with the Old Czechs in 1890 after concluding that
Rieger and Mattuš had, by endorsing the Agreement of that year,
jeopardized Bohemian state rights and the future of the Czech
national movement. Neither man believed that he had compromised
his principles or his patriotism by changing so readily from one
party to another. Both men continued to regard the Old and
Young Czech parties as branches of the same national movement
with loyalty to the movement clearly transcending any allegiance
to either of its constituent parties.

Jakub Škarda was taciturn and reserved, in contrast to his
open and gregarious colleague Trojan. Born in 1828, Škarda made
a name for himself in Prague city government, beginning in 1860,
and after 1865 as editor of the prestigious law journal *Právník*
(The lawyer). More than any other Young Czech he advocated
"politics step by step," that is to say working patiently from
one small achievement to another until one had put together a
considerable reform. His good business sense and widespread
governmental experience helped him amass a considerable fortune
in industrial stock. His work in preparing the series of laws
on local and district government, approved by the Bohemian Diet
and the Belcredi administration in 1864, made him one of the
founding fathers of Czech provincial and district self-government.
At the same time his three-volume *Sbírka zákonů rakouských* (Collection of Austrian laws) won recognition as the best guide in
Czech to commercial and criminal law.[58] An intellectual of
retiring nature, Škarda made few public appearances. His
political activity, unlike that of Trojan and the more colorful
Grégr brothers, received little public attention. But in the
self-governmental institutions which he helped to establish and
in the "step-by-step politics" which he sought to follow, he

left an ineradicable mark upon all future programs and actions
of the Young Czech party, whether acknowledged or not.

Jan Kučera, a lawyer of radical liberal convictions, succeeded Karel Sladkovský in 1880 as chairman of the party executive committee and as a party delegate to the Reichsrat.[59] He
had already won acclaim for having served as defense attorney
to many of the Czech newspapermen prosecuted during Governor
Koller's repression of the Czech national movement. He never
forgave the Habsburgs for having authorized the imposition of
unjust fines and imprisonment at that time, nor did he ever
cease criticizing the Old Czechs for not having more forthrightly resisted Koller's policies. As chairman of the party executive committee, Kučera helped guide the Young Czechs to decisive
electoral victories over the Old Czechs in the fourth-curial
diet elections of 1889 and in the parliamentary elections of
1891. Throughout his long chairmanship, the executive committee
remained a bastion of radical liberalism.

Two younger lawyers who came to the party in the eighties,
Josef Herold and Bedřich Pacák, soon won enviable reputations
as leading parliamentary spokesmen and public speakers during
the 1889 and 1891 electoral campaigns. Herold in this respect
quite appropriately lived up to his name. His reputation as a
public speaker owed much to his patriotic appeals, graphic anec-
dotes, and concentration upon simple topics. Later generations
will find his speeches in large part unintelligible unless pre-
faced by some study of the issues at hand. As a student leader,
Herold became a politically active patriot through association
with the tábor movement and with Josef Barák and Julius Grégr.
At one time or another he served, like Jakub Škarda, on the
boards of almost all important Czech patriotic associations and
had helped found both the Sokol in his native Vršovice and the
Central School Foundation. He first won election to the diet in
1883 and to the Reichsrat in 1888 and long served on the Young
Czech executive committee and as mayor of the wealthy Prague
suburb of Vinohrady.

Bedřich Pacák, nicknamed Bedřich the Short because of his stature, distinguished himself as a leading party spokesman for
civil liberties.[60] Such activity derived in part from his imprisonment in 1868 for the "treasonable activity" of having organized several tábor demonstrations. Upon his release from
prison in 1871, after serving three years of a five-year term,
he took up political journalism while completing his law degree.
In 1883, he established his own law practice in Kutná Hora and
beginning in 1889 regularly won reelection to the Bohemian Diet
and the Reichsrat from the Čáslav and Kutná Hora districts. His
correspondence indicates that his prison experience occasioned
no lasting hatred of Germans or the imperial authorities; but
that experience, along with his training in the law, helped increase his impatience with anyone who, like publicists from the
Neue Freie Presse or the Foreign Office, judged Austria-Hungary

more on the liberal wording of its laws than on their authoritarian enforcement. Pacák's many speeches on behalf of civil rights and representative government were characterized by their attention to factual detail and avoidance of inflammatory rhetoric. Pacák never indulged as did the Grégr brothers or Kramář in histrionics or hyperbole, and his cautious actions were in keeping with his temperate words.

Three of the four party mavericks were lawyers. Jan Vašatý, an outspoken radical and Russophile, showed so little respect for party discipline that he became the principal Young Czech troublemaker. Count Václav Kounic, a titled great landowner of radical political convictions, joined the Young Czechs during the eighties and carried on in the Thurn-Taxis tradition. His fellow aristocrats and a number of Czechs, including Eim and Stašek, thought him to be slightly crazy, though generous and of good will. Toward the end of his life, he sought to help improve wages and working conditions for miners and to advance the emancipation of women. Jakub Scharf was the only Jew ever elected to the Bohemian Diet as a Young Czech; he represented the predominantly Jewish Josefov district in Prague and also served as an intermediary between the party and the Czech Jewish community. He belonged to that growing minority of Jews in Prague who believed that their interests would best be served by identifying themselves as Czechs instead of as Germans. The fourth maverick, the Prague glovemaker Václav Březnovský, rivaled Vašatý in making intemperate and inopportune remarks. In 1863 he had been briefly imprisoned for having helped Josef Barák organize Czech volunteers in Kraków to fight in the Polish insurrection. His occasional anti-Semitic statements to some degree undermined Scharf's efforts and embarrassed the Young Czech party, which had always refused to endorse anti-Semitism. He nonetheless remained a popular enough figure in many lower middle-class sections of Prague to win election repeatedly to the diet and the Reichsrat.[61]

Few entrepreneurs or independent businessmen participated in parliamentary activities of the party, but many served as local trusted men and on the Board of Provincial Trustees where they constituted at least a third of the membership. This gave business interests ample voice in the management of party affairs. Many of the Czech business representatives in the diet and the Reichsrat were chosen by the Prague, Pilsen, and České Budějovice chambers of commerce. Entrepreneurs like Václav Formánek from Hradec Králové, Max Hájek, a cavalry veteran of the Italian wars and representative of the Pilsen Chamber of Commerce, and Josef Wohanka, chairman of the Prague Chamber of Commerce after 1895 and director of the Živnobanka, typically contributed little to parliamentary politics and made little name for themselves in public life apart from their work in industry. Nonetheless, strong endorsement of business enterprise could be found among all leading party members from Julius Grégr and Ervín Špindler

to party chairman Emanuel Engel, who in 1903 candidly stated
that twenty more Czech millionaire industrialists would better
serve the national cause than the best legislation on language
rights.[62]

The eighth and last group to join the Young Czech party in
time for the parliamentary electoral campaign of 1891 were the
younger scholars and writers who organized themselves in 1886 as
the Realists. Most prominent among them were Josef Kaizl and
T. G. Masaryk, professors respectively of political economy and
philosophy at Charles-Ferdinand University, and Karel Kramář, an
independently wealthy young lawyer who like Kaizl had studied in
Germany and been influenced in his economic views by the professorial "socialists of the chair." Other Realists included František Drtina, a prolific professor of philosophy and pedagogy,
Antonín Rezek, a promising young historian at Charles-Ferdinand
University, and Antonín Zeman, a young writer from the Krkonoše
and upper Jizera valley who wrote under the name of Antal Stašek.[63] The Realists chose "reasoned and honest politics" as the
motto for their weekly paper Čas (Time), which made informed
criticism of public issues and advocated extensive social and
institutional reform, in contrast to the Manchester liberalism
espoused by both Old and Young Czechs. To their mind, political
"realism" did not call for expedient adaptation to current exigencies but for the steadfast and intelligent application of
long-range policies designed to anticipate future needs.[64]

The Realists had first banded together in 1886 in defense of
their professorial colleague, Jan Gebauer, who, defying fervent
public sentiment, had proved the allegedly medieval Czech
Králové Dvůr and Zelená Hora manuscripts to have been forged
rather than "discovered" in 1817 and 1818 by the Czech romantic
poet Václav Hanka. When both Young and Old Czech leaders, including Julius Grégr and F. L. Rieger, chose to defend the authenticity of the manuscripts, many students and younger intellectuals concluded that any men who sanctioned intellectual dis-
honesty in the name of patriotism could not be trusted to serve
as national political leaders. The Realists therefore entered
Czech politics in hopes of improving it through the practical
application of scholarship as well as informed social concern.

Kaizl and Masaryk each brought to politics a critical intelligence, broad erudition, and mastery of a new scholarly discipline. Kaizl taught the first courses in political economy at
Charles-Ferdinand University and understood the complexities and
problems of modern industrial society as well as any contemporary. Masaryk introduced the discipline of sociology and the
study of British empiricist philosophy to Austrian and Czech
universities. He had written as his doctoral dissertation a
sociological study of suicide, whose rising rate he attributed
to the dislocation and insecurity created by modern industrial
society and to a loss of religious belief. This study began
Masaryk's lifelong effort to regulate and democratize the modern

state for the welfare of all and to restore to man a faith in
himself based upon the Judeo-Christian tradition. Kramář,
though intellectually inferior to his elder and more learned associates, nonetheless contributed considerable intelligence,
good will, and oratorical ability to the common cause.

The Realists generally agreed that a modern industrial society required a measure of state intervention to deal with social
and economic ills, as well as new forms of political organization, including a party which would bring the millions of citizens soon to be enfranchised into a moral and mutually advantageous relationship with the state. Better education and extended civil liberties would help citizens more fully develop their
abilities and acquire a greater sense of political responsibility. The Realists aimed eventually to create a progressive and
truly national party which would consider the needs and appeal
to the mutual interests of all social classes in working to establish a just and orderly society. Such a party would reject
all outmoded political slogans and come to grips with pressing
social and nationality questions. In their opinion, neither
Young Czechs nor Old Czechs offered any realistic and positive
program for resolving serious contemporary problems. They detested the patriotic chauvinism of the former often expressed in
the *Národní listy* and had reservations about the latter's ongoing alliance with the conservative great landowners. Although
they endorsed some aims and ideals of social democracy, they did
not support that movement because of its advocacy of revolution
and what they discerned to be its excessively materialistic, de-
terministic, and collectivist outlook.

The Realists continued to think that the advancement of national unity and social reform required in the long run the establishment of a new political party but recognized that short-
term exigencies required immediate reform of the existing party
system. Initially, they believed the National party to be more
susceptible to reform than the Young Czechs because of its affin-
ity with the learned professions and its nearly three decades of
preeminence in Czech politics. Moreover, they thought that recent Young Czech electoral victories in the fourth curia had awa-
kened Old Czechs to the need for broadening their constituency
and advocating political reform, whereas the Young Czechs, emboldened by victory, persevered in using the time-honored radical
tactics and slogans.[65] Close personal ties also drew the Realists toward the Old Czechs. Rieger's son-in-law, Albín Bráf, was
their colleague and contemporary; and both Josef Kaizl and his
uncle, Edmund Kaizl, had won election to the Reichsrat as Old
Czechs in 1885. Only after the Old Czechs capitulated to German
Liberal and imperial demands in signing the Agreement of January
1890 did the Realists begin seriously to consider concluding an
alliance with the Young Czechs.

The Progressive movement of Czech youth, which worked closely
with the Young Czechs from 1889 until its suppression by the

imperial authorities in 1893, grew out of educational reform efforts initiated by university students in 1887.[66] Most of these students had grown up in middle-class or lower middle-class families, and more than four out of five had come from districts outside of metropolitan Prague.[67] As a self-styled "new generation" (*nová generace*), they began trying in 1887 to establish a student newspaper and to improve secondary and higher school curricula and student living conditions by working through the Academic Reading Society (Akademický čtenářský spolek), the authorized social and cultural organization to which almost half of all Czech university students belonged.[68]

After the university repeatedly refused to sponsor or support an independent student newspaper, the law students Antonín Čížek and Alois Rašín and the philosophy students Antonín Hajn and Karel Stanislav Sokol established in May 1889 the *Časopis českého studentstva* (The journal of Czech students) as a private corporation: Sokol became the owner and publisher, thanks to the requisite capital provided by his family and father, Young Czech deputy Josef Sokol. At first, the editors concentrated primarily on student life while occasionally commenting on any public issues that directly affected its improvement.[69] For example, they advocated such reforms as repeal of the draconian 1851 imperial disciplinary code for universities and reduction of rote memorization in secondary and higher school curricula. At their invitation, T. G. Masaryk became the first faculty contributor to the journal. His "several thoughts on the goals of Czech students," which appeared in the second issue, contended that students could best serve their nation by living up to the old virtues of honesty and hard work and by acquiring the skills with which they could best serve their fellow citizens.[70] The student journalists and reformers organized around the *Časopis českého studentstva* first referred to themselves as a "Progressive movement" (*Pokrokové hnutí*) in the fall of 1891. At other times, with no sense of contradiction or impropriety, they designated themselves either as a "faction" (*směr*) or as a "party" (*strana*), understood to be a partisan group as opposed to a political party.[71]

Efforts by Progressive students to achieve their aims by politicizing the Academic Reading Society soon aroused the wrath of university and imperial officials, including Governor Alfred Kraus, who disbanded it on August 24, 1889, for having engaged in a series of "provocative" and illegal political acts. The last straw had been publishing a letter sent to fellow students in France which praised French revolutionary and republican traditions in commemoration of the one-hundredth anniversary of the Sorbonne.[72] The Progressives responded by winning several elections between November 1889 and March 1890 to take control of "Slavia," the student association that had taken the place of the recently dissolved Reading Society, a control which they would retain until ousted by governmental intervention in the fall of

1893. The Young Czechs immediately granted fiscal backing to
Slavia, thus further cementing their ties to the Progressive
students. The Old Czechs, who had heretofore discouraged student participation in national politics, now found themselves
isolated from the mainstream of student life. To reassert their
influence at the university, they challenged Slavia and its
Young Czech sponsors by helping establish the rival Society of
Student Friends (Spolek příznivců studentstva). But this organization attracted little support, primarily because of Old
Czech identification with the repressive policies of Governor
Kraus and Minister-President Taaffe.[73]

During the spring and summer of 1890, the Progressive students turned decisively toward preoccupation with public as opposed to university affairs and did so in association with the
Young Czech party. The Progressive program of May of that year
dealt primarily with improving student life, including curtail-
ment of the university's right to impose nonjudicial punishment
and to restrict student political activity. But it also proposed that students participate in national politics with an aim
to advancing civil liberties, national autonomy, and social as
well as educational reform.[74] In July, the Progressives published a supplementary program for student participation in national politics during the summer recess.[75] Both the May and
July programs reflected a decidedly reformist and Young Czech
outlook, especially in advocating the advancement of Bohemian
state rights and opposition to the Agreement of 1890. Each program also revealed a certain political naiveté which would continue to characterize the Progressive movement, especially in
self-congratulatory pronouncements, in sometimes equating youth
with virtue, and in unwarrantedly expecting public gratitude and
support.

The *Časopis českého studentstva* supported the successful Young
Czech electoral campaigns of 1889 for the Bohemian Diet and 1891
for the Reichsrat, in hopes that liberal and anticlerical programs could thereby be realized.[76] Progressive association with
the Young Czech party dated back to May 1887, when representatives Engel, Kounic, Vašatý, and Edvard Grégr sponsored bills in
the Reichsrat to authorize public demonstrations by the Sokol
and to abolish German-language examinations in the Czech Law Faculty at Charles-Ferdinand University. Progressive students had
not only long favored both measures but simultaneously supported
the four Young Czechs against the Old Czech majority, which had
expelled them from the Czech club of delegates. Student demonstrators enthusiastically greeted Edvard Grégr upon his return
by train from Vienna and smashed out several windows in the offices of the Old Czech journal *Politik* (Politics). At that
time, the Old Czech party made the first of many charges that
the Young Czechs played the demagogue to student Progressives
only in order to exploit them as political pawns.[77] Progressive
youth allied with the Young Czech party during the diet elections

of July 1889 and continued this association by protesting the
dissolution of the Academic Reading Society after August 1889,
by helping to raise funds to build a Hus monument in Prague, and
by opposing the Agreement of 1890.[78] The Young Czechs cemented
this association by giving direct subsidies to Slavia and indirect support to the *Časopis českého studentstva*.[79] On the eve
of the March 1891 Reichsrat election, that journal, under editor
Antonín Hajn, endorsed all Young Czech candidates and issued a
five-point program spelling out what it expected their party to
accomplish. This closely resembled the Young Czech electoral
platform in advocating "resolute opposition" to the Taaffe government, the advancement of civil liberties and Bohemian state
rights, and cooperation with like-minded Slovenian, Polish, and
Ukrainian parties. It differed only in advocating universal
suffrage for all citizens regardless of sex instead of universal
manhood suffrage.[80]

The Agreement of 1890 and the 1891 Reichsrat Elections

The Young Czechs, after reestablishing their independent club
of Reichsrat delegates in January 1888, entered a hard-fought
contest with the Old Czech party that ended in their overwhelming victory thirty-eight months later. The Young Czech party
platform of 1889 endorsed those of 1874 and 1879 and added
planks on tariffs and fiscal policy more responsive to the interests of the peasantry and the newly enfranchised five-gulden
voters. The party's revival of a state rights program and demands for an independently Czech policy in Vienna challenged both
Old Czech dependence upon the Taaffe government and German attempts to destroy the political unity of Bohemia. The Bohemian
Diet elections of July 1889 confirmed the strength of the newly
established alliance between the Young Czech party and Alfons
Št'astný's Peasant Union as the party won thirty of thirty-nine
Czech seats in the fourth curia and emerged for the first time
as a serious challenger to Old Czech hegemony. The party's
having won thirty-nine of ninety-seven Czech mandates in three
curias alarmed the emperor as well as the Old Czechs and the
government. In July 1889, he reportedly told an Old Czech delegate from Moravia that "a lot of strange customers have come to
the surface, and we must take energetic measures against them."[81]
    The fourth-curial Young Czech victory wrought consternation
in Old Czech ranks and brought a hostile reaction from the
Taaffe government, which opted for its time-honored policy of
trying to strike down a popular challenge before considering
whether or not to accommodate to it. Baron Alfred Kraus, the
governor of Bohemia whose firm rule had failed to prevent Young
Czech electoral success, resigned, to be replaced on September 7,
1889, by Count Francis Anthony Thun-Hohenstein, at age forty the
ablest of the wealthy young conservative great landowners and
noted for his broad knowledge of politics and aristocratic

demeanor. Thun had come from and married into the finest of Bohemian noble families; he was the eldest son of Count Frederick
Thun, late friend of Bismarck and one-time Austrian ambassador
to St. Petersburg, the nephew of Count Leopold Leo Thun, patron
of the Czech National Revival and the Czech National party, and
the son-in-law of Prince Charles of Schwarzenberg. From his
father-in-law and uncle and from several years as a conservative
great landowner in the diet and Reichsrat, he had learned the
intricacies of Czech and German politics in Bohemia and took office as governor in the expectation of breaking Young Czech radicalism without alienating the Taaffe government's Old Czech supporters. Thun was known to be a firm and conscientious administrator who would not shy away from the selective use of force to
preserve imperial authority. Authoritarian acts and stylish
dress earned Thun the nickname of "Gigerle ["dandy"] Alba," as
his tallness gave rise to the more affectionate appellation
"Francis the Long."[82]

Governor Thun soon moved to suppress the forces threatening
the old order in politics: the radical Young Czechs, the Progressive students, and the peasantry. He followed up Kraus's
closure of the Academic Reading Society and ban on Sokol proces-
sions by instituting heavy fines and frequent confiscations
against the Czech patriotic press and by revoking the charter of
the Peasant Union, for its allegedly illegal participation in
political activity, and seizing its weekly newspaper, the *Selské
noviny*, which Alfons Šťastný soon revived and published largely
at his own expense.

In Moravia, Young Czech success in elections to the Bohemian
Diet encouraged Moravian liberal and peasant organizations to
plan a challenge to the Old Czechs. After the governor of that
province on February 1, 1890, responded by disbanding the Peasant Union of Moravia, the Young Czechs extended fiscal and
journalistic support to Josef Vychodil, head of that union, and
to Adolf Stránský, chairman of the Moravian liberals.[83]

Neither Taaffe nor Thun believed that suppression of peasant
and student organizations would alone suffice to reestablish
political stability. It would also be necessary for parties
which favored the existing social order to compose their differences on nationality and constitutional issues. With this aim
in mind, Taaffe assembled representatives from his government
and the Old Czech, German Liberal, and two great landowning parties in Vienna on January 4, 1890, to hammer out an agreement on
the questions of nationality and language in Bohemia. All agreed
to exclude the Young Czechs, whose radical views and popular ties
would likely cause them to oppose the goals of the negotiations.
The Old Czechs also hoped that an agreement which would promote
national harmony in Bohemia would help their party by undercut-
ting the appeal of radical Young Czech nationalism.

The Agreement drawn up by representatives of the five parties
in Vienna between January 4 and 19 in essence aimed at dividing

most institutions of government according to nationality. The
proposal to suspend the Stremayr ordinances in the predominantly
German districts of Bohemia would have the effect of establishing two systems of administration and justice, one for the predominantly Czech districts, in which both languages would be
utilized in external service, and one for the predominantly German districts, in which Czech need not be so used. The Provincial School Board, the Provincial Agricultural Council, and the
Superior Court and Court of Appeals in Prague were to be divided
into Czech and German sections. In areas of mixed nationality,
the borders of judicial districts were to be redrawn wherever
practicable to include the smallest possible number of citizens
of the minority nationality, and no knowledge of Czech would be
required of officials in predominantly German areas. Moreover,
the Bohemian Diet would be divided into two national curias, each
having veto power in matters of national interest, and a third
for the great landowners. This insured that the German minority
of 35 percent would continue to have proportionally greater representation than the Czech majority of almost 64 percent and
allowed the great landowners to retain the balance of power.
The same divisions would apply to the Provincial Executive Council, in effect preventing that body from effectively overseeing
the treatment of Czech minorities by district self-governmental
boards in predominantly German areas. In return for making so
many concessions to the Germans, the Czechs were promised no
more than a new chamber of commerce in eastern Bohemia, to be
located in either Hradec Králové or Pardubice. The Young Czechs
feared that points of the Agreement not only compromised Bohemian state rights but also signaled German intentions to initiate
a territorial division of Bohemia in accordance with the German
manifesto of December 26, 1886.

The five parties to the Agreement--the Taaffe government, the
German Liberals, the conservative and the constitutional great
landowners, and the Old Czechs--believed that this proposal to
settle aspects of the long-standing conflict between Czechs and
Germans would strengthen their own political position while un-
dercutting that of their radical Young Czech and German nationalist opponents. Taaffe could thereafter expect the German Liberals to cease boycotting the Bohemian Diet in return for his having upheld the authority and German character of imperial administration in Bohemia. The German Liberals, led by Ernst von Plener, feared eventual Czech political preponderance in Bohemia
and sought by dividing provincial administration and justice according to nationality to insure German dominance in all areas
where Germans comprised a majority of the population and German
strength in those areas where Germans comprised a minority. In
abandoning some of the more far-reaching aims of the 1882 Linz
Program and thereby incurring the wrath of German radicals, the
German Liberals could claim to have made some concessions to the
Old Czechs in the interests of a compromise agreement. At the

same time they could satisfy almost all of their electors by
continuing to uphold the December 1886 Manifesto and by noting
that in settling for less than the entire Linz Program they gave
up nothing more than unrealistically ambitious aims, whereas the
Old Czechs, in endorsing the Agreement, had paved the way for
amendment of the Stremayr ordinances in favor of the Germans.
The conservative and the constitutional great landowners, led
respectively by Bohemian Grand Marshal George of Lobkowicz and
Count Joseph Oswald Thun-Salm, preserved their class privileges
through curial representation in the Bohemian Diet and could be
assured of having an influential voice in any future dispute between Czechs and Germans. The Old Czechs, having lost seats to
Young Czechs in the 1889 diet elections, sought to maintain
their traditional dominance of Czech politics by excluding their
rivals from the negotiation of what was expected to be a successful agreement. In doing so, the Old Czech leaders F. L.
Rieger and Karel Mattuš did not at all foresee the almost unanimous rejection of the Agreement of 1890 by the Czech electorate.
Even the emperor's belated recognition of Czech cultural and
scientific achievement on January 23, 1890, by authorizing the
formation of the Czech Academy of the Emperor Franz Joseph for
Sciences, Literature, and the Arts, did little to prevent the
decline of public confidence in the Old Czech party.

The Agreement or *punktace*, published on January 27, 1890,
after ratification by each party to the negotiations, constituted a set of proposals subject to approval by the Bohemian Diet
which were intended to dampen both nationality conflict and popular agitation for political and social reforms. The authors of
the Agreement deliberately excluded from the negotiations all
parties which represented large numbers of disfranchised citizens. They did not realize that on account of extensive social
change and aroused popular aspirations, binding political agreements could no longer be reached by the procedures of 1879, when
Clam-Martinic, Rieger, and Taaffe had hammered out the terms by
which the Old Czechs had agreed to support the Iron Ring in exchange for specific concessions. In 1890, no such agreement between leading representatives of the government, the national
upper middle classes, and the nobility could automatically expect to sway a five-gulden electorate moved by national pride
and a desire for greater civil freedom and economic opportunity.
Czechs from all walks of life had after three decades of constitutional rule and two decades of universal primary education come
to demand a share in making important political decisions.

The Czech Social Democrats, disfranchised by curial voting,
preoccupied with preparations for the 1890 May Day, and still
suffering from the effects of governmental persecution during
the eighties, took little interest in the Agreement of 1890,
which they believed to be an issue of concern only to the privileged classes. On the other hand, both the nascent peasant
movement and the Young Czech party, recent victors in the 1889

elections, found much to oppose in the Agreement and recognized
that public opinion stood behind them.[85]

Gustav Eim, Vienna correspondent for the *Národní listy*, closely followed the negotiation of the Agreement of 1890 and through
his daily dispatches became the first reporter to demonstrate
the extent to which its implementation would harm Czech national
interests. Along with Julius Grégr and other party members, Eim
criticized the Agreement as a thinly disguised attempt to increase the political privileges enjoyed by the Bohemian German
minority and to prevent the Czechs from ever exercising political
influence in Bohemia in proportion to their numbers. The Young
Czechs also pointed out that ratification of the Agreement would
endanger the civil liberties and material interests of Czechs
residing in predominantly German districts. These Czechs had
never exercised as many civil rights as did Germans in predominantly Czech areas, and some had no access to teachers, judges,
and jurors who could speak their language.[86] The Agreement proposed an administrative and judicial division of Bohemia according to nationality that would destroy forever Czech hopes of
realizing a national autonomy based on Bohemian state rights and
comparable to that enjoyed by the Poles in Galicia. Granting
each nationality its own curia in the Bohemian Diet would inevitably lead to legislative stalemate and allow imperial authorities to rule by default, especially since the Agreement preserved
the political privileges of the great landowners and the authoritarian powers of the imperial administration. In sum, the Agreement posed a serious threat to Czech civil liberties, to the advancement of popular participation in politics, and to Czech aims
for greater national autonomy.

Rieger, Mattuš, and Zeithammer not only encountered strong
Young Czech opposition to the Agreement of 1890 but unexpectedly
failed to acquire the unanimous consent of their own party. On
January 26, 1890, the Czech club voted to endorse the Agreement
after Rieger promised that a forthcoming amendment would make
Czech an internal official language in all predominantly Czech
areas. Alois Pravoslav Trojan and Karel Pippich walked out of
the club meeting rather than vote for party acceptance of the
Agreement, while Jakub Škarda abstained. The defection of elder
statesmen Trojan and Škarda offset much of the encouragement Rieger received from the thirty-four delegates voting in his favor.[87]
Trojan and Pippich wrote articles questioning Rieger's ability
to realize the acceptance of Czech as an internal official language in predominantly Czech areas and charged that Bohemian
state rights might have been compromised by the Agreement. They
published these articles in the *Národní listy* after Rieger refused to provide space in the Old Czech daily *Hlas národa*.[88]
The extent to which the Old Czechs had compromised themselves became evident when Minister of Justice Schönborn began on January 31 to issue decrees implementing points 6, 7, and 8, by

ordering the delineation of judicial districts and the division
of the two higher courts according to nationality.

Throughout the summer Rieger tried in vain to persuade Taaffe
to make Czech an official internal language in the predominantly
Czech districts but received no governmental backing whatever
for this his promise of January 26 to his party. His request
was turned down by none other than the emperor himself. As a
result, the Czech electorate had even less reason to endorse Old
Czech candidates and the Agreement of 1890 but had new grounds
to doubt the efficacy of Rieger's much-vaunted influence in
Vienna.[89]

The government further discredited the Old Czechs by involving
them willy-nilly in its attempts to buy off Czech opposition to
the Agreement of 1890. With the approval of the Old Czechs,
Minister-President Taaffe authorized Governor Thun to grant up
to ten thousand gulden in subsidies to Czech newspapers which
backed the government's policies.[90] Thus the Old Czech party,
while still claiming to lead the nation, diminished its popularity by supporting the very government that had closed down the
two leading Czech peasant unions and that sought to control the
press through bribery or confiscation. In this light, Edvard
Grégr's denunciation of the Old Czechs for having sold out the
national movement did not appear very far off the mark.[91]

Popular opposition to the Agreement of 1890 enabled the Young
Czechs to create the majority coalition which ended Old Czech
hegemony in Czech politics. Alfons Št'astný and Jan Rataj endorsed the Young Czechs even more strongly after the authorities
closed down their Peasant Union and that of Vychodil and Tvrdík
in Moravia. After February 1890, many Old Czech politicians and
self-governmental officials transferred their allegiance to the
Young Czech camp, including some like Karel Adámek and Alois
Pravoslav Trojan who had been Young Czechs during the seventies.
Seven other Old Czech delegates to the Reichsrat, including
Jakub Škarda, declared that they would seek reelection indepen-
dently of the National party and thereby insured that the Young
Czechs would run no one against them.

Only gradually did the Czech Realists come around to endorsing
the Young Czech opposition to the Agreement of 1890. As late as
April of that year, Karel Kramář on behalf of himself and his
colleagues published an article in *Čas* which justified the Agreement on the grounds that it would help promote better relations
between Czechs and the Bohemian Germans. On March 27, the Realists had broken off negotiations for an alliance with the Old
Czechs; but not until summer did they realize the extent to which
the Old Czechs had aroused public hostility and undermined their
own authority by continuing to endorse the Agreement. In July,
Čas printed a letter from Kramář, on vacation in Russia, in which
he explained how more careful reflection had led him to accept
the Young Czech view of the Agreement.[92] Kramář's change of mind

may be attributed to study of critical commentary on the Agreement, including a long letter from his Realist colleague František Drtina in Paris, and to a change in perspective wrought by his travels in Russia.[93] By fall, all Realists recognized that they could successfully enter politics only in association with the Young Czech party and delegated Kramář, their colleague closest in spirit to party views, to open negotiations for an electoral alliance.

The Realists, after having long underestimated popular opposition to the Agreement of 1890, decided to come to terms with the Young Czech party in order to maintain their political effectiveness and as much of their 1889 program as possible. Only to the extent that they recognized they would have to meet the Young Czechs more than halfway in any negotiations can their behavior in 1890 be termed opportunistic. Tactfully and without being self-righteous, Young Czech chairmen Tilšer and Kučera worked to bring the Realists as well as renegade Old Czechs into an enlarged Young Czech party. Direct negotiations between the three Realists and the Young Czechs Tilšer, Kučera, and Julius Grégr led to the signing of a pact on December 13, 1890, whereby Kaizl joined the party as a member of the board of trustees, Masaryk as a member of the executive committee, and Kramář as a member in good standing. All three won party endorsement as candidates for the Reichsrat. Both *Národní listy* and *Čas* praised the agreement as a contribution to political reform and national progress and chose to consider the once-lively manuscripts controversy as a scholarly issue on which any party member could freely express an opinion.[94]

December 1890 saw the Young Czech party grow from a small radical nucleus into a coalition party embracing all segments of Czech society except the working class as the Realists followed Old Czechs and the Peasant Union leaders into its ranks. This growth reflected the increasing popular opposition to Old Czech policies and indicated probable Old Czech defeat in the March 1891 parliamentary elections from Bohemia. Moreover, the more-than-twofold increase in Young Czech party members drew the party away from its radical national and agrarian origins and toward the urban upper middle class and university intelligentsia, two groups which had traditionally supported the Old Czechs. This enormously strengthened the party on the eve of the forthcoming elections while creating the possibility of serious intra-party disputes in the future.

The parliamentary elections of March 2 and 4, 1891, resulted in an overwhelming Young Czech victory in Bohemia, where the party swept thirty-seven of the thirty-nine Czech seats, including three of four in the second curia, seventeen of eighteen in the third, and all seventeen seats in the fourth. Alois Pravoslav Trojan, the only Young Czech comparable in age, experience, and popular veneration to F. L. Rieger, defeated him by 883 votes to 10 in Prague's New Town district.[95] The three Czech chambers

of commerce gave to Young Czech candidates 39 of the 66 votes
cast, or 59.1 percent. In the third or urban curia, Young
Czechs received 22,552 votes, or 57.3 percent, of 39,160 cast.
Of 9,058 electoral votes cast in indirect elections in the fourth
or rural curia, they won a total of 5,291, or 58.2 percent. In
Moravia, where the Young Czechs had not yet established a party
organization, the Old Czechs won all eleven Czech seats. But
the liberal and anticlerical Czechs of that province, encouraged
by the Young Czech landslide in Bohemia, began to organize under
the leadership of Adolf Stránský for the eventual overthrow of
the Moravian Old Czechs.[96]

Through its victory in Bohemia, the Young Czech party acquired
new problems as well as new responsibilities. That it owed this
success to the votes of less than 10 percent of the Czech adult
male population in Bohemia illustrated the degree to which the
party represented the interests of the urban middle class and the
wealthier independent farmers.[97] With the best of intentions,
the party would find it difficult to live up to its campaign promise to represent the interests of the entire nation. It also
remained to be seen whether this new coalition party founded in
opposition to the Agreement of 1890 could maintain and enact a
positive political program comparable to its liberal, anticlerical, and patriotic electoral platforms of 1889 and 1891.[98] This
task would be very difficult, since it would have to be undertaken without the parliamentary allies on whom the Old Czechs relied as a partner in the Iron Ring.

The Zenith of Young Czech Radicalism

The years 1891 to 1894 mark a distinct period in the development of the Young Czech party. For the first time, it was the majority party and a coalition of diverse groups instead of a radical and closely-knit minority opposition. Though outnumbered by the new agrarian, Old Czech, and Realist recruits, the radical leadership and popular institutions of the party still had the upper hand. Theirs had been the moral leadership in 1891, and it was perforce to them that the party initially looked for guidance. The Young Czechs had won their great electoral victory essentially on a negative issue--opposition to the Agreement of 1890-- which had been defined by political foes. It remained to be seen whether the different elements in the party could now agree upon a positive and comprehensive program.

The Young Czechs in Parliamentary Opposition

The principal domestic issues of the early nineties were set forth in the Young Czech platforms of 1889 and 1891 and in the two opening addresses of the Young Czech delegates to the Reichsrat in April 1891. The first address succinctly restated the party's intention to work for the realization of Bohemian state rights in accordance with the sense of the imperial rescript of September 12, 1871. The second, essentially a gloss on the party platform, proclaimed Young Czech willingness to cooperate with other parties in matters of mutual concern, particularly in the extension and firmer guarantee of civil and nationality rights.[1] The party pressed for extension of the franchise, greater internal improvements, continued subsidies to industry and agriculture, tax relief for Bohemia, and general tax and currency reform. While in opposition to the Taaffe government on many issues, it participated constructively in the committee work and housekeeping chores of the diets and Parliament in hopes of strengthening those institutions. In the Bohemian Diet, the party's main task was to defeat the Agreement of 1890. In the Reichsrat, its efforts to effect liberal reforms culminated on March 17, 1893, in its presentation of Jan Slavík's bill for direct, equal, secret, and universal manhood suffrage.

The defeated Old Czechs, notably Rieger, Bráf, Mattuš, Randa, and Zeithammer, expected the newly victorious Young Czech party to founder or revert to Old Czech policies after it tried to oppose the imperial government without the aid of the conservative great landowners. The German Liberals, disconcerted by the

overwhelming Young Czech victory and disappointed that the Agreement of 1890 had eluded their grasp, drew close to the Taaffe
government they had once condemned for having governed the Germans in favor of the Slavs, that is to say, for having showed
them less favoritism than they believed to be their due.

The conservative great landowners, though stunned by the overwhelming defeat of their heretofore dependable Old Czech allies,
could take comfort in the fact that one of their own, Francis Anthony Thun, occupied the governor's office and that they still
controlled enough seats in the diet and on the Provincial Executive Council to play off the Young Czechs against the Germans.
Like the Old Czechs, they expected the Young Czech coalition to
disintegrate upon failing to realize its extravagant campaign
promises and intended to exploit the divisions within its ranks,
many confident that given time and repeated frustrations, the
Young Czech party would have no choice but to return to the now-
discredited policies of Rieger and become their ally. The aim
of the conservative great landowners, defined in letters by
Charles Buquoy, Prince George Lobkowicz, and the Schwarzenbergs,
father and sons, was to hold the line against the Young Czechs,
eschewing the more provocative forms of harassment employed by
the governor when backed by an Old Czech majority, until the
Young Czechs became amenable to persuasion or until the tension
between the doctrinaire radicals and those favorably disposed to
compromise divided the party. The conservative great landowners
still believed they understood "their Czechs" and generally continued to talk of them in condescending terms, alternately sympathetic and contemptuous. But the Young Czech victory of 1891
introduced notes of bewilderment and newly found respect.[2]

The emperor and the imperial authorities remained hostile to
the Young Czechs, judged political merit among Czechs by the degree of subservience to imperial interests, and were determined
to grant few concessions. Taaffe and his entourage expected
lasting Czech gratitude for favors reluctantly conceded a decade
ago and could never fathom why the Czechs so vehemently rejected
the Vienna Agreement of 1890.[3] Young Czech opposition had been
stronger than the government had bargained for and, incapable of
learning from experience, it would continue to underestimate the
party. It would also be surprised to find that the Young Czechs
represented only the surface of popular radicalism and discontent.

Victory in the March 1891 elections began an auspicious year
for the Young Czechs. On May 15, the great Centennial Exhibition
opened in Prague, marking the one-hundredth anniversary of Leopold II's coronation as king of Bohemia. The exhibition revealed
to the world the material and cultural wealth of the Czech people
and their remarkable achievements in agriculture, industry, and
the arts during the first three decades of constitutional rule.[4]
It remained an almost exclusively Czech affair because the Germans, although invited, refused to participate in great numbers.

Some Czechs entertained short-lived hopes that Emperor Franz Joseph would now agree to be crowned king of Bohemia in Prague in keeping with his unfulfilled promises of 1861 and 1871. But Governor Thun had trouble persuading the emperor to come to Prague at all, much less to be crowned.[5] Franz Joseph's fleeting appearance in September occasioned no outpouring of affection, as it led to two bomb scares and to Czech crowds that studiously refrained from singing the imperial anthem. These crowds expressed hostility toward the monarchy rather than the emperor himself, who was still generally respected despite his pronounced lack of understanding and sympathy for the Czech people.

The Young Czech coalition acquired greater strength and confidence as its delegates worked together to defeat every attempt by Taaffe and his supporters to win parliamentary authorization for the Agreement of 1890. They did so with much encouragement from local political organizations, especially in areas where Czechs constituted a minority of the population. In the Bohemian Diet, during March 1892, the Young Czechs mustered enough support from Old Czech delegates to prevent passage of a series of German Liberal bills designed to implement several points of the 1890 Agreement, including the redrawing of boundaries in four Bohemian judicial districts. Meanwhile, Taaffe and Governor Thun had refused to investigate alleged German harassment of the Czech minority in Liberec and in Most and had even confiscated editions of the *Národní listy* that described problems in those cities. This caused still more Old Czech delegates to realize that Czech cultural and political institutions in predominantly German areas would be jeopardized if the Agreement of 1890 ever became law. Moreover, most Old Czechs recognized that if they did not withdraw their endorsement of that agreement they would risk total defeat in diet elections scheduled three years hence. Therefore, on April 1, 1892, the Old Czechs and the conservative great landowners announced their decision to cease supporting all attempts to persuade the diet to endorse any or all points in the 1890 Agreement.[6] Governor Thun dared not dismiss the diet and call new elections for fear that the Young Czech party would capture all remaining Old Czech seats in a victory as decisive and lopsided as that in the Reichsrat elections of 1891.

The rejection of the Agreement of 1890 by a vast majority of diet delegates in April 1892 led the German Liberals and the Taaffe government to try to impose particular points of that agreement piecemeal and by administrative fiat. That same month, the imperial Minister of Justice, Count Friedrich Schönborn, ordered the drawing of new boundaries for the district court in Teplice, intending thereby to set a precedent for redrawing other judicial districts and for allowing the Taaffe government to implement other points of the 1890 Agreement one by one over the head of the diet. The Young Czechs responded on May 5, 1892, by introducing a bill in Parliament indicting Count Schönborn for having exceeded his authority under the constitution.[7] Since

this proposal, prepared by František Tilšer, was sure to win a
majority of votes, Taaffe backed down rather than precipitate a
constitutional crisis. Nonetheless, he and the German Liberals
did not give up trying to impose the Agreement. As late as October 1893, when his government was on the verge of collapse,
they tried unsuccessfully to get authorization from the Reichsrat to establish a new judicial district in Trutnov. These renewed attempts to circumvent the majority opposition in the diet
even at the risk of provoking a constitutional crisis not only
failed but so intensified Czech distrust of the Germans that representatives of the two nationalities found it increasingly
difficult to come to any agreement on the language issue.[8]

After being blocked in all attempts to implement the Agreement of 1890, the government and the Germans retaliated by har-
assing certain patriotic Czech institutions and individuals. In
May 1892, the Minister of Public Instruction, Baron Paul von
Gautsch, banned the Komenský tercentenary festivities in Czech
public schools on the grounds that such patriotic celebrations
would endanger public order. On August 4, 1892, Minister-
President Taaffe obtained Alois Pražák's resignation as Minister
without Portfolio for Czech Affairs (Ministr krajan) in a second
empty gesture to placate the Germans. Pražák had never been beloved in Social Democratic or in Young Czech circles: as acting
Minister of Justice, he had enforced Taaffe's antisocialist laws;
and for three decades he had opposed universal suffrage and maintained Czech political ties to the great landowners in Moravia.
But the circumstances of Pražák's resignation made him a national
hero overnight. Neither his dismissal nor governmental banning
of celebrations in honor of the tercentenary of Komenský's birth
ever advanced the German cause; in fact, these gratuitous in-
sults served only to anger Czechs in all parties.[9]

Pražák's forced resignation unexpectedly strengthened the
Young Czechs by driving many disillusioned Moravian Old Czech
deputies into the ranks of Adolf Stránský's Moravian People's
party. This increased the size of the National Liberal club of
Reichsrat delegates, to which both Young Czech and People's party delegates belonged. The People's party became strong enough
to dispense with Young Czech subsidies, and Stránský transformed
his biweekly *Moravské noviny* (Moravian news) into the daily
Lidové noviny (People's news) as a first step toward establishing liberal and anticlerical politics in Moravia on a firm foundation.[10] Stránský and Josef Tuček, along with Josef Vychodil,
founder and chairman of the Peasant Union for Moravia, accepted
appointments to the executive committee of the Young Czech party
in Prague.[11] The dismissal of Pražák also stiffened the resolve
of the Peasant Union, which thereafter in league with the
People's party and the Political Association for Northern Moravia, tried to overcome Old Czech and aristocratic opposition to
suffrage extension and tax relief for the peasantry. The latter
organization, founded at Olomouc on February 13, 1892, aimed to

advance political and social reform in the seven northernmost
Moravian districts.[12] Thus, by attempting to apply the Agreement of 1890 in Bohemia, the Old Czechs, German Liberals, and
conservative great landowners helped bring about the demise of
Old Czech preponderance in Moravia as well as in Bohemia.

Young Czech proposals to found new Czech higher schools and
to increase the use of Czech in the civil service foundered in
the face of intransigent German and imperial opposition. These
proposals, which henceforth remained principal tenets of Young
Czech programs, included the establishment of a Czech university
in Moravia and a Czech gymnasium in Opava, Silesia, and the
amendment of the Stremayr ordinances to include Czech as well as
German as the internal official language of the imperial civil
service in Bohemia and Moravia.[13]

Young Czech efforts to extend civil rights and to work harmoniously with other Slavic delegates to the Reichsrat coalesced
in the Spinčić affair of July 1892. Vjekoslav Spinčić, a Croatian parliamentary delegate, had been suspended from employment
as a professor at the state normal school in Gorica for having
publicly advocated, in Zagreb, the union of Dalmatia and Istria
with the kingdom of Croatia. All Slavic delegates in the Reichsrat banded together to defend both Spinčić and freedom of speech.
On behalf of the Young Czech party, Bedřich Pacák and Karel Kramář excoriated Minister of Public Instruction Gautsch for having
upheld Spinčić's suspension. To take away the livelihood of any
man, much less that of a parliamentary delegate, for expressing
new or unpopular opinions directly violated the spirit if not
the letter of the law; this action further illustrated the fact
that while "civilized" Western nations upheld freedom of speech,
"feudal" Austria still arbitrarily violated civil rights despite
its constitutional window dressing.[14] Although Gautsch could
uphold the suspension of Spinčić on strictly legal grounds, moral
victory belonged to the protesting Slavic delegates. Spinčić won
fame and honor throughout Slavic Cisleithania as a martyr to
Habsburg oppression and continued to speak his mind in the
Reichsrat after being repeatedly returned by a large majority of
constituents. Cooperation between Slovenian, Croatian, Ukrainian, and Czech delegates in defending Spinčić and in obtaining
Taaffe's promise to fund Slovene grammar schools in southern
Styria led directly to the formation of a "Slavic coalition" on
November 24, 1893, at the behest of the Young Czechs.

Debates on the annual budget in the Reichsrat and the diets
gave all opposition parties their best opportunity to criticize
government policy and to try to change it by attempting either
to cut or to reject the budget. During the Reichsrat budget debates of December 16, 1891, Edvard Grégr created a sensation
throughout the empire by fervently denouncing discriminatory
Habsburg policies against the Czechs:

Gentlemen, the majority of the Czech people feel

themselves to be discontented and downtrodden in this state.
In fact, they feel themselves to be on alien and hostile
ground [shouts of "that's the way it is," from Young Czech
delegates], in a Babylonian captivity, as it were. . . . Although Austrian statesmen still remain blind and deaf to the
just requests and grievances of the Czech nation, there is
great need and demand for justice and for compliance with
moral precepts! We await and are preparing ourselves for the
time of their coming.[15]

Moderate Young Czechs often found such condemnatory speeches
embarrassing; but Grégr only reflected growing popular impatience
with the political status quo, given the unprecedented Young
Czech electoral victory, the government's continued attempts to
implement the Agreement of 1890, and the successful Prague Centennial Exhibition. Even Julius Grégr was concerned about this
impatience and cautioned his editors to avoid arousing unwarranted popular expectations.
    Disagreement among Young Czechs on policies and tactics re-
flected the interests of at least seven different party groups
which had coalesced in opposition to the Agreement of 1890 and
which generally disagreed on economic and social issues while favoring the extension of national and civil rights. Four groups
had founded the party and upheld it since 1874: editors and reporters of the *Národní listy* and of liberal district newspapers,
led by Julius Grégr, Josef Anýz, Karel Tůma, and Servác Heller;
the sugar beet farmers and prosperous peasants of Podřipsko, the
Jizera valley (Pojizeří), and parts of the middle Labe valley
(Polabí), represented by Ervín Špindler, the Jandas, and Emanuel
Hrubý; the liberal commercial and industrial middle class of the
third curia, whose principal spokesmen were Gabriel Blažek, Josef
Herold, and Bedřich Pacák; and the five-gulden voters of that
curia, primarily tradesmen, artisans, or teachers, whose champions included František Tilšer, Jan Slavík, Edvard Grégr, Jan
Kučera, and Edvard Brzorád. Three new groups increased party diversity and differences of opinion. The Realists, Kaizl, Kramář,
and Masaryk, still sought to stand apart from factional disputes
while trying to persuade the party to adopt their program of
1890.[16] The former Old Czech cadres, led by self-governmental
officials like František Schwarz, Karel Adámek, Blažej Mixa,
František V. Veselý, and Jakub Škarda, controlled more district
boards than did the original Young Czechs. They could also, together with Kaizl and Kramář and Young Czech stalwarts Pacák and
Herold, generally insure party support for legislation favoring
urban business interests. Peasant smallholders, represented by
such organizations as Alfons Šťastný's Peasant Union, remained
the party's largest potential constituency but because of curial
voting could not exercise influence in proportion to their
numbers.
    With regard to tactics as well as party policy, Young Czechs

divided into broad categories, radical liberals and moderate liberals, reflecting the fact that the party itself was the product of both the popular and the privileged institutions of Czech society. This division corresponded on a larger scale to that between the Grégr brothers and Ervín Špindler in the pre-1891 radical party.[17] Radical views continued to hold sway in the editorial offices of the *Národní listy* and pragmatism in the clubs of parliamentary delegates. The former concentrated on arousing popular support by appeals to patriotism in hopes that a stronger party could persuade Parliament and the government to approve its liberal program. The moderates shared the same hopes but did not meanwhile rule out compromise with imperial or provincial authorities in order to win small concessions advantageous to their constituents. During the years 1891 to 1894, the radicals generally dominated the party executive committee under Jan Kučera, thanks in large part to their having organized the victories of 1889 and 1891, and held their own on the party board of trustees under chairman Gabriel Blažek. Conflict between radicals and moderates usually resulted in a standoff and never became too heated because they agreed on important issues like opposing the Agreement of 1890 and extending civil rights. Chairman-elect Engel's tactful management of the party clubs of delegates and Gustav Eim's moderating influence on the *Národní listy* helped keep intra-party conflict within bounds and hold the disparate groups together till the end of the nineties.[18]

The three Realist converts to the Young Czech cause initially tried to stand apart from traditional party factions and to serve as peacemakers. They also attempted to moderate the traditionally popular radicalism that advocated parliamentary opposition until the government agreed to enact state rights reforms, favoring instead limited cooperation to test in every way the government's capacity for gradual reform. Masaryk remained the most principled Realist and the closest in political opinion to the student Progressives and to Social Democracy. Kaizl and Kramář continued to view and advertise themselves as conciliators and experts who stood above party factions. Eim recognized this in noting that the ambitious young Kramář practiced "at being a Rieger."[19] Both Kaizl and Kramář soon perceived that the mayors and delegates from district boards representing commerce and industry would eventually gain the upper hand in deciding party policies. Moreover, their endorsement of state support for private enterprise reinforced their growing social ties to the upper middle classes, who managed the financial and industrial institutions of Czech society. Masaryk's view of Kaizl as the "Old Czech Realist" and of the more fervently patriotic Kramář as the "Young Czech Realist" and himself as the "true Realist" was therefore not far off the mark.[20]

Young Czech agreement on most political objectives did not preclude differences of opinion on what constituted proper party organization and tactics. One such disagreement concerned how

best to broaden the base of party support. In accordance with
their 1890 program, the Realists advocated building a genuinely
popular national party which would truly reflect and respond to
the interests of Czechs from all social classes. Such a party
would have to establish positive goals and patiently organize
and politically educate a mass electorate; it should not, like
the Old Czechs, cater primarily to an elite electorate or, like
the Young Czechs, rely excessively upon radical slogans and a
predominantly negative response to public issues defined by political opponents. The Young Czechs had proved themselves to be
much more adept at arousing popular fervor than in organizing
and directing it. For example, they appeared unable to take
full advantage of their great electoral victory of March 1891 or
to retain the Progressive allies whom they had acquired in 1890.
Masaryk, and to a lesser degree Kaizl and Kramář, recognized
that Progressives and Social Democrats appealed to constituencies outside the Young Czech party and could only be expected to
collaborate with it if it promoted the interests of their constituents. To do this, the party would, in Masaryk's opinion, have
to rely less upon privileged classes and institutions and qualify
its radicalism and state rights principles, changes which a majority of party members appeared unwilling to accept.

Given the diversity of opinion in the party, disputes inevitably arose concerning the proper limits of party discipline and
the extent to which the party could permit public debate of disputes within its ranks. A tight discipline, like that of the
Old Czechs against which the radical Young Czechs had rebelled,
was generally deemed necessary if the new coalition were to
function effectively in the diet and the Reichsrat. Jan Vašatý,
the only party delegate consistently to flaunt party discipline
and to attack party policies through his radical weekly Vyšehrad,
was censured by the party board of trustees on September 6, 1891,
and ultimately expelled in October 1896 to no one's regret.

T. G. Masaryk alone vigorously advocated having serious public
debates on political issues on which opinion within the party remained divided. He contended that free and open debate would
strengthen rather than weaken the party and attract the support
of other groups, notably Social Democracy and the Progressive
movement, which might otherwise be repelled by the closed nature
and iron discipline of the party. Masaryk presented these views
at meetings of the party executive committee and club of Reichsrat delegates and in the weekly Čas (Time) and monthly Naše doba
(Our era) which he used as forums for criticizing party shortcomings. His May 28, 1892, editorial in Čas called for the
transformation of the Young Czech coalition into a genuinely national People's party, and that of September 3, 1892, asked for
a broader discussion of public issues within party ranks. In
criticism of policy, Masaryk caused the greatest consternation
in party ranks by his campaign in Čas against "demagogic radicalism" and by his Strakonice speech of September 22, 1891,

exposing the many "fantasies and fables" entertained by the
party about Russia, which contrary to popular hopes took little
interest in the Czech national struggle.[21]

The fact that Masaryk worked openly and spoke candidly did
not endear him to many party figures. A few even considered him
to be a troublemaker like Vasatý. His breadth of knowledge and
great self-confidence reinforced a professorial manner and a tone
of moral superiority which antagonized several party colleagues,
notably the Grégrs and Gustav Eim. Kaizl and Kramář for this
reason and for his solicitous care of students appropriately referred to him in private correspondence as the "shepherd." Despite party admonitions to the contrary, Masaryk continued to
speak his mind publicly on important issues, even disagreeing
with party policy on occasion. While party leaders believed
this to be detrimental to party solidarity, Masaryk believed it
necessary to mitigate popular distrust of the party's secrecy in
reaching its decisions.

Besides intra-party debate on organization and tactics, serious differences of opinion persisted on certain political issues,
primarily those relating to economic policy. In the period 1891
to 1894, measures for currency and tax reform supported by industrial and commercial interests found able spokesmen in Herold,
Kaizl, and Kramář. Other colleagues, notably Adámek and Schwarz,
joined them to vote against a proposal to limit stock speculation
by placing a 2 percent tax on all stock exchange transfers, on
the grounds that such a small step toward reform would be useless
as long as the entire system were not overhauled. These grounds
appeared specious to spokesmen for agrarian, small commercial,
and peasant interests, who welcomed any legislation that would
restrain speculators. The decision to place Austro-Hungarian
currency on the gold standard also divided the party as most delegates from fourth-curial districts voted with the party majority for the measure only after having been overruled by vote of
the parliamentary club.[22]

As the first flush of enthusiasm after the electoral victory
of 1891 began to fade, all Young Czechs recognized that the party
would face serious problems and severe trials in the future.
This would be particularly true on those issues where the coalition party was obliged to hold if not extend its newly won popular constituencies.

On the ever serious agrarian question, where declining prices,
particularly of sugar beets, and higher taxes had helped bring
most of the peasant organizations of Bohemia into line behind the
Young Czechs in 1889 and 1891, the party had to reconcile its
traditional partiality to the interests of industry, commerce,
and middling landholders with its wish to retain its newly acquired allies among the smaller and poorer landholding peasantry.
A mutual anticlericalism, liberalism, and opposition to the great
landowners could not long unite the likes of František Tilser,
Ervín Špindler, and Alfons Št'astný.

In the Dual Monarchy, the social question, nationality conflict, and Habsburg authoritarianism were the three most serious
issues of the day. This was especially true in the Czech lands,
where extensive industrialization had produced an impoverished
and increasingly dissatisfied urban proletariat. On the social
question and on the related issue of universal manhood suffrage,
the Young Czechs not only had to overcome deep divisions within
their own ranks but hoped to come to some sort of understanding
with the Czechoslavonic Social Democratic party and the student
Progressive movement. Given the importance of interaction between the Young Czech party and these movements in conditioning
Czech political development during the nineties, they should be
surveyed before discussing party policies and actions with regard to the social question and the campaign for universal direct, equal, and secret manhood suffrage.

The Young Czechs and Social Democracy

Social Democracy had been a popular and potentially powerful
political force in the Czech lands ever since the establishment
of the first trade unions in Cisleithania by Czech and German
workers of northern Bohemia during the 1860s. Cordial cooperation between Czechs and Germans in the pursuit of common interests contributed to the advance of unionization, while the economic insecurity and severe physical and psychological hardships
endured by every working man accounted in large part for the
priority initially placed by unions on improved working conditions and greater pay and security in employment.[23] Desire for
knowledge and an intellectual curiosity were evident in the primarily self-educated leadership, notably Lev J. Palda and Josef
Boleslav Pecka, and in the many workers' societies for self-
improvement and for the education of their children.[24]

By its allegiance to international socialism, Czech Social
Democracy demonstrated its belief that the social question could
be resolved only within an international framework. It also reaffirmed the Czech Hussite and radical democratic traditions and
always argued that Czech workers had as much right to cultivate
their own national culture as did the workers of any other nationality.[25] In keeping with these principles, it always contended that no lasting solution to the nationality question in
Central and Eastern Europe could be achieved apart from a solution to the social question.[26] Most Czech workers hesitated a
long time before joining the Socialist International founded in
1864, and many did not join at all, primarily because in their
view it showed too little concern for the problems peculiar to
small nations in Central and Eastern Europe. Nonetheless, Czech
workers numbered among the first Slavic-speaking adherents of
that organization, which finally added a Czech section in New
York in the spring of 1871.[27] The following year at its congress
in The Hague, the International called for the formation of

socialist workers' parties among all peoples but did not, as
many Czechs had wished, specifically mention the Slavic peoples
of Austria-Hungary.

On April 5, 1874, Czechs numbered ten among the seventy-four
delegates to the congress at Neudörfl which established a unified Austrian Social Democratic party based on the platform of
the International and the Eisenach program of German Social Democracy.[28] The party preamble stated that "national differences
offer no hindrance to the common struggle for social liberty"
and reflected the victory of those delegates led by Andreas
Scheu who called for a union of socialists of all nationalities
within Austria. Their opponents, notably Heinrich Oberwinder,
slandered Scheu for his efforts, calling him a Pan-Slav and an
instrument of Bakunin. The founding of an autonomous Czechoslavonic Social Democratic party on April 7, 1878, at Prague-Břevnov
further attested to the continuing popularity of socialism among
Czech workers and to the tolerance and acceptance of nationality
differences within the all-Austrian party.[29]

Systematic oppression of socialists and anarchists by the
Taaffe government after 1884 shattered the unity and effectiveness of Austrian Social Democracy and forced many of its leaders
into prison or exile, including the Czechs Gustav Habrman and
Josef Boleslav Pecka and the Bohemian German Josef Peukert.[30]
The simultaneous enactment of legislation providing for factory
inspection and limited social welfare measures did nothing to
allay class conflict. A relaxation of the severe governmental
prosecution, which even Taaffe came to recognize as counterproductive, facilitated the work of the Hainfeld Congress in 1889
in reestablishing a unified Austrian Social Democratic party in
association with the newly founded Second International. Dr.
Viktor Adler, a Viennese Jewish physician and a politician of
courage and ability and formerly a German nationalist, emerged
as the leading figure in the new party. He and the moderate majority distrusted anarchism and advocates of violent revolution.
They preferred instead a disciplined mass party which looked to
German Social Democracy for leadership and example and which
concentrated on social and economic issues.[31]

The nineties began auspiciously with an impressive display of
working-class strength and solidarity at the 1890 May Day celebrations throughout Cisleithania; but serious differences of
opinion among the various nationalities within the movement remained unresolved. At Hainfeld, Adler and other party leaders
made no attempt to establish any official policy on the nationality question in order not to risk a public debate between
Czechs and Germans which might divide or embarrass the party.
German workers already feared economic and cultural competition
from the growing Czech minority in northern Bohemia, and some
supported the Pan-German and anti-Semitic forces of Georg von
Schönerer. Many Czech workers believed that they did not exercise an influence within the all-Austrian Social Democratic

party commensurate with their strength and numbers in the Cisleithanian labor force. Moreover, many thought that the pre-
ponderantly German higher party officials had an inadequate appreciation of the additional discrimination a working man might
encounter in Cisleithania by virtue of speaking Czech or another
Slavic language. The independent Czech patriotic and socialist
paper, *Naše obrana* (Our defense), later *Volnost* (Freedom), which
appeared in April 1890 and sought to capitalize on this discontent, received encouragement and subsidies from the Young Czechs.
Editors of Czech Social Democratic papers at their August 1890
meeting in Brno refused to recognize *Naše obrana* as a party paper largely on account of its Young Czech orientation. At the
end of June 1891, in Vienna at the second all-Austrian Social
Democratic party congress, heated debate arose between Czech and
German delegates on the extent to which the party should be de-
centralized to accommodate nationality differences. A majority
of Czech delegates remained dissatisfied at the unwillingness of
that congress to move in a federalist direction, and a small
faction led by Jan Vávra and *Naše obrana* editors Jan Wurstiál and
Václav Sedmidubský angrily walked out to build up their own independent Czechoslavonic *National* Social Democratic party.[32] This
faction won very little support in its efforts to fill the gap
between middle-class parties and Social Democracy and is remembered primarily as a short-lived forerunner of the more successful Czech National Socialist party established seven years later.
In 1891 as in 1898, the vast majority of workers in Cisleithania,
regardless of nationality, remained loyal to Social Democracy and
tried to compose their differences of opinion within its framework.

In struggling to realize universal suffrage, civil rights, and
social justice, members of the Czechoslavonic Social Democratic
party recognized that their inferior status in society derived
from their being Czechs as well as workers.[33] On December 26,
1893, in České Budějovice, the party at its third congress reas-
serted the autonomous status within Austrian Social Democracy
which it had enjoyed from its founding in 1878 until its suppression by Taaffe in 1884 and which it had reaffirmed in principle
at its Brno congress of December 1887.[34] During the last week
of March 1894 in Vienna, the fourth all-Austrian Social Democratic party congress acknowledged the Czechoslavonic Social Democrats as an "independent party within the party" and with Czech
support rejected anarchism once and for all in favor of continuing a policy that resembled the moderate Erfurt program of German Social Democracy.[35] Through their autonomous party, Czech
Social Democrats sought to maintain their national heritage on
the one hand and their commitment to socialist internationalism
and all-Austrian working-class solidarity on the other. These
efforts belied frequent charges by both Old and Young Czechs
that Czech Social Democratic leaders were foreign hirelings or
traitors to the national cause.

In the summer and fall of 1893, Czech Social Democrats proudly published two letters from Friedrich Engels in which he expressed understanding and sympathy for their work, reemphasized the international character of socialism, and called for greater unity among Czech and German workers against common class enemies, the great landowners and capitalists. In his second letter, Engels expressed regret that advanced age did not permit his learning Czech and again evinced somewhat greater appreciation of Czech efforts to build socialism than did the leadership of the Austrian party. So pleased were the Czech Social Democrats to have Engels's tribute and encouragement that they did not note the extent to which he had in other statements agreed with the aims and activities of the Viennese party leadership. In future years they would often cite his letters when chastised by Vienna for refusing to accept German Social Democracy as their model or to subscribe to the notion that socialism could only be achieved within the framework of a reformed Habsburg Monarchy.[36] An increasing number of strikes during the nineties, culminating in those by miners at Ostrava in 1896 and in the northern Bohemian coal fields in 1900, indicated the success of Social Democracy and its trade unions in organizing workers to combat economic exploitation.[37] The Social Democratic struggle for civil rights, including universal suffrage and protection from arbitrary police action, continued to enjoy widespread support in Czech society.

The Young Czechs had observed the rapid growth of Social Democracy among the Czech working class with a mixture of sympathy and foreboding. To their mind its politically awakening and organizing the Czech masses served the best interests of the nation as a whole. But they could not accept its aim to abolish private ownership of the means of production, its belief in an irreconcilable class struggle, and its allegiance to an international workers' association. In its programs of 1874, 1889, and 1891, the Young Czech party acknowledged the legitimacy of working-class aspirations for a share in the cultural and material wealth of Czech society.[38] This position resembled that of Czech Social Democracy on enough points that it was possible for each party to view the other as a potential ally. After their formal break with the Old Czechs in December 1874, the Young Czechs repeatedly proposed to Czech Social Democrats that they cooperate in advancing specific interests such as increasing the number of eligible voters and removing limitations on freedom of speech, the press, and assembly. During the summer of 1874, the Young Czechs had also attempted without success to transform the *Dělnické listy* (Workers' news) into another party paper.[39] The imperial police kept records on the several temporary agreements that Young Czechs and Czech Social Democrats concluded during the summers of 1882 and 1887 and discerned, correctly enough, that this concord had been facilitated by a mutual interest in

extending civil liberties and the use of the Czech language in
civil and governmental affairs.[40]

In its attempt to suppress Social Democracy by suspending
trial by jury and applying the antisocialist laws of 1886, the
Taaffe government encountered in Edvard Grégr and other Young
Czech delegates some of its few outspoken opponents among
middle-class parties. On June 5, 1886, in the Reichsrat, Grégr
charged that Taaffe, by trying to eradicate socialism, was sti-
fling the very force that worked for orderly and constructive
reform and thereby gave truly dangerous extremists an opportunity
to manipulate popular discontent. In such trying times every
delegate had "a duty to be a socialist" in order to hasten the
advent of universal manhood suffrage as well as to curb emergency
antisocialist legislation before it endangered those few liberties still enjoyed by middle-class citizens.[41] Though Grégr had
not expected to sway the clerical and conservative majority to
his point of view, he expressed delight at having been able to
show his "democratic colors."[42] On December 19, 1888, the Young
Czechs voted with other parties of the left in an unsuccessful
attempt to have the Reichsrat request imperial reinstatement of
trial by jury. The Old Czechs again voted with the Iron Ring of
the Right to uphold the status quo. Like their colleague and
Acting Minister of Justice, Alois Pražák, they believed that the
maintenance of public order and morality required enforcement of
all emergency laws; and most, like F. L. Rieger, also feared
that the Czech national movement would be irreparably weakened
if Czech workers continued to embrace Social Democracy.[43]

Czech Social Democrats appreciated Young Czech efforts to repeal the antisocialist laws and reestablish trial by jury, as
they also welcomed endeavors to abolish the newspaper tax stamp
and to wrest from imperial authorities firmer guarantees for
freedom of speech and assembly. But they did not consider these
efforts sufficient grounds for joining a party beholden to business and farming interests as a junior partner, for that is exactly what they would have been, given curial voting procedures.
Most Czech Social Democrats regarded the Young Czechs as less
dangerous class enemies than the great landowners, German Liberals, and clerical-conservatives who had helped the imperial authorities repress the workers' movement. But Young Czechs always opposed Social Democratic views on private property and on
the primacy of internationalism. On these two issues there
could be no agreement between the parties.

The Social Democratic allegiance of Czech workers, which so
disturbed Young Czechs, engendered interest and understanding
among the Czech students and intellectuals who began in 1889 to
organize themselves politically as a Progressive movement. This
developing community of interest between workers and students
caused great consternation in Young Czech ranks. Many party
leaders continued to entertain hopes of having the working class

accept their tutelage, and most had assumed that the younger intelligentsia would gratefully take its place in the lower echelons of the party. Moreover, they realized that their preponderance in national politics could be endangered if a permanent
alliance between Progressives and Social Democrats ever came to
pass.

Progressive Politics and the Younger Generation

So many future leaders of the Young Czech and other Czech political parties entered politics through the Progressive movement of the nineties that a knowledge of its history is a prere-
quisite for understanding Czech political development from 1890
to 1918. Leaders of this movement wished to institute a thoroughgoing reform of Czech society which would entail making
Czech culture more modernist and more international in character
as well as introducing extensive political and social reforms.
This helps explain why the great flowering of Czech culture
which began during the nineties and continued through the 1920s
developed hand-in-hand with Progressivism and Social Democracy
and thrived despite sporadic imperial efforts to suppress all
political movements of the left. It also helps explain why the
Young Czechs, so closely identified with defense of the forged
manuscripts and with the system of *Honoratiorensparteien*, could
not on the morrow of their greatest electoral victory become political mentors to the younger generation.[45]

The generation of Czech intellectuals come of age by 1890,
the first to be wholly educated in Czech public schools and a
Czech university, generally favored the modern and the avant-
garde in European culture and those political principles, whether
liberal, democratic, or socialist, that often transcended parochial Czech interests. These views stood in marked contrast to
the more nationalistic outlook of their fathers' generation,
among whose foremost spokesmen was Julius Zeyer, master of the
epic poem, the folk legend in verse, and the supernatural tale.
In an 1889 letter to his friend and fellow writer, J. V. Sládek,
Zeyer expressed privately what many of his generation uttered
publicly: the younger generation, having grown up without memory of Habsburg oppression in the fifties, sixties, and early
seventies, could no longer appreciate the Czech nation's need to
struggle for survival. Zeyer reported on having attended with a
young Czech companion, V. V. Zelený, celebrations in honor of
Mickiewicz at his grave in Montmartre:

> The speaker cried: "Poland is not dead, she may be severe-
> ly wounded, but she is not dead—*elle a incessament le cauche-
> mar de ses assassins. . . .*" And we Czechs? We now have no
> such nightmare, and do we not therefore thank God that this
> dear Austria has been granted to us? I see this every day in
> Zelený. Those of his generation have grown up in Cisleithania

and have already ceased to be Czechs. If this situation
lasts yet another twenty years, thank goodness I won't be
around to see it.[46]

Younger intellectuals repeatedly asserted that this and similar views of the older generation erred principally in considering one generation's perception of the Czech question to be the
only valid one. Confident in the future of the Czech nation,
more confident perhaps than their fathers who had known harder
times, the generation of the nineties sought to revitalize Czech
culture and democratize Czech politics. In this effort they reaffirmed and strengthened a tradition of active political involvement by the Czech intelligentsia dating from the National
Revival and 1848. Far from denying the validity of earlier patriotic endeavors, as some of their elders asserted, the young
intellectuals consciously sought to build upon the achievements
of the past. All honored the revolutionaries of 1848 and the
tábor leaders of the late sixties and believed themselves obliged
to exhaust all constitutional and nonviolent means in resisting
the authoritarian supranational state in the name of national
autonomy, civil liberties, and social justice. Contrary therefore to the fears of the older generation, the younger intelligentsia's rejection of the old order in Czech politics and culture constituted no acceptance of the political status quo in
Cisleithania. The Habsburg Monarchy remained for them the principle obstacle to reform, especially after it struck down their
political organizations in sloppily contrived "conspiracy" trials and jailed them as it had jailed their fathers during the
sixties and seventies and their grandfathers in 1848.
The younger Czech Progressive intellectuals of the nineties
complemented their work for political and social reform with efforts to bring Czech literature, arts, and scholarship abreast
of the most modern trends in European culture. Prolific and popular Czech poets of an older generation, like the sentimental
nationalist Svatopluk Čech and the cosmopolitan Jaroslav Vrchlický, proudly hailed the arrival of this young and confident generation, only to find their own works subjected to severe scruti-
ny by younger literary and social critics like František V.
Krejčí, František X. Šalda, and Jindřich Vodák. Most younger
writers sought to give Czech literature a more universal appeal
and make it more fully reveal the complexity of human motives
and the relationship of man to society.[47] They impartially attacked both the *Ruch* and *Lumír* schools, criticizing very sharply
the naively romanticized and clumsily wrought patriotic and Pan-
Slavistic themes of traditional *Ruch* literature epitomized by
the works of Alois Jirásek, Eliška Krásnohorská, and Svatopluk
Čech. They also had little liking for the eclectic and Parnassian poetry of Vrchlický and others of the *Lumír* group. The
younger writers often looked for inspiration to French symbolism
and to the psychological and social realism of the Russian novel,

thereby continuing the emancipation of Czech culture from both
parochialism and German tutelage begun by their elders. Two of
the younger poets who began composing original and subtle verse
in the French symbolist manner, the impressionist Antonín Sova
and the mystic Otakar Březina, occasionally turned from an evo-
cation of purely personal themes to a consideration of the great
political and intellectual crises of the nineties that so helped
to mold their contemporaries.[48]

Many Czech intellectuals, particularly those of the younger
generation, shared the widespread concern in Europe and America
for the apparent social and moral disintegration of Western civilization. T. G. Masaryk in 1881 published his treatise *Der
Selbstmord als sociale Massenerscheinung der modernen Civilisation* (Suicide as a social mass phenomenon of modern civilization),
a pioneering sociological and psychological study of this disintegration, which resembled and foreshadowed in many respects
Freud's *Studies in Hysteria* of 1895 and Durkheim's *Suicide* of
1897.[49] Petr Bezruč's *Slezské písně* (Silesian songs) reflected
in verse a deep concern for the material and cultural deprivation
endured by Czech workers and peasants. Another Czech poet, J. S.
Machar, upheld the tradition of Havlíček and Neruda in his ironical political commentary and in his superb poetic satire of
Young Czech leadership, *Boží bojovníci* (The warriors of God).[50]
At the turn of the century, several fine novels, including *Santa
Lucia* by J. Vilém Mrštík, *Ivův román* (Ivo's novel) by Antonín
Sova, and *Prosinec* (December) and *Konec Hackenschmiduv* (The end
of Hackenschmid) by Viktor Dyk, portrayed sensitive heroes who
sought to overcome the discrepancy between ideals and reality in
Czech society by participation in collective struggles for political and social justice.[51] These fictional heroes of complex
character, like many of their prototypes in the Progressive movement, acted on the basis of firm and carefully thought-out convictions, not on the basis of simplistic slogans.[52]

The intention of young intellectuals to reform both Czech culture and political life is most clearly revealed in the "Manifesto of Czech Modernists" of October 1895 signed by twelve of
the leading younger Czech writers. Therein they denounced the
use of "empty" patriotic slogans in politics as they rejected
all decadence and dilettantism in literature and the arts and
condemned the neglect of social problems and public education by
the existing middle-class parties:

> As we want individualism in literature, so do we demand it
> in politics. Politics will be implemented by industrious in-
> dividuals who have the interests of the community at heart.
> The measure of individuality will be in direct proportion to
> the level of self-denial: nothing for the self alone, every-
> thing for the task.
>   In politics, we want first of all to be with the people in
> the full sense of the word. . . . Do we include working-class

Czechs as party of the nation even when they declare themselves to be internationalist? Of course we do. Neither
the Young Czech nor the Old Czech party has any special claim
to represent the nation or its interests. Parties may change,
but the nation remains.[53]

The Modernists and other young intellectuals in the Progressive movement believed that material prosperity and the arts and
letters could contribute little to building a just society so
long as all Czechs could not exercise certain fundamental
civil rights and so long as Czech workers and peasants remained
politically disfranchised and without equal opportunities for
material or cultural enrichment. Antonín Hajn, František Modráček, and Antonín Pravoslav Veselý, among other young intellectuals associated with the Progressive movement, contended that the
Czech nation could advance only by struggling for political democratization and extensive social reform as well as for civil
liberties and national autonomy and considered the dynasty to be
the principal obstacle to any reform. Despite severe political
setbacks and in some cases imprisonment during the nineties, the
younger Progressives maintained their liberal, socialistic, and
humanitarian principles. After 1897 they would help create new
political parties and ultimately play an important part in establishing an independent Czechoslovakia.[54]

Beginning in the nineties, the predominantly confident mood
of Czech intellectuals contrasted sharply with a mood of anxiety
and despair widespread among their German-speaking counterparts.
This contrast continued despite a sensitivity to contemporary
social problems and an emphasis upon artistic refinement shared
by both groups. Czech literature as well as politics generally
reflected confidence in the ability and good will of ordinary
citizens and their determination to work together to build a
better future, whereas the pessimism and self-infatuation so prevalent in German Austrian literature, notably in the works of
Ferdinand von Saar and Hugo von Hofmannsthal, reflected the increasing isolation and insecurity of the landed aristocracy
and the cultivated urban upper middle class.[55] The Czechs welcomed the very social and political changes feared by the Austrian elite and could therefore face the future with confidence
instead of trepidation.

The Young Czechs and the Progressive Movement

Leaders of the Progressive movement had, from 1889 onward,
generally supported Young Czech programs and had endorsed Young
Czech candidates in the diet elections of July 1889 and the
Reichsrat elections of March 1891. They had also gratefully accepted Young Czech subsidies for Slavia and indirect fiscal and
moral support for the *Časopis českého studentstva*, without becoming subservient to party dictates. Both the Young Czechs and

the Progressives had joined forces out of self-interest as well
as common loyalty to liberal and patriotic political ideals.
The Young Czechs had desperately needed allies in order to over-
turn Old Czech hegemony and advance civil liberties and Bohemian
state rights. Given restricted suffrage and an authoritarian
government, the Progressives had looked upon the Young Czechs as
the political party most likely to open the way to extensive social, political, and educational reform.[56]

From March 1891 onward, leaders of the Progressive movement
urged the victorious Young Czechs to persevere in trying to
carry out their program of political reform and radical opposition to the Taaffe government.[57] At the same time, the Progressives began in at least three ways to depart markedly from traditional Young Czech policies by advocating the transformation
of society through the emancipation of women, the enfranchisement and organization of labor, and the advancement of Slavic
solidarity through cooperation with radical young Poles, Ukrainians, and Southern Slavs. By continuing to support equal rights
and opportunities for women, the Progressives up to 1914 distinguished themselves from most Young Czechs as well as all Old
Czechs. The Progressives advocated both social and sexual
equality in large part to strengthen national solidarity and
hasten the achievement of national autonomy. Eliska Krásnohorská, a fervent patriot and long-time crusader for women's rights
who had contributed an article to the second issue of the
Časopis českého studentstva advocating the pursuit of knowledge
for its own sake, helped set the tone for future articles and
editorials by the Hajn brothers and other Progressives favoring
the emancipation of women.[58] Progressives unanimously agreed on
the need to eliminate the double standard for men and women in
social relationships but disagreed among themselves on what sort
of single standard to adopt. One faction, jokingly called the
"partisans of morality" and led by Antonín Hajn, asked that "pre-
marital chastity" apply to men as well as women. The larger so-
called "immoral party" endorsed "free love" for both sexes.[59]

The student Progressives recognized a potentially powerful
political force in the tens of thousands of Czech workers who
had assembled for the 1890 May Day celebrations. Many Progressives aimed to help the workers improve their education and increase their wages as well as win the right to vote. Like Antonín Hajn, many also thought that working-class indifference toward Czech national emancipation could be attributed primarily
to a lack of Old and Young Czech concern about the social question: national emancipation and social reform had to advance
hand-in-hand if they were to advance at all.[60] Progressives
thus generally sympathized with many aims of Social Democracy as
well as with those of the Young Czech party but without giving
their allegiance wholeheartedly to either camp. Few had wholly
trusted the latter party since its leaders had obdurately defended bogus manuscripts in the interests of national pride.

And most remained wary of Social Democratic internationalism and belief in irreconcilable class conflict. Therefore, they preferred to constitute themselves as an independent political movement nominally allied to the Young Czech party.

The leaders of the Progressive movement promoted Slavic solidarity within the Dual Monarchy by cooperating with leaders of comparable movements among younger Poles, Slovaks, Ukrainians, and Southern Slavs. They began by sending three delegates to Kraków at the invitation of Polish students to help celebrate on July 4, 1890, the transfer of Mickiewicz's remains from Montmartre to the Wawel and to discuss means of facilitating future political collaboration.[61] The Poles had originally planned to hold an assembly of progressive Slavic youth, but this had to be cancelled at the behest of the authorities. Nonetheless, the discussions at Kraków between Czech and Polish students led directly to the convening of the First Congress of Slavic Progressive Youth in Prague on May 17, 1891, at the time of the Centennial Exposition and in defiance of a governmental ban. Representatives elected to the permanent central committee of the congress included future political leaders of prominence like the Slovak Pavel Blaho, the Ukrainian Ivan Franko, the Serb Dušan Peleš, the Croat Ante Radić, and the Poles Stanisław Bądzyński and Franciszek Nowicki.[62] Besides endorsing extensive social and institutional reform, the congress proposed ultimately to establish a progressive political party that would cut across national and ideological lines. At the Second Congress of Slavic Progressive Youth, held in Vienna during June of the following year, a majority of delegates, including most Poles and Ukrainians and the Czechs led by F. V. Lorenz and Antonín Pravoslav Veselý, approved a program which closely resembled that of Social Democracy.[63] The two congresses revealed a widening rift between the Progressive movement and a Young Czech party which criticized the First Congress for having taken an "anti-Russian" turn, given the preponderance of Polish and Ukrainian delegates, and which regarded the Second Congress as an unwarranted capitulation to Social Democratic influence.[64]

The program adopted by the Prague Congress of Slavic Progressive Youth on May 19, 1891, spelled out several policies to which the Czech Progressive movement and its successor parties would continue to adhere. The congress had succinctly proclaimed its "opposition to any sort of rule by nation over nation, sex over sex, and class over class." Its program called for the reconstitution of the Dual Monarchy as a federation of autonomous nations based on ethnicity and natural human rights rather than upon the historic crown lands. Fraternity and cooperation among all Slavs would help each Slavic nation realize its unique identity and destiny. The program also advocated direct, equal, secret, and universal suffrage and pledged to carry out social reform in association with representatives of the working class.[65]

Given the continuing importance of the Progressive movement

and its successor parties in Czech politics up to 1918, one must take account of its interesting and very complicated development, including its many internal divisions and the frequency with which its successors broke up and recombined.[66] From 1887 through 1893, the movement and its constituent organizations developed in three phases. The first, ending in 1889, primarily encompassed organizational groundwork and emphasis upon university affairs. The second phase through 1891 brought a shift to participation in national politics as Young Czech allies and an emphasis upon Slavic solidarity culminating in the two congresses of Slavic youth. The third phase during 1892 and 1893 brought increasing political activism and advocacy of social reform as well as growing disagreement with the Young Czech party. This activism grew most directly out of dissatisfaction with inequality and injustice in contemporary society and with governmental harassment initiated by Governor Thun. The first severe blows came in the summer of 1892, when Thun dissolved the progressive Sladkovský Society and when the Academic Senate of the university dismissed four students and reprimanded another for having helped draw up the "collectivist" plank endorsed by the Second Congress of Slavic Progressive Youth in Vienna. Progressives who had heretofore doubted the need for direct political action now joined the majority in organizing public demonstrations by workers and students and in stepping up editorial attacks on the authoritarian state and upon Young Czech political timidity and lack of social concern. This phase culminated in Progressive support of the Social Democratic and Young Czech campaigns for universal manhood suffrage.

Progressives generally agreed upon all points in the program of May 19, 1891, but disagreed on their order of priority and on the best means of putting them into practice. By the summer of 1892, these disagreements led to an informal division of the Progressive movement into two large groups--university youth on the one hand and working-class youth on the other--each of which contained several factions. To be sure, throughout the early nineties common interests still far outweighed any differences of opinion.[67] Among the university-student youth who comprised the original Progressive movement, two factions began to emerge. One, guided by Alois Rašín and Karel Stanislav Sokol, gave state rights policies some precedence over social reform and sought to maintain a closer affiliation with the Young Czech party. Members of the larger faction, including the Hajn brothers, Antonín Čížek, and František Vahalík, likewise considered themselves to be the "left wing" of the Young Czech party but thought that national autonomy should be based on natural rather than historical state rights and could only be achieved along with the emancipation of workers and women. A second group of Progressives, whose leaders often came from peasant or working-class families, stood closer to Social Democracy than to Young Czech radicalism. These "left" Progressives increasingly gave precedence to

proletarian interests and ultimately split into three subfac-
tions. One, including František Modráček and František Soukup,
soon joined the Czechoslavonic Social Democratic party. Members
of the second, who did not become Social Democrats until 1897,
called themselves Progressive Socialists and criticized Social
Democracy primarily for what they believed to be its excessively
materialistic and dogmatic doctrine. Their leaders included Jan
Ziegloser and the Veselý brothers, Antonín Pravoslav and Josef.
The third subfaction, whose principal spokesman was Václav J.
Klofáč, upheld the tradition of Josef Barák and the Young Czech
left of the seventies. It objected to Social Democratic neglect
of Czech national aspirations and resembled the *Naše obrana*
group in trying to steer a middle course between the Young
Czechs and Social Democracy.[68]

Journalism continued to serve as the cutting edge of the Progressive movement. The *Časopis českého studentstva* ceased publication with its twenty-first issue on December 17, 1892, but
was replaced within two months on the one hand by a new journal
managed by younger students, the *Časopis pokrokového studentstva*
(The journal of Progressive students), and on the other hand by
the weekly *Neodvislost* (Independence), edited by Antonín Hajn,
and the fortnightly *Nové proudy* (New currents) under editor
Josef Škába and publisher Karel Stanislav Sokol.[69] The latter
two journals, with circulations of 1,500 and 600 respectively,
remained closer to the Young Czech party in orientation than any
others affiliated with the Progressive movement, despite their
publication of some works critical of party policies, notably
J. S. Machar's satirical poem *Magdalena* which appeared in *Nové
proudy* and in which a poor but reformed prostitute is humiliated
and never forgiven by self-righteous and respectable Czech society.[70] This journal's debates with Social Democratic papers and
advocacy of historic state rights also led to lively debate within the Progressive movement.[71] In its inaugural issue of December 1892, *Neodvislost* claimed to represent the "left wing" of the
Young Czech party and announced its intention to guide the party
leftward by advocating nothing less than internal independence
for the Czech lands within the monarchy and firm resistance to
the authoritarian state until that independence was achieved.[72]
Like Edvard Grégr, editor Antonín Hajn defined radicalism as
getting to the "root" of any problem and working tenaciously to
resolve it without succumbing to either fanaticism or fatigue.
Logically, no compromise appeared possible between the Czechs
and the Dual Monarchy as presently constituted: any Czech efforts to work with imperial authorities toward its minor amelio-
ration or reform would likely do no more than prolong its use
as an instrument of political oppression. By unequivocally sub-
stituting natural for historical state rights, Hajn and his associates had in effect adopted certain radical Young Czech ideas
long identified with Edvard Grégr and František Tilser and reissued them in a more modern and cogent form. Identification of

Neodvislost with Young Czech radicalism was reinforced by its receiving cash subsidies from the party treasury and sponsorship by many leading party radicals, including Václav Březnovský, Heřman Janda, Richard Purghart, Josef Sokol, and Dr. Josef Šíl.[73]

A third important Progressive journal, the monthly *Rozhledy* (Outlooks), appeared in January 1892 under the editorship of Josef Pelcl and with a lead editorial by Antonín Hajn.[74] It served as the principal literary and cultural review of the Progressive movement and as the long-needed competitor of the conservative and academic monthly *Osvěta*, long identified with Old Czech politics and the national tradition in literature. *Rozhledy*, whose circulation reached 1,800 by 1895, generally looked more favorably upon Social Democracy and Masaryk's Realism than did either *Neodvislost* or *Nové proudy*. Its greater tolerance of differing political opinions helped attract as contributors many of the abler young writers, including the brilliant literary critic F. X. Šalda, the philosophic idealist Jan Vorel, the sometime satanist and anarchist poet S. K. Neumann, the Marxist cultural critic F. V. Krejčí, and the progressive Moravian lawyer Václav Choc.[75] *Rozhledy* often attacked the Young Czechs for stressing historical as opposed to natural state rights and for neglecting social and educational problems. Its sympathy with Social Democracy, its publication of the Modernist Manifesto, and its advocacy of thoroughgoing political reform reinforced the growing leftward orientation of Progressive politics. Among its aims, considered utopian at the time, were equal rights for women, tuition-free schools, public accountability of state officials, a progressive income tax, and replacement of the imperial army by a citizens' militia.[76]

By 1891, Antonín Čížek, K. S. Sokol, Alois Rašín, Josef Škába, A. P. Veselý, and the Hajn brothers had emerged as the principal leaders of the Progressive movement. The ablest theoretician and most prolific journalist of the lot was Antonín Hajn, the eldest son of a carpenter from the village of Solnice in eastern Bohemia. He stood barely over five feet tall and was of delicate build but healthy constitution. A high forehead, fierce countenance, and bright piercing eyes more than compensated for his small facial features. Most photographs taken after his release from prison in 1895 reveal a studied and excessively self-conscious pose of toughness and hauteur. Political satirists like Jaroslav Hašek and cartoonists like Josef Lada delighted in exaggerating or poking fun at Hajn's distinctive appearance and diminutive height as well as at his fervently held political convictions. Given to prodigious activity, Hajn wrote nearly half the articles in the *Časopis českého studentstva*, most of them unsigned, as well as in its successors *Neodvislost* and *Samostatnost*. He excelled in polemical journalism and in editorial planning, but intellectual arrogance and difficulty in understanding popular psychology rendered him largely unfit for practical politics. His scathing criticism of Habsburg

authoritarianism and Czech timidity in politics as well as his
coupling the cause of national autonomy to that of social reform
won him widespread respect if not affection in Czech intellectual and political circles.[77] As editor of the *Časopis českého
studentstva* from October 1890 to November 1892 and of *Neodvislost* after February 1893, he demonstrated his independence of
the party line by defending Czech Social Democracy against Young
Czech charges that it neglected national problems and by denouncing occasional anti-Semitic remarks by certain Young Czechs as
unwarranted and as inimical to the Czech national cause. Hajn
admired his former teacher of philosophy, T. G. Masaryk, for his
honesty and courage of conviction but disagreed strongly with
many of his political and philosophical views. In a series of
articles for *Neodvislost* and *Rozhledy* during 1893, Hajn not only
rejected Masaryk's plea for Progressive moderation in political
activism but regarded his humanitarian ideals as too abstract
and tolerant to guide Czech politics under authoritarian rule.[78]

Alois Hajn resembled his older brother only faintly in appearance, personality, and political outlook. Almost equally active in journalism and in the Progressive movement and just as
tenacious in defending his convictions, Alois possessed greater
stature, a more genial disposition, and a concrete as well as an
abstract liking for the common people. At the university, he
became a vigorous advocate of natural as opposed to historical
state rights and an independently minded disciple of Masaryk,
whom he would join in 1905 to help form the People's Progressive
party.[79]

The lawyer and economist Alois Rašín became the most formidable leader of those Progressive youth who maintained close ties
to the Young Czech party. He did so not only by intellectual
brilliance and organizational skill but by virtue of greater age
and experience. Born in October 1867, he was one or two years
older than most of his compatriots.[80] Like Antonín Hajn, he was
short in stature even by Czech standards and came from the same
social milieu: his father, a baker and farmer in Nechanice, resembled the Hajns' father in being a village tradesman of peasant origin from eastern Bohemia. Despite an early bout with
tuberculosis, Rašín remained robust in constitution and hard as
nails. His broad knowledge and rapier wit intimidated those few
associates with whom he did not become friends. A vigorous po-
lemicist, he regularly contributed articles and editorials to
Nové proudy and *Neodvislost* and other Progressive journals.[81]
He thought analytically with an eye for pithy or colorful detail
and gave no quarter to shoddy scholarship or opinions unrelated
to facts. In 1891, he received his doctorate in jurisprudence,
after having been Josef Kaizl's ablest pupil. Like his mentor,
he simultaneously pursued careers as a theoretical economist and
a practicing politician and by 1908 ranked among the leading
Czechs in both fields.[82] Ironically, this radical imprisoned
for "conspiracy" in 1894 distinguished himself not only as an

establishmentarian Young Czech after 1906 but as the first finance minister of the Czechoslovak Republic and the man most responsible for putting its currency on the gold standard.[83]

Antonín Čížek, a law student and private secretary to the
Young Czech club of diet delegates, and Karel Stanislav Sokol, a
philosophy student and son of the Young Czech Reichsrat deputy
Josef Sokol, served as the principal emissaries between the Progressive movement and the Young Czech party. Čížek, like Sokol,
had grown up in a Young Czech household, having been raised by
the Julius Grégrs after the untimely death of his lawyer father.
Personality and character as well as connections facilitated
Čížek's and Sokol's work as intermediaries. Both were of a
genial and gregarious nature, talented in public speaking and
enormously popular with their fellows. Both also worked in progressive journalism as writers and editors and in Sokol's case
as publisher. Though each possessed a physical stature and social graces that Hajn and Rašín did not, neither had the extraordinary discipline and energy that made their colleagues such
productive as well as perspicacious political writers.[84] Both
died prematurely, Čížek at thirty-one in 1897 and Sokol at
fifty-four in 1922. Besides his publication of the *Časopis českého studentstva* and nearly three decades of activity in Progressive politics, Sokol is best remembered as the founder and
editor of the monthly *Kronika*, a critical "chronicle" of political events from 1903 to 1914, and of the "Educational Library"
(Vzdělávací biblioteka), which from 1890 to 1912 published inexpensive Czech classics and translations from foreign literature
including Mill's *On the Subjection of Women*, Tolstoy's *Kreutzer
Sonata*, and Flaubert's *Madame Bovary*.[85]

Three Progressives who worked closely with Čížek and Sokol
were Josef Škába, Václav J. Klofáč, and Prokop Grégr, the son of
Julius Grégr. As a medical student and Čížek's closest friend,
Prokop Grégr became associated with the Progressive movement and
entertained hopes of someday guiding the *Národní listy* and the
Young Czech party toward a more popular political orientation.[85]
Klofáč, an erratic student and the son of an impoverished tailor
from Německý Brod, began in 1890 to write for the *Národní listy*
and participated in Progressive politics from 1889 until the
summer of 1892. By temporarily withdrawing from school and political life at that time, he did not become involved in the Progressive demonstrations of 1893 or in the subsequent *Omladina*
"conspiracy" trials.[87] Josef Škába served as the last editor of
the *Časopis českého studentstva* and the first of *Nové proudy*.
He also first suggested and helped popularize use of the Polish
song "The Red Flag" among Czech students and workers and even
arranged for its translation into Czech. Along with Rašín,
Sokol, and Antonín Hajn, he was one of four Progressives whom
imperial prosecutors indicted in January 1894 as "intellectual
originators" of the alleged *Omladina* conspiracy. His continuing
advocacy of Czech minority interests led the North Bohemian

National Union (*Národní Jednota severočeská*) to appoint him as
its secretary in 1900 and chairman in 1910.[88]

Several score of Czech students, who opposed what they deemed
to be the excessively left-wing outlook of the Progressive movement as well as its pretensions to represent the views of all
students, organized themselves in 1892 as the Independent Party
of Czechoslavonic Students (*Strana neodvislého studentstva českoslovanského*). They tried to advance a program of nationalism,
conservatism, and anti-Semitism, primarily through their two
short-lived publications, the *Časopis studentstva českoslovanského* (Journal of Czechoslavonic students) during the spring and
summer of 1893 and the *Studentský sborník strany neodvislé* (The
student magazine of the Independent party) for three years beginning in May 1894. But they won so little university or public support for their program that they gave the Progressive
movement only negligible opposition.[89]

Working-class Czech youth organized their own Progressive Socialist association and monthly journal, *Omladina* (Youth), on
September 28, 1891, in the mining and industrial city of Kladno.[90] They maintained their primary allegiance to Social Democracy while establishing close informal ties with the Progressive youth in Prague in the belief that all citizens would benefit if reform-minded youth cooperated in trying to achieve mutually acceptable goals.[91] Such goals included seeking an end to
the exploitation of nation by nation or class by class and a
guarantee of equal rights and free education for all citizens
regardless of class or nationality. They defined their relationship to Social Democracy as follows:

> Recognizing that among all political parties, the Social De-
> mocratic party alone is qualified to rectify social relation-
> ships, to assure the necessities of life and the welfare of
> both humanity and the individual, and to restore justice and
> freedom to all, we profess our adherence to this party and
> declare ourselves to be radical (energetic) socialists. . . .
> We recognize the merits of the older fighters for the idea of
> Social Democracy, from whom we do not wish to dissociate our-
> selves.[92]

After establishing close ties to the Progressive movement,
this *Omladina* group, which included many future Social Democrats
and Progressive Socialists, likewise sent delegates to the Second
Congress of Slavic Progressive Youth in Vienna. Besides editors
F. V. Lorenz and Antonín Pravoslav Veselý, the leading contributors to *Omladina* were Josef Myslík, a future editor of *Právo
lidu* and Social Democratic publicist, Josef Skalák, Czech trans-
lator of Bakunin and Bebel and a future administrator of the
Communist *Rudé právo* (Red justice), and František Modráček, who
joined the *Omladina* staff in 1893 after having served time in
Vienna for agitation as a "communist anarchist."[93]

The leading Progressive Socialist was Antonín Pravoslav Veselý, a typesetter by trade from Jičín, who in 1892 helped organize many Progressive demonstrations and in June 1893 as editor
transformed the monthly *Omladina* into the biweekly *Pokrokové
listy* (Progressive news). A forthright and courageous journalist,
he rose swiftly to become a recognized leader of the whole Progressive movement. Though largely self-educated, he could hold
his own in any political or literary debate. All close associates have testified to his kindness and honesty, and there is no
evidence of his ever having had any personal enemies. Imprisonment with other *Omladina* "conspirators" at Bory in 1894 and 1895
stifled neither his courage nor his love for journalism; he even
had to serve extra time for bringing out a clandestine prison
newspaper. During his imprisonment for eight months, he con-
tracted tuberculosis which led to his early death in March 1904,
making him in death as in life the Karel Havlíček of his generation. Tens of thousands of mourners turned his funeral into a
great public demonstration for the socialist and humanitarian
ideals for which he had lived.[94]

Cooperation between students and workers in the Progressive
movement occurred to such an unprecedented degree that it cannot
adequately be explained either by student enthusiasm for Social
Democratic ideas or by strong national consciousness on the part
of many workers. Progressives like A. Pravoslav Veselý and sympathetic observers like T. G. Masaryk emphasized the fact that
many students in the higher schools and the university came from
peasant or working-class families at most one or two generations
removed.[95] Most students, including many from middle-class families, believed that the nation would be strengthened by developing mutual understanding between all social classes and by
giving workers a better education and a fair share of the national wealth. Many also understood proletarian problems from childhood experience as well as from study and believed that a common
background of poverty and exploitation gave young workers and
students some grounds for mutual understanding and political cooperation. Only a few feared that by fraternizing with the working class they would themselves become proletarians. Few also
shared the distrust and dislike of Social Democracy expressed by
their Young Czech sponsors. At the same time, most Progressive
working-class youth did not, as did their Social Democratic elders, look with misgiving upon the growing influence of highly
educated young Progressive "bourgeois intellectuals" in the
workers' movement. In Prague and other large cities, students
often frequented the same inexpensive restaurants and beer halls
as workers and, having often grown up under similar conditions,
were separated by no social barrier save that which a university
education would likely impose. The great Czech impressionist
poet Antonín Sova, who came from a poor peasant family in the
south Bohemian town of Pacov, has accurately described many effects of this experience:

At the time when I wrote *Stormy Sorrows* [*Vybouřené smutky*, 1897], I truly lived from "day to day" like a hardened proletarian, glad to have what little I did have and often having to go hungry. If I went to a wedding or to a funeral, I had to wear a black coat borrowed from a friend in better circumstances. Later when I was able to buy a coat for myself, I in turn lent it to needy friends for their weddings and for their funerals. In all of this personal tribulation and discontent was concealed the germ of impersonal suffering. Only through this experience did I come to see in true perspective the lives of those who oppress others and the lives of those who are oppressed. And so I have tried to find a poetic form for conveying the universality and collective nature of human suffering.[96]

The fine system of Czech public schools established since May 1869 also helped to break down class barriers and misunderstandings and further provide a common experience for younger workers and students. That the working-class youth of the nineties enjoyed the benefit of eight or more years of formal schooling which had been denied to their fathers also helped account for the many well-read and articulate spokesmen in their ranks, of whom the Veselý brothers were the most outstanding examples. On the other hand, most Young Czechs had come through primary and secondary schools before 1869, when German and clerical dominance obtained. As pupils they had constantly to assert their national pride and identity against German schoolmasters and classmates who treated them as inferiors. Given this experience, most could not comprehend the camaraderie between young workers and students or their acceptance of internationalism.

Cooperation between Czech students and workers who sought to advance extensive political reform began in politics, journalism, and public demonstrations and culminated in support of the 1893 Young Czech proposal for universal, direct, equal, and secret manhood suffrage to the lower house of the Reichsrat. Young intellectuals and working men served together on the editorial boards of the progressive journals *Omladina* and *Rozhledy* and later on the staff of Social Democratic papers and periodicals. The first in a series of memorable joint demonstrations for national solidarity and social reform occurred on February 1, 1891, as delegations of students and workers laid wreaths on the grave of Augustin Smetana, early nineteenth-century Czech philosopher and foe of clericalism.[97] On July 6, 1892, exactly 477 years after Hus's martyrdom at Constance, young workers and students assembled at the site of the Bethlehem Chapel to sing the Czech national anthem and "The Red Flag" (*Rudý prapor*). A memorial procession to the White Mountain battlefield on November 8, 1892, marked a day of national mourning for the two-hundred-seventy-second anniversary of the end of Bohemian independence. To honor the Taborite Hussites who fell in battle at Lipany in

1434, Czech students and workers on June 1, 1893, there unfurled red flags as well as banners bearing the Hussite chalice and re-affirmed their intention to work for social justice.[98]

Increasing political activism by workers and students during 1892 and 1893 helped stimulate a growing radicalism within the Young Czech party. To be sure, most Young Czechs disliked criticism of their party by *Rozhledy* and *Neodvislost* for alleged intellectual sterility and inadequate efforts on behalf of social reform. And they took alarm at what they perceived to be the increasingly rash actions and left-wing ideas of their nominal allies in the Progressive movement. But, at the same time, many Young Czechs began more vigorously to urge adoption of universal manhood suffrage and extended civil liberties not only in the public interest but in part to dampen youthful revolutionary fervor and channel youthful energies into working for reform through established laws and institutions. As massive popular demonstrations for universal suffrage in the summer of 1892 indicated widespread support for electoral reform, Young Czech lawyers Pacák, Slavík, and Stránský took the lead in drafting a party-sponsored bill for universal manhood suffrage in elections to the lower house of the Reichsrat. Editorials as well as demonstrations helped persuade a party largely predisposed to favor universal manhood suffrage to endorse it wholeheartedly, as most former Old Czechs, including Adámek, Schwarz, and František V. Veselý, came to accept this traditionally radical Young Czech proposal which they had rejected as formulated by Karel Sladkovský nineteen years before.[99]

From the Campaign for Universal Suffrage to the *Omladina* Trials

After intra-party debates from February 18 to March 16, 1893, almost all Young Czechs had come to believe that universal suffrage offered the only feasible way to bring Czech Socialists and Progressives into their parliamentary system, where their radical tactics might be blunted and their cooperation with the Young Czechs on matters of mutual concern might be won.[100] All now recognized what Tilšer, Jan Slavík, Adolf Stránský, and the Grégr brothers had long contended: universal suffrage would benefit the Slavic peoples of Cisleithania by giving them representation more in conformity with their numerical majority and by diminishing the strength of the great landowners and German parties in Parliament.[101] Furthermore, most leading Young Czechs, including Herold, Špindler, and Edvard Grégr, believed that the new voting order would likely win allegiance of the working class to the national cause.[102] Antonín Hajn and Alois Rašín of the Progressive movement concurred; but Alfons Šťastný came out against the measure, surprising those who had overestimated his democratic proclivities. He preferred instead proportional representation that would continue to favor landholding peasants at the expense of landless rural laborers.[103]

On March 17, 1893, Jan Slavík presented the Young Czech bill
for direct, equal, secret, and universal manhood suffrage to the
Reichsrat.[104] The clerical and conservative majority immediately rose in opposition, as did the German Liberals, who denounced
it as an invitation to mob rule.[105] Despite this setback, the
Young Czechs continued to press for the bill's adoption, thereby
performing a signal service for the parties of the left heretofore excluded from the Reichsrat by curial voting. In bringing
about cooperation between all popular Czech political movements,
the 1893 struggle for universal manhood suffrage marked the ze-
nith of Young Czech radicalism.

Though discouraged by the hostile reception of Slavík's bill,
Young Czechs, Social Democrats, and Progressives were heartened
by the Belgian Parliament's April adoption of universal suffrage
in the face of a general strike.[106] The Austrian Social Democratic party now proposed direct, equal, secret, and universal
suffrage for all citizens over twenty-one regardless of sex and
demonstrated on its behalf throughout Cisleithania. Governmental
reaction came swiftly and severely. After a demonstration by
some thirty thousand in Brno on June 18, 1893, the authorities
handed out sentences totaling fifteen years and eight months to
forty-six ringleaders, six men receiving terms in excess of one
year. Despite continued police repression, the demonstrations
increased in size and frequency through the summer, becoming especially turbulent in the Czech lands, where the alliance between Social Democratic youth and the Progressive movement led
to patriotic rallies in favor of universal suffrage and against
the dynasty.[107] On May 15, 1893, St. John's day, a group of students and workers celebrated by draping a huge noose around the
neck of the statue of Emperor Franz I on the Vltava quay and by
trying unsuccessfully to topple the statue of St. John Nepomuk
from the Charles Bridge into the Vltava River.[108] These pranks,
the former regarded by the authorities as highly provocative,
occurred as delegates to the Bohemian Diet engaged in several
days of stormy controversy over Taaffe's attempt to redraw the
boundaries of the Trutnov judicial district in accordance with
the Agreement of 1890. On May 16 and 17, the Young Czechs obstructed all business of the diet by performing such undignified
acts as throwing ink wells and emptying wastebaskets. This led
to the diet's being dismissed until fall.[109] Sporadic acts of
vandalism perpetrated for the most part by teenage rowdies occurred throughout the summer and included the destruction of
German signs and dual-language street markers.[110] The tearing
down or defacing of imperial emblems especially annoyed the authorities and even alarmed the emperor and Minister-President
Taaffe, who pressed Governor Thun to put an end to all disturbances.[111]

Youthful fervor and discontent on the one hand and increasing
government rigidity on the other reinforced one another to create a highly charged emotional atmosphere in Prague by late

summer. Spontaneous demonstrations continued, with the largest
taking place on August 17, 1893, the eve of the emperor's
birthday, as groups of students and young workers, almost all
without ties to the Progressive movement, disrupted a concert in
honor of the emperor by shouting and distributing handbills
which called for revolution and the overthrow of the monarchy.
These demonstrators drowned out the imperial anthem by singing
"The Red Flag" and after the concert followed the band as it
left the Old Town Square. On the way down Celetna Street, they
smashed all windows in the Noble's Casino. After breaking
through a police cordon at the Powder Tower, they pursued the
band across Joseph Square and all the way back to its barracks
in suburban Karlín, where they dispersed after shouting "Long
live anarchy!" Other groups committed such sporadic acts of
violence as destroying several street lamps and breaking windows
at the city jail on Charles Square. Because the unprepared police appeared unable to restore public order, Governor Thun dispatched dragoons to disperse the remaining rioters: by early
morning, silence reigned.[112] Mass arrests of leading left-wing
Progressives and other suspects and rabble-rousers followed,
totaling thirty-eight by September 10 and including A. P. Veselý,
František Modráček, and S. K. Neumann. Also in this group were
Bořivoj Weigert, a nineteen-year-old typesetter, and Jan Ziegloser, an eighteen-year-old carpenter's helper, on whose hectograph
many of the inflammatory handbills appeared to have been printed.[113]

The events of August 17 had caught the governor by surprise;
but, expecting more trouble on September 12, the twenty-second
anniversary of the imperial rescript of 1871, he put the Prague
garrison on alert and called in police reserves from outlying
districts. He knew that the Young Czech party had planned a
series of 120 public demonstrations throughout Bohemia in favor
of state rights; already at Lužec nad Vltavou on September 3,
Edvard Grégr and K. Stanislav Sokol had delivered speeches highly
critical of the Taaffe government and imperial authority.[114]   On
September 12, a private patriotic gathering of nearly 600 Czechs
assembled, after obtaining requisite police permission, on Žofín
Island in the Vltava with the expectation of hearing speeches by
Edvard Grégr, Václav Březnovský, Alois Rašín, and other prominent radicals which would ask that the rescript be honored and
Bohemian state rights be restored. But Police Commissioner
Nostitz von Lichtenstern refused to allow the meeting to take
place. While his police and dragoons blocked all exits from the
island, he broke up the meeting after pulling Edvard Grégr off
the podium where he was trying to begin his speech. The police
herded the participants off the island and arrested several for
unruly conduct. That evening, some disgruntled participants
complained that the Young Czech organizers had too meekly sur-
rendered to the commissioner's demands. Many more went home or
to small private gatherings.[115]   But others engaged in small

demonstrations to protest Lichtenstern's action, including the
smashing of plaster busts of their imperial majesties at the
restaurant U Choděru.[116]   In response to the events of September 12, Governor Thun promptly declared a state of emergency
(*výjimečný stav*) in Prague and five adjacent districts which was
to last for more than twenty-six months. He immediately suspended freedom of assembly and trial by jury, prohibited seventeen political associations, including the Young Czech party,
from carrying on activities in the area, and required 213 organizations to give three days' advance notice of any meeting
and all others to give at least two days' notice. He closed
down eight newspapers, all of them Czech, and required twenty
others, nineteen of them Czech, to submit copy to the police at
least three hours before going to press.[117] More mass arrests
of young workers and Progressives followed, including established
journalists and leaders like Alois Rašín and Antonín Hajn. With
the help of anonymous letters and police informers, notably the
glovemaker Rudolf Mrva, the governor's office fabricated an alleged *Omladina* "conspiracy" of 729 members in two branches and
on January 15, 1894, brought 76 young men to trial on charges
ranging from riotous behavior to high treason.[118]

Taaffe, who had to date ruled longer than any Cisleithanian
minister-president, did not survive the crises which he had
helped provoke by reactionary "divide-and-rule" policies. On
October 10, 1893, with Prague and vicinity still under a state
of emergency and almost seven months to the day after Jan Slavík
had introduced the Young Czech bill for universal manhood suffrage, Taaffe and Finance Minister Emil Steinbach asked the
Reichsrat to approve their watered-down version of Slavík's
bill. The new bill retained curial voting, by granting universal manhood suffrage only to the third and fourth curias, and kept
the "electoral geometry" which gave more representation to German
than to non-German districts.[119] Like the introduction of
several social-welfare measures in the eighties, the new voting
bill sought to buy off the masses, who were still believed to
harbor great affection for the monarchy, by halfway measures
after systematic oppression had been tried and found wanting.
The Young Czechs, Moravian Old Czechs, Christian Socialists,
Ukrainians, several German nationalists, and two German democrats,
Ferdinand Kronawetter and Engelbert Pernerstorfer, constituted
the minority which voted for the measure. Ernst von Plener and
the German Liberals joined the old conservative-Catholic alliance
on October 25 in voting it down.[120] The Taaffe government, shaken by popular demonstrations and unable to pass this bill, collapsed after more than fourteen years in office. On November 11,
1893, Franz Joseph accepted Taaffe's resignation and on the morrow appointed a government headed by Prince Alfred Windischgrätz
and backed by the parliamentary coalition which had twice rejected universal manhood suffrage. The Reichsrat voted 185 to 73 on
December 12, 1893, to uphold Governor Thun's declaration of

martial law in Prague.[121] Czechs unhappily noted that the new
minister-president was, appropriately enough, the grandson of
Field Marshal Alfred Windischgrätz, the conqueror of revolutionary Prague in June of 1848.

The *Omladina* Trials and Their Consequences

The Windischgrätz government gave Governor Thun a carte
blanche to continue his efforts to smash the Progressive and
socialist movements among Czech youth. Before he had finished
preparing his case against the *Omladina* group, two working-class
Czech youths avenged the seventy-six incarcerated Progressives
by murdering police informer Rudolf Mrva in his Malá Strana
apartment on December 23, 1893. The Czech press and all Czech
political parties quickly denounced the crime. As Josef Soukup
later aptly put it, the Mrva case was "the one tare among the
wheat."[122] The official government paper *Prager Zeitung-Pražské
noviny* charged that the Young Czechs stood behind the "political
murder" of Mrva, a charge which the party emphatically denied on
December 29. That same day the government's desire to implicate
both Young Czechs and Progressives in the murder became evident
as Antonín Čížek, leading Progressive and secretary of the Young
Czech club of delegates, was arrested and along with five other
defendants charged with murder and conspiracy to commit murder.[123]

The trial of the seventy-six alleged *Omladina* conspirators,
which did not include the six charged with the Mrva murder, opened on January 15, 1894, before a military tribunal closed to the
public. Charges ranged from lese majesty to conspiracy to commit
high treason and from creating public disorder to advocacy of
revolution. Fifty-five of the defendants were under age twenty-
one; and fifty-two were workers, including ten typesetters besides Antonín Pravoslav Veselý and Bořivoj Weigert. Among prominent Progressives in the dock were Antonín Hajn, František Modráček, Alois Rašín, Karel Stanislav Sokol, and Josef Škába. Various attorneys, including Adolf Stránský and Karel Baxa, defended
the seventy-six against great odds in proceedings where circum-
stantial evidence, anonymous letters, and paid informers sufficed
to win sixty-eight convictions and prison sentences totaling more
than ninety-six years.[124]

The trial of the six defendants in the Mrva case came as an
anticlimax. On March 20, 1894, František Dragoun and Josef Kříž
as the convicted murderers and Otakar Doležal as their accom-
plice received sentences of ten years each. Antonín Čížek and
the other two defendants were acquitted for lack of evidence.[125]

The Young Czech party, banned from meeting in Prague, and the
Národní listy, crippled by three-hour pre-censorship, took no
concerted stand in favor of the *Omladina* "conspirators." The
party published a broadside with some phrases deleted by censorship, challenging the government's grounds for imposing a state
of emergency and condemning the draconian measures taken against

Czech newspapers and political organizations. It offered no
concrete plan to compel Governor Thun to rescind his actions.[126]
Meetings of the party executive committee and clubs of delegates
in September and the annual meeting of the party trustees at
Pardubice on October 8, 1893, endorsed the policy of watchful
waiting advocated by Chairman Engel and Kaizl, among others, in
the expectation that the government would soon exhaust its fury.
Vigorous intervention on behalf of the imprisoned Progressives
might well hurt both their cause and the party's position. Meanwhile, the government would only harm its reputation at home and
abroad if it resorted to more severe measures.[127] Eim and Stránský, among the minority, contended that the party ought to assume
responsibility for its "left wing" in this time of crisis. Eim
also objected to the party trying to take credit for the heroism
of the Progressive demonstrators while remaining silent and doing
next to nothing to help the accused.[128] A number of party members including Breznovský, Kramář, Purghart, and Josef Sokol
visited the defendants in the New Town prison where they awaited
conclusion of the pretrial investigation. Edvard Grégr, Pacák,
Kramář, Janda, and Vašatý, among others, also criticized the
government's brutal overreaction in speeches to the Reichsrat.
Although these individual expressions of sympathy were appreciated, they could not disguise the impotence of the Young Czech
party at this time of crisis.[129]

Two Young Czechs dissociated themselves enough from the party
to win the lasting gratitude of the *Omladina* group. Defense attorney Adolf Stránský to the best of his ability argued the innocence of the "conspirators" before the special military court.
Masaryk's long opposition to aimless radicalism and lack of social responsibility in party policy culminated in a serious political dispute with Julius Grégr--the Šromota affair--and in
disappointment at the party's having disclaimed responsibility
for the *Omladina* youths whom they had earlier encouraged in
their radical behavior.[130] He resigned his party mandates to
the diet and the Reichsrat on September 25, 1893, and stepped up
his criticism of the party through *Čas* and his new monthly review, *Naše doba* (Our era). Most student Progressives had not
appreciated Masaryk's earlier criticism of their radicalism and
reliance on street demonstrations, but his break with the Young
Czechs now revealed him to be one of the few politicians with an
understanding, if not always friendly, view of their cause.

Governor Thun's suppression of the Progressive movement by
means of the *Omladina* trial momentarily halted the political activities of the younger generation and demonstrated again the
hostility of the Habsburgs toward any genuinely liberal and democratic reforms. A disillusioned but not disheartened younger
generation redoubled its efforts to revitalize Czech culture
while it awaited the coming of a better day to resume its political activities.

Thun's continuation of the state of emergency for twenty-six

months crippled the *Národní listy* as the voice of radical opinion. Proscription of public political life in the capital compelled the Young Czech party to conduct its affairs from outlying areas where it could rely on strong district organizations.
The Habsburgs had no desire to strangle completely Czech political life by closing down the diet and district and communal self-
governing bodies. Such repression, as of the diet in 1913, would
have meant a temporary halt in tax collection and government
services until an expanded police force and bureaucracy could
take over. The Young Czech party therefore survived the dark
years of 1894 and 1895 in the very self-governmental institutions which most determined its fundamentally undemocratic character and its close ties to the privileged commercial and landholding classes. This in turn hastened the eclipse of the already discredited party radicalism.

The Young Czech party leadership sympathized with the plight
of the imprisoned *Omladina* "conspirators" but still resented
their past attacks on its integrity and courage. During the
trials, the party had done little to defend its young and self-
proclaimed "left wing," regarding the *Omladina* affair as a serious but temporary political crisis. The moderate Young Czechs
still did not abandon hope of someday coming to terms with Vienna. Once the government's fury had been spent and its limits of
coercion defined, they reasoned, it would offer terms for reconciliation on which they could negotiate. Meanwhile popular Czech
ire and frustration in the face of government oppression found
an outlet in ostentatious celebration of the Franco-Russian Entente concluded in January 1894.[131]

The younger generation would not be satisfied with a policy
either of cautiously outwaiting oppression or of effusive but
ineffective Francophile or Russophile demonstrations. To them,
the *Omladina* trial and the defeat of universal suffrage constituted a serious social and moral crisis whose dimensions transcended politics. They began to question not only the desirability of Young Czech policies and actions but the validity of
the very system of politics on which it rested. For solutions
to pressing contemporary problems they commenced to look beyond
the patriotic, commercial, and self-governmental institutions
through which Czech political and material progress had occurred
during the preceding generation. Though Young Czech radicalism
had been discredited, a new radical generation had been formed
which constituted a greater danger to the Habsburgs because it
aspired to establish genuinely popular political parties aiming
at social as well as political reform. The Young Czech party's
preponderance in national politics survived by several years
the *Omladina* trials, but its claim to moral leadership had been
tarnished. By its ambivalence during those trials, the party
lost its last chance to attract the younger generation in any
appreciable numbers and thereby to become a truly national

party. Though younger Progressives and Social Democrats immediately criticized the party, the extent to which it had lost the
confidence of its national constituency would only gradually
become apparent.

Responsible and Active Political Work

Prospects for all Czech political parties looked bleak as the Young Czech board of trustees assembled for its annual meeting at Nymburk on September 23, 1894. That a state of emergency still obtained in Prague and outlying suburbs helped dictate the choice of Nymburk, a city thirty miles east of Prague, as the meeting site. Governor Thun had silenced or intimidated Czech political movements within the capital and was preparing decrees to circumscribe the autonomy of Czech public schools. The imperial government of Prince Alfred Windischgrätz and a Reichsrat majority dominated by the German Liberals continued to sanction the governor's dictatorial acts. Forty-six of the sixty-eight *Omladina* "conspirators" still remained in Bory prison; and the campaign for universal manhood suffrage, launched with such great expectations by Young Czechs and Social Democrats nearly eighteen months before, lay in shambles, despite some continued demonstrations in its favor by Social Democrats outside of central Bohemia.

The Nymburk Resolution

In assembling at Nymburk, the Young Czech trustees and delegates came to a typical town in the area of their greatest electoral support, the fertile Labe valley north and east of Prague. The site of a district board, a district captaincy, and an imperial court, Nymburk served as the principal trading and food processing center for prosperous small and middle farmers of the Poděbradsko district. Its prosperity depended primarily upon the two industries which had most improved the status of the independent Czech peasant during the past three decades, brewing and the refining of beet sugar.[1] A city of over seven thousand inhabitants, Nymburk lay along the Labe River halfway between the lower Labe districts of Podřipsko and Mělnicko and the districts on middle Labe tributaries around Čáslav and Hlinsko which had traditionally sent radical Young Czech delegates to the Reichsrat. It numbered among the middle Labe districts, including Kolín, Kutná Hora, and Pardubice, in which until 1889 the Old Czech party had won its largest rural following.[2] In June of that year the Young Czechs had won all fourth-curia diet seats from the Poděbradsko area, in which Nymburk was located, and in March 1891 captured all parliamentary representation after the traditionally Old Czech district boards announced their support of Young Czech candidates. Many city notables

remained Old Czechs at heart, even though they recognized that
the electoral defeats of 1889 and 1891 had ended National party
supremacy.[3] Nymburk therefore proved to be an appropriate place
in which Young Czechs could meet to consider reviving certain
Old Czech policies.

Besides circumventing the prohibition on political meetings
in areas under state of emergency, the choice of Nymburk put the
party gathering on ostensibly neutral ground and prevented
charges against the party trustees for having shown favoritism
to any person or faction in choosing the site. The city, while
typical of those electing Young Czechs after 1889, belonged to a
different voting district in each of the four diet and three
Reichsrat curias in which Czechs could vote and could count no
party delegates or prominent leaders among its citizens. Furthermore, in no way could the congress in Nymburk either by its
moderate resolutions or by its location be described as a provocation of the Germans. Nymburk stood farther from the language
frontier than any Czech city of comparable size except Kolín and
Kutná Hora, and no serious nationality conflict had occurred in
the districts of Nymburk and Poděbrady, where Czechs numbered
99.77 percent of the population.

The Young Czech board of trustees assembled at Nymburk to
unify and strengthen a party badly shaken by the *Omladina* trials
and overwhelmed by the governor's dictatorial decrees. The
trustees intended to reconfirm their ruling at Pardubice on October 8, 1893, against the party radicals led by Edvard Grégr
and Josef Fort who wished the party to oppose the state of emergency more forcefully.[5] Moreover, they were prepared to endorse
the "Prague Proposal" (Pražský traktát), that moderate program
drafted by Josef Herold and approved by the party clubs of delegates at their joint meeting in Prague on July 14, 1894.[6] At
that time, the two clubs had also jointly endorsed a parliamentary policy of "opportunistic" as opposed to "destructive" opposition, thereby discouraging further inflammatory denunciations
of the imperial government like those made in the Reichsrat by
Edvard Grégr, Václav Březnovský, Josef Sokol, Václav Šamánek,
and Jan Vašatý on April 11 and 12, 1894.[7] Identical differences
of opinion on party ideology and tactics reappeared at Nymburk
in September; but so thoroughly had the moderate majority con-
solidated its position in the intervening months that approval
of the Prague Proposal by the Nymburk assembly was a foregone
conclusion.[8] A majority of moderates, led by Engel, wished to
restrain the radicals without driving them from the party, recognizing that Julius Grégr had for so long been the principal
public spokesman of the party that any open conflict with him
would seriously harm party rapport with the electorate.[9] A minority of moderates, including Kaizl and Kramář, wanted to be
rid of the radicals altogether.

Chairman Engel and Gustav Eim, ably seconded by Adámek,
Herold, Pacák, Kaizl, Kramář, and Václav Škarda, directed the

campaign for a "responsible and active" parliamentary policy.[10]
This policy, broadly conceived, advocated active opposition only
until the imperial government and other parties became willing
to support measures long favored by the party. Meanwhile, the
party would support any bill which would benefit the whole monarchy without harming Czech interests. Such a policy was designed to strengthen Parliament and help sustain the institutions
of self-government which served as the best guarantors of limited
Czech political autonomy and civil liberties. Eim and Engel emphasized the practical advantages of such a "muscular" and "active" policy, especially the possibility of winning concessions
from the government in return for backing it on issues which did
not compromise the party's liberal principles. Kaizl and Kramář
cited the Realist program of 1890 in seconding Herold's and
Pacák's call for moderation in parliamentary opposition and in
insisting that the party show itself responsible and worthy of
imperial respect.[11] All moderates welcomed the support of that
old fox in Czech politics, Jakub Škarda, now sixty-six and ill,
who had backed what proved to be the winning party as an Old
Czech in the sixties and eighties and as a Young Czech in the
later seventies and again after 1890. In reply to charges of
political opportunism, he always maintained, with considerable
justification, that he had consistently supported whatever Czech
party worked most effectively for reform through established institutions.[12]

Jakub Škarda's eldest son Václav, aged thirty-three, had
meanwhile joined the ranks of the party moderates. On January 7,
1894, he had won election as a Young Czech to the diet from the
third-curial electoral district that included Mladá Boleslav and
Nymburk, replacing the Old Czech stalwart, Karel Mattuš, who had
resigned in September of the previous year. This brilliant and
established young lawyer had taken first place in the law examinations at Charles University in 1882 and received his doctorate
of jurisprudence the next year at age twenty-one. After joining
the party in 1892, he continued to serve as editor of the prestigious law journal *Právník*, to manage his own law firm, and to
give legal advice to Czech self-governmental and patriotic institutions. From his father, he had since childhood learned the
ins and outs of Czech politics. In 1892, before having run
for the diet or Reichsrat, he became a member of the party administrative subcommittee responsible to Jan Kučera. At Nymburk
he won election to the party executive committee and to the
chairmanship of its electoral subcommittee. In the latter capacity he would serve as the chief organizer of the party's landslide victories in the diet elections of 1895 and Reichsrat
elections of 1897. Škarda's letters to party associates were
businesslike and to the point and contained very little of the
gossip and intrigue that characterized those of his colleagues
Eim, Kaizl, and Kramář. While Václav Škarda succeeded his
father in the political arena, his younger brother, Vladimír,

looked after family business interests, rising eventually to become chairman of the board of the Czech Industrial Bank and of
Českomoravská-Kolben-Daněk, which after 1919 stood second only
to Škoda as a Czech producer of machine tools and transportation
equipment. Like their father, the two brothers also worked for
many years as executives in various Czech patriotic organizations, Vladímir for example serving as a director of the Central
School Foundation.[13]

Defining the proper relationship of the Young Czech party to
Progressives and radicals within and without its ranks constituted the most difficult task of the moderate majority in preparing
for the Nymburk congress. Most moderates had expressed publicly
as well as privately their sympathy for the plight of the *Omladina* youth; but most also believed that Progressive association
with Social Democracy would help undermine the existing order of
society, including the very governmental and private institutions by which the Czechs had risen from a peasant to a middle-
class society. Furthermore, Progressive ties to doctrinaire
Young Czech radicals appeared to endanger the unity and future
electoral appeal of the party, and Progressive antidynastic demonstrations and revolutionary slogans had apparently diminished
what little imperial good will Old and Young Czechs had gradually won through years of responsible participation in the Taaffe
government. Many more years of patient and responsible toil
would be required for the party to regain the respect of rival
parties and of the imperial authorities.[14] Among the Young
Czechs who had witnessed 1848 or the tábor movement of 1868, the
older radicals best understood the impatience and enthusiasm of
youth for implementing long-overdue reforms.[15] On the other
hand, all moderates equated radicalism with political immaturity
and contended that radical preponderance in Czech politics from
the 1891 Reichsrat elections to the *Omladina* trials had done in-
estimable harm to the Czech national cause.[16]

Although the moderate majority agreed to dissociate themselves from the Progressive movement and to discipline the party
radicals, they moved hesitatingly to achieve these ends. They
first announced that members of the Progressive movement who
still considered themselves to be members of the party's "left
wing" might attend Nymburk "as journalists with an advisory
vote."[17] But the majority leaders soon changed their minds and
required any Progressive who wished to attend to pledge unconditional support to the moderate party program. The party publicly explained that it had changed to this procedure in order to
conform to the existing by-laws which prohibited nonaffiliated
persons from taking part in party debates.[18] Though this explanation was technically correct, the party moderates had instituted a loyalty oath primarily because, knowing certain radical
party members to be in close touch with Progressive leaders,
they feared that the presence of unrepentant Progressives at
Nymburk would embolden the party radicals and perhaps stampede

the party trustees into endorsing radical proposals.[19] The stir
created by the radical Reichsrat speeches of April 11 and 12 had
hardly subsided when Edvard Grégr and Josef Sokol, father of the
imprisoned Progressive Karel Stanislav Sokol, resumed their advocacy of unremitting opposition to the government in speeches
before large and enthusiastic crowds in traditionally Young
Czech electoral districts.[20] Meanwhile, Adolf Stránský, chairman of the affiliated Moravian People's party and one of two defense attorneys for the *Omladina* "conspirators," had in *Lidové
noviny* charged the Young Czech majority with moving too hastily
to sever ties with the idealistic and radical youth whom it had
once encouraged. Party moderates dispatched their best speakers
to counter any charge that the party had erred in making discretion the better part of valor. Among those sent out, Karel Kramář, already noted for his forensic skills, proved himself to be
one of the ablest public spokesmen. His speech of April 1, 1894,
published in the *Lidové noviny*, countered Stránský by reiterating that the Progressives deserved censure for having acted
rashly in leading public demonstrations and airing unorthodox
views on social reform and Bohemian state rights.[21] From this
debate a lasting coolness arose between Stránský and Kramář
based primarily on political differences of opinion but assuming
after 1900 a personal character as Kramář out of expediency began to take a more tolerant view of anti-Semitism.

The manner in which the Young Czech party dissociated itself
from the Progressive movement as well as the act of dissociation
led to deep and abiding distrust of party leaders by left-wing
critics within as well as outside the party. These critics included T. G. Masaryk, *Čas* editor Jan Herben, and the Progressives who in February 1894 began publishing the *Radikální listy*
(Radical news) in Kolín.[22] The hypocrisy and calculated opportunism which they so often attributed to moderate Young Czech
leaders cannot adequately explain the latter's hesitancy and va-
cillation in taming party radicals and in ousting the Progressives. Many Young Czech moderates acted as they did because
they so well understood and to a degree sympathized with radical
and Progressive views. Most believed that the nation's best interests required severing all ties between the party and the
Progressive movement. At the same time, many also felt a sense
of solidarity with the *Omladina* prisoners and regretted having
encouraged their demonstrations and radical manifestoes from
1890 until the antidynastic riots of September 1893. Almost all
party members, including Chairman Engel, believed that continued
"responsible" behavior by the party would best assure an end to
the state of emergency and a pardon for the imprisoned *Omladina*
"conspirators." Ironically, two of the three hostile groups
this moderation was supposed to impress, the imperial authorities and the German Liberals, did not fundamentally change their
mistaken view of the Young Czechs as malcontents, radicals, and
troublemakers. No moderation of any sort on the part of the

Young Czechs could ever satisfy German and Viennese expectations
that Czechs loyally serve the emperor and accept German supremacy in Cisleithania. So vigorously did the *Neue Freie Presse*
champion the interests of the dynasty and the German upper middle
classes that it never fully understood either the grounds for
Czech discontent or the extent and nature of conflict between
the various Czech political factions. Only the conservative
great landowners recognized after Nymburk that the Young Czech
party had for the first time since the early eighties become
amenable to cooperation with the right, thereby opening the way
to a revival of a parliamentary majority of conservatives, clericals, and Slavs.[23]

"The Resolution on the Program and Progress of the Party"
adopted by the moderate majority at Nymburk disavowed radicalism,
including further support of the Progressive movement, and committed the Young Czechs generally to "responsible and active political work" and, when appropriate, to "dignified and serious
opposition" to any imperial government. This, the Nymburk Resolution, after reaffirmation by the party trustees on September 28,
1897, remained until 1914 the most definitive statement of party
parliamentary policies and also, until modified by the eighth
party congress of March 1907, continued to define internal party
organization and relations with other political parties.[24]

The resolution contained three parts. The first presented a
party program which reaffirmed and supplemented those of 1889
and 1891. The second obliged the party to employ more pragmatic
and moderate tactics than those employed from the 1891 Reichsrat
elections to the *Omladina* trials. The third defined the party's
relationship and policies toward other political parties and
factions. Given the fact that the Nymburk Resolution immediately occasioned intra-party debate and thereafter enormously influenced party development, it deserves to be carefully studied in
content and in style.[25]

The first part of the resolution announced that the party
stood "irrevocably behind its program set forth in the electoral
proclamations of 1889 and 1891" and that any future "elaboration"
of this program had to be approved by the clubs of delegates and
the party executive committee.

The second part enumerated eight guidelines for electoral and
parliamentary tactics:

1. The National Liberal party discerns in the policies of
   the present government a fundamental resistance to Czech
   political, national, and social aspirations. Consequent-
   ly, the relationship of Czech delegates to the government
   can only be that of a party in opposition. The government's rejecting even the most minimal Czech requests,
   its strengthening of Germanization and centralization, its
   imposing a state of emergency, and its sanctioning the
   persecution and restrictions imposed on all areas of life

by the administrative authorities require that the parliamentary representatives of the party come out in decisive
parliamentary opposition and persist therein so long as
there are no policies established to the satisfaction of
the Czech nation.

2. The party considers that such policies should include
sincere steps by the government toward the realization of
a state rights compromise with the Czech kingdom, a reform of the unjust electoral system in the Czech lands,
and the realization of equality before the law by the introduction of Czech as the internal official language in
law courts and in political administration.

3. . . . The dignity and seriousness of opposition demands absolute unity in the conduct and in the speeches of delegates and manly discipline and unconditional solidarity from
delegates, journalists, and all followers of the party.

4. Parliamentary opposition must also be supported by a consistent, comprehensive, and harmoniously organized opposition movement of the nation itself. It is essential
that cooperation between delegates and the people be increased, that mutual trust be strengthened, and that any
breaking of this mutual trust be most resolutely rejected.

5. With regard to justifiable demands by the nation in cultural and economic matters, the party believes that its
tactics of opposition to the government will be neither
impaired nor prejudiced by its efforts to achieve such
demands by parliamentary means or through government institutions. The party's parliamentary delegation must be
empowered to judge for itself which governmental proposals, even those of an unpolitical nature, may be rejected
solely and purely on political grounds because of their
effect in strengthening the existing system and which
proposals may be considered on their merits because of
obvious advantages which the nation and each of its social strata would be able to appreciate.

6. We affirm that the parliamentary opposition has the duty
to vote for parliamentary committees and that delegates
of the party should serve on these committees in accordance with the guidelines established in (5) above. It is
possible to accept only reports regarding those bills
which fundamentally do not prejudice or concern Czech
affairs.

7. Such parliamentary and oppositional tactics require that

debates within the clubs of delegates do not generally
and especially do not prematurely become public knowledge
unless publicity is acknowledged by the parliamentary delegation to be to its advantage. Party delegates and
journalists are obliged not to discuss needlessly in public and least of all on the basis of unauthorized or un-
verified information the internal business of the party
and its parliamentary clubs.

8. Self-governing Czech corporations, political and other
associations, as well as every single member of the party
are obliged in all matters to defend self-government,
civil and political liberties, and language rights recognized by law and to observe them in all dealings with
those who intrigue against our national program and
standpoint of opposition. The executive committee is authorized to extend aid and support in all cases involving
abridgement of these political rights.

The third part of the Nymburk Resolution redefined the Young
Czech relationship to other Czech political parties and signaled
a retreat from the very liberal state rights programs of 1889
and 1891. The resolution confirmed the autonomous status of the
People's party in Moravia, which continued to send three representatives to the Young Czech executive committee but otherwise
retained a separate organization. Each party set its own policies with regard to electoral campaigns and editorials, but any
change in tactics or platforms of one party which might affect
the other required consent of both executive committees.
The Young Czechs at Nymburk also sought to reassure potential
allies on the right that their party endorsed constructive politics and moderate goals. In an overture to the conservative
great landowners, they denied that there could be any "danger
for the Czech nation in the formation of a Conservative party in
Bohemia" so long as "that party would accept as a basis of its
platform the Czech national and state rights program and thereby
increase the ranks of the Czech opposition." They also warned
the conservative great landowners to expect no effective support
from a defeated and moribund Old Czech party, while proclaiming
that they "had not ruled out cooperation with conservative or
Old Czech cadres in national and local questions." Progressive
and Social Democratic critics could thereafter with some justification charge the Young Czechs with having rehabilitated the
supposedly discredited Old Czech policy of alliance with the
conservative great landowners. However, the Young Czechs reaffirmed their anticlerical principles and stated that "the creation of a separate Czech clerical party constitutes a danger for
the Czech nation and for its continued cultural progress."
The opening sentence in that section of the Nymburk Resolution

dealing with the proper relationship between the Young Czechs
and the Progressive movement set the tone for all statements
that followed:

> The National Liberal party as a popular, progressive, and
> modern party welcomes every progressive movement among our
> younger generation, provided of course that each submits in
> every respect to the platform and leadership of the National
> Liberal party.

The Young Czechs denounced the independence and radicalism of
the Progressives as self-defeating and detrimental to the national movement and asked that the Progressives join them in re-
storing national political unity on the basis of Bohemian state
rights. The party expressly dissociated itself from any claims
by Progressives to be its "left wing."

The Young Czechs defined their relationship to Czech Social
Democracy in similarly condescending terms: "The National Liberal party has by its program firmly expressed its intention to
attend to social reform and to the material and spiritual elevation of all people, including the working class, from the
standpoint of humanity as well as for national interests." The
party reviewed its long and honorable record of advocating universal suffrage and civil liberties and reaffirmed its responsibility as the foremost national party to support insofar as possible the interests of all classes in Czech society. It specifically promised "to support the working class in endeavors to
obtain political rights and an improvement in its social and material conditions and to take pains to insure that the national
idea is strengthened in working-class circles to the greatest
possible degree."[26]

In conclusion the Young Czechs reiterated their intention to
make no alliance with any party which supported the Windischgrätz government and to make common cause with every party opposed to what they deemed to be undesirable government policies.

At Nymburk, the board of trustees modified party structure in
the interests of strength and unity and control by "responsible"
moderate leaders. The board gave greater responsibilities to
the clubs of delegates, including the authority to make all tactical decisions except the opening of direct negotiations with
the minister-president. Existing by-laws made the executive
committee accountable for all actions to the board of trustees.
To aid this committee, the trustees set up five subcommittees
staffed by moderate party members to handle party organization,
elections, finance, publications, and national economy. At the
sixth party congress in Prague on September 29, 1896, the moderates completed their reorganizational work by enlarging the
executive committee from thirteen to thirty-two members, thereby making it for the first time thoroughly moderate and

"responsible" and ending its interminable and counterproductive disputes with the party clubs of delegates.[27]

At Nymburk, the Young Czech radicals lost forever their predominance in the party, as the trustees not only endorsed the Prague proposal of July 14, 1894, but disavowed those strongly antidynastic speeches given by the radicals during the April session of the Reichsrat. The radicals, including the Grégr brothers, Anýž, Fořt, Slavík, Sokol, Březnovský, and the Jandas, stayed in the party, hoping to influence policy and restrain the moderate leadership if it became too flexible in negotiations with the authorities. All looked back upon the electoral victories of 1889 and 1891 and the campaign for universal suffrage in 1893 as the party's period of greatest achievement. They resented having been caricatured by younger politicians like Kaizl and Kramář as "doctrinaire radicals." Rather they believed their radicalism and distrust of imperial authority to have been the proper responses to repeated disappointments and oppression. They prided themselves on having kept liberalism alive during difficult times and on having transmitted the heritage of Havlíček and Sladkovský to the younger generation.[28] More disconcerting to the radicals than Kramář's superficial criticism were the charges by Václav Škarda and by T. G. Masaryk that they had practiced an opportunistic policy to a greater extent than anyone had imagined.

Young Czech radical ranks were further diminished before and after Nymburk as four old stalwarts passed from the scene. Václav Kratochvíl, the founder of Young Czech and peasant politics in Podřipsko and mentor of Ervín Špindler and Václav Janda, died on August 4, 1893. After Jan Kučera's death on January 17, 1895, the party chose Jan Podlipný to fill his offices as chairman of the party executive committee and as member of the Provincial Executive Council. A serious paralytic illness forced Julius Grégr's retirement from active politics in the spring of 1894; within thirty months he would be dead. František Tilšer at age seventy announced his retirement from politics on March 2, 1895, on grounds of advanced age and dissatisfaction with party opportunism since Nymburk. The two leading Young Czech creators of "politics by stages" (*etapová politika*) of the 1870s which so foreshadowed the "responsible and active" Nymburk policies, Alois Pravoslav Trojan and Jakub Škarda, had died respectively on February 9, 1893, and December 31, 1894, their policies apparently vindicated.

The Young Czech party emerged from Nymburk with its program, tactics, and organization established essentially as they would remain until the 1906 attempt to transform it into a mass political party. Critics of Nymburk charged that reaffirmation of the 1889 and 1891 programs could not be reconciled with the new image of "responsibility" and that to pretend otherwise was hypocrisy.[29] The party moderates countered by arguing that only

responsible and active political work could in present circumstances bring about implementation of civil liberties, equality
of the Czech language with German, and Bohemian state rights.
They further contended that responsible and active policies were
no less than a contemporary version of the politics by stages
practiced so well by Jakub Škarda, A. P. Trojan, and the Grégr
brothers since the seventies. On one point moderates and their
radical and Progressive critics could generally agree: whether
or not the traditional liberal and national principles of the
Young Czech party would be compromised by the Nymburk Resolution
would depend upon how the party put it into practice.

The Nymburk Resolution clearly delineated the policy of responsible and active opposition which Young Czechs would follow
for two and a half years until agreeing to support the Badeni
government in April 1897. During those years the Young Czechs
directed their attention primarily to three questions. The
first concerned the party's relationship to the successive Windischgrätz, Kielmansegg, and Badeni governments until "policies
acceptable to the Czech nation" were established. The Young
Czechs helped maintain the parliamentary "Slavic Coalition,"
pushed for universal suffrage, civil liberties, and language
rights, and protested harsh imperial restriction of the press.
The second concerned the domestic political crisis in Bohemia,
where the party sought to have the state of emergency lifted
from Prague and to make the governor responsible to the diet.
In any case, the party could look forward to diet elections in
1895 in which it could expect to capture most remaining Old
Czech seats. The third problem concerned the party's relationship to rival Czech political movements in view of the decision
at Nymburk to go it alone unless these rivals would cooperate on
terms set by the party.

The Nymburk Resolution and its implementation occasioned a
free-wheeling journalistic debate between party leaders and
their Progressive and radical opponents on the nature of the
Czech question as well as on particular social, economic, and
political issues. This debate continued unabated until the
break-up of the Young Czech coalition in 1898 and 1899. Because
the debate concerned party actions as well as policies, it must
be understood in the context of the Young Czech opposition to
Governor Thun and the Windischgrätz government.

Opposition to the Windischgrätz Government

Young Czech opposition to the coalition government of Prince
Alfred Windischgrätz put the Nymburk Resolution to its first
test.[30] Even after adopting a moderate stance, the Young Czechs
could still expect no favors from this government of German Liberals, Polish and Bohemian great landowners, and the conservative and clerical Hohenwart Club, which had endorsed Governor
Thun's continuing the state of emergency in Prague.[31]

Windischgrätz, a leading constitutional great landowner, relied
heavily in his cabinet on Count Friedrich Schönborn, whom he retained as Minister of Justice, and on two German Liberals who
remained steadfast opponents of the Czech national movement, Finance Minister Ernst von Plener and Minister of Commerce Gundacker Wurmbrand.[32]

In addition to passing the annual budget, the Windischgrätz
government had as its primary tasks the resolution of the long-
standing political crisis in Bohemia, extension of the franchise
for the Reichsrat, to which Taaffe had committed the emperor in
principle, and reform of tax laws, the 1862 press law, and the
penal code. Save for the latter two reforms and the 1894-95
budget, the government failed to achieve any of its objectives.
It never functioned effectively because all parties of the coalition had come together only in opposition to universal suffrage
and could never agree on a positive program. Windischgrätz,
moreover, did not provide forceful leadership, giving rise to
adverse judgments like that of Charmatz, who claimed that "this
overgrown feudal aristocrat was also a petty politician and an
insignificant man."[33]

At the behest of the German Liberals, Windischgrätz made a
final attempt to enact administratively the Agreement of 1890 by
reviving Taaffe's and Schonbörn's plan to create new Bohemian
judicial districts by government fiat. But parliamentary opposition, in which the Poles and conservative great landowners
voted with the Young Czechs and the Southern Slavs, compelled
him to abandon the project on February 13, 1894.[34] Ironically,
the Agreement of 1890, so unfavorable to Czech interests, had been
initiated by an Iron Ring government supposedly ruling "against
the Germans" and abandoned by a coalition government ruling ostensibly in the German interest.

Young Czech efforts to organize a united Slavic opposition to
the Windischgrätz government met with an immediate partial success. On November 23, 1893, the Moravian Old Czechs led by
Josef Fanderlík declared their opposition to the Windischgrätz
government, enabling the Young Czechs on the following day to
bring together a Slavic coalition comprising all Czech delegates
from Bohemia and Moravia, regardless of party, and the Yugoslav
Club recently founded by the eleven Slovenian and Croatian delegates who had withdrawn from the Hohenwart Club.[35] Among the
Slavic delegates, only the Polish Kraków Conservatives continued
to uphold the government and stand apart from the new coalition,
whose formation Kramář exaggeratedly termed "one of the greatest
moments in the life of the Slavs in Austria and of the Slavs in
general."[36]

The Young Czechs maintained their long-standing commitment to
the eventual achievement of universal manhood suffrage by supporting the government's electoral reform bill of February 26, 1894,
which merely proposed to add a fifth and "universal" curia of
forty-three delegates to the four existing curias while leaving

"electoral geometry" intact. After Windischgrätz's German and
Polish allies voted down the bill, the Young Czechs, led by
Kaizl and Slavík, renewed their efforts to persuade the parliamentary electoral committee to put a more democratic electoral
reform bill on the agenda and again endorsed the Social Democratic campaign for universal suffrage.[37] After declaring that
he would not be intimidated by any mass street demonstrations,
Windischgrätz submitted a second proposal for a fifth curia
which met with predictable defeat. Meanwhile, the Young Czechs
also pressed for a wider franchise to the Bohemian and Moravian
diets, resulting in the introduction of proposals for electoral
reform to the Bohemian Diet on January 11, 1895, by Herman Janda
and to the Moravian Diet on January 31, 1895, by Adolf Stránský
and Josef Vychodil.[38] Both proposals were ultimately voted down
by the great landowners and the German Liberals.

Bedřich Pacák led the Young Czech campaign to win immunity
from prosecution for citizens who published parliamentary
speeches in languages other than German.[39] On February 6, 1894,
Minister of Justice Schönborn interpreted basic state law no. 141
and the 1862 press law to mean that henceforth only speeches in
German would enjoy the customary immunity from prosecution under
laws restricting freedom of speech and of the press. His specious interpretation stated that since the law provided only for
the publication of German speeches in the "Stenographic parliamentary record," only those speeches should have immunity.
Schönborn's interpretation was a step toward the recognition of
German as the official language of Cisleithania and another attempt to abridge the civil liberties of non-Germans, against whom
the authorities already enforced the law in a discriminatory
manner. The government followed up the interpretation by twice
confiscating the *Národní listy* for having reprinted Czech
speeches of April 10, 1894, and February 12, 1895, and by seizing the October 10 edition of the *Radikální listy* for having
printed excerpts from Jan Kaftan's speech of October 1, 1894.

The Young Czechs advocated immunity for speeches in all languages on principle and because the publication of Czech
speeches provided an important means of appealing to the electorate.[40] In view of Schönborn's reasoning, they added to these
demands an amendment to have all Reichsrat speeches printed in
the language in which they were given. After Parliament's rejection of Pacák's proposals of November 28 and December 12,
1894, and February 27, 1895, to overrule Schönborn, the Young
Czechs made immunity of speeches a campaign issue until its acceptance in modified form two years later.[41]

The Young Czechs sought every opportunity to defend and extend
civil liberties. On May 28, 1894, Gustav Eim tried unsuccessfully to persuade the Reichsrat to pass a more liberal revision
of the 1862 press law than the mere abolition of caution money.[42]
The Young Czechs nonetheless voted for this modest reform and
for the government's subsequent bill to reduce the types of

crimes subject to capital punishment. On November 12, 1894, the coalition voted down a Young Czech bill introduced by Karel Kramář to prohibit parliamentary deputies from simultaneously working for the imperial civil service. The party had expected its bill if passed to insure that no deputy would serve more than one party or constituency or be directly susceptible to imperial pressure.[43]

The Young Czechs encouraged efforts to present a case for the national cause abroad, recognizing that most foreigners formed opinions on Cisleithanian affairs by reading Viennese and government newspapers uniformly hostile to Czech interests. In America, the party continued to find ample support among Czech-Americans, notably from the Bohemian National Committee and from Tomáš Čapek, publicist and chairman of the Bank of Europe in New York, which helped channel funds back to the Czech lands and to Slovakia.[44] In 1894, Karel Hipman began to publish in Prague the French-language periodical, *La Nation Tchèque*, which featured essays by leading Czech writers on many aspects of contemporary life.[45] T. G. Masaryk and Karel Kramář, among others, contributed articles to Viennese and German publications, notably *Zeit* (Time). The Habsburg police closely watched Czech activities abroad and suspected all to be of a treasonous nature, especially the international gymnastics meets attended by the Sokol and its Young Czech chairman Jan Podlipný.[46]

The traditional state rights program appeared to most Young Czechs in a particularly attractive light, given the continuing state of emergency in Prague and Governor Thun's rule by decree. In both the Bohemian Diet and the Reichsrat, they introduced bills to make the governor responsible to the diet rather than solely to the emperor. This proposal was regarded by the authors and by its leading spokesmen, Karel Kramář in the diet and Gustav Eim in the Reichsrat, as a matter of utmost practical concern and also as a first step toward the future realization of Bohemian state rights. A majority in each legislative body, including Old Czechs, German Liberals, and conservative great landowners, opposed the proposal, thus sparing imperial authorities the trouble of having to quash this proposed abridgement of the emperor's authority. On January 31, 1895, after Kramář's diet speech advocating the limitation of gubernatorial powers, a heated exchange occurred between Franz Thun and the Young Czechs. Thun announced that he would not allow diet delegates to discuss Kramář's proposal because it touched upon imperial prerogatives. The Young Czechs so took umbrage at this and at Thun's speaking only in German that they interrupted him with catcalls and cries of "Speak Czech!"[47]

The Young Czechs next attempted, likewise without immediate success, to have the Reichsrat declare invalid Governor Thun's decrees aimed at destroying the autonomy and the patriotic spirit of Czech schools. These decress, issued on March 8, 1895, required all schools within eight days to fly the black and yellow

imperial colors and forbade any display or wearing of the national colors and insignia. A supplemental decree ordered the
creation of a teaching staff loyal to the emperor and the Catholic Church and the firing of teachers who espoused patriotic or
liberal ideas.[48] Governor Thun topped off everything by a tactless but heartfelt remark to complaining teachers, "If you do
not obey orders, I shall break your necks."[49] After the diet
was dismissed on February 16, the Young Czechs took their protest to the Reichsrat, where on April 25, 1895, Josef Sokol presented an "urgent proposal" (pilný navrh) that the decrees be
nullified. On April 27, the proposal was rejected by a majority
of delegates, including the conservative great landowners, who
stood by their colleague Governor Thun.[50]

Upon exhausting all other means of parliamentary opposition
and frustrated by repeated defeats, the Young Czechs decided to
obstruct Parliament. On May 21, 1895, in opposing Minister Plener's tax bill which favored upper middle-class and German interests, party delegates led by Pacák, Kaizl, and Brzorád began
to obstruct parliamentary business by repeatedly having twenty
or more members exercise their right to call a ten-minute recess.[51] Some party members, notably Eim and Kramář, opposed
this obstruction on tactical grounds and hoped to come to an understanding with the Germans to amend parliamentary rules of
procedure to disallow the practice. All parties soon discovered
that obstruction could temporarily be effective in either covert
or overt form. The former entailed procedural modifications
like roll call votes and prolonged discussion of every item on
an agenda. The latter included filibusters and the frequent
calling of ten-minute recesses. By hurling inkwells during
their obstruction of the Bohemian Diet on May 17, 1893, the
Young Czechs set one of several bad precedents for future ob-
structions of last resort.[52]

Neither Young Czech opposition nor obstruction brought down
the Windischgrätz government on June 17, 1895: its own German
Liberal allies did so by withdrawing their support because the
minister-president had endorsed the establishment of a Slovene
gymnasium in Celje (Cilli), a small and predominantly German
town in southern Styria which served as the commercial and governmental center for a predominantly Slovene commune of 38,000
inhabitants.[53] Rather than uphold any "scheme" to "destroy the
German character" of Celje, the German Liberals deserted Wind-
sichgrätz on June 14, four days after the parliamentary finance
committee approved including the Slovene gymnasium in the annual
budget. Windischgrätz, who no longer commanded a parliamentary
majority, resigned three days later with only four positive accomplishments to his credit: the 1894-95 budget, the abolition
of caution money in press censorship, a reduction in the number
of felonies subject to capital punishment, and the purchase of
several private Cisleithanian railway lines for incorporation
into the state system.[54]

Windischgrätz had not expected the German Liberals to carry out their threats of resignation and had supported funding the Celje gymnasium both as a just measure and as one necessary to obtain enough votes from the Slavic Coalition to pass the annual budget. His principal backers, the Hohenwart Club, voted to fund the school as a gesture of friendship to their clerical Slovene compatriots. Moreover, since Taaffe had as minister-president already promised government funds for the Celje school, Windischgrätz felt obliged to honor a fellow nobleman's commitment.[55]

Why did the German Liberals attach such great importance to Celje that they would cavalierly topple a government in which they held three cabinet posts and which had generally upheld their interests? The emperor was at a loss to explain such "petty behavior," which Ernst Plener later attributed to "inexperience" in parliamentary government.[56] A single Slovene gymnasium represented no threat to German culture nor any attempt to Slavicize German youth, Liberal claims to the contrary. But the establishment of that school would, by upholding the principle of equal rights for all nationalities, embolden every Slavic-speaking citizen and thereby ultimately endanger German political preponderance in Cisleithania. More importantly, the German Liberals could afford to risk bringing down this or any government because they knew that in the absence of Parliament the civil bureaucracy could be expected to rule in their favor. The Czechs, on the other hand, recognized that a breakdown in parliamentary government would probably lead to the reinstatement of authoritarian rule as in 1868, 1871, and 1893. This helps explain why the Czechs, who chafed under second-class citizenship and discriminatory law enforcement, usually cooperated much more readily with imperial governments through the Reichsrat than did the privileged Germans.

Franz Joseph took the advice of the great landowners and planned to appoint the Polish Count Kazimierz Badeni as the next minister-president. Since the emperor did not wish to relieve Badeni as governor of Galicia before the diet elections in September or to have him assume office in the midst of the Celje controversy, he appointed a caretaker government headed by Count Erich Kielmansegg, a former governor of Lower Austria. Meanwhile, in the name of the Young Czech party, Josef Herold asked the Reichsrat to approve the Celje school and thereby recognize every citizen's right to be educated in his native language. František Schwarz, Jan Kaftan, Gustav Eim, and Edvard Grégr used the continuing debates on Celje and the budget as a pretext for reminding the government that it could expect to obtain no lasting domestic peace until it guaranteed equal rights to all citizens regardless of nationality. Approval of the Celje proposal would be a step in the right direction. On July 20, Kielmansegg finally won parliamentary approval for the annual budget, including funds for the Celje gymnasium. By agreeing to vote for that

budget, the Young Czechs had on June 11, 1895, obtained imperial
confirmation of Herman Janda as chairman of the Czech Provincial
Agricultural Council. Kielmansegg resigned in September as
minister-president to make way for Count Kazimierz Badeni, who
took office with a clean slate on October 2, 1895.[57]

Debate on the Czech Question

Progressive and Social Democratic critics of the Young Czech
party found little to praise in the limited achievements of its
responsible and active opposition to the Windischgrätz government. They continued to contend that the party had erred in
dismissing its "left wing" at Nymburk and reviving moderation in
politics and association with the nobility. Moreover, they
thought minor changes in party organization and tactics inadequate to facilitate any resolution of serious social and political issues. Only a complete reordering of Czech politics on a
democratic basis could insure progress and stability in years to
come.

The Young Czechs customarily dismissed criticism from the left
as deficient in understanding of practical politics and existing
political institutions. Party leaders like Gustav Eim and Václav
Škarda believed that after several years of day-to-day political
experience, the younger left-wing intellectuals would "descend
from Olympus" and view problems much as did their elders. These
Young Czechs invited all to join the party who sought to achieve
national autonomy and civil liberties through patient and responsible work.[58]

Professor T. G. Masaryk emerged in 1895 as the most formidable
critic of Young Czech policies. In that year he published three
works which together provided the first thorough and comprehensive philosophical discussion of the Czech question and which
challenged the fitness of the Young Czech party to lead the nation out of its present crisis. The first and principal work,
Česká otázka: snahy a tužby národního obrození (The Czech question: struggles and aspirations of the National Revival), a
treatise on the meaning and goals of the Czech nation, appeared
in the spring of 1895. Two supplementary works appeared in the
fall: K šestému červenci: naše obrození a naše reformace (On
the sixth of July: our revival and our reformation), an essay
on Jan Hus as a positive inspiration to Czechs of all succeeding
generations, and Naše nynější krise (Our present crisis), a
gloss on Česká otázka and a direct attack upon the aims and tactics of the Young Czech party.[59]

In "The Czech Question," Masaryk took the first steps toward
creating a positive and comprehensive Czech national ideology--
or as he called it, a philosophy--which offered both a critical
interpretation of the past and a guide to political action.[60]
Masaryk built upon and acknowledged his debt to the leaders of
the National Revival, especially Palacký and Havlíček. He sought

to find a "purpose" in the Czech experience, that is to say to
resolve whether or not the continuing existence of a small
people living in the heart of Europe made any "sense." Masaryk
contended that the cultivation of a peculiarly national identity
for its own sake had no justification and asked that Czechs work
toward positive and universal goals to avoid the pitfall of allowing nationalism to degenerate into hatred of the foreigner.

Nationalism threatens us more than we realize. We too often
look at our national life negatively. We interpret our historical goal as an eternal antagonism against the Germans and
cannot properly comprehend and value our necessary and positive mission. We don't know how to work without taking the
foreigner into account.[61]

Masaryk believed he had found such a positive goal in the
ideal of humanity embodied in the thoughts and deeds of the Hussites and Czech Brethren and revived and practiced by the leaders
of the National Revival, notably Dobrovský, Kollár, Palacký, and
Havlíček. Only such a positive goal could justify continuing to
struggle for national autonomy and civil rights, and only by living up to these ideals could the Czech nation continue to prosper.
    Masaryk did not explicitly define his notion of humanity
in the Česká otázka or in K sestému červenci except to describe
its predominantly Hussite and Reformation origins and its rein-
forcement by the Enlightenment. In later works, he further discussed this ideal and also ways in which it might contribute to
the emancipation of small nations.[62] But, in the Česká otázka,
his most cogent definition of humanity appeared as follows:

The ideal of humanity proclaimed by Dobrovský and Kollár, the
ideal of our revival, has for us Czechs a deep national and
historical meaning--through humanity, a complete and genuine
concept, we are bound to our finest period in the past.
Through humanity we leap across the spiritual and moral sleep
of several centuries. Through humanity we have to march in
the vanguard of human progress. Humanity means for us our
national task created for and bequeathed to us by our Bohemian Brethren. The ideal of humanity is the whole justification of our national life.
    This, our Czech ideal of humanity, is not romantic enthusi-
asm. Of course, humanity without consistent effort and performance is dead. The ideal of humanity requires that we systematically in all things, everywhere, and at all times reject evil in our own and in foreign inhumanity, and in society and in its cultural, religious, political, and national
institutions--in a word, in everything. Humanity is not sen-
timentality, but work and more work.[63]

Masaryk's Naše nynější krise: pád strany staročeské a

počátkové směrů nových (Our present crisis: the fall of the Old
Czech party and the beginning of new trends) responded to critics of the *Česká otázka* by more clearly defining the ideal of
humanity and its importance in guiding political conduct.[64]   If
the Czech struggle for national autonomy were to make sense and
be successful, Masaryk contended, it would have to adhere to
this ideal which had in large part inspired the achievements of
the Hussites and the Awakeners. After demonstrating his sympathy for the Progressive youth, Masaryk admonished them as he
had done before 1893 to temper their fervent and justifiable enthusiasm for national emancipation and social reform by pursuing
a more patient and disciplined program of work and inquiry.
Moral reformation would have to accompany any lasting political
reform and precede any revolutionary action.

Masaryk argued that the present crisis arose primarily because the Czech national movement, which comprised both Old and
Young Czech parties, could no longer effect the necessary political and institutional adjustments to social change. Therefore, the 1891 collapse of the Old Czechs entailed the decline
of the Young Czech party as well. The Nymburk Resolution signaled no hopeful departure from the errors of the past but simply confirmed that the Young Czechs could not help but perpetuate Old Czech policies.[65]   Masaryk's view of Nymburk as an endorsement of the policies and tactics long used by the majority
party of the middle-class Czech national movement closely coincided with that of Young Czech stalwart Václav Škarda, who believed Nymburk to be the desirable and logical continuation of
the "politics step by step" first advocated by Young Czechs
during the seventies and adopted after 1879 by the Old Czechs.[66]

Masaryk's critique of the Young Czech party in *Naše nynější
krise* and his attempt through *Česká otázka* and *K sestému červenci* to establish the basis for a national ideology provoked
the Young Czech party into replying with a philosophical and
equally learned justification of its policies. This the party
had never before attempted, despite Masaryk's request in June
1891 that it be done by the executive committee. It had heretofore drawn its inspiration uncritically from nineteenth-
century liberalism, a belief in scientific progress, and the
Czech National Revival.

Great breadth of knowledge and critical intelligence qualified Josef Kaizl as the Young Czech best able to defend his
party against the learned and polemical attacks by T. G. Masaryk.[67]   The two professors and former political associates engaged in a serious and high-minded debate on the meaning of
Czech politics and history, and Kaizl never publicly implied, as
did less informed critics, that Masaryk opposed Young Czech policies primarily because of the unpleasant circumstances surrounding his departure from the party.[68]

Kaizl's *České myšlenky* (Czech thoughts), a lucid and informed
criticism of *Česká otázka, Naše nynější krise* and *K sestému*

červenci, appeared in May 1896. This essay, the most thorough
and informed philosophical discussion of the principles of Young
Czech politics ever written, arose typically enough as a response to outside stimuli, as had many of the party policies it
defended. In marked contrast to Masaryk's work, *Česká otázka*,
which aimed at nothing less than justifying the existence and
future advancement of the Czech nation, *České myšlenky* sought
primarily to justify the principles and policies of the Young
Czech party. In this sense, Kaizl's work was much less comprehensive but also more readily understood, given its emphasis on
the practical as opposed to the desirable and on understanding
the present in light of the past instead of illuminating those
past problems and achievements which would best help Czechs prepare for the future.

Kaizl commented favorably upon Masaryk's breadth of vision and
stimulating questions before critically examining several of his
more important ideas and arguments. He very sharply criticized
Masaryk for not precisely defining what he meant by "humanity,"
that vague and abstract term by which he sought to justify and
give a sense of purpose to the Czech nation.[69] Kaizl also questioned Masaryk's belief that the ideals of the Hussites and the
Bohemian Brethren had strongly influenced the Czech National Revival. To his mind, it had been stimulated primarily by the
liberalism and nationalism of the later Enlightenment and its
representatives, Rousseau and Herder. In particular, Kaizl
thought that Masaryk had overestimated the influence of Protestantism on Palacký and that Josef Jungmann, the Awakener whose
works best revealed the influence of the Enlightenment, was a
much more typical representative of the Revival than Masaryk had
implied.

Kaizl contended in his second chapter that Masaryk had over-
emphasized the extent to which the Old Czech party grew out of
the National Revival. To his mind, the Old Czech party by forming a political alliance with the "oligarchical party of the nobility" had turned away from the ideals of Palacký and Havlíček
which the Young Czechs would later recover.[70] Neither Kaizl nor
Masaryk really came to grips with the fact that Palacký had supported Rieger in making that very alliance. But Masaryk more accurately described the continuity between Palacký's work in furthering the Revival before 1848 and his leadership of the Old
Czech party after 1860, pointing out that Palacký viewed the
Czech question as the task (*úkol*) of a small nation to build the
necessary material and political as well as cultural bases for
its survival.[71]

In his third chapter, Kaizl argued that Masaryk had exaggerated the gravity of "the present crisis" and erred in viewing
the Young Czechs and Old Czechs as part of the same political
movement. To the contrary, Kaizl praised the Young Czechs for
having reaffirmed Havlíček's liberalism and abandoned any formal
alliance with the nobility.[72] Whereas Masaryk expected that an

opportunistic Young Czech party beholden to a privileged electorate would repeat Old Czech mistakes, Kaizl believed this
party to be a progressive force by virtue of its liberalism and
loyalty to the ideals of 1848.[73]

The fourth chapter of *České myšlenky* replied to Masaryk's
criticism of the Young Czech party for its unrepresentative
character and inadequate dedication to democracy and social reform. Kaizl there defended Young Czech liberalism for having in
large measure helped achieve the "political, social, and economic emancipation of the third estate and political equality for
all people."[74] Moreover, the liberal Young Czech programs of
1889 and 1891 together with the Nymburk Resolution had improved
upon as well as continued the programs of Palacký and Havlíček,
constituting "to date the most comprehensively composed national
and humanitarian program."[75]

Masaryk and Kaizl agreed that Czech politics should rest on
liberal and anticlerical principles and should further civil
liberties and the work of the National Revival. They disagreed
in assessing the accomplishments and prospects of liberalism and
in defining the relationship of the Young Czech party to the
Progressive movement and to Social Democracy. Kaizl considered
socialism to be an aberration of that liberalism which had guided the Czech movement for national emancipation in both its political and economic aspects, whereas Masaryk, without denigrating the past achievements of liberalism, believed it to have
been superseded by democracy and socialism and therefore to be a
blind alley insofar as future political programs were concerned.[76] Kaizl did not question the fact that liberalism everywhere appeared to be in decline. Many of its principal faults,
including lack of self-discipline and party loyalty as well as
reliance on abstract and inflammatory rhetoric, he argued, had
first appeared in the Young Czech radicalism of the sixties and
seventies, epitomized by the Grégr brothers, and had reappeared
among contemporary youth in the radical progressivism represented by Antonín Hajn. But the Young Czech party, having overcome
this "decadent radicalism" at Nymburk, could now be expected to
achieve liberal programs in a pragmatic and responsible manner.[77]

Contemporary politicians and scholars closely followed the
erudite debate between Kaizl and Masaryk.[78] All commented favorably on Masaryk's breadth of vision and stimulating inquiries,
but the majority held Kaizl's work in higher esteem because of
what they discerned to be its superior clarity and objectivity
and its penetrating criticism. The Progressive editor of
Rozhledy, Josef Pelcl, criticized the doctrinaire and intensely
"Puritanical" tone of *Naše nynější krise* and the attendant dangers of self-righteousness and self-deception.[79] Antonín Randa,
Jiří Pražák, and Bohuslav Rieger, the foremost Czech legal scholars and long-time Old Czechs, likewise took Masaryk to task for
the imprecision of his terminology, his underestimation of self-
government, and his neglect of institutional and legal history.

Historians equally critical of Masaryk's work included Antonín
Rezek, a Young Czech and close friend of Kaizl, Jaroslav Goll,
the dean of contemporary Czech historians and founder of a historical school which sought to understand Czech history in relation to larger European developments, and his most brilliant pupil, Josef Pekař.[80] Like Kaizl, all contended that Masaryk exaggerated the influence of ideas in history, especially those of
the Hussite and Czech Protestant reformers. Subsequent scholarship has upheld in detail few of Masaryk's interpretations of
the National Revival or of the Hussite and Czech Protestant traditions, while recognizing the extent to which these challenging
interpretations have stimulated or informed many fine scholarly
studies.[81] Whereas Kaizl's brilliant work is remembered as a
timely but not timeless essay in political criticism, Masaryk's
three works of 1895, despite many flaws, have served as the
point of departure for other perceptive studies of the Czech
question.

Contemporaries recognized that the essays of Masaryk and Kaizl
dealt primarily with the nature and course of Czech politics and
only incidentally with the Czech past. Kaizl more fully understood contemporary law and political institutions and took a
less present-minded view of the past. But Masaryk proved to be
the better prophet. If he overestimated the power of ideas and
moral values in history, Kaizl underestimated them, not least of
all the strength of Masaryk's own ideals.

Whereas Kaizl received greater support from contemporary politicians and scholars, Masaryk won a larger following among the
younger intelligentsia. Those imprisoned after the *Omladina* trials especially could not share Kaizl's rather optimistic assessment of the prospects for social reform under Young Czech leadership, and few disagreed with Masaryk's view that the Nymburk Resolution constituted a partial revival of Old Czech policies.
In his eighteenth letter smuggled out of Bory prison, A. Pravoslav Veselý spoke for many of his imprisoned associates when he
criticized those "Old Czechs painted over and now called Young
Czechs" who had sold out the Progressives in order to follow an
opportunistic policy.[82] Even young Progressives like Hajn and
Pelcl and young Social Democrats like Bohumír Šmeral who could
not accept Masaryk's abstract notions of humanity and his Protestant outlook welcomed his broad view of the present crisis
and his penetrating questions about the sense of Czech history.
Like Masaryk, they believed this crisis to be so serious that it
could not be satisfactorily resolved within the existing political framework. In this respect their Manifesto of the Czech
Modernists of October 1895 resembled Masaryk's view of the impending demise of the political system represented by the Old
Czech and Young Czech parties:

We take a more affirmative and confident view of the Czech
national question than do our elders. We are not afraid for

our language. The Czech people have for so long been con-
scious of their nationality that no power in the world can
force them to relinquish it. Its preservation is thus not
our aim, but only the means to a higher goal. We condemn
therefore the brutality that is perpetrated under nationalistic slogans by the German parties as we would condemn any
such activity if it were to be perpetrated by our own parties.
We also condemn political parties that cultivate and exaggerate the nationality question only in the interests of staying
in office and thereby annihilate the finest assets of the nation. We shall try to come to an understanding with our German fellow countrymen not at the conference table or parliamentary negotiations but on the basis of our common humanity
and of bread-and-butter issues. We are prepared to deal with
the fact that the old parties will deliberately use this issue to arouse the masses against us--this pressure we shall
endure. Those whose thought is based on the principle of
honesty do not have to stamp their feet or shout or boast.
     With regard to the social question, we above all want to
be with the people. . . . The Young Czech parliamentary delegates of today have become the representatives of the Czech
bourgeoisie and of a part of the peasantry. . . . The Young
Czech party, while still considering itself to be a popular
party, has forgotten its [liberal] mission and has conformed
to prevailing opinion and to circumstances. . . . Parties
must become the means to social progress and not an obstacle
to such progress.[83]

     Besides *Česká otázka* and the Manifesto of the Czech Modernists,
the most widely read and discussed work critical of the post-
Nymburk Young Czech party was Josef Svatopluk Machar's superb satirical poem *Boží bojovníci* (The Warriors of God).[84] Published
serially and partially in *Rozhledy* beginning in October 1895 and
in its entirety in the fall of 1896, this mock-epic poem took
its title from the first line of the greatest Hussite battle
hymn and purported to be the long-lost Vinohrady manuscript un-
earthed in that prestigious late nineteenth-century upper middle-
class suburb of Prague where many leading Young Czechs made
their homes. The poem's alleged editor, Dr. Č. Folklor, praised
it as a work worthy of comparison with such Czech masterpieces
as the Green Mountain and Queen's Court manuscripts and such international favorites as the *Iliad* and the *Neibelungenlied*.
     The Vinohrady Hussites who set forth to do battle for their
country markedly resembled the Young Czech party leadership, including "bloody Tůma," Sybilla-Eim, "schismatic Kaizl," and
Pacák, "sword at his side riding in from Kutná Hora." While
talking like seasoned and aggressive warriors, these Hussites
postponed expedition after expedition at the slightest excuse
and never engaged the enemy in a decisive battle. In the end
they pinned all hopes upon their rescue by the Polish hosts

under Hetman Kazimir Neplaval.[85] Machar wittily caricatured the
well-known idiosyncracies of party leaders in addition to making
light of the Nymburk policies and the obvious discrepancies between Young Czech ideals and practices. Not least of the notions satirized was the Young Czechs' glorification of the Hussite past and their attempts to appropriate this glory for party
interests and self-esteem.

   Boži bojovníci aroused both amusement and anger among party
members and the general public. Many critics condemned Machar
as a perfidious and irreverent man for denigrating the Hussite
past, while others resented his satirizing that verbose and pom-
pous style in which Vrchlický and Zeyer wrote many of their
epic poems. Like most party members, Chairman Engel enjoyed
each installment immensely and even found amusing the references
to "sergeant-manipulator of encampments, Angel."[86] Gustav Eim
recognized a good political journalist when he saw one and
wished that he could acquire Machar for the *Národní listy*.
Adolf Stránský noted with amusement how his children used to embarrass his wife by reading aloud at mealtime the passages about
Hussite Stránský deserting home and family in Moravia to help
defend his embattled compatriots in Bohemia. Josef Kaizl numbered among the few party members who did not take kindly to
being satirized. After studiously reading each installment, he
would ask Machar to explain why he had made no reference to a
mutual friend: "Why isn't Kramář in it?"[87]

   Masaryk's attempt to provide an ideology of the Czech question can best be appreciated if viewed in relation to contemporary Czech politics and political theory. His effort corresponded in many particulars to that of leading Czech Progressives
and Social Democrats of the nineties, who also wished to recon-
stitute politics on a democratic and socialist basis. Like all
Social Democrats and many Progressives, he sought to overcome
narrowminded nationalism and to establish higher national goals
than those of political autonomy and material progress. Similarly, he contended that national autonomy as well as attendant
civil liberties should be derived from "the natural rights of
man" instead of from historical Bohemian state rights which
aimed to legitimize Czech national autonomy on the same basis as
existing class privileges and imperial prerogatives. Like all
politicians, Masaryk recognized the importance of self-
governmental institutions in furthering the Czech struggle for
national emancipation. But, like the parties of the left, he
wished to democratize these institutions, in contrast to the
Young Czechs, who regarded them as a guarantor of upper middle-
class preponderance in local government and as the first step
toward eventual imperial recognition of Bohemian state rights.[88]

   Masaryk was also not alone in seeking to explain the development of an autonomous Czech nationality on other than materialistic grounds and in this effort repeatedly acknowledged his
great intellectual debt to Kollár and Palacký. The poets Viktor

Dyk and Otakar Březina presented mystical interpretations of
Czech national identity which resembled the views on French nationalism then advanced by Maurice Barrès and Charles Péguy.
These poets viewed national consciousness as a fundamental, powerful, and enduring force all but inaccessible to scientific inquiry or interpretation, and in Dyk's view difficult, if not impossible, for a foreigner to comprehend. Masaryk and the Czech
left generally had little liking for Dyk's obscurantism or
Březina's mysticism.[89]

Masaryk created through his many pre-war writings an ideology
of the Czech question in the sense of providing certain ration-
ally determined principles as a guide to moral renewal and practical action. To the making of this ideology and to the conduct
of public affairs, he brought a crusading temperament as well as
a critical mind. He derived his ideology in large part from the
great literary and historical works of Czech Romanticism but
critically reinterpreted these works to serve the profoundly
changed Czech society of the later nineteenth century. Masaryk's
preeminence as an ideologist of the Czech question did not
therefore arise from his having singly developed an entirely new
ideology. Instead, he was the first to combine old and new
ideas into one comprehensive if not entirely consistent national
ideology. He also first sought to define the aims and methods
of Czech politics primarily in terms of enduring moral principles
like "humanity," "democracy," and "work." Not until the First
World War did Masaryk's national ideology win widespread acceptance; it then became the principal guide for those Czechs and
Slovaks who aimed to establish an independent Czechoslovak
state.[90]

In asking that Czech politics be based on certain moral principles, Masaryk forcefully argued that any political system not
based on these principles would, regardless of its organization
and aims, soon degenerate into an unstable system sanctioning
the exploitation of one group by another. He therefore criticized the Young Czech party not only for its inadequate advocacy
of political and social reform but for its refusal to recognize
any moral imperatives above those of national and individual interests. To make responsible and active political work an end
in itself was to take a short-sighted and superficial view of
"the Czech question" and to underestimate the gravity of "the
present crisis." Masaryk also leveled charges of materialism
and opportunism against Marxian socialism in his informed and
otherwise sympathetic 1898 study *Otázka sociální: Základy
marxismu sociologické a filosofické* (The social question: the
sociological and philosophical bases of Marxism).[91] But the
Czech Social Democrats, unlike the Young Czechs, continued to
regard Masaryk as a friendly critic and in 1907 and 1911 by
their endorsement insured his election to the Reichsrat from the
Moravian district of Valašské Meziříčí.

Masaryk thought no politics of morality to be possible

without "work," which he defined essentially as individual effort undertaken cooperatively to achieve social goals. In arguing this point, his 1898 theoretical essay, *Jak pracovat* (How to work), complemented his earlier writings on the Czech question.[92] By continuing to publish scholarly works on social and political issues, by fighting for unpopular causes where moral issues were involved, and by founding an independent People's party in 1900, Masaryk gave credence to his opinion that politics required patient, morally informed, and socially responsible labor.

Masaryk's justification of the Czech struggle for national emancipation on the grounds of its embodying ideals of democracy, Protestantism, and humanity closely resembled Polish messianism, his disclaimers notwithstanding. To be sure, his views differed markedly in content from the notion that Poland was "the Christ of nations" and "the easternmost bastion" of Western civilization. But each national ideology resembled the other in both form and intent--to foster the moral regeneration and material welfare of the nation and to provide guidance in practical politics.[93]

Masaryk's views on humanity, morality, and work in politics can be appreciated only if considered in relation to the serious crisis in Czech politics during the nineties. If not so considered, they may appear to be no more than high-minded cant. That this was not the case is evident from Masaryk's untiring efforts to put his ideals into practice. His willingness to take a principled and unpopular stand on controversial issues was first demonstrated by his defense of Jan Gebauer in the manuscripts controversy of the eighties and by resignation of his parliamentary mandates and membership in the Young Czech party in September 1893. He continued to take courageous stands by demanding repeal of Leopold Hilsner's conviction in 1899 of Jewish ritual murder, by supporting in 1908 Ludwig Wahrmund's right to academic freedom at the University of Innsbruck, and by defending at Zagreb in 1909 the Croats and Serbs tried for treason on the basis of bogus evidence.[94]

Any attempt to establish a political ideology, much less an ideology of the Czech question, was foreign to both the Young Czech and Old Czech parties. That they had based their programs on liberal principles as well as national interests indicates that they were not the shallow pragmatists caricatured by their opponents. But by having built their party and policies upon self-governmental and commercial institutions, the Young Czechs became too intimately involved in day-to-day political compromise and came to have too much at stake in acquiring material wealth and public office to create any ideology which would jeopardize or seek to undermine the established order. Theirs was a policy of pragmatism, that of using all legal and institutional means at their disposal, however inadequate, to try to effect reforms. That the success of this policy depended

upon continuing imperial good will only gradually became apparent to all.

It was not at all evident in 1895 that the moralist and practical idealist Masaryk would within a generation emerge as the
founder of an independent Czechoslovakia or that his pre-war
writings would in retrospect be regarded as prophecy. As 1895
drew to a close, most Czech voters still believed that Josef
Kaizl and the Young Czechs offered the best way out of the present crisis. Responsible and active political work had after all
contributed to the demise of the Windischgrätz coalition; and
the caretaker Kielmansegg government had smoothed the way for
the succession in October 1895 of a new "savior" of the monarchy,
the tough and respected Polish Count Kazimierz Badeni, known to
be open-minded on the Czech question and willing to cooperate
with the Young Czechs on mutually advantageous terms.

The Young Czechs and the Badeni Government

Count Kazimierz Badeni took office as minister-president of Cis-leithania under apparently favorable circumstances. After six years of political turmoil, the authorities and privileged classes looked forward to a revival of the status quo as it had existed under Taaffe during the eighties. The new minister-president fa-vored and could be expected to follow Taaffe's policy of forming a government of professional administrators that would rule with parliamentary consent. During nine years as governor of Gali-cia, Badeni, a Kraków conservative without democratic inclina-tions, had won recognition as a tough, fair, and able executive. He aimed to treat all nationalities equitably insofar as pos-sible, believing this to be the only policy that could insure domestic order. But because he had done little to eliminate dis-criminatory laws against Ukrainians in Galicia, Czech politi-cians, like many others, were initially quite skeptical of such talk about fair play.

The Badeni Government

Badeni gave a decidedly professional and nonpartisan tone to his administration by filling cabinet posts primarily with ca-reer civil servants, among whom two were Poles, Minister of Fi-nance Leon Biliński and Minister for Galician Affairs Edvard Rittner. Poles thus held four of ten Cisleithanian ministries, since Badeni became Minister of the Interior as well as minister-president.[1] German civil servants took charge of three minis-tries, with Hugo Glanz-Eich as Minister of Commerce, Paul Baron von Gautsch as Minister of Worship and Public Instruction, and Johann Count Gleisbach as Minister of Justice. The great land-owners Johann Count Ledebur-Wicheln and Walter Count von Welser-heimb respectively became Minister of Agriculture and Minister of Defense. In January 1896, Badeni created the new post of Minister of Railways, to which he appointed Field Marshal Emil Ritter von Guttenberg.

Badeni appealed to many nations and diverse groups in Cis-leithania for other reasons than his unquestionable honesty and administrative ability. In an empire increasingly divided ac-cording to national loyalties, he retained the cosmopolitan out-look that had long characterized the aristocracy.[2] He was a great landowner, a Catholic, and a Polish nobleman of distant Italian origin. Great landowners throughout Cisleithania be-lieved he could be trusted to look after their interests, though

the Bohemian nobility would have preferred to have one of their
own take office. Badeni's ancestry made him especially appealing to Poles and Italians, and his tolerance in religious matters helped him get along with the freethinking and anticlerical
Young Czechs. By firmly and fairly governing Galicia, he had
earned the respect and confidence of the predominantly German
civil service. And the army high command gratefully remembered
his having kept Galicia calm during the Russian war scare of
1888 arising from the Bulgarian crisis. Badeni had ruled Galicia with a heavy hand, while treating Poles and Ukrainians equitably in accordance with laws that favored the former. He had
also tried to conciliate the Ukrainians by granting small concessions and had brought the great Ukrainian historian Mychajlo
Hruševs'kyj from Kiev to Lvov in an attempt to play off the
Ukrainian party against the Old Ruthenians.[3]

On most counts, Badeni was a better minister-president than
his generally bad press and poor reputation among German historians would indicate.[4] Contemporary German papers, notably the
Neue Freie Presse, disliked him as they had the senior Gołuchowski during the sixties, for what he was--a Slav and a great
landowner--as well as for what he stood for--federalism and
equal rights for all nationalities. The *Národní listy* and radical Young Czechs consistently denounced him as the "Machiavellian" who systematically corrupted Czech politicians through
minor concessions or unfulfilled promises. Against such accusa-
tions stands favorable testimony to his character and ability by
politicians as diverse in viewpoint as the Young Czech journalists Josef Penížek and Gustav Eim and the German Catholic conservative leader Theodor Kathrein, who served as speaker of the
lower house of the Reichsrat.[5]

Badeni relied not only on his extensive knowledge of the empire and long experience in its administration, but on close personal contact with political leaders among most nationalities
and interest groups. He preferred to prepare legislative proposals quietly and in concert with trusted friends, sounding
them out for advice on important issues before announcing his policies to the press or to Parliament. Badeni's thus working secretly through friends and confidants earned him the largely un-
deserved reputation of a Machiavellian or a schemer. This practice did not suit him for democratic politics, but the Habsburgs
never intended that politics in Cisleithania should be run in a
democratic manner. Badeni's confidants included Gustav Eim
among the Young Czechs, Oswald von Thun-Salm among the constitutional great landowners of Bohemia, and Johann Ledebur-Wicheln
among the conservative great landowners.[6] He brought with him
from Kraków to Vienna two trusted advisors and career civil servants, the German Liberal Ernst von Koerber and the ennobled Galician Jew Heinrich Ritter von Blumenstock-Halban.[7] Halban's
presence and Badeni's three recommendations that the emperor not
confirm Karl Lueger's election as mayor of Vienna gave rise to

unfounded charges in the German press that Badeni had become a
creature of the Rothschilds. Actually the minister-president
was by conviction strongly opposed to anti-Semitism and considered Lueger a troublemaker.[8]

Badeni would be the last minister-president to serve any
length of time without ever resorting to article 14; and unlike
the German bureaucrats who served after him as minister-
presidents, he showed no contempt for the non-German nationalities or for the majority in Parliament.[9] He keenly appreciated
the intensity of national pride and rivalries and the consequent
danger to Austria-Hungary of becoming involved in foreign wars,
but he underestimated both German national pride and German hostility to parliamentary rule.[10]

Three important long-standing and unresolved issues confronted the Badeni government. It had to achieve the extension of
the franchise which had eluded Taaffe and Windischgrätz and to
which the emperor had committed himself in principle. It would
have to dampen if not end the smoldering conflict between Czechs
and Germans in Bohemia which had been inflamed by the Agreement
of 1890 and by Governor Thun's humiliation of the Czechs. Finally, it would be required to win parliamentary approval for
renewal of the decennial tariff agreement with Hungary due to
expire in 1897. To govern as he intended with the consent of
Parliament, Badeni had to put together a majority in time to ra-
tify the new agreement. This gave him less than two years in
which to win the confidence of Czechs and Germans that would be
necessary to assure ratification.

Badeni attempted by his first acts as minister-president to
restore Czech confidence in imperial authority and to reassure
the Germans that his government would not harm their interests.
On October 11, 1895, he lifted the state of emergency that had
subjugated Prague and environs since September 12, 1893, and on
October 18 granted amnesty to the eleven *Omladina* "conspirators"
still in Bory prison. His October 22 speech to Parliament promised a prompt electoral reform which would blunt demands for
universal suffrage while preserving almost intact the privileges of curial voting. After professing "complete trust in the
Czech nation," he recognized "the traditional and historically
established position of the German nation" in Cisleithania and
praised the German culture "which had enlightened all other nations." The Young Czechs recognized that Badeni's gestures of
good will, even if they did no more than restore the status quo
of 1893, could open the way to serious negotiation. But the
party first had to defend its record in the November elections
to the Bohemian Diet.[11]

Two other developments in October 1895, besides Badeni's
lifting the state of emergency, marked a continuously growing
Czech national self-confidence. The large and impressive Czech
Ethnographic Exhibition (Národopisná výstava), which attracted
more than two million spectators, completed its sixth and final

month in Prague. This exhibition both continued and complemented the equally successful Jubilee Exposition of 1891, by including Czechs from Moravia and Silesia as well as the kingdom of
Bohemia and by placing greater emphasis upon Czech folk art and
the arts and letters as opposed to achievements in commerce, industry, and farming. On October 13, representatives from Czech
commercial and self-governmental institutions met in Prague's
Old Town Hall to found the Czech Society for National Economy
(Česká národohospodářská společnost) in order to institutional-
ize and perpetuate the cooperation and sense of national unity
which had grown out of their work in putting on the great expo-
sitions of 1891 and 1895. The society aimed not only to further
cooperation between Czech business and industry in the three
crown lands but to increase economic development generally and
thereby indirectly advance the achievement of political autonomy. It also sought to popularize among all classes of Czech society the ideals of "national economy" and self-help, including
the slogans "buy Czech" and "each to his own" ("Svůj k svému).
Thereby the society expected not only to promote the national
welfare but to combat "utopian" Social Democratic ideals. Young
Czechs, including Adámek, Fořt, and Kaizl, predominated among
the organizers and speakers at the congress, though spokesmen
from diverse parties attended, including Václav Choc from the
Progressive camp and the Social Democrats Josef Steiner and
Vilém Černý, who asked that greater emphasis be placed on social
as opposed to national welfare.[12]

The Diet Elections of 1895 and 1896

The sixth Young Czech party congress, which met in Prague
from September 25 to 29, 1895, prepared a platform, a list of
candidates, and a vigorous campaign for the November elections.
Chairman Engel expected the party to win at least twenty-one of
the thirty-one seats still held by Old Czechs and anticipated
even less competition from independent Agrarians and Progressives, thanks in large part to highly restrictive four-curial
voting.[13] The party platform differed from that of 1889 only in
minor respects. It proclaimed the party to be "patriotic" and
"responsible," promised to combat the worsening agrarian crisis,
an issue overlooked at Nymburk, and argued that responsible and
active political work in the Bohemian Diet and the Reichsrat
would bring tax relief and internal improvements of benefit to
all classes.[14]

The Old Czechs offered nothing new to the electorate, as they
continued to wait for the Young Czech coalition to break up
through internal conflict or under external pressure. Most district boards which had backed the Old Czechs in 1891 had meanwhile gone over to the Young Czechs, satisfied that radicalism
had been overcome at Nymburk. F. L. Rieger steadfastly refused
to endorse any extension of suffrage to the diet or to

Parliament because it would be a "heresy against state rights."
Instead, he refurbished old plans for indirect elections to the
Reichsrat by the provincial diets, which would revive the status
quo previous to April 2, 1873; but the party knew better than to
make such a proposal to the electorate.[15] The Old Czech party
congress of November 3 and 4, 1895, in Prague accepted Rieger's
and Karel Mattuš's recommendations that the party not campaign
actively for seats in the diet.[16] This decision demoralized the
incumbent Old Czech deputies, many of whom were already resigned
to defeat and gave the Young Czechs a landslide victory by default. Whether Old Czechs chose to run as independents or under
the Old Czech banner, they could count only on help from local
party cadres and in some instances on backing from rudimentary
Catholic political organizations.

Competition of a more serious nature came from discontented
agrarian and radical elements within the Young Czech party. In
the end, only one radical, Josef Horák, editor of the *Čáslavské
listy*, declared an independent candidacy to the diet. But the
powerful Peasant Union had announced in April 1895 that it would
support an independent slate of peasant candidates in the fourth
curia, including founder Alfons Št'astný, chairman Jan Rataj,
and M. Vondrovic and Jan Erhart.[17] Rataj, who held the diet
seat from Písek which he had won as a Young Czech in 1889, could
be expected to retain it in the forthcoming election, while
Št'astný posed a serious threat running in his home district of
Tábor.[18]

Since Nymburk, Št'astný had through the *Selské noviny* criticized Young Czech neglect of peasant interests in the diet and
in Parliament. The agrarian crisis which had helped bring the
Peasant Union into the Young Czech camp had grown worse as the
same forces--intensive mechanized agriculture at home and increasingly stiff competition from the Americas--continued to
overwhelm the already debt-ridden Czech smallholder.[19] Under
these circumstances, liberal and national Young Czech programs
no longer aroused much enthusiasm among the peasants of south
Bohemia. The Peasant Union issued a straightforward three-point
program on April 28, 1895, in anticipation of the diet elections:[20]

1. To demand that the traditional rights of the lands of the
   Bohemian Crown be restored.
2. To demand that equality of rights be granted to the Czech
   nation.
3. To defend the interests of the peasant class in order
   that greater weight be given to the agricultural elements
   in public life.

The Bohemian Diet elections of November 20 to 26, 1895, went
according to the fondest Young Czech expectations. Party candidates took eighty-nine of ninety-seven Czech seats, a total

which increased to ninety when Josef Horák, who had run independently, returned to the fold.[21] For the first time, the Young
Czechs became the largest party in the diet, exceeding the con-
servative great landowners at seventy seats and the German Lib-
erals at fifty-four.[22] The Old Czechs retained only three of
their former thirty-one seats: the České Budějovice Chamber of
Commerce could not refuse reelection to its Old Czech chairman,
Antonín Effmert, while backing from the Buquoy family and the
Catholic clergy helped elect two others from south Bohemia,
J. Baar in urban Třebon and August Zátka in rural Budějovice.
Otherwise, the Catholic vote had little effect, and all clerical
candidates ran a poor third or fourth. The Social Democrats,
too, made a predictably poor showing in the few third-curial
districts where they chose to run; the tailor Karel Dědic, for
example, won 63 votes against 708 for the incumbent Josef Anýz
in the district including Beroun, Borovice, and Rokycany, while
Josef Steiner received only 13 of 1806 votes cast in Prague's
New Town (Nové Město) district.[23]

The elections brought the first victory of an independent
Progressive candidate. The *Radikální listy*, a Progressive weekly established in Kolín in February 1894, with Young Czech subsidies, to carry on for the Prague Progressive press shut down
by Governor Thun, helped elect the *Omladina* trial defense lawyer
and Progressive Karel Baxa.[24] The other Progressive candidate,
Jan Klecanda, who had revived his radical weekly *Vyšehrad*, ran
second in the fourth-curial district including Železný Brod and
Rieger's home town of Semily. Encouraged by Baxa's victory and
Klecanda's good showing, the Progressives, including many of the
recently amnestied *Omladináři*, assembled in Kolín on December 21,
1895, to consider forming an independent political party. Not
only did a majority of delegates, including Rašín, Sokol, and
Škába, recently returned from Bory, reject such a step as premature, they also criticized editors Antonín Čížek and Jan Tre-
bický for having published articles excessively critical of the
sixth Young Czech party congress and for having supported Baxa's
candidacy against Young Czech J. V. Kalaš. After Čížek, Tre-
bický and Jaroslav Preiss resigned from the editorial board, the
majority approved appointment of Antonín Hajn as editor-in-chief.
The delegates voted to endorse the Young Czech policy of opposition to the Badeni government but to work independently of the
party.[25]

Only the unexpectedly good showing made by independent Agrarian candidates marred the Young Czech victory. Peasant Union
chairman Jan Rataj easily won reelection from Písek and Vodnany.
Although three other Agrarian candidates fared badly, Alfons
Šťastný squeaked through with a one-vote margin in his home
district of Tábor, Vožice, and Soběslav, only to have the authorities and the Young Czech party agree to void the election
on grounds of possible error or fraud. But in a new election on
December 23, 1896, Šťastný again defeated Young Czech Hynek

Lang, this time by eleven votes.[26] That the Young Czechs had
agreed to let the authorities invalidate his first election,
question his electors' honesty, and keep him from office for a
year made Št'astný and his union even less willing to renegotiate any return to the parent party. Though the Peasant Union
candidates won only two seats, the Young Czechs took alarm because they recognized that curial voting registered only a small
part of widespread peasant discontent.[27] Št'astný and Rataj had
won in districts where few union members could meet the five-
gulden tax requirement to vote.

The Young Czech party responded to the potentially dangerous
defection of its south Bohemian allies in the Peasant Union by
helping to establish during the next fifteen months three new
peasant organizations which primarily served the more prosperous
peasants in the intensive agricultural areas of central and
eastern Bohemia. Chairman Engel personally took a hand in this
work, for he had always believed that the party could not maintain its predominance without the agrarian support it too often
took for granted. He and the Young Czech delegates representing
fourth-curial parliamentary or diet districts believed that the
party's advocacy of industrial, commercial, and scientific progress would appeal to farmers who used modern techniques and who
owned their own food-processing and marketing facilities, if not
to the impoverished and tradition-minded peasantry of south Bohemia.[28] The founders and first chairmen of these new organizations were Young Czech party members who later won seats as parliamentary delegates. On February 9, 1896, Stanislav Kubr, a
farmer from Kneževes, helped establish and chaired the Central
Bohemian Peasant League (Středočeská Selská Župa). František
Udržal, a farmer from Dolní Roveň, and Mayor J. V. Markalous of
the Pardubicko District Board organized in June and incorporated
in October 1896 the Peasant Political Union in Pardubice (Politická selská Jednota v Pardubicích), which served all east Bohemian districts. Št'astný immediately denounced both organizations as tools of the Young Czech party for keeping agrarian interests subordinate to those of the middle class. Meanwhile the
Central Bohemian Peasant League, encouraged by Engel, began to
unite the smaller Bohemian peasant organizations, excepting
Št'astný's Peasant Union, into a single association.[29] This led
to the assembly of peasant leaders in Prague on February 27,
1897, which formed the Association of Czech Agriculturalists
(Sdružení českých zemědělců) under the chairmanship of Stanislav
Kubr.[30] The Association served as a clearinghouse and spokesman
for local peasant cooperatives and savings and loan associations
of central and western Bohemia. It fully repaid Young Czech efforts on its behalf by helping party candidates sweep fifteen of
seventeen fourth-curial parliamentary seats in the elections of
March 1897.[31]

The diet elections of October 1896 in Moravia also brought
returns favorable to Young Czech interests. Stránský's People's

party won a plurality of Czech seats for the first time, taking
seventeen seats in the third and fourth curias as opposed to
thirteen for the National, or Old Czech, party and five for the
clerical parties. An electoral agreement between Stránský and
the Old Czechs against both clericals and Germans in large measure contributed to the victory.[32] Two of the five clerical
mandates went to the leaders of the newly founded Czech Catholic
National party (Katolická strana národní)--Mořic Hruban, a former Old Czech, and Antonín Cyril Stojan, professor of theology
at the Catholic university in Olomouc.[33] Cooperation between
the People's party and the Moravian Old Czechs after Nymburk had
contributed to the formation of the Catholic National party,
much as the 1891 Old Czech defeat in Bohemia led Czech Catholics
to establish the first independently Catholic and Christian Socialist movement in accordance with *Rerum novarum*. Devout Catholics in the Old Czech ranks could not accept compromise with
Stránský's strident Young Czech anticlericalism, just as the
Progressive Moravian youth would find it hard to go along with
Stránský's politically expedient alliance with his former Old
Czech conservative opponents.

The impressive Young Czech landslide in the November 1895
elections followed by Stránský's success in Moravia appeared to
vindicate the policies adopted at Nymburk. The Bohemian Old
Czechs had ceased to be formidable competitors, while most Moravian Old Czechs had come to terms with Stránský. The challenges
from Agrarians and Progressives in Bohemia and from the Catholic
National party in Moravia were seemingly checked. The electoral
returns clearly demonstrated to the emperor and Badeni that Governor Thun's repressive measures had outlived their usefulness.
If the government wished to end Young Czech opposition, it would
have to grant more concessions to the Czech nation.

The Making of the Young Czech Alliance with Badeni

During the sixteen months from the November 1895 diet elections through the March 1897 Reichsrat elections, Badeni and the
Young Czechs gradually came to an understanding. Both sides had
to make sacrifices. To please Badeni and his allies, the Young
Czechs had to come to terms with the great landowners and thereby risk further loss of radical, progressive, and agrarian support. Badeni in turn could only grant those concessions to the
Czechs which would not alarm his conservative and German Catholic backers.

Three acts of the Badeni government after the elections of
1895 helped persuade the moderate majority of the Young Czech
party that mutually advantageous cooperation with the minister-
president might be possible. On January 6, 1896, he accepted
Count Francis Thun's resignation as governor of Bohemia, replacing him with Count Karl Coudenhove, and approved repeal of the
draconian May 6, 1895, school decree.[34] Two months later,

Badeni restored the immunity of non-German parliamentary
speeches to legal prosecution.

Almost all Czechs greeted Thun's departure with rejoicing,
and many accepted the Young Czechs' claim that it attested to
the efficacy of the Nymburk Resolution. The German liberal and
radical press uniformly regarded the dismissal of Thun as an admission of weakness on the part of the government or, worse yet,
as a surrender to the Young Czechs. Both opinions were mistaken.
After Badeni became minister-president, Thun himself recognized
that he had lost all effectiveness as governor and could only embarrass attempts to restore harmony and normality to political
life. In October 1895, Badeni refused his first offer to resign,
having underestimated the degree of Czech hostility toward Thun,
whom he respected and wished to retain as a governor. But,
prodded by Young Czech moderates, he soon realized that no reconciliation with the Czechs would be possible so long as the man
who ruled for two years by state of emergency remained in office.[35]

Badeni's first three months in office persuaded Young Czechs
that he would be a more acceptable minister-president than Windischgrätz or Taaffe. Official party policy toward his government continued to be responsible and active opposition in accordance with the Nymburk Resolution; but by January 1896, party
members had split three ways on the question of adopting a new
policy: those in favor, those opposed on principle, and those
opposed for the time being.

A small group, led by Gustav Eim, Badeni's friend and advisor,
and including Josef Herold and Karel Kramář, favored negotiations
toward a mutually advantageous alliance. Herold wrote to Eim on
January 9, 1896, expressing his willingness to negotiate and to
do all that he could "to see that things develop in a reasonable
way."[36] Kramář joined them in hopes of winning Badeni's confidence and becoming an indispensable intermediary between imperial
authorities and the party. Eim's efforts to win over other colleagues had to date proved less productive. On December 6, 1895,
he had brought Badeni and Edvard Grégr together to discuss political differences of opinion. He did not expect Grégr to become
a supporter of Badeni but could at least be sure than an informed
Edvard Grégr would be a fair-minded opponent and raise no charges
of conspiracy. Moreover, Badeni would better appreciate the rea-
sonableness of Young Czech moderates after having talked to
Grégr. The exchange went as expected: in reply to Badeni's inquiry about the price for party cooperation, Grégr demanded the
full implementation of Bohemian state rights beginning with gubernatorial responsibility to the diet.[37] Eim and Herold believed Grégr's demands to be unrealistic, primarily because Badeni had no authority whatsoever to abridge imperial prerogatives. They also recognized that the Habsburgs had only implemented extensive constitutional reforms after defeat in foreign
wars or under great external pressure. Since Austria-Hungary at

that time neither faced nor sought foreign conflicts, the Czechs
would not help their cause by making demands which no minister
could reasonably be expected to grant.[38]

The second party group, which comprised most radicals including Edvard Grégr, Václav Březnovský, Jan Vašatý, Josef Fořt, Jan
Slavík, Václav Šamánek, and Edvard Brzorád, distrusted Badeni
and did not believe that any minister-president, no matter how
well-intentioned, could be relied upon to enact reforms through
Parliament when he held office only at the discretion of the emperor. Even if Badeni could be held to his word, would the emperor back him? Why be lured into supporting a government which
could give little or no assurance of implementing any point in
the party's program?[39] Moreover, the more experienced party radicals, including Grégr, Slavík, and Adolf Stránský, did not,
like many of their colleagues, regard the removal of Thun as a
panacea. The Czechs were rid of an exemplary authoritarian
civil servant but not of the system which produced his kind and
enabled them to rule arbitrarily.[40]

Since the radicals could not be expected to support Badeni,
Eim and Herold concentrated on winning over the third group,
those uncommitted moderates comprising a majority of delegates,
among whom the most influential figures were Chairman Engel,
Kaizl, Pacák, and Škarda. The moderates recollected the Old
Czech experience with Taaffe and therefore did not wish to commit themselves to supporting Badeni without first being assured
that some reforms long desired by the party would be forthcoming.[41] Furthermore, Badeni's creation of a railway ministry in
January 1896 without parliamentary authorization led them to
doubt his professed desire to rule with consent of Parliament.
When the new Minister of Railways, Emil Ritter von Guttenberg,
eliminated Czech as one of the administrative languages of the
railway system, the moderate Young Czechs had no choice but to
attack the government's policies in Parliament.[42] The price
which the moderates now demanded for ceasing opposition to the
government was nothing less than full equality for the Czechs in
all aspects of public life in Cisleithania.[43]

The three-way division of Young Czech opinion on policy toward the government still remained when Badeni introduced to the
Reichsrat on February 6, 1896, his proposals for electoral reform. In a bill similar to the two put forward by the Windischgrätz government, he proposed to add a fifth curia of seventy-two
seats based on universal manhood suffrage and to lower the tax
requirement in the third and fourth curias from five gulden to
four. Otherwise, the existing four-curial system would remain
intact. The reform would triple the size of the electorate by
adding at least five million new voters. But elections would
still be indirect in the fourth and fifth curias and the newly
enfranchised voters would elect very few delegates in comparison
with the established curias, as table 18 in the appendix, on
Reichsrat representation, shows.[44]

Young Czech party radicals agreed with Progressives and Social Democrats in regarding the reform as at best an "incomplete" measure which gave little more than the illusion of popular representation while retaining all discrimination in favor
of class, wealth, and German nationality.[45] The great debate
within the Young Czech party on whether or not to support Badeni's franchise reform occurred in the club of parliamentary delegates on March 25 and 26, 1896. After a stormy debate, party
members agreed to press for universal suffrage independently of
the Badeni government and if that failed to vote for Badeni's
bill.[46] Jan Slavík reintroduced to the Reichsrat his bill for
direct equal, secret, and universal manhood suffrage in April
1896, only to have it again defeated.[47] Badeni's electoral reform bill passed on May 7 by a vote of 234 to 19 with only two
Young Czechs voting against it. The two, Edvard Grégr and Václav
Šamánek, returned respectively to Libochovice and to Prague's New
Town to explain to their electors that they voted against the
bill to try to prevent Badeni from enacting the small reforms by
which he intended, like Taaffe, to accustom the Czech nation to
settling for "crumbs." But public opinion, including *Čas*, accepted the electoral reform as a desirable halfway measure.[48]

Two events in the fall of 1896 helped draw all Young Czechs
together and overshadowed their disagreement on party policy toward the Badeni government. On September 23, 1896, the party
executive committee voted to establish a new minority defense
fund and to publish brochures describing the problems of Czech
minorities in predominantly German areas of Bohemia and Moravia.
This supplemented contributions earlier raised for the North Bohemian National Union, the Šumava National Union, and their
counterparts in Moravia. In a speech on October 3, 1896, Adolf
Stránský noted that minorities should continue to work ardently
for self-improvement and deserved the support of every Czech.[49]

The death of Julius Grégr on October 4, 1896, found Young
Czechs united not only in mourning but in praise of his achievements and character, which had once been controversial topics.
All helped make his funeral into a great manifestation of Czech
patriotism that they hoped would redound to the party's advantage. Representatives from other Slavic nations attended the
funeral along with practically all prominent Czech literary and
political figures.[50] F. L. Rieger, whose political quarrels
with Grégr dated back to 1863, hesitated before deciding to attend. "If I go to the funeral I shall have to say something
that will feign the sorrow that I do not feel, and if I don't go
people will say that I am irreconcilable to the very grave."[51]

Julius Grégr's will bequeathed his majority share in the ownership of the *Národní listy* to its editorial staff, which included his son Prokop, Karel Tůma, Servác Heller, and Gustav Eim.
Other political parties, including the Old Czechs and the Catholics, tried to buy the paper, but the new managers refused to
sell it and announced that it would continue to be an independent,

liberal, and patriotic journal affiliated with the Young Czech
party. The editors could no more agree on how best to implement
this policy than they had agreed in the past. The struggle continued between Eim, who wished the paper to support an agreement
between the Young Czech party and Badeni, and Josef Anýz and
Karel Tůma, who wished the party to remain in opposition to the
government. With Julius Grégr no longer around to decide in
favor of radicalism, the paper gradually assumed a more moderate
tone despite protests by Tůma and Anýz. The way had opened for
the journal's transformation from an independent ally of the
Young Czech party into an organ effectively controlled by the
moderate party leadership. Until this occurred in 1908, political debates on the editorial board corresponded almost exactly
to those in the executive committee and the clubs of delegates
of the Young Czech party.[52]

The passing of Julius Grégr not only led to renewed demonstrations of party solidarity and patriotic fervor but facilitated the making of a political understanding between the Young
Czechs and the conservative great landowners, the very act which
he had so long opposed. On November 6, 1896, Prince Charles of
Schwarzenberg proposed such an understanding to the Young Czechs
which, when accepted in December, opened the way to their joint
collaboration with the Badeni government.[53]

By early November 1896, the Young Czech party had, after its
"strategic pause" during the spring and summer, firmly committed
itself to a policy of overcoming "aimless radicalism" within its
ranks and exploring mutual interests with the conservative great
landowners and the Badeni government. Its having thus revived
National party policies of the Taaffe era was further revealed
by its coming to terms with the Old Czechs in Bohemia and Moravia and by its expulsion of Jan Vašatý, its most radical delegate. In Bohemia, the Young Czechs had reached an understanding
with the Old Czechs before the many October elections of officials for communal self-governmental bodies. In Moravia, the
People's party, largely at Stránský's behest, had concluded an
electoral agreement with the Old Czechs before the diet elections of late October, in which their combined slate had against
clerical opposition won thirty of thirty-five Czech seats in the
third and fourth curias. The People's party had adopted more
moderate policies in order to acquire the Old Czech support that
proved to be decisive in several close victories over clerical
candidates in the rural fourth curia. Finally, on October 28,
1896, the Young Czech party expelled Jan Vašatý, thereby demonstrating its responsibility and respectability to prospective
allies on the right and serving notice to the remaining party
radicals that they should henceforth help the majority make responsible and active politics a continuing success. For eight
years, the moderates had patiently endured Vašatý's violations
of party discipline. Occasional reprimands had not kept him in
line, but the moderate majority waited to expel him until it was

politically advantageous to do so. His naively enthusiastic
praise of Russia and denunciations of imperial ministers had at
least the one redeeming feature of making other party firebrands
like Edvard Grégr or Václav Březnovský look mild by comparison.[54]

The last holdouts among the moderate party majority capitulated as the terms for supporting Badeni were revealed on December 17, 1896. The minister-president proposed nothing less than
the issuance of ordinances, subject to parliamentary approval,
that would realize the Young Czech quest for the equal validity
of the Czech and German languages in the internal and external
service of the imperial bureaucracy in Bohemia and Moravia. At
the emperor's behest, all departments of the bureaucracy concerned with defense or taxation would continue to carry on business exclusively in German. But, with these exceptions, which
might also include the state railway system, Badeni could offer
Czechs a means of acquiring preponderance within the judicial
and administrative branches of imperial civil service in Bohemia
and Moravia and thereby exercising political influence commensurate with their wealth and numbers. The moderate Young Czech
majority regarded the enactment of these proposals as a logical
step toward national autonomy. Nonetheless, the party agreed to
collaborate with Badeni only after the March 1897 Reichsrat
elections and after several stormy sessions of the party parliamentary club in which moderates overruled those radicals who
still distrusted Badeni and considered his proposed reforms to
be halfway measures at best.[55]

Gustav Eim died on February 7, 1897, while vacationing in
Florence and at the very moment when a majority in his party appeared likely to conclude that alliance with the Badeni government which he had tirelessly advocated. This gifted journalist
had always thought it possible to reconcile Czechs and Germans
of good will and to realize Czech national and liberal aims
through representative institutions, however weak and imperfect.
After Nymburk, he had increasingly become known as an "opportunistic politician from head to toe" while retaining his reputation as a liberal-minded patriot and the greatest Czech political commentator of his generation.[56] Citizens from all walks of
life mourned his passing at a less ostentatious funeral than
that given Julius Grégr. The most appropriate and enduring tribute to Eim's memory was that large memorial volume of his political essays and editorials, *Politické úvahy*, compiled by Josef
Penížek.[57]

No one man could fill Eim's many party functions, and his
death, like that of Julius Grégr, accelerated extensive changes
within the party. Though Josef Penížek ably carried on as Vienna correspondent for the *Národní listy*, the paper would never be
the same without Eim's inimitable dispatches. Grégr's passing
had so eased the tension between *Národní listy* editors and party
parliamentary delegates that there was no need for anyone to
succeed Eim as the principal go-between or peacemaker between

those groups. No Young Czech ever surpassed Eim's intimate
knowledge of so many imperial statesmen or his understanding of
the pathways to limited political influence in Vienna. The pro-
fessionalization of party operations, authorized by Engel and
implemented by executive committee chairman Václav Škarda, soon
terminated the casual procedures which had facilitated Eim's
acting on his own as a power broker or party spokesman. Moreover, as the emperor and his advisors after 1900 gave increasingly less emphasis to placating or buying off a parliamentary
majority, opportunities diminished for the sort of backstage negotiations at which Eim had excelled.

The November 1896 Young Czech agreement with the conservative
great landowners implied eventual acceptance of an alliance with
Badeni and indicated that the Young Czechs were about to embark
on a course similar to that taken by the Old Czechs after 1879,
when they had supported the Taaffe government in return for obtaining the Stremayr language ordinances, extended suffrage, and
a separate Czech university. Party radicals never ceased to
point out that Rieger had received no more than minor concessions
once Taaffe had fulfilled his part of the bargain: by settling
for a language law that changed the status quo less than did the
1880 Stremayr ordinances, the party would obligate itself to
pursue an opportunistic policy offering no more than crumbs from
the parliamentary banquet table. Moderates, on the other hand,
contended that the Czech nation had grown so much stronger since
the eighties that their party could for the first time bargain
from a position of strength.[58]

Party radicals steadfastly argued against the party's concluding any alliance with Badeni, particularly when doing so would
require it to cease advocating universal manhood suffrage and to
endorse Prince Frederick of Schwarzenberg's candidacy in České
Budějovice. Kaizl, Kramář, and other moderates who favored the
agreement denounced their radical colleagues for adhering to
"shopworn doctrines of the sixties" in a situation that required
flexibility and compromise. Engel and Pacák spoke more temper-
ately in suggesting that party members accept the alliance as a
necessary risk by which, win or lose, they could claim to have
exhausted every legal opportunity to advance the national interest.[59] More experienced in Cisleithanian politics than Kaizl
or Kramář, they were more sceptical of imperial promises and
less willing to sacrifice party unity or principles for any anticipated tactical success. Nonetheless, like Eim and Josef Holeček, they also advocated association with Badeni on the grounds
that party collaboration with Polish noblemen and clerical Slovenes would constitute a "Slavic policy." Indeed, from their
return to the Reichsrat with Rieger in 1879 until their endorsement of Neo-Slavism before 1914, moderate Young Czechs often supported conservative parliamentary coalitions in the name of Slavic solidarity.

By concluding its November agreement with the conservative

great landowners, the Young Czech party confirmed all charges
made since Nymburk by Masaryk and the Progressives that it aimed
to revive the discredited Old Czech policy of alliance with the
Bohemian nobility and a conservative imperial government. None
other than the venerable F. L. Rieger commended the party for
its remarkable change of heart. Speaking to the Political Association of the Labe Region (Politický spolek polabský) in Kolín
on January 10, 1897, he happily reported that the Czech nation
in pursuit of Bohemian state rights would once again benefit
from the guidance of "our aristocracy" and "our clergy."[60]
Among the more vocal critics of this policy was Čas editor Jan
Herben, who charged the Young Czech party with committing the
cardinal Old Czech error of expecting to advance national objectives in association with powerful and established forces of the
old regime. Neither nobility nor clergy, much less the imperial
government, could ever have Czech interests at heart. Both Herben and Masaryk contended that in the hard times to come, Czechs
should rely primarily on themselves and concentrate on building
a better-educated and more democratic society in which all citizens would have a stake in continuing national emancipation and
social reform.[61]

Like Masaryk and Herben, Czech Progressives increasingly opposed the gradual Young Czech drift toward the right. Most Progressives had throughout 1896 argued against any premature establishment of political parties independent of the Young
Czechs. But in February 1897, they began to organize such parties in preparation for the March Reichsrat elections.

The Growing Rift between Young Czechs and Progressives

The successor parties to the Progressive movement profoundly
influenced Czech politics up to 1914. Initially, they reflected
growing popular dissatisfaction with the Young Czech revival of
Old Czech policies. At the same time, Young Czech moderates
sought to dampen this discontent and to vindicate their responsible and active post-Nymburk policy by trying to win Badeni's
support for revised language laws and other concrete reforms.
Subsequently and more importantly, the two Progressive parties
founded in 1897, and their successor after 1908, the State
Rights Progressive party, helped accelerate the democratization
of Czech politics and ultimately contributed many leaders to the
wartime struggle for Czechoslovak independence.[62]

The establishment of an independent Czech Radical Progressive
party in April 1897, in opposition to the Young Czechs, grew out
of a long-standing dispute between Czech Progressives on whether
highest priority should be assigned to state rights or social
reform. This dispute erupted into open conflict on February 13,
1897, as Progressives began planning strategy for the March parliamentary elections. A majority, comprising Antonín Čížek,
Antonín Hajn, František Soukup, and others who gave precedence

to social reform, argued against supporting any Young Czech candidates in the new fifth curia because it should rightfully be-
long to Social Democracy. The outvoted Progressive minority,
headed by Alois Rašín, Karel Baxa, and K. Stanislav Sokol, contended, like the Young Czechs, that all parties should compete
equally for fifth-curia seats. On February 28, Rašín and Sokol
and a majority of shareholders in the Independence Cooperative
(družstvo "Neodvislost") which published the *Radikální listy*
retaliated by ousting Antonín Hajn as its editor, by refusing to
print the majority Progressive resolution of February 13, and by
endorsing several fifth-curial Young Czech candidates. The majority Progressives then brought out their own weekly *Samostatnost* (Independence) on April 3, 1897, with Antonín Hajn as
editor-in-chief, but were too late to influence the March
Reichsrat elections. These conflicts of February decisively
split the Progressive movement and left personal ill-will between former compatriots lasting up to a decade.[63]

During 1895 and 1896, some working-class Progressives and
former associates of the journal *Omladina* had joined the Czechoslavonic Social Democratic party, especially after its autonomy
had been recognized by the Fifth Congress of Austrian Social Democracy in April 1896. A larger group of these Progressives,
including A. Pravoslav Veselý and František Modráček, had after
October 1895 constituted themselves as an independent Progressive Socialist faction (*směr*) and published the fortnightly
Pokrok (Progress) in Kolín. In March 1897, they gave unqualified
support to the fifth-curial candidates of Social Democracy despite reservations about its excessively materialistic and collectivist attitudes and its doctrinaire belief in the inevitabi-
lity and desirability of revolution. Modráček, especially, had
come to advocate policies based on evolutionary as opposed to
revolutionary change, much as did Eduard Bernstein and the Social Democratic revisionists in Germany. Leaders of the Czechoslavonic Social Democratic party, notably Josef Steiner, chairman of the Workers' Political Club in Prague, not only solicited
the unqualified support of Progressives but believed that the
Progressive movement had reached a "watershed" where its adherents would either uphold private enterprise and Young Czech politics or wholeheartedly participate in efforts to build a socialist society. Should any large number of Progressives choose
the former course, as indeed happened, Social Democracy could
expect to gain many recruits among their other-minded colleagues.[64]

The dispute between Progressives on whether or not to endorse
Social Democratic fifth-curial candidates reflected a deeper difference of opinion concerning the social question and the policies of the Young Czech party. The cordial relations between
Progressive factions before and during the imprisonment of the
Omladina "conspirators" indicates that their formal split in
1897 primarily concerned policy and had little to do with

personality conflict or personal ambition. The majority radical
Progressives around *Samostatnost* believed that the social question had to be resolved before any lasting progress could be
made toward realizing Bohemian state rights or resolving the nationality conflict between Czechs and Germans. In this regard,
Čížek and Hajn opposed the recent Young Czech alliance with the
nobility and expected little good to come of Badeni's concessions on the language issue. Rašín and Sokol, though critical
of Young Czech "opportunism," continued to give priority to Bohemian state rights and support Young Czech candidates while
maintaining a policy of watchful waiting with respect to the
party's cooperation with Badeni.[65] The antidynastic and anticlerical views of both Progressive camps nonetheless continued to
identify them as progeny of Young Czech radicalism.

On April 4, 1897, Čížek, Hajn, and Soukup from Bohemia and
Václav Choc and František Vahalík from Moravia convened the congress of 154 Czech Progressives which established the independent Radical Progressive party (Radikálně pokroková strana) for
all Czech lands. The party issued a program reaffirming its opposition to the policies of the Young Czechs and the *Radikální
listy* group. It advocated achieving Bohemian state rights on
the basis of natural rights and popular sovereignty, but gave
priority to resolving the social question. Its specific reform
proposals included transformation of the imperial army into a
popular militia. At an August 22, 1897, congress in Olomouc,
the Moravian members of the party, led by Choc, proposed to establish universal suffrage to the diet and to rid politics and
education of clerical influence.[66] All Radical Progressives emphatically ruled out association with the Young Czechs, while
Rašín, Sokol, and the *Radikální listy* still hoped to transform
that party into a broadly based organization representing popular interests. The Radical Progressive party lost three of its
best administrators and public spokesmen with Čížek's death on
June 3, 1897, and the subsequent withdrawal of Soukup to Social
Democracy and Choc to the Czech National Socialists. That the
party thereafter lacked charismatic leaders contributed in part
to its remaining a small party of the intelligentsia.[67]

The formation of the "Young Moravia" movement by the younger
Moravian Czech intelligentsia in opposition to the post-Nymburk
collaboration of Adolf Stránský's People's party with the Moravian Old Czechs corresponded to the revival of the Progressive
movement in Bohemia. The Hodonín "Congress of the younger Moravian generation" (*sjezd mladší generace moravská*) on September 6
and 7, 1896, constituted itself as the Young Moravia movement
and declared its intention to promote social reform as the "left
wing" of the People's party. The movement elected the young
lawyers and publicists from Nový Jičín, František Derka and
František Vahalík, to be co-chairmen and issued a manifesto in
which it pledged to help the People's party overcome its "inadequate" concern for the working class and become a truly "popular"

234 The Young Czechs and the Badeni Government

party.[68] The omission of any reference to the agrarian question by a movement claiming to represent all people in a predominantly rural province was a serious shortcoming.[69] In content as in style, the program of the Hodonín congress resembled an abstract "Manifesto of Czech Modernism:"

> Our political program must in truth be popular and respond to the demands of all classes and strata of the nation and must bind together these heretofore variously and frequently conflicting classes in a single political body, which will be a healthy organism conscious of its goals.[70]

At its Brno congress of December 27, 1896, Young Moravia severed all ties with the People's party and announced that it would support candidates of its own choosing in the forthcoming parliamentary elections under the new five-curial system. It elected a thirteen-member executive committee including Derka, Vahalík, and Václav Choc, reaffirmed the Hodonín manifesto, drew up a ten-point program, and declared itself to be a "party of social reform but not a socialist party."[71] Young Moravia opposed collectivization but favored selective expropriation of property for the welfare of the community. Other points included tuition-free education, tax reform, and equal rights for women, including universal suffrage.

In the parliamentary elections of March 1897, Young Moravia backed the veteran Brno Social Democrat, Josef Hybeš, in the fifth curia against People's party candidate František Müller.[72] Hybeš won, to the consternation of Stránský and the People's party leadership, who, like the Young Czechs several years before, began to denounce the younger intelligentsia for having abandoned national ideals.

The Parliamentary Election of 1897

The active opposition and growing independence of the Czech Progressives constituted only one among many problems facing the Young Czech party as it prepared for the parliamentary elections of March 12 through March 20, 1897. Based on its performance in the November 1895 diet elections, the party had every expectation of winning all but one or two seats in the second, third, and fourth parliamentary curias. Thanks to universal manhood suffrage in the new fifth curia, where Czechs predominated in eleven of seventy-two electoral districts, Social Democratic candidates were expected to do well, despite indirect elections. Moreover, the Young Czech party could expect many Czech voters in the fourth and fifth curias to register their disapproval of its steadily rightward drift since the Nymburk congress. Especially the recent party alliance with the conservative great landowners was bound to be an important issue not only in Bohemia but in more conservative Moravia, where the People's party had prepared a joint slate of candidates with the Old Czechs.

The Young Czech pre-electoral proclamation of February 20, 1897, in comparison with its counterparts of years past, was decidedly bland, despite its reaffirmation of the party programs of 1889 and 1891.[73] It was also quite conciliatory in tone in objecting to certain imperial as well as German policies and in protesting abridgement of civil rights and limitations on the use of Czech language in many areas of government in Bohemia and Moravia. The proclamation committed the party to parliamentary opposition until the government demonstrated by "substantial deeds" rather than by "words" and "friendly gestures" its trust in the Czech people. For the first time the party did not advocate universal suffrage in an electoral program. While this omission pleased the conservative great landowners and potential allies to the right, it embarrassed the party, which had to reconcile this omission with its reaffirmation of the '89 and '91 programs which endorsed universal suffrage. Even straightforward Young Czechs like Chairman Engel found it difficult to explain this omission. When asked point blank for an answer after his March 4 speech in Jílový, he replied:

> Gentlemen, we delegates didn't do it. Rather we inquired of our trustees whether we shouldn't have universal suffrage in our program. Their answer was voiced negatively. Consequently, it was the Czech nation itself which made the decision.[74]

Chairman Engel thus quite candidly admitted that the Young Czech trustees believed themselves uniquely qualified to define the national interest. In doing so, he confirmed what had long been alleged but never explicitly proven by all Social Democrats as well as by Masaryk and Herben and by the Progressives of *Samostatnost*.[75]

In an all-out effort to defeat the Social Democrats in the fifth curia, the Young Czechs withdrew some of their more popular delegates from normally safe seats in the third and fourth curias to run in their home fifth-curial districts against relatively unknown Social Democrats. This group included Heřman Janda in Podřipsko, Karel Adámek in Hlinsko, Josef Doležal, mayor of Lomnice nad Popelkou, in the upper Labe valley, Václav Formánek of Kutná Hora in Polabí, and Chairman Engel himself in the district including Benešov, Vinohrady, and Kolín. In the city of Prague, where the Social Democrats were expected to make their best showing, thanks to direct elections and large numbers of workers, the party ran the ever-popular Václav Březnovský.

The Young Czechs won a victory in the 1897 Reichsrat elections which exceeded all expectations as they swept sixty of seventy Czech seats in Bohemia and Moravia, an increase of twenty-three over 1891, and thus became the largest party represented in Parliament.[76] Table 19 for the Bohemian elections, in the appendix, shows that the party won forty-five of fifty Czech

seats in the second through fifth curias. In Moravia, the joint
slate of People's party and Old Czech candidates took fifteen of
the seventeen Czech districts, with one seat going to the Social
Democrat Josef Hybeš and one to the Catholic National candidate
Antonín Cyril Stojan.

The Young Czechs took great pleasure in their unexpectedly
strong showing in the fifth curia, where they won nine of eleven
mandates and 57.8 percent of the electoral votes, thanks primarily to peasant support and to indirect elections. Chairman
Engel rolled up the largest Young Czech plurality in the fifth
curia, winning 526 electoral votes to 106 for his Social Democratic opponent and 18 for the Christian Socialist. In municipal Prague, where direct voting applied, Václav Březnovský defeated the Social Democratic candidate, Karel Dědic, by a surprisingly large margin in a run-off election after the clerical
candidate had been eliminated. In fact, Dědic polled 720 fewer
votes in the second election than in the first, when he had come
within 998 votes of Březnovský out of 34,650 cast. The Young
Czech run-off victory may be explained primarily by the fact
that the clerical press and 3,142 Catholic voters preferred the
fervently anticlerical Březnovský to Dědic. The press attributed Dědic's unexpected loss of votes to his having received
very vocal German-Jewish support and to his use of electoral
placards printed in German as well as in Czech.[77] Voters in Bohemia elected only two Social Democratic candidates, Karel Vrátný from the Pilsen region and Josef Steiner from the district
including Smíchov, Kladno, and Louny. Social Democrats won just
one contest in Moravia and two in Silesia, sending Josef Hybeš
from Brno and Petr Cingr and Arnošt Berner to the Reichsrat.

Voting in other Bohemian curias went as expected, with the
Young Czechs electing thirty-six of thirty-nine candidates.
Prince Frederick of Schwarzenberg, a joint candidate of Old Czechs
and clericals unopposed by the Young Czechs, won in urban Budějovice. Jan Vašatý avenged his ouster from the party by winning
rural Písek; and the independent agrarian František Šrámek carried rural Budějovice. Šrámek came over to the Young Czech camp
in the following year to increase their Reichsrat delegation to
sixty-one members.[78]

The results of the 1897 parliamentary elections outside the
Czech lands had equally great importance for the future of Czech
politics. They demonstrated that popular mass parties had come
to stay, as ten German along with five Czech Social Democratic
delegates won election from the fifth curia and the number of
Christian Socialists doubled from fourteen to twenty-eight. The
potential allies of the Young Czechs on the language issue, the
conservative great landowners and the Polish club, returned with
their delegate strength undiminished at twenty and fifty-nine
respectively. The German Liberals, who now called themselves
the Free German Alliance (Freie deutsche Vereinigung), took a
dreadful beating at the hands of the more radically nationalist

German parties and the two clerical parties, the Christian Socialists and the Catholic People's party (Katolische Volkspartei). Their poor handling of the Celje affair and identification with upper middle-class interests contributed to the decline of their parliamentary representation to fourteen seats
from the one hundred eight held by the "United German Left" in
1891. Meanwhile, Otto Steinwender's German People's party
(Deutsche Volkspartei) increased its delegates from seventeen to
thirty-eight, and Georg von Schönerer's German National Party
added one seat to its original four. The German Progressive
party (Fortschrittspartei), which broke away from the Liberals
after the Celje fiasco, won thirty-six seats. This shift in
German party strength did not bode well for the Czechs, because
most of the new German delegates were even less disposed than
the outgoing Liberals to regard the Czechs as equals.[79]

After their decisive electoral victory, the moderate Young
Czech architects of Nymburk resumed the negotiations with Badeni
which had been suspended during the election. Both sides were
under increasing pressure to find a mutually acceptable agreement. The moderates needed concessions on the language issue to
fulfill their campaign promises and to demonstrate to the party
radicals that the politics of compromise would work. Since Badeni wished to govern with Parliament, he needed Young Czech
votes to pass the annual budget and to renew the ten-year customs union. Moreover, he recognized that an agreement on the
language issue would strengthen the moderate Young Czech majority, thereby blunting Czech radicalism and retarding the growth
of Social Democracy.

The Badeni Language Ordinances

Three days after the March elections, the Young Czechs met
with Badeni to work out the final agreement by which they would
support his government in return for a revision of the Stremayr
language ordinances. Engel, Adámek, Brzorád, Herold, Kaizl,
Kramář, and Pacák represented the party at the all-day meeting
on March 23, to which Badeni also invited three cabinet ministers, Biliński, Gautsch, and Gleispach. To the afternoon session of the March 23 meeting, Badeni invited four representatives from German parties, Alois Funke, Julius Lippert, Ludwig
Schlesinger, and Karl Schücker.[80] Czechs and Germans could
agree neither on the ends to be negotiated nor on the way in
which negotiations should be conducted. The Germans insisted
that any talks include discussion of dividing electoral curias
and provincial administration according to nationality. The
Young Czechs would not accept this revival of the Agreement of
1890 and stood by their original aims. They also contended that
revision of the existing language ordinances should remain a
matter between the Czechs and the government, while the Germans
insisted on being a party to all decisions. When the Czechs and

Badeni would not accept their proposals, the four German representatives ceased to participate in the talks and complained
about not having been consulted sooner. Badeni's decision not
to include the Germans before March 23 may have been a tactical
error but not one that would have altered the course of events.
Up to that time, he and the Young Czechs had engaged only in exploratory talks and reached no binding agreement, and it is unlikely that German participation would have changed anyone's
opinion. The Czechs would not abandon Bohemian state rights or
their efforts to make Czech equal to German as an internal official language.[81]

Those Young Czechs still reluctant to support the government
had been temporarily reassured by the party's presentation of a
list of long-standing party demands to Badeni on March 31, 1897,
including abolition of the newspaper tax stamp, subsidies for
agriculture, tax reform, a Czech university in Moravia, and a
Czech gymnasium in Opava, Silesia. The party could not expect
Badeni to realize all demands at once, having offered him unqualified support in return for revised language ordinances.
The majority nonetheless preferred to reassert these demands
publicly in order to reassure the electorate that party cooperation with Badeni did not imply abandonment of national and liberal objectives. Kaizl and Kramář, who since Eim's death regarded themselves as the unofficial party spokesmen and confidants of Badeni, objected to this presentation, believing that
these demands, though well known, would both alarm the Germans
and embarrass the government.[82] The discussion of these demands
revealed two important currents of opinion in the party, the majority that still gave priority to pleasing the electorate and a
minority led by Kaizl and Kramář that put dealings with the
minister-president and the government ahead of dealings with the
electorate in hopes of realizing greater concessions in the end.

What provisions for a language ordinance for Bohemia and Moravia did Badeni and the Young Czechs find mutually acceptable?
In lengthy negotiations between March 23 and 31, 1897, the Young
Czechs agreed to accept much less than their original demand for
the elevation of Czech to full equality with German in the internal bureaucratic service. The proposed ordinances applied
only to the ministries of Interior, Justice, Finance, Trade, and
Agriculture. In accordance with imperial wishes, they did not
affect the exclusive use of German in the Ministry of Defense or
the existing regulations for language in the state railway system, the postal and telegraph service, and state-owned industrial
enterprises, which provided for the use of Czech only as an external language in certain areas.[83] In applicable departments,
the internal official language (*vnitřní úřední jazyk, innere
Amtssprache*) would be Czech as well as German but the internal
service language (*vnitřní služební jazyk, innere Dienstsprache*)
would remain solely German. This meant that the Young Czechs
had settled for a less extensive use of the Czech language in

Bohemia and Moravia than that of Polish in Galicia or than that
requested by patriotic Czech liberals on April 6, 1848.[84]

The difference between the internal official language and the
internal service language should be reviewed. The internal official language within any single branch of the bureaucracy applied to all written or oral communications pertaining to cases
in which officials dealt with the public. The internal service
language was that used to carry on all other business within one
branch and included all inter-office correspondence relating to
internal administrative matters. For communications between the
various branches of the bureaucracy and between any branch of
the bureaucracy and its central office in Vienna, the exclusively German innermost service language (*nejvnitřnější služebni
jazyk, innerste Dienstsprache*) applied.

The proposed ordinances represented an advance for the Czechs
over the existing Stremayr ordinances in essentially three respects. Paragraph 7 defined the status of Czech and German as
internal official languages and assured every Czech and German
citizen who might deal with the civil service that all transac-
tions and records would be in his native tongue. The official
language pertaining to any case would be that first used by a
citizen upon the opening of the case. Paragraph 10 specifically
assured the accused in any trial that all oral proceedings and
written transcripts would be in his language and that testimony
given in another language would be translated for him. The
third change stipulated that within four years knowledge of both
languages would be required of all civil servants in those
branches of the bureaucracy subject to the ordinances. Civil
servants already in service at that time who demonstrated good
faith in trying to comply would then be given up to seven years
to remedy any shortcomings.

The practical advantages of these limited reforms to every
Czech citizen of Bohemia and Moravia was readily apparent, particularly to peasant and working-class Czechs, who usually did
not command fluency in German. The third provision assured
Czechs for the first time that public officials in all parts of
the two provinces would be able to speak their language and also
tended to favor the employment of Czechs in the bureaucracy,
since any Czech there employed already knew both languages
whereas present and prospective German civil servants would in
almost all cases have to learn Czech.

Badeni had driven a hard bargain with the Young Czechs to get
them to end their six-year opposition to the imperial government.
Both he and his advisors among the constitutional and conservative great landowners were pleased at having acquired at a moderate price Young Czech support for the annual budget and the
all-important renewal of the decennial tariff agreement with Hungary.[85] In the process they had defused Young Czech radicalism,
harnessed the more responsible elements of the party to service
to the state, and widened the rift between the Young Czechs and

the Czech Social Democrats and Radical Progressives to the left.

The assurance of good relations with Russia also enabled Badeni to move more confidently toward conciliating the Czechs. He believed, as had Taaffe, that the Germans would be less likely to succumb to already-exaggerated fears of Pan-Slavism or to oppose small concessions to the Czechs if reassured of Russia's peaceful intentions. Unknown to the public, Foreign Minister Gołuchowski was by early April preparing to conclude an agreement with Russia to put the Balkans "on ice" in order to diminish tensions between the two powers which had built up since the Bulgarian crisis of 1885 and the failure in 1887 to renew the Three Emperors' Treaty of 1881.

The state visit of Emperor Franz Joseph and Foreign Minister Gołuchowski to St. Petersburg on April 27, 1897, became the occasion for signing the Austro-Russian agreement on the Balkans.[86] Both emperors pledged to uphold the status quo in that area; and in the event of Ottoman defeat or internal disruption, both sides agreed to seize no additional territories and to assure insofar as possible an equitable division of spoils among the independent Balkan kingdoms. The agreement reaffirmed Austria-Hungary's special privileges in Bosnia-Hercegovina in accordance with the treaty of Berlin. Badeni believed that this assurance of peace abroad would enable him to guide his language ordinances and renewal of the decennial Austro-Hungarian customs union safely through the Reichsrat. Seldom had a minister-president been so mistaken.

The December agreement between the Young Czechs and the conservative great landowners was officially announced to the public on March 27, 1897, by a joint declaration in which eighty-three parliamentary delegates from the Czech lands pledged to support the September 23, 1879, State Rights Manifesto drafted by Count Jindřich Clam-Martinic. This manifesto, which reaffirmed the indivisibility and autonomous rights of the Czech lands, had constituted the basis for agreement between Old Czechs and the Bohemian nobility to support the Taaffe government. The sixty Young Czech signatories of the new agreement also declared their adherence to the liberal party programs of 1889 and 1891 without explaining the several points on which these programs contradicted the manifesto. The independents Jan Vašatý and František Šrámek and the two Czech Catholic delegates Antonín Cyril Stojan and Prince Frederick of Schwarzenberg joined them and the nineteen conservative great landowners in signing the document. Eighty-three signatories had in effect publicly affirmed their return to the policies of 1879. One logical step remained: to come to terms with the imperial government and the parties of the right as Clam and Rieger had done eighteen years before.[87]

The only Czech parliamentary delegates who did not sign the State Rights Manifesto were the five Czech Social Democrats, Arnošt Berner, Petr Cingr, Josef Hybeš, Josef Steiner, and Karel

Vrátný, who countered on March 30, 1897, with an Anti-State
Rights Proclamation (Protistátoprávní prohlášení) drafted primarily by Antonín Němec. The five denounced Young Czech policies and alliance with the nobility and demanded that antiquated
and ineffectual Bohemian state rights demands be renounced in
favor of equal rights for all nationalities in Austria-Hungary.

We the undersigned Social Democratic delegates of the
Czech nation offer the following proclamation against the manifesto of the Young Czech party and the club of Bohemian
conservative great landowners.
As conscientious representatives of the Czech people [Oho!]
and as Social Democrats we stand united with the Social Democrats of other nations in Austria on the basis of equal rights
for all nations [Bravo!]. We protest in our capacity as
Czechs and as Social Democrats against the exhumation of yel-
lowing historical privileges and documents [Oho! applause].
We are sons of our time and demand modern institutions for
ourselves and all nations of Austria.
We therefore demand the abolition of all privileges based
on birth or property [applause].
We protest the attempt to deceive our people by offering
them illusory national and economic advantage [cries of
"Shame" and applause].
We protest against the attempt to distract the attention
of the great masses of politically, economically, nationally,
and culturally oppressed Czech people from their material and
spiritual distress and to entice them to accept the erroneous
way of state rights fantasy [protests and applause].
At the same time we express our conviction that we shall
be able to reach an understanding with our German fellow countrymen, who are our brothers, only when the bourgeois cliques
that today dominate in some areas are in their selfishness
fully recognized and seen through [cries of Ah! Ah!].
We know that the Czech working-class people as well as the
German are today the prey of a gold-hungry bourgeoisie [calls
of "Jews!"] and a domineering feudal nobility [quite right!].
We know that these two classes constitute the greatest obstacle to the political, material, and cultural development
of our, the Czech, people.
In conclusion, we reaffirm our belief that the liberation
of our people from dishonorable political chains, from social
servitude, and from national oppression can only occur
through the victory of socialism [applause], to which we are
dedicated as sons of our time and of our people [vigorous
applause].[88]

The Czech Social Democratic proclamation caught both the
Young Czechs and the Austrian Social Democratic leadership by
surprise. The former had anticipated no Czech outcry in

Parliament against their renewal of the Old Czech alliance with
the Bohemian nobility. The latter had had nothing to do with
the resolution: Viktor Adler wished to eschew all controversial
statements on the nationality question, fearing in this case
that the Young Czechs would use the speech as an opportunity to
attack Social Democracy.

As expected, the *Národní listy* and other Young Czech papers
condemned the Social Democratic proclamation as at worst a calculated insult to national ideals, at best a lamentable lack of
patriotism, and in any case as a statement which could be used
to advantage by the Germans.[89] To be sure, the German and
German-Jewish press seized the opportunity to quote parts of the
proclamation as an argument against autonomy for the Czech lands
and, as was their custom, ignored the points about "equal rights"
and "modern institutions" for all nationalities.[90] On April 11,
a gathering of Czech workers and tradesmen in "Slavic Prague,"
led by Alois Simonides, František Kváča, and some former associates of *Naše obrana*, also expressed their disapproval of the
Anti-State Rights Proclamation as a denial of the nationality of
Czech workers in the name of a socialist utopia and as a sell-
out to the German-Jewish Social Democratic leadership.[91]

The proclamation received more thorough and objective discussion from most Czech Progressive papers, including *Samostatnost*
and *Rozhledy*, which praised the Czech Social Democrats for their
courage and patriotism but believed that they had erred in entirely writing off Bohemian state rights as a viable program.
T. G. Masaryk in an April 16, 1897, interview with the *Neue
Freie Presse* gave qualified approval of the statement, having
been among those suggesting its presentation to Parliament.
While it agreed with his view of natural rights as the proper
basis for Czech national autonomy, Masaryk, like the Progressives,
only wished to see historical state rights subordinated to natural rights, not to have them written off entirely.[92] In *Čas*,
Jan Herben published the Social Democratic proclamation side-by-
side with excerpts from Edvard Grégr's famous 1876 *Open Letter
to F. L. Rieger* in which he claimed that historical state rights
without the institutional means to enforce them "were not worth
a pipe of tobacco."[93] That these statements agreed in most essentials indicated how far in twenty-one years the Young Czech
party had moved away from its original position on state rights.

Badeni welcomed renewal of the 1879 State Rights Manifesto by
the Young Czechs and conservative great landowners because it
formalized their decision to cooperate with each other and with
his government. On March 31, 1897, the Young Czech party promised to cease opposing him in the Reichsrat in return for his
issuing new language ordinances for Bohemia and Moravia. Some
party members, including Kaizl and Kramář, wanted Badeni to retain a "free hand" in relation to all parties.[94] All hopes for
this vanished when Chairman Engel at an April 4 gathering of representatives of the Polish club, Southern Slavic Catholics,

German Catholics, Christian Socialists, Romanians, and conservative great landowners responded affirmatively to their request
that the Young Czechs join them in trying to form a parliamentary majority of the right in support of Badeni. In making the
announcement Engel disregarded the guidelines of the party parliamentary commission, which in accordance with Badeni's wishes
favored an agreement with the minister-president rather than
with any party or coalition of parties. Engel followed his own
and what he believed correctly to be the majority opinion within
the club of delegates and mistakenly believed that the Polish
club in proposing the coalition enjoyed Badeni's confidence.[95]
Kaizl, worried lest Badeni think himself betrayed, sent Kramář
to assure him that the party intended no plot against him and
that the two of them had nothing to do with Engel's statement.[96]
On April 6, the party club of delegates sanctioned Engel's decision, which allowed the party to help form a majority of the
right on April 25, 1897.[97] The revival of the rightist majority
confirmed what leftist critics of the Young Czechs had long suspected: the party had in return for small concessions revived
the Old Czech policy of supporting the imperial government in
league with the great landowners.[98] Announcement of negotiations to form the majority on April 4 and confirmation of that
majority on April 25 also aroused old German fears of a parliamentary coalition that would try to rule against them.

Badeni's majority coalition formed only after Franz Joseph
had, on April 4, 1897, expressed confidence in the minister-
president and his program. Under fire from the German "left,"
Badeni had, on April 2, tendered his resignation because of his
uncertainty whether or not he still enjoyed imperial favor.
This uncertainty had grown primarily out of the emperor's request of March 29 that Badeni maintain a government unbeholden
to any parliamentary majority. But, to the Germans' disappointment, the emperor reaffirmed his trust in the Badeni government
while reminding all parties that it remained responsible solely
to him.[99]

On April 5 and 22 respectively, Badeni issued new language
ordinances for Bohemia and Moravia, confident that he enjoyed
the support of the emperor as well as a majority in the Reichsrat. He presented them as revisions of the long-established
Stremayr ordinances and as the fulfillment of article 19 of the
December Constitution.[100] Though technically within the law,
his having issued ordinances instead of presenting a bill to the
Reichsrat gave German parties an excuse to make an issue of his
action on constitutional grounds. But, by having acted so
promptly to fulfill a long-standing Young Czech demand, he
helped persuade many party radicals to join the moderate majority in endorsing responsible and active politics.[101] On April 26,
the Young Czech executive committee overwhelmingly approved
party participation in a right-of-center parliamentary coalition after overruling all objections by the few radicals who

still held views similar to those expressed by Edvard Grégr in
his famous "pipe of tobacco" speech of 1874.[102] Criticism by
Czech Social Democrats and Progressives likewise did not affect
the predominantly optimistic outlook of almost all Young Czechs.
Their party, now the largest in the Reichsrat as well as in the
Bohemian Diet, appeared to be on the threshold of achieving
another step toward realizing Bohemian state rights and thus its
greatest success.

No one anticipated the extent or vehemence of the German reaction.

The Constitutional Crisis of 1897-1899

Minister-President Badeni's language ordinances of April 1897
for Bohemia and Moravia initiated a two-and-one-half-year constitutional crisis in Cisleithania that saw the breakdown of the
parliamentary system as established in the 1860s and rioting and
street violence on a larger scale than at any time since 1848.
The crisis shook the Habsburg state to its foundations and compelled changes in both its domestic and foreign policy. For the
first time in three decades, observers at home and abroad began
to reckon seriously with the possibility of the monarchy's disintegration. Prolonged constitutional crisis led the Czechs to
reorder their domestic politics and to seek greater cooperation
with peoples outside the monarchy.

The Badeni language ordinances did not in themselves cause
this crisis but did provide the issue that intensified the long-
standing conflict between Czechs and Germans and that dramati-
cally revealed the long-apparent constitutional weaknesses of
the authoritarian Habsburg state. This chapter will delineate
the nature and events of this crisis as well as its immediate
effect upon the Czech question in its domestic and international
aspects. The next chapter will discuss the great turn-of-the-
century reorientation of Czech politics, which entailed the disintegration and decline of the Young Czech party.

The *Furor Teutonicus*

The ultimately violent German response to the Badeni language
ordinances popularly came to be known as the *furor teutonicus*.
But not all German parties responded to promulgation of the ordinances in the same way.[1] The old conservative-Catholic leadership which had been the mainstay of the Taaffe and Windischgrätz governments stood by Badeni and the parliamentary majority
of the right to the very end. The German Christian Socialists,
who had voted to fund the Celje school in 1895, did not immediately declare against Badeni, whom they had to date supported.
The predominantly German Social Democratic leadership took no
immediate action, seeking to avoid taking any stand on the language issue, which they regarded primarily as a quarrel of the
bourgeoisie and which might exacerbate tension between Czech and
German workers. The German nationalist parties, including the
Liberals, the Progressives, the Schönererites, and the People's
party, attacked the language ordinance for Bohemia in Parliament
on April 9, 1897, four days after its issue. The anti-Semite
Georg Ritter von Schönerer, who avowed neither loyalty nor respect for the "rotten" Habsburg state, denounced the ordinances

in more intemperate language than other German nationalist politicians but by no means led the opposition. He merely helped to
inflame a public opinion already hostile to greater use of non-
German languages in the civil service and which in the March
1897 elections had already registered its support for the more
radically nationalist parties.

German efforts to prevent Parliament from approving the Badeni ordinances occurred in two stages. The ninety-three delegates from German nationalist parties began their opposition on
April 9 by using all parliamentary means, including a proposal
to quash the ordinances. After Parliament refused to consider
this bill by 209 votes to 145, they began on April 14 to obstruct parliamentary business. Upon the defeat of their proposal to impeach Badeni on May 8, by a vote of 203 to 163, they encouraged their followers to take to the streets in an effort to
bring down the Badeni government.[2] They did not need to remind
the public that the German left had wrecked the Windischgrätz
government for a less direct infringement of traditional German
prerogatives and a less serious insult to German self-esteem.

The Germans used two principal arguments against the ordinances, one denouncing the ordinances as an "anti-German" measure and the other objecting to the manner in which they had
been issued. The former inflamed tensions between Czechs and
Germans, while the latter led to a constitutional crisis that
discredited the already-weak Cisleithanian Parliament.

The four German nationalist parties claimed the ordinances to
be an insult to "superior" German culture and a political threat
to every German in Cisleithania. Many papers falsely charged
that Czech would become the sole language of administration and
that all officials would have to learn Czech. These hysterical
responses admitted no sober discussion of the ordinances on the
basis of their merits and faults and no consideration of the
preponderance the Germans enjoyed by virtue of wealth and numbers over the Czechs in Cisleithania as a whole. German papers
very rarely reported that the ordinances still gave German pre-
ference over Czech in Bohemia and Moravia as the sole interde-
partmental and internal service language for all departments and
the sole internal official language in several departments.

Delegates of the Liberal and German People's parties, notably
Otto Steinwender, also raised constitutional and procedural objections to the ordinances. They contended that some sort of
compromise between Czechs and Germans was inevitable, so long as
the German minority retained a privileged status, and that certain provisions of the ordinances might have been acceptable had
Badeni presented them to the Reichsrat as a bill rather than as
ordinances and had he more considerately consulted the Germans
before forming a majority.[3] This objection may be largely discounted in view of the German Liberals' refusal ever to accept
Czechs as equals, their exclusion of the Young Czechs from the
Vienna negotiations of 1890, and their attempts to impose

the Agreement of 1890 by administrative fiat over the head of
the Bohemian Diet. Moreover, the attachment which the German
national parties suddenly developed for parliamentary procedures
was nothing short of extraordinary: since the later 1880s, they
had consistently denounced any attempts at parliamentary rule
and called for "a government above the nationalities." When
Francis Thun would as minister-president in 1898 present language
proposals less representative of Czech wishes to a parliamentary
committee for consideration, the Germans would find them no less
objectionable. Furthermore, the Germans exaggerated the admit-
tedly abrupt way in which Badeni issued the ordinances, though
they had grounds for objecting to his excessive secrecy in drawing up the original proposals. The German party leaders invited
to consider tentative drafts of the ordinances had refused to discuss the matter on any terms but their own, although Badeni had
already persuaded the Young Czechs to back down on some demands.

All rhetoric aside, what were the principal German objections
to the Badeni ordinances? Germans recognized that enactment of
the ordinances would preclude any dreams of transforming Cisleithania, less Galicia and Dalmatia, into a German national
state.[4] The Czechs, by gaining greater influence in the civil
service, could exercise political power in the Czech lands more
in proportion to their superior wealth and numbers. A precedent
would be set for the elevation of Slovene to the status of an
internal official language in the bureaucracy of Carniola and
Styria. What most frightened the Germans was Badeni's allowing
the creation of a parliamentary majority of Slavic and clerical
parties. If this majority, established primarily to renegotiate
the customs union with Hungary, also enabled Badeni to rule
without the Germans, clearly the language ordinances would not
be the last assault on the privileges enjoyed by the German and
German-Jewish minority.

So intensely did Germans in all Cisleithanian provinces oppose
the language ordinances that within a month most German Christian
Socialists and the German Social Democratic leadership joined the
German nationalists in obstruction of Parliament. The Christian
Socialist deputies gave in because German public opinion against
the ordinances ran almost as strongly in Vienna and the Alpine
lands as in Bohemia and Moravia.[5] The case of the Austrian Social Democratic party is more complicated. Both Czech and German
Social Democratic delegates announced their support of the obstruction on May 18, arguing that Speaker Kathrein had in one instance violated parliamentary rules of order and that the Badeni
government represented reactionary interests.[6] Both objections
were consistent with socialist principles and past behavior.
That Chairman Viktor Adler had endorsed the 1882 Linz program of
German nationalism before his conversion to Social Democracy and
still wished to maintain German cultural and political preponderance in Cisleithania also cannot be questioned. In his advocating obstruction of Parliament, one can only say that Adler's

German patriotism reinforced his democratic and socialist principles. To allege, as some Czechs have done, that Adler led the Social Democratic party into opposition solely because of his pro-German views is to overstate the case.

Badeni prorogued Parliament for the summer on June 2, 1897, German obstruction having stopped all normal business, and brought Czech and German leaders together to negotiate a mutually acceptable revision of the ordinances. No agreement was reached. The Young Czech delegation headed by Bedřich Pacák offered to reduce the number of officials required to know both languages and to increase the time allowed to learn a second language but insisted on the designation of Czech as an internal official language.[7] Pacák and Herold reiterated their arguments from parliamentary debate that the Czechs had neither the desire nor the means to oppress the Germans. But the Germans refused all Czech concessions because they would not recognize the Czech language as equal to German under any circumstances.

The summer recess also signaled intensified efforts by Germans at home and abroad to prevent parliamentary ratification of the ordinances.[8] German national deputies returned home to participate in popular street demonstrations which in outlying districts of Bohemia and Moravia frequently led to violence against Czech persons and property. In northern Bohemia crowds sang the the Imperial German national anthem, toasted Kaiser Wilhelm II, flew the German national colors, and asked for help from Germans across the frontier. Mass demonstrations in adjacent Saxony and Silesia and expressions of sympathy in the Imperial German press indicated that appeals for assistance by the German minority in the Czech lands would not go unanswered.

By the summer of 1897 in Imperial Germany, newspapers and political and fraternal organizations representing a broad segment of society were taking an increasing interest in supporting the German minority of Cisleithania.[9] Most important among these organizations was the Pan-German League (Alldeutsches Verband) which on June 27, 1897, denounced the Badeni language decrees as "a menace directed against the alliance between the German Empire and Austria-Hungary" and encouraged German obstruction of Parliament and rioting against the Badeni government.[10] These acts merely intensified the intervention in Cisleithanian affairs begun by the League after its founding in 1891. Drawing its membership largely from professors and educators and its financial support from industrialists and army officers as well as professional men, this organization worked to expand Imperial German influence overseas, to maintain German hegemony in Central and Eastern Europe, and to include all Germans within a Greater Germany.[11] To this end it mobilized popular support in Germany for the Germans of Austria-Hungary and in 1894 adopted a resolution in favor of the aims of the German nationalist parties in Bohemia.[12] Pan-German publicists regarded Czechs, Slovenes, and Slovaks as inferior peoples whose culture might justifiably be annihilated in the interests of German expansion.[13] In contrast, no such threats or brutal language came from the embattled Czechs, who decried the Pan-German intervention while steadfastly holding to their goal of friendship and equal rights.[14] The Imperial German government gave tacit approval to the intervention of the Pan-German League and two years later would itself intervene to secure the downfall of Minister-President Francis Thun, the continuator of Badeni's policies.[15]

The riots between Czechs and Germans in 1897 caught the leaders of Austrian Social Democracy, at their own admission, by surprise and found them without any official policy on the nationality question. While Czech and German workers fought one another in Pilsen, Most, Kladno, and Prague, Viktor Adler declared Social Democracy neutral and without responsibility in the nationality conflict, which he denounced as a creation of the bourgeoisie. But on May 18, 1897, he had already announced Social Democratic support of the German parties obstructing Parliament. Such policies could scarcely inspire among Czech workers much confidence in the perspicacity or neutrality of the Viennese leadership.[16]

Austrian Social Democratic support of German parliamentary obstruction adversely affected party unity. At its sixth party congress in Vienna during June 1897, the Social Democratic party reorganized as a federation of semi-autonomous parties according to nationality. Most Czech trade unions had already withdrawn from the central all-Austrian union organization on January 31, 1897, and established an autonomous Czechoslavonic Trade Union Commission.[17]

In the eyes of many Czechs and at least one German critic, Friedrich Stampfer, Adler and his associates had chosen to uphold the status quo of German minority preponderance in Cisleithania. By denying Czechs equal rights with Germans in Bohemia and Moravia, Stampfer argued, Social Democracy had not only neglected legitimate interests of Czech workers but had let pass an opportunity to carry out political reforms in cooperation with the Young Czechs which would help strike at authoritarian imperial power and the privileges of the ruling classes. Karl Kautsky replied by accusing Stampfer of "opportunism" and by equating Young Czech advocacy of Bohemian state rights with German anti-Semitism, an allegation without basis in fact.[18]

Kautsky and Adler, respectively the foremost Marxist theoretician and the foremost Austrian Social Democratic leader of their era, had dedicated themselves to the eradication of social and political injustice. How then can one account for their supporting the German obstruction of the Reichsrat in 1897? Adler had entered politics as a German nationalist before his conversion to socialism in 1883. But neither he nor Kautsky, as some opponents alleged, consciously wished to favor one nationality at the expense of another. And Kautsky, a native of Prague who had observed Czech cultural and national progress, no

longer accepted Marx's post-1848 division of national movements
into progressive--German, Polish, and Hungarian--and reaction-
ary--Czech, Slovak, and Southern Slavic--groups.[19] The two
Marxists nonetheless took for granted the superiority of German
culture and underestimated the popular roots and appeal of nationalism. Moreover, Austrian Social Democracy owed its organization and its ideology to the parent German party, and its German and German-Jewish leaders in Vienna looked to that party for
guidance.[20]

The reconvening of the Reichsrat in September 1897 brought no
end to conflict in the lower house or to German riots and street
demonstrations. In fact, encouraged by German party leaders and
by Mayor Karl Lueger of Vienna, German mobs took to the streets
in ever greater numbers to try to intimidate the Badeni government. Under this unrelenting pressure, the situation in the
Reichsrat went from bad to worse. Schönerer, Wolff, and the
German anti-Semites continued to surpass all other German delegates in inflammatory invective and advocacy of violence. So
annoyed did Badeni become with Schönerer's boorishness that in
typically aristocratic fashion he challenged "Ritter Georg" to a
duel. The ensuing shoot-out on September 25, in which Schönerer
slightly wounded the minister-president, vindicated Badeni's
honor and made Schönerer even more popular among his lower
middle-class followers. The duel was quite in character for Badeni, who from first to last tried to apply the methods of the
old regime to contemporary politics. It had taken him a long
time to realize that in dealing with the German opposition he
was not dealing with gentlemen or with men who would compromise
on any proposal that might limit their own privileges.

Given the intensity of the summer riots and the breakdown of
secret negotiations between Czechs and Germans, Badeni weighed
three possible alternatives for handling the expected German attempts in the fall to obstruct the Reichsrat and to continue
street demonstrations. He could persevere in his present course,
maintaining his parliamentary majority and outlasting German obstruction while hoping for renewed secret negotiations to bear
fruit. Second, he could supplement this policy by selective application of article 14 to enact the language ordinances, pass
the annual budget, and extend the customs union with Hungary until a more amenable Reichsrat would give its support. Third, he
could, were the emperor willing, carry out the coup d'état advocated by several of his ministers and by the Young Czech delegates Kaizl and Kramár. This coup envisioned imperial abrogation
of the law of April 2, 1873, which had set up direct elections
to the Reichsrat, and the election of a new Reichsrat by the diets in accordance with the provisions in force before that date.[21]
The new legislature elected under these provisions could be expected to return an even larger majority of the right. In favoring this proposal, Kaizl and Kramár requested what Rieger and
Zeithammer had long desired. Both also revealed a distaste for

constitutional rule and a dependence on the imperial authorities
rather than on the Czech people. This clamor for a coup d'état
found no support among the moderate and responsible Young Czech
party leaders like Engel, Pacák, Herold, Václav Škarda, and Jan
Slavík, who joined the Social Democrats and party radicals in rejecting any unconstitutional procedures.[22]   How could one expect
language ordinances achieved by force or chicanery to have any
validity? They believed that strength and safety lay in the institutions of self-government, however inadequate, and the Cisleithanian constitution, however poorly enforced. To sanction
extra-legal measures against the Germans would be to lose a superior moral posture and to invite retaliation later.

Badeni, still determined to rule with the support of a majority in the Reichsrat, ruled out any resort to a coup d'état and
considered the use of article 14 to be both less desirable and
more dangerous than continuing to seek parliamentary sanction for
pending legislation and decrees. From police reports, he learned
of the many public demonstrations against his language ordinances
in Imperial Germany and of growing collaboration between the Pan-
German League and German nationalist groups in Bohemia.[23] Faced
with a situation fast approaching open revolt at home and subjected to the most massive foreign intervention in Austrian internal affairs since Franz Joseph had asked the Russians to
crush the Hungarian revolutionaries in 1849, Badeni was severely
constrained in his efforts to restore law and order. He dared
not order the police or army to fire on unruly mobs of middle-
class German citizens. The one instance in which the police had
panicked and opened fire had resulted in the death of a German
demonstrator in Graz and led only to greater rioting. Badeni
could do very little about intervention from Imperial Germany
because that state was Austria-Hungary's only reliable ally and
the stronger partner. He could only hope to ride out the crisis
while his majority in the Reichsrat found some means to cope
with unruly minority obstruction.[24]

Theodor Mommsen's open letter to the *Neue Freie Presse* published on October 31, 1897, fanned the flames of anger and revolt in the Reichsrat and in the streets. A world-renowned professor of history at Berlin, noted for his history of Rome, and
an outspoken German liberal during the sixties, Mommsen's words
carried great weight in the German-speaking world. The *Neue
Freie Presse* expressed its appreciation and approval of this address "to the Germans of Austria," which it featured on the
front page of the morning edition. Mommsen's opinion that Cisleithania belonged within the sphere of Germanic culture and
that the Badeni language ordinances should at all costs be opposed came as no surprise. On July 19, 835 Imperial German university professors had signed an open letter to the rector of
the German university in Prague stating that they would stand by
their Austrian brothers until the hateful ordinances were repealed.[25] The unexpected in Mommsen's letter was its arrogant

and brutal attitude toward the Czechs and its call for violence
to put them in their place:

> We [Germans] had believed the unity of Germany and Austria
> to be finally assured. And now the [Czech] apostles of bar-
> barism are at work to bury the German achievements of half a
> millenium in the abyss of their *Unkultur*. . . .
> *Be united!* That is the first word.
> And the second word is: *be tough!* The Czech skull is im-
> pervious to reason, but it is susceptible to blows. On ac-
> count of untimely softness, much in Austria has become evil
> and rotten. Everything is at stake; to be overcome means an-
> nihilation. German Austrians cannot emigrate from the Mark,
> which they have brought to flower materially and culturally,
> as the Jews can emigrate from Russia. Whoever gives in must
> be given to understand that he will Czechize either his child-
> ren or at least his grandchildren. Be tough! That is the
> second word.[26]

The Czech response to Mommsen's letter began with justifiable
outrage at his ignorance and rudeness and ended with thoughtful
reappraisal of the Czech relationship to a German culture which
no longer appeared so worthy of emulation or respect. All evidence indicated that the learned Mommsen had proclaimed views
typical of the German professorial class, giving rise to a disturbing thought: what must uneducated Germans be thinking? On
November 2, the *Národní listy* noted that at last "everyone can
see at first hand the horrible beastliness and barbarousness of
thought . . . which characterizes the apex of German education
and German scholarship. How can the German-speaking world place
any trust in such a man?"[27] On November 6, *Čas* condemned "the
barbarous outburst of the German spirit which reeks of blood and
iron."[28] Antonín Sova addressed a long poem to Mommsen in which
he scolded the professor for setting aside out of blind hatred
all notions of humanity and scholarship and for forgetting that
a truly great German, Martin Luther, had acknowledged indebtedness to Hus and the Hussites.[29] Even the young and conserva-
tively inclined Czech historian Josef Pekař condemned Mommsen in
no uncertain terms for his misapprehension of the Czech past.[30]
     After further reflection, Czechs began to reassess the rela-
tionship of Czech to German culture in the light of Mommsen's
words and other comparable statements from politicians and professors in both Cisleithania and Imperial Germany. Emanuel Engel and Edvard Grégr, among other Young Czechs, had often publicly acknowledged Czech indebtedness to German schools, German
technology, and German arts and letters, as well as recognizing
that German would likely remain the international language for
Czechs. Although many Bohemian Germans continued to look upon
and treat Czechs as inferior people, most Czech writers and politicians had continued to expect something better of the Germans

in Imperial Germany.[31] The violent German resistance to the
Badeni ordinances and the Mommsen letter put an end to that.
Among those who began the reassessment were retired Young Czech
chairman František Tilšer, emeritus professor of descriptive geometry at the Prague Technical Institute, and former Young Czech
delegate T. G. Masaryk. Tilšer, writing in the *Národní listy* on
December 14, 1897, coupled his criticism of the Mommsen letter
with an attack on the whole Kantian tradition in German philosophy.[32] How could Czechs any longer take seriously the German
idea of freedom? In this article Tilšer anticipated his 1901
work *Kdo hlásá pravdu: Kant či Lamarck a Monge?* (Who speaks the
truth: Kant or Lamarck and Monge?) in which he favorably contrasted methods of the exact sciences to the "chimerical meta-
physics of Kant."[33] He reiterated his opinion that a thorough
knowledge of mathematics and geometry would enable youth to see
through crude political slogans and to recognize the arrogance
and lack of clarity in German idealistic philosophy since Kant.
T. G. Masaryk, in his 1898 lectures at Charles University on
"The Ideals of Humanity" and "How to Work," also strongly criticized the German idealist tradition in philosophy and urged
Czechs to seek guidance from the West in scholarship and politics. Czechs should also continue to cultivate the strong social basis of their own thought as opposed to the selfish and
self-destructive individualism in German philosophy typified by
Kant, Stirner, and Nietzsche.[34]

The Mommsen letter helped inflame debate and reinforce German
obstruction of Parliament during November, as its words were often repeated or paraphrased by German delegates. German professors who prided themselves on being above politics thus contributed to popular hysteria as much as did the politicians they
affected to scorn. In the Chamber of Deputies on November 24,
1897, fisticuffs and the throwing of inkwells began after the
German Progressive and university professor Emil Pfersche
threatened the Czech and Polish delegation with violence while
waving a knife.[35] Meanwhile, secret talks had been under way
since November 20 between a Young Czech delegation headed by
Pacák and a German contingent including Alois Funke, Gustav
Gross, and Anton Pergelt. Many hoped that these representatives
would hammer out a last-minute compromise on the language question, but their negotiations broke down on the same points as
did those of the summer.[36]

Badeni continued to reject all pleas that he invoke article 14.[37] Instead he concurred with the parties of the right
and the Young Czech club of delegates, who proposed that the
Chamber of Deputies authorize its speaker to expel unruly deputies for three days and allow the deputies by majority vote to
dismiss any obstreperous colleague for up to thirty days with
forfeiture of pay. On the morrow, in a stormy session, Count
Julius Falkenhayn won parliamentary approval for this measure,
which would bear his name. A majority of delegates, including

Kramář, rejected Emanuel Engel's amendment to prohibit the use
of force in expelling deputies and to use instead a ten-minute
recess after which offending deputies would not be readmitted.[38]
Kramář, unlike the more experienced and principled Young Czech
leaders, had no scruples about using force. On the twenty-sixth,
in his capacity as acting speaker he asked the police to remove
eight German deputies who had engaged in violent obstreperous
acts. The police did their duty amidst cries from the floor of
"police rule" and denunciations of Kramář as a "traitor" and "a
Russian in disguise." So violent did the protest become that
Speaker David Abrahamowicz had to adjourn Parliament for the
day.[39] The anti-Semitic Christian Socialist mayor of Vienna,
Karl Lueger, then announced that he could no longer guarantee
law and order in the capital and continued to encourage the rioters. Badeni had to tell the emperor that the police could no
longer protect lives and property in Vienna without military
support.[40]

Another stormy parliamentary session on November 27 and additional street riots forced Badeni's resignation on the twenty-
eighth. He thus became the third imperial minister-president to
be retired by mob action and the first since Metternich and Fic-
quelmont in 1848. He retired from public life to his estate in
Galicia, asking only to be remembered by the words of St. Matthew: "I came not to destroy the laws but to fulfill them."[41]

On November 30, 1897, Franz Joseph appointed a caretaker government headed by Baron Paul von Gautsch that ruled without Parliament and amended the Badeni ordinances to the satisfaction of
neither Czechs nor Germans, by requiring Czech as the internal
official language only in predominantly Czech and mixed districts. Meanwhile Germans throughout Cisleithania celebrated
Badeni's ouster by singing patriotic German songs and vowing to
preserve the largely German character of the western crownlands.

Beginning on Monday, November 29, Czechs in Prague and several
other Bohemian cities began to attack German demonstrators and
property. By their spontaneity and size, the riots caught Czech
political leaders and imperial authorities by surprise. Badeni's
dismissal did not alone spark the violence. In Žatec (Saaz), a
predominantly German district seat forty-five miles west north-
west of Prague, a German mob celebrated Badeni's dismissal by
mauling Czech citizens, demolishing the headquarters of the local
Czech Society (Česká beseda), smashing out windows in the Czech
school, and scrawling threats like "Death to the Czechs" (*Tod
gegen die Tschechen*) in public places. Similar German attacks
on Czech property and persons occurred in other North Bohemian
towns where Czechs constituted a minority, including Jablonec,
Děčín-Podmokly, Ústí nad Labem, Teplice, Most, Chomutov, and
Cheb (Eger).[42] Telegraphic reports of the violence in Žatec and
elsewhere reached Prague on the twenty-ninth just as the German
Student Association (Burschenschaft) at the University began
marching in honor of Professor Emil Pfersche, the knife-wielding

parliamentary obstructionist. These coinciding events triggered
nearly four days of the most severe and widespread rioting by
Czechs since 1848 and led to the beating of German student demonstrators, the desecration of imperial flags, the vandalizing
and looting of German and German-Jewish stores, and the stoning
of homes of some German politicians. Governor Coudenhove, who
had responded with restraint toward earlier German rioting,
promptly and with imperial approval called up troops to help the
police restore order in Prague. On December 1, street demonstrations and sporadic violence continued despite separate appeals for disciplined and peaceful action by F. L. Rieger and
Jan Podlipný, Young Czech mayor of Prague, and despite the arrival of imperial dragoons from Brandýs nad Labem. On Thursday,
December 2, Coudenhove finally restored order by declaring martial law and ordering troops to charge demonstrators with fixed
bayonets or to fire over their heads. From all accounts, the
predominately German soldiers and policemen relished the opportunity to manhandle Czechs and injured by blows or by bayonet
and sabre over two hundred rioters and some eighty-six innocent
bystanders. Typically enough, imperial press releases and *Neue
Freie Presse* reports exaggerated the extent of rioting by Czech
workers and alleged without evidence that Czech intellectuals
and politicians had egged them on.[43]

Few Czech party leaders anticipated the riots of late November and early December and were initially at a loss to explain
what had happened. Prominent Czech Social Democrats as well as
Old Czechs and Young Czechs like Anýž, Herold, and Podlipný,
urged all Czechs "not to lose their heads" or to respond violently to German provocation, while at the same time asking Coudenhove not to employ excessive and therefore counterproductive
force. Jan Herben thought it strange that Czechs had demonstrated so vigorously for Badeni, to whom they owed nothing and
who had only succeeded in resurrecting the parliamentary majority
of the right.[44] But such rational arguments appealed to few
Czechs after eight months of German opposition culminating in
the three related developments of late November: Badeni's forced
resignation, German violence against Czechs in Žatec and other
North Bohemian towns, and the subsequent riots by Czechs in
Prague and elsewhere. These help explain the intensity and extent of civil disturbance, as does Badeni's having come to symbolize the promise of fair play for the Czech nation within the
Habsburg Monarchy.

In comparison with French or American labor violence of the
late nineteenth and early twentieth centuries, the Czech riots
of late November and early December 1897 were quite tame indeed.
Many observers, including the new French consul in Prague, Alfred
Méroux de Valois, reported that the Czechs on this as on other
occasions were rather "timid" rioters.[45] In part, the fact that
the riots caused no loss of life and fairly little property damage was due to efforts by Czech businessmen and politicians to

discourage violence. Neither before nor during the riots did
these men urge demonstrators to attack persons or property. At
most, some viewed the riots as a deplorable though justifiable
reply to repeated German provocations.

With the passage of time, increasing numbers of Czechs began
to view the November and December rioting as courageous patriotic activity. Immediately after the riots, few Czechs held such
views except for those younger workers and intellectuals come of
age in the nineties who had participated in or approvingly witnessed the rioting. Spontaneous retaliation against German violence and imperial indifference thus in time came to symbolize
something heretofore in doubt: Czech willingness to resort to
violence in defense of life and liberty. Viktor Dyk's novel
Prosinec (December), written in 1905, remains, despite its partisan patriotism, the most penetrating assessment of how events
during and immediately preceding that month influenced the younger intelligentsia. A lively discussion of the riots by Dyk's
five principal characters reveals each to hold different political views and the author to favor the romantic nationalist, Kopulent, who tries to persuade his friends that Czechs, by resorting to violence, had demonstrated a capacity for national revolution. Hackenschmidt, who epitomizes the gilded and sophisticated youth of the nineties, considers any advocacy of revolution to be horrible if not bizarre. The Social Democrat Brez-
nicka thinks it amusing that anyone should explore the consequences of Badeni's fall: there would be no more than the usual
"angry voters, telegrams, manifestoes, official demonstrations,
and singing the national anthem." The Realist Hilarius tries to
dissuade Kopulent from endorsing revolution and sees in the
riots only a repetition of the events of 1848, 1868, and 1893:

"Don't you know the history of the past few years? Do you
want to have 1893 all over again and then 1894? I'm simply
not going to get involved in that sort of business. The
problem is quite different if defined as a question of power.
We will give up. We are weak."

To this Kopulent replies: "What does it mean to be weak?
Chiefly to feel that way." This young writer, who longed for
national greatness and abhorred Czech material enslavement to
Vienna, argued that the fall of Badeni at least had the virtue
of making Czech youth recognize the humiliatingly inferior status of their nation within the Dual Monarchy and also their ability and responsibility to effect improvements.[46]

Twenty years later, from the perspective of impending Austro-
Hungarian defeat in the First World War, Dyk characterized the
November and December riots by Czechs as a popular and spontaneous national uprising which in retrospect might be seen as the
harbinger of Czechoslovak independence:

December 1897 had no well-defined aims or historical

character. Its hero was the *street* [*ulice*]. . . . It was
spontaneous and assumed an appearance beyond reproach: the
street showed its teeth. It was a mixture of people of both
sexes and of various social classes, types, and characters
who together constituted the unified, defiant and combative
street.[47]

The Young Czechs and the Thun Government

In retrospect, the fall of Badeni appears to mark the end of
constitutional government in Cisleithania and of imperial reliance on the great landowning nobility to manage domestic affairs.[48] But in December 1897, Czechs, Germans, great landowners, and the emperor did not regard any important issue, including that of language, to have been resolved by Badeni's
dismissal. The extent of the conflict and crisis would only become apparent in October 1899, after two more imperial governments had tried and failed to resolve the nationality question
by parliamentary means. Before considering the manifold reaction within Cisleithania and abroad to this extended constitutional crisis, it is necessary to review its principal events up
to the time when the Badeni language decrees were officially
withdrawn.

Despite the magnitude of the debacle in 1897, all parties
still attributed it primarily to personal or party shortcomings
instead of to an anachronistic political system. German complaints about Badeni's procedural errors or partisan policies
were at bottom only special pleading. The German nationalist
parties would never accept a majority Reichsrat decision contrary
to their interests. All their talk of "a government above the
parties" was simply a euphemism for authoritarian rule by the
imperial bureaucracy. Young Czech leaders, notably Engel,
Herold, and Pacák, thought that Badeni had aroused popular distrust by conducting affairs of state too secretly and still believed an open and honest compromise between Czechs and Germans
to be both desirable and possible.[49] A few Young Czechs, like
Kramář and Kaizl, and proponents of a strong central government,
like Ernest von Koerber, argued that success could have been obtained if only Badeni had acted more forcefully or employed article 14.[50] On the other hand, politicians as different in
their political opinions as Edvard Grégr, Jan Herben, Josef
Kaizl, and Francis Thun concurred in adversely judging Kramář's
behavior as acting speaker of the lower house. Only Kaizl knew
fully of Kramář's fanciful vision of a coup d'état carried out
by the emperor and Badeni for the benefit of the Young Czechs,
but Kramář's actions had revealed to all a disturbing ruthless-
ness and willingness to rely on imperial use of authoritarian
measures to achieve Czech ends. Jan Herben aptly remarked that
"to the degree that he rises in rank in Parliament, he does not
rise in the esteem of his colleagues."[51] Long before the downfall of Badeni, Edvard Grégr had distrusted Kaizl and Kramář and

tried to restrain them by vigorous public criticism.[52] Former
governor Francis Thun concurred that Kramář had ruined all
chances of winning parliamentary approval for the Badeni language ordinances and hurt his party's reputation.[53] Josef
Kaizl, who had absented himself from Parliament with a conveni-
ent illness, also expressed reservations about Kramář's maturity
and capacity for good judgment, even likening him to Vašatý on
one occasion.[54]

The conservative great landowners contended that Badeni failed
in part because he lacked an intimate understanding of the nationality conflict in the Czech lands, implying that only a
nobleman from their own ranks could lead Czechs and Germans to a
satisfactory agreement. The emperor, likewise disappointed by
Badeni's performance, looked for a stronger and better-informed
man, perhaps no longer mindful that Badeni himself had been
touted as a strong man and savior of Austria.

All leading politicians agreed that the next minister-
president could only be Count Francis Anthony Thun, living in
semi-retirement at Děčín since his forced resignation from the
governorship of Bohemia in January 1896. The conservative great
landowners recognized Thun to be their ablest representative,
and he otherwise qualified for the highest government office by
his understanding of the many-faceted nationality conflict in
Bohemia and his ability to keep the Czechs in line and tactfully
handle the Germans. He had, after all, smashed Czech radicalism
as governor of Bohemia and thereby helped transform the Young
Czech party into a responsible and moderate organization. His
loyalty to the emperor, his imposing and aristocratic demeanor,
and his Germanophile sympathies, as opposed to the Czechophile
reputation of most other conservative great landowners, could be
expected to impress the German bureaucracy and upper middle
class. Thun, in sum, appeared to be the only man who could perpetuate the old order of government.

On March 7, 1898, at the emperor's request, Thun relieved
Paul von Gautsch as minister-president to form a government
which had as its principal tasks those that had frustrated Badeni: a peaceful solution to the nationality conflict in the
Czech lands and the renewal of the customs union with Hungary.
Thun gave posts to German conservative-clericals, Poles, and
both parties of great landowners. The emperor retained Gołuchowski as Foreign Minister and at Thun's recommendation chose Josef
Kaizl as Finance Minister.[55]

Thun proposed to modify the time-honored governing procedures
of Taaffe and Badeni in light of recent experience. While wishing to govern if possible by a parliamentary majority, he did
not rule out the use of article 14. He also did not wish to
create a permanent majority which would exclude the German nationalist parties. By appointing four ministers from the Chamber
of Deputies and two from the upper house of the Reichsrat, he
gave his cabinet a more parliamentary complexion than those of

Taaffe and Badeni, in which career civil servants had predominated. Finally, Thun decided to present revisions of the Badeni
language ordinances as amended by Gautsch to Parliament as a
bill rather than as an ordinance, seeking thereby to win the support of any delegates who had objected to the Badeni ordinances
on constitutional or procedural grounds. Despite intentions to
rule with Parliament, Thun would use article 14 on twenty-eight
occasions during his nineteen months in office, including emergency renewal of the customs union.

The difficult straits in which the Young Czech found themselves was evident in their support of a minister-president who
had earlier as governor of Bohemia ruled them with an iron
hand. Kaizl entered the Thun cabinet without official party endorsement, but Chairman Engel and most other party leaders did
not object to having him so strategically placed. In fact,
Kaizl's great influence in the cabinet gave rise to German talk
of a "Thun-Kaizl government."[56] With Thun, the party took what
would be its last opportunity to carry out responsible and active policies in cooperation with the conservative great landowners. Young Czech support of Thun on fiscal and other particular issues resulted in their receiving in 1899 two long-sought
concessions: a technical high school in Brno and a six-year
Czech gymnasium in Opava, Silesia, the first Czech institution
of higher education in that province. But the Germans again
managed to defeat in Parliament any authorization to establish a
Czech university for Moravia at Brno.

Although Thun enjoyed full support from the conservative
great landowning nobility, he could not overcome German intransigence on the language issue to arrange a compromise between
Czechs and Germans. He prepared a bill in June 1898 that would
have made Czech an official internal language only in purely
Czech, predominantly Czech, and mixed nationality districts. Of
the 219 Bohemian judicial districts, the bill designated 76 to
be exclusively German, 6 to be predominantly German, 15 to be
mixed, 8 to be predominantly Czech, and 114 to be purely Czech.
Thun first presented it for consideration to a committee of conservative great landowners, Germans, and Czechs. Upon German
refusal to accept this watered-down version of the Badeni ordinances, Thun dissolved the committee in July 1899 and decided
not to submit the bill to Parliament.[57]

While the Young Czechs persevered in their alliance with Thun
in hopes of salvaging something of their 1897 program, the German national and liberal parties, emboldened by their overthrow
of Badeni, refused every compromise offered by Thun on the language question. On Whitsun 1899, these German parties reiterated old demands that German predominance be guaranteed in Cisleithania, thus reaffirming the 1882 Linz program and the Progressive party platform of 1895 in all essentials. Principal demands included the following: (1) "Austria" as the official
name of Cisleithania, (2) German as the official language of

communication, (3) closer and irrevocable alliance with Imperial Germany, and (4) a privileged status for German in all crown lands except Galicia and Dalmatia.[58] The Whitsun program expected the impossible in demanding that non-Germans accept second-class citizenship. It exacerbated the existing nationality conflict and foreclosed almost all possibility of compromise between the privileged German minority and the Slavic majority. It offered the Habsburg Monarchy internal peace and stability only on German terms.

After repeated demonstrations against Thun and Kaizl by the German minority in Cisleithania and complaints from the Imperial German ambassador, Count Philip Eulenburg, the emperor forced Thun's resignation on October 2, 1899, and thereafter approved repeal of the Badeni ordinances as amended by Gautsch.[59] His decision to give priority to German interests, or in Eulenburg's words, "to turn to Germandom," thus ended what several German historians have defined as the last attempt to govern Cisleithania by parliamentary majority "against the Germans."[60] Czechs in Prague and in other cities took to the streets to protest the eradication of Badeni's work as in December 1897 they had demonstrated against his dismissal. The authorities swiftly brought the turmoil under control by declaring a state of emergency in riot areas and reinforcing the Prague garrison.[61] The debacle of Young Czech politics was now complete.

The Demise of the Old Order

The fall of Badeni and Thun confirmed the demise of the old Austria dominated by dynasty and aristocracy and put an end to serious talk of reform by federalization. After 1900, the emperor chose as minister-presidents only high-ranking bureaucrats and relied to a much greater extent on rule by decree. Badeni and Thun, the last great landowning nobles to serve as minister-president in Cisleithania, were men of exemplary ability and character--honest, forthright, and fearless--and justifiably regarded by contemporaries as the ablest representatives of their class.[62] Had "strong men" of integrity, authoritarian demeanor, and Christian conscience been able to make the Cisleithanian constitution work, Badeni and Thun would have done so. Their greatest shortcomings, like those of their Hungarian counterparts, Counts Gyula Andrássy and Kálmán Tisza, were those of their class. All four followed the traditional governing methods of the aristocracy and, given their prejudices and ties to class interest, could never fully comprehend modern problems or popular aspirations to equality.

The eclipse of the conservative great landowners and the decline of the Old Czech and Young Czech parties naturally went hand in hand. Except for the years 1891 to 1896, the majority Czech party had always been associated with the Bohemian nobility on terms comparable to those established by Palacký, Rieger,

and Clam-Martinic in 1861. Recognition that the great landowners could no longer provide effective support outside of provincial politics increased the disorientation in Old Czech and
moderate Young Czech ranks. Where could the Young Czechs now
turn but to the imperial bureaucracy itself? Kaizl had entered
the Thun government as Thun's collaborator and in the expectation of influencing policy. With Kramář's and Škarda's blessing,
Antonín Rezek, an able professor less learned and articulate
than Kaizl, joined the Koerber government in 1900 as a supplicant
for crumbs.[63]

During the late nineties, older Young Czech leaders had given
way to younger men. Julius Grégr died in October 1896, followed
by Gustav Eim in February. Edvard Grégr, his "theatrical radicalism" discredited, had ceased to be the leading party spokesman
after Nymburk but continued to hold mandates in Parliament and
the diet.[64] Since entering politics in 1860, the Grégr brothers
had honestly and consistently upheld liberal ideals and Czech
national interests, though Edvard stated that if forced to
choose between the two he would give priority to the latter.[65]
The Grégr brothers made their greatest contribution to Czech political life by helping to perpetuate the bonds between liberalism and Czech nationalism first forged by Havlíček and Sladkovský. But their shortsightedness toward certain social problems
and their opposition to new trends in politics and scholarship
indicated that by the mid-nineties they had largely outlived
their political effectiveness. Ervín Špindler, Karel Adámek,
and František Schwarz maintained Young Czech political preponderance respectively in Podřipsko, Hlinsko, and the Pilsen region;
but, the day of parties of the notables having passed, they
could no longer exercise great influence in national or in Cisleithanian affairs. Jan Slavík, the leading party campaigner
for universal manhood suffrage, resigned his mandates to the
Reichsrat and the Bohemian Diet in the spring of 1898 in the
belief that he would compromise his liberal principles were he
to remain a party delegate.[66] In retirement, František Tilšer
viewed with misgiving Young Czech collaboration with Thun in return for small concessions whose implementation could not be
guaranteed.[67] Party radicals likewise found the new opportunism
hard to take. Some, like Václav Šamánek, ran independently for
reelection; others, like Edvard Grégr and Josef Fort, remained
in the party to resist the new order as best they could.[68]

Emanuel Engel's resignation as chairman of the party club of
parliamentary delegates in 1900 and his decision not to seek reelection to the Reichsrat in 1901 signaled not only the passing
of Young Czech preponderance in Czech political life but also
the passing of an era in which the middle-class Czech national
parties almost completely dominated Czech politics. Engel's
ability to stand apart from serious intra-party conflicts on issues or between personalities made him the ideal peacemaker, and

his devotion to the party was as unwavering as his view that men
of education and wealth should exercise political leadership in
Czech society, albeit with due regard for the opinions of the
poor and the disfranchised.[69] He continued to serve the party
as chairman of the party club of delegates in the Bohemian Diet
until 1908. That Engel recognized his responsibility for implementing the active and responsible policies that failed in the
debacle of 1897-99 accounted in large part for his pessimistic
outlook after 1900. This pessimism was accentuated by the apparent intention of both Habsburgs and Cisleithanian Germans to
make no compromise with the Czechs on serious nationality disputes and to deny them full equality before the law.[70] As a
Czech patriot and an admirer of German science and culture, Engel had been most profoundly disturbed by the Mommsen letter,
the German riots, and the uncompromising Whitsun Demands which
indicated that the Germans would never recognize the Czechs as
equals. His disillusionment and pessimism in 1900 resembled
that of Rieger in 1891. Engel had as chairman staked his reputation on negotiating a fair agreement with the imperial authorities and the Germans and was more disturbed by the unhappy turn
of events than most other leading Czech politicians. More perspicacious politicians like Masaryk had discerned the probable
failure of responsible and active policies as early as 1893,
whereas more unscrupulous politicians like Kaizl, Kramář, and
Škarda saw in the debacle not so much a tragic failure to compromise as another opportunity to be exploited for personal advancement, in this case rebuilding the disorganized and disoriented Young Czech party.

As Germans within and without Austria-Hungary tried to maintain that bulwark of German preponderance in Central and Eastern
Europe, they inevitably came into conflict with the aspirations
of the smaller non-Germanic peoples of the monarchy but not with
the dynastic and supranational principles upon which the state
based its authority. High-ranking and influential German politicians and civil servants, notably the future foreign minister
Alois Lexa von Aehrenthal, argued that to maintain Austria-
Hungary as a great power and uphold the prerogatives of the dynasty would require greater centralism and deference to German
predominance in Cisleithania.[71]

Ever more fearful of losing their privileged status, the Germans were the sole nation within the monarchy that had anything
to gain from a more centralized and more authoritarian state,
whether *Rechtsstaat* or *Polizeistaat*. This had been evident
since the rule of Schmerling and became especially obvious during the nineties as the Germans toppled three imperial governments in succession--those of Windischgrätz, Badeni, and Thun.
Unlike the other nationalities of Cisleithania, the Germans had
few qualms about disrupting or destroying parliamentary institutions, because they believed imperial rule by decree to be often
preferable to rule in consultation with the Reichsrat. Since

the days of Schmerling, the interests of the predominantly German state apparatus and those of the German and German-Jewish upper middle class had gradually come to coincide as that privileged class compromised its liberal principles out of fear of the Slavic majority and Social Democracy. Moreover, the popular German parties, excepting Social Democracy, had little attachment to liberal political principles, supported majority or constitutional government only as long as it governed in their favor, and readily succumbed to demagogic anti-Semitic and anti-Slavic leaders of the type of Leuger and Schönerer.

The Austrian Social Democratic leaders, dedicated as they might be to international socialism, could not overcome their belief in the desirability of continuing German cultural and political preponderance in Austria-Hungary generally and in the Social Democratic party in particular. In this case Marx's rather mechanistic and increasingly dated interpretation of the revolution of 1848 coincided with their views and gave them the sanction of ideological orthodoxy. Some of the more perceptive German Social Democrats like Friedrich Stampfer and Otto Bauer tried to point out the progressive aspects of various Slavic national movements, particularly the Czech, but their efforts did not change the views of the majority of party leaders.

After 1899, the Habsburgs could only hope to retain their authority if they placated the outraged and powerful Cisleithanian German minority, which, unlike the Slavic majority, was willing to support a centralized and authoritarian state and accept an Imperial German alliance that would maintain Austria-Hungary as a bastion of German political and economic preponderance in Central and Eastern Europe. For this, the Habsburgs paid the price of further alienating their Slavic subjects and compelling them to look increasingly abroad for salvation.

The resignation of the Thun government at imperial request much disturbed the Young Czech party and temporarily isolated it in Cisleithanian politics except for Old Czech and Southern Slavic ties. The party could no longer very easily expect to implement a program in collaboration with its recent allies, the Polish aristocracy and the great landowners of Bohemia, who had lost their leading position in Cisleithanian politics. The Young Czechs, having failed to achieve any fundamental extension of civil and nationality rights through radical opposition in the early nineties or through opportunistic cooperation in the later nineties, stood publicly discredited and internally divided. Their constituents from the peasantry, the lower middle class, and the intelligentsia withdrew to form respectively the Agrarian, National Socialist, and State Rights Radical parties.[72]

Since the emperor had asked for the resignations of Badeni and Thun despite their support by a parliamentary majority, political parties could entertain few expectations of ever achieving their objectives through alliance with other parties. Before 1897, imperial governments had been able to win parliamentary

approval of budgets and the decennial customs union with Hungary
in return for limited concessions to certain parties. After
1900, Franz Joseph made less pretense of deferring to the wishes
of the Reichsrat. His future appointees as minister-president,
using methods refined by Ernst von Koerber, generally ruled by
invoking article 14 if a parliamentary majority could not be obtained. This being the case, those moderate and liberal Young
Czechs most dedicated to parliamentary politics like Engel,
Slavík, and Stránský gradually gave way to those like Kaizl,
Kramář, and Škarda who favored adjusting to circumstances and negotiating directly and independently with the imperial authorities, a variation of the time-honored "policy of stages" to be
known as "positive politics." Not coincidentally, the advocates
of parliamentary rule also had the closest ties to agrarian interests and wished the party to remain a coalition of diverse interest groups. The positivists, by inclination as well as necessity, became more exclusively the representatives of Czech banking and industrial interests. Pacák, who surprised many colleagues by endorsing positive policies, succeeded Engel as chairman of the club of parliamentary delegates, where he tried to
mediate between the opportunistic majority and the few doctrinaire liberals like Josef Fořt and Edvard Grégr who still remained within the party.

Few Czechs after 1899 looked to the emperor for support. Demonstrations by Czech radicals in 1893 had been punished by the
declaration of a state of emergency and the *Omladina* trials, but
violence by Germans in 1897 had been rewarded by the dismissals
of Badeni and Thun. To most Czechs the conclusion was inesca-
pable. In any future crisis, the emperor, the heir apparent,
and the bureaucracy could be expected to defer to the interests
of Berlin and the German minority in Cisleithania.[73]

As the nineties drew to a close, most Czechs, regardless of
political persuasion, recognized that the very foundations of
the monarchy as well as their relationship to it had been irrevocably shaken. In fact, many realized with a curious mixture
of hope and foreboding that the survival of the monarchy could
no longer be taken for granted and that they had best adjust
their aims and tactics accordingly. Few Czech parties wholly
gave up efforts to reform the monarchy, but, at the same time,
most preferred to rely primarily on programs of self-help and
democratization at home and to seek new allies within the monarchy and abroad.

T. G. Masaryk expressed the new mood in a letter to Karel
Kramář on January 9, 1899:

You are fighting for Austria! I am not. Palacký said that
we were here before Austria and that we shall be here after
Austria has gone, but whereas for Palacký that was only a
phrase, I want that to become a fact.[74]

Czech Relations with Other Slavic Peoples
at the Turn of the Century

The defeats and growing isolation experienced by the Czechs
from 1897 to 1900 led to a twofold reorientation of Czech politics. First, Czechs founded new political parties that encouraged popular participation in politics and pressed for extensive
social and political reforms. Second, recognition that the dynasty and aristocracy could not defend them against German attacks led the Czechs to seek closer association with like-minded
peoples at home and abroad. In struggling for equal rights and
national autonomy, the Czechs occasionally obtained Polish support and at almost all times enjoyed the backing of Ukrainians,
Slovaks, and Southern Slavs, all of whom recognized that any
Czech gains could serve as precedents for their own. The Hungarians had also long acknowledged the importance of the Czech
example for their own subject nationalities and feared that approval of the Badeni language ordinances might lead to pressure
for the enactment of similar measures in Hungary.[75]
The downfall of the Thun government ended the Young Czechs'
short-lived parliamentary alliance with the Polish nobility as
it weakened their old association with the conservative great
landowners.[76] The fall of Badeni nonetheless had occasioned
three great demonstrations of Polish-Czech solidarity in response
to the German riots of 1897. The December 12, 1897, congress of
Slavic parliamentary delegates in Kraków, where Brzorád, Pacák,
and Stránský represented the Young Czechs, adopted a four-point
program pledging delegates to work for improvements in the following areas: cultural development, political and nationality
interests, the preservation of parliamentary institutions, and
firmer guarantees for civil rights.[77] At the centenary celebrations for Palacký in Prague and Mickiewicz in Kraków in the summer of 1898, Czechs and Poles again reaffirmed their willingness
to cooperate in resisting German aggression.
Ironically, parliamentary and extra-parliamentary cooperation
between Czechs and Poles reached its acme at the very moment
when the dismissal of Thun ended all opportunities to revive a
parliamentary majority of the right. The Polish democrat
Franciszek Smolka and his son Stanisław had long been the strongest advocates in the "Polish Circle" of an alliance with the
liberal Young Czechs. In his 1898 brochure, *Polen, Böhmen und
Deutsche* (Poles, Czechs, and Germans), the son argued forcefully
for Czech and Polish cooperation against the common German danger and recognized the Mommsen letter to be as much an insult to
Polish sensibilities as to Czech.[78] After 1900 the only notable
examples of Czech-Polish cooperation occurred among parties of
the left. The Social Democrat Petr Cingr won four elections
over his German nationalist opponent from Silesia to the Parliament from 1897 to 1911, thanks to support from Czech, Polish,

and German workers. Czech and Polish Progressives sporadically renewed ties established at the three congresses of Slavic Progressive Youth during the early nineties.

Three issues continually hindered cordial cooperation between Czech and Polish parties: Poles resented the sustained sympathy and support among Czech parties of the left for the Ukrainian minority in Galicia; they likewise resented the aggressive support Young Czechs and Czech National Socialists gave to Czech minorities in predominantly Polish areas of Silesia; and they disliked the traditionally Russophile views of most Czech politicians. On a nonpolitical basis, cooperation between Czech and Polish cultural societies continued and was in many respects reinforced by the growing collaboration between student, professional, and patriotic groups among the two peoples.[79] But, all things considered, the Czechs found greater mutual interests and opportunities for cooperation among the Slovaks and Southern Slavs than with the Poles in the decade preceding the First World War.

By 1900, Slovaks and Czechs could look back on a century of mutual assistance in advancing one another's national and cultural development. Slovaks like Šafařík and Kollár had contributed greatly to the success of the Czech National Revival, and František Palacký had in 1848 first publicly proposed uniting Czechs and Slovaks within a Czechoslavonic region of a federalized Austria. Cooperation which had traditionally been limited primarily to individuals or literary and scientific societies began in the nineties to include political cooperation as well.[80]

Prominent among the organizations furthering Czech and Slovak cooperation, and to which Young Czechs contributed individually, were Detvan, the Slovak self-help association in Prague, and the Association of Czechoslovak Unity (Spolek Československé Jednoty). Founded in 1882 Detvan encouraged Czech and Slovak understanding through lectures and exhibits and raised funds to support Slovak students in Prague and Slovak elementary education in Hungary.[81] Its first chairman, Jaroslav Vlček, a leading Slovak literary historian and close friend of Masaryk, sought to acquaint the Czech intelligentsia with the distinctiveness and richness of Slovak culture. Among the Slovak students sponsored by Detvan during the nineties were Milan Rastislav Štefánik and Vavro Šrobár. The Association of Czechoslovak Unity, set up in 1896 by Czechs and Slovaks, including Jan Smetaný and Vavro Šrobár, proposed to defend Czech and Slovak nationality interests in areas where they had come under attack and to raise funds for promoting Slovak education and closer cultural ties between Czechs and Slovaks. By 1898, the association had established three hundred lending libraries with 30,000 volumes in the Czech lands and Slovakia.[82]

The Young Czech party took relatively little interest in the Slovaks, in comparison with other Czech parties like the Social Democrats, who gave moral and material support to the autonomous

Slovak workers' movement, or the Progressive Realists Karel
Kalál, František Pastrnek, and František Taborský, who publicized the plight of the Slovaks under Hungarian rule and who
helped maintain contacts between Czechs and Slovaks formed during the congresses of Progressive Slavic youth during the early
nineties.[83] Young Czech demands for historical Bohemian state
rights offered nothing to the Slovaks and even implied autonomy
for the Czechs while leaving the Slovaks under Hungarian rule.
Young Czech anticlericalism also prevented any close ties with
the Slovak National party or with the clerical People's party.
After 1900, the Czech industrial and banking interests which
backed the Young Czech party looked to Slovakia primarily for
opportunities in business and investment and only incidentally
for cultural exchange and political cooperation. The Young
Czechs from time to time in the Reichsrat denounced the more
flagrant incidents in the Hungarian oppression of the Slovak national movement, notably closing the Matica slovenská (Slovak
Foundation) and confiscating its funds in 1875 on trumped-up
charges of Pan-Slavist agitation, and the Černova massacre of
October 27, 1907, in which Hungarian gendarmes killed fifteen
Slovaks by firing on a crowd which peacefully petitioned to have
their Slovak pastor, Father Andrej Hlinka, restored in lieu of
his appointed successor. But beyond protests in response to
events, the Young Czechs had no well-defined or positive policy
to encourage political cooperation between the Czech and Slovak
peoples. The Young Czech program of Neo-Slavism introduced after the turn of the century dealt only indirectly with Slovakia
and then viewed it primarily as the vital link between the
Czechs and the Eastern Slavs.
   The programs and ideas of the Czech Progressive movement
spread to Slovakia primarily through younger Slovak intellectuals who had studied in Prague during the nineties. The leading
political group among the Progressive Slovaks called themselves
"Hlasists" (hlasiste) after their monthly journal Hlas (The
voice), founded in Ružomberok in 1898 by the medical doctors
Pavel Blaho and Vavro Šrobár. In many respects their dedication
to both medicine and politics arose from the same desire to
serve their people in a socially useful occupation that had
moved the doctors Grégr, Engel, and Šamánek in Bohemia a generation earlier. The Hlasists enjoyed the fiscal and moral support
of T. G. Masaryk and Jan Herben in setting up their journal and
continued to receive aid and encouragement from them and from
other Czech Progressive groups. After the Hungarian authorities
imprisoned Šrobár in 1906 for having engaged in unauthorized political "agitation" in trying to win election to the Hungarian
Parliament, Masaryk helped publicize this and other acts of Hungarian injustice and in one of several letters to Šrobár wrote
that, despite incarceration, "your authority increases." These
acts helped commend Masaryk to the Slovaks, much as his 1909 defense of the Serbs and Croats tried in Zagreb on false charges

or treason commended him to the Southern Slavs. The *Hlas* group
and other young reform-minded Slovak intellectuals like Jaroslav
Vlček sought to establish Western democratic and anticlerical
politics on the Czech model in Slovakia under very difficult
circumstances and at the same time cultivate a distintively Slovak national identity.[84] They worked with Czech Progressives to
encourage greater interdependence and understanding between
their peoples which implied no subordination of one to the
other. Though small in numbers and lacking the popular appeal
of the Slovak National party or the much larger clerical Slovak
People's party, the *Hlas* group laid the foundations for the wartime cooperation between Czechs and Slovaks which led to an independent Czechoslovakia. At the same time, Masaryk and his
Progressive party proved to be much more influential in forging
ties between Czechs and Slovaks than the powerful Young Czech
party, whose strident anticlericalism repelled Slovak Catholics
and whose ties to urban industrial interests and efforts to
achieve national autonomy on the basis of historic state rights
appeared especially suspect to all Slovak parties. Not only had
the Slovaks never been part of any historic Bohemian kingdom,
but the Hungarians used a similar historical state rights argument to deny national autonomy to the Slovaks. For the same
reasons, the Young Czech party came to have a very limited appeal to most Southern Slavic citizens of the Habsburg Monarchy.

Mutual experiences and interests during the nineties helped
provide a firmer and more popular basis for political coopera-
tion between Czechs and Southern Slavs. Since the early 1800s,
Czechs had identified with and given limited support to the
Serbs and Bulgarians who fought for liberation from the Ottoman
Empire. Beginning in the eighties, Czech delegates to the
Reichsrat often allied with the Slovenes, who represented a na-
tion having a similar class structure and political problems.
The division of the Slovene National party into "Old" and
"Young" factions resembled the Czech example, as did the Slovene
adoption of tábor demonstrations to protest the 1867 Compromise
with Hungary. The Young Czechs continued to cooperate with
Croat and Slovene parties in the Reichsrat, having joined them
in the 1893 Slavic coalition and having given timely backing to
the former in the Spinčić affair and to the latter during the
Celje controversy. The Slovenes joined the Czechs in supporting
the Badeni language ordinances, heightening German fears that
the ordinances would set a precedent for Slovenian becoming the
equal of German in the civil service of Carniola and Styria.

After 1895, the Czech and Southern Slavic Progressives worked
closely together toward mutual goals, exchanging ideas and providing moral support through conferences, journals, and exchanges
of correspondence, and thereby laid the groundwork for the wartime collaboration between Czechs and Yugoslavs which brought
about independence for Czechoslovakia and Yugoslavia.[85] The
three congresses of Slavic youth in the early nineties revealed

common aspirations and similar experiences among Czech, Polish, and Southern Slavic Progressives in Cisleithania, Hungary, and Bosnia-Hercegovina. Repression of Croatian student demonstrations against Hungary and the monarchy in 1895 followed the same pattern as the *Omladina* trials. The younger Southern Slavic Progressives, like their Czech counterparts, rejected the unproductive state rights programs of middle-class parties like the Croatian Party of Rights in favor of a nationality and social program based on "natural rights." All Slavic progressive parties, Czech as well as Southern Slavic, condemned Stjepan Radić's 1902 endorsement of Austro-Slavism and reliance on imperial good will. Czech Progressives supported the program of the Serbo-Croatian Coalition based on the Croatian Rijeka resolution of October 1905 and the Serbian Zadar resolution. In 1908, all Czech parties except the clericals and Young and Old Czechs joined the Southern Slavic parties in opposition to Austrian annexation of Bosnia-Hercegovina, thereby setting a precedent for Czechoslovak and Yugoslav cooperation during the First World War.[86]

In contrast to the concrete steps by Czech Progressives and Social Democrats toward advancing Slavic solidarity, the Young Czech party's revival of Slavic reciprocity under the name of Neo-Slavism, announced with much fanfare in May 1908, seldom passed beyond the level of rhetoric. Largely at Kramář's prodding, the party adopted this program in response to its loss of domestic influence after the introduction of universal suffrage in the Reichsrat and to diminishing confidence in Russia after her defeat by Japan and as a protest against German and Austro-Hungarian imperialism in the Balkans. The first Neo-Slavic congress assembled in Prague on July 7, 1908, with an agenda limited primarily to cultural and economic affairs. Kramář proclaimed that loyalty to the monarchy and Slavic reciprocity were compatible goals. All plans for Slavic cooperation, including a Slavic press bureau, came to naught. This congress and a second held at Sofia in July 1910 fostered personal contacts which in the long run facilitated international cooperation.[87] The manifestly Russophile tone of the congress alienated the Ukrainians and insured that only those Poles would come who, like Dmowski, desired cooperation with Russia. Talk of establishing an entente between Austria-Hungary and Russia aroused the opposition of progressives and socialists among all nationalities. They had no liking for either Habsburgs or Romanovs and feared that such an entente would restrain the Serbs and Bulgarians if not lead to indirect support of the Ottoman Empire. In the eyes of the Czech left, Kramář's enthusiasm for the Russians confirmed their perception of his hostility to popular sovereignty and democratic institutions.

Czech Russophilism, imperial fears of Pan-Slavism notwithstanding, offered no serious threat to the integrity of the Habsburg Monarchy. Russia time and again proved unwilling to aid the Czechs and studiously refrained from acts that might be viewed as intervention in the internal affairs of the monarchy. The Young Czechs seldom talked in terms of Pan-Slavism or Pan-Russism, recognizing that this could only reinforce exaggerated Viennese fears of Pan-Slavic conspiracy. At the same time, they favored establishing cordial relations between the Dual Monarchy and Russia, not only for the sake of Slavic solidarity but in the belief that a better relationship would facilitate maintaining peace and developing profitable trade including the export of Czech manufactured goods to Russia.[88]

Czech Serbophilism was a different matter. Any expression of sympathy by Czechs for the small, sovereign, and embattled Serbian national state could be construed as opposition to imperial foreign policies. After the turn of the century, as the Habsburgs increasingly came into conflict with Serbia, traditionally Serbophile Czech sympathies were especially strong among Czechs of the National Socialist and the various progressive parties. Many of these Czechs clearly recognized that their nation could expect little help from Czarist Russia and that only with the Southern Slavs did they share a mutual interest in resisting the authoritarian rule as well as the imperial expansion of Austria-Hungary. In Czech eyes, any Serbian shortcomings in cultural refinement were more than compensated for by the courageous Serbian resistance to the Turks and then to the Habsburgs. The Czech press in the Czech lands and in America celebrated the victories of Serbian, Bulgarian, and Russian armies over the Turks in 1876-78 and thereafter deplored the Austro-Hungarian military occupation of Bosnia-Hercegovina.[89] Czech solidarity with the Serbs again became very evident after the Austro-Hungarian annexation of Bosnia-Hercegovina in 1908, especially in the refusal of all Czech parties, except the Old and Young Czechs, to vote for additional arms appropriations and in the antimilitaristic demonstrations organized by the Czech National Socialist Youth.

Many Czech parties and politicians of the left and center increased their cooperation with Serbian leaders from Bosnia and from Serbia after 1912 in response to increasing efforts by the Habsburgs to maintain authoritarian rule at home and to extend their and Imperial German influence in the Balkans. Just as the Habsburgs moved to limit Serbian and Montenegran gains during the Balkan wars of 1912-13, so they moved with the St. Ann's Patent of May 1913 to limit Czech powers of self-government by dismissing the Bohemian Diet and replacing its elected Provincial Executive Council by an administrative commission responsible solely to Vienna.[90] When Austria-Hungary attacked Serbia on July 28, 1914, very few Czechs supported that action.

Antonín Hajn summed up as well as any Czech progressive the importance of the Serbian example to Czech politics in his January 1905 polemic against the Young Czech "positive" policies of compromise with Vienna:

It was quite clear to the half-barbarian Serbs at the beginning of the nineteenth century that their freedom depended
solely upon their own courage and willingness to make sacrifices and not at all on the magnanimity of the Turks. Today
a party of the more advanced Czech intelligentsia quite seriously and selfishly pursues the latter course, believing that
to realize Bohemian state rights, we must wait until the German attitude changes and there will be less chauvinism, less
intolerance, and less arrogance. . . .

Let us visualize ourselves standing with such company before the Europe which already knows our arts and our sciences.
Behold the nation which does not want to be free! Look at
the nation which does not dare to be free! Good riddance to
the nation that believes it does not need to be free! We are
a nation of beggars [národem žebráküv]. How often do we not
neglect our state rights struggle because our economic
strength is still inadequate? Formerly we claimed we had to
strengthen the nation economically in preparation for the
next fight against centralism. This is the very same argument being used today against progressive state rights policies . . . and so today we are still a nation of beggars--only
not beggars for material goods but beggars for moral goods.
In no way do we lack gold and silver in our conflict with Vienna, but we do lack manliness and courage, perseverance and
self-sacrifice in political struggles.[91]

The Great Powers and the Czech Question

The constitutional crises of 1897 to 1899 in Austria-Hungary
aroused the interest of the great powers in the Czech question
and its probable influence upon Austro-Hungarian foreign policy.
Successful Imperial German intervention to bring about the dismissal of Minister-President Thun suggested that Austria-Hungary
had become so dependent on Germany that it could no longer pretend to carry out an independent foreign policy. Diplomatic representatives of France, Germany, and Russia and influential
foreign publicists recognized that the political crises in the
Czech lands affected the European balance of power as well as
the internal stability of the Habsburg Monarchy.[92]
The Young Czechs became the predominant Czech party at a time
when Imperial Germany had intensified its overseas expansion and
support for German minorities in Eastern Europe. Wilhelm II's
dismissal of Bismarck, the expiration of the 1887 Russo-German
Reinsurance treaty, and the founding of the Pan-German League in
1891 promised a more forceful German foreign policy and helped
cement a Franco-Russian entente by the end of 1893. The German
Foreign Office took an increasing interest in the Czech question
after Young Czech electoral victories in 1891 and expressions of
sympathy for France and Russia. The domestic policies of Badeni
and Thun aroused Imperial German fears that a Slavic and clerical

parliamentary majority would endanger the Triple Alliance and
led to intervention to help secure the dismissals of Badeni and
Thun. Wilhelm II echoed Eulenburg's criticism of the policies
of the Thun government and expressed his fear of Austria being
transformed into a "Roman Catholic and Slavic state."[93] After
1900, the German government, sensitive to foreign charges of intervention in Austrian affairs, officially dissociated itself
from Pan-German activities abroad; but it had already contributed
to the overthrow of two Cisleithanian minister-presidents. And
Franz Joseph, succumbing to pressure abroad and at home, came to
accept Aehrenthal's and Eulenburg's opinions that German preponderance in Cisleithania and rule by the Magyar nobility in Hungary were the most effective means of assuring German domination
of Central Europe and the preservation of dynastic prerogatives
in Austria-Hungary.

In June 1898, Czechs used the centennial celebration of Palacký's birth as an international forum to advocate again Slavic
solidarity and to publicize their continuing struggle against the
furor teutonicus. They welcomed the presence of scholars and
newspapermen from the various Slavic nations, including three
prominent Galician Poles and Russian delegates from the Universities of Moscow and St. Petersburg. A gathering of the Slavic
journalists present endorsed greater civil liberties, especially
freedom of the press, and laid the groundwork for future cooperation and periodic assemblies. In the name of the St. Petersburg
Academy of Science, the Grand Duke Constantine sent a telegram
of greetings in which he praised Palacký's contributions to Czech
national autonomy.[94] On June 19, Russian General V. V. Komarov,
representing the St. Petersburg Slavic Benevolent Association,
gave a speech that proclaimed Germans to be the common enemy of
all Slavs, thereby arousing anxiety among Bohemian Germans and
imperial officials and embarrassing some Young Czech moderates.[95]
Austrian Foreign Minister Gołuchowski did not regard the more
extensive ongoing intervention by Pan-German League officers in
the same light as that by Constantine and Komarov because Germany
remained Austria-Hungary's only reliable ally and enjoyed support
from most higher Habsburg officials.

The April 1897 agreement between Russia and Austria-Hungary
to maintain the status quo in the Balkans and Russia' paramount
concern at that time with problems in Central Asia and the Far
East indicated that Russia had no desire to stir up trouble in
the Balkans or Central Europe.[96] Moreover, Russia had never intervened directly in Habsburg affairs unless invited, as in 1813
and 1849, by the Habsburgs themselves. Although the Russian
government took an active interest in the Ukrainians of eastern
Galicia and indirectly aided the Serbian underground in Bosnia-
Hercegovina, it had done nothing to encourage the Czechs during
the constitutional crises of the 1860s, 1871, or the 1890s.[97]
In fact the Russians were alarmed lest Czech and Southern Slavic
gains within the monarchy drive the emperor and the Cisleithanian

Germans into ever greater subservience to Germany.[98] The scrupulous Russian aloofness contradicted all Viennese and German propaganda. Pan-Slavist followers of Danilevsky included a Czechoslovak state in their grandiose visions of a reorganized Europe beholden to Russia, but their doctrines exercised little influence beyond intellectual circles and were never endorsed by the imperial Russian government. Slavism and Russophilism remained popular sentiments among the Czech people but never provided the ideological basis for any Czech political party.[99] Nonetheless, Austrian and Hungarian police continued to use Pan-Slavist conspiracies as a pretext for harassment or repression of Slavic cultural, political, and national organizations.[100]

Although the reports of the Russian ambassador in Vienna after 1897 indicate Russian apprehension concerning Pan-German activities in Cisleithania, there is no evidence of official Russian intervention on behalf of the Slavs of Austria-Hungary. In fact, Eulenburg himself reported in 1899 that the Russian ambassador in Vienna believed the smaller Slavic nationalities to be more content in Austria-Hungary than they would be in Russia and that their grievances could be satisfied by greater autonomy in a federalized Habsburg Monarchy.[101]

French and Russian concern over Pan-German intervention and internal instability in Austria-Hungary led to French Foreign Minister Théophile Delcassé's trip to St. Petersburg in August 1899 to insure the continuation of the Franco-Russian Entente in the event Austria-Hungary disintegrated or left the Triple Alliance. Both powers extended their 1893 entente to include preservation of the European balance of power and agreed to put their military convention of 1891 into effect should the monarchy collapse.[102] After the German parliamentary obstruction and summer riots of 1897, the French established a consulate in Prague which thereafter kept the Quai d'Orsay well informed on Czech politics and after 1900 actively encouraged commerce between Bohemia and France.[103] The Russians never took such steps.

The first French consul, Alfred Méroux de Valois, a veteran of twenty-six years in the foreign service including eight years as consul in Trieste, soon acquired great understanding of, if not great sympathy for, the Czech national cause; and, with the approval of the French Foreign Minister, he maintained a careful neutrality in word and deed at official functions and declined to appear at any pro-French demonstrations by Czechs. He was never taken in by effusive Young Czech demonstrations in favor of France and Russia, which he believed, correctly enough, to be undertaken to influence public opinion by distracting attention from Young Czech impotence at home by appearing to have support abroad.[104]

Neither the Young Czech party nor the French government ever considered the other to be an ally in undermining Austria-Hungary. While the Young Czechs sought primarily to win domestic political advantages by Francophile demonstrations, the French consulate

wished primarily to ascertain the effects of the conflict between Czechs and Germans on Austro-Hungarian foreign policy. The
French feared that domestic unrest and constitutional crises in
Austria-Hungary would strengthen the hand of Imperial Germany in
directing Habsburg foreign policy.[105]

French journalists and scholars shared the concern of the
French foreign office over the political crises in the Czech
lands and their effect upon the stability of the monarchy. Comprehensive studies of Pan-German ambitions and Austrian problems
published by René Henry and André Chéradame just after the turn
of the century aroused French concern about the Czech question
and the future of Austria-Hungary.[106] The article by Charles
Benoist in the November 1899 Revue des Deux Mondes on "Europe
without Austria" attracted widespread attention.[107] Scholars
like Ernest Denis and Louis Leger had already created a fine
literature in French on many aspects of Czech society and history. The Czech Sokol and French gymnastic groups frequently exchanged visits during the nineties, alarming Imperial Germany as
well as the Habsburgs, but the Austrian police never discovered
any activities more subversive than mutual declarations of brotherhood and admiration.[108] The French also exchanged commercial missions with Prague with a view to increasing trade.[109]
If the growing fraternization among French and Czech intellectuals, businessmen, gymnasts, and politicians aimed only at promoting better understanding between the two peoples and in no
way sought to undermine Austria-Hungary, it did help prepare the
climate of opinion for Franco-Czech cooperation during the First
World War.

Count Francis Lützow did more to popularize Czech history and
literature in Great Britain before 1914 than any other man. After serving as an Austro-Hungarian diplomat in London during the
later seventies, he spent many winters in Britain actively promoting Czech business ventures, sporting events, and cultural
affairs. His principal publications, including Bohemia: A Historical Sketch and A History of Bohemian Literature, date from
the turn of the century. His leading predecessor in such work
had been Albert Henry Wratislaw, a scholar and Anglican bishop
whose forbears had come to Britain from Moravia in 1770. From
the fifties through the eighties, he informed his fellow citizens of Czech problems and achievements through several books
and many articles. British interest in Czech and Slovak politics quickened after 1900 as Henry Wickham Steed, the Vienna
correspondent for the Times of London, and R. W. Seton-Watson,
the Scots journalist and scholar, published critical and penetrating studies of problems facing the Dual Monarchy and its
peoples.[110] Czechs and Norwegians had followed one another's
similar political struggles with great interest through to the
achievement of Norwegian independence in 1905.

Franz Joseph's capitulation to German intransigence convinced

most Czechs that few reforms and little understanding could be
expected from Vienna and that they should reemphasize national
self-help and seek aid abroad as well as at home. Karel Kramář
attracted international attention by an 1899 article in the
Revue de Paris and a 1902 article in *The National Review* in
which he clearly delineated the threat posed by Pan-German intervention to the Slavic peoples of Austria and to an independent Austrian foreign policy. He proposed the gradual internal
reform of Austria-Hungary and redirection of its foreign policy
away from the Triple Alliance.[111] In doing so, he spoke for
many Young Czechs and for all those Czechs who looked to Russia
for moral support and hoped against all hope for a restoration
of an Austro-Russian alliance.

Those Czech Social Democrats, Progressives, and Realists, like
T. G. Masaryk, who advocated friendship with Russia, wanted that
relationship to be based on reciprocity and mutual understanding.
But first of all, they sought to maintain the predominantly Western orientation of Czech culture and politics and at times cultivated close ties to the United States. Masaryk owed his first
acquaintance with the United States to his American wife, Charlotte Garrigue, and became well known in American academic and
business circles and in Czech-American communities primarily
through his publications and his having lectured in the United
States in 1902 and 1907. Social Democratic ties to the United
States remained especially strong, primarily because most Czech
immigrants were poorer workers or peasants.[112] Many leaders of
Czech Social Democracy had also resided there in exile, like
Josef Boleslav Pecka and Gustav Habrman, while others like František Soukup and Vojta Beneš visited to report on the activities
of Czech communities in America.[113] In contrast to Czech Social
Democrats, the Young Czechs showed very little interest in or
understanding of the United States, in keeping with typical upper middle-class prejudices of that time, and ignored its foreign policy except to condemn American sympathy for Japan during
the Russo-Japanese war.

T. G. Masaryk also recognized the dangers created by the Imperial German intervention in 1897 to 1900, but unlike Kramář
and many Young Czechs, he did not pretend to expect salvation
from abroad. He recognized the limits of foreign sympathy in
aiding the Czech cause, which he did not cease to regard as a
matter that could only be resolved by the Czechs themselves.
These views he cogently set forth in his Velím speech of June 23,
1901, and in his letters to the *Národní listy* of January 10 and
September 29, 1901:

The *Czech question* is not merely an internal matter of this
empire. Everyone who grasps the *danger of Pan-Germanism* sees
the triumph of Czech interests as the firmest guarantee for
the international balance of power in Europe. Our difficult

struggle for justice in this land and for the security of our
nation has won us the sympathy of fair-minded foreign public
opinion. It is necessary that we recognize that no one is
going to help us. . . . Even though we must rely solely on
our own strength, the sympathy of the cultured nations gives
us an uncommon moral strength.[114]

The Young Czechs and the Successor Parties

The fall of the governments of Badeni and Thun led to a transformation of Czech politics through the disintegration of the heretofore predominant Young Czech party, the reorganization of Czech
Social Democracy and the two Czech clerical parties, and the founding of five new political parties. The latter five, founded by or
with the help of former Young Czechs, perpetuated the liberal, nationalistic and anticlerical views of their parent party but surpassed it in encouraging popular participation in politics and in
trying to resolve serious social and economic problems. Because
of this, they were better able to put pressure upon the Habsburgs
and the Cisleithanian Germans. Two of the five new parties--the
Agrarians and the National Socialists--constituted themselves as
mass parties and won over most Young Czech constituents among respectively the landowning peasantry and the lower middle class.
The other three--the State Rights Radicals, the Radical Progressives, and the People's party or "Realists"--were mainly parties
of progressive intellectuals that tried to win popular support.

The creation of five new parties after 1897 as well as the continued growth of Czech Social Democracy and the two Czech clerical
parties may be attributed primarily to three causes, the first explaining why a multi-party system was likely to emerge and the second and third why it emerged exactly when it did. First the increasing differentiation of social classes and occupational groups
in Czech society facilitated the development of parties or associations representing particular classes or interests, beginning
with the founding of Czech Social Democracy in 1878 and the various Czech agrarian unions during the 1880s. Second, every extension of suffrage both responded to and encouraged popular advocacy of economic, political, or religious programs, with the
introduction of a fifth curia in 1896 enabling Czech Social Democrats to elect in 1897 their first delegates to the Reichsrat and
encouraging the formation of political parties that appealed directly to the millions of newly enfranchised proletarian and rural
voters. Third, the Young Czech party failed during the nineties
to resolve pressing social, economic and political issues to the
satisfaction of its constituents, many of whom from 1897 onward
left the party after observing that not only radicalism but responsible and active politics had been tried and found wanting.

Because the five new parties grew at the expense of the Young
Czech party while furthering many of its programs, any attempt to
assess the influence of the Young Czechs of the nineties on subsequent Czech political development should be preceded by a

comprehensive survey of the new parties during their formative
years. It is especially important to observe the growth of the
Agrarian and National Socialist parties, whose success dealt a
fatal blow to the preeminence of the parent Young Czech party.
Such a survey should help account for the steady decline of
Young Czech fortunes up to 1914 and assist in understanding
Young Czech predominance during the nineties in historical per-
spective.

New departures in imperial policies as well as the many unresolved national and social conflicts conditioned the development
of the Young Czechs and their successor parties. After 1900,
Franz Joseph no longer tried to rule strictly in accordance with
the constitution, as successive minister-presidents from Ernest
von Koerber to Karl Stürgkh, using methods created and refined
by the former, invoked article 14 to tax and legislate by decree
if parliamentary majorities could not be obtained.[1] Members of
Czech parties held cabinet appointments in the governments of
Koerber, Gautsch, Beinerth, and Beck, but their power to influence government policy was minimal.[2] The only important reforms
of the decade came either at the provincial level of self-
government, like the Moravian Agreement of 1905, or in partial
response to pressure from abroad, like the 1907 introduction of
universal manhood suffrage to the lower house of the Reichsrat.[3]
Economic development continued apace; but the social question,
the conflicts between nationalities, and the struggle for civil
rights came no closer to resolution. Despite the odds against
success, all democratically inclined parties still sought to influence imperial policy by parliamentary means and, though increasingly apprehensive about Austria-Hungary's survival, continued to work for its reform whenever practicable.

The Dual Monarchy had been fortunate in 1897 to 1898 that
its constitutional crises occurred at a time when it had reached
agreement with Russia to keep the Balkans "on ice." In the decade before the First World War, its annexation of Bosnia-
Hercegovina and its attempts to intimidate Serbia and extend its
influence in the Balkans could hope to succeed only so long as
Russia had not recovered from defeat by Japan and the 1905 revolution. Continuing tension with Serbia meanwhile strengthened
the hand of those in Vienna advocating preventive war as a solution to the monarchy's ever more pressing problems at home and
abroad.

In Bohemia from the turn of the century to the First World
War, the nationality conflict remained as far from resolution as
ever.[4] On the issue of language, Czechs would agree to nothing
less than the Badeni language ordinances as amended by Gautsch,
and Germans to nothing less than the status quo if they could
not realize their Whitsun program of 1899. On this, the issue
that had helped win every election of the nineties, the Young
Czechs ceased to have room for maneuver. The dismissals of Badeni and Thun indicated that the emperor would uphold the

privileges of the German minority at home and defer to Imperial
German interests abroad.

The many proponents of universal, direct, and equal manhood
suffrage achieved limited success in 1907 with its adoption for
the lower house of the Reichsrat. But privileged interests with-
stood efforts in 1905 to introduce universal suffrage to the provincial diets in the three Czech lands, efforts supported only
by Czech parties of the left--the Social Democrats, the National
Socialists, the three Progressive parties, and the Moravian
People's party. Only in Moravia, as part of the Agreement of
1905, did a limited extension of the franchise occur. Some
Young Czechs, notably Jan Podlipný, favored universal suffrage
to the Bohemian Diet, but a majority led by Karel Kramář preferred instead the addition of a fifth and universal curia.
Speaking in favor of the majority proposal on October 24, 1905,
the Agrarian delegate Karel Prášek argued for "universal proportional suffrage" and against opening the floodgates to Social
Democracy.[5] The provincial captain of Silesia expressed a view
typical of great landowners and imperial officials when speaking against the 1905 proposal in Silesia: "God forbid that universal suffrage ever be applied to the diet; for if that should
happen it would have to be extended to the communes, which would
bring reddest anarchy and ruin to the state."[6]

The Moravian Agreement (*pakt*) of November 27, 1905, had manifold effects on the development of Czech political parties.
This agreement, the law in Bukovina of May 26, 1910, and the reform bill in Galicia of February 14, 1914, constituted the only
successful attempts to broaden the franchise for the diets and
to moderate conflict between nationalities in the various Cisleithanian crown lands.[7] The agreement enlarged the third and
fourth curias of the Moravian Diet, added a fifth curia for all
heretofore disfranchised men over twenty-four, and divided all
three curias according to nationality. The great landowners retained their privileged position in the first curia, with greater representation awarded to entailed estates. The Germans held
de facto control of the chambers of commerce and also had proportionally 7 percent greater representation than Czechs in the
third, fourth, and fifth curias than their numbers would warrant.
The Provincial Executive Council was likewise divided according
to nationality and class with four seats assigned to the Czechs,
two to the Germans, and two to the great landowners. The provincial captain who chaired that body continued to be appointed
by the governor. Imperial officials were to be appointed insofar as possible in the same ratios as the national divisions of
the curias. A comparison of the representation in the Moravian
Diet before and after the agreement of 1905 indicates the nature
of this reform.[8]

Old Czech and Czech clerical delegates in the Moravian Diet
voted for the agreement in order to preserve the privileges of
wealth and social status while increasing Czech representation

and to try to dampen nationality conflict. The German delegates,
who had less at stake than those in Bohemia, accepted an agreement that weighted the balance between nationalities in the Germans' favor. Representatives of the People's, the Progressive,
the Agrarian, and the Social Democratic parties, opposed the
agreement as a halfway measure that retained curial suffrage and
favored the propertied classes, Germans generally, and great
landowners. Since these parties were virtually excluded from
the diet by curial voting, save for the People's party opposition led by Adolf Stránský, they protested the agreement primarily by editorials and public demonstrations. On November 16,
1905, as the diet met to accept the agreement, the governor de-
ployed dragoons to protect diet delegates from the crowds demanding universal manhood suffrage.[9]

The Moravian Agreement had consequences unforeseen by the
right. It encouraged continuing cooperation among the four parties that had opposed it while increasing their representation
by its small extension of the franchise. These parties, organized in 1911 as a Moravian Progressive Bloc, defeated the clericals and Old Czechs in a majority of contests in the Reichsrat
elections of 1911 and in the fourth- and fifth-curial diet elections of 1913.[10] The introduction of a broader franchise in Moravia than in Bohemia together with the absence of district
boards helped give the former province more democratic self-
government. This in turn accentuated differences in organization and in policy between the Young Czechs and their former allies, the Moravian People's party. There could be no compromise
between the two on the issues of franchise reform and alliance
with Masaryk and the Social Democrats.

Division on many issues did not preclude mutual interests
among the Young Czech party and its five successor parties. All
advocated extension of civil liberties and concurred on assign-
ing high priority to nationality issues, especially language
rights and schools, and on honoring the heritage of 1848 and the
National Revival. All agreed in opposing clerical parties and
in considering Marxism to be an inadequate guide to political
theory and practice. This did not preclude enduring sympathy
with the workers' movement on the part of former Young Czechs
like T. G. Masaryk of the People's Progressive, or "Realist,"
party and many former participants in the Progressive movement,
now leaders of the Radical Progressive and State Rights Radical
parties. Given the lively interaction between these parties and
the Social Democratic and clerical parties, it is helpful to
survey the development of the latter two parties before returning
to the Young Czechs and their successor parties.

Social Democracy

The nineties brought only moderate gains to Austrian Social
Democracy while revealing serious conflicts of interest between

workers of different nationalities within its ranks. Though
denied universal suffrage, the party won limited access to Parliament through the new fifth curia in 1896 and had been able to
expand its network of newspapers after the 1899 repeal of the
newspaper tax stamp. But these and other advances appeared to
have been partially offset by riots between Czech and German workers at the time of German demonstrations against the Badeni language ordinances in 1897. Joint demonstrations and manifestoes of
solidarity by Czech and German Social Democrats during the same
year indicated the persistence of good will and common class interests among workers regardless of nationality but did not entirely erase the tensions and distrust engendered by the rioting
or overcome the widening rift between the Czech rank and file
and the Viennese party leadership.[11]

The nationality issue overshadowed all others as a newly federalized Austrian Social Democratic party convened its first
general party congress at Brno in September 1899. Delegates
there adopted a program calling for the democratization and federalization of Austria, by which self-governing districts determined according to nationality would replace the historic
crown lands and administer all educational and cultural affairs
in addition to those matters already reserved to self-government.
This Brno program, as it came to be called, advocated too much
federalization to suit the Germans and too little to satisfy the
Slavic nationalities. It offered only long-range ideal goals
rather than any practical means of overcoming authoritarian imperial rule and existing conflicts between nationalities. Nonetheless, it constituted a genuine effort at compromise and helped
hold the Austrian Social Democratic party together for another
twelve years.[12]

Widespread popular support, understanding of working-class
aspirations, and an intelligent and humane leadership made Social Democracy a potentially powerful force in Cisleithanian politics. But several serious weaknesses prevented the movement
from ever fully realizing its potential. A passivity at times
of crisis, evident in the party's indecision and unwillingness
to take a stand during the riots of 1897 and the Hilsner ritual-
murder trial of 1899, arose largely from a mistaken belief on
the part of some Viennese leaders, like Karl Renner, that history or the Habsburgs would achieve for Austrian Social Democracy what it could not achieve for itself. Many contemporary Social Democrats, notably Friedrich Stampfer, Alfred Meissner, and
Lev Winter, contended that an uncritical acceptance of Marxian
theory derived from the Western European and German experience
after mid-century had blinded the Viennese leadership to the
popular nature of national movements among the smaller peoples
of Central and Eastern Europe. Attempts to apply these theories
mechanistically to Cisleithanian politics inevitably led to conflict among nationalities within the Austrian Social Democratic
party, a conflict in turn exploited by interests hostile to

socialism in any form.[13] Adler and Renner continued to look to
German Social Democracy for guidance and to advocate a narrowly
conceived "internationalism" that sought to reform and preserve
the Habsburg Monarchy and accepted German preponderance in both
party and state.[14] Most Czech and other Slavic Social Democrats
in the monarchy wanted an international socialism that would
guarantee the equality and fraternity of all nations, large and
small. Many Czech Social Democrats, like Habrman, Modráček, and
Veselý, who had endured imprisonment or exile during the eighties or nineties, came to believe that few social or democratic
reforms could be instituted and safeguarded unless the monarchy
were first destroyed.

The 1901 Reichsrat fifth-curial electoral returns indicated
continuing discontent with Social Democratic policies among the
Czech working class, as Czech Social Democrats won no seats from
Bohemia and returned only Josef Hybeš from Brno and Petr Cingr
from Moravská Ostrava.[15] After April 1898, tens of thousands of
dissatisfied Czech Social Democrats had joined the newly founded
National Socialist party of Václav Klofáč and Alois Simonides.
Many German workers in Bohemia defected after 1904 to the mili-
tantly nationalist German Workers' party (Deutsche Arbeiterpar-
tei) of Hans Knirsch, a forerunner of Nazism and an outspoken
foe of Jewish capital and Czech labor.[16]

The introduction of universal manhood suffrage to the lower
house of the Reichsrat in 1907 temporarily revived Social Democratic hopes and confidence in parliamentary government. But
the anticipated realignment of Cisleithanian politics on the
basis of class rather than nationality did not occur. Having
achieved representation in one house in proportion to their numbers, the mass parties, all organized on the basis of nationality as well as class or ideology, were not to be satisfied by one
belated and partial reform. The law gave rural areas greater
per capita representation than cities and awarded 45 percent of
the seats to Germans, who comprised only 36 percent of the population. The upper house of the Reichsrat, enlarged by new appointees, continued to serve as a check upon the popularly elected lower house and to be dominated by life appointees of the
emperor, higher Church officials, and hereditary members from
the aristocracy and royal family. Both houses of the Reichsrat
remained as powerless as ever to hold imperial ministers accountable or to circumvent an imperial veto. Furthermore, the
retention of curial voting to provincial diets and district
boards and of class voting in communal self-government preserved
the political privileges and powers of great landowners, notables, and the upper middle class.[17]

Unable to command a majority in an almost powerless Parliament or to overcome nationality conflict within its own ranks,
Austrian Social Democracy foundered. Disagreement on the proper
organization of trade unions led to a formal split between the
autonomous Czechoslavonic Social Democratic party and the

Austrian Social Democratic party, the former advocating unions
organized according to nationality and the latter a central
trade union for all of Austria-Hungary. After the 1910 Copen-
hagen Congress of the Second International condemned the Czechoslavonic party for its views, a small group of Czech Social Democrats calling themselves Trade Union Centralists formed a separate party with encouragement and funds from Viktor Adler and
German Social Democracy.[18] These Centralists and the parent
Czech Social Democrats, now called "Autonomists," ran separate
slates of candidates in the 1911 Reichsrat elections in which
the latter won twenty-five seats, one more than in 1907, while
the former elected only Petr Cingr. Collaboration between Czech
Social Democrats, the Moravian People's Progressive party, and
Masaryk's Progressive party, initiated during the 1911 elections
in Moravia, continued until the war, reflecting a growing community of interest among all Czech parties of the left.[19]

Widespread discontent among Czech workers with Austrian Social
Democratic support of German obstruction in 1897 foreshadowed
both the split between Czech and Austrian Social Democracy in
1911 and the division of Czech Social Democrats after 1914 into
two camps, Austro-Marxists and advocates of independence. Those
Czech Social Democrats who had earlier experienced Habsburg prosecution, notably Habrman, Modráček, and Soukup, led in the
fight for independence. The slightly larger and avowedly Austro-
Marxist group, dominated by Bohumír Šmeral, an opportunist ideologue and editor of *Právo lidu*, opposed the work of Masaryk and
the Czech Secret Committee (*tajný výbor*), better known as the
Mafia, in the expectation that the Central Powers might win the
war and in any event because of a belief that workers' interests
would better be served in a reformed monarchy than in small and
independent national states.[20] At the eleventh congress of the
Czechoslavonic Social Democratic party in December 1913, Šmeral
had also prophetically remarked that any impending break-up of
Austria-Hungary could unleash a new Thirty Years War in which
Bohemia would again be the seat of conflict.[21]

The Church in Politics

By the turn of the century, the Catholic Church in the Czech
lands had not only lost ground to Protestantism, anticlerical
liberalism, and socialism but faced a revolt from within by Catholics who placed concern for national and social issues before
deference to the Church hierarchy or the Habsburgs. Even the
various Christian Social and conservative Catholic political
parties of Cisleithania were organized according to nationality
and could not always agree on policy. The Church could no longer unite Catholics of different nationality and social origins in
loyalty to an Austrian Church and to the Habsburg Monarchy.

Efforts by the younger Czech intelligentsia to reorient and
revitalize culture and politics reinforced corresponding attempts

by Czech clergymen to reform the Catholic Church and to involve
it politically in trying to resolve contemporary social and nationality problems. The Church hierarchy in the Czech lands
prior to 1918 corresponded to the ordering of preindustrial society, with almost all high Church offices, including the arch-
bishoprics of Prague and of Olomouc, held by the landed nobility.
Czechs of peasant or middle-class origin predominated at lower
levels of the hierarchy, especially as priests in Czech parishes.
Widespread anticlericalism in Bohemia and parts of Moravia indicated that many Czechs associated the Church, traditionally a
pillar of the monarchy, with Habsburg absolutism and the Counter
Reformation rather than with the contributions of several Catholic priests, notably Balbín and Dobrovský, to the Czech National
Revival.[22] The influence of religion in Czech society remained
proportionally stronger in Moravia than in more highly institu-
tionalized and secularized Bohemia and accounted in large part
for the growth of genuinely popular Catholic political movements
among Moravian Czechs.

Both Christian Socialism and Catholic modernism, two attempts
to accommodate the Church to social and intellectual change, had
greatly influenced Czech political development by the turn of
the century. While Christian Socialism constituted a mass political movement based on the doctrines of *Rerum novarum*, the
Catholic modernist movement, encouraged by Pope Leo XIII's 1879
encyclical *Aeterni patris*, sought to challenge moribund Church
institutions and dogmas and to spread the influence of Catholicism by using modern arts and literature as vehicles for Christian thought.[23] Through journals like *Nový život* (The new life)
and *Bílý prapor* (The white banner), Czech modernists attempted
to demonstrate the compatibility of Catholicism and modern European culture and aroused sympathetic interest, though little
support, among the Czech intelligentsia.[24] Czech modernists and
parish priests in the Unity of Catholic Clergy (Jednota katolic-
kého duchovsenstva), organized in 1902, sought to democratize
Church institutions and to involve priests in resolving the social and economic problems of their parishioners. But the Austrian Church hierarchy, including the archbishop of Prague, Leo
Skrbenský z Hříště, discouraged reform and applauded the condemnation of modernism by Pope Pius X on September 8, 1907, and the
subsequent dissolution of the Unity of Catholic Clergy.[25] Many
Czech modernists, including Emil Dlouhý-Pokorný, František Loskot,
and Bohumil Zahradník-Brodský, left the Church rather than submit
to papal authority and later helped establish the independent
Czechoslovak Church in 1919.[26] Another, Josef Svozil, rose to
prominence in the National Union for Southwest Moravia and in
the Czech National Socialist party as chief editor of its daily,
České slovo (The Czech word).[27] Those who remained priests,
like Jindřich Šimon Baar and Xaver Dvořák, would in 1918 revive
the Unity of Catholic Clergy and help the Roman Church come to
terms with the Czechoslovak Republic.[28]

The experience of František Loskot, a young parish priest from Jablonec nad Jizerou, illustrates the dilemma faced by many Czech Catholics in trying to relate their Catholic faith to the political and social crises of the nineties.[29] Loskot became actively involved in the modernist movement and in Czech reform politics of the Krkonoše region. He responded to the 1897 German violence against Czech minorities in northern Bohemia by becoming a leader in the North Bohemian National Union and by publishing a pamphlet titled *Jste Čechové!* (You are Czechs!), in which he urged all countrymen to defend the persecuted Czech minorities in north Bohemia.[30] After papal condemnation of modernism, Loskot left the Church, believing that he could not reconcile the Catholic faith with his concern for social and nationality problems. He continued to oppose the authoritarianism of Church and state through teaching and journalism and after 1918 became one of the founders and first bishops of the Czechoslovak Church.

Protestantism, the faith of most Czechs before the Thirty Years War, could by 1890 claim no more than 300,000 adherents in the three Czech lands, at least one-third of whom were Czechs.[31] The extension of freedom of organization and public worship to Protestants and Jews in 1861 found most Czech Protestants of the Reformed faith and most German Protestants of the Lutheran, these two having been the only Protestant confessions recognized by the 1781 Edict of Tolerance. Differences between Czech and German Protestants became more pronounced later in the nineteenth century as nationality conflict discouraged cooperation. This became evident even within the Gustavus Adolphus Society, an association formed to assist Protestants in Austria irrespective of nationality. Czech Protestant ministers and seminarians rarely received a cordial welcome at the German Faculty of Protestant Theology in Vienna, the sole Protestant seminary in Cisleithania. As a result, many, like Jan Blahoslav Kozák and Josef Hromádka, studied abroad, primarily in Western Europe, where they forged lasting ties with British, French, Swiss, and Dutch Protestantism. Still others found in Imperial German seminaries an acceptance that had been denied them in Vienna.[32]

By the turn of the century, Czech Protestantism, which had once appeared on the verge of extinction, had grown to number almost one hundred congregations, its revival having been aided by its identification with the national heroes Hus and Komenský. In February 1905, all Czech Protestants joined to form a central coordinating body, the Constance Union (Kostnická Jednota), to direct common endeavors and provide an antidote to the parochialism and lack of confidence which characterized many individual congregations.[33] This organization laid the groundwork for the establishment in December 1918 of the Evangelical Church of Czech Brethren (Českobratrská církev evangelická), a single Czech Protestant church uniting Czechs of both Reformed and Lutheran persuasions and supporting Czechoslovak independence.

Czech Protestantism prior to 1914 never developed into a disruptive force comparable to the *Los von Rom* movement organized among Cisleithanian Germans in 1898 by Karl Hermann Wolf and Georg von Schönerer and aided by Lutheran churches in Imperial Germany.[34] Czech Protestants seldom became involved in politics because of preoccupation with strengthening their small congregations and caution instilled by centuries of Habsburg oppression.[35] Protestant influence in Czech political life manifested itself primarily through leaders of Protestant faith, including Palacký and Kollár during the National Revival and T. G. Masaryk and Jan Herben beginning in the 1890s. Both Masaryk and Herben shared the anticlerical views of Social Democrats, Young Czechs, and Agrarians and attacked the Catholic Church as a pillar of Habsburg authoritarianism and as past oppressor of the Hussites and Bohemian Brethren. Their Protestant faith also encouraged them to try to establish moral foundations for a democratic society and to condemn Young Czechs for their opportunism and materialistic outlook.[36] Protestant clergymen exercised their greatest influence on pre-war Czech politics by helping to secure Masaryk's election in 1907 and 1911 to the Reichsrat from the heavily Protestant Valasské Meziřící district of Moravia. This support, together with that of the Social Democrats and Moravian People's Progressives, enabled Masaryk to defeat his Catholic opponent in two very close contests.[37]

Traditional Young Czech anticlericalism and powerful peasant and working-class movements prevented the development of strong Czech Catholic parties in Bohemia. Encouraged by Pope Leo XIII's 1891 encyclical *Rerum novarum*, the Czech Catholic clergy of Bohemia and Moravia had started to organize politically during the nineties as the strength of their traditional political patrons, the great landowners and the Old Czechs, began to wane. A Catholic political movement first formed in Bohemia after the Old Czech defeat of 1891 as study of electoral returns and discussion with Old Czechs persuaded clergymen that replacement of Old Czech cadres by an avowedly Catholic party would win popular acceptance for clerical and conservative policies and eventually diminish Young Czech support.[38] But Catholic candidates failed to win any seat to the Bohemian Diet in 1895 and 1901. Even the reorganized Christian Socialist party of 1904 succeeded in sending only one delegate to the diet in 1908 and in 1913. Clerical candidates from Bohemia won election to the Reichsrat for the first time under universal suffrage in 1907, taking seven seats and 11.9 percent of the vote. But all these seats were lost in 1911 due to an electoral agreement between the Agrarians and Czech Social Democrats not to split the anticlerical vote in strongly Catholic districts.[39] The Catholic movement in Bohemia, weakened by internal discord and repeated electoral defeats, then split three ways to form the Conservative People's party (Konservativní strana lidová) the Christian Social party, and the Catholic National party.[40]

A very different situation obtained in Moravia, where Czech clerical parties found their principal support among a devoutly Catholic population in rural areas. In the spring of 1896, Moric Hruban, formerly an Old Czech, and Antonín Cyril Stojan, Th.D., there established the Catholic National party (Katolická strana národní), which in October acquired five mandates to the Moravian Diet and in the following year sent Stojan to the Reichsrat. Hruban remained party chairman until 1918 and first won election to the Reichsrat in 1901. While the Catholic National party served wealthier and more conservative Czech Catholics, the Christian Social party for Moravia and Silesia (Křest'ansko-sociální strana), founded in 1894 and reorganized on a popular basis in 1899, appealed to Catholic peasants, tradesmen, and workers, seeking to combat liberalism and Social Democracy and to resolve the social question in accordance with *Rerum novarum*. Under the able leadership of Jan Šrámek, a young parish priest, this party and its local affiliates for political education and economic self-help enjoyed great success throughout rural Moravia. In 1902, Šrámek set up a Catholic trade union (Všeodborové sdružení křest'ansko-sociálního dělnictva), which grew by 1914 to 410 branches and 32,000 members.[41]

A 1905 alliance between Šrámek and Hruban preserved the dominance of the Christian Social and Catholic National parties in Moravia until their narrow defeat by the Moravian Progressive Bloc of Agrarians, People's Progressives, and Social Democrats in the Reichsrat elections of 1911 and in the fourth- and fifth-curial diet elections of 1913. The gradual decline of clerical influence in Moravia may be attributed to a growing conservatism in both Catholic parties as well as to the coordination of anti-clerical forces by the Progressive Bloc. The 1905 alliance and Pope Pius X's 1907 condemnation of modernism by *Pascendi gregis* strengthened the hand of conservative elements within the allied clerical parties at the expense of those more sympathetic to social change and Czech nationality interests. Both parties continued unequivocally to demand equal rights for all nationalities within Cisleithania and tried to promote the well-being of their constituents within the limits prescribed by Catholic doctrine. But at the same time they favored unity of church and state and publicly professed loyalty to the Habsburgs. They aroused further opposition by their endorsement of the 1905 Moravian Agreement and by their refusal to support any extension of the franchise that would impair the privileged position enjoyed by great landowners and the higher Catholic clergy in the Moravian Diet. They attacked the patriotic Sokol association primarily because of its avowedly secular and at times anticlerical orientation and promoted without much success a competing Czech Catholic gymnastics organization, the Orel (Eagle).[42] While favoring the use of the Czech language in all Czech schools and the establishment of a Czech university in Brno, they continued attempts to reinstitute clerical control over

secular and state-supported elementary education. And, as the
Juda case of 1905 in Moravia would show, even a modernist journal would go to great lengths to persuade provincial authorities
to suppress published remarks hostile to the Church.[43] Given
such conservative policies, the two Czech clerical parties could
not in the end prevail against the parties of the Progressive
Bloc, which favored extensive social and political reforms and
resolutely opposed authoritarian Habsburg practices and aristocratic privilege.

All Czech clerical parties and their affiliates in Bohemia
and Moravia remained independent of comparable parties among the
Germans of Cisleithania and found a greater community of interest
with Slovene and Polish Catholics. In fact, after the debacle
of 1897, the Czech and Slovene clerical parties seldom made
political agreements with German Catholics of the Christian Social or Catholic People's parties.[44] Extension of the franchise
and intensification of nationality conflict had entirely precluded any return to the conservative-Catholic coalition of the
Taaffe era. The division of Cisleithanian Catholic parties according to nationality remained even more pronounced than the
corresponding division of Austrian Social Democracy.

The devotion of Czech clerical politicians to both Catholicism and Czech national interests ultimately proved stronger
than any devotion to the monarchy or the Austrian Church hierarchy. In 1918, Hruban, Stojan, and Šrámek, after some hesita-
tion, joined the Revolutionary National Assembly (Revoluční národní shromáždění) and afterward played leading roles in the
politics of the First Czechoslovak Republic.[45]

The Agrarian Party

Loss of peasant support was the most severe blow to Young
Czech preponderance in Czech politics at the end of the nineties.
On October 13, 1898, the powerful Young Czech peasant affiliate,
the Association of Czech Agriculturalists (Sdružení českých zemědělců), declared its independence because the party had neglected agrarian interests and failed to implement its national
and liberal program by supporting the Badeni and Thun governments.[46] The Association thereby followed the precedent of the
Peasant Union of Bohemia (Selská jednota pro Království české)
whose chairmen, Alfons Šťastný and Jan Rataj, had run independently of the Young Czech party in 1895 to win election to the
Bohemian Diet. Within twenty months, the Association, led by
estate owners Stanislav Kubr and Karel Prášek, increased its
membership over ninefold to 18,362.[47] While readily endorsing
Young Czech liberalism, patriotism, and anticlericalism, it had
reserved to itself "freedom of action in all economic questions"
primarily because of Young Czech collaboration with the conservative great landowners and initiation of legislation favoring
banking and industry.[48] Once the Association declared its

independence of the party, the Young Czechs could no longer
count on that agrarian support which had assured their preponderance in Podřipsko and the Ohře valley during the seventies
and eighties and their electoral victories of 1889 and 1891
throughout rural Bohemia over the Old Czechs. Moreover, since
the working class had never accepted Young Czech tutelage, withdrawal of peasant support from the party, coinciding with the
transfer of lower middle-class allegiance to the Czech National
Socialists, prevented any future reconstitution of the party on
a popular basis.

That the Association of Czech Agriculturalists rather than
the Peasant Union established an ascendancy among the various
Czech peasant organizations in Bohemia helped determine the progressive character of Czech agrarian politics as well as accelerate the decline of the Young Czech party. Differences between
the two organizations were in part reflected by their names.
Šťastný's Union, like the Moravian Peasant Union, proudly retained the adjective "peasant" (selská) to identify itself,
while Czech middling farmers (střední sedlaci) and estate owners
(statkáři) in the Association preferred the more modern and dignified title "agriculturalists." The name of each organization
rather accurately described its rank and file in addition to reflecting the outlook of its founders. The Peasant Union principally served peasant smallholders in southern Bohemia who generally lacked the fiscal independence and entrepreneurial spirit
of the Czech farmers from central and eastern Bohemia who predominated in the Association. While the Union usually sought to
improve farming techniques even if that required transformation
of traditional rural life, the Association more actively encouraged scientific agriculture and the adoption of capitalistic as
well as cooperative institutions and practices.[49] Both organizations advocated higher agricultural tariffs, more easily ob-
tainable farm credit and an overhaul of what they considered to
be discriminatory rates of farm taxation and insurance. But,
from 1897 to 1899, the Association as opposed to the Union thought
that farmers might best deal with these and other agrarian issues
with the help of the Young Czech party. Since the Young Czechs
had never enjoyed great popularity in rural southern Bohemia,
they suffered only small losses from the defection of the Peasant
Union. But the departure and continuing success of the Association, whose leaders and rank and file came principally from those
rural party strongholds in Podřipsko and the Labe and Ohře val-
leys, dealt the Young Czech party a blow from which it would
never recover. A typical leader of the Association and former
Young Czech, like Prášek and Kubr, was Emanuel Hrubý, secretary
of the Agrarian party and editor of its weekly Obrana zemědělců
(Defender of the agriculturalists). He had entered politics in
the late eighties as editor of the liberal Young Czech weekly
Hlasy z Podřipska (Voices from Podřipsko) in Libochovice and supported Young Czech politics until 1898.[50]

From 1899 to 1905, a single Czech Agrarian party grew out of the various independent Czech agricultural organizations in Bohemia, Moravia, and Silesia, largely in response to a growing desire among Czech farmers to advance common political and economic interests through an organized political party of their own. This development was also stimulated by the anticipated introduction of election by universal suffrage to the lower house of the Reichsrat and by a realization that agrarian interests could no longer be effectively served by peasant affiliation with a Young Czech party increasingly dominated by a privileged urban upper middle class. Growing consciousness of class solidarity as well as specific economic interests also encouraged Czech farmers to try to elect fellow agriculturalists to the diets and Reichsrat as opposed to the lawyers or professional men who more often than not had been the Young Czech candidates in rural electoral districts.

On January 6, 1899, the Association of Czech Agriculturalists, under the leadership of former Young Czechs Hrubý, Kubr, and Prášek, former Old Czech Jan Antonín Prokůpek, and Antonín Švehla, Sr., formed an independent Czech Agrarian party for Bohemia (Česká strana agrární) which included the Association as an autonomous affiliate.[51] The new party grew rapidly, absorbing Šťastný's Peasant Union and weekly newspaper, *Selské noviny*, in October 1900, the Regional Union of Central Bohemian Economic Societies (Župní jednota hospodářských společenstev středočeských) in 1902, and František Udržal's East Bohemian Union (Východočeská jednota) in 1905. In May 1905, the Bohemian party joined the newly formed Agrarian party of Moravia and Silesia to create a unified Agrarian party for all the Czech lands.[52]

That the newly united Agrarian party would within three years command the largest Czech delegation in both the Reichsrat and the Bohemian Diet may in large part be explained by the fact that both parties to the merger had arisen from flourishing grassroots peasant organizations. Party leaders had only to coordinate the efforts of these organizations, including the thousands of agrarian cooperatives and credit unions established after 1873, with a view to achieving mutual political goals. As the Bohemian party to the merger had developed out of the Association and the Peasant Union, so had the Moravian and Silesian party arisen from the Czecho-Moravian Peasant Association for Moravia (Českomoravský spolek selský pro Moravu), founded in Olomouc in September 1883 by J. J. Tvrdík and Josef Vychodil, and its successor after 1892, the Peasant Union for Moravia.[53] During the nineties, the several Czech peasant associations had dealt primarily with local issues and had depended upon the Young Czech party in Bohemia and the People's party in Moravia to advance agrarian interests in the provincial diets and in the Reichsrat. Such policies had conformed to the traditionally parochial peasant outlook but, more importantly, had been fostered by curial voting, which restricted peasant representation in the

diets and the Reichsrat, and by the newspaper tax stamp, which
retarded the growth of an agrarian press. Seldom had Czech farmers and peasants ever lacked intelligent or able leadership or
an understanding of their own problems and aspirations.[54] Once
the peasants had won permission to establish a press and institutions for self-help and political advancement, they had to
wage a never-ending struggle against the imperial authorities to
achieve parliamentary representation and freedom from governmental harassment. Given the addition of a fifth curia to the Reichsrat and the growing number of farmers who qualified to vote in the
fourth curia of the diet, the various peasant organizations by
the turn of the century no longer needed to depend upon a political party dominated by other social classes. An independent
agrarian party would not only more effectively serve peasant interests than could the Young Czechs but would win more seats in
the Reichsrat once universal suffrage replaced curial representation.

The newly united Czech Agrarian party soon transformed itself
into a popular political organization with affiliates and branches
in all predominantly Czech rural districts and communes. The
party leadership initially sought to satisfy all Czech farmers,
but especially those with middling to large estates, and to keep
its ideological distance from Social Democracy on the left and
from the Catholic Church and the great landowners on the right.
Agrarian landowners, regardless of wealth, resolutely opposed
Social Democratic proposals for abolition of private ownership
of land and for unionization of landless rural laborers, and
most continued to espouse anticlericalism and oppose any party
alliance with their former masters, the great landowners.[55] Beyond agreement on these and on most tariff and credit questions,
the difference in interests between small holders and larger estate owners precluded harmony within the party. Party leaders,
drawn primarily from the Association of Czech Agriculturalists,
in which estate owners and middling farmers had predominated,
talked of following a middle way but usually deferred to their
own interests.[56] On January 18, 1903, the Bohemian party had
adopted a program that reflected the anticlericalism and peasant
conservatism of Šťastný as well as fears of popular sovereignty
on the part of estate owners like Karel Prášek, Stanislav Kubr,
and Jan Dvořák.[57] That program proposed to extend curial suffrage to include all landowning peasants but exclude the rural
and urban proletariat.[58]

At the first congress of the united Czech Agrarian party in
December 1905, the more democratic party elements, led by Antonín Švehla, Jr., from Hostivař, Bohemia, and by František Staněk
and almost all delegates from Moravia, overwhelmed the right
wing and largely repealed the conservative program of 1903. The
party reaffirmed Šťastný's ardent anticlericalism and praise of
peasant ties to soil and homeland but not his scepticism about
modern technology and institutions and his strident advocacy of

atheistic freethought. The party gave priority to the interests of the small and medium landholders who predominated among
the Czech peasantry--interests often identical to those of the
estate owners--promoted scientific agriculture, and for the
first time came out in favor of universal suffrage. This program received further impetus during the next three years as
Šťastný's retirement and Kubr's death in a railway accident
hastened the transfer of party leadership to younger and more
progressive men who had entered politics during the nineties.
Antonín Švehla, Jr., a vigorous young man of thirty-five known
as an able organizer and master at compromise, won election in
1908 as chairman of the Agrarian delegation to the Bohemian Diet
and in 1909 as chairman of the party executive committee. He
was ably seconded by František Staněk, party vice-chairman and
head of its delegation to the Moravian Diet, and František
Udržal, chairman of the party delegates in the Reichsrat, who
had until 1903 been an outspokenly liberal Young Czech. The
three men respectively represented as well as personified three
of the largest constituencies in the party: the recently enfranchised and well-educated middling farmers determined to advance
their interests in the political arena, the rural Moravian Czechs
with a long tradition of cooperative endeavor and political activism, and the prosperous liberal-minded farmers of central,
northern, and eastern Bohemia who had heretofore constituted the
backbone of the Young Czech party in rural districts.

The three new chairmen sought to arouse greater popular support for the Agrarian party by further "democratizing" its platforms and organization.[59] To emphasize the unity of agrarian
interests, the party adopted the slogan, "The countryside is one
big family."[60] It added a daily, *Venkov* (The Countryside), to
its several weeklies and regional publications in 1906 and set
up its own publishing firm in 1907. Party affiliates expanded
by 1912 to include a bank and at least 2,150 producers' and consumers' cooperatives and even an organization of Agrarian Women
and Girls (Organisace agrarních žen a dívek).[61] In accordance
with the 1905 merger, a central executive committee in Prague
directed the manifold activities of the party through executive
committees in each province and branches in all predominantly
Czech rural communes. The continuing independence of spirit of
party affiliates and cooperatives helped insure that the party
remained responsible to the rural electorate.

"Democratization" of policies and party organization helped
the Agrarians achieve electoral success. In 1907 they became
the largest Czech party in the Reichsrat and in 1908 the largest
Czech party in the Bohemian Diet.[62] The Agrarians swept the
fourth or rural curia, while the Young Czechs could not win
enough seats in the urban second and third curias against their
National Socialist and Progressive rivals to overcome the Agrarian lead.

Agrarian victories in the 1907 Reichsrat elections enabled

Karel Prášek to succeed Young Czech Bedřich Pacák in the Bech
government as Minister without Portfolio for Czech Affairs
(Ministr krajan). In the 1901 Reichsrat elections, the Agrarians had won six seats in the fifth curia and ranked second only
to the Young Czechs in number of Czech representatives from all
curias. Under universal suffrage in 1907 and 1911, they outpolled all Czech parties except Social Democracy but sent more
delegates to the Reichsrat than the Social Democrats because of
the greater representation given rural as opposed to urban electoral districts.[63] The Agrarian politicians who had entered politics under the tutelage of the Young Czechs thus eclipsed
their parent party as the leading Czech parliamentary delegation.
Thereafter in seeking electoral agreements with the Agrarians,
Young Czechs had to approach them as equals.

Agrarian success came more slowly in Moravia, where the party
labored against powerful Catholic opposition, winning there only
four of its twenty-eight seats in the 1907 Reichsrat elections.
In 1911, under Staněk's leadership, the Agrarians of Moravia
moved to the left, joining the Social Democrats and the liberal
Moravian People's Progressives to form a Moravian Progressive
Bloc directed against the united Czech clerical Christian Social
and Catholic National parties. Victories by the Progressive
Bloc in the 1911 Reichsrat and 1913 diet elections attested to
the wisdom of this policy and to the success of Staněk and his
associates in establishing the party in Moravia "on a firm liberal and popular basis."[64]

The success of "democratization" in winning votes and in creating a mass Agrarian party organization led to the secession in
1911 of some larger estate owners, led by Karel Prášek and Isi-
dor Zahradník, who in December 1911 founded their own small party, the Independent Association of the Bohemian Countryside
(Neodvislé sdružení venkova pro království České). The departure of these conservatives further confirmed Švehla's leadership as well as the popular character of the Agrarian party.[65]
Beginning in 1912, the party began to take a livelier interest
in Slovak affairs, entering into agreements with Slovak peasant
associations for greater Czech investment in rural Slovakia and
for the training of 145 Slovak students in Czech agricultural
schools.[66] At the same time, the party worked in concert with
other Czech parties through the National Council on matters of
mutual interest like protesting imperial closure of the Bohemian
Diet in May 1913.[67]

Mass party organization and electoral victories complemented
continuing efforts by Agrarian party leaders to insure the fiscal independence of Czech landholders as both producers and consumers.[68] Toward this end, the party helped coordinate the ac-
cumulation of capital by the thousands of local agrarian cooperatives and credit unions. The success of these efforts led the
party and its affiliate, the Central Union of Czech Economic
Societies (Ústřední jednota českých hospodářských společenstev),

to establish in February 1911 their own Agrarian Bank (Agrární
banka) capitalized at 2 million crowns. The new bank served as
an independent central bank and clearinghouse for the various
party affiliates and the many local agrarian savings and loan
associations. Meanwhile, with a view to influencing national
banking and credit policies, the party and its affiliates had
begun to buy shares in leading Czech banks which held extensive
mortgages on or liens against farms. Experience in management
of the "Slavic" insurance bank that it helped found in 1909 encouraged the party to set up its own, and the first Czech, mutual insurance company in 1911.[69] Investments of the Agrarian
Bank were directed not only toward improving agricultural production but toward helping Czech agrarian organizations acquire
greater control over the principal food-processing industries,
especially distilleries and breweries, fertilizer plants, tan-
neries, mills, and beet sugar refineries. By December 1914, the
Agrarian Bank, with capital stock of 4 million crowns and total
assets in excess of 22 million crowns, was ninth in size among
all Czech banking institutions.[70]

As the Živnobanka had assured the fiscal independence of
Czech industry and Czech patriotic associations from Viennese
capital, so did the Agrarian Bank help free Czech agrarian organizations from dependence upon Czech as well as Viennese industrial and commercial banks. Foremost among these remained
the Central Union of Czech Sugar Beet Growers (Ústřední jednota
českých reparů). Having acquired considerable fiscal autonomy
and after 1907 the largest Czech delegation in the Reichsrat,
the Agrarian party could bargain directly with imperial governments for tax relief and subsidies to landowners. Fifty-two
million crowns in relief thus flowed into Bohemia, 37 million
into Polabí alone.[71] To insure that these subsidies were used
to further agrarian needs, the party's Czech delegation in the
Bohemian Diet secured a majority of seats on the body responsible
to the Provincial Executive Council for disbursing all such funds,
the Czech section of the Provincial Agricultural Council (Český odbor zemské zemědělské rady). Young Czech loss of preponderance on this body as well as their loss of the fourth curia of
the Bohemian Diet to the Agrarians by 1908 reduced Young Czech
influence in rural Bohemia to zero. This hurt the party badly
and left it more than ever beholden to commercial and industrial
interests.

The Czech Agrarian party was a successful response to specific economic needs and to a growing class consciousness among
Czech peasants, who realized that their interests and aspirations would not be served by subordination to either Young Czechs
or great landowners. In organization and in policy, the party
more closely resembled agrarian parties in the smaller Western
nations of Denmark, Norway, and Switzerland than those elsewhere
in Eastern Europe. Like most peasant parties, the Czech Agrarian
party opposed policies favorable to big business and sought to

curtail privileges of the aristocracy. But, thanks in part to
its Young Czech heritage, it sought to extend civil liberties
and Bohemian state rights and, unlike Croatian, Slovenian, or
Slovak peasant movements, it became an avowedly anticlerical
party. Besides upholding the material interests of Czech farmers, the party advocated broader suffrage, greater authority
for local and provincial self-government and full equality of
the Czech language with German in the civil service in Bohemia
and Moravia. By resolutely defending the principle of private
property and the interests of landholders, large and small, the
party often neglected the needs of the landless rural poor.
Nonetheless, it contributed to the growing democratization of
Czech political life by encouraging peasant participation in politics, by criticizing authoritarian imperial practices, and by
seeking to diminish domination of provincial and district self-
government by notables and men of wealth. Its great popular
support among Czech peasants precluded the successful establishment of any Cisleithanian peasant party under Catholic or imperial auspices as well as any reassertion of Young Czech influence
in the Bohemian countryside.

The Czech National Socialist Party

The Czech National Socialist party (Strana národně sociální)
captured the next-to-largest share of the original Young Czech
constituency, competing with the Young Czechs for the four-
gulden vote in the third curia while the Agrarians overwhelmed
them in the fourth. An assembly of Czech workers and tradesmen
in Prague from April 9 to 11, 1898, founded this party under the
leadership of Vaclav J. Klofáč, veteran of the Progressive movement and an editor of the Národní listy, and Alois Simonides,
editor of Český dělník (The Czech worker) and a draper by trade.[72]
The party preached patriotism along with social reform in the
tradition of Josef Barák and Naše obrana, capitalizing on Czech
working-class discontent with the pro-German bias of Austrian
Social Democracy and on lower middle-class dissatisfaction with
Young Czech deference to banking and industrial interests and
participation in the Thun government. It promised to promote the
material welfare of the working and lower middle classes and to
win greater civil liberties for all citizens, including "the reordering of the Czech state on the broadest democratic basis in
province, region, district, and commune: the will of the majority must unconditionally receive public expression."[73] The party
did not hold class conflict to be irreconcilable and therefore
expressed willingness to collaborate with middle-class parties
under favorable circumstances. In contrast to the proletarian
internationalism of Social Democracy, the Czech National Socialists emphasized Slavic solidarity and usually ended party meetings with the singing of "Hej Slovane."[74]
The National Socialist party first revealed its strength by

winning four seats in the 1901 fifth-curial elections to the
Reichsrat, as the working-class strongholds of Kladno, Slany,
and Smíchov chose Klofáč and the Czech Social Democrats failed
to carry any districts. A comparison of fifth-curial returns in
1901 with those of 1897 shows that the National Socialists took
almost as many seats and votes away from the Young Czechs as they
did from Social Democracy.[75] Under universal suffrage in 1907,
they increased their representation to nine seats in alliance
with the smaller Radical Progressive and State Rights Radical
parties.

At their third party congress in September 1902, the National
Socialists adopted a comprehensive program based upon patriotic,
democratic, anticlerical, and socialist principles, supplement-
ing the programs of 1898 and 1901 and replacing the hastily prepared and at times demagogic manifestoes on which they had often
heretofore relied. The program of the third congress constituted the basis for all pre-war party platforms. It advocated
guaranteed civil liberties, universal suffrage for women as well
as men, and greater autonomy for all peoples of Cisleithania,
while eschewing anti-Semitism and promising to oppose the authoritarian Koerber government. The preamble asserted that the
party "originated on the one hand in opposition to German oppression of the Czech nationality and on the other hand in opposition to contemporary legal and social injustices in the Czech
lands."[76] It reiterated traditional views that national and social liberation must go hand in hand, that class conflicts could
be reconciled, and that the Slavic peoples should stand together.
The red carnation became a popular party symbol, providing a
fragrance that nicely complemented the flowery speeches of party
leaders. "Equality among nations and equality in the nation"
proved to be a very effective slogan.[77]

Václav Choc, Alois Simonides, and Jan Vorel, able political
veterans of the nineties, took the lead in establishing an extensive organization and in providing intellectual leadership
for the National Socialist party. Václav J. Klofáč, an accom-
plished rabble-rouser of amiable nature and undisciplined intellect, became the party's chairman and leading spokesman. His
stirring speeches, his common touch and unfailingly courteous
and unaffected demeanor, and his genuine affection for his constituents best account for his great popularity. Having come
from a poor tailor's family, he intimately understood poverty
and working-class aspirations. He had grown up in Havlíček's
home town of Německý Brod and from an early age had idolized the
great journalist. His heroes as a young man were Josef Barák
and the Grégr brothers, who by example led him to make a career
of journalism and become an editor of the *Národní listy* in 1890
at the age of twenty-two. Klofáč always remained a man of much
greater style than substance and an enormously popular figure
with the party rank and file. Of all Czech politicians after

the turn of the century, he best perpetuated traditional Young
Czech radicalism.[78]

All but excluded from district and provincial self-government
by curial voting, the National Socialists, like the Social Democrats and Agrarians, concentrated on winning Reichsrat elections
and on building up an extensive party organization at all levels,
including trade unions, newspapers, and special auxiliaries.
One such auxiliary, the National Socialist Youth (Národně soci-
alistická mládež), directed by Emil Špatný, Alois Hatina, and
Matěj Teichman, led antimilitarist demonstrations in January and
March 1909 which resulted in mass arrests and strengthened the
radical and antidynastic sentiments of younger party members.[79]
The National Socialist Youth had organized not only to protest
military conscription and high expenditures on armaments but to
demonstrate their sympathy with Serbia in resisting Austro-
Hungarian imperialism in the Balkans. In 1908, National Socialist deputies in the Reichsrat united with T. G. Masaryk, Czech
Social Democrats, and Czech State Rights Progressives in speaking against the imperial annexation of Bosnia-Hercegovina and in
castigating Kramář and the Young Czechs for refusing to join
them in opposition.

The National Socialist party strongly reaffirmed its socialist nature in preparation for the 1911 Reichsrat elections, believing that it could thus best prevail against its more conservative competitors, the Young Czechs and the State Rights Progressives.[80] Like other Czech parties of the left, it condemned
the Bohemian state rights program as a subterfuge for maintaining the preponderance of notables and men of property in district and provincial government.[81] The elections vindicated the
party's leftward stance and revealed growing popular dissatisfaction with state rights parties, as the National Socialists
won 28 percent more votes than in 1907 and outpolled the Young
Czech party by a margin of 1.7:1. That they could amass only
27 percent as many votes as Czechoslavonic Social Democracy indicated that they had not made enormous inroads into the working-
class vote.[82] By 1912, they operated fifty-one trade unions
with 72,076 members, a daily, České slovo (The Czech word), and
several monthlies including Česká Demokracie (Czech democracy)
and Sociální Reforma (Social reform). Like the Young Czech party, they received little support from Moravia, where in 1911
they won only 2.2 percent of the vote and one of their fourteen
Reichsrat seats and where two years later only 3,400 of their
83,384 members resided.[83]

In Bohemia, the Czech National Socialist party held the balance of power between the Young Czechs and the Social Democrats
in parliamentary elections from urban and industrial districts.
The Young Czechs could defeat the Social Democrats only by agreeing with the National Socialists to run a single non-Marxist
candidate in any district. This the latter were often reluctant

to do, for they could generally outpoll the Young Czechs in such
districts and had no fear of the Young Czech and Social Democratic parties ever combining against them. As it had always
done, the National Socialist party drew as many votes away from
Young Czechs as it did from Social Democrats and revealed itself
in theory and in practice to be an heir of later nineteenth-century Young Czech radicalism.

People's Progressives in Moravia

After 1899, the Young Czechs gradually lost their Moravian
ally, the People's party, as a growing number of differences on
policy led to a formal break in 1907. While the Young Czechs
became more dependent upon industrial and banking interests after 1900, the People's party grew closer to the Moravian parties
of the left. Its merger with the Moravian Progressives in 1909
and formation of the Moravian Progressive Bloc in 1911 with the
Agrarians, Social Democrats, and Masaryk's Progressives reduced
Young Czech influence in Moravia to nil.

How did the formal split between Young Czechs and the People's
party come about? Young Czech adoption of "positive policies"
after the fall of Badeni and Thun led Stránský and the Moravians
to begin disengagement from their parliamentary and electoral
alliances with the Young Czechs.[84] Other serious issues already
divided the parties, notably the People's party's continuing advocacy of popular sovereignty in communal and provincial self-
government in opposition to the Young Czechs who after 1895 continued to rely on unrepresentative district boards and ceased
trying to eliminate curial suffrage to the diets.[85] Moreover,
given the retarded industrialization of Moravia, Czech commercial and banking enterprises were not strong enough to dominate
the People's party. In contrast, therefore, to a Young Czech
party increasingly beholden to big business interests, the People's party remained a party of anticlerical small businessmen
and farmers.[86] Czech efforts to overcome German opposition to
the establishment of a Czech university in Moravia led to a tactical conflict between the Young Czechs and Stránský.[87] The
former wished to propose its establishment to Minister-President
Koerber and to the Reichsrat in an amendment to a bill requesting revival of the Badeni language ordinances in modified form.
The People's party believed enactment of language reforms to be
unlikely and therefore wished to negotiate separately for the
university the Moravian Czechs had so long desired. The Young
Czechs' condescension toward the People's party only exacerbated
the situation, as they sought to keep the People's party as the
subordinate ally it had of necessity been during the nineties
and to limit its growing independence in policies and action.

The campaign of the Moravian left against the Moravian Agreement of 1905 further widened the rift as the People's party discovered its natural allies to be the Agrarians and Social

Democrats rather than the Young Czechs, whose power to influence
events in Moravia was minimal and whose identification with
privileged classes in Czech society made association with them a
liability in running a campaign against the Christian Socialists
or in forming an alliance with Agrarians and Social Democrats.[88]
Stránský also did not receive anticipated Young Czech support in
the Juda case of January 1906, in which Professor Karel Juda was
taken to court by Catholic clergymen for having published remarks critical of the Church in a brochure describing the exhibition of František Kupka's art in Prostějov.[89] Meanwhile, the
People's party grew stronger by extending its control over communal and municipal self-governing boards heretofore run by a
wealthy German minority: Hranice, Kroměříž, Prostějov, Uherské
Hradiště, and Vyškov thus came under Czech administration.

The progressive Moravian student organizations under František
Vahalík and Václav Choc which had broken with the People's party
in 1896 to form Young Moravia (Mladá Morava) and the liberal political associations which had merged to form the independent
Moravian Progressive party (Moravská strana pokroková) between
1900 and 1905 rejoined Stránský and the People's party in 1909
to form the decidedly liberal and progressive Moravian People's
Progressive party (Lidová strana pokroková).[90] The associations
whose challenge to Stránský's alliance with the liberal Moravian
Old Czechs and the Bohemian Young Czechs finally led him to opt
for a more leftward orientation included the Organization of
Progressive Work (Organisace pokrokové práce), the Anticlerical
League in Moravia (Antiklerikální liga na Moravě), and the Political Association for Northern Moravia in Olomouc (Politický spolek
pro severní Moravu v Olomouci), chaired by Richard Fischer, and
its province-wide successor, the Progressive Political Union for
Moravia (Pokrokový spolek politický pro Moravu), formed in November 1902.[91] The new People's Progressive party moved further to
the left in 1911 by joining Agrarians, Social Democrats, and Masaryk's Progressives in the Progressive Bloc to overthrow clerical preponderance in the Moravian Reichsrat elections of that
year and in the diet elections of 1913.[92] In the Reichsrat, Masaryk, already allied to the State Rights Progressives of Bohemia, continued to be the principal intermediary between Czech
politicians of progressive persuasion in Bohemia and Moravia.

Successors to the Progressive Movement

Two among the seven new Czech parties at the turn of the cen-
tury--the Radical Progressives and the State Rights Radicals--
were the heirs of the center and right wings of the Progressive
movement, and two others founded in 1900 described themselves as
"progressives"--the Moravian Progressive party and T. G. Masaryk's People's, later Progressive, party. All were essentially
parties of the intelligentsia which tried with little success to
attract a popular following. Their leaders had with few

exceptions entered politics during the nineties in association
with the Young Czech party or with its Moravian ally, the People's party, and all continued to uphold anticlerical and liberal principles after breaking with the parent party on social,
nationality, and economic questions. The limited electoral success of the various progressive parties cost the Young Czech
party few votes. Rather, these parties harmed it in the long
run by attracting many younger intellectuals, particularly journalists and writers, who would be prominent politicians of the
future. In the heyday of the *Národní listy*, the progressive intelligentsia and journalists had often supported the Young
Czechs. The younger progressives of the nineties, though dis-
trustful of the party, had nonetheless tried to work with it for
constructive change until the *Omladina* trials, followed by the
crises of 1897 to 1899, shattered the illusions of any who imagined that extensive social and political reforms could be
achieved under its auspices.

The Radical Progressive party (Radikálně pokroková strana) and
the more moderate State Rights Radical party (Radikálně státoprávní strana) were the successors respectively of the post-1895
center and right wings of the Progressive movement. The former
party, founded on April 4, 1897, by the Hajn brothers, Antonín
Čížek, Antonín Hubka, and Antonín Kalina, gave the social question precedence over state rights, opposed Young Czech collaboration with the Badeni and Thun governments, and became a resolute foe of anti-Semitism, clericalism, and the authoritarian
imperial bureaucracy. Former leaders of the Progressive right,
Alois Rašín and Karel Stanislav Sokol, formed the State Rights
Radical party on February 19, 1899, after an unsuccessful attempt to assume positions of leadership in the Young Czech party
in order to radicalize its policies. They were soon joined by
many leading Czech intellectuals, among them the composer Víte-
slav Novák and the poet and novelist Viktor Dyk, who demanded
radical nationalism and state rights and a national leadership
of the intelligentsia and who opposed the policies of both the
Young Czechs and the new mass parties.[93]

Neither successor to the Progressive movement proved strong
enough to survive more than eleven years on its own, thanks in
large part to limited membership, lack of electoral appeal, and
fratricidal competition for the same small intellectual constituency. Loss of key personnel also diminished each party's
strength. Čížek's death, Václav Choc's defection to the National Socialists, and František Soukup's becoming a Social Democrat
soon left the Radical Progressives with few popular leaders.
The party was further weakened in 1905 when Alois Hajn and the
staff of the journal *Osvěta lidu* (Enlightenment of the people)
left to join T. G. Masaryk and his People's party in forming the
Progressive party (Pokroková strana). Alois Rašín left the State
Rights Radical party in 1906 to help Kramář, Pacák, and Škarda

reorganize the Young Czech party to compete for mass support in anticipation of the advent of universal manhood suffrage. Bereft of leaders, including most of the more factious ones, and of the figures who fought each other most, the two progressive parties allied with the National Socialists to run a joint slate of candidates in the 1907 Reichsrat elections.[94] The seven seats won primarily benefited the National Socialists, further demonstrating that the two progressive parties could help make or break a larger party but could not become one on their own.

On April 20, 1908, the remnants of the Radical Progressive and the State Rights Radical parties merged to form the State Rights Progressive party (Státoprávně pokroková strana), which advocated full civil rights for all citizens regardless of class, sex, or nationality and the realization of national independence on the basis of natural rather than Historical Bohemian state rights. To insure the "healthy" development of the nation, it aimed "to integrate the Czech people and the Czech intelligentsia into one indivisible and unbreakable whole!"[95] The party, whose principal spokesmen were Antonín Hajn, Karel Baxa, Viktor Dyk, Antonín Kalina, and the radical journalist Lev Borský, promulgated an uncompromisingly anticlerical, radical national, and antidynastic program. Its party organization, based on local cadres and an elected executive committee, resembled that of the Young Czechs more than that of the mass parties.[96] The State Rights Progressives opposed the positive policies of Kramář and the Young Czechs, accused Masaryk and Herben of being too conciliatory toward the Germans, and asked that the nation follow the leadership of the enlightened and progressive intelligentsia rather than Agrarian and National Socialist leaders who catered to short-sighted and uninformed popular desires. They formed a more positive opinion of Masaryk after 1908 when at the Zagreb treason trials he publicly exposed the stupidity and deceit of the Austrian Foreign Office. After the 1911 Reichsrat election, in which the State Rights Progressives won four seats, they joined the Czech Progressive party to form a united parliamentary club with T. G. Masaryk as chairman and supported the Moravian People's Progressive party in its disputes with the Young Czechs.[97]

The State Rights Progressives were to be found with the Social Democrats, the National Socialists, and Masaryk's Progressives in the vanguard of the Czech movement for women's rights.[98] These parties, in contrast to the Young Czechs, Agrarians, and clerical parties, all advocated universal suffrage and full equality before the law for women as well as men. Women who had been active in the Progressive movement of the early nineties included Karel Stanislav Sokol's sister Bohuslava, Antonín Hajn's future wife Liduška, and Beta Rajchlová. Charlotte G. Masaryk had like her husband encouraged women to participate in politics, an activity not yet considered genteel by upper middle class Czech society. Františka Plamínková of the National Socialist

party and Tereza Nováková, editor of Ženský svět (Woman's world),
also numbered among the leading crusaders for women's rights
after the turn of the century.[99]

The absence of any strong indigenous Czech anti-Semitic movement was to a degree due to the vigilance of Czech Social Democrats and various Czech progressives. The virulent anti-Semitism
so popular among the Viennese and the Catholic Germans of the
Alpine lands had no counterpart among the Czechs, whose success
in modern agriculture, industry, and finance had all but prevented the emergence of wealthy Jewish merchants or moneylenders
against whom popular animosity might be aroused. The predominantly liberal and democratic orientation of Czech politics further militated against widespread acceptance of anti-Semitism.
And most Czech politicians recognized that their struggle to
acquire equal rights with the Germans in Cisleithania could not
be advanced by trying to deny Jews equality and protection under
law.[100]

The occasional outbursts of Czech anti-Semitism usually accompanied popular demonstrations against German privileges or parliamentary obstruction in which Jews were attacked for having
sided with the Germans. This became especially apparent during
the Kladno riots between Czech and German workers in 1897 and in
Czech demonstrations opposing repeal of the Badeni and Gautsch
language ordinances.[101] Likewise, the anti-Semitic overtones of
the Czech "each to his own" (svůj k svému) movement in Moravia
arose largely from boycotts against German merchants or Jewish
merchants professing German nationality.[102] Anti-Semitism, propagated by Czech Catholic publicists like Rudolf Vrba and up to
1896 by the independent student journal Studentský sborník
strany neodvislé (Student journal of the Independent Party),
aroused very little support.[103] Vrba received only 20 of the
683 electoral votes cast in fifth-curial elections from the
Hradec Králové district to the Reichsrat in 1897.[104]

The Grégr brothers, despite having published several demagogic anti-Semitic attacks on Jewish Social Democrats in the
Národní listy, had consistently opposed attempts to include an
anti-Semitic plank in Young Czech party platforms or to create
an independent Czech anti-Semitic party. More importantly, any
anti-Semitic remarks in the Národní listy or other journals were
immediately condemned by the Czech Social Democratic and progressi
papers. The Národní listy in its inaugural issue had in fact
come out strongly for equal rights for Jews.[105] Young Czech delegate to the diet Jakub Scharf, a Prague Jewish lawyer, helped
found the Czech Jewish National Union (Národní jednota česko-
židovské) and tried unsuccessfully to win Prague's predominantly
Jewish Josefov quarter for the party ticket.[106] He was also
among the first to encourage Prague Jews to shift party allegiance from German to Czech, a gradual shift that occurred more
slowly among Jews of higher social strata.[107]

Where Sladkovský and the Grégr brothers had officially

eschewed anti-Semitism, the turn-of-the-century party of Kramář, Pacák, and Škarda, particularly in its satirical journal *Šípy* (Arrows), exploited latent anti-Semitic sentiments among the Czechs by making demagogic attacks upon the Jewish management of the *Neue Freie Presse* and upon Czech Social Democracy, whose weekly *Právo lidu* (The rights of the people) they usually called in a play on words *Právo židů* (The rights of the Jews).[108] Attacks on the German Jewish leadership of Austrian Social Democracy for Germanophile views may have been justified during the nineties, but charges that Czech Social Democracy had sold out to the Jews had no basis in fact. Czechs had long criticized the *Neue Freie Presse* for its support of imperial foreign policy and its contemptuous attitude toward the aspirations of the Slavic nationalities. Racial slurs against its owners and editors were therefore unnecessary as well as in bad taste.[109]

During the crises of 1897 to 1899, T. G. Masaryk and the Czech Radical Progressives, notably Alois and Antonín Hajn, emerged as the most outspoken foes of anti-Semitism in Cisleithania.[110] They opposed anti-Semitism on principle and argued that any Czech who tried to make a scapegoat of Jews disgraced himself and did the national cause a disservice. In October 1899, Masaryk became the first politician in all of Cisleithania to defend a poor itinerant Czech Jew, Leopold Hilsner, against trumped-up charges of ritual murder. Before Masaryk's public protest, neither the *Neue Freie Presse* nor the Austrian Social Democratic leadership had considered it expedient to declare publicly in Hilsner's defense. Masaryk's courageous stand won the gratitude of Jews the world over and the eventual support of Czech public opinion.[111]

Czech Progressive and Social Democratic politicians at the turn of the century helped sustain liberal political traditions by refusing to allow anti-Semitism to poison Czech public life. Every leading Czech party except the clericals thus benefited from the participation and support of Czech Jews. Among those who entered politics at the turn of the century and rose rapidly to positions of leadership in their respective parties were Jakub Scharf of the Young Czechs, Adolf Stránský of the Moravian People's party, Otakar Frankenberger of the Agrarians, Evžen Štern, a Czech Progressive turned Social Democrat, and Františka Plamínková, a National Socialist deputy and tireless campaigner for women's rights.[112] By contrast, widespread anti-Semitism in Vienna and in predominantly German areas of Cisleithania rather effectively excluded Jews from all but the German Liberal and Social Democratic movements. Karl Lueger and Georg von Schönerer actively popularized and encouraged anti-Semitism, thereby willy-nilly helping to prepare the way for Hitler.[113] Thanks in large part to the courage and vigilance of its progressive and Social Democratic founders, the Czechoslovak Republic would survive its first twenty years relatively untroubled by the vicious anti-Semitism that helped cripple democratic political

institutions in many of the newly independent Central and Eastern
European states.

T. G. Masaryk and the Progressive Party

In his 1895 study *Naše nynější krise* (Our present crisis),
T. G. Masaryk had argued that the political crisis following the
Omladina trials did not reflect the decline of the Czech nation
but merely the failure of an outmoded political system represented by the Old Czechs and their Young Czech successors.[114] After
having frequently reiterated this opinion, he asserted in his
April 1903 Hradec Králové speech that the disintegration of the
Young Czech party, by discrediting Bohemian state rights and the
last vestiges of "compromising" Old Czech tactics, had at last
made possible the reorientation of Czech political life on the
basis of natural rights and democratically constituted parties
responsible to the people.[115] In accordance with such aims, Masaryk on April 1, 1901, founded the Czech People's party together
with the professor of philosophy and pedagogy František Drtina,
the economist Josef Gruber, and the professor of political economy Cyrill Horáček. Four years later, the party reorganized itself as the Czech Progressive party (Česká strana pokroková)
when joined by Alois Hajn and other Radical Progressives from
the journal *Osvěta lidu*. The party based its program upon democratic and anticlerical principles and sought the greatest possible political independence for the Czech nation within the
framework of the monarchy. It advocated extension of women's
rights, the education of an intelligent citizenry, and bringing
political influence, prosperity, and culture within the reach of
all social classes.[116] Toward these ends it sought to introduce
universal suffrage and popular sovereignty to every level of
self-government.[117]

The Czech Progressives, often referred to as Realists, won
few elections, sending Masaryk and Drtina to the Reichsrat in
1907 and Masaryk alone in 1911. But they acquired widespread
support among the Czech intelligentsia and made electoral agreements with the State Rights Progressives, the Moravian People's
Progressives, and the Czech Social Democrats. Without the latter two parties having agreed not to oppose him, Masaryk could
not have twice won mandates to the Reichsrat from the Valašské
Meziříčí district of Moravia.[118] Moreover, the Realists aided
progressive forces among the Slovaks and Southern Slavs, thereby
helping to lay the groundwork for the wartime cooperation between Czechs, Slovaks, and Yugoslavs.[119]

Masaryk had long supported most working-class aspirations but
could not, as he explained in his 1898 work "The Social Question," accept the excessively materialistic Marxist interpretation of man or the risks of dictatorship implicit in revolution
as defined by Marxism.[120] Thanks in part to his humble origin
and experience as an "outsider" in Czech politics, Masaryk

showed greater respect and affection for ordinary people than
did most Czech intellectuals, especially those who prided themselves on having risen above the masses as well as those who
claimed to know what was best for the common people. Masaryk's
untiring advocacy of universal suffrage and women's rights, his
intelligent and constructive criticism of Marxist doctrines, and
his willingness to talk directly to disfranchised workers in
1891 and 1893 had won him the respect of most Czech Social Democratic leaders. Nor would his arguing the case for Hilsner in
1899 or for the striking miners of north Bohemia in 1900 be forgotten. Even Bohumír Šmeral, principal ideologue of the more
doctrinaire wing of Czech Social Democracy, distinguished between Masaryk's party and the other "bourgeois" parties. Šmeral
did not regard Masaryk and his associates as class enemies like
the others because they provided "a way-station on the road to
socialism" for those intellectuals who were "too intelligent or
too honest" to support the "bourgeois" parties and who sought a
deeper understanding of social problems.[121] He nonetheless considered such activity to be inadequate and asked the intelligentsia to do what Masaryk had warned them not to do: suspend
critical judgment in the interests of promoting a worthy cause.

More than any other man, Masaryk introduced the politics of
morality to Czech political life. Through teaching and politics
he tried to demonstrate that love of country should be based on
critical understanding rather than unreasoning emotion and persuaded many Czechs, though by no means a majority, that politics
should rest on moral and humanistic principles as well as on material and nationality interests. His works *Česká otázka* (The
Czech question), *Naše nynější krise* (Our present crisis), and
Karel Havlíček provided the first comprehensive discussion of
the political, cultural, and historical aspects of the Czech
question. Therein Masaryk maintained that the small Czech nation in the heart of Europe could best justify its existence by
living up to its democratic and humanistic traditions dating
from the fourteenth century. By presenting the Czech National
Revival as a continuation of work begun by the Hussites and Bohemian Brethren, he helped free Czech politics from psychological dependence upon Bohemian state rights and other traditions
associated with the Habsburg Monarchy. To a greater degree than
his contemporaries, particularly those among the Young Czechs,
Masaryk recognized the importance of ideology in politics, especially for a small people under adverse circumstances that
could not in his view prevail unless it had a true notion of
where it had been and a clear plan for future action.

Like many of his Progressive and Social Democratic rivals,
Masaryk wanted to bridge the gap between ideals and reality in
Czech society. Concern for serious contemporary problems guided
his principal intellectual ventures from the 1881 treatise on
suicide to his classic study of Russian philosophy, history, and
religion written after the 1905 revolution.[122] He attracted a

large and loyal following not only through his lectures and
works but through strength of character and the patient political labor by which he tried to realize his ideals of democracy
and religious humanism. Though many have disagreed with Masaryk's political philosophy and some have doubted his integrity,
no one has questioned his courage.[123] In defending Gebauer,
Hilsner, Wahrmund, and Pribećević, he stood four times against
public opinion when expediency would have dictated silence.

By word and deed, Masaryk strengthened the liberal and Western orientation of Czech political life and at the same time
furthered Czech friendship for Russia by arguing that such amity
should rest on mutual criticism and understanding rather than on
naive adulation. He helped nurture growing Czech ties with the
Slovaks and Yugoslavs through working with their more radical
and progressive leaders toward common goals in domestic and foreign affairs. Like other Czechs, he recognized that the smaller
Slavic peoples had already benefited by cooperative endeavors
and that given increasing German belligerence, they would have
to rely on one another more in the future.

Masaryk further influenced Czech politics by bringing to it a
world outlook, which had heretofore been wanting. He thought
that the Czech question, like the social question, could be resolved only within a European framework. Czech politicians had
hitherto thought almost exclusively in terms of advancing specifically Czech interests, as Viennese or imperial officials
thought almost exclusively in terms of imperial interests. By
viewing both Czech and Austrian imperial problems in a world
perspective, Masaryk could readily relate them to the interests
of the great powers and of the United States. During the First
World War he was thus prepared to persuade Allied leaders that
the dissolution of the Habsburg Monarchy would contribute to a
more lasting European peace and serve their own national interests as well as those of the Czechs, Slovaks, Poles, and Yugoslavs.

The Young Czechs may have helped develop the economic and political preconditions for Czechoslovak independence, but they
did not aim at achieving it. Masaryk first made the attempt to
establish an independent Czechoslovakia. For his success in
this attempt as for his courage in adversity before and after
1914 Czechs have always been grateful.[124]

The Democratization of Czech Politics

The period from 1898 to 1914 witnessed the democratization
and leftward movement of Czech politics as the once-predominant
Young Czech party declined in the face of two steadily growing
established mass parties, Christian Socialism and Social Democracy, and the founding of two new mass parties, the Agrarians
and National Socialists, and three parties of the intelligentsia.
Czech parties after 1900 were organized both as national parties

and as parties representing particular classes or interest groups. Organization according to class or interest reflected the growing diversification of Czech society and the inability of any one party or policy to satisfy a majority of groups. Party organization according to nationality and the establishment of the Czech National Council (Národní rada česká) in June 1900 to coordinate activities of all parties in matters of national concern reflected the interest of all Czechs in furthering national aims and demonstrated that Czechs like other Slavs in the monarchy regarded the nation as the proper basis for political and economic organization. Even those parties that maintained close ties to supranational organizations upheld Czech interests. Social Democrats as well as Roman Catholic clergy in the Habsburg Monarchy found it necessary to organize their respective parties according to nationality.

The democratization and leftward movement in organization and policy which characterized the mass parties and parties of the intelligentsia weakened the Old and Young Czechs and the clerical parties. The formation of the Moravian Progressive Bloc in 1911 ended clerical hegemony among the Czech parties in Moravia. Despite a temporary setback in 1897, the Czechoslavonic Social Democratic party continued until 1914 to be the largest and most popular Czech party. By giving greater emphasis to its "socialist" programs, the National Socialist party won increased representation in 1911. And the Agrarian party gave greater support to the small and middling farmer and advocated universal manhood suffrage to the lower house of the Reichsrat, after its capture by the more democratically minded elements headed by Švehla, Staněk, and Udržal. Generally the Czech parties of the left helped free the Czech national movement from dependence upon the emperor and the great landowners by advocating greater national autonomy within the monarchy on the basis of natural rights rather than Bohemian state rights.

The new parties undertook to become democratic in organization as well as in policy. Veterans of the Progressive movement recognized that the failure of their radical demonstrations in 1893 could be attributed to their disorganization and lack of popular support as well as to authoritarian police power. As State Rights Progressives, they added organizational discipline to enthusiasm and made accountability of the imperial bureaucracy to Parliament a cardinal political aim. The four mass parties attempted to arouse popular support by relying upon a permanent political organization of local branches and auxiliary organizations like trade unions, youth groups, and self-help societies rather than relying almost exclusively upon parliamentary politics and a party press as did the Old and Young Czech parties. Their building mass party organizations largely apart from parliamentary institutions may be attributed to their exclusion from provincial and district self-government by curial voting. The parties of the intelligentsia, all progeny of the

Young Czechs, could not compete with the mass parties in an extensive organization or in popular appeal but did design their programs to educate and to appeal to all classes of society.

The movement to the left in Czech politics was accompanied by a growing resistance among all Czech parties except the Young Czechs, Old Czechs, and clericals to Habsburg expansion in the Balkans. In 1908 as in 1900 and 1901, Masaryk's Progressive party, the State Rights Progressives, the National Socialists, and to a degree the Agrarians numbered among the most fervent opponents of Austrian militarism and imperialism. This in turn intensified cooperation between Czech political parties and those of Southern Slavic peoples.[125] Czech Social Democracy maintained its internationalist outlook while refusing to subordinate itself to German preeminence in the Austrian Social Democratic party. The National Socialists acquired marked Serbophile sympathies, while veterans of the Progressive movement established ties with the younger intelligentsia among the Southern Slavs which later served the causes of Czechoslovak and Yugoslav independence. T. G. Masaryk's defense of the Croatian and Serbian subjects of the empire charged with treason at Zagreb exposed the deceit of the Austrian Foreign Office and further demonstrated to most Czechs the need for closer cooperation between the smaller Slavic peoples in the future. By contrast, efforts by Kramář and the Young Czechs to revive Slavic solidarity in the form of Neo-Slavism produced little more than stirring rhetoric and two inconclusive Slavic congresses, the first at Prague in 1908 and the second at Sofia in 1910.

The decline of the liberal Young Czech party, the emergence of mass parties, and the democratization and leftward movement of Czech politics corresponded to political developments in Scandinavia and Western Europe. By contrast, the newer Austrian German nationalist and clerical parties rejected liberalism and succumbed to anti-Semitism and racism. With the coming of the First World War, an increasingly democratic and liberal Czech political tradition helped win widespread understanding and support in the Western parliamentary democracies for Czechoslovak independence.

The Czech political parties, policies, and leaders that emerged from the crises of the nineties were essentially those of the First Czechoslovak Republic. When the opportunity came to overthrow the Habsburg dynasty, the political as well as the social and economic bases for an independent and democratic Czechoslovakia would be present.

11

Epilogue

1901 marked the end of Young Czech predominance in Czech politics. In that year of Kaizl's death and Engel's retirement from
the Reichsrat, the party lost ten seats in the Reichsrat and
twenty-two in the Bohemian Diet, five of the former and nineteen
of the latter to the Agrarians alone.[1] Pursuing "positive politics" for the first time since the fall of the Thun government
on October 2, 1899, the party had begun to cooperate on certain
specific issues with the Koerber government, despite objections
by Edvard Grégr, Josef Fořt, and others of a dwindling radical
minority.[2] What turned out to be the last public demonstration
of Young Czech radicalism had occurred during November and December 1899 when the party had filibustered and otherwise non-
violently obstructed Reichsrat proceedings in retaliation for
the repeal of the Badeni-Gautsch language ordinances by Minister-
President Count Manfred Clary-Aldringen, Thun's successor and
former governor of Styria. This obstruction had helped a right
majority in the Reichsrat force Clary's resignation on December 21, 1899, primarily because he, having promised to rule
without invoking aritcle 14, could not obtain approval for the
annual budget or the overdue decennial tariff renewal with Hungary.[3] The party had continued in opposition to the short-lived
caretaker government of Heinrich Ritter von Wittek and initially
to that of Ernst von Koerber, who took office on January 19,
1900. But, moderate Young Czechs committed the party irrevocably in 1901 to positive politics as they had found opposition to
be unproductive and as their constituents called for increased
public works projects and government subsidies, given the worsening of an economic recession that had begun in 1900.   In 1901
as well, the party renwed its ties to the right, thanks largely
to executive committee chairman Václav Škarda who arranged a
pact with the Old Czechs to avoid cutthroat competition in the
September diet elections.[4] To no one's surprise, therefore, on
December 28, 1901, Old and Young Czechs entered the Bohemian
Diet as a united Czech Club prepared to resume cooperation with
the conservative great landowners on the basis of all three parties having in February 1901 reaffirmed their support for Bohe-
main state rights as they had done in 1879.
     Young Czechs observed with satisfaction that the Agrarian and
National Socialist parties also promoted economic growth and advocated extending national autonomy on the basis of Bohemian
state rights. Imperial authorities could take no comfort from
the fact that these parties proved to be not only as intransigent

309

as the Young Czechs on state rights and language questions but
more demanding on economic issues.[5] Because of this and because,
like the Social Democrats, the two new parties represented a mass
as opposed to an elite constituency, they proved to be potentially a much greater threat to imperial prerogatives and to privileged interests than the Young or Old Czechs had ever been.
After ten years as the leading Czech party, therefore, the Young
Czechs had on balance succeeded in advancing to a limited degree
civil liberties and national autonomy and in strengthening the
Czech national movement by broadening its popular support, even
at the cost of irretrievably weakening their own party.

The thirteen years preceding the First World War saw the
steady decline of the Young Czech party as it tried to realize
state rights and liberal programs and to maintain an important
if no longer predominant position in Czech political life. The
Czech National Council (Národní rada česká), which the party
helped establish in June 1900, served effectively as the clearinghouse and coordinating body for all Czech political parties
except Social Democracy on questions of national importance, including economic growth, language and civil rights, and Slavic
solidarity. Up to 1914, Young Czechs remained the strongest influence on the Council primarily by virtue of their greater political experience and connections to leaders in business, self-
government, and patriotic and cultural institutions. This preeminence was reflected by the fact that Young Czechs provided
all Council chairmen beginning with Engel in 1900 and continuing
with Herold in 1903, Jaromír Čelakovský in 1908, and Jan Podlipný
from 1909 to 1914.[6] Until 1914, the Young Czech party also dominated Czech district boards and chambers of commerce in Bohemia
and the second and third curias of the Bohemian Diet. But in the
Reichsrat after January 1907, the party dropped to fourth among
Czech parties in total votes received and to third in number of
deputies. In 1911, the party slipped further to sixth in votes
and to a tie for third in number of seats.[7] Like the Old Czech
party in decline during the late eighties, the Young Czech party
after 1901 proved ever more ready to cooperate with the imperial
authorities, seeking in Vienna to win through positive politics
limited concessions from the governments of Koerber, Beck, and
Bienerth that would restore its popularity and influence at
home.[8] Given continuing imperial deference to German interests,
this policy became one of diminishing returns. The attempt by
the party and the Czech National Council to revive Slavic reciprocity as Neo-Slavism, beginning with the Neo-Slav Congress of
July 1908 in Prague, met with little success. Young Czechs, especially Karel Kramář, had hoped that Neo-Slavism would bolster
Russia in the aftermath of defeat by Japan besides compensating
the party for its loss of domestic influence by providing an international forum to promote Czech exports and to help coordinate in the Reichsrat the Slavic delegations recently enlarged
by universal manhood suffrage.[9]

By 1906, the retirement of long-time party leaders, notably
Blazek, Engel, Edvard Grégr, and Slavík, and the defection of
more agrarian, radical nationalist, and intellectual party members to the successor parties, brought to the fore new recruits
like František Fiedler, Alois Rašín, and Zdeněk Tobolka to join
stalwarts like Herold, Pacák, Škarda, and Kramář in leading the
Young Czech party through years of retrenchment and attempted
reform. Josef Herold succeeded Emanuel Engel in 1903 as chairman of the Czech National Council and until his death in April
1908 served as a leading party spokesman and as mayor of suburban Vinohrady. Bedřich Pacák, that consummate, cautious, and
matter-of-fact lawyer, who had translated Machiavelli's *Il Prin-
cipe* into Czech, took over from Engel as chairman of the parliamentary club of delegates in 1900. Few who saw him in 1906 re-
splendent in a gold-braided waistcoat as the imperial Minister
without Portfolio for Czech Affairs would have remembered that
thirty-five years before he had just been amnestied after spend-
ing three years in prison for revolutionary agitation. In that
office from June 1906 to November 1907, he proved to be what he
had always been, a tireless advocate of civil liberties and of
Czech economic and cultural interests. Václav Škarda ably continued to serve as chairman of the party's executive committee
and in 1908 succeeded Engel as chairman of the party club of delegates to the Bohemian Diet. In recognition of Škarda's tact,
moderation, and high social status, the emperor in 1907 appointed him a life member of the upper house of the Reichsrat, along
with the Old Czechs Bráf, Mattuš, Randa, and Zeithammer. Until
his death in March 1912, Škarda belonged to that small elite of
Prague society in which few Young Czechs besides Engel had moved
with ease and from which the rough-hewn Grégr brothers, among
others, had been excluded.

Two younger men, Alois Rašín and Zdeněk Tobolka, and one recent recruit, František Fiedler, rose to positions of importance
in the turn-of-the-century Young Czech party. After Kaizl's
death, Fiedler became the party's expert on economics, a task
which he shared with Rašín after 1906. Professor of law and social science at the Czech Technical Institute in Prague and after
1904 professor of administrative science and Austrian administrative law at Charles-Ferdinand University, Fiedler had a theoretical and practical knowledge of self-governmental institutions
equaled only by the great legal scholars Bohuslav Rieger and Antonín Randa. Before winning election in 1901 to the Bohemian
Diet and to the Reichsrat as a Young Czech, Fiedler had served
from 1883 to 1898 as drafting clerk for the Provincial Executive
Council. Author of learned studies on Cisleithanian political
institutions and a well-known work on the decennial customs
agreement between Cisleithania and Hungary, he often spoke on
behalf of the party during renegotiation of the customs agreement of 1907.[10] Up to 1914, he strongly advocated positive politics, but his devotion to the Dual Monarchy became very

apparent after 1914, when he, in contrast to most Czech politicians, worked to preserve the Monarchy while trying to obtain
greater autonomy for the Czechs within it.

Efforts by Herold, Kramář, Pacák, and Škarda, beginning in
1906, to reorganize the Young Czech party as a mass party did
not succeed but did help rejuvenate the party and bring back
Alois Rašín, a veteran politician of great courage and intellect.
The failure of his State Rights Radical party to win any seats
in the Reichsrat election of 1901 and the gradually declining
circulation of the *Radikální listy* severely tried Rašín's devotion to the politics of principle. Unlike the Hajns, Sokol, or
Dyk, who championed unpopular causes and small parties from un-
shakeable inner conviction, Rašín could not be satisfied unless
he could take a hand in making public policy. Like many State
Rights Radical compatriots, he distrusted the untutored judgment
of common men. Rather than continue trying to uplift and lead
the masses through radical splinter parties and journals, he,
like Tobolka, chose to try to make the Young Czech party a progressive and popular force in politics.[11]

Zdeněk Tobolka in 1906 was a free-lance historian and an administrator of the Charles-Ferdinand University library. As a
student in 1896, he had helped turn the *Studentský sborník* away
from anti-Semitism and in 1900 had helped Masaryk found the
Czech People's party, serving as its first secretary. Viktor
Dyk, in his novel *Prosinec*, made Tobolka the model for the
thoughtful Hilarius, who believed that discretion was the better
part of valor. Tobolka, like Rašín, came to the Young Czech
party expecting to help make public policy and already disillusioned by what he saw as petty bourgeois National Socialists,
Progressive ideologues, and parochial Agrarians. An indefati-
gable journalist and historian, he contributed greatly to the
quality and success of the Young Czech monthly *Česká revue* (Czech
review) and edited much of the comprehensive five-volume encyclopedia of Czech politics, *Česká politika*, which in many respects
reflected Young Czech views. His three-volume edition of the
Kaizl papers appeared between 1909 and 1914 as a tribute to Kaizl
and as a documentary justification of positive politics. This
solid work of scholarship, despite its showing Kaizl and especially Kramář to best advantage, is still the outstanding published collection of materials on the Young Czech party. Advancing quite rapidly in the party thanks to backing by Kramář,
Tobolka won election to the Reichsrat in 1911 and to Václav
Škarda's seat in the Bohemian Diet in 1913. Throughout the
First World War, he was a leading Czech proponent of compromise
and cooperation with Austria-Hungary.[12]

After the untimely death of his mentor Kaizl in August 1901,
Karel Kramář emerged on his own as a leading party figure and
assumed the role once played by Edvard Grégr as firebrand and
parliamentary tribune of the party. His forceful and flamboyant
speeches, like those of Grégr or Herold, somewhat unnecessarily

angered political opponents while encouraging supporters. Unlike Grégr and Fořt, Kramář prided himself on having eschewed
radicalism and doctrinaire civil libertarianism and on being
prepared to cooperate constructively with the imperial authorities. His views on social policy, derived in part from the German "socialists of the chair," appeared forward-looking in contrast to the Manchester liberalism espoused by some older party
members like Adámek and Schwarz. His competent if undistinguished publications on history and politics commanded some respect, despite occasional self-serving statements and a style
at times characterized by verbosity and imprecision.[13] A man of
vitality, personal charm, and great ambition, he worked to revive the Young Czech party and to become not only its leader but
that of the nation as well. Much though he enjoyed public acclaim, he had the good sense to avoid sycophants and to surround
himself with independently minded assistants. It was largely
through his offices that able young men like Rašín and Tobolka
and later František Hlaváček and Vladimír Šís were brought into
the party. Kramář outlived his prominent contemporaries Herold,
Pacák, and Škarda to become by 1912 the uncontested head of the
Young Czech party.[14]

Kramář, like Julius Grégr, whom he had in turn opposed and
honored, had serious flaws in character which frustrated his aim
to become, as had Palacký and then Rieger, the acknowledged
leader of the nation. As acting speaker of the Reichsrat during
the Badeni crisis, he had aroused apprehension and mistrust
among colleagues and opponents which never wholly dissipated.
Though not devoid of humor, he took himself and his career quite
seriously and could on occasion be ungracious in victory and re-
sentful in defeat. His boundless ambition and insatiable taste
for political intrigue, in contrast to men like Edvard Grégr,
Antonín Hajn, and T. G. Masaryk who usually fought their political battles publicly, further aroused popular distrust and were
to serve neither Kramář nor his party well. Nonetheless, even
opponents who expressed reservations about his politics or his
character never questioned his patriotism.

Kramář denigrated, as Young Czechs often did, Masaryk's efforts to reconcile Czechs and Germans, his debunking of naive
Pan-Slavist or Neo-Slavist enthusiasm, and especially his efforts
to effect the moral regeneration of the Czech people. Masaryk
looked to the West for guidance, put his trust in the common
people, and sympathized with Social Democratic aspirations. Kramář expected help from Russia, looked out for the interests of
wealthy Czechs, and sanctioned demagogic attacks on Czech Social
Democracy for allegedly lacking patriotism or selling out to
the Jews. His occasional references to the peasant as the backbone of Czech society did not temper his belief that most Agrarians were devoted to parochial interests and limited in understanding the high finance and international relations on which
he considered himself, with some justification, an expert. The

profound differences in political opinion between Kramář and Masaryk were reflected in their social origins and style of life. Masaryk came from a poor coachman's home. Kramář was the pampered scion of a prosperous self-made middle-class family in Vysoké nad Jizerou where his father owned a mill and lumberyard. Masaryk and his American-born wife, Charlotte Garrigue, lived with their five children in comfortable circumstances and gave generously of their limited time and funds to poor students and to newly established progressive and Social Democratic journals. The independently wealthy Kramář married in 1900 a rich Russian heiress, Naděžda Nikolajevna Chludová. The childless couple vacationed annually at their palatial villa "Barbo" in the Crimea, where they enjoyed the company of Russian middle-class and gentry society. They also built for themselves in Prague an equally magnificent villa on the old St. Thomas bastion overlooking the nearby Hradčany, home of Czech kings from the early Middle Ages to the seventeenth century. Kramář relished playing the role of politician and patron *en grand seigneur* and won the trust and affection of many wealthy Czechs, despite his speeches which called faintly for political democratization and social reform. The mass Czech electorate similarly discounted Kramář's populist rhetoric. Actions spoke louder than words.

Kramář was an honest Czech patriot and an advocate of Slavic solidarity, amorphous as his ideas may have been and however much he allowed patriotism to mask private and commercial interests. He often conjured up visions of a federated and less authoritarian Austria-Hungary, which would grant rights to its Slavic majority equal to those enjoyed by the German and Hungarian minorities. Like Young Czechs past and present, he urged fellow citizens to be "positive, realistic, and active" in working through established institutions, however imperfect, to realize Bohemian state rights. Unlike Fiedler or the Old Czechs Goll and Zeithammer, he had no genuine devotion to Austria-Hungary, though he did on occasion foretell a glorious future for the Monarchy. More often he assailed imperial oppression before large crowds in small Bohemian towns. So ardently did Kramář argue these two tacks that he would later be mistakenly viewed by some as "an Austrian politician" and by others as "the true instigator of the World War."[15] In fact, Kramář perpetuated the time-honored Young Czech practice of speaking boldly while acting circumspectly. The coming of the First World War found him prepared to sit tight in hopes of a Russian victory. In 1915, the Austro-Hungarian authorities foolishly made a hero of him by incarcerating him for high treason when in fact he had done no more than forthrightly defend Czech interests and engage in petty and inconclusive intrigues with Russian friends and in exploratory talks with Masaryk and the Czech Secret Committee.

The Young Czech party under the leadership of Herold, Kramář, Pacák, Rašín, and Škarda became more outspokenly the representative of the privileged urban upper middle class after it lost

the peasantry and lower middle classes to the Agrarians and National Socialists respectively and most of the intelligentsia to
the several progressive parties. Given these losses and the introduction in January 1907 of universal manhood suffrage to the
lower house of the Reichsrat, the Young Czechs had no choice but
to try to rebuild their party along lines similar to the mass
parties. Their efforts were too little and too late. Young
Czechs had nonetheless endorsed extension of the franchise, believing it to be in the national interest while recognizing it
would diminish their influence. For this sacrifice, few expected that they would receive many peasant and working-class votes,
for fifth curial voting since 1896 had shown that most newly enfranchised voters would support Social Democratic or Agrarian
candidates. On balance the party sought to advance its own and
the national cause by enfranchising the masses to fight for
Czech interests in the Reichsrat while continuing to exclude the
masses from politics at home through curial voting for the diets
and district boards.

The end of Young Czech preponderance in Czech politics accentuated the party's dependence upon unrepresentative commercial
and self-governmental institutions. Under three-class voting in
communes and four-curial voting for district boards and the Bohemian Diet, the party in Czech areas kept control of all urban
and some rural communes, all district boards, and the second and
third curias of the Bohemian Diet. But the party's poor showing
under universal manhood suffrage proved that its claim to represent the whole nation had no basis in fact.

Agreement on several policies continued to unite the Young
Czechs and the successor parties, including promotion of economic growth, Czech language, Czech schools, the interests of
Czech minorities, and efforts to transform Austria-Hungary into
a more liberal and federalized constitutional state. Such agreement did not preclude serious differences of opinion on tactics
as well as on other policies. For example, Young Czech positive
politics came increasingly under fire from these parties, who
thought that cooperation between any imperial government and the
Young Czech party would probably be effected at their expense.
And as efforts by the National Socialists, Masaryk's Progressives, and the Social Democrats to extend the franchise to provincial and district self-government ran into Young Czech opposition, these parties began to argue that defense of Bohemian
state rights ought not to entail perpetuation of the privileged
status of upper middle-class Czechs.

The positive politics, highly touted by Kramář as a new departure, were, as their chief executor Pacák and architect Škarda recognized, no more than a refurbishing of the responsible
and active politics adopted at Nymburk in 1894 with one important
change: Young Czechs no longer entered an imperial government
as individuals, as had Kaizl and Rezek under Engel's chairmanship, but with party endorsement, as did Fort, Fiedler, and

Pacák. Indeed, positive politics did successfully win modest
concessions from imperial governments in return for Young Czech
support on tariffs, taxes, or military budgets. These concessions, whether internal improvements, tax reform, government
subsidies for industry and agriculture, or aid to disaster areas,
were usually administered in Bohemia by the Provincial Executive
Council through the district boards controlled by the Young
Czechs. All citizens benefited indirectly from certain such
concessions like railway and canal construction or flood relief.
But others, notably tax reductions for industry without lowering
high taxes on staple goods, hurt propertyless workers and peasants. In any case, parties not represented on the unrepresentative Provincial Executive Council and district boards had
little voice in the distribution of imperial or provincial funds
or in the planning of projects to be undertaken with local tax
monies. The Social Democrats and the National Socialists therefore argued that concessions for material improvements, no matter how beneficial to the public, usually strengthened and perpetuated the privileges of the propertied and educated classes.
On this issue there was no possibility of compromise between the
Czech left and the upper middle-class Young Czech and Old Czech
parties.

To compensate for their relative political weakness in Cisleithania, Young Czechs in cooperation with the Prague and Pilsen chambers of commerce used the newly acquired Czech economic
muscle to further Slavic solidarity while opening new markets,
as the export of Czech capital and industrial products to the
Balkans and Slovakia went hand in hand with Czech political ambitions. Meanwhile, Czech banks and savings and loan institutions, so important in achieving fiscal independence for Czech
cultural and political institutions, grew increasingly powerful
and prosperous and, apart from the locally owned savings and
loan associations, came more effectively under the control of
the privileged upper middle classes.

Rašín, Fiedler, and Kramář, like their mentor Kaizl, opposed
all Social Democratic panaceas proposing economic growth through
public ownership of the means of production and a redistribution
of wealth. These men, who had helped put Austria-Hungary on the
gold standard in 1892, always argued that Czech prosperity and
progress required financial stability, rational application of
science and technology, individual initiative, and a prosperous
monarchy. They deplored the riots of 1897 primarily because of
resulting property damage and economic dislocation. Like the
German socialists of the chair under whom Kaizl and Kramář had
studied, most Young Czechs came to favor state intervention to
implement social welfare measures to promote national strength
and harmony. Behind all decisions on policy lay the assumption
that men of education and wealth should run business and local
self-government and would promote the general welfare of the
country while promoting their own.

The party leadership gradually overcame the last radical
holdouts in the party, already weakened by the loss of their
constituency to the National Socialists. Edvard Grégr in semi-
retirement was revered by all factions as an elder statesman.
To be rid of Josef Fořt, the party arranged his appointment as
Minister of Commerce in the Beck cabinet.

The control of the Young Czech party by banking and industrial interests was greatly furthered in 1908 when Kramář and his
wealthy backers bought the *Národní listy* from Prokop Grégr and
the staff who were no longer able to make up its deficits from
their own pockets.[16] The former tension between the radical *Národní listy* and the moderate party leadership all but vanished
as Kramář brought into line the last group to resist positive
politics within the party. That editorial bastion of radical
liberalism and nationalism became a spokesman for commercial and
industrial interests. This completed the eclipse of the Young
Czechs as a party that tried to represent popular interests and
act in accordance with liberal principles as well as expediency.
The *Národní listy* continued to pay tribute to Julius Grégr and
retained many veteran editors, including Anýž, Tůma, and Heller.
But the price for changing editorial policy was a waning popular
influence and loss of intellectual preeminence best reflected by
the growing circulation of the new mass party dailies, *Venkov*
and *Právo lidu*. Stránský's *Lidové noviny* eventually became the
foremost liberal voice.

The Young Czechs at times turned to their advantage the radical tactics and programs of the new popular parties of which
they heartily disapproved. Kramář pointed out to successive
minister-presidents that governmental concessions to the Young
Czechs would prevent Social Democracy and antidynastic parties
from winning even greater popular support, much as Kaizl and
Pacák had tried to wheedle concessions from Minister-President
Thun in 1898 and 1899 by reporting their talks and exchanges of
letters with radical Czech opponents.[17] Kramář and Tobolka also
exaggerated the extent and intensity of radicalism in the Young
Czech party to make their positive politics appeal all the more
responsible by comparison.

For forty years, the Young Czech party played an important
and largely constructive part in Czech and in Cisleithanian politics before giving way to parties more representative of popular interests and aspirations. These years, despite a series of
severe political defeats for the Czech nation, were generally
ones of economic and cultural progress. To complement this advance, the Young Czech party encouraged industrial and agricultural development and campaigned tirelessly for political autonomy, civil liberties, universal manhood suffrage, secular national schools, and equal rights for all nationalities. Although
it remained short-sighted on the social question, it helped
transmit the heritage of the Czech National Revival and the
ideals of 1848 to its more democratic successor parties. A

measure of the party's devotion to liberal principles and to the
national interest was its continuing advocacy of liberal and
democratic reforms that would clearly spell an end to its preeminence in Czech politics. It helped give Czech politics of
the later nineteenth and early twentieth centuries its characteristic features: radicalism at home and conciliation in Vienna, vigorous speech-making and courageous journalism, an uncompromising defense of national and civil liberties, and a willingness to compromise or negotiate on bread-and-butter issues. Much
as the party denounced the ties of Czech politics to the Bohemian
nobility and much as it tried to become more democratic in character, it could never escape the conservative influence of the
Rieger-Clam-Martinic alliance or the self-government institutions
established in the sixties. The party ended in 1914 as it began,
an elite or cadre party of solid citizens and notables based upon
the highly unrepresentative institutions of district and provincial self-government. But it nonetheless served as the party of
transition between the elite national parties of the sixties
through the eighties and the mass political parties which arose
during the nineties. In its refusal to settle for second-class
citizenship for the Czech people within Austria Hungary and in
its adherence to the program of Bohemian state rights, the party
kept alive the struggle for political and cultural self-
determination. It aimed to transform the Habsburg Monarchy, not
destroy it. But the monarchy proved incapable of peaceful transformation and in the end chose violence instead of reform. Defeat of the Central Powers and the dissolution of the Habsburg
Monarchy made possible the creation of an independent Czechoslovakia, which all Czechs could justifiably regard as the crowning
achievement of their National Revival.

The achievement of national independence and the institution
of social and land reforms left the State Rights Progressives
without a program and they had nowhere to go except back to the
parent Young Czech party. Together, the Young Czechs and State
Rights Progressives emerged in 1919 as the party of Czechoslovak
National Democracy, which became the rallying point for banking
and business interests and for the nationalist intelligentsia
opposed to Social Democracy, the leftward orientation of Masaryk
and Beneš, and Agrarian willingness to compromise with the Germans. It was a party whose time had passed, ranking sixth in
popularity, well behind the Agrarians, Social Democrats, National
Socialists, Communists, and Catholics.

Political success is usually transitory and especially so
among the smaller peoples of Central and Eastern Europe. The
worth of politicians has therefore often been measured in terms
of their honesty, decency, and devotion to national and democratic principles as well as in terms of their political success.
The Young Czech party produced no national leaders comparable in
ability, deeds, or popular esteem to Palacký, the father of his
country, or to T. G. Masaryk, the President-Liberator. It did

produce able political tacticians and formidable political pole-
micists who manipulated and at times modified existing political
ideas and institutions and who, despite many shortcomings,
played a constructive and prominent part in Czech and Cisleithanian politics. Among them assuredly were Adámek, Eim, Engel,
and the Grégr brothers; Kaizl, Kramář, Pacák, Rašín, and Sladkovský; and Trojan, Slavík, the two Škardas, and Špindler. Few
Czechs have ever held the Young Czech party in great affection
or esteem; but as the dominant Czech political party during one
decade and as a leading force in three others, with achievements
for the most part constructive, its important place in Czech and
Cieleithanian history remains secure.

APPENDIX

Table 1

Population of Cisleithania

Nationality According to *Umgangssprache*	Population in Thousands				Percentage of Total Population			
	1880	1890	1900	1910	1880	1890	1900	1910
Total Population								
German	8,009	8,462	9,171	9,950	36.75	36.05	35.78	35.58
Czech	5,181	5,473	5,955	6,436	23.77	23.32	23.23	23.01
Polish	3,239	3,719	4,252	4,968	14.86	15.84	16.59	17.76
Ukrainian	2,793	3,105	3,382	3,519	12.80	13.23	13.19	12.58
Slovenian	1,140	1,177	1,193	1,253	5.23	5.01	4.65	4.48
Serbian and Croatian	564	645	711	788	2.59	2.75	2.78	2.82
Italian	669	675	727	768	3.07	2.88	2.84	2.75
Romanian	191	209	231	275	0.88	0.89	0.90	0.98
Hungarian	10	8	10	11	0.05	0.03	0.04	0.04
Total Slav	12,917	14,119	15,493	16,964	59.25	60.15	60.44	60.65
Total Pop.	21,796	23,473	25,632	27,968	100.00	100.00	100.00	100.00
Bohemian Population								
Czech	3,470	3,644	3,930	4,242	62.40	62.37	62.19	62.66
German	2,054	2,159	2,337	2,468	36.99	36.95	36.98	36.45
Other	37	40	52	60	0.66	0.68	0.83	0.89
Total	5,561	5,843	6,319	6,770	100.00	100.00	100.00	100.00

Table 1--*Continued*

Nationality According to *Umgangssprache*	Population in Thousands				Percentage of Total Population			
	1880	1890	1900	1910	1880	1890	1900	1910
Moravian Population								
Czech	1,507	1,591	1,727	1,868	70.00	70.00	71.36	71.79
German	629	664	675	719	29.22	29.21	27.89	27.63
Other	17	18	18	15	0.78	0.79	0.75	0.58
Total	2,153	2,273	2,420	2,602	100.00	100.00	100.00	100.00
Silesian Population								
Czech	126	130	146	180	22.30	21.45	21.47	23.78
German	269	282	297	326	47.61	46.53	43.68	43.06
Polish	155	178	220	235	27.43	29.37	32.35	31.04
Other	15	16	17	16	2.66	2.65	2.50	2.12
Total	565	606	680	757	100.00	100.00	100.00	100.00

Sources: Figures are from Richard Charmatz, *Deutsch-österreichische Politik* (Leipzig, 1907), pp. 84-85; Zdeněk Tobolka, ed., *Česká Politika* (Prague, 1906), 1:234; *Statistisches Handbuch des Königreiches Böhmen*, 2d ed. (Prague, 1913), pp. 14-15; Karel Adámek, *Z naší doby* (Velké Meziříčí, 1890), 4:86-87; Josef Pazourek, ed., *Ottův obchodní slovník* 3 vols. (Prague, 1912-24), 1:436-38, 2:553, 3:1206-7; Jan Vyhlídal, *Naše Slezsko* (Prague, 1900), pp. 18-19; *Ottův slovník naučný*, vol. 28, articles "Čechy," "Morava," and "Slezsko."

Table 2

Division of the Population in Cisleithania According to
Language and Economic Activity in 1910

Nationality According to *Umgangssprache*	Percentage of Total Population	Type of Work Done by the Gainfully Employed including Family Members			
		As Percentage of the Total Labor Force			
		Agriculture	Industry	Commerce, Transport	Bureaucracy, Army, Liberal Professions
German	34.8	21.6	47.9	46.3	46.9
(Those living in Czech lands)	(12.2)	(6.5)	(20.9)	(14.3)	(13.8)
Czech	22.5	17.9	31.6	20.6	23.1
Polish	17.3	21.5	10.2	20.2	13.7
Ukrainian, Slovene, Serbian, Croatian	19.5	34.1	4.3	5.4	8.9
Others: Magyar, Romanian, Italian, etc.	5.9	4.9	6.0	7.5	7.4
Total	100.0	100.0	100.0	100.0	100.0

Source: Pavla Horská, "Structure économique et sociale des pays
tchèques au début du XXe siècle en comparaison des autres pays de
l'Europe centrale," *Communications Mezinárodní Konference k 50. Výročí
Československé Republiky* (Prague, October 11-15, 1968), p. 59, gives
this table. Information in it is derived from *Österreichische Statistik*
NF 3/1.

Table 3A

Population Growth in the Czech Lands by Areas, 1857-1910

Area	Population in Thousands					
	1857	1869	1880	1890	1900	1910
(1) Depressed Agricultural	2,027	2,132	2,221	2,219	2,256	2,325
(2) Intensive Agricultural	1,343	1,422	1,580	1,647	1,723	1,971
(3) Older Industrial	2,215	2,391	2,522	2,606	2,702	2,751
(4) New Industrial	1,371	1,597	1,876	2,168	2,664	3,005
Total	6,956	7,542	8,199	8,640	9,345	10,052

Source: Ludmila Kárníková, *Vývoj obyvatelstva v českých zemích
1754-1914* (Prague, 1965), pp. 348-51. The population of Polish
Cieszyn is not included.

Table 3B

Noble and Peasant Holding of Arable Land in Bohemia, 1791 and 1891

Class	1791		1891	
	Thousands of Hectares	Percentage	Thousands of Hectares	Percentage
Nobles	1,853	41.5	1,677	33.8
Peasants	2,614	58.5	3,289	66.2

Source: *Ottův slovník naučný*, 6:422.

Table 3C

Population Growth of Czechs and Germans in
Three North Bohemian Districts, 1880-1921

Three North Bohemian Districts	Percentage of Total Population Speaking Czech or German[a]									
	1880		1890		1900		1910		1921	
	German	Czech	German	Czech	German	Czech	German	Czech	German	Czech
Most (Brüx)[b]	86.31[c]	13.68	74.42	25.57	68.73	31.25	72.17	27.81	52.77	46.47
Teplice-Šanov (Teplitz-Schönau)	94.77	5.21	93.95	6.05	89.65	10.35	87.05	12.91	76.70	22.70
Duchcov-Bílina (Dux-Bilin)	88.82	11.18	86.75	13.25	82.88	16.99	73.99	25.74	61.17	38.62

Sources: *Statistický lexikon obcí v Čechách* (Prague, 1923), pp. xiii-xviii, and *Statistische Handbuch des Königreiches Böhmen* (Prague, 1913), pp. 16-17.

a. 1880-1910 according to *Umgangssprache (obcovací jazyk)*; in 1921 by declaration of nationality.

b. In 1910 the total population of each district was as follows: Most (Brüx): Germans, 75,342; Czechs, 25,056; Teplice-Šanov (Teplitz-Schönau): Germans, 86,679; Czechs, 12,851, Duchcov-Bílina (Dux-Bilin): Germans 61,572; Czechs 21,420.

c. The percentage of the total population speaking languages other than Czech or German was as follows: Most (Brüx): 1880-.01; 1890-.01; 1900-.02; 1910-.02; 1921-.76; Teplice-Šanov (Teplitz-Schönau): 1880-.02; 1910-.04; 1921-.60; Duchcov-Bílina (Dux-Bilin): 1900-.02; 1910-.04; 1921-.60.

Table 4A

Distribution of the Agricultural Labor Force
in Cisleithania in 1910

Nationality According to *Umgangssprache*	Distribution among 1,000 Persons				
	Independent Producers	Administrative Help	Workers	Day Laborers	Members of Families Helping
German	294.0	4.4	276.9	92.1	332.6
Czech	304.7	3.9	273.4	90.0	328.0
Polish	308.4	3.4	87.9	60.0	540.3
Ukrainian	316.2	0.2	53.6	58.9	571.1
Slovene	293.5	0.4	134.1	60.0	512.0
Serbian and Croatian	296.4	0.1	29.6	9.1	664.8

Source: Pavla Horská, "Structure économique et sociale des pays tchèques au début du XXe siècle en comparaison des autres pays de l'Europe centrale," *Communications Mezinárodní Konference k 50. Výročí Československé Republiky* (Prague, October 11–15, 1968), p. 60, gives this table. Information in it is derived from *Österreichische Statistik* NF 3/1.

Table 4B

Distribution of the Nonagricultural Labor Force
in Cisleithania in 1910

Nationality According to *Umgangssprache*	Distribution among 1,000 Persons				
	Self-Employed	Clerks	Industrial Workers	Day Laborers	Members of Families Helping
German	341.7	59.8	421.6	47.0	129.9
Czech	326.1	35.0	427.0	55.3	156.6
Polish	351.2	28.2	172.2	57.2	391.2
Ukrainian	330.9	5.5	77.4	59.0	527.2
Slovene	348.2	15.3	217.9	52.7	365.9
Serbian and Croatian	309.5	12.3	79.1	14.1	585.0
Italian	380.2	48.3	243.3	58.4	269.8
Romanian	316.3	12.6	81.1	205.0	385.0
Magyar	303.3	8.3	48.2	112.4	527.8
Total Population	337.7	38.7	310.8	53.4	259.4

Source: Pavla Horská, "Structure économique et sociales des pays
tchèques au début du XXe siècle en comparaison des autres pays de
l'Europe centrale," *Communications Mezinarodní Konference k 50. Výročí
Československé Republiky* (Prague, October 11-15, 1968), p. 65, gives
this table. Information in it is derived from *Österreichische
Statistik* NF 3/1.

Table 5

Distribution of Officials in Central Offices in Vienna, January 1, 1914

Central Office	Total officials	Germans	Poles	Czechs	Slovenes, Croats, & Serbs	Italians	Hungarians	Romanians	Ukrainians and Ruthenians
Ministry of Foreign Affairs	832	396	49	55	52	37	229	14	-
Ministry of War	614	419	18	91	29	5	42	8	2
Administrative Court of Justice	75	53	7	10	3	1	1	-	-
Presidium of the Ministerial Council	48	31	10	4	3	-	-	-	-
Ministry of Interior	259	187	19	31	10	5	3	1	3
Ministry for Worship & Public Instruction	152	109	13	17	5	3	1	-	4
Ministry of Justice[a]	197	77	48	31	19	7	-	2	13
Ministry of Finance	295	224	28	24	10	7	-	1	1
Ministry of Commerce	2073	1915	15	128	10	5	-	-	-
Ministry for Public Works	763	613	35	99	12	1	-	1	2
Ministry of Railways	515	406	37	67	2	2	-	1	-
Ministry of Agriculture	148	117	13	16	2	-	-	-	-
Ministry of Provincial Home Defense	322	225	16	80	1	-	-	-	-
Total	6293	4772	308	653	158	73	276	28	25

Source: Information from Hermann Münch, *Böhmische Tragödie: Das Schicksal Mitteleuropas im Lichte des Tschechischen Frage* (Berlin, 1949), p. 542.

a. With the Highest Court of Justice and the General Procurator

330

Table 6

Division of Personal Income in the Dual Monarchy in 1911

Areas Now In:	Share of Personal Income	Share of Population	Ratio of Income to Population
Austria	19.2	12.9	1.48
Czechoslovakia (Czech lands)	28.9	20.3	1.42
Poland, U.S.S.R., Romania (Galicia and Bukovina)	10.9	18.1	0.60
Yugoslavia	5.7	6.5	0.87
Total Cisleithania	64.7	57.8	1.117
Hungary	14.8	15.4	0.96
Czechoslovakia (Slovakia)	5.8	7.2	0.80
Romania	7.3	10.6	0.68
Yugoslavia	6.8	8.4	0.80
Austria (Burgenland)	0.6	0.6	1.00
Total Transleithania	35.3	42.2	0.84
Total Dual Monarchy	100.0	100.0	1.00

Source: This table is taken from Peter Hanák, "Die bürgerliche Umgestaltung der Habsburger-Monarchie und der Ausgleich" in *Der österreichisch-ungarische Ausgleich 1867: Materialien (Referate und Diskussion) des internationalen Konferenz in Bratislava 28.8.--1.9 1967*, edited by Anton Vantuch and L'udovít Holotík (Bratislava, 1971), p. 348. I have corrected the addition of figures in columns one and three.

Table 7

Landholding in Cisleithania in 1900 in Millions of Hectares

Province	Farm Land		Smaller Farms			Great Landed Estates				
	Total Area	Of This Forests	Total Area	Percentage Total Area	Of This Forests	Total Area	Percentage Total Area	Of This Forests	Of This Entailed	Number of Entailed
Lower Austria	2.0	0.8	1.5	75	0.5	0.5	25	0.3	0.13	72
Upper Austria	1.2	0.4	0.9	75	0.3	0.3	25	0.1	0.06	20
Salzburg	0.7	0.23	0.4	57	0.07	0.3	43	0.16	----	--
Tyrol, Vorarlberg	2.9	1.1	2.2	76	0.8	0.7	24	0.3	0.0009	1
Styria	2.2	1.1	1.7	77	0.7	0.5	23	0.4	0.02	30
Carinthia	1.0	0.5	0.8	80	0.3	0.2	20	0.2	0.07	15
Carniola	1.0	0.4	0.8	80	0.3	0.2	20	0.1	0.05	10
Istria, Goriza, Trieste	0.8	0.23	0.7	88	0.2	0.1	12	0.03	0.001	19
Dalmatia	1.3	0.41	1.2	92	0.4	0.1	8	0.01	0.005	36
Bohemia	5.2	1.5	3.5	67	0.5	1.7	33	1.0	0.6	58
Moravia	2.2	0.6	1.7	77	0.2	0.5	23	0.4	0.2	19
Silesia	0.5	0.18	0.3	60	0.04	0.2	40	0.14	0.02	5
Galicia	7.9	2.0	4.8	61	0.3	3.1	39	1.7	0.05	11
Bukovina	1.1	0.4	0.6	55	0.1	0.5	45	0.3	0.03	1
Total	30.0	9.85	21.1		4.71	8.9		5.14	1.2369	297

Sources: Figures from *Statistische Monatsschrift, 1900*, pp. 125ff.
Table adapted from that in Richard Charmatz, *Deutsch-österreichische Politik* (Leipzig, 1907), p. 260. Totals computed by author.

Table 8A

Landholders in Bohemia in 1896

Classification of Holder[a]	Size in Hectares	Number of Holdings	Percentage of Total No. Holdings	Total Hectares	Percentage of Total Holdings
Peasant Dwarfholder	0-1	484,885	55.84	131,203	2.58
	1-2	109,148	12.57	155,748	3.07
Peasant Smallholder	2-5	109,544	12.61	346,794	6.84
Middling Farmer	5-20	124,309	14.31	1,328,804	26.19
Large Farmer	20-50	36,119	4.16	1,013,505	19.98
Large Farmer or Estate Owner	50-100	2,849	0.33	188,363	3.71
Estate Owner	Over 100	1,548	0.18	1,908,948	37.63
Total		868,402	100.00	5,073,365	100.00

Sources: Information for this table taken from table in Rudolf Franěk, *Některé problemy sociální postavení rolnictva v Čechách na konci 19. a počátkem 20. stoleti* ("Rozpravy," vol. 77, no. 6; Prague, 1967), p. 19, and from *Statistisches Handbuch des Königreiches Böhmen* (Prague, 1913), p. 184. See table 8B for more complete data, table 9 for comparison with Moravia, and table 7 for a comparison with other crown lands in Cisleithania. Franěk remains the most complete work to date on its subject. The use of Leninist terminology to describe later nineteenth-century agricultural classes in the Czech lands usually obfuscates rather than clarifies the question of rural class relationships. For example, see Jan Havránek, "Die ökonomische und politische Lage der Bauernschaft in den böhmischen Ländern in den letzten Jahrzehnten des 19. Jahrhunderts," *Jahrbuch für Wirtschaftsgeschichte*, pt. 2 (Berlin, 1966): 96-136; and Jurij Křížek, *T. G. Masaryk a česká politika: politické vystoupení českých "realistu" v letech 1887-1893* (Prague, 1959).

a. The Czech terms "peasant" (*sedlák*), "farmer" (*rolník*), and "agriculturalist" (*zemědelec*) were often used interchangeably, but as a general rule contemporaries more often than not followed the above distinctions. A "parcelholder" or "dwarfholder" was any peasant with

Table 8A--*Continued*

less than one or two hectares of land. The distinction between large
farmers and estate owners varied from district to district, but an
estate was usually defined as any farm in excess of 50 to 100 hectares
in which all land was in one parcel and under one management, as defined by the *Ottův slovník naučný*, 24:11-12. For purposes of clarity
and consistency all terms used in the paper shall correspond to the
above listing, but the reader should remember they do not define fixed
categories. These divisions correspond to those used by official
statisticians of Imperial Germany, as reported in Richard Charmatz,
Deutsch-österreichische Politik (Leipzig, 1907), p. 273.

Table 8B

Landholding in Bohemia in 1896

Size of Holdings in Hectares	Number of Holdings	Percentage of Total No. Holdings	Total Hectares	Percentage of Total Hectares
0-0.5	373,088	42.96	50,439	0.99
0.5-1	111,797	12.87	80,764	1.59
1-2	109,148	12.57	155,748	3.07
2-5	109,544	12.62	346,794	6.84
5-10	62,963	7.25	454,136	8.95
10-20	61,346	7.06	874,668	17.24
20-50	36,119	4.16	1,013,505	19.98
50-100	2,849	0.33	188,363	3.71
100-200	772	0.09	104,406	2.06
200-500	380	0.04	116,143	2.29
500-1000	141	0.02	101,748	2.00
1000-2000	104	0.01	150,567	2.97
2000 or more	151	0.02	1,436,084	28.31
Total	868,402	100.00	5,073,365	100.00

Source: Information from a table in *Statistisches Handbuch des Königreiches Böhmen* (Prague, 1913), 2:184. Percentages of total number of holdings were computed from these figures.

Table 9

Landholding in Moravia in 1900

Size of Holdings in Hectares	Number of Holdings	Percentage of Total No. Holdings	Total Hectares	Percentage of Total Hectares
0-0.5	356,917	56.84	48,232	2.2
0.5-1	80,079	12.75	58,029	2.7
1-2	60,846	9.69	85,642	3.9
2-5	53,599	8.54	170,212	7.8
5-10	33,911	5.40	243,122	11.1
10-20	28,259	4.50	403,723	18.5
20-50	12,634	2.01	350,929	16.1
50-100	1,088	0.17	72,416	3.3
100-200	287	0.05	38,198	1.8
200-500	151	0.02	46,411	2.1
500-1000	60	0.01	42,611	2.0
1000-2000	43	0.01	63,075	2.9
2000 or more	73	0.01	558,625	25.6
Total	627,947	100.00	2,181,225	100.0

Source: Percentages were computed from official figures in *Ottův slovník naučný* (Prague, 1909), 28: 973-74.

Table 10

The Nine Largest Czech Banking Institutions in 1914

Bank	Capital Stock in Thousands of Crowns
The Tradesman's Bank (Živnostenská banka)	80,000
Czech Industrial Bank (Česká průmyslová banka)	40,000
The Central Bank of Czech Savings Banks (Ústřední banka českých spořitelen)	25,000
Prague Credit Bank (Pražská úvěrní banka)	25,000
The Savings and Loan Institution (Záložní úvěrní ústav)	15,000
Moravian Agrarian and Industrial Bank (Moravská agrární a průmyslová banka)	12,000
Land Bank (Pozemková banka)	9,000
Czech Bank (Česká banka)	8,000
Agrarian Bank (Agrární banka)	4,000

Source: Figures for this table were taken from Antonín
Pimper, *České obchodní banky za války a po válce* (Prague,
1929), p. 39.

Table 11

Production in the Czech Lands of Certain Items as a Percentage
of Total Cisleithanian Production, 1880-1900

Year	Bohemia	Moravia	Silesia	Czech Lands
Hard Coal				
1880	55.4	10.8	27.6	93.8
1890	41.7	12.8	38.1	92.6
1900	32.7	13.5	42.7	88.9
Soft Coal				
1880	73.4	1.1	0.0	74.5
1890	79.5	0.7	0.0	80.2
1900	80.6	0.9	0.0	81.5
Pig Iron				
1880	48.9	27.8	6.8	83.5
1890	19.5	58.1	5.2	82.8
1900	14.0	63.4	13.0	90.4
Sugar Beets				
1880/81	68.69	25.55	4.28	98.52
1889/90	64.87	28.96	4.42	98.25
1899/1900	61.31	32.67	2.67	96.65
Beer				
1880/81	44.67	8.70	1.91	55.28
1889/90	44.34	8.55	2.44	55.33
1899/1900	46.10	10.22	2.14	58.46

Source: Table taken from Oldřich Říha and Július Mésároš, eds.,
Přehled Československých dějin (Prague, 1960), vol. 2, pt. 1,
p. 504.

Table 12

Mining of Hard and Soft Coals in the Czech Lands

Year	Production in Millions of Tons	Number of Miners
1819		1,672
1828	0.13	
1830	0.16	
1840	3.27	
1850	4.03	
1851		11,970
1857		19,448
1860	4.18	
1870	8.42	37,012
1880	9.58	49,794
1889		66,845
1890	15.5	70,021
1900	20.07	
1910	24.72	
1913		97,458
1919	27.6	

Sources: Information for this table is from a table in *Školní atlas československých dějin* (Prague, 1959), p. 30, and from Ludmila Kárníková, *Vývoj uhelného průmyslu v českých zemích do r. 1880* (Prague, 1960), p. 352.

Table 13

Sugar Beet Production in Bohemia

Year	Refineries	Production in Tons
1841	52	947
1854	96	3,790
1860		47,000
1863	114	94,219
1871		184,500
1873	159	
1880		329,000
1890		450,000
1891	133	
1913	100	700,000

Source: Information for this table taken from a table in
Školní atlas československých dějin (Prague, 1959), p. 30.

Table 14

Growth of the Forty Largest Cities in the Czech Lands to 1910

City and Rank in 1910	Prov.	Area	Population to Nearest Thousand						
			1829 -34	1850 -51	1869	1880	1890	1900	1910
1. Prague (Praha, Prag) and suburbs "Velká Praha"	Bc	Ig	89	136	276	356	444	506	673.2
2. Brno (Brünn) including "Velké Brno"	Ms	Ig	34	61	95	109	134	164	201.5
3. Moravská Ostrava, Sleszká Ostrava and suburbs "Velká Ostrava"	M&S (Mn)	I	1	4	24	40	66	121	156.3
4. Plzeň (Pilsen) and suburbs	Bw	I	9	11	24	42	55	80	99.1
5. Liberec (Reichenberg) and suburbs	Bn	T	10	13	34	42	48	57	65.0

Source: Data for this table was taken from various tables in Ludmila Kárníková, *Vývoj obyvatelstva v českých zemích 1754-1914* (Prague, 1965), pp. 78-101, 112-19, 143-82, 218-69. Mrs. Kárníková used official census data and statistics in preparing her tables.

Notes: Abbreviations: Provinces: B-Bohemia, S-Silesia, M-Moravia
n-north, s-south, e-east, w-west, c-central
Areas: A - Intensive agricultural areas
D - Depressed agricultural areas
T - Older manufacturing area dominated by textile industries
I - New industrial area dominated by iron, steel, machine products
g - Important governmental center
ND - No Data

Names of cities with German majorities or large German minorities given in two languages.

Table 14--*Continued*

City and Rank in 1910	Prov.	Area	Population to Nearest Thousand						
			1829 -34	1850 -51	1869	1880	1890	1900	1910
6. Karviná-Orlová (Karwin)	S (Mn)	I	1	3	8	22	30	48	63.7
7. Ústí nad Labem (Aussig) and suburbs	Bn	I	2	3	16	24	38	54	63.0
8. Teplice-Šanov (Teplitz-Schönau) and suburbs	Bn	I	3	8	12	24	33	49	57.0
9. České Budějovice (Budweis) and suburbs	Bs	D	7	12	17	25	32	45	54.0
10. Olomouc and suburbs	M	A	10	11	19	33	37	45	50.5
11. Kladno and suburbs	Bc	I	1	ND	15	21	28	35	41.8
12. Most (Brüx) and suburbs	Bn	I	2	4	7	15	23	33	39.6
13. Opava (Troppau) with Katerinky	S (Mn)	Tg	8	13	20	25	30	34	38.2
14. Karlovy Vary-Rybare-Stará Role (Karlsbad-Fischern)	Bw	I	3	ND	13	16	20	29	35.1
15. Prostějov	Ms	A	7	11	16	18	21	25	31.5
16. Jablonec nad Nisou (Gablonz)	Bn	T	3	4	7	9	15	21	29.5
17. Cheb (Eger)	Bw	T	9	11	13	17	19	24	26.7
18. Jihlava (Iglau)	Ms	D	13	18	20	22	24	24	26.0
19. Chomutov (Komotau) with Horní Ves	Bn	I	4	4	7	12	15	20	24.9

Table 14—*Continued*

City and Rank in 1910	Prov.	Area	Population to Nearest Thousand						
			1829 -34	1850 -51	1869	1880	1890	1900	1910
20. Děčín-Podmokly (Tetschen-Bodenbach)	Bn	T	1	3	8	11	15	20	24.1
21. Varnsdorf (Warnsdorf)	Bn	T	ND	5	13	15	18	21	23.2
22. Hradec Králové and suburbs	Be	A	3	9	10	15	17	19	22.8
23. Těšín (Ceiszyn) (Teschen)	S (Mn)	I	6	6	10	13	15	19	22.5
24. Aš (Asch)	Bw	T	5	6	9	13	16	19	21.9
25. Přerov	Mn	A	4	6	7	11	13	17	20.7
26. Pardubice	Be	A	4	5	8	10	12	17	20.6
27. Znojmo (Znaim)	Ms	D	5	7	10	12	15	16	18.8
28. Sokolov-Chodov-Loket (Falkenau-Chodau-Elbogen)	Bw	I	ND	5	8	10	13	17	18.6
29. Frýdek-Místek	Mn	I	ND	6	9	10	12	15	18.5
30. Žatec (Saaz)	Bc	A	5	6	9	10	13	16	17.1
31. Kroměříž	Ms	A	6	8	10	12	12	14	16.6
32. Kolín	Bc	A	6	6	8	12	14	15	16.5
33. Mladá Boleslav	Bc	A	5	5	9	10	12	13	16.3
34. Trutnov (Trautenau)	Be	T	2	3	8	11	13	15	16.1
35. Kutná Hora	Bc	A	8	10	13	13	14	15	15.6
36. Písek	Bs	D	5	6	9	11	11	14	15.5

Table 14--*Continued*

City and Rank in 1910	Prov.	Area	Population to Nearest Thousand						
			1829 -34	1850 -51	1869	1880	1890	1900	1910
37. Litoměřice (Leitmeritz)	Bn	A	4	6	10	11	11	13	15.4
38. Dvůr Králové nad Labem	Be	T	4	5	6	7	9	11	15.1
39. Šternberk	Mn	D	9	12	14	14	15	15	14.6
40. Klatovy	Bw	D	6	6	8	10	11	13	14.4

Table 15

Young Czech Leaders Grouped According to Occupation

Occupation	1888 Provincial Trustees	1889 Board of Trustees	1889 Diet	1895 Diet	1897 Reichsrat	1901 Diet
Lawyer	4	11	7	19	8	13
Medical Doctor	3	6	3	5	3	4
University Professor	-	2	1	3	2	4
High School Teacher	1	1	-	1	2	1
Ag. School Director	-	2	2	1	1	-
Farmer (rolník)	3	13	10	28	8	15
Estate Owner (statkář)	-	7	6	6	1	1
Miller	2	2	-	2	1	2
Businessman	6	9	3	13	10	9
Engineer	-	1	1	2	1	2
Architect	1	1	-	-	-	-
Journalist	-	4	4	2	1	2
Protestant Minister	1	1	-	-	-	-
Self-Governmental Official	-	-	-	5	5	8
Independently Wealthy	-	1	1	2	1	1
Other	-	1	1	1	1	4
Total	21	62	39	90	45	66

Sources: Information came from PNP, Engel papers, Zemští důverníci: zvolení organisačním sjezdem národní strany svobodomyslné, April 11, 1888; Jaromír Váňa, *Volby do říšské rady v království Českém roku 1897* (Prague, 1897), pp. 70-71; Michael Navrátil, *Almanach sněmu království Českého (1895-1901)* (Prague, 1896), passim; and Michael Navrátil, *Nový český sněm (1901-07)* (Tábor, 1902), pp. 189-90.

Table 16

Diets of the Czech Lands

Province	Total Members	Ex-Officio	Curias				
			I.	II.	III.	IV.	V.
Bohemia	242 (241)[a]	6 (5)[a]	70	15	72	79	-
Moravia	151 (100)[b]	2 (2)	30 (30)	6 (6)	40 (31)	53 (31)	20 (-)
Silesia	31	1	9	2	10	9	-

Sources: Table adapted from tables in Zdeněk Tobolka, ed., *Česká politika* (Prague, 1907), vol. 2, pt. 1, p. 761; and Edmund Bernatzik, *Die österreichischen Verfassungsgesetze*, 2d ed. (Vienna, 1911), p. 847.

a. Before 1882 when the rector of the new Czech university became an ex-officio member.

b. Moravian figures in parentheses show representation before the Moravian Agreement of 1905.

346

Table 17

Bohemian Diet Elections in Predominantly Czech Districts, 1883-1908

Party	Curias			Total (97 Seats)
	II. (8 Seats)	III. (40 Seats)	IV. (49 Seats)	
1883 Election				
Young Czechs	-	4	6	10
Old Czechs	8	36	43	87
1889 Election				
Young Czechs	-	9	30	39
Old Czechs	8	31	19	58
Changes in Party Affiliation during 1890 and 1891				
Young Czechs				59
Old Czechs				31
Škarda Group				7
1895 Election				
Young Czechs	7	37	46	90[a]
Old Czechs	1	1	1	3
Agrarians	-	-	2	2
Radical Progressives	-	1	-	1
Independent (Blažej Mixa)	-	1	-	1
1901 Election				
Young Czechs	4	38	24	66
Old Czechs	4	1	1	6
Agrarians	-	-	21	21
Radical Progressives	-	-	2	2
State Rights Radicals	-	1	1	2

347

Table 17--*Continued*

Party	Curias			Total (97 Seats)
	II. (8 Seats)	III. (40 Seats)	IV. (49 Seats)	
	1908 Election			
Young Czechs	6	30	2	38
Old Czechs	2	2	-	4
Agrarians	-	-	43	43
State Rights Progressives	-	5	-	5
Catholic People's	-	-	1	1
People's Progressives ("Realists")	-	-	1	1
Independent Young Czechs	-	2	-	2
Independent State Rights Candidates	-	1	1	2
Independent	-	-	1	1
Candidate of All Czech Parties	-	1[b]	-	1[b]

Sources: Information in this table is taken from Michael Navrátil, *Almanach sněmu království Českého (1895-1901)* (Prague, 1896, passim; Michael Navrátil, *Nový český sněm (1901-07)* (Tábor, 1902), passim; and *Statistisches Handbuch des Königreiches Böhmen*, 2d ed. (Prague, 1913), pp. 54-55.

a. Includes Josef Horák, who ran independently but soon returned to the party, and Jan Vašatý, who ran as a Young Czech but who was expelled from the party in October 1896.

b. This candidate won a seat formerly held by a German, thus increasing the total number of Czech seats in the third curia to 41 and the total number of Czech seats in the diet to 98.

Table 18

Curial Voting to the Lower House of the Reichsrat, 1879 to 1897

Curia	Deputies Elected	No. of Voters	No. of Voters per Deputy
1879--Ten-Gulden Tax Required in Third and Fourth Curias			
1. Great Landowners	85	4,768	56
2. Chambers of Commerce	21	515	25
3. Municipalities	118	196,993	1,669
4. Rural Communes	129	1,290,733	10,006
1891--Five-Gulden Tax Required in Third and Fourth Curias[a]			
1. Great Landowners	85	5,402	64
2. Chambers of Commerce	21	583	28
3. Municipalities	118	338,500	2,869
4. Rural Communes	129	1,387,572	10,756
1897--Four-Gulden Tax Required in Third and Fourth Curias[b]			
1. Great Landowners	85	5,431	64
2. Chambers of Commerce	21	556	26
3. Municipalities	118	493,804	4,185
4. Rural Communes	129	1,505,466	11,670
5. Universal Curia	72	5,004,222	69,500

Sources: Tables adapted from Viktor Adler, *Aufsätze, Reden und Briefe* (Vienna, 1929), 20:23-30; and from Richard Charmatz, *Deutsch-österreichische Politik* (Leipzig, 1907), p. 38.

Note: Direct elections occurred in the first, second, and third curias. Indirect elections occurred in the fourth and fifth curias. Eligible voters chose electors, generally one elector to every 25 voters in the fourth curia and one elector to every 120 voters in the fifth curia.

a. In accordance with imperial law no. 142 of October 4, 1882.

b. In accordance with imperial law no. 168 of June 14, 1896, which also added a fifth or universal curia for all men over twenty-four previously disfranchised residing in their district at least six months.

Table 19

1897 Reichsrat Elections in Predominantly Czech Districts of Bohemia

| Party | Total | Curias | | | | | | | |
| | | II. | | III. | | IV. | | V. | |
		Deputies Elected	%o of Vote	Deputies Elected	%o of Vote	Deputies Elected	%o of Electoral Vote[a]	Deputies Elected	%o of Electoral Vote[a]
Young Czechs	45	4	85.1	17[b]	74.8	15	73.9	9	57.8
Joint Candidates, Old Czechs-Clericals	1	-	2.7	1	15.8	-	11.5	-	3.7
Independents	2	-	--	-	2.4	2[c]	13.6	-	5.3
Social Democrats	2	-	--	-	2.9	-	0.2	2	33.2
Anti-Semites	-	-	--	-	0.8	-	--	-	--
Germans and Others	-	-	12.2	-	3.3	-	0.8	-	--
Total	50	4	100.0	18	100.0	17	100.0	11	100.0

Source: Information for this table came from Jaromír Věňa, *Volby do říšské rady v království Českém roku 1897* (Prague, 1897), pp. 12-13, 28-29, 48-49, 66, 70-72.

a. Indirect elections occurred in the fourth and fifth curias. Percentages shown are of those ballots cast directly for candidates by the electors, each of whom had earlier been chosen by the eligible voters in his district. In the fourth curia in the predominantly Czech districts of Bohemia, 175,256 voters chose 7,589 electors of whom 7,298 or 96.4 percent participated in the election of Reichsrat delegates. In the fifth curia, the comparable figures were 827,475 voters and 6,673 electors of whom 6,371 or 94.3 percent cast ballots.

b. Bedřich Prince Schwarzenberg elected.

c. František Šrámek, independent agrarian, and Jan Vašatý, independent, elected.

Table 20A

1897 Curial Elections to the Reichsrat from Bohemia

Curia	No. of Deputies	No. of Voters	Number of Voters per Deputy	Direct Taxes Paid in Gulden	Amount of Taxes per Deputy
1. Great Landowners	23[a]	444	19	4,714,635	204,984
2. Chambers of Commerce	7	190	27	---	---
3. Municipalities	32	108,517	3,391	13,290,120	415,316
a. Predominantly Czech	18	62,293	3,461	9,030,455	501,692
b. Predominantly German	14	46,224	3,302	4,259,665	304,262
4. Rural Communes	30	288,713 (12,509)[b]	9,624 (417)	12,827,140	427,571
a. Predominantly Czech	17	175,256 (7,589)	10,309 (446)	8,008,635	471,096
b. Predominantly German	13	113,457 (4,920)	8,727 (378)	4,818,505	370,654
5. Universal Curia	18	1,348,020 (11,226)	74,890 (624)	---	---
a. Predominantly Czech	11	827,475 (6,673)	75,225 (607)	---	---
b. Predominantly German	7	520,545 (4,553)	74,363 (650)	---	---

Source: This table and the following three tables are based on the author's computations from figures in Jaromír Váňa, *Volby do říšské rady v království Českém roku 1897* (Prague, 1897), passim.

a. Including 6 from entailed estates.

b. Figures in parentheses denote the number of electors chosen by voters in indirect elections.

Table 20B

Curial Distribution of Taxes, Population, Voters, and Deputies for
1897 Reichsrat Elections in Bohemia: All Districts

		Third Curia	Fourth Curia	Fifth Curia
A.	Total Direct Taxes Paid in Gulden	13,290,120	12,827,140	---
B.	Total Population, 1890	1,356,364	4,411,546	5,770,954
	1897 Estimate			5,980,510
C.	Eligible Voters	108,517	288,713 (12,509)[a]	1,348,020 (11,226)
D.	Number of Deputies	32	30	18
E.	Number of Voters per Deputy	3,391	9,624 (417)	74,890 (624)
F.	Direct Taxes in Gulden per Deputy	415,316	427,571	---
G.	Number of Citizens per Deputy	42,386	147,052	320,609

a. Parentheses denote number of electors chosen by eligible voters
in indirect elections.

Table 20C

Curial Distribution of Taxes, Population, Voters, and Deputies for
1897 Reichsrat Elections in Bohemia: Predominantly Czech Districts

		Third Curia	Fourth Curia	Fifth Curia
A.	Total Direct Taxes Paid in Gulden	9,030,455	8,008,635	---
B.	Total Population, 1890	794,810	2,626,382	3,498,217
	1. 1897 Estimate	865,810	2,743,950	3,655,170
	2. Czechs, 1897	809,707	2,697,787	3,523,426
	3. Germans, 1897	56,103	46,163	131,744
C.	Eligible Voters	62,293	175,256 (7,589)[a]	827,475 (6,673)
D.	Deputies Chosen	18	17	11
E.	Number of Voters per Deputy	3,461	10,309 (446)	75,225 (607)
F.	Direct Taxes in Gulden per Deputy	501,692	471,096	---
G.	Number of Citizens per Deputy	44,156	155,434	318,020
	1. Number of Czech Citizens per Deputy	44,984	158,693	320,311

a. Parentheses denoted number of electors chosen by eligible voters
in indirect elections.

Table 20D

Curial Distribution of Taxes, Population, Voters, and Deputies for
1897 Reichsrat Elections in Bohemia: Predominantly German Districts

		Third Curia	Fourth Curia	Fifth Curia
A.	Total Direct Taxes Paid in Gulden	4,259,665	4,818,505	---
B.	Total Population, 1890	562,261	1,769,164	2,272,737
	1. 1897 Estimate	594,500	1,792,986	2,325,340
	2. 1897 Czechs a. *Umgangssprache*	27,346	268,160	340,275
	b. By Declaration	55,855	325,475	
	3. 1897 Germans a. *Umgangssprache*	567,154	1,524,826	1,985,065
	b. By Declaration	538,645	1,467,511	
C.	Eligible Voters	46,224	113,457 (4,920)[a]	520,545 (4,553)
D.	Deputies Chosen	14	13	7
E.	Number of Voters per Deputy	3,302	8,727 (378)	74,363 (650)
F.	Direct Taxes in Gulden per Deputy	304,262	370,654	---
G.	Number of Citizens per Deputy	40,162	136,090	324,677
	1. Number of German Citizens per Deputy a. *Umgangssprache*	40,511	117,294	283,581
	b. By Declaration	38,475	112,885	

a. Parentheses denote number of electors chosen by eligible voters
in indirect elections.

Table 21A

January 1901 Five-Curial Reichsrat Elections
in Predominantly Czech Districts of Bohemia

Party	Curiae										Total	
	II		III		IV		V					
	Deputies Elected	Change since 1897	Deputies Elected	Change since 1897	Deputies Elected	Change since 1897	Deputies Elected	Change since 1897	Deputies Elected	Change since 1897
Young Czechs	4	--	17	--	11	(-4)	7	(-2)	39	(-6)
Joint Candidates Old Czechs-Clericals	--	--	1	--	--	--	--	--	1	--
Agrarians	--	--	--	--	6	(+5)	--	--	6	(+5)
Independents	--	--	--	--	--	(-1)	--	--	--	(-1)
National Socialists	--	--	--	--	--	--	4	(+4)	4	(+4)
Social Democrats	--	--	--	--	--	--	--	(-2)	--	(-2)
Total	4	--	18	--	17	--	11	--	50	--

Sources: *Naše doba* (1901), 8:278-81; Adolf Srb, *Politické dějiny národa českého od počátku doby konstituční*, 2 vols. (Prague, 1926), 2: *Od r. 1879 do r. 1918*, pp. 253-54.

Table 21B

The Effect of Czech National Socialist Candidacies on the
Young Czech and the Social Democratic Parties in the
Fifth-Curial Parliamentary Elections of 1901 in
Predominantly Czech Electoral Districts of Bohemia

District	Party of Candidate Elected in 1897	Party of Candidate Elected in 1901	1897-1901 Net Decline of Young Czech Votes	Net Decline of Social Democratic Votes
I. Praha (Prague)	Yg.Cz.	Yg.Cz.	5579	6176
II. Smíchov-Kladno	S. D.	Nat.Soc.	270	158
VII. Mladá Boleslav	Yg.Cz.	Yg.Cz.[a]	(1) 79 (2) +26	186
X. Jičín	Yg.Cz.	Nat.Soc.	172	115
XI. Hradec Králové	Yg.Cz.	Yg.Cz.[a]	(1) 223 (2) 173	98
XII. Litomyšl	Yg.Cz.	Nat.Soc.[a]	(1) 167 (2) 83	28
XIII. Čáslav	Yg.Cz.	Yg.Cz.	81	7
XIV. Kolín	Yg.Cz.	Yg.Cz.	140	40
XV. Tábor	Yg.Cz.	Yg.Cz.	131	29
XVI. Budějovice[b]	Ger.Lib.	Ger.Prog.	---	46
XVII. Písek	Yg.Cz.	Yg.Cz.[a]	(1) 152 (2) 56	142
XVIII. Plzeň (Pilsen)	S. D.	Nat.Soc.	196	208
Total			(1) 7190 (2) 6855	7233

Source: Computations for table made from figures in František Soukup,
Druhé volby v páté kurii a sociální demokracie (Prague, 1901).

a. Run-off election: (1) first election, (2) run-off.

b. The Social Democrats ran Němec in 1897 and Vaněk in 1901 against
German candidates. There were no other Czech candidates.

Table 22A

Czech Party Representation in the Lower House of the Reichsrat
under Universal Suffrage in 1907

Party	Number of Votes Received	Total Seats	Percentage of Votes and Number of Seats					
			Bohemia		Moravia		Silesia	
			%/o	No.	%/o	No.	%/o	No.
Social Democrats	389,960	24	39.8	17	30.7	5	65.9	2
Agrarians	206,784	28	22.0	23	15.8	4	14.5	1
Clericals	182,500	17	11.9	7	29.8	10	----	-
Young Czechs and Moravian People's Party	116,524	19	11.3	14	11.4	5	2.2	-
Old Czechs	32,524	6	1.4	2	6.7	4	----	-
National Socialists ⎤	75,101	9	10.3	9	1.1	-	17.4	-
Radical Progressives ⎟ a	9,899	-	0.6	-	----	-	----	-
Radical State Rights Party ⎦	7,879	-	0.5	-	----	-	----	-
People's Progressives ("Realists")	14,704	2	0.9	1	2.4	1	----	-
Without Party Affiliation	----	2	1.3	1	2.1	1	----	-
Total	1,035,875	107	100.0	74	100.0	30	100.0	3

Sources: This table and the following one were adapted from information
in *Statistisches Handbuch des Königreiches Böhmen*, 2d ed. (Prague, 1913),
p. 56; Miroslav Buchvaldek et al., *Dějiny Československa v datech*
(Prague, 1968), pp. 464-65; Oldřich Říha and Július Mésároš, eds.,
Přehled československých dějin (Prague, 1960), vol. 2, pt. 1, pp. 1000
and 1012; and Richard Fischer, *Pokroková Morava 1893-1918* (Prague, 1937),
2:318.

a. Electoral agreement ("kartel") of Czech State Rights Democracy.

Table 22B

Czech Party Representation in the Lower House of the Reichsrat
under Universal Suffrage in 1911

Party	Number of Votes Received	Total Seats	Percentage of Votes and Number of Seats					
			Bohemia		Moravia		Silesia	
			%	No.	%	No.	%	No.
Czech Social Democrats[a]	357,263	25	36.5	14	26.5	11	35.5	-
Centralist Social Democrats	19,367	1	0.2	-	2.5	-	33.8	1
Agrarians[a]	257,714	38	26.4	30	18.9	6	24.5	2
National Socialists	95,906	14	9.7	13	2.2	1	---	-
National Catholics ⎤ [b] Christian Socialists ⎦	127,992 83,124	7	11.9	-	36.6	7	---	-
Young Czechs	56,673	14	9.8	14	---	-	---	-
Moravian People's Progressives	34,443	4	---	-	8.5	4	---	-
State Rights Progressives	20,916	2	2.4	2	---	-	---	-
Old Czechs	9,872	1	0.4	1	2.1	-	---	-
Progressives ("Realists")[a]	10,168	1	0.7	-	1.5	1	---	-
Without Party Affiliation	10,802	1	2.0	1	1.2	-	6.2	-
Others[c]	14,931	-		-		-		-
Total	1,099,171	108	100.0	75	100.0	30	100.0	3

a. In Moravia only, these parties formed "the Progressive Bloc."

b. The clerical parties ran a joint slate of candidates.

c. Includes the Tradesmen's party of Moravia with 3,199 votes, the Czech National party in Silesia with 1,893 votes, and *Zählkandidaten* in three provinces with 9,839 votes.

Table 23

Three-Class Voting in Královo Pole in 1902

Class	Number of Notables	Number of Taxpayers	Total Tax Value in Crowns	Delegates Elected
I	10	20	27,996.28	10
II	27	136	21,484.77	10
III	None	1,328	23,045.35	10
Total	37	1,484	72,526.40	30

Source: *Naše obec: Jubilejní číslo k 100 vyroči pamatného roku 1848* (Brno, 1948), p. 29.

Table 24

Representation in the Moravian Diet before and after 1905

Curia	Members Before November 1905	Members after November 1905
Ex-officio (Prince-Archbishop of Olomouc and Bishop of Brno)	2	2
I. Great Landowners	30 (Including 5 from entailed estates)	30 (Including 10 from entailed estates)
II. Chambers of Commerce	6	6 (Germans *de facto*)
III. Municipalities	4 for Brno 27 for other cities	20 Germans 20 Czechs
IV. Rural Communes	31	14 Germans 39 Czechs
V. Universal Curia	None	6 Germans 14 Czechs
Total	100	151

Sources: See chap. 10, n. 8.

Notes

Introduction

1. These are sometimes referred to as "cadre" parties, especially by Marxist scholars. See the discussion in Maurice Du-
verger, Political Parties, trans. B. and R. North, rev. ed. (New
York, 1959). The best sociological study of Czech and other European political parties before 1914 remains Edvard Beneš,
Strannictví: sociologická studie (Prague, 1912). On political
theory and political parties at the turn of the century, see
T. G. Masaryk, "Politika vědou a uměním," in Česka politika, ed.
Zdeněk V. Tobolka (Prague, 1906), 1:1-31. On political parties
and parliamentary politics in the same era see Bohumil Baxa,
Parlament a parlamentarism (Prague, 1924).

2. All studies of later nineteenth-century Czech politics
begin with Srb and Tobolka. Adolf Srb's Politické dějiny národa
ceského od roku 1861, 2 vols. (Prague, 1899-1901) is a solid
documentary narrative of parliamentary and provincial politics.
All citations are to this work and not the 1926 abridgement of
similar title. Zdeněk V. Tobolka's Politické dějiny ceskoslo-
venského národa od r. 1848 až do dnešní doby, 4 vols. in 5
(Prague, 1932-37), is a long, informed, and sprawling account
primarily concerned with parliamentary politics and with Czech-
imperial relations and partisan to the Young Czechs. Tobolka's
edition of the papers of Josef Kaizl, Z mého života, ed. Zdeněk
Tobolka, 3 vols. in 4 (Prague, 1908-14), remains the best and
most complete printed collection of source materials on the
Young Czech party, despite the fact that Tobolka edited them to
show the more moderate Young Czechs to best advantage. An important collection of statistical and documentary materials
appears in Young Czech Karel Adámek's topical account of Czech
advances in industry, agriculture, education, politics, and
general culture, Z naší doby, 4 vols. (Velké Meziříčí, 1886-90).
The largest collection of published articles and memoranda on
the Progressive movement is Antonín Hajn's Výbor prací, 3 vols.
(Prague, 1912-13), much of it critical of the Young Czechs. On
political developments in Moravia before and after the turn of
the century, the best collection of source materials, most of
them published, is Richard Fischer, Pokroková Morava, 1893-1918,
2 vols. (Prague, 1937).

3. Edvard Grégr, K objasnění našich domácích sporů (Prague,

1874); Edvard Grégr, Naše politika: Otevřený list panu dru. Fr.
L. Riegrovi, 2d ed. (Prague, 1876); Gustav Eim, "O nas pro nás,"
in Politické úvahy, ed. Josef Penížek (Prague, 1898), pp. 7-168,
a series of articles originally published in 1885; Josef Kaizl,
České myšlénky (Prague, 1896); Václav Škarda, "Politika etapová
a základní názor strany svobodomyslné na českou politiku," Česká
Revue, vol. 2, no. 2 (1898):536-51; Karel Kramář, Poznámky o české politice (Prague, 1906); Karel Kramář, "Od vstupu Čechu na
risské radu až do pádu strany staročeské" and "Za vedení národní
strany svobodomyslné," in Česká politika, ed. Zdeněk V. Tobolka
(Prague, 1909), 3:448-795; T. G. Masaryk, Naše nynější krise:
pád strany staročeské a počátkové směru nových (Prague, 1895);
T. G. Masaryk, Nynější krise a desorganisace mladočeské strany:
Organisujme se ku práci (Prague, 1903); T. G. Masaryk, Politická
situace: Poznámky ku poznámkám (Prague, 1906).

4. On Masaryk, see the selection of works in the bibliography. Other works on the later nineteenth century include the
collection of articles by Albert Pražák, O národ (Prague, 1946);
and Karel Kazbunda, "Krise české politiky a vídeňská jednání o t.
zv. punktace roku 1890," ČČH, vol. 40 (1934):80-108, 310-46,
491-528, and vol. 41 (1935):41-82, 294-320, 514-54.

5. Representative works in the first category include an excellent survey by Ludmila Kárníková on demography, Vývoj obyvatelstva v českých zemích 1754-1914 (Prague, 1965); works by
Pavla Horská-Vrbová on industrial and technological development:
Český průmysl a tzv. druhá průmyslová revoluce, Rozpravy, vol.
75, no. 3 (Prague, 1965); Hlavní otázky vzniku a vývoje českého
strojírenství do roku 1918 (Prague, 1959); and Počátky elektrisace v českých zemích, Rozpravy, no. 71, no. 13 (Prague, 1961);
and articles by Jaroslav Purš on the industrial revolution:
"The Industrial Revolution in the Czech Lands," Historica 2
(1960):183-272; "The Situation of the Working Class in the Czech
Lands in the Phase of the Expansion and Completion of the Industrial Revolution (1849-1873)," Historica 6 (1963):145-238; and
"The Working-Class Movement in the Czech Lands in the Expansive
Phase of Industrial Revolution," Historica 10 (1965):67-158.
Works on class conflict in the nineties include Jan Havránek,
Boj za všeobecné, přímé a rovné hlasovací právo roku 1893, Rozpravy, vol. 74, no. 2 (Prague, 1964); Jan Havránek, Hornická
stávka roku 1900 v severočeském hnědouhelném revíru, Rozpravy,
vol. 63, no. 2 (Prague, 1953); Jurij Křížek, "Krise cukrovarnictví v českých zemích v osmdesátých letech minulého století a její
význam pro vzrůst rolnického hnutí," ČsČH, vol. 4 (1956), no. 2,
pp. 270-98, no. 3, pp. 417-47; vol. 5 (1957), no. 3, pp. 473-506;
vol. 6 (1958), no. 1, pp. 46-59; and Jurij Křížek, T. G. Masaryk
a česká politika: Politické vystoupení českých "realistů" v
letech 1887-1893 (Prague, 1959). Among Zdeněk Šolle's many important works on the workers' movement are Dělnické hnuti v

českých zemích: koncem minulého století (1887-1897) (Prague,
1954); Internacionála a Rakousko (Prague, 1966); "Die Sozialdemokratie in der Habsburger Monarchie und die tschechische
Frage," Archiv für Sozialgeschichte 6-7 (1966/67):315-90; and
"Die tschechische Sozial demokratie zwischen Nationalismus und
Internationalismus," Archiv für Sozialgeschichte 9 (1969):181-
266. Other useful works are cited in footnotes and the bibliography. The enormous literature on these topics is listed in
Josef Macek, Václav Husa, and B. Varsik, eds., 25 ans d'historiographie tchécoslovaque, 1936-1960 (Prague, 1960), and in the
bibliographies of Czechoslovak publications on history beginning
with the calendar year 1955 and titled Bibliografie ceskosloven-
ské historie za rok 19-- (Prague, 1957 to date).

6. Heretofore unexamined evidence included many police reports and the correspondence of many political leaders.

7. Ernest Denis, La Bohême depuis la Montagne Blanche,
2 vols. (Paris, 1903), is a survey which, however dated and partisan in some respects, still numbers among the most informed and
perceptive interpretations of its subject. Robert W. Seton-
Watson, A History of the Czechs and Slovaks (London, 1943), and
S. Harrison Thomson, Czechoslovakia in European History, 2d ed.
(Princeton, 1953), are two short surveys which view the First
Czechoslovak Republic as the logical and desirable end of Czech
and Slovak history. The most complete survey to date in German
is the multivolume collection of chapters by several authors
edited by Karl Bösl, Handbuch der Geschichte der böhmischen
Länder, 4 vols. (Stuttgart, 1966-70). Volume 3, which covers the
period from 1848 to 1918, should especially be noted. Reference
should also be made to selected articles in the Jahrbuch des Collegium Carolinum, 12 volumes to date (Munich, 1960-1976).

8. Oscar Jászi, The Dissolution of the Habsburg Monarchy
(Chicago, 1929); Robert A. Kann, The Multinational Empire: Na-
tionalism and National Reform in the Habsburg Monarchy, 1848-
1918, 2 vols. (New York, 1950); C. A. Macartney, The Habsburg
Empire, 1790-1914 (New York, 1969); Arthur J. May, The Habsburg
Monarchy, 1867-1914 (Cambridge, Mass., 1951); A. J. P. Taylor,
The Habsburg Monarchy, 1809-1918 (London, 1948); Hugo Hantsch,
Die Geschichte Österreichs, 2d ed., 2 vols. (Graz, 1953) and
Gestalter der Geschicke Österreichs (Innsbruck, 1962); Louis
Eisenmann, Le compromis austro-hongrois de 1867 (Paris, 1904);
Victor Tapié, Monarchie et peuples du Danube (Paris, 1969); Erich
Zöllner, Geschichte Österreichs von den Anfängen bis zur Gegen-
wart, 2d ed. (Munich, 1966); C. Daicoviciu and Miron Constantin-
escu, eds., La désagrégation de la Monarchie Austro-Hongroise
1900-1918 (Bucharest, 1965).

9. Johann Wolfgang Brügel, Tschechen und Deutsche: 1918-1938

(Munich, 1967); Hermann Münch, Böhmische Tragödie: Das Schicksal
Mitteleuropas im Lichte des Tschechischen Frage (Berlin, 1949);
and Elizabeth Wiskemann, Czechs and Germans: A Study of the
Struggle in the Historic Provinces of Bohemia and Moravia, 2d ed.
(London, 1967).

10. J. F. N. Bradley, "Czech Pan-Slavism before the First
World War," SEER, vol. 40, no. 94 (December 1961): 184-205, a
useful essay based primarily on reports and opinion of imperial
officers; Bruce M. Garver, "The Reorientation of Czech Politics
in the 1890's: A Step Toward an Independent Czechoslovakia?"
Communications: Conférence internationale du 50e anniversaire de
la République Tchécoslovaque (Prague, 11-15 October 1968), pp.
43-113, the published first draft of a paper to have been presented at this conference, which did not take place, is revised
in this book; three fine articles by Otakar Odložilík, "Na
predělu dob," Zítřek 2 (1943): 30-68; "Enter Masaryk: A Prelude
to His Political Career," JCEA, vol. 10, no. 1 (April 1960):
21-36; and "Russia and Czech National Aspirations," JCEA, vol.
22, no. 4 (January 1963): 407-39; Stanley Z. Pech, "F. L. Rieger:
The Road from Liberalism to Conservatism," JCEA, vol. 17, no. 1
(April 1957): 3-23; Stanley Z. Pech, "Passive Resistance of the
Czechs, 1863-1879," SEER, vol. 36, no. 87 (June 1958): 434-52;
S. Harrison Thomson, "T. G. Masaryk and Czech Historiography,"
JCEA, vol. 10, no. 1 (April 1950): 37-52; and "Thomas Garrigue
Masaryk--Philosopher in Action," University of Toronto Quarterly,
vol. 18, no. 4 (1949): 328-39; H. Gordon Skilling discusses "The
Partition of the University in Prague," SEER, vol. 27, no. 69
(1949): 430-49, and surveys the Czech relationship to Vienna in
"The Politics of the Czech Eighties," in The Czech Renascence of
the Nineteenth Century, ed. P. Brock and H. G. Skilling (Toronto,
1970), pp. 254-81; Stanley B. Winters, "The Young Czech Party
(1874-1914): An Appraisal," Slavic Review, vol. 28, no. 3
(September 1969): 426-44, a short study of the party based on
selected printed sources which compares its legislative accomplishments in Bohemia with its stated objectives.

11. Three dissertations on specific aspects of later nine-
teenth-century Czech politics are Karen Johnson Freeze, "The
Young Progressives" (Ph.D. diss., Columbia University, 1974);
Stanley B. Winters, "Karel Kramář's Early Political Career" (Ph.D.
diss., Rutgers University, 1965); and Stanley Z. Pech, "F. L.
Rieger" (Ph.D. diss., University of Colorado, 1956).

12. These include the private papers of important party leaders, notably those of Chairman Emanuel Engel which contain the
party archives for the nineties, and of their political opponents.
The extensive records of the provincial, secret, and municipal
police contain reports on party activities and policies. Political pamphlets, newspapers, memoirs, and published correspondence

provide information on every aspect of party development.

13. Eugene N. Anderson, The Social and Political Conflict in
Prussia, 1858-1864 (Lincoln, Neb., 1954); Maurice F.
Neufeld,
Italy: School for Awakening Countries: The Italian Labor Movement in Its Political, Social, and Economic Setting from 1800 to
1960 (Ithaca, N. Y., 1961); Carl E. Schorske, German Social Democracy, 1905-1917: The Development of the Great Schism (Cambridge, Mass., 1955); John Vincent, The Formation of the Liberal
Party, 1857-1868 (London, 1966); Ludwig Bergsträsser, Geschichte
der politischen Parteien in Deutschland (Berlin, 1932); and
Theodore Zeldin, The Political System of Napoleon III (London,
1958).

14. On parties in political development see Karl W. Deutsch,
Nationalism and Social Communication: An Inquiry into the Foundations of Nationality, 2d ed. (Cambridge, Mass., 1966); Duver-
ger, **Political Parties**; Joseph LaPalombara and Myron Weiner, eds.,
Political Parties and Political Development (Princeton, N. J.,
1966). On parties in developing countries, see Gabriel A. Almond
and James S. Coleman, eds., The Politics of the Developing Areas
(Princeton, N. J., 1960); C. E. Black, The Dynamics of Moderni-
zation: A Study in Comparative History (New York, 1966); Samuel
P. Huntington, Political Order in Changing Societies (New Haven,
Conn., 1968); and James S. Coleman and Carl G. Rosberg, Jr.,
Political Parties and National Integration in Tropical Africa
(Berkeley, Calif., 1966).

15. On nationalism, see Carleton J. H. Hayes, The Historical
Evolution of Modern Nationalism (New York, 1948); Hans Kohn, The
Idea of Nationalism: A Study in its Origin and Background (New
York, 1944); Friedrich Meinecke, Weltbürgertum und Nationalstaat,
7th ed. (Munich, 1928); and Boyd C. Shafer, Nationalism: Myth
and Reality (New York, 1955). On Pan-Slavism, see Alfred Fischel,
Der Panslawismus bis zum Weltkrieg: Ein geschichtlicher Überblick (Stuttgart, 1919); and Hans Kohn, Pan-Slavism: Its History
and Ideology, 2d ed. rev. (New York, 1960). Works which have set
the tone for Marxist histories or studies of nationalism and national development are Lenin, "The Right of Nations to Self-
Determination" (1914), and J. V. Stalin, "Marxism and the National Question" (1913), available in English translation (New York,
1942). The former work appears in a new translation in Robert
Tucker, ed., The Lenin Anthology (New York, 1975), pp. 153-180.

16. Leonard W. Doob, Patriotism and Nationalism: Their
Psychological Foundations (New Haven, Conn., 1964), and H. Duijker
and N. Frijda, National Character and National Stereotypes (Am-
sterdam, 1960) discuss this problem.

Chapter 1

1. The literature in Czech on the National Revival is rich
and enormous. Among the best recent general surveys is Josef
Kočí, Naše národní obrození (Prague, 1960). Other works are
listed in the several useful bibliographical guides in English
on Czech and Slovak history, including Paul L. Horecký, East
Central Europe: A Guide to Basic Publications (Chicago, 1969);
Rudolf Sturm, Czechoslovakia: A Bibliographic Guide (Washington,
1967); Josef Kočí and Jiří Koralka, "The History of the Habsburg
Monarchy (1526-1918) in Czechoslovak Historiography since 1945,"
AHY 2 (1966):198-223; Josef Anderle, "Major Contributions of
Czechs and Slovaks to Austrian and Hungarian History, 1918-1945,"
AHY 6-7 (1970-71):169-220; Otakar Odložilík, "Modern Czechoslovak
Historiography," SEER 30 (1952):376-90; Macek et al., 25 ans; and
Bibliografie československé historie.

A fine and growing body of studies in English is available on
the Czech National Revival. The reader will first want to con-
sult the recent collection of seventeen articles edited by Peter
Brock and H. Gordon Skilling, The Czech Renascence of the Nineteenth Century: Essays presented to Otakar Odložilík in Honour
of his Seventieth Birthday (Toronto, 1970). See also the two
books on nineteenth-century Czech literature by Milada Součková,
The Czech Romantics (The Hague, 1958) and The Parnassian Jaroslav Vrchlický (The Hague, 1964), and chap. 6 in Deutsch, Nationalism and Social Communication. Among the more interesting articles are Otakar Odložilík, "The Czechs on the Eve of the 1848
Revolution," Harvard Slavic Studies 1 (1953):179-217; George
Pistorius, "Two Paradoxes of Czech Literary Evolution," in The
Czechoslovak Contribution to World Culture, ed. Miloslav Rechcigl
(The Hague, 1964), pp. 639-43; and two studies by René Wellek in
his collected Essays on Czech Literature, introduced by Peter
Demetz (The Hague, 1963), "The Two Traditions of Czech Litera-
ture," pp. 17-31, and "Mácha and English Literature," pp. 148-78.

2. Two of the most thorough Young Czech works reflecting this
viewpoint are Karel Adámek, Z naší doby, 4 vols. (Velké Meziříčí,
1886-90), and Josef Kaizl, České myšlenky (Prague, 1894). Specific citations from these works will be found in subsequent chapters.

3. F. X. Šalda, "Problem malého národa," in Soubor díla F. X.
Šaldy, ed. Karel Jíše (Prague, 1947-63), vol. 14: Kritické projevy 5, 1901-1904, ed. Emanuel Macek (1951), p. 51.

4. A readable but at times fairly superficial intellectual
history of "Czech nationalism in the nineteenth century" is František Červinka, Český nacionalismus v XIX. století (Prague, 1965)
An excellent introductory survey in English on Czech and Slovak
nationalism in historical perspective is Joseph F. Zacek,

"Nationalism in Czechoslovakia," in Nationalism in Eastern Europe, ed. Peter F. Sugar and Ivo J. Lederer (Seattle, 1969), pp. 166-206.

5. Two of the many Young Czechs who often looked to the past for inspiration were Julius Grégr and Josef Herold. See, as examples, LANM, Julius Grégr papers, file titled "Vyrovnání 1889-90," notes on the importance of Jan Hus for Young Czech politics; and a speech on George of Poděbrady by Josef Herold, O králi Jiřím Poděbradském, Reč proslovená pri slavnosti odhalení pomníku krále Jiřího Poděbradského v Poděbradech, dne 15 srpna 1896 (Prague, 1896). Such views on Hussite Tábor were expressed by the foremost peasant leader in southern Bohemia, Alfons Šťastný, O doplnení naseho národního programu (Prague, 1872), pp. 40-48; several articles of 1869 and 1870 in Dělník (The Worker) by Josef Boleslav Pecka, the leading Czech Social Democrat of the seventies, are excerpted or cited in Šolle, "Die tschechische Sozialdemokratie," pp. 185-87.

6. No English term adequately renders "Matice," which is derived from "matrix," but "foundation" is most descriptive of the functions of the several Matice organizations. The exact year in which the Royal Society of Sciences was founded is still uncertain. The date most often cited is 1771, though 1769, 1770, and 1774 have also been proposed. The most thorough work on the origin of the society yet published is Jaroslav Prokeš, Počátky České spolecnosti nauk do konce XVIII. stoleti, vol. 1: 1774-1789 (Prague, 1938). An excellent survey in English is Mikuláš Teich, "The Royal Bohemian Society of Sciences and the First Phase of Organized Scientific Advance in Bohemia," Historica 2 (1960):161-81.

7. Some Czech and Slovak awakeners, like Šafařík and Kollar, were products of German universities, notably Halle and Jena. See the excellent studies by Herbert Peukert, Die Slawen der Donaumonarchie und die Universität Jena, 1700-1848 (Berlin, 1958), and by Eduard Winter, Die tschechische und slowakische Emigration in Deutschland im 17. und 18. Jahrhundert (Berlin, 1955).

8. "Contact and conflict (stýkání a potýkání)" are Palacký's words. The most thorough study of Palacký's thought and works in Czech remains Josef Fischer, Myšlenka a dílo Frantiska Palackého, 2 vols. (Prague, 1926-27). A largely uncritical but competent biography is Václav Řezniček, Frantisek Palacký: Jeho zivot, pusobeni a význam, 3d ed. (Prague, 1912). A very fine recent study is Joseph Frederick Zacek, Palacký: The Historian as Scholar and Nationalist (The Hague, 1970).

9. Jan Neruda, Literatura (Prague, 1966), 3:253, reprinting

on pp. 248-53 his feuilleton in Národní listy of September 25, 1887.

10. Lumír took its name from a hero in Hanka's forged manuscripts (Rukopisy). Ruch, almost untranslatable, means great "activity and commotion." Osvĕta means "enlightenment." One should take care not to exaggerate the differences between Ruch and Lumír, especially since some literary figures contributed regularly to both journals. On the development of the two groups, see Arne Novák, Přehledné dějiny literatury české (Prague, 1946), pp. 678 ff. The most thorough study of Lumír remains Ferdinand Strejček, Lumírovci a jejich boje kolem roku 1880 (Prague, 1915). On Lumír, see also Jan Jakubec and Arne Novák, Geschichte der čechischen Literatur (Leipzig, 1907), pp. 307-26. On Ruch, which appeared from 1879 through 1888, see Ferdinand Strejček, O Svatopluku Čechovi (Prague, 1908), pp. 94-98.

Julius Zeyer, 1841-1901; Jaroslav Vrchlický, 1853-1912; Svatopluk Čech, 1846-1908; Václav Vlček, 1839-1908; Jan Neruda, 1834-1891; Josef Václav Sládek, 1845-1912.

11. Braniboři v Čechách (1862-63). Smetana, 1824-84; and Dvořák, 1841-1904.

12. The Czechs had always believed Charles-Ferdinand University to have been primarily a Czech institution, despite its gradual Germanization after 1621. They endorsed the division (rozdvojení) of the University in 1882 as the best solution only after the Germans on the faculty had shown themselves unwilling to give very many concessions to the Czechs within the existing framework. After 1918 the separate Czech insitution officially became Charles University. On the division of 1882 and attendant problems, see Karel Kazbunda, Stolice dějin na pražské universitě: Od obnovení stolice dějin do rozdělení university (1746-1882), vol. 2: Doba jazykového utrakvismu (1848-1882) (Prague, 1965). Still useful is Jaroslav Goll, Rozdělní pražské university Karlo-Ferdinandovy roku 1882 a počátek samostatné university české (Prague, 1908). See also the two excellent surveys in English: Otakar Odložilík, The Caroline University 1348-1948 (Prague, 1948), and H. Gordon Skilling, "The Partition of the University in Prague," SEER, vol. 27, no. 69 (1949):430-49. The National Theater is discussed in chap. 4 below.

13. On working-class interest in and sponsorship of schools, see Josef Cach, Otázky výchovy a vzdělání v počátcích českého dělnického hnutí (Prague, 1958). On progress in rural and in agricultural schools, see F. V. Moravec, "Úkoly samosprávy v našem programu kulturním," Škola našeho venkova 8 (1904):94, 172, 216, 256, 301, 350, 395ff.

14. "Analphabeten," Handwörterbuch der Staatswissenschaften, 2d rev. ed., 1:294.

15. Ottův slovník naučný, 6:192.

16. Jan Šafránek, Za českou osvětu: Obrázky z dějin českého školství středního (Prague, n.d. [ca. 1900]), p. 161.

17. Establishment of a university in Brno came only after the establishment of the First Czechoslovak Republic.

18. Good general discussions include Frank Wollman, Slavismy a antislavismy za jara národu (Prague, 1968); Edvard Beneš, Úhavy o slovanství: hlavní problémy slovanské politiky (London, 1944; 2d ed., Prague, 1947); Miloš Weingart, Slovanská vzájemnost (Bratislava, 1926); and the several articles in Jiří Horak, ed., Slovanská vzájemnost, 1836-1936: Sborník prací k 100 výročí vydání rozpravy Jana Kollára o slovanské vzájemnost (Prague, 1938). See also the surveys by S. Harrison Thomson, "A Century of a Phantom: Panslavism and the Western Slavs," JCEA, vol. 11, no. 1 (April 1951):57-77; and Bradley, "Czech Pan-Slavism."

19. The Czech journalist Karel Kálal in 1896, cited by Július Mésároš, ed., Dejiny Slovenska (Bratislava, 1968), 2:512.

20. Andrej Mráz, "Česko-slovenské kultúrne vzt'ahy v druhej polovici 19. storočia do roku 1918," O vzájomných vzt'ahoch Čechov a Slovákov, ed. L'udovít Holotík (Bratislava, 1956), pp. 177-88; and Jaroslav Vlček, Dejiny literatúry slovenskej (Turčanský Sv. Martin, 1923), pp. 386-89.

21. On the Polish influence on the Czech National Revival, see chaps. 3 by M. Kudělka and 4 by Václav Žáček in Češi a Poláci v minulosti, ed. Václav Žáček (Prague, 1967), pp. 92-121 and 122-94.

22. Masaryk, Česká otázka, pp. 20-27; Edvard Beneš, Úvahy, pp. 56ff. The two general surveys of Pan-Slavism in Western languages, Fischel, Panslawismus, and Kohn, Pan-Slavism, never clearly distinguish between the types of Slavism or Pan-Slavism or between Pan-Slavism as a literary and as a political movement. Fischel's work reflects Imperial German governmental and public opinion at the time of the First World War. Kohn's superficial study often relies uncritically on Fischel and other journalistic or propagandistic German works.

23. A comprehensive discussion is Nicholas Riasanovsky, Russia and the West in the Teaching of the Slavophiles: A Study of Romantic Ideology (Cambridge, Mass., 1952).

24. Danilevsky's principal work Russia and Europe (1871) was translated into Czech. See discussion in Beneš, Úvahy, pp. 70-76, and Kohn, Pan-Slavism, pp. 190-208.

25. Beneš, Úvahy, pp. 79-80; Hugh Seton-Watson, The Russian Empire, 1801-1917 (Oxford, 1967), pp. 445-51.

26. Bradley, "Czech Pan-Slavism," cites Austrian police files and reports to the Ministry of Foreign Affairs. Fischel, Panslawismus, sees conspiracies in the most innocent literary relationships.

27. Wollman, Slavismy, pp. 47-72.

28. The 1848 Czech revolution is the subject of a voluminous literature in Czech and of a fine work in English by Stanley Z. Pech, The Czech Revolution of 1848 (Chapel Hill, 1969). Other English works which include discussions of Czech events are François Fetjö, ed., Opening of an Era, 1848: An Historical Symposium (London, 1949); Lewis Namier, 1848: The Revolution of the Intellectuals (New York, 1946); Priscilla Robertson, Revolutions of 1848: A Social History (New York, 1952); and William L. Langer, Political and Social Upheaval, 1832-1852 (New York, 1969). SEER 26 (1948) contains an excellent series of articles on the Czechs, Slovaks, and other Slavic peoples during the revolutionary upheavals of 1848-49.

29. "Manifest českého Národního výboru o žádovcím spojení zemí Moravské a Slezské s korunov Českov, dne 6 maje 1848," in Boj za právo: Sborník aktů politických v věcech státu a národa českého od roku 1848, ed. Jan M. Černý, 2 vols. in 1 (Prague, 1893), pp. 183-88.

30. Palacký, Spisy drobné, 1:20. The text, "Psaní do Frankfurta dne 11. dubna 1848," appears on pp. 17-22. An English translation by Otakar Odložilík appears in SEER 26 (1948):303-08. See also the discussion of this letter by Stanley Z. Pech, "The Czechs and the Imperial Parliament," in Brock and Skilling, Czech Renascence, pp. 202-14.

31. The text of the September 7, 1848, decree in photocopy is in Vladimír Klimeš, Česká vesnice v roce 1848 (Prague, 1949), between pages 408 and 409. Joseph II had abolished personal servitude (servage de l'homme or Liebeigentum) in 1781 but had regularized and retained the manorial labor dues (robota or corvée) owed by peasants by virtue of land tenure.

32. On law no. 253 of November 20, 1852, and its effects, see the discussion by Josef Gruber, "Živnostenská společenstva a spolky," Obchodní Sborník, no. 9, pt. 3 (1899):3-25, especially

pp. 23-25. On the effects of civil government, see Jan Heidler, Počátky ústavního života v Rakousku od r. 1848-1870 (Prague, 1914), a lucid brochure.

33. Josef Matoušek, Karel Sladkovský a český radikalism za revoluce a reakce (Prague, 1929), pp. 87-91.

34. On the Slavic Congress, see Otakar Odložilík, "The Slavic Congress of 1848," The Polish Review 4 (1959):3-15; see also the definitive Congress proceedings with commentary in Václav Žáček, ed., Slovanský sjezd v Praze 1848 (Prague, 1958), and the account by Zdeněk V. Tobolka, Slovanský sjezd v Praze roku 1848 (Prague, 1901). On the Imperial Constituent Assembly at Kroměříž, see Otakar Odložilík, Na Kroměřížském sněmu 1848 a 1849 (Prague, 1947), especially pp. 38-42, and "A Czech Plan for a Danubian Federation, 1848," JCEA 1 (1941):253-74.

35. See the discussion by Jan Kříž, "Státoprávní politika od r. 1848 po Badeniho," in Státoprávní politika, ed. Antonín Hajn, Antonín Hubka, and Ladislav Machač (Prague, 1903), pp. 78-108.

36. Josef Hybeš, Křížová cesta socialismu (Prague, 1920), reprinted in Zdeněk Šolle, ed., Průkopníci socialismu u nás (Prague, 1954), pp. 132-273, quotation, p. 174.

37. The most severe of these setbacks occurred during the years 1849 to 1852, 1862 to 1864, 1867 to 1868, and 1871 to 1873 and are discussed in chaps. 2 and 3.

38. See table 1 in the appendix for comparative population figures. The following comparative account of development in Bohemia and Moravia considers the average level of development in each province. One can always find exceptions to the average. For example, the economic and cultural development of the Czech communities in the large Moravian industrial centers of Brno and Moravská Ostrava proceeded at a faster pace than that of the Czechs in certain of the poorer districts in South Bohemia.

39. No works in German or West European languages have to date taken adequate account of Moravia in assessing the development of Czech politics. Similarly, no works have taken adequate account of Czech politics in Bohemia below the provincial level. I am indebted to Professors Otakar Odložilík and Zdeněk Šolle for suggesting to me that the Young Czech party cannot be understood apart from developments in Moravia. On the history of Moravia generally through the nineteenth century, see Rudolf Dvořák, Dějiny Moravy, in 2 vols. (Brno, 1902).

40. A complete account of the literary awakening in Moravia is Miloslav Hýsek, Literární Morava v letech 1849-1885 (Prague,

1911). On the Moravian Foundation see H. Traub, Dějiny Matice moravské (Brno, 1911), pp. 7-17ff.

41. A valuable general survey of the development of progressive politics in Moravia is Richard Fischer's Pokroková Morava, 2 vols. (Prague, 1937). A superb account of the development of the Czech national movement in Olomouc which considers all topics in the context of Czech politics generally is Julius Ambros's Z malých kořenů: vzpomínky a úvahy z vývoje českého národního života v Olomouci (Olomouc, 1912). Both Fischer and Ambros were the observers of many of the events that they objectively discuss. Useful accounts of politics in specific Moravian cities include A. V. Musiol, Soudní okres Hranický: vývoj v letech 1900 až 1935 (Hranice, 1936); František Šujan, Dějepis Brna, 2d ed. (Brno, 1928), especially pp. 402-80; Rudolf Hurt, Dějiny města Vracova (Vracov, 1969), pp. 142-74; Matouš Václavek, Dějiny města Vsetína a okresu Vsackého (Vsetín, 1901); and Andělín Grobelný, "Národně politický život v Ostravě a na Ostravsku v 2. polovine 19. století," in Ostrava: Sborník příspevků k dejinám a výstavbě města (Ostrava, 1967), 4:147-81.

42. On general developments, see Andělín Grobelný, ed., K otázkám dějin Slezska (Ostrava, 1956), and Antonín Grund, "Selzsko v době českého obrození a jeho místo v českém literárním vývoji 18.-19. století," in Slezsko, český stát a česká kultura (Opava, 1948).

43. See table 1 in the appendix.

44. Ignát Hořica, Pamatujte na Slezsko! Úvahy a feuilletony (Prague, 1895); Ignát Hořica, Poslední řeč poslance Ignáta Hořice, proslovená v poslanecké sněmovně dne 12 brezna 1902 (Prague, 1902); and Josef Kudela, O Slezsku (Prague, 1909).

45. See tables 22A and 22B in the appendix.

46. See table 11 in the appendix. On railway mileage, see Jurij Křížek, "La crise du dualisme et le dernier compromis austro-hongrois," Historica 12 (1966):88. On Czech industrial development generally, see Horská-Vrbová, Český prumysl; Purš, "Industrial Revolution;" and Československá Vlastivěda, vol. 9: Technika, ed. Jaroslav Veselý (Prague, 1929). On the coal industry, see Ludmila Kárníková, Vývoj uhelného prumyslu v českých zemích do r. 1880 (Prague, 1960).

47. The relative prosperity of the Czech lands in comparison with the rest of Austria-Hungary is clearly indicated by appended table 6 on the division of personal income in the Dual Monarchy. The Czechs stood second only to the Germans in self-employed persons and in income per capita. The relatively

advanced development of Czech society is further evident in appended tables 2, 3, and 4 showing the distribution of the labor force among the various nationalities. In 1900, the Czech lands, with 36 percent of the population of Cisleithania, employed 53 percent of all industrial workers.

48. A comprehensive account of the "national industry" is in Václav Vilikovský, Dějiny zemědělského průmyslu v Československu (Prague, 1936), pp. 340ff. See also table 11 in the appendix and Purš, "Industrial Revolution," pp. 219-28. The invention during the early sixties by Čeněk Daněk of machinery to clean and slice beets and by Hugo Jelínek and Julius Robert of new methods of sugar extraction led to the establishment of Czech sugar refineries under both corporate and cooperative management. Daněk's firm alone built eighty-six new sugar factories in the decade after 1862, and its export of refining equipment abroad as well as sales at home soon made it one of the larger Czech corporations. So rapidly did the new factories process sugar that for seven years the production of beets could not keep pace with the demand. By 1883, the Dual Monarchy produced over one-quarter of all European beet sugar, with the Czech lands accounting for over 98 percent of the Cisleithanian production by 1881. In the fifties, most sugar beet farming and processing had been done by the great landowners, whereas by the eighties Czech independent farmers, by increasing the yield on existing holdings and by buying additional land, had taken over the bulk of production. Their success attested to the economic superiority of the independent small and middle holdings over the large estates.

49. The Daněk firm in Karlín dated from 1860, the Czech-Moravian Works in Libeň from 1871, and Kolben and Co. in Vysočany from 1896. These three enterprises merged after 1918 to form Českomoravská-Kolben-Daněk (ČKD).

50. In Mladá Boleslav, Václav Laurin and Václav Klement pioneered in the production of motorcycles in 1898, began producing automobiles in 1906, and by 1911 had become the largest automotive and cycle manufacturers in Austria-Hungary. See Edvard Maška, "Václav Klement: průkopník českého automobilismu," in České postavy (Prague, 1940), 2:215-35.

51. Antonín Hajn, "Státoprávní politika v přítomnosti i budoucnosti," in Hajn, Hubka, and Machač, eds., Státoprávní politika, pp. 153-57.

52. Austria-Hungary never tried to regulate cartels by civil law as in Great Britain or by criminal law as in American antitrust legislation. Rather, it sought to regulate solely through administrative measures, thus disallowing any legal action against trusts by aggrieved citizens or private parties. This,

in effect, gave the cartels a free hand so long as they paid
taxes and lived up to the provisions in their charter from the
government. Austro-Hungarian as opposed to American and British
practices are more fully discussed by Friedrich Kleinwächter,
"Kartelle," Handwörterbuch der Staatswissenschaften, 5:39-45.
The growth of cartels in Austria-Hungary in relation to imperial
politics is described by Jurij Křízek, Die wirtschaftlichen
Grundzüge des österreichisch-ungarischen Imperialismus in der
Vorkreigszeit (1900-1914) (Prague, 1963), pp. 26-31.

53. See table 10 in the appendix. The financing of sugar
refineries and the interest on mortgaged beet acreage enabled
the Živnobanka to recover rapidly after the depression of 1873.

54. Karel Adámek, Z naší doby, 1:68ff.

55. Antonín Pimper, České obchodní banky za války a po válce
(Prague, 1929), pp. 25-41, on pre-war investments and activity
of Czech banking.

56. The ratio of percentage of banking stock held to percentage of the total Cisleithanian population was 1.02:1 for the
Czechs and 1.83:1 for the Germans. The Czech banking system,
though small in comparison with Viennese banks, which held 65.75
percent of Cisleithanian banking stock, far overshadowed banks
in all other provinces, which held only 10.68 percent. The
capital investments in Czech banks reached 226 million crowns by
1913, far more than the 138 million crowns in German banks in
the Czech lands. See Zdeněk Šolle, "Kontinuität und Wandel in
der sozialen Entwicklung der böhmischen Länder 1872 bis 1930,"
in Aktuelle Forschungsprobleme um die Erste Tschechoslowakische
Republik, ed. Karl Bosl (Munich, 1969), p. 33.

57. See table 3A in the appendix, based on data in Kárníková,
Vývoj obyvatelstva, pp. 348-51. The population of Polish
Cieszyn is not included.

58. The agrarian situation in South Bohemia is discussed
with ample statistical data in Vladimír Havel, "Rozdělení pozemkové drzby v obvodu Obchodní Komory Česko-Budějovické," Jihočeský kraj: Revue věnovaná studiu a řešení jihočeské otázky, vol.
2, nos. 8, 9, 10 (1911):296-302, 332-43.

59. O. Frankenberger and J. O. Kubíček, Antonín Švehla v
dějinách československé strany agrární 1899-1929 (Prague, 1931),
pp. 20-21, 47-48.

60. See table 14 in the appendix and the discussion of these
industries in Přehled československých dějin, vol. 2, pt. 1: 1848-
1918, ed. Oldřich Říha and Julius Mésáros (Prague, 1960), pp. 307-1

61. Purs̆, "Industrial Revolution," pp. 198-218, on textile industry.

62. Figures from table 3A in the appendix. Development of new industries is delineated by Horská-Vrbová in Strojírenství and Poc̆atky elektrisace and in a central European setting in her Kapitalistická industrializace a stredoevropská spolecnost (Prague, 1970), pp. 26-29.

63. Antonín Bohác̆, O c̆eské otázce mens̆inové (Olomouc, 1910), pp. 10-14.

64. On this and as source for table 3B in the appendix, see Heinrich Rauchberg, Der nationale Besitzstand in Böhmen (Leipzig, 1905), 1:67, 463, 490; and Statistische Handbuch des Königreiches Böhmen (Prague, 1913), pp. 16-17.

65. The classic work on migration is Rauchberg, Der nationale Besitzstand, 2 vols. (Leipzig, 1905); by accepting the Umgangssprache as the criterion for nationality he underestimated the size of Czech minorities and slightly exaggerated the effects of Czech migration in creating the mixed-language areas. See criticism in Antonín Bohác̆, "Národní rozhranic̆ení v C̆echách ve svĕtle statistiky," Nas̆e doba, 15 (1908):368-73 and 439-48. A discussion of migration based primarily on Rauchberg is Andrew G. Whiteside's Austrian National Socialism before 1918 (The Hague, 1962), pp. 37-50. An excellent recent study of the question is Harald Bachmann's "Sozialstruktur und Parteientwicklung im nordwestböhmischen Kohlenrevier vor dem Zusammenbruch der Monarchie," Bohemia: Jahrbuch des Collegium Carolinum 10 (1969):270-86.

66. See tables 16 and 18 in the appendix. Curial suffrage is discussed in chaps. 2 and 4 below.

67. Miloslav Volf, Nas̆e dĕlnické hnutí v minulosti (Prague, 1947), p. 79.

68. Purs̆, "Situation," and "Working-Class Movement."

69. C̆eská politika, 4:918-20.

70. Jan Havránek, "Social Classes, Nationality Ratios and Demographic Trends in Prague, 1880-1910," trans. R. F. Samsour, Historica 13 (1968):171-208.

71. Zdenĕk S̆olle, Dĕlnické stávky v C̆echach v druhé polovinĕ XIX. století (Prague, 1960).

72. Otto Bauer, Die nationalitäten Frage und die Sozial-

demokratie, 2d ed. (Vienna, 1924), pp. 259-60 and 450. Friedrich Stampfer, "Für das böhmische Staatsrecht," Die Neue Zeit,
vol. 17, no. 1 (1899):275-78.

73. Also contributing to Polish and Hungarian success was
the fact that relatively few Germans resided in Hungary or Galicia, in contrast to the minority of two and one-half million in
the Czech lands which always opposed greater autonomy for the
Czechs.

74. Česká politika, 4:36.

75. František Wenzel, Dějiny založen a družstevního podníkání
na Moravě do roku 1885 (Prague, 1937), thoroughly traces this development. For German agrarian parties see Richard Charmatz,
Deutsche-osterreichische Politik (Leipzig, 1907), pp. 257-88. On
law no. 70, April 9, 1873, see Zákonník rissky (1873), pp. 273-89.

76. Šolle, "Kontinuität und Wandel," p. 34.

77. See table 9 in the appendix.

78. These terms and categories are explained and the relationships between the different groups in rural society are delineated in tables 8 and 9 in the appendix. The principal
source, Rudolf Franěk, Některé problémy sociálního postavení
rolnictva v Čechách na konci 19. a počátkem 20. století, Rozpravy,
vol. 77, no. 6 (Prague, 1967), and other sources are discussed
in notes to table 8A in the appendix. The narrow legal definition of the great landowning class helped perpetuate its political privileges by preventing newly landed nouveaux riches from
buying their way into the first curia unless they purchased "recorded estates." In fourteen of seventeen Cisleithanian provinces, great landowners eligible to vote in the first curia
were defined as those families holding either entailed estates
or estates inscribed on the provincial land records (Zemské
desky or Landtafeln). Trieste had no first curia, and in the
two provinces where land records did not exist, Dalmatia and the
Vorarlberg, property qualifications excluded all but a few families from the first curia. Franz Günther, Der oesterreichische
Grossgrundbesitzer: Ein Handbuch für den Grossgrundbesitzer und
Domainebeamten (Vienna, 1883), pp. 34ff.

79. This class, an exception to the generally independent
and prosperous peasantry in the Czech lands, had little social
mobility as well as low wages. Its status and problems are well
discussed by Oldřiška Kodedová, Postavení zemědelského proletariátu v Čechách koncem 19. století , Rozpravy, vol. 77, no. 7
(Prague, 1967).

80. See table 3C in the appendix based on data in Ottův
slovník naučný, 6:422. The relatively high productivity of
modern intensive agriculture among Czech peasants and farmers is
further reflected in table 4A in the appendix, which shows that
in comparison with the rural labor force elsewhere in Cisleithania, relatively few members of rural Czech or German families
helped in agricultural work.

81. Franěk, Některé problémy, pp. 17-23, clearly delineates
these changes but does not distinguish between the sizes of estates over fifty hectares in showing changes in land ownership.

82. On the Netherlands, David Mitrany, Marx Against the Pea-
sant: A Study in Social Dogmatism (New York, 1951), p. 38. On
Denmark, Frederic C. Howe, Denmark, A Cooperative Commonwealth
(New York, 1921), pp. 21-25. On Belgium and Imperial Germany,
J. Conrad, "Agrarstatistik," in Handwörterbuch der Staatswissenschaften, 1:128-31. On European agriculture generally after the
turn of the century, see Rudolf Rolíček, Agrární politika
(Prague, 1912). By the 1890s, socialist leaders like Eduard
David in Germany and Jules Guesde and Jean Jaurès in France began to challenge Marx's doctrine that industrial progress would
gradually ruin the peasant smallholder and lead to the concentration of land in larger units. In his classic work on Die
agrarischen Fragen in Verhältnis zum Sozialismus (Vienna, 1899),
Fredrich Hertz argued, beginning on p. 81, that "the technical
superiority of large-scale agricultural production has no relationship to the technical superiority of large-scale concentration in industry." The economists J. Conrad and Eduard David at
the turn of the century contended that many advantages enjoyed
by great estates derived not from economic superiority but from
political privileges, including disproportionate parliamentary
representation, easier access to state credit, and exemption
from paying certain taxes to local self-government. See J. Conrad, "Agrarpolitik," in Handwörterbuch der Staatswissenschaften,
1:120-25; and Eduard David, Sozialismus und Landwirtschaft (Berlin, 1903), 1:692-94.

83. See, for example, the discussion of the Moravian Peasant
Union during the eighties in Obrtel, Moravští sedláci, pp. 235-63.

84. See tables 8 and 9 in the appendix.

85. The Schwarzenbergs held over 176,000 hectares, the
Colloredo-Mansfelds 58,000, and Count Valdstein 47,000. Thirty-
eight families held 996,400 hectares. Franěk, Některé problémy,
p. 19.

86. These families included those already owning estates in
other Habsburg crown lands like the Liechtensteins,

Windischgrätzes, Thuns (Thun-Hohenstein and Thun-Salm), and
Clams (Clam-Gallas and Clam-Martinic) and those from abroad like
the Buquoys, Colloredo-Mansfelds, and Schönborns. The few Catholic families of the original Bohemian nobility that did not revolt, notably the Černíns, Lobkowiczes, Kinskýs, Kolovrats,
Kounices (Kaunitzes) and Sternberks, had been handsomely rewarded for their loyalty. Other great landowning families, like the
Auerspergs, Belcredis, Taaffes, and Clary-Aldringens, received
estates in the Czech lands for services rendered to the Habsburgs in later wars.

87. Michal Navrátil, ed., Nový český sněm (1901-07) (Tábor,
1902), pp. 152-53, 163.

88. Forty-six members of the forty Bohemian families elected
16, or 6.6 percent, of the 242 delegates to the Bohemian Diet.
In Moravia nobles from entailed estates elected 5, or 5 percent,
of the 100 delegates until the 1905 Agreement, which gave them 10,
or 6.6 percent, of the 151 delegates. Statistisches Handbuch des
K. Böhmen, p. 184; Česká politika, vol. 2, pt. 1, pp. 909-10;
Josef Holeček, Česká šlechta: Výklady časové i historické
(Prague, 1918), pp. 60-66.

89. See table 16 in the appendix. In Moravia after 1905,
great landowners held 20 percent of the diet seats.

90. See table 18 in the appendix. For example, 444 great
landowners elected 23, or 28.8 percent, of all delegates to the
Reichsrat from Bohemia in 1879; and each great landowner's vote
exceeded by 178 times that of an urban upper middle-class citizen, and by 507 times that of a prosperous farmer.

91. Karel Sladkovský, Výklad voleb zástupců dle práva a
spravedlnosti (Prague, 1875), pp. 4-7, 64-66, 75.

92. Tobolka, Politické dějiny, 2:15-18, 37-43, and Holeček,
Česká šlechta, pp. 28-33.

93. Typical statements by Young Czechs on this issue were
Bedřich Pacák, Několik slov pravdy k jazykovému nařízení (Prague,
1897), pp. 43-56; Adolf Stránský, Řeč pronesená v středu 25 října 1899 (Brno, 1899), p. 25; Edvard Grégr, "Empire and Language,"
in Europe in the Nineteenth Century: A Documentary Analysis of
Change and Conflict, vol. 2: 1870-1914, ed. Eugene N. Anderson,
Stanley J. Pincetl, Jr., and Donald J. Ziegler (Indianapolis,
1961), pp. 131-33, 151-53.

94. The appended tables 20C and 20D on curial representation
to the Reichsrat in the 1897 election show that one German delegate in the third curia represented 3,302 voters as opposed to

one Czech representing 3,461 voters. In the fourth curia, the
Germans held a similar advantage, electing one delegate for
8,727 voters while the Czechs elected one for every 10,309 voters.

95. In retrospect, one may appreciate the problems of the
Germans in the Czech lands. Although a minority of no more than
one-third of the population, they had long been accustomed to
ruling the Czechs; and many of them had acquired false notions
of racial and cultural superiority. One cannot, of course, excuse German arrogance toward and ignorance of their Slavic neighbors. And educated Reich Germans like Theodor Mommsen often
showed greater arrogance and ignorance than did most of the Bohemian Germans. Historians should, nonetheless, avoid drawing
what may appear to be obvious parallels between the German riots
against the Czechs during the later nineties and German aggression in two world wars. Each successive conflict exacerbated
existing tensions; but only after the years 1933 to 1938 and under Reich German influence did the Germans in the Czech lands
assume an uncompromisingly hostile attitude toward the Czechs.
By the same token, the brutal Nazi occupation of Czechoslovakia
accounts for the Czech expulsion of almost all Sudeten Germans
after 1945. Before 1938, no Czech seriously advocated such an
expulsion. General studies of the problems of the Germans in
the Czech lands are Brügel, Tschechen und Deutschen; Münch,
Böhmische Tragödie, the most dated; and Wiskemann, Czechs and
Germans, pp. 29-67. See also Andrew G. Whiteside, "The Germans
as an Integrative Force in Imperial Austria: the Dilemma of
Dominance," and Erich Zöllner, "The Germans as an Integrating
and Disintegrating Force," pp. 157-200 and 201-233 respectively
in AHY, vol. 3, pt. 1 (1967).

96. German surnames among prominent Czech politicians as
well as among Czechs generally were not unusual, like the Old
Czechs Rieger and Zeithammer, the Young Czechs Engel and Schwarz,
and the Social Democrats Habrman and Steiner. Likewise, Bohemian
German and Viennese political leaders sometimes had Czech names.

97. Peter C. J. Pulzer, The Rise of Political Anti-Semitism
in Germany and Austria (New York, 1964), is a good up-to-date
survey. See especially pp. 236-46 and 295ff.

Chapter 2

1. In fact, during the preceding century the Habsburgs had
seldom undertaken extensive political and institutional reform
unless compelled to do so by revolution at home and abroad, as
in 1848, or by military defeat, as in wars against Frederick the
Great and Napoleon. Recognizing thereafter that long wars might
lead to the disintegration of their empire, the Habsburgs fought

short ones, capitulating to the French and Piedmontese after the
second battle in 1859 and to the Prussians after the first defeat in 1866.

2. It is here possible only to survey briefly the making of
dualism by way of introduction to Czech politics during the seventies. Anyone interested in works which more comprehensively
elucidate events and problems of the sixties is advised to begin
with the recently published collection of articles edited by Anton Vantuch and L'udovít Holotík, Der österreichisch-ungarische
Ausgleich 1867: Materialien (Referate und Diskussion) der internationalen Konferenz in Bratislava 28.8-1.9. 1967 (Bratislava,
1971). Questions of imperial foreign policy are concisely and
clearly delineated in Fritz Fellner, Der Dreibund, 2d ed. (Vienna, 1960). Still helpful are the informed but occasionally
partisan older works by Louis Eisenmann, Le compromis austro-
hongrois de 1867 (Paris, 1904), Josef Redlich, Das österreichische Staats- und Reichsproblem, 2 vols. (Leipzig, 1920-26),
and Zdeněk Tobolka, Politické dějiny, 2:1-285. On the role of
the Council of Ministers in the constitutional crises see Helmut
Rumpler, Ministerrat und Ministerratsprotokolle 1848-1867: Be-
hördengeschichtliche und aktenkundliche Analyse (Vienna, 1970),
which also serves as the introduction to a projected multivolume
publication of the protocols of the imperial ministerial councils. Antonín Okáč, Rakouský problém a list Vaterland 1860-1871,
2 vols. (Brno, 1970), thoroughly studies the ideas and activities of the conservative great landowners of Bohemia and Moravia
during the decade of constitutional crisis. A cogent survey by
Macartney, Habsburg Empire, pp. 495-568, reflects the use of
Hungarian sources. Still indispensable to any study of constitutional questions is Edmund Bernatzik, Die österreichischen
Verfassungsgesetze mit Erläuterungen (Vienna, 1911). Other
works which have informed this section include Richard Charmatz,
Österreichs innere Geschichte von 1848 bis 1895, 3d ed. (Leipzig, 1918); Bedřich Hlaváč, František Josef I: Život, povaha,
doba (Prague, 1933); Jászi, Dissolution; Kann, Multinational Empire; Josef Redlich, Kaiser Franz Joseph von Österreich (Berlin,
1928); Taylor, Habsburg Monarchy; and the articles in AHY 3
(1967).

3. After having suppressed all revolutionary or reform-
minded organizations by 1851, the authoritarian and highly centralized Bach-Schwarzenberg regime had taken tentative steps toward meeting several demands of the 1848 revolution on terms acceptable to the dynasty. These steps occurred primarily in governmental and economic organization, confirming the abolition of
feudal dues and the replacement of manorial by civil administration and authorizing formation of limited-liability corporations
to finance and manage industrialization and improved communication. These steps having been taken and the obedience of a

centralized civil bureaucracy to the monarchy assured, the Habsburgs could after Solferino somewhat more confidently proceed to
reintroduce representative governmental institutions and a measure of civil liberty.

4. In accordance with imperial ordinance no. 57 of March 5,
1860, the text of which appears in Bernatzik, Verfassungsgesetze, pp. 217-22.

5. The Hungarians revived some of the April laws of 1848 and
reestablished their county committees of that year. The Poles
advanced demands for the political autonomy and territorial integrity of Galicia. Serbs, Croats, and Slovenes formed their
own national committees which aimed to advance national self-
determination. Slovaks assembled at Turčiansky Svätý Martin on
June 6-7, 1861, to issue a memorandum reiterating the requests
for national autonomy and civil liberties adopted at Liptovský
Svätý Mikuláš in May 1848. The Czech Sokol and Národní listy
are discussed in chap. 4 below.

6. German historians generally like Germans of the early
1860s have evaluated the Schmerling government more positively
than have Czechs. See, for example, Charmatz, Österreichs innere Geschichte, 1:48-64 and Reinhold Lorenz, "Anton Ritter von
Schmerling (1805-1893) and Alexander Freiherr von Bach (1813-
1893)," in Hantsch, ed., Gestalter, pp. 407-30.

7. The most complete essay to date on the Czechs and Belcredi is Karel Kazbunda's "Česká politika na počátku éry Belcrediho," ČČH, vol. 39, no. 1 (1933):102-19. Antonín Okáč's
Rakouský problém gives a comprehensive account of the Belcredis
in politics during the sixties. After that time, Richard (1823-
1902) served on higher imperial courts and in the upper house of
the Reichsrat. Egbert (1816-94) remained head of the conservative great landowners in Moravia until shortly before his death.
The former Belcredího třída in Prague is now the Třída obranců
míru.

8. On the Compromise generally see Josef Kaizl, Vyrovnání
s Uhry r. 1867 a 1877 (Prague, 1886), and František Fiedler,
Rakousko-Uherská vyrovnání po roce 1878 (Prague, 1903). On the
economic provisions and consequences of the Compromise, see
Jászi, Dissolution, pp. 185-212, and Ivan T. Berend and György
Ránki, "Economic Factors in Nationalism: The Example of Hungary
at the Beginning of the Twentieth Century," AHY, vol. 3, pt. 3
(1967):163-88. On the attempts to negotiate a customs union for
central Europe, see Hans Rosenberg, "The Struggle for a German-
Austrian Customs Union, 1815-1931," SEER 14 (1935-36):332-42.
On the Delegations, see Bernatzik, Verfassungsgesetze, pp. 339ff.

9. So-called because each adherent wore a tulip in his lapel.

10. By 1907, forty years later, the percentage of Germans had declined to 36 percent.

11. The discussion that follows is drawn primarily from Eisenmann, Le compromis; Jan Slavík, Nová draha české politiky: Časová úvaha o dvou větách z ústavy (Prague, 1899); and Eugene N. Anderson and Pauline R. Anderson, Political Institutions and Social Change in Continental Europe in the Nineteenth Century (Berkeley, 1967), pp. 66-78.

12. One might further divide proposals to reorganize the Dual Monarchy into essentially four categories: authoritarian federalism, democratic federalism, authoritarian centralism, and democratic centralism. The classic authoritarian federalist solution contemplated autonomous powers for provincial diets based on highly restricted curial suffrage: its principal proponents were the territorial nobility and the wealthy middle classes among the various non-Germanic nationalities. Liberal politicians among the various Slavic nationalities, most notably the Young Czechs, advocated federalist solutions that guaranteed both national autonomy and democratic practices, including universal manhood suffrage and freedom of speech, association, and assembly. All advocates of a centralized unitary state run largely by the imperial bureaucracy harked back to the system of Schmerling and included most middle-class Germans, most higher imperial officials, and a number of German noble families. The leadership of Austrian Social Democracy, on the other hand, generally favored a centralized and democratic monarchy which would deny arbitrary authority to the bureaucracy and dynasty while guaranteeing civil rights for all citizens and cultural autonomy for all nationalities.

13. Solomon Wank makes this point clearly in his perspicacious essay on "Foreign Policy and the Nationality Problem in Austria-Hungary, 1867-1914," AHY, vol. 3, pt. 3 (1967):37-56.

14. The phrase "two-tracked" is attributed to Count Kazimierz Badeni by Albín Bráf, "O některých starších a novějších projektech rakouských v příčině samosprávy," p. 193, from an offprint of a lecture of February 25, 1897, which does not cite the original source of publication. The text of law no. 44, which established the two-tracked system in its final form, appears with commentary in Bernatzik, Verfassungsgesetze, pp. 469-73. Law no. 8, which authorized the establishment of communal self-governing bodies throughout the empire, is discussed in chap. 4.

15. The highest provincial official on the bureaucratic "track" was called the governor in all but five crown lands--

Silesia, Carinthia, Carniola, Salzburg, and the Bukovina--where
he held the title of Crown Land President (zemský president,
Landespräsident). One governor was responsible for both the
Tyrol and the Vorarlberg and another for Trieste, Gorizia, and
Istria, making a total of fourteen chief executives for the seventeen crown lands. The governor was responsible to the emper-
or through the Cisleithanian Minister of Interior for most duties and through the Ministries of Agriculture, Defense, and
Worship and Public Instruction for almost all the rest. Comprehensive discussions of the political administration will be
found in Dobroslav Krejčí, "Nynější organismus rakouské správy
zeměpanské," Česká politika, vol. 2, pt. 2, pp. 77-254.
Powers of the district captain are outlined on pp. 83-85. A
shorter discussion appears in Jan Janák, Vývoj správy v českých
zemích v epose kapitalismu (Prague, 1965), pp. 79-120.

16. Cisleithania contained 324 district captaincies, of
which 89 were in Bohemia, 30 in Moravia, and 7 in Silesia. Each
captaincy comprised two to four judicial districts and had boundaries so drawn that it shared no judicial district or commune
with another captaincy. In thirty-three of the larger Cisleithanian cities, including six in Moravia and Prague and Liberec
in Bohemia, a magistrate directly served the governor's office
in lieu of a district captain and acted as spokesman for a council of officials. Among the most important duties of each captaincy was the supervision of elections to the diets and local
self-governmental bodies, including approval of voting lists,
establishment of dates and polling places, and the handling of any
complaints. Other duties included the promulgation and enforcement of imperial laws, maintenance of fire and police protection,
collection of statistical data on population, trade, farming,
and manufacturing, the surveillance and control of all organizations, publications, and theatrical and musical productions,
overseeing tax collection, military recruitment, and state public welfare programs, state inspection of business, industry,
and agriculture, and supervising the maintenance of important
highways and waterways. In practice, the district captain acted
as the executive arm of the state in all matters not specifically
reserved to other imperial officials.

17. Police reports will be found for Bohemia in SÚA, fond PM,
for Moravia in SA Brno, fond PM, and for these and other imperial
crown lands in HHSA, Information Bureau of the Ministry of Foreign Affairs, and in VA, Presidium of the Ministry of Interior.
A representative selection from the second Taaffe government
(1879-93) is published in Arthur Skedl and Egon Weiss, eds., Der
politische Nachlass des Grafen Eduard Taaffe (Vienna, 1922).
Reports of the municipal Police Administrative Boards in Prague
and Brno are to be found in SÚA, fond PŘ (policejní ředitelství)
Prague, and in SA Brno, fond PR Brno.

18. Secret police reports on politics in the Czech lands are
in SÚA, fond PMT. A comprehensive study of the imperial police
and bureaucracy has yet to be written. Redlich, Staats- und
Reichsproblem, and most other historians using only German-
language sources have given the police and bureaucracy fairly
high marks. This has not been the case with historians who have
used sources in other languages and who have not made the mistake of assuming that the emperor and the police were "above politics." Šviha will be discussed in chap. 10. On Sabina, see
Jakub Arbes, "Karel Sabina: Volné crty z literárně politické
pathologie," Naše doba 2 (1895):506 and continued in series; and
Jaroslav Purš, K případu Karla Sabiny (Prague, 1959).

19. Among others, Josef Redlich, Zustand und Reform des
oesterreichischen Verwaltung: Rede gehalten in der Budgetdebatte
des Reichsrates vom 26 Oktober 1911 (Vienna, 1911), pp. 36ff.
The work by Ignaz Beidtel, Geschichte der österreichischen
Staatsverwaltung, 1740-1848, 2 vols. (Innsbruck, 1896-98), partly
history and partly memoirs, is an invaluable guide to the actions
and attitudes of Vormärz bureaucrats. Anderson and Anderson,
Political Institutions, pp. 166-237, discusses the bureaucracies
in all principal European states, including Austria-Hungary.

20. "Ein Absolutismus gemildert durch Schlamperei," cited in
Jászi, Dissolution, p. 165. See also Jászi's comments on pp. 163-
69 and those by Henry Wickham Steed, The Habsburg Monarchy, 3d
ed. (London, 1914), pp. 73-90 on "bureaucracy," pp. 90-98 on
"police," and pp. 95-105 on "justice."

21. This topic is discussed at length in chap. 4.

22. On the distribution of officials by nationality, see
Table 5 in the appendix.

23. Comprehensive studies of the language question in its
legal and political aspects are Adolph Fischel, Das österreichische Sprachenrecht, 2d ed. (Brno, 1910); K. G. Hugelmann, ed.,
Das Nationalitätenrecht des alten Oesterreich (Vienna, 1934);
and Edvard Koerner, "Národnostní a jazyková otázka v Předlitav-
sku," in Česká politika, 1:340-469. Solid shorter studies by
Young Czechs are Josef Herold, O české řeči úřední (Prague,
1909); Pacák, Několik slov; and two Reichsrat speeches by Josef
Kaizl on May 8, 1897, and January 21, 1898, reprinted in Z mého
života, 3:601-11 and 696-707. A brief survey is Peter Burian,
"The State Language Problem in Old Austria (1848-1918)," AHY 6-7
(1970/71):81-103. Generally helpful are the texts of imperial
language laws and the Reichsrat debates concerning them, for
example SPHA, 16th Session, 1900, supplements 604 and 606.

24. It is necessary at this point to discuss in some detail

the important laws that comprised the Cisleithanian Constitution because no book or article in English on the Habsburg Monarchy, with the exception of Macartney, Habsburg Empire, gives them more than cursory treatment; and even Macartney does not point out the self-contradictory and fundamentally antidemocratic nature of the laws.

25. Young Czechs were nonetheless, on balance, primarily critical of those German Liberals and constitutional great landowners who had helped establish the December Constitution and the May Laws, especially for their part in supporting imperial suppression of the Czech national movement in 1868-69 and in 1871-73. See Eim Politické úvahy, pp. 38-59 from "O nás pro nás," and pp. 265-75, the article "Kníže Karlos Auersperg," especially pp. 268-69 and 272-73. For a favorable Young Czech account of the school laws introduced primarily by German Liberals in 1868 and 1869, see Adámek, Z nasí doby, 2:5-6. Adámek, 1:36-40, is nonetheless, on balance, like Eim and other Young Czechs, highly critical of most German Liberal policies.

26. The complete texts of law no. 40 and no. 41 of April 2, 1873, will be found in Zákonník říšský, rok 1873 (Vienna, 1873), pp. 161-92.

27. On law no. 141 and its amendment by subsequent laws, see Bernatzik, Verfassungsgesetze, pp. 390-422. For the sake of conformity and clarity, all page references to imperial laws will be either to Bernatzik or to Zákonník říšský. Another useful reference work on Austrian constitutional law is Ludwig Gumplowicz, Das oesterreichische Staatsrecht (Verfassungs- und Verwaltungsrecht): Ein Lehr- und Handbuch (Vienna, 1891).

28. All biographies and studies of the emperor attest to this, including Redlich, Franz Joseph, and Hlaváč, František Josef I.

29. On laws no. 143, no. 144, and no. 145, see Bernatzik, Verfassungsgesetze, pp. 427-39 for the German text and commentary.

30. The employment of article 14 is discussed in chaps. 9 and 10.

31. For complete texts of laws no. 143 and no. 144, see Zákonník říšský, rok 1867 (Vienna, 1867).

32. Jan Šafránek, Školy české. Obraz jejich vývoje a osudů, 2 vols. (Prague, 1913, 1919), 2:175-79, 223-49, 304-13, and 432-38.

33. The text of law no. 142 is in Bernatzik, Verfassungsgesetze, pp. 422-27. The second paragraph of article 19 reads,

"Die Gleichberechtigung aller landesüblichen Sprachen in Schule, Amt und öffentlichem Leben wird vom Staate anerkannt." The first and third paragraphs are translations by Macartney, Habsburg Empire, pp. 562-63.

34. Remarks on the unenforceability of the law are in the letter from Karel Kramář to Bedřich Pacák, dated May 1907, in the Pacák papers, LANM. See also Eim, Politické úvahy, pp. 447-48 from Eim's Reichsrat speech of May 28, 1894.

35. Bernatzik, Verfassungsgesetze, pp. 503ff., on law no. 60 of May 5, 1869. Corporate bodies could exercise the same right of appeal or petition as any private individual provided they had been chartered by the government.

36. Imperial suppression of Czech political activity and civil rights by emergency decree is well documented by Jakub Arbes in Plác koruny České neboli Persekuce lidu českého v letech 1868-1873, 2d ed. (Prague, 1894) (hereafter Arbes, Plác); Persekuce lidu českého v letech 1869-1873. Dodatkem k druhému vydání spisu "Plác koruny České" (Prague, 1896) (hereafter Arbes, Persekuce), the second edition of Plác forming a companion to Persekuce which contains an index for both works; and J. Ex. hrabě František Thun z Hohensteina, c. k. místodržící v království českém: Kritika úřadní činnosti Jeho Excellence (Smíchov, 1895). A more recent treatment is Karel Malý, Policejní a soudní perzekuce dělnické třídy v druhé polovině 19. století v Čechách (Prague, 1967). These may be supplemented by police reports noted above. Events of the seventies, eighties, and nineties will be discussed in subsequent chapters. The longest peacetime state of emergency in the Czech lands, that maintained by Governor Thun in Prague and five adjacent districts from September 12, 1893, until November 15, 1895, is discussed in chap. 6.

37. Bernatzik, Verfassungsgesetze, p. 425. The Czech text appears and is discussed in Arbes, Thun, 2:264ff.

38. Karel Malý, Policejní perzekuce, pp. 166-89, also demonstrates by citing police reports the extent to which postal and customs authorities exceeded the broad powers granted to them by the Schmerling press law and by law no. 60.

39. See Zákonní říssky, rok 1862 (Vienna, 1863), for text of the law. Available official correspondence relating to it from SÚA, PM 1860-1870, 8/4/15/30. The law of December 17, 1862, went into effect on March 9, 1863. Imperial law no. 122 of May 17, 1852, had reestablished preventive censorship in fact but not in theory. Such censorship was deemed to have been abolished by the Imperial Patent of March 15, 1848.

40. A fine comparative study of censorship in continental European states during the nineteenth century will be found in Anderson and Anderson, Political Institutions, pp. 244-72.

41. A cogent and comprehensive discussion of the growth of the Czech press in spite of the law of December 17, 1862, appears in the twelve-page introduction to František Roubík, Bibliografie časopisectva v Čechách z let 1863-1895 (Prague, 1936). A brief discussion of the problems of censorship is given by Milena Beránková, Český buržoasní tisk v druhé polovině 19. století (Prague, 1964), pp. 82-84. A thorough and informed evaluation of imperial press laws is the May 28, 1894, Reichsrat speech by Young Czech journalist and delegate Gustav Eim, which appears as "Řeč promluvená 28. května r. 1894 v poslanecké sněmovně o návrzích výborových na částečnou změnu zákonův o časopisectvu," in Eim, Politické úvahy, pp. 440-62. Perceptive eyewitness comments from 1897 by Mark Twain appear in "Stirring Times in Austria," in Literary Essays, Author's National Edition of the Writings of Mark Twain, vol. 24 (New York, 1918), pp. 200-02.

42. Roubík, 1863-1895, p. xii.

43. SÚA, PM 8/1/17/1, no. 1779.

44. On this tax and on the importance of its repeal for Czech journalism and politics see the report in Naše doba 7 (1899/1900):285-87. Similar taxes had been abolished in Great Britain in 1853, in Germany in 1874, and in France in 1881.

45. Skedl and Weiss, Taaffe, pp. 477-78, letter from Minister-President Taaffe to Governor Thun of January 1890 and Thun's reply of February 5, 1890.

46. Josef Anýž, "Několik vzpomínek z persekuce Národních listů," in Půl století "Národních listů:" Almanach (Prague, 1911), p. 41.

47. Roubík, 1863-1895, p. xiii.

48. Eim, Politické úvahy, pp. 457-58, and Gustav Kolmer, ed., Parlament und Verfassung in Oesterreich (Vienna, 1902-14), 3:430ff.

49. SPHA 11, 30 October 1891, p. 2803, speech by Young Czech Bedřich Pacák.

50. These efforts are outlined in Antonín Hajn, "Pilný návrh na ochranu českého tisku," in Výbor prací 1889-1909 (Prague, 1912-13), 3:142-46.

51. Arbes, Thun, 1:258-61ff.

52. The development of the Czech, especially the Young Czech, press is discussed in chap. 4 below.

53. This theme appears in almost all Young Czech addresses, many of which are cited in later chapters.

54. The standard work on the history of Bohemian state rights to 1848 is Josef Kalousek's České státní právo (Prague, 1871; 2d rev. ed., 1892), from which all subsequent work must begin. František Palacký defined state rights in relation to the Habsburg Monarchy in his 1865 work, "Idea státu rakouského," in Palacký, Spisy drobné, 1:209-67. Karel Mattuš wrote several short accounts for political purposes, among them Historické právo a národnost co základové státního zřizení říše Rakouské (Prague, 1867) and Několik myšlének o českém státu (Prague, 1870).

55. Thun's interesting account of his encounter with the emperor on the subject of Bohemian state rights is reported by Albín Bráf in his memoirs, Život a dílo, vol. 1: Pameti (Prague, 1922), pp. 3-4.

56. František Cyrill Kampelík, Stav Rakouska a jeho budouc-nosti (Hradec Králové, 1860), pp. 69-92, discusses German hostility toward and ignorance of the Czechs in 1860.

57. The Czech conservative and Catholic historian W. W. To-mek tells in his memoirs, Pameti z mého ziwota (Prague, 1904-05), 1:470-71, how at the suggestion of Count Leo Thun he helped bring Rieger and Clam together.

58. As reported by A. Pravoslav Veselý, "Dr. Fr. Lad. Rieger," Zář, vol. 7, no. 11 (March 12, 1903).

59. Albín Bráf in Česká politika, vol. 2, pt. 2, p. 256.

60. See Národní listy, January 8, 1863; March 29, 1863; June 23, 1865; June 10, 1865; and January 11, 1865. For general comments see Karel Adámek, Státoprávní základy národnosti (Prague, 1862), and the excellent article by Valentin Urfus, "Český státoprávní program na rozhraní let 1860-1861 a jeho ideové složky," Právněhistorické studie 8 (1962):127-72. Note Zdeněk Tobolka's opinion on Rieger in Česká politika, 3:205.

61. These themes appear in most of Palacký's historical writings and also in the series of eight articles on "the idea of the Austrian state" published in Národ during April and May of 1865 and republished in Palacký, Spisy drobné, 1:206-67. In

providing historical justifications for their political programs, Czechs like Palacký and the legal historian Josef Kalousek did what many European political leaders did throughout the nineteenth century. On such doctrines as a European practice, see Stanley Mellon, The Political Uses of History (Stanford, 1958).

62. František Ladislav Rieger, Příspěvky k listáři, ed. Jan Heidler (Prague, 1924-26), 2:176 (hereafter Rieger-Heidler, Příspěvky); Kampelík, Stav Rakouska, pp. 106-14; P. Hanuš Nadlabský, "Náš ústavní život před rokem a nyni," Obecné listy, vol. 2, no. 3 (January 17, 1862). On Clam-Martinic's decision, see Reiger-Heidler, Příspěvky, 1:138, no. 361, letter from Rieger to Vilém Gabler, December 10, 1860.

63. This argument is fully developed in chap. 4.

64. A typical argument of this case is Zeithammer's speech of December 28, 1861, in Příbram to the congress of the Agricultural Union of the Prague region, printed in Obecné listy, vol. 2, no. 1 (January 3, 1862).

65. Jiljí V. Jahn, František Ladislav Rieger: Obraz životopisný (Prague, 1889), pp. 221ff.

66. The Czechs believed the law insured equal rights for both languages. František Ladislav Rieger, Řeči a jednáni v zákonodárných sborech, ed. Josef Kalousek, 4 vols. (Prague, 1883-88), 3:300-12, including Rieger's speech of May 21, 1864, and subsequent debate. German delegates to the Bohemian Diet repealed this law in 1868, taking advantage of the first boycott of that body by the Czech delegates.

67. The Seven Weeks War brought Prussian troops into Prague during July of 1866 after their defeat of the Austrian army under Field Marshal Benedek at Sadowa. The Prussians had intended to encourage revolt by the Czechs and the Hungarians if Austria proved to be a resolute foe and had even employed the 1848 veteran and radical democrat J. V. Frič to try to rouse the former. When the swift Austrian capitulation rendered appeals to revolt unnecessary, the Prussians promptly withdrew from Bohemia.

68. Karel Kazbunda, "Kolem dubnového sněmu českého z r. 1867," ČČH 38 (1932):285-346.

69. Edvard Grégr, Denník, 2 vols. (Prague, 1908, 1914), 1:131, diary entry for March 30, 1867. SA Litoměřice, branch at Zitenice, correspondence of Jiří Kristián z Lobkovic, letters from Johann A. Schwarzenberg, dated March 6 and March 16, 1867. I wish to thank Mr. Josef Křivka, archivist at Žitenice, for

pointing out the importance of this and related material in the
Lobkowicz archives.

70. Police reports on the diet in SÚA, PMT, 1866-1916, no. 8,
GP 1867, Report of the Prague Chief of Police to the Governor,
dated February 22, 1867.

71. Bernatzik, Verfassungsgesetze, pp. 1087-91 for German
text. Srb, Politické dějiny, 1:220-23 for Czech text, pp. 229-35
for text of Moravian declaration, p. 235 for the minority report
of the Moravian Diet opposing this resolution, and pp. 235-36 for
the majority report of the Silesian Diet opposing the text.

72. Piotr S. Wandycz, "The Poles in the Habsburg Monarchy,"
AHY, vol. 3, pt. 2 (1967):278.

73. Václav Čejchan and Josef Macek, eds., Dějiny česko-
ruských vztahů, 1770-1917 (Prague 1967), 1:212-22, and Milan
Prelog, Pouť Slovanů do Moskvy roku 1867 (Prague, 1931), authori-
tatively discuss the Moscow pilgrimage. The role of Grégr and
the Young Czechs in that event is discussed in chap. 3 below.

74. These events are discussed in Odložilík, "Russia and
Czech National Aspirations," and Karel Kazbunda, "Ke zmaru
českého vyrovnání," ČČH 37 (1931):512-73. The text of the December 1870 manifesto is in Srb, Politické dějiny, 1:312-17.

75. These appeals are discussed in chaps. 9 and 10 below.

76. Count Alfred Potocki served as minister-president from
April 1870 to April 1871. On the secret negotiations, see Kazbunda, "Ke zmaru."

77. Schäffle, a former professor at the university in Tübingen, numbered among the few articulate German advocates of a
federated Austria in which all nationalities would enjoy equal
rights. Schäffle argued primarily from expediency and as a
Swabian and Protestant could take a more detached and objective
view of problems in the monarchy than could Austrian-German
burghers, scholars, or noblemen. Habietinek and Jireček will be
discussed in chap. 3.

78. Thomson, Czechoslovakia, p. 217, had this translation.
Czech text in Srb, Politické dějiny, 1:329-30.

79. Czech text given in Srb, Politické dějiny, 1:341-47.
German text in Bernatzik, Verfassungsgesetze, pp. 1097-1109. A
Slavic minority in the Silesian Diet also favored the articles.

80. Odložilík, "Russia and Czech National Aspirations,"

demonstrates Russian refusal to meddle in Austrian internal affairs on the basis of extant printed and archival sources and also shows that Rieger erred in asserting that Russia intervened against the Czechs.

81. The first promise was made April 13, 1861.

82. "Idea státu Rakouského," in Palacký, Spisy drobné, 1:266. This work, reprinted on pp. 209-67, originally appeared as a series of eight articles in Národ from April 9 through May 16, 1865.

83. On relations between Czechs and Slovenes, see Fran Zwitter, "The Slovenes and the Habsburg Monarchy," AHY, vol. 3, pt. 2 (1967):172-73. On Slovaks, see František Bokes, ed., Dokumenty k slovenskému národnému hnutiu v rokoch 1848-1914, 2 vols. (Bratislava, 1962), 1:449-54, quotation on p. 450: "narod slovenský program federalistov tak, ako dosial' stojí, prisvojit' si naskrze nemôže."

84. Polish Czech relations in as well as outside the Habsburg Monarchy are discussed by Václav Žáček, Češi a Poláci, 2:246-82, and indirectly by Wandycz, "The Poles," and Lands of Partitioned Poland, and by Henryk Wereszycki, "The Poles as an Integrating and Disintegrating Factor," AHY, vol. 3, pt. 2 (1967): 287-313.

85. Developments in Hungary, generally beyond the scope of this book, are discussed in English by Macartney, Habsburg Empire; by R. W. Seton-Watson, Racial Problems in Hungary (London, 1908), and Corruption and Reform in Hungary: A Study of Electoral Practice (London, 1911); and by two articles in AHY, vol. 3, pt. 1 (1967): pp. 234-59, George Barany, "Hungary: The uncompromising Compromise," and pp. 260-302, Péter Hanák, "Hungary in the Austro-Hungarian Monarchy." See also the recently published history of Slovakia, L'udovít Holotík and Július Mésáros, eds., Dejiny Slovenska, vol 3: Od roku 1848 do roku 1900 (Bratislava, 1968).

86. Jiří Kořalka, "Some Remarks on the Concepts of Nationalism and Internationalism," Historica 13 (1966):209-16, and Peter F. Sugar, "External and Domestic Roots of Eastern European Nationalism," in Sugar and Lederer, Nationalism in Eastern Europe, pp. 3-54, discuss this point. The marked differences between the national movements of small nations and those of large nations or empires are seldom thoroughly accounted for by works in English or German or other Western languages.

87. In some respects Czech economic interests were as well served by the Habsburg Monarchy as by the Czechoslovak Republic;

but prospects of economic advantage within the monarchy in no
way compensated for the lack of national independence or extensive civil liberties. Within the monarchy, Czech investment and
trade were confined largely to Cisleithania, since economic dis-
parities and conflicts between the two halves of the monarchy
made that state a free-trade area in theory much more than in
practice.

Chapter 3

1. Karel Sladkovský, Výbor z politických řečí a úvah, ed.
Servác Heller (Prague, 1899), speech of March 10, pp. 45-61, and
of March 20, pp. 67-72; Tomek, Paměti, 2:63-64; Rieger, Řeči,
3:89-99. The vote went 149 to 52 against the bill. On unequal
representation see tables 16, 18, and 20A.

2. Rieger, Řeči, 3:167-71. The conservative German vote
made the difference between the votes of 1863 and 1864.

3. Národní listy, June 8, 1863; October 22, 1863; June 23,
1865; and the report of the Prague chief of police to the governor dated February 17, 1867, in SÚA, PMT 66-16, no. 7.

4. Rieger, Řeči, 2:21-25, 3:259-60; Jahn, Rieger, pp. 92-96;
and Srb, Politické dějiny, 1:12-19.

5. The text of the proposal is in Rieger, Řeči, 3:99-101.

6. Pražák-Kaminíček, Paměti, vol. 2, no. 8, pp. 15-16, letter of Š. Dvořák to Alois Pražák, June 7, 1863, from Prague.
Dvořák estimated that had all twenty-one been present, eleven
(including four Moravians) would have voted against Rieger.

7. The text of this memorandum, dated June 17, 1863, is in
Srb, Politické dějiny, 1:41-47.

8. Rieger, Řeči, 3:233-34.

9. The text of the Declaration of August 22, 1868, appears
in Srb, Politické dějiny, 1:220-27. Accounts of the events surrounding this declaration will be found on pp. 216-19 and 227-29;
in Mattuš, Paměti, pp. 57-63; and in Tobolka, Politické dějiny,
2:162-71.

10. The memorandum of the Czech delegates to the emperor,
dated August 30, 1870, will be found in Srb, Politické dějiny,
1:281-84; the supplementary historical justification for Bohemian state rights which was appended to the memorandum appears on
pp. 285-97.

11. The declaration of National party delegates drawn up on November 25, 1872, and presented to the diet on November 27, announcing their forthcoming withdrawal from that body, appears in Srb, Politické dějiny, 1:412-15. A petition to the emperor from the same delegates, dated December 31, 1872, appears on pp. 422-24.

12. Václav Škarda, "Politika etapová" and "O národní straně svobodomyslné," in Výbor statí a řecí Dra. Václava Škardy, ed. Miloslava Sísová (Prague, 1912), pp. 101-14. See also Josef Fort, Ven z přítmí! Českých snah pohnutky, cíle a cesty (Prague, 1905), another classic Young Czech statement on politics of the present and the immediate past. See especially chap. 8, "positivní politika," pp. 161-95.

13. Pražák-Kameníček, Paměti, vol. 2, no. 6, pp. 12-14, a letter from Mezník to Pražák of May 16, 1863, explained that the Moravian Czechs would not join Rieger in passive resistance because they expected to advance their interests through an alliance with the Moravian nobility, thus maintaining a majority in the Moravian Diet.

14. Rieger-Heidler, Příspěvky, vol. 1, no. 416, Rieger to J. Grégr (ca. November 1863), pp. 159-60. See also the general survey of events in Václav Žáček, ed., Češi a Poláci, 2:259-62, and Tobolka, Politické dějiny, 2:339-49.

15. Rieger-Heidler, Přívspěvky, vol. 1, no. 412, Šimáček to Rieger, August 1, 1863, p. 155. Jahn, Rieger, pp. 168-80; and Adolf Srb, František Šimáček (Prague, 1910), pp. 44-66.

16. Like the National party leadership, the Young Czechs remained Russophiles and participated in the 1867 pilgrimage to Moscow but, as Havlíček had done, strongly criticized imperial Russian autocracy.

17. E. Grégr, Denník, 1:110, entry for January 10, 1864.

18. Jahn, Rieger, p. 179. Karel Tůma, Život Dra. Julia Grégra (Prague, 1896), pp. 161-64ff.

19. Trojan (1815-93), Rieger (1818-1903), Tilšer (1825-1913), E. Grégr (1827-1907), J. Grégr (1831-96), Sladkovský (1823-80), Mattuš (1836-1919), Zeithammer (1832-1919).

20. Rieger's patronizing attitude toward the common people and their leaders is best revealed by his low estimation of Josef Barák and by his refusal to attend Barák's funeral. Rieger perceived Barák's lack of great intellect and broad vision but could not appreciate his achievements as a popular journalist

and politician. Rieger-Heidler, Příspěvky, vol. 2, no. 508,
p. 218, diary entry of Rieger's daughter Marie Červinková for
November 15, 1883.

Jahn, Rieger, a partisan work designed to show Rieger to best
advantage and in many respects a typical campaign biography, remains the most complete account. Two articles very critical of
Rieger have appeared in English: Stanley Z. Pech, "F. L. Rieger:
The Road from Liberalism to Conservatism," JCEA, vol. 17, no. 1
(April 1957):3-23; and idem, "Passive Resistance of the Czechs,
1863-1879," SEER, vol. 36, no. 87 (June 1958):434-52. Odložilík's "Enter Masaryk" describes the social and political prominence enjoyed by Rieger in the eighties, and "Na předělu dob"
gives a fair, critical, and generally sympathetic portrayal of
Rieger and his policies. Karel Mašek et al., Od kolébky Riegrovy:
Almanach ve prospěch zřízení Riegrovy mohyly na Kozákove (Prague,
1900), contains several interesting pieces, among them Karel
Mattuš, "František Ladislav Rieger: několik slov jeho a o něm,"
pp. 5-9, and a poem by Bohdan Kaminský, "Památce Riegrově,"
pp. 3-4.

21. Albín Bráf, Život a dílo, vol. 1: Paměti (Prague, 1922),
pp. 123-44 on Mattuš and Rieger. Other information on party
figures in the index. Jan Neruda, Podobizny (Prague, 1952),
2:33-36 on Zeithammer. Mattuš became one of the first Old
Czechs to favor an "active" policy after 1871.

22. Srb's Šimáček is the standard biography. On Skrejšovský
and the journalistic wars of the seventies, see the anonymous
pamphlet Skrejšovský a družstvo "Politik" (Prague, 1878). See
also Arbes, Persekuce and Plác.

23. On the strength of Zátka's Old Czech cadres in Budějovice after 1891, see the exchange of correspondence between
Young Czech party chairman Emanuel Engel and Vojtěch Holanský,
leading Young Czech representative in Budějovice, PNP, Engel
papers, 6s85, Holanský to Engel, April 19, 1892, and reply
April 21, 1892.

24. These were among the adjectives most frequently employed
by the Old Czech press, notably Pokrok and Politik, to describe
Young Czech policies and motives. Pokrok (Progress) became Hlas
národa (The voice of the nation) in March 1886 and continued as
a daily to try to rival the Národní listy. The Old Czech journalists and scholars were František Šimáček (1834-85); J. S.
Skrejšovský (1837-1902); Albín Bráf (1851-1912); and Bohuslav
Rieger (1857-1907).

25. Srb, Pclitické dějiny, 1:239-40. Arbes, Persekuce,
pp. 91-97, 275-311.

26. On Ruch and Lumír, see above, chap. 1. On Engel in Ruch, see Strejček, O Svatopluku Čechovi, pp. 94-98. Engel published a fine selection of his lyrical and patriotic poems, Básně (1867).

27. Tobolka, Politické dějiny, 2:356-57; Tomek, Paměti, is an invaluable source on the conservative Catholic faction among the Old Czechs.

28. On Catholic conservatives, aside from Tomek, Paměti, and the various works by Rudolf Vrba listed in the bibliography, see Okáč, Rakouský problém, for the sixties. On problems of the nineties see the short, retrospective, partisan and anonymous article from a Catholic perspective, "Deset let české politiky," in Alétheia 3 (1899):157-60.

29. Josef Václav Frič (1829-90) is best revealed in his memoirs, completed only to his thirtieth year, through the fifties, Paměti do třiceti let, 4 vols. (Prague, 1886-87), an invaluable source on Czech politics of 1848 and the early fifties. Frič's many political articles of the same period, some of which were written and published in exile, will be found in Josef Václav Frič, Spisy, vol. 1: Politické clanky z let 1847-1864, ed. Otto Šimáček and Božena Šimáčková (Prague, 1956). Frič's articles and observations on literary and political associates are published as J. V. Frič, Naši předchůdci, ed. Karel Cvejn (Prague, 1953). A selection of his poetry appears in J. V. Frič, Písně z bašty a jiné básně, ed. Karel Cvejn (Prague, 1952).

30. Barák's (1833-83) lectures were published after his death by Jan Podlipný and Václav Řezníček, Přednásky Josefa Baráka (Prague, 1884-86). On Barák's character and influence, see Antal Stašek, Vzpomínky (Prague, 1925), pp. 368-77. Jan Neruda's works are available in a number of collected editions. His interesting sketches of Czech political as well as literary figures appear in Podobizny 1873-1891, 4 vols. (Prague, 1951-57).

31. Jakub Arbes (1840-1914) is remembered for his many short stories and novels, including Kandidáti existence first published in 1878 and dedicated to J. V. Frič, as well as for his thorough documentary accounts of governmental persecution of the Czech press and National and Social Democratic political parties, Plác and Persekuce and Thun. Arbes as well as Jan Neruda (1834-91) will be discussed at greater length in chap. 4.

32. Thurn-Taxis (1833-1904) came from a noble family of Italian origin (della Torre e Tassis) which had first entered Habsburg service in the twelfth century. From 1880 to 1892 he served as an administrator and legal advisor to successive Bulgarian governments and retired thereafter to a family estate near Dresden, where in his declining years he renounced his

princely title to become a simple Freiherr. On Thurn-Taxis, see
Ottův slovník naučný, 25:404-05, and Okáč, Rakouský problém. On
Hlahol, see Zdeněk Nejedly, Dějiny pražského Hlaholu (Prague,
1911).

33. Tůma, Život J. Grégra, pp. 184-88.

34. On Edvard Grégr's opinions, see his published diary,
Denník, 1:131, 163-65, and manuscript diary, PNP, Edvard Grégr
papers, for the section on his "audience with the Czar," which
does not appear in its entirety in the published version.

35. E. Grégr, Denník, 1:168-69, diary entry of June 12, 1867,
upon his return from Moscow. V. V. (Vincenc Vávra?), Pout' Slo-
vanův do Ruska roku 1867 a její význam (Prague, 1867), published
by the Grégrs.

36. On Rieger's discussions with the French, see Rieger's
exchange of letters with A. Lefaivre, seven letters, from November 1870 through February 1871, and the summary of a letter from
Emile Picot to Rieger, dated February 12, 1871, in Rieger-
Heidler, Příspěvky, 1:214-20.

37. On Rieger's basing domestic policy on anticipated changes
in Austro-Hungarian foreign policy, see Odložilík, "Na předělu
dob," and Tobolka, Politické dějiny, 2:314ff.

38. The most fully developed radical Young Czech interpretation of Havlíček (1821-56) will be found in Karel Tůma's biography, Karel Havlíček Borovský: nejslavnější publicista českého
národa (Kutná Hora, 1883), and his edition of selected works in
three volumes, Vybrané spisy Karla Havlíčka Borovského (Kutná
Hora, 1886-87). Other important Young Czech tributes to Havlíček include Edvard Grégr's speech on the unveiling of the Havlíček monument in Vysoké nad Jizerou on August 23, 1891; and
speeches by Václav Škarda and Prokop Podlipský on November 8,
1896, at an assembly of the Young Czech party in the National
Museum in Havlíček's honor. These and other tributes to Havlíček appear in Antonín Hajn, ed., Národ o Havlíčkovi (Prague,
1936). Hajn's collection indicates the extent to which almost
all Czech political parties, from the Old Czechs to the Social
Democrats, have claimed Havlíček as a predecessor. Only the
clerical parties have not so claimed him. Marxist historians,
while admiring him, have tended to downplay his criticism of
Russia and his uncompromising defense of civil liberties. See
also the bibliographical commentary by T. G. Masaryk, who claimed
Havlíček as a progressive and realist in his Karel Havlíček:
snahy a tužby politického probuzení, 2d ed. (Prague, 1904),
pp. 9-15. Masaryk accurately noted that "Mr. Tůma made a radical
of [Havlíček]--to be sure a radical of the eighties--and

confiscated him for his own political faction. Tůma's biography
of Havlíček and selections from his writings are indeed original—he made Havlíček out to be exactly the opposite of what he
actually was: a responsible opponent of radicalism." Zdeněk
Tobolka's edition of Havlíček's political writings, Karla Havlíčka politické spisy, 3 vols. in 5 (Prague, 1900-03), remains
the standard. A solid scholarly study is Emanuel Chalupný, Havlíček: prostředí, osobnost a díla (Prague, 1929). Barbara
Kohák Kimmel has written an article on "Karel Havlíček and the
Czech Press before 1848," in Brock and Skilling, Czech Renascence, pp. 113-30.

39. Edvard Grégr, Řeč Dr. Ed. Grégra při slavnosti odhalení
pamětní desky K. Havlíčka na jeho úmrtním domě v Praze II v Hav-
líčkove ul. dne 15. května r. 1870 (Prague, 1870).

40. This argument appears in many Young Czech pamphlets of
the seventies, including, notably, E. Grégr, K objasnění and
Otevřený list. See also Eim, Politické úvahy, "O nás pro nás,"
pp. 7-163. The importance of the institutions of self-government
(samospráva) to Young Czech politics is discussed in chap. 4.

41. For detailed accounts of the above events, see Srb, Politické dějiny, 1:216-29; Mattuš, Paměti, pp. 57-63; and Tobolka,
Politické dějiny, 2:162-71. On the debate of March 31, 1867, see
E. Grégr, Denník, 1:137-39. The Young Czech argument against
boycotting the diet is well-expressed in the series of articles
entitled "Political Independence" published in Národní listy,
March 15, 17, and 18, 1867.

42. See the excellent and thorough article by Jaroslav Purš,
"Tábory českých zemích 1868-1871 (Příspěvek k problematice národního hnutí)," ČsČH 6 (1958):234-66, 446-70, and 661-90. On
tábory in the Krkonoše and Pojizeří areas, see Stašek, Vzpominky,
pp. 259-72. On the general political context, see Fort, Ven z
prítmí!, pp. 115-20. On Moravia, see Jan Janák, "Táborové hnutí
na Morave v letech 1868-1874," Časopis Matice moravské 77 (1958):
290-324. On Silesia, see Andělín Grobelný, Slezsko v období
národních táboru v letech 1868-1871 (Ostrava, 1962). An account
of a typical youth tábor held on Prague's Letna on May 16, 1869,
and its resolutions is in PNP, Servác Heller papers, 12s83,
"Tábor Omladiny československé na Letné."

43. Podřipsko literally means "the area under Říp" and included the self-governmental districts of Mělník and Roudnice
nad Labem. Recognition of Říp as a patriotic site is indicated
in fiction, memoirs, and unpublished writings. For example, see
Sokol Archives, Tomáš Černý papers, Diary, Folder 3, p. 5, describing a Sokol outing to Říp, May 29, 1865.

44. Protocol quoted in Srb, Politické dějiny, 1:207-08, and in Národní listy, May 11, 1868, p. 1; it is discussed in Purš, "Tábory," p. 242ff.

45. On the emperor becoming worried and upset, see Karel Kazbunda, "Pokusy rakouské vlády o české vyrovnání," ČČH, 27 (1921):122, who used the cabinet meeting reports before they burned in 1927.

46. Arbes, Plác, pp. 208, 391-92; Arbes, Persekuce, pp. 49-50 on Janda and Kratochvíl, pp. 36, 422-23 on others. Pacák was condemned to five years' imprisonment for treason; Černý to four and one-half years; Tůma to three years; and Barák to one and one-half years. On the persecution of tábory leaders generally, see also F. M. Hájek, Zápisky vysockého omladináře politického vězně F. M. Hájka, ed. Jaroslav Skrbek (Prague, 1936). Taaffe's first term as minister-president lasted from September 8, 1868, until February 1, 1870.

47. Purš, "Tábory," pp. 265-66, using materials from police reports in SÚA and contemporary newspaper accounts for details. On Oul, see Cyrill Horáček, Počátky českého hnutí dělnického (Prague, 1896), pp. 30-65. Imperial officials contended that the political activity of the "democratic opposition" within Oul violated laws governing nonpolitical associations.

48. Purš, "Tábory," pp. 663-65.

49. PNP, Eim papers, 3aG31, E. Grégr to Eim, January 7, 1885.

50. On the meeting of November 23, 1873, and its consequences, see E. Grégr, K objasnění, pp. 50-52, from the Young Czech perspective, and Rieger-Heidler, Příspěvky, 2:26-28, letter of Rieger to Karel Mattuš, dated December 24, 1873, for a justification of Old Czech actions.

51. Eim, Politické úvahy, 117. "Sedm Makkabejců" and "sedm Švábů." "Švábi," an uncomplimentary Czech term for Germans, means both "Swabians" and "cockroaches." "Švábi" is from the German "Schwabe." The best American equivalent is "Krauts."

52. Srb, Politické dějiny, 1:400-10; Česká politika, vol. 2, pt. 1, pp. 628-31.

53. See the Young Czech party program of December 27, 1874, article 6, which promised relief from the depression through governmental assistance to commerce, industry, and agriculture. For the general effects of the depression of 1873-96 see the excellent article by Hans Rosenberg, "Political and Social Consequences of the Great Depression of 1873-1896 in Central Europe,"

Economic History Review, vol. 13, no. 1 (1943):58-73. For specific effects on the Czech lands, see Adámek, Z naší doby, 4:185ff.

54. Rieger-Heidler, Příspěvky, vol. 2, no. 72, p. 30, excerpts from a letter of Alois Pražák to Rieger dated January 23, 1874.

55. E. Grégr, K objasnění, pp. 52-65. Rieger-Heidler, Příspěvky, 2:11-12, letter from Rieger to Zeithammer dated September 28, 1872, indicates that Young Czech fears were not groundless. Tilšer, Ve službě panstva, indicates how such fears continued into the eighties.

56. Šolle, Internacionála, passim, and "K počátkům dělnického hnutí v Praze," ČsČH, vol. 5, no. 4 (1957):664-87.

57. This congress is described in Tůma, Život J. Grégra, pp. 248-49. The above quotation, intended to be ironical, appears in Palacký's critique of the newly founded Young Czech party, "O roztržce v národu českém," in his Spisy drobné, 1:421.

58. See the introductory remarks by Servác Heller in Sladkovský, Výbor, pp. 5-7 and 8-20, the latter the eulogy from Národní listy, March 5, 1880.

59. Hardship in Habsburg prisons contributed to his premature death; Neruda, Podobizny, 1:182-83.

60. Matoušek, Sladkovský, thoroughly traces this development, pp. 59-75, 138-44.

61. Sladkovský, Výklad.

62. F. Schulz, "Vincenc Vávra (1824-1877): Nekrolog," Osvěta 7 (1877):795-96. Vávra's memoirs appeared posthumously, Zápisky starého osmačtyřicátníka, ed. Jaroslav Schiebel (Kutná Hora, 1889).

63. Works which appraise Purkyně's political and cultural contributions to Czech society as well as his scientific achievements include K. Chodounský, Jan Evangelista Purkyně: Působení jeho pro rozvoj české kultury (Prague, 1927); Jan Kepl, Jan Evangelista Purkyně a Průmyslová Jednota (Prague, 1937); and Jarmila Pstoníčková, Jan Evangelista Purkyně (Prague, 1955).

64. On Grégr's scientific career, see the short accounts in Psotníčková, Purkyně, pp. 36-39; Ottuv slovník naučný, 10:459; and "Dr. Edward Grégr," The Bohemian Voice, vol. 1, no. 8, p. 1 (Omaha, April 1, 1893).

65. The principal sources on Edvard Grégr are his diary,
published and edited through 1889 in two volumes by Zdenek Tobolka as Denník, and complete in manuscript form in PNP, Edvard
Grégr papers. Also important are the large collection of his
letters to his brother Julius which remain in LANM, Julius Grégr
papers, and the large selection of his correspondence with Alfons Šťastný published in Traub, Ze života Alfonse Šťastného.
Tobolka's editing of the diary appears to have been done with
political as well as personal considerations in mind. Materials
in the diary after 1890 are highly critical of Kramář and other
Young Czech leaders of the post-1906 era to whom Tobolka was beholden and whose politics Tobolka then supported. Also, later
diary materials would have embarrassed too many persons in public life at the time of the publication of Denník. The Tobolka
papers in PNP shed no light on the precise grounds for editing
Denník as it was done. The principal political writings of Edvard Grégr, revealing for his personality and style as well as
political opinions, are cited frequently in the text and are
listed in the bibliography.

The Grégrs' father was a forest surveyor (lesný geometr) who
gave both his sons an appreciation of scientific achievement and
nature as well as national pride. Julius also acquired from his
father a love of hunting. Julius Grégr is discussed at length
in chap. 4.

66. Remarkably little has been written about Tilšer, one of
the most influential Young Czechs during two decades. His work,
Ve službě panstva, most cogently and thoroughly expresses the
radical Young Czech distrust of the conservative great landowners; and the Pravda o vyrovnání, which he coauthored and approved
for publication, makes the most complete exposition of the Young
Czech case against the Agreement of 1890.

67. Biographical data drawn primarily from entries in Ottův
slovník naučný and Michael Navratil, ed., Almanach českých práv-
niků (Prague, 1904). On Janda, see Stašek, Vzpomínky, pp. 532-33.
Persecution of peasant organizations is documented in Arbes, Plác
and Persekuce. These and important party figures of later decades are more thoroughly discussed in chap. 5 below.

68. Texts are in V. Škarda, Program 1897, pp. 18-23; Program
Národní strany svobodomyslné (Prague, 1912); and Tůma, Život J.
Grégra, pp. 249-54. All stress is in the original text.

69. E. Grégr, K objasnění, pp. 34-36, prints the proclamation. The manifesto is reprinted in Srb, Politické dejiny,
1:467-68. The twenty-eight signatories of the Proclamation of
November 28, 1873, are listed by Tůma, Život J. Grégra, p. 244.

70. V. Škarda, Program 1897, p. 20, ". . . uznání a

uskutečnění samostatností a samosprávy zemí českých na základě platného a neporušitelného statního práva."

71. By this they meant universal *manhood* suffrage.

72. The eighth and final paragraph, to be discussed below, dealt in a general way with party organization.

73. Masaryk, Desorganisace, p. 38. ". . . jsme [Češi] jazykově nejvíce cítili svou politickou porobu."

74. The English equivalent would be "a tinker's damn" or "a hill of beans." Edvard Grégr, Naše politika: Otevřený list panu dru. Fr. L. Riegrovi (Prague, 1876), p. 10.

75. Edvard Grégr, K objasnění (1874) and later Slovo osudné (1883).

76. [Edvard Grégr], Má-li se jíti na sněm? (Prague, 1873), pp. 23-25, 27, 29. Edvard Grégr, Politické rozjímání před volbami do řísské rady (Prague, 1879), pp. 6-13.

77. Tilšer, Ve službě panstva, is the classic statement of this position.

78. E. Grégr, K objasnění, p. 8.

79. Národní listy, July 5, 1876. Jednání na druhém valném sjezdu národní strany svobodomyslné odbývaném dne 7 listopadu 1875 (Protocols of the second Young Czech party congress, November 7, 1875) (Prague, 1875), pp. 7ff.

80. LANM, Julius Grégr papers, "Ve sporu zájmů národních a liberálních museji ustoupiti zájmy liberální," letter of Edvard Grégr to J. Grégr, November 19, 1879. He thought the likelihood of having to make such a choice was increased by the recent decision of Young and Old Czechs to participate in the Reichsrat in association with Taaffe's newly formed "Iron Ring" parliamentary majority. Edvard Grégr expressed much the same conviction in his letter to Julius of January 28, 1884: "we [Young Czechs] must be liberal but also be more resolute on national issues than the Old Czechs." This letter is also in LANM, Julius Grégr papers.

81. The six board members from Podřipsko were Edvard Černický from Sedlec, Antonín Herites from Vodňany, Václav Janda from Budohostice, Václav Kratochvíl from Lounky, Antonín Nedoma from Vraňany, and Gustav Švagrovský from Roudnice. To these might be added Josef Barák, an editor of the Národní listy and then also the publisher of the Mělnické listy. The other elected

board members were Antonín Čížek, Julius Grégr, Arnošt Hnízdo,
Jan Jeništal, Jan Kučera, Stanislav Majer, František Schwarz,
Karel Sladkovský, Jan Strakatý, František Tilšer, Emanuel Tonner,
and Vincenc Vávra. The seven diet delegates were Edvard Grégr,
Jakub Hruška, Antonín Husák, Adolf rytíř z Maiersbachu, Robert
Nittinger, Josef Pražák, and Alois Pravoslav Trojan, all of whom
also served on the board. E. Grégr, Denník, 2:5-7, 15-18, diary
entries for September 15 and December 28, 1874.

82. Šťastný, O doplnění našeho národního program.

83. Barák, Přednásky, lecture no. 8, pp. 13-14 and 17. Jan
Podlipný, the Young Czech mayor of Prague during the nineties,
underlined the quoted lines and other passages in his copy.

84. See platforms of 1874 and 1879 in V. Škarda, Program 1897,
and platform of 1889 in Národní listy, June 25, 1889. Kramář,
before joining the party, expressed similar opinions to Julius
Grégr in his letter of November 18, 1890, LANM, Julius Grégr
papers. Kaizl's letter to Kramář of November 17, 1890, cites
Špindler's opinion that Old and Young Czech labels mattered little
given mutual interests. See too Kaizl's last letter to Pacák,
dated August 11, 1901, which stresses common goals and interests
in light of the recent Old and Young Czech electoral agreement.

85. The statement (dated September 14, 1874) of the Young
Czechs upon returning to the Bohemian Diet follows the entry for
September 15, 1874, in the Grégr diary, Denník, 2:6-7.

86. E. Grégr, K objasnění, p. 11.

87. Palacký, Spisy drobné, 1:411-26.

88. See, for example, the oversimplified argument in E. Grégr,
K objasnění, pp. 39-46.

89. Palacký in his Spisy drobné, 1:422, contended that Sladkovský and Julius and Edvard Grégr wished to play at being
"saviors" of the nation. He thought their attitude to be "away
with Palacký and Rieger. Long live Sladkovský and Grégr."

90. On the negotiations with Taaffe and his representatives
leading to the joint return of Old and Young Czechs to the
Reichsrat and subsequent cooperation with the Taaffe government,
see National party and Moravian Old Czech aims and expectations
discussed in a series of letters from Rieger to Pražák, in Pražák-Kameníček, Paměti, 2:212-14, letter of July 22, 1879; pp.
219-20, letter of August 15, 1879; pp. 227-31, letter of August 22, 1879; and pp. 234-37, letter of August 26, 1879. See
also Rieger-Heidler, Příspěvky, 2:118-19, letter from Smolka to

Rieger, July 13, 1879, and pp. 125-56, letter from Rieger to
Zeithammer, September 13, 1879.

91. On negotiations generally see Gustav Eim, part 15 of
"O nás pro nás," in his Politické úvahy, pp. 127-51, especially
on the renewed cooperation between Old and Young Czechs. On
Young Czech reservations concerning this cooperation see Rieger-
Heidler, Příspěvky, 2:123-34, letter from Rieger to Zeithammer
dated September 10, 1879, and Zeithammer's reply of the following
day. See also and more importantly LANM, Julius Grégr papers,
letters of Edvard Grégr to Julius dated March 2, 1880, and especially November 19, 1879, that expresses fear that Young Czech
participation in a coalition with the Old Czechs and the Right
would lead to a "weakening" and "disintegration" of the party
and to a decline of Czech liberalism generally. The best antidote in Edvard Grégr's opinion would be for Young Czechs to
"make evident in the Reichsrat at the earliest possible moment
their liberal and Slavic convictions."

92. A chronological account of the Taaffe government which
concentrates on activities in the Reichsrat and is based almost
exclusively on German sources is William A. Jenks, Austria under
the Iron Ring, 1879-1893 (Charlottesville, Va., 1965). See Gustav Eim on "Taaffe," in his Politické úvahy, pp. 277-88, for a
critical but sympathetic portrait. For a discussion of Czech
parliamentary politics during the Taaffe era, see Skilling, "The
Czech Eighties."

93. Kazbunda, Do rozdělení university, pp. 220ff.

94. "Čtvrtstoletí české techniky," Naše doba, vol. 2, no. 10
(July 1895):958.

95. On Czech politics in the early Taaffe era see Tobolka,
Politické dějiny, vol. 3, pt. 1, pp. 19-48, 94-100; Adámek, Z
naší doby, 4:5-184; and Eim, Politické úvahy, pp. 151-63,
"Čechové--na řískou radu."

96. These shifts are explained by Alois Pravoslav Trojan,
Dr. Pravoslav Alois Trojan ke svým voličům a krajanům i všem
Čechům (Prague, 1888), and Karel Adámek, Památce Dr. Aloise
Pravoslava Trojana (Chrudim, 1910), and idem, Z mých styků s dr.
Aloisem Pravoslavem Trojanem v letech 1879 až 1893 (Chrudim,
1910). On the 1890 shifts of party allegiance, see below,
chap. 5.

97. Paragraph 8 of the 1874 program, V. Škarda, ed., Program
1897, pp. 22-23. The number of trustees thereafter varied.

98. V. Škarda, ed., Program 1912, pp. 5-6.

99. J. Kretší, Stručný památník Klubu národní strany svobodomyslné. Na oslavu pětadvacetileté činnosti, 1873-1898 (Prague,
1898). See also Česka revue 1 (1898):1017-21.

100. PNP, Engel papers, 6s83, notebook 7, minutes, sixty-
eighth meeting of the party executive committee, August 20, 1891;
ninth meeting, March 8, 1890; meeting of January 1891. Rules for
delegates, "Stanovy Klubu neodvislých poslanců českých v radě
říšské," are in LANM, Julius Grégr papers.

101. PNP, Engel papers, 6s82, "Zemští důvěrníci: zvolení organisačním sjezdem národní strany svobodomyslné, 11. dubna 1888."

Chapter 4

1. From Karel Pippich's speech in honor of Karel Adámek's
seventieth birthday and forty-fifth year as mayor of the Hlinsko
district self-governmental board, in Čenek Jezdík et al., eds.,
Adámkův den v Hlinsku: 13 března 1910 (Hlinsko, 1910), p. 13.
  I have followed custom in translating samospráva or Selbstverwaltung as "self-government." Its powers did not begin to approach those of self-government in Britain or in the United
States; "self-administration" more accurately describes Selbstverwaltung in relation to the American experience.

2. No works in western European languages have dealt with the
question of communal and district self-government in the Czech
lands before 1914. General works on the monarchy have ignored it.
The literature in Czech on the subject is enormous, reflecting its
importance in Czech political and institutional history. A partial listing of works will be found in Jan Schmitt, ed., Příruční
seznam české literatury (Prague, 1916), pp. 939-61. Of great interest are the many articles in the leading periodical devoted to
self-government, Samosprávný obzor, which first appeared in 1879
and continued until the First World War. Among these articles
are Karel Adámek, "Z dějin okresních zastupitelstev," vol. 30
(1908):101-16 (from 1864 to 1867), 129-46 (through 1894), and
193-221 (through 1907), the most thorough history of the very important district self-governmental boards in Bohemia; the numerous articles published in vol. 27 and vol. 28 commemorating the
fortieth anniversary of the establishment of self-government in
various Bohemian districts; the article by Frantisek Fuksa on
self-government at the 1891 Exposition in Prague, "Samospráva na
zemské jubilejní výstavě," vol. 13 (1891):97-101, 129-37, and
193-207; and the article by the editors on the importance of statistics for self-government, "O statistice v samosprávě," vol.
14 (1892):97?115. Jakub Škarda was a founder and editor.
  Albín Bráf wrote the article on "self-government" for Česká
politika: "Samospráva," vol. 2, pt. 1, pp. 255-351. Especially
pertinent to developments in the Czech lands are pp. 255-65 on

the concept of self-government, pp. 300-44 on the situation in Austria-Hungary, and the general bibliography on pp. 345-51.

Aspects of the first sixty years of self-government are discussed in the memorial volume published in 1925 by the Association of Czech Districts and the Association of Czechoslovak Cities (Svaz českých odresů a Svaz československých měst v Československé republice), edited by Otakar Klapka et al., Šedesát let československé samosprávy (Prague, 1925). Especially pertinent to the pre-war years is the topical discussion of the development of district self-government, pp. 8-57.

Standard legal texts and commentaries on laws for the Czech lands are indispensable to any understanding of self-government, as is the Zákonník říšský. Among the former are those written and edited by Jiří Pražák, professor of Austrian public law at Charles-Ferdinand University: Jiří Pražák, ed., Zákony z oboru ústavy obecní a zemské které k potřebe studujících vysokých škol a praktiků sestavil Jiří Pražák, 2d ed. (Prague, 1904) (hereafter cited as Zákony); and Rakouské právo ústavní, vol. 2: Ústava zemská, 2d ed. (Prague, 1901) (hereafter cited as Ústava); and the work by secretary of the Pilsen District Board of Representatives and long-time Young Czech delegate to the diet and the Reichsrat, František Schwarz, ed., Výklad zákona obecního pro království české ze dne 16. dubna se všemi jeho zákonními změnami až do nejnovější doby . . . (Prague, 1877) (hereafter cited as Výklad).

Among the best contemporary discussions of self-government are the mimeographed university textbook by Jan Janák, Vývoj správy v českých zemích v epose kapitalismu, vol. 1: Období 1848-1918 (Prague,1965), and the history of Czechoslovak government and law recently published by the Slovak Academy of Sciences, Leonard Bianchi, ed., Dejiny štátu a práva na území Československa v období kapitalizmu 1848-1945, 2 vols. (Bratislava, 1971). The thesis of this chapter, written in 1969 and 1970 and published by University Microfilms in 1971, is confirmed by the latter work. Edvard Táborský surveys local government under the First Czechoslovak Republic in "Local Government in Czechoslovakia, 1918-1948," SEER, vol. 10, no. 3 (1951):202-15, and in Czechoslovak Democracy at Work (London, 1945). Anderson and Anderson, Political Institutions, pp. 117-24, discuss communal self-government in Austria-Hungary. Several of Josef Redlich's works, including Staats- und Reichsproblem, discuss this issue from a Viennese perspective.

3. Self-government was established in Galicia by the statute of 1861. Imperial law no. 18 of March 5, 1862, applied in other lands and provinces. For its application in the Czech lands and its text, see Schwarz, Výklad, pp. 33ff., and J. Pražák, Zákony, pp. 97-104. The text also appears in Zákonník říšský (1862). For commentary and discussion see also Bráf, "O některých starších a novějších projektech rakouských v příčine samosprávy," a

lecture of February 25, 1897 (Prague, 1897), pp. 193ff., and
"Samosprávy," Česká politika, vol. 2, pt. 2, pp. 255-66, "Český
pojem samosprávy: Definice její právní a politické." See also
Karel Adámek, Z naší doby, 1:19-30, on the importance of self-
government to civil liberties and national autonomy.

4. Law no. 7 established districts and district voting com-
missions. Law no. 27 established a District Board of Representatives in each district. For texts and discussion, see Schwarz,
Výklad, pp. 14-14, 288ff., 308ff.; J. Pražák, Zákony, pp. 1-35,
134-52; Bohuslav Rieger, "K vývoji samosprávy okresní" and "O
vedoucích myšlenkách naší samosprávy," in Drobné spisy, ed.
Karel Kadlec (Prague, 1915), 2:609-17 and 618-27; and Josef
Žalud, "Aforismy o samosprávě a reformě samosprávy," Samosprávný
obzor 28 (1906):321-31 and 353-58.

5. The text of the Moravian provincial law of March 15, 1864,
with commentary, appears in J. Pražák, Zákony, pp. 65-96, and in
Zákonník Říšský (1864). Moravian and Silesian law are also discussed by Janák, Vývoj správy, 1:134ff.

6. Scholarly and objective studies of the advantages and
disadvantages of regional government are Jaroslav Macek and
Václav Žáček, Krajská správa v českých zemích a její archivní
fondy (Prague, 1958), especially pp. 27-36, and Klub konceptního
úřednictva, Krajská zastupitelstva (Prague, 1910).

7. Prague and Liberec (Reichenberg) in Bohemia; Opava (Troppau), Bilsko (Bielsko), and Frýdek in Silesia; and Brno, Jihlava
(Iglau), Kroměříz, Olomouc, Uherské Hradiště, and Znojmo (Znaim)
in Moravia.

8. J. Pražák, Zákony, pp. 7ff. On the question of the powers of self-government in relation to the imperial administration, see Rudolf Krejčí, "O úpravě obvodů okres. zastupitelstev,"
Samosprávný obzor 28 (1906):15-17 and 65-67. On the development
of self-governmental authority, see Karel Adámek, "Z dějin okresních zastupitelstev," Samosprávný obzor 30 (1908):101-16 and 129-
46. On the importance of self-government to rural districts and
to agriculture see "V. B.," "Zájmová společenstva zemědělská a
samospráva," Samosprávný obzor 28 (1906):54-57, 76-82, and 97-99.

9. Josef Fomann, ed., Zpráva obce král. města Plzně o činnosti správy obecní od roku 1897 (Pilsen, 1900), discusses in detail
and with statistics all aspects of self-government in Pilsen.
The same applied to other larger cities, including Olomouc. See
Rostislav Bartocha, JuDr. Jan Ostádal; kulturní a národohospodářský budovatel moravský, 1864-1927 (Olomouc, 1937), Richard Fischer, Jan Drlík, et al., Deset let práce na Olomoucké radnici 1918-
1928 (Olomouc, 1928); and Julius Ambros, Z malých kořenů.

10. August Sedláček, Dějiny královského krajského Města
Písku nad Otavou, 2 vols. (Písek, 1928-30), 2:379ff, 403ff, on
the circumstances peculiar to Písek. On the question of urban
planning and beautification, see for example the discussion and
debate at the Third Congress of Czech Cities held in Klatovy on
August 21 to 23, 1909, Třetí sjezd měst z království českého
v král. městě Klatovech ve dnech 21.-23. srpna 1909: Stenografický protokol o jednání sjezdovém (Prague, 1909), especially
speeches and discussion, "Estetika měst," pp. 69-94, and "Stavi-
telství měst," pp. 119-52. On a successful example of later
nineteenth- and early twentieth-century Czech city planning see
Alois Kubiček and Zdeněk Wirth, Hradec Králové: Město českých
královen (Hradec Králové, 1939), chapter on "Ulrichův Hradec,"
pp. 85-95. Mayor Ulrich of Hradec Králové was a Young Czech.

11. Statistics on self-governmental bodies in Bohemia, including income and expenditures, may be found in pertinent publications of the kingdom of Bohemia or occasionally in articles for
the Samosprávní obzor. For statistics for the year 1891, see
František Fuksa, "Samospráva na zemské jubilejní výstavě." For
the finances of the kingdom of Bohemia and of its cities with a
population over 5,000 for the year 1896, see Dobroslav Krejčí,
ed., Die Finanzen des Landes und der grösseren Ortsgemeinden in
Böhmen für das Jahr 1896, vol. 2, pt. 3 of Mittheilungen des
Statistischen Landesamtes des Königreiches Böhmen (Prague, 1900).
For statistics on employment, including jobs and wages, for self-
government in Bohemia, see Jan Auerhan, Honorovaní orgánové
místní samosprávy v království Českém z konce roku 1908, s dodat-
ky o zřízencích okres. zastupitelstev z r. 1909 a o orgánech zemské samosprávy z l. 1890 a 1911 (Prague, 1914), vol. 2, pt. 2 of
Zprávy Zemského Statistického Úřadu království Českého. Each of
the above works, like all those published by the Provincial Statistical Office, appeared in both Czech and German editions. On
the budgets of communal self-government in Bohemia in 1912 with
special reference to the situation in Moravia and Silesia and to
district and provincial finances during the period 1896 to 1936,
see the thorough study by Albín Oberschall, Výdaje a příjmy obcí
v Čechách r. 1912 se zvláštním zřetelem k poměrům na Moravě, ve
Slezsku a k okresním a zemským financím v období 1896-1936
(Prague, 1938). The above works are but a representative sample
of the many available. For a listing of the literature on the
period before 1914, see Schmitt, Příruční seznam.

On the fiscal scandal in Horní Bělá, see the article "Obrázek
pěkné samosprávy," in Čas, vol. 10, no. 38 (September 19, 1896):
595-98. Čas both supported the extension of self-governmental
powers and criticized self-governmental institutions for their
unrepresentative character. Therefore its editor and reporters,
like those of other left-of-center journals, delighted in exposing any traces of corruption in self-government. Given the
press's readiness to expose shortcomings on the one hand and

imperial intervention in the event of shortcomings on the other,
self-governmental institutions by and large operated honestly
and within the limits of the law. District captains generally
proved as unwilling to protect self-governmental bodies from
criticism by the press as they were eager to confiscate newspapers which criticized shortcomings in imperial administration.

12. On the Zemský výbor, see J. Pražák, Ústava, pp. 139ff;
Česká politika, vol. 2, pt. 1, pp. 785-98, "Zemský výbor" by
Dobroslav Krejčí; and the introduction, pp. 1-15, by Aleš Chalu-
pa to the inventory of the Zemský výbor archives in LANM, Aleš
Chalupa, ed., Zemský výbor v Čechách: 1791-1873, 2 vols., and
Zemský výbor v Čechách: 1874-1928, 2 vols. (Prague, 1959).

13. Národní listy, January 12 through 19, 1891, Eim's dispatches from Vienna, and František Schwarz, "Samospráva ve světle
nových politických události, "Samosprávní obzor 13 (1891):1-4.
Many cases of conflict between district boards and the district captain arose from the latter attempting to define narrowly
and enforce strictly what constituted proper self-governmental
activity for the good of the district or local community. One
such case involved fund-raising and donations totaling 200 gulden
by the district board of Mladá Boleslav for building the Hus monument in Prague, a project begun in November 1889 and supported by
the Národní listy and the Young Czech party. The board voted on
December 27, 1889, to give the 200 gulden from district self-
governmental funds to the committee in charge of building the
monument. The district captain on January 18, 1890, overruled
the board, citing imperial laws which required that funds raised
locally be used for the "good" of the community. The case turned
on the question of whether or not building a monument to Hus in
Prague would benefit the citizens of the Mladá Boleslav district.
The regional court on February 18, 1890, decided against the
board's contention that the captain had acted illegally in halt-
ing their contribution. The governor's office upheld the court,
citing primarily imperial law no. 79 of July 25, 1864. The
board remained dissatisfied and continued to encourage private
fund-raising efforts throughout the district for a cause which
was quite popular when first proposed and which became even more
popular after the district captain's January action. This case
and others similar to it were criticized by Young Czech candidates in the Reichsrat elections of March 1891 and in the elections to the Bohemian Diet in 1895. See the thorough discussion
of this case by "F. B.," "O zápovědi, aby provedeno bylo usnesení
okresního zastupitelstva, kterým věnován byl příspěvek na postavení pomníku mistra Jana Husi v Praze," Samosprávní obzor 13
(1891):53-57, and by František Schwarz, "Lze-li obecné vzdělávací
zájmy národa pokládati za vnitřní záležitosti okresu?" Samosprávní obzor 13 (1891):101-05.

14. The proceedings of each congress were published. These
are among the best sources on the activities and problems of
self-governmental institutions generally as well as on their efforts at cooperation and widening areas of mutual self-interest.
The proceedings are also an excellent source for any topic on
urbanization or urban development. For the first congress, held
at Kolín on October 27, 1907, see Stenografický protokol jednání
sjezdového: Sjezd českých měst království Českého v Kolíně
(Kolín, 1907). On the second congress, held in Prague from September 26 to 28, 1908, see Druhý sjezd českých měst v Praze 26.-
28. září 1908: Stenografické protokoly o jednání sjezdu (Prague,
1908). On the third congress, held in Klatovy from August 21 to
23, 1909, see Třetí sjezd. On the fourth congress, held in
Prague from October 15 to 17, 1911, see Čtvrtý sjezd českých
měst z království českého v královském hlav. městě Praze ve
dnech 15.-17. října 1911: Zápis o jednání sjezdovém (Prague,
1911).

15. See nn. 2 and 3 above on the law of March 5, 1862. Popular enthusiasm for the introduction of communal self-government
is indicated by the reports and editorials in Obecné listy: Politický týdenník (Community news: a political weekly) (published
in Prague): "Slovo o zevnější upravě a ozdobě obcí," pp. 89-90
on February 21, 1862; "Nový zákon obecní," pp. 146-47 on
March 28, 1862; and "Ještě něco o zevnější úpravě a ozdobě českých obcí," pp. 160-61 on April 4, 1862.

16. For details, see J. Pražák, Zákony, pp. 27ff.

17. See table 23 in the appendix. Figures for this table
were obtained from Naše obec (1948), Jubilejní číslo k 100.
výročí památného roku 1848, p. 29.

18. See discussion of the debates in chap. 2 and the effects
of the law in chap. 1 above.

19. Anderson and Anderson, Political Institutions, pp. 121ff.,
compare developments in the various continental European countries.

20. For sources on the Provincial Executive Council (Zemský
výbor), see n. 12 above.

21. Janák, Vývoj správy, p. 135; and Zákonník Říšský (1864).

22. F. L. Rieger, Řeči, 4:81-83. Mattuš, Historické právo
and Paměti, pp. 46-50. See LANM, Protocols of the Young Czech
parliamentary club MČS, 26. V. 1880. Sources on Czech district
boards, which clearly indicate their wide range of activities,
include František Bareš, Paměti města Mladé Boleslavě (Mladá
Boleslav, 1920), 2:181-277; two works on Hlinsko and its foremost

self-governmental leader, the Young Czech Karel Adámek, Památka
činnosti okresního zastupiltelstva hlineckého and Jezdík, ed.,
Adamkův den v Hlinsku; František Schwarz, Jubilejní spis. Čtyri-
cet roků činnosti okresního zastupitelstva plzeňského (Pilsen,
1905); Ferdinand Vlček, Město Dobřany v historii a v době pří-
tomné (Pilsen, 1932), pp. 59-78; Sedláček, Dějiny Písku, vol. 2,
chaps. 7 and 8; and František Pavlík, ed., Památník města Královských Vinohradů (Prague, 1929), pp. 29ff.

23. On activities of the District Board of Representatives
in the Hlinsko district, see Památka čtyřicetileté činnosti
okresního zastupitelstva hlinského, 1865-1905 (Chotěbor, 1905).
On the activities of district boards generally, see Adámek,
"Z dějin okresních zastupitelstev." On Schwarz and on his work
in the Pilsen district, see Karel Jonáš, O životě a činnosti
Františka Schwarze: K jeho čtyřicetiletému úřednickému jubileu
(Pilsen, 1905), and "Ch.," "František Schwarz: Jeho jubileum a
činnost," Samosprávný obzor 28 (1906):33-42, both works celebrating and assessing Schwarz's forty years of service as a self-
governmental official. The Schwarz papers may be found in the
Archive of the City of Pilsen (Městský archiv v Plzni).
     Self-government later served Czech agrarian politicians as an
entry to politics and as a political base in predominantly rural
areas. See, for example, the account of Stanislav Kubr's early
career in politics, V. Chundela, Stanislav Kubr: Zakladatel
české strany agrární, sedlák a politik (Příspěvek k dějinám zemědělského hnutí) (Prague, 1933), pp. 41-43.

24. These data supplement those on professions of party members in table 15 in the appendix, which lists as self-governmental officials or as journalists only those men who held no other
employment. This data, unlike that in table 15, is approximate,
since biographical information does not indicate whether or not
the remaining fifteen parliamentary and thirty-seven diet delegates served in local government or not. Some may have done so;
therefore figures in the text should be considered to be low estimates. Sources used for this data are Michael Navrátil, Almanach sněmu království českého, 1895-1901 (Prague, 1896); Michael
Navrátil, Nový český sněm (1901-07) s životopisy a podobiznami
(Tábor, 1902); Michael Navrátil, Almanach českých právníků
(Prague, 1904); and Ottův slovník naučný, vols. 1-28.

25. Fischer, Pokroková Morava, 2:276-83 and 344ff.

26. Exchange of correspondence between the two is in LANM,
Julius Grégr papers; individual letters will be cited below.

27. Přehled, vol. 7, nos. 13 and 14 (December 18, 1908),
"Samospráva po stránce mravní," pp. 246-47; "Z hlasů o budoucnosti českého života politického," an attack on Kramář and the Young

Czechs, pp. 248-49; ibid., no. 20 (February 5, 1909):349-52.
Social Democratic criticism of unrepresentative Young Czech control over local and district self-government appears in a speech
by František Soukup, cited in part in his Revoluce práce, 1:773.
See also the section on "self-government" in Program české
strany pokrokové (Prague, 1912), pp. 136ff.

28. Starosta Václav Dobrovský, reformátor obce Nezdarovské
(Prague, 1890). The original text appeared in 1877 in the journal Posel z Prahy. Schwarz's articles include "Samospráva ve
světle," "Lze-li zájmy pokládati," and "Jazyková rovnoprávnost v
samosprávném životě," Samosprávní obzor 14 (1892):33-40; and "Co
vadí výkonům samosprávních opatření v obci a okresu?" (1892):
161-70, a lecture delivered in Tábor on September 10, 1892.

29. Působení Václava Dobrovského jako okresního starosty
(Prague, 1890).

30. Josef Dobiáš, Dějiny královského města Pelhřimova a jeho
okolí, 2 vols. (Pelhřimov, 1927-36); Zdeněk Nejedlý, Litomyšl,
tisíc let života českého města, 2 vols. (Prague, 1954); Sedláček,
Dějiny Písku; Wacslaw W. Tomek, Dějepis města Prahy, 12 vols.
(Prague, 1892-1906); Jindřich Vancura, Dějiny někdejšího král.
města Klatov, 2 vols. in 4 (Klatovy, 1927-36); František Teplý,
Dějiny města Jindřichova Hradce, 2 vols. in 7 (Jindřichův Hradec,
1927-34).

31. On the theory of národní hospodářství, see Alois Rašín,
Národní hospodářství, 3d ed. (Prague, 1922), and Josef Kaizl,
Národní hospodářství (Prague, 1883). On the development of com-
merical institutions in the Czech lands, see Adámek, Z naší doby,
1:45-102.

32. Čas, vol. 10, no. 37 (September 12, 1896):589.

33. See table 18 in the appendix.

34. A typical manual is František Šimáček, Zákon o svépomocn-
ných spolcích (Prague, 1873). Figures on the growth of agricultural cooperatives are in Antonín Blažek and Bohumír Treybal,
Zemědělské družstevnictví v království českém (Prague, 1913),
pp. 68-71. On savings and loan associations and their development, see Josef Schreyer, Dějiny svépomocných záložen českých
(Prague, 1891). Schreyer was at that time secretary of the
Union of Czech Savings and Loan Associations.

35. The text of the law is in Zákonník říšsky (1873), pp.
273-89, law no. 70 of April 1873. Ladislav František Dvořák's
ed., Družstevní zákony československé (Prague, 1924), also
presents the text of the law, pp. 21-48, with commentary, pp. 19-

21, and the two most important pieces of supplementary legislation, decree no. 74 of the Minister of Justice, dated May 25,
1895, pp. 49-56, and law no. 133 of June 10, 1903, pp. 57-81,
with commentary. For the latter, see also Zákonník rísský (1903),
pp. 409-21.

36. Josef Nožička, Jan Antonín Prokůpek: Apoštol hospodářského pokroku a národní svornosti (Prague, 1939), pp. 56-67 and
94ff. The development of peasant political associations is discussed in chap. 5 below.

37. Program 1912, as well as the above cited programs, reveals such appeal to commercial interests. The development of
commercial institutions is discussed in chap. 1 above.

38. On the budget debates of 1897 and 1899, see chaps. 8 and
9 below. On the 1892 currency reform advocated by the Young
Czechs, see Kaizl's speech of May 24, 1892, in the lower house
of the Reichsrat, reprinted in Kaizl, Z mého života, 3:163-65.
For a discussion of the currency reform, see Fiedler, Vyrovnání,
pp. 244-52, and Steed, Habsburg Monarchy, pp. 137-41. On the
problem of the decennial tariff debates generally, see Kaizl,
Vyrovnání, pp. 26-50, and Fiedler, Vyrovnání, pp. 146ff., 255ff.,
and 269ff. On the desire of Czech business interests for political tranquillity in 1897, see chaps. 8 and 9 below.

39. See tables 15, 16, and 18 in the appendix.

40. Patriotic and literary journals had already contributed
to the success of the National Revival and to the political awakening of the Czech people during the 1848 revolution. See Kimmel, "Havlíček," and the discussion of Karel Havlíček in chap. 3
above.

41. Chap. 2 above indicates how the Národní listy, like all
Czech liberal and socialist papers, regularly faced enormous
fines, confiscation of offending issues, intermittent pre-
censorship, and imprisonment of its editors, including such
Young Czech stalwarts as the Grégr brothers, Josef Anýz, and
Karel Tůma.

42. Figures from Roubík, 1863-1895, pp. xiiiff.

43. For example, Our Voices (Naše hlasy) and Our News (Naše
listy).

44. See discussion of 2,479 Czech and German newspapers published in Bohemia between 1863 and 1895 in Roubík, 1863-1895,
pp. xivff.

45. After 1867, the paper often charged F. L. Rieger with having retreated from the principles he so well stated in the paper's first edition. "Constitutional independence," translated from "ústavní samostatnost," refers more accurately to "the greatest possible constitutionally guaranteed independence within Austria."

46. Roubík, 1863-1895, lists circulation figures under entry for each newspaper. Figures for Čas and Selské noviny are for 1890 and that for Čech is for 1896.

47. Národní listy, January 10 and September 9, 1901.

48. Hálek (1835-74), Heller (1845-1922), and Smetana (1824-84). Antonín Šilhan, "Bedřich Smatana v Národních listech," in Půl století Národních listů, pp. 112-16.

49. Neruda (1834-91). Národní listy, January 16, 1890. On Neruda's early political activity, see Ivan Pfaff, Jan Neruda a české demokratické hnutí v letech šedesátých (Prague, 1963).

50. Národní listy, May 1, 1890.

51. The court proceedings and official correspondence concerning the trial and sentencing of Julius Grégr are contained in Tiskový soud Dra. Julia Grégra redaktora Národních listů v měsíci červnu r. 1862 (Prague, 1862). Several months after becoming editor of the Národní listy, Julius Grégr received his first official "warning" for publishing an article on "the fall of Gaeta" in praise of Garibaldi. Národní listy, vol. 1, no. 49 (1861).

52. Masarykův slovník naučný, 2:1059.

53. Sladkovský, Výklad.

54. Grégr's defense of the manuscripts published as Na obranu rukopisu královédvorského a zelenohorského, 2d ed. (Prague, 1886).

55. LANM, Julius Grégr papers, envelope marked "punktace."

56. The most comprehensive studies on Julius Grégr are Tůma, Život J. Grégra, and Josef Holeček, Tragedie Julia Grégra (Prague, 1914). On the Omladina trial, see chap. 6 below.

57. Anýž (1852-1912). See "Několik vzpomínek," in Národní listy, 1861-1941: Jubilejní sborník (Prague, 1941), pp. 70-71; and Navrátil, Nový sněm, pp. 216-19.

58. Tůma (1843-1917). Tůma's principal works on the Národní listy are Život J. Grégra and "Padesát let boje a práce," in Půl století Národních listů, pp. 9-35. On Belgium's struggle for liberation from the Habsburgs, Ze života malého národa (Prague, 1874). On the Irish national movement, Potlačený národ: obraz osudův lidu irského pod cizovládou britskou (Kutná Hora, 1882). On the American war of independence, O boji amerického lidu za samostatnost (Prague, 1872). His many biographies include O Jiřím Washingtonu, zakladateli svobody americké (Prague, 1872); Léon Gambetta: obraz života i povahy jeho (Kutná Hora, 1883); Apoštel svobody: živopis italského vlastence Massiniho, 2d ed. (Prague, 1897); Josef Garibaldi, bohatýr svobody (Prague, 1908); and Bojovníci za svobodu: Washington, Mazzini, Manin, Cavour, Gambetta, Gladstone, de Potter, John Brown, 2d ed. (Prague, 1901).

59. See the appreciation by Josef Penížek in the introduction to Eim, Politické úvahy, pp. 3-4. The most complete biography is Michael Navrátil, Gustav Eim: geniální publicista a vynikající politik (Prague, 1923).

60. Eim, Politické úvahy, and Servác Heller, Z minulé doby: našeho života národního, kulturního a politického, 5 vols. (Prague, 1916-23).

61. On his drinking problem, see PNP, Eim papers, letter from Engel to Eim, September 26, 1893: "I have only one little favor to ask of you: *Don't go back to your old ways!* Above all, lay off *all* remedies for the nerves whatever they may be—alcohol, nicotine, hypnotism, etc. If you don't sleep one night, be patient—you'll make it up the next night." Other Engel letters, for example that of December 29, 1895, contain similar advice. Engel was the personal physician to many party members as well, and it is a measure of the trust and affection in which the chairman was held that he could speak so frankly to proud men like Eim.
Ill will existed between Masaryk and Eim. Eim detested the Puritanical and sometimes intellectually arrogant professor so much that he could not appreciate his greatness. Masaryk's adverse comments on Eim in Politická situace: Poznámky ku poznámkám (Prague, 1906), pp. 15-18 and 31-35, point out the journalist's many faults but ignore some of his good points.

62. This correspondence is collected in PNP, Eim papers. Many Eim letters exist in other collections of papers, especially PNP, Engel papers; LANM, Pacák papers; and LANM, Julius Grégr papers.

63. This phrase occurs throughout the German press at that time and in the correspondence of Ernst von Plener, HHSA, Plener papers.

64. Národní listy, January 2 through January 18, 1890, Eim's telephonic dispatches from Vienna to the Národní listy.

65. V. Škarda, Program 1897, p. 16.

66. On Špindler, see chap. 5 below.

67. PNP, Eim papers, Emanuel Engel to Eim, September 26, 1893, p. 3.

68. Národní listy, January 1, 1861. Tobolka, Politické dějiny, 2:64ff. prints a facsimile of this issue.

69. See tables 17 and 19 in the appendix.

70. LANM, Pacák papers, Eim to Pacák, no. 16, February (?), 1894, complaining of Anýz, who charged him with lack of patriotism.

71. LANM, Julius Grégr papers, letters from Eim to Julius Grégr of March 28, 1895, December 1, 1895, and undated from early 1896, on the dispute between him and Anýz.

72. Josef Horák, editor of the Čáslavské listy, was also a Young Czech deputy in the Bohemian Diet.

73. PNP, Engel papers, 6R80, folder "Z listů Dra. Stránského s doklady," Strásnký to Engel, March 1, 1890, January 25, 1891, March 18, 1891, September 24, 1891, and Engel to Stránský, March 26, 1890 and October 5, 1891, detail the relationship and the subsidy and include annual balance sheets for the Lidové noviny enclosed to justify a continuing subsidy. The subsidy ended after the March 1891 Reichsrat elections, and Stránský prospered on his own.

74. The influence of the press on other Czech parties corresponded closely to that of the Národní listy on the Young Czechs. The Czech agrarian and socialist press preceded the Agrarian and Czechoslavonic Social Democratic parties as representatives of popular interests. Newspaper editors played an important part in the formation of all parties. For example, Antonín Hajn, editor of Časopis českého studentstva (Journal of the Czech students) and Samostatnost (Independence), and Václav J. Klofáč, a former junior editor of the Národní listy, took the lead in founding respectively the Radical Progressive and National Socialist parties. Antonín Němec, editor of Právo lidu (The rights of the people) in Prague, and Vlastimil Tusar, editor of Rovnost (Equality) in Brno, were among the most important Czech Social Democratic leaders before and after the First World War.

75. Article 24 of imperial law no. 134 of November 15, 1867, on associations, which remained in effect after article 12 of imperial law no. 142 on "the general rights of the citizen" guaranteed freedom of association subject to existing restrictions. Bernatzik, Verfassungsgesetze, p. 385.

76. The differences between political and nonpolitical associations followed the requirements of law no. 134, articles 29 through 34. In the absence of any clear-cut distinction between political and nonpolitical organizations, the authorities were empowered to make that distinction in accordance with article 35. Bernatzik, Vergassungsgesetze, p. 385.

77. The Royal Bohemian Society of Sciences is discussed in chap. 1; see also Jaroslav Prokeš, Počátky, and Mikuláš Teich, "The Royal Bohemian Society of Sciences and the First Phase of Organized Scientific Advance in Bohemia," Historica 2 (1960):161-82. The classic work on the National Museum is Josef Hanuš, Národní museum a naše obrození, 2 vols. (Prague, 1921-23).

78. The most complete institutional histories are still Karel Tieftrunk, Dějiny Matice české (Prague, 1881), and Hugo Traub, Dějiny Matice moravské k šedesátiletí jejímu (Brno, 1911). Publications and board directors of the Matice česká are listed in Antonín Grund, ed., Sto let Matice české, 1831-1931 (Prague, 1931). The social background is discussed in František Kutnar, Sociálně myšlenková tvárnost obrozenského lidu: Trojí pohled na český obrozenský lid jako příspěvek k jeho duchovním dějinám (Prague, 1948); and in Kočí, Naše národní obrození, chap. 8. For Serbian model see Vasa Stajić, "The Centenary of the 'Matica Srpska," SEER 6 (1927-28):593-602.

79. On the history of the theater see Jan Bartoš, Dějiny národního divadla, vol. 1: Národní divadlo a jeho budovatelé, ed. Jaroslav Jelínek (Prague, 1933); and on its art and architecture, see Antonín Matějček, Národní divadlo a jeho výtvarnici (Prague, 1934). On its operas, see Zdeněk Nejedlý, Dějiny opery Národního divadla, 2 vols. (Prague, 1935; 2d ed., 1949), and Josef Bartoš, Prozatimní divadlo a jeho opera (Prague, 1938), the latter concerning the provisional theater before the 1880s. A complementary work is Jan Bartoš, Prozatimní divadlo a jeho činohra (Prague, 1937). The two authors were brothers. Other important histories of the National Theater include Otakar Fischer, Činohra Národního divadla do r. 1900 (Prague, 1933), and Václav Tille, Činohra Národního divadla od r. 1900 do převratu (Prague, 1936). A classic study of the early theater in the Czech lands is Jan Vondráček's Dějiny českého divadla, 2 vols., 1: Doba obrozenská 1771-1824 (Prague, 1956); 2: Doba předbřeznová 1824-1846 (Prague, 1957). See also Vladimír Štěpánek, Počátky velkého národního dramatu v obrozenské literatuře (Prague, 1959). A study

in English of the building of the National Theater is Stanley
Buchholz Kimball's Czech Nationalism: A Study of the National
Theatre Movement, 1845-83 (Urbana, Ill., 1964). A thorough critical review of this book is by George P. Springer in The Western Humanities Review, vol. 19, no. 4 (Autumn 1965), pp. 371-73.

80. On the struggle between Young Czechs and Old Czechs, see
Jan Bartoš, Prozatimní divadlo, pp. 167-96, and idem., Dějiny
divadla, 1:121ff. See also Jan Bartoš, Budování Národního divadla: Legenda a skutečnost (Prague, 1934), pp. 9ff; this short
work is a reply to Karel Stoukal's criticism of the Dějiny divadla in the ČČH.

81. Kimball, Theatre, pp. 135-50, on the building campaign
and data. On the 1868 celebration, see Jaroslav Benda, ed., Za-
ložení Národního divadla 1868: Vydáno na pamět padesátého výročí (Prague, 1918); and Kimball, Theatre, pp. 80-114.

82. The translation of the second line is by Springer, Western Humanities Review, pp. 372-73. Kimball, Theatre, p. 87,
gives the Czech text but an unintelligible translation.

83. Česká politika, 5:403-33, on the Matice školská, including a brief history and statistical data. See also the general
and informed discussion of Czech minority schools in ibid.,
pp. 335-90. The most comprehensive published account to date of
the Matice školská is the memorial volume issued on the fiftieth
anniversary of its founding, Padesát let Ústřední Matice školské,
1880-1930. Pamětní list vydaný na oslavu půlstoleté činnosti
Ústřední Matice školské v Praze (Prague, 1931), 135 pages plus
numerous charts. This work clearly indicates the extent and nature of the foundation's work over fifty years. A collection of
stories, poems, and illustrations in honor of the twenty-fifth
anniversary of the Matice is Ústřední Matici školské na oslavu
25 l.-činnosti-1880-1905 (Prague, 1905). On the development of
schools generally in the Czech lands, see Adámek, Z naší doby,
2:1-153. The German Schulverein originated in the southern Tyrol
and in 1880 became an organization for all of Cisleithania.

84. On the Matice opavská, see Jan Vyhlídal, Naše Slezsko
(Prague, 1900), pp. 76ff.

85. Ottův slovník naučný, 28:990.

86. For examples of interaction between party and foundation,
see PNP, Engel papers, 6s85, "Klub poslanců strany svobodomyslné,"
Executive Committee of Ústřední matice školska (hereafter cited
as ÚMŠ) to Young Czech party club of delegates, July 20, 1890;
E. Engel to ÚMŠ in reply, August 1, 1890; Executive Committee of
ÚMŠ to club of Young Czech party, April 14, 1892; reply of E.

Engel, April 16, 1892, reaffirming Young Czech support of ÚMŠ
and its works in the national interest.

87. LANM, Julius Grégr papers, letters of Jaromír Čelakovský
to J. Grégr during the eighties and early nineties. Čelakovský
was a Young Czech delegate to the Reichsrat and the diet before
his election in 1891 to the chairmanship of the Central School
Foundation.

88. E. Grégr, Denník, 1:171-73, on reasons for founding the
Matice lidu in 1867. On the Academic Reading Society, see Osvěta, vol. 4, no. 17, for earlier history. See chaps. 5 and 6 for
the events of 1889.

89. Popular estimates of 800,000 according to Umgangssprache
and 1,000,000 according to private Czech censuses made by Antonín Boháč, O české otázce menšinové (Olomouc, 1910), pp. 9-10,
15ff. The problems of the Czech minority are discussed also in
Antonín Boháč, Boj o české menšiny (Prague, 1909); Jan František
Svoboda, Jihočeské menšiny: Vývoj kulturní, národností a školský (České Budějovice, 1925); and the two years of the Menšinová
Revue, vols. 1 and 2 (1911/12 and 1913/14).

90. On Unions, see Emanuel Rádl, Válka Čechů s Němci (Prague,
1928), pp. 147-52; Menšinová Revue, vol. 2, no. 10, pp. 450-51ff.
On the National Union for Southwestern Moravia, see Pamětní list
k jubileu 20 letého trvání Národní Jednoty pro Jihozápadní Moravu (Brno, 1906). This volume, commemorating twenty years of the
Union's activity, contains statistics and retrospective articles
along with the original call for the Union's founding published
by the Orel in Telč on May 1, 1886.

91. Vyhlídal, Naše Slezsko, pp. 98-100.

92. Reported in Boháč, O otázce, pp. 6ff., and Boháč, Boj,
pp. 3ff.

93. For example, the Ladies Division of the North Bohemian
National Union (Dámský odbor Národní jednoty severočeské) in the
central Bohemian district seat of Nymburk, population 7,000, had
during its first sixteen years (1894-1910) raised 28,850
crowns, most of which went to the Czechs in the north Bohemian
town of Bezděčín u Liberce. The Nymburk branch of the Central
School Foundation had 433 members and had raised 70,000 crowns
in twenty-four years for minority schools. See F. Kulhánek and
F. Mikolášek, Královské město Nymburk v přitomnosti a minulosti
(Nymburk, 1911), p. 24.

94. Ottův slovník naučny, 28:985.

95. Antonín Hubka, Menšinová práce: K jubileu dvacetiletého trvání Nár. Jednoty Pošumavské (Prague, 1904), p. 294.

96. Ibid., p. 388 for figures.

97. For example, see the speech by the Young Czech Reichsrat delegate Josef Sokol on "The Foundations of Our National Existence" to the North Bohemian National Union in Dvůr Králové, "O podminkách národní naší existence (Prague, 1896).

98. Pavlík, Památník města Královských Vinohradů, pp. 50-54.

99. LANM, 6T90, Parliamentary club correspondence, "došlé věci, 1896-7," letter from the Šumava National Union to the party executive committee, dated February 8, 1897, and others in "dosle věci, 1898-99." LANM, Julius Grégr papers, correspondence with A. Pravoslav Trojan during the eighties. PNP, Engel papers, letters to the chairman of the club of party delegates from 1892 to 1899 from various private organizations, including the National Unions and the Central School Foundation.

100. LANM, Václav Choc papers, box 321, No. 138/47, North Bohemian National Union to Choc. Also F. S. Frabša, ed., 40 let čs. strany národně socialistické v Liberci (Liberec, 1946), pp. 29-30.

101. On the role of the Sokol in Czech politics, see the essay by Edvard Šmejkal, Tyrš v politickém zápase českého národa (Brno, 1932). A short history of the Sokol's first twenty-five years is Josef E. Scheiner's Dějiny Sokolstva v prvém jeho pětadvacetiletí (Prague, 1887); a catechism designed to popularize the Sokol's task of moral and physical education is Milan Fucík's Sokolstvo a naše doba (Prague, 1897). Typical of the histories of individual Sokol organizations is Jindřich Lepa, ed., Šedesát let tělocvičné jednoty Sokol I. na Smíchove (Prague-Smíchov, 1928). Contacts with and growth of Sokol branches in the United States are discussed in Josef Scheiner's Sokolská výprava do Ameriky roku 1909 (Prague, 1909).

102. On slogans, see V. H. Brunner and Renata Tyršova, eds., Jindřich Fügner, 1822-1922: K stým narozeninám prvého starosty pražské tělocvičné jednoty Sokol (Prague, 1922).

103. Renata Tyršova, ed., Dra. Miroslava Tyrše: Úvahy a pojednání o umění výtvarném (Prague, 1901), 1:5-13, for reproductions of original Manes drawings and designs.

104. Miroslav Tyrš, "Jindřich Fügner: Nárys života, zjevu, a povahy," speech of November 16, 1882, in Sokolské úvahy a

řeči Dra. Miroslava Tyrše, ed. Josef Steiner, 3d ed. (Prague, 1919), pp. 174-88.

105. Brunner and Tyršová, eds., Jindřich Fügner, 1822-1922, plates 65-68.

106. L. T. Demay, "Un exemple: les Sokols," Les Marches de l'Est 4 (1912/1913):842.

107. In Silesia, where there were six chapters with 410 members by 1899, 72 percent of exhibitor-performers were workers. See Vyhlídal, Naše Slezsko, p. 102.

108. On the Brno demonstrations, see Šujan, Dějepis Brna, pp. 453-55. On the Prague exercises of 1912, see the special edition of Cizinecký Ruch (nos. 4-18) issued in fifteen numbers between May 27 and July 12, 1912, and titled VI. Slet Všesokolský 1912 v Praze slovem i obrazem, ed. A. Melichar (Prague, 1912), 416 pp. On foreign participation and commentary, see this work and also Česká demokracie 4 (1912):85.

109. Státní museum československé tělesné výchovy a sportu v Praze, oddělení archivní dokumentace, holds copies of reports on the Sokol by the Information Bureau of the Austrian Ministry of Foreign Affairs (hereafter IB). Ibid., the Jan Podlipný papers, folder No. 8, contain the correspondence of the Prague Sokol with French gymnastic organizations from 1890 to 1912. On the famous exercises in Paris in June 1889, see Národní listy supplement to the June 13, 1889, issue.

110. Ibid., IB files on the surveillance of Sokols in America. On Bavarian police reporting on Czech Sokols en route to France, see 1903/4 IB 892, enclosing Bavarian police report from Munich, July 7, 1892. Ibid., Copy 1585/4, IB, telegram from Berlin dated June 2, 1892, from Count Széchényi: "Kaiser Wilhelm beauftragte mich auf dem gestrigen Hoffeste in Potsdam, seiner Dank für die gegenüber den czechischen Turnerverein-ergriffenen Massregeln zu übermitteln, wodurch die Dinge sehr vereinfacht worden wären."

111. Miloslav Spáčil and Ladislav Roubal, eds., Přehledný seznam archivalié, dokumentů a sbírek, vztahujících se k činnosti bývalého Sokola Pražského (Prague, 1958), pp. 1-9, gives a brief history of the Sokol organization.

112. This is evident from an examination of correspondence in the Sokol Archives at Státní museum československé tělesné výchovy a sportu v Praze, and of party correspondence in PNP, Engel papers.

113. On Tyrš and the Sokol, see Albert Pražák, Dr. Miroslav Tyrš: Osvobozenský smysl jeho díla (Prague, 1946); L. Jandásek, Život dr. Miroslava Tyrše (Prague, 1924, 1932); and František Táborský, ed., Paní Renáta Tyršova: Památník na počest jejích sedmdesátých narozenin (Prague, 1926).

114. Others included Jan Jand'ourek, businessman in Lomnice nad Jizerou, František Klouček, lawyer in Jičín, and Jan Jaroš, wealthy farmer from Čáslavky u Černožic.

115. Podlipný served as chairman of the party executive committee until 1897, when he was succeeded by Václav Škarda.

116. An interesting but excessively laudatory biography of Jan Podlipný by Vácslav Řezníček, JUDr. Jan Podlipný, jeho život a působení (Prague, 1924), describes the mood of crowds at Sokol parades and the charisma of Podlipný.

117. That Podlipný used his activity in the Sokol to further his political career was also noted by the French consul in Prague, Alfred Méroux de Valois, Archives diplomatiques, Autriche-Hongrie, NS 26, dispatches of Valois of June 26 and July 2 and 18, 1901.

118. Tyrš, "Navrh opětné volby Dr. Tomáše Černého za starostu Sokola pražského: Řeč o valné hromadě dne 22. října roku 1879," in Tyrš, Sokolské úvahy a řeci, ed. J. Steiner, pp. 189-90. The Tomáš Černý papers are in the Sokol Archive.

119. On the Sokol and Social Democracy, see Jan Havránek, "The Development of Czech Nationalism," Austrian History Yearbook, vol. 3, pt. 2 (1967):259.

120. Archives diplomatiques, Autriche-Hongrie, NS 26, dispatches of Valois of June 26 and July 2 and 18, 1901.

121. This problem is very objectively assessed by Chairman Emanuel Engel in his September 26, 1893, letter to Gustav Eim. PNP, Eim papers, 3aG31.

Chapter 5

1. On Taaffe, see chap. 3 above. Tobolka, Politické dějiny, vol. 3, pt. 1, offers a solid study of Czech parliamentary politics during the Taaffe era. Srb, Politické dějiny, 1:573-768, contains many of the most important political statements or programs of the same period. Skilling, "The Czech Eighties," discusses the Czech relationship to the Taaffe government. Jenks, Iron Ring, provides the most complete account in English of Taaffe's years as Minister-President in a chronological narrative

based almost exclusively on German sources and dealing primarily
with parliamentary politics in Vienna. Charmatz, Österreichs
Innere Geschichte, 2:40-94, is cogent and witty, sometimes at
the price of oversimplification. Macartney, Habsburg Empire,
pp. 611-61, briefly surveys the Taaffe years and, pp. 687-739,
developments in Hungary during the same era.

2. The assassination of Czar Alexander II of Russia in March
1881, as well as the apparent success of Bismarck's antisocialist
legislation initiated in 1878, contributed to Taaffe's decision
to embark upon a similar policy in Cisleithania. On the early
governmental prosecution of the Czech workers' movement, see
Robert Maršan, Československá sociální demokracie v prvím sesti-
letí své činnosti (1878-1884) ve světle zpráv policejních
(Prague, 1923), a work based upon and extensively quoting the
contents of imperial police reports. On Taaffe's discriminatory
legislation after 1884 directed against Social Democrats and Anarchists, see K. Malý, Policejní a soudní perzekuce, pp. 203-63,
and also the contemporary work by Czech Social Democrat Josef
Hybeš, Křížová cesta socialismu (Brno, 1900; 2nd ed., 1920), reprinted in Šolle, Průkopníci, pp. 139-273. A thorough account in
German will be found in the third volume of Ludwig Brügel's classic, Geschichte der österreichischen Sozialdemocratie, 5 vols.
(Vienna, 1922-1925).

3. Taaffe's program of social legislation proved to be much
less comprehensive than that initiated by Bismarck. The text of
law no. 117 of June 17, 1883, appears in Zákonník říšský (1883),
pp. 396-99, "Zákon o zrizování dozorcu živnostenských."

4. On Karel Adámek's speech in the Reichsrat on May 17, 1884,
see SPHA, IX, 12, 916-20. See also a similar argument based on humanitarian grounds as well, in his Z naší doby, 3:269ff., especially 279-82. Adámek, who had entered politics as a Young Czech
in the seventies, returned to that party in 1890. On law no. 115
of June 21, 1884, see the text in Zákonník říšský (1884), pp. 367-
68, "Zákon o zamestnávání mladistvých delníku a zenštin, pak o
denní pracovní době a o nedělním klidu při hornictví." Children
under age twelve could not work in the mines at all; those between
the ages of twelve and fourteen could do so only with parental
permission and if their health would not be impaired. Men under
sixteen and women under eighteen might be employed only if such
employment would not harm their health. The total daily hours of
labor for any person in the mines was limited to ten, with up to
two more hours allowed for transit time to and from the pits.

5. The text of law no. 22 appears in Zákonník říšský (1885),
pp. 35-51. This extensive and thorough piece of legislation complemented or revised various laws and decrees dating back to December 20, 1859. Children from twelve to fourteen could work in

factories up to eight hours per day if their health would not be
thus impaired. Children under twelve could not be employed in
factories. Factory labor in any twenty-four-hour period was limited to eleven hours. Work books continued to be authorized for
laborers, this a feature much appreciated by employers. The text
of law no. 11 of December 28, 1887, appears in Zákonník říšský
(1888), pp. 1-14, "Zákon o pojišt'ování dělníku pro případ úrazu,"
providing accident insurance for industrial workers to be administered at the provincial level by a state insurance agency in
each land or province with ten percent of the cost born by the
insured. See SPHA, IX, 2, 523ff., for Adámek's speech of May 21,
1886. This law, first proposed in December 1884, met with heavy
opposition in the Reichsrat from the German Liberals who advocated administration from Vienna with costs born exclusively by
employers and with similar coverage for agricultural workers.

6. On the results of the elections to the Bohemian Diet in
early July 1889, see Navrátil, Almanach sněmu 1895-1901, pp. 59-
79, and table 17 in the appendix below. Table 16 indicates the
unrepresentative character of this and other Cisleithanian diets.

7. František Tilšer led the Young Czech attack on this bill.
See his speech of April 14, 1883, strongly anticlerical in tone
and upholding the separation of church and state, in SPHA, IX,
10, 145-49. Clerical attempts to restore Catholic influence in
the public schools repeatedly failed during the eighties and
nineties, thanks in large part to German Liberal as well as
Young Czech opposition. Young Czechs continued to differ from
Old Czechs in vigorously upholding secular schools and the participation of teachers and students in patriotic celebrations.
See for example Eim's article, "Od oposice ke kapitulaci!" which
discusses shortcomings in Old Czech and governmental policy
toward the schools under Minister of Worship and Public Instruction Baron Paul Gautsch, in Národní listy, March 15, 1888, supplement.

8. On the Hus controversy, see the comprehensive article by
Albert Pražák, "Banda lupicův a žhářů," which appeared in Čas in
1920 and is reprinted in Albert Pražák, O národ (Prague, 1946),
pp. 24-37. All liberal-minded Czech newspapers immediately criticized Schwarzenberg, including Národní listy, November 26,
1889. On the same day the Neue Freie Presse in an article on
"the new Hussites" pointed out the increasingly anticlerical
direction Czech politics would likely take under radical Young
Czech leadership. The committee organized to build the Hus monument in Prague publicly announced its intentions on December 3,
1889, in Národní listy; it included among its fifteen members
the Young Czechs Ervín Špindler, J. V. Frič, Servác Heller, Jan
Neruda, and the Grégr brothers. After the Provincial Executive
Council contributed to erecting the Hus plaque on December 28,

1889, Schwarzenberg resigned from the board of directors of the
National Museum. In contrast to the self-governmental institutions which gave continuous support, imperial officials, including several district captains, interfered with fund-raising efforts. See chap. 4 above, n. 13.

9. The text of law no. 142, of October 4, 1882, appears in
Zakonník říšský (1882), pp. 549-53, "Zákon, jímž mění se některá
ustanovení volebního řádu do říšské rady." Both Young and Old
Czechs supported extension of the franchise. Among the most
pointed debates on this bill in the Reichsrat was that of March
18, 1882, in SPHA, IX, 7 525-55. The enfranchisement of "five-
gulden" voters for diet elections in Bohemia, authorized by the
diet on May 5, 1885, became law on May 20. The franchise was
likewise extended in Silesia on January 1, 1887, but despite persistent attempts by Czechs in Moravia it was never authorized by
the diet of that province. The absence of a five-gulden vote
in Moravia helps explain the relative weakness there of liberal
and anticlerical Czech political parties. See, for example, the
two proposals for reform of representation and the franchise in
Moravia submitted for the National party by František Šrom in
December 1885 and on October 23, 1890. Alois Pražák had proposed
a similar reform as early as October 12, 1871. All were defeated.

10. Returns were carried by the Národní listy in the March 5,
1891, "extra" edition, and on March 6, 1891, in the regular edition. For a discussion of the returns, see below, this chapter,
and Národní listy, March 8, 1891, and Čas, March 23, 1891.

11. The growth in the Czech population and Czech advances in
agriculture and industry are discussed in chap. 1 above.

12. Edvard Grégr in opposition to the Wurmbrand bill spoke
in the lower house of the Reichsrat on January 26, 1884. See
SPHA, IX, 11, 182-93. An English translation of this famous
speech, "Speech in Behalf of the Czech Language," appears in
Anderson, Pincetl, and Ziegler, Nineteenth Century, 2:129-53.
See also Edvard Grégr, Slovo osudné: Časová úvaha o jazykových
poměrech našich od Dra. Edvarda Grégra (Prague, 1883). In favor
of the bill, see Plener's speech of January 28, 1884, SPHA, IX,
11, 217-34, reprinted in Ernst von Plener, Reden (Stuttgart,
1911), pp. 272-303, a very thorough presentation of the German
position. The bill took its name from the German Liberal stalwart who first introduced it, Count Gundacker Wurmbrand (1838-
1901), a delegate from the second curia, the chamber of commerce,
in Graz, Styria. Polish delegates, among other Slavs, also
strongly opposed Wurmbrand's bill, as Otto Hausner and Ritter
von Grocholski spoke for their delegation on January 24, 1884,
SPHA, IX, 11, 122-34ff. The second bill to make German the official state language was introduced by Max Freiherr Scharschmid

von Adlertreu (1831-1905), a delegate from the first curia of
the Pilsen region and owner of a large estate at Trnova u
Zbraslavě, Bohemia. The vote against the Wurmbrand bill on January 29, 1884, was 186 to 155. See SPHA, IX, 11, 282-85.

13. On the Linz program, see Münch, Böhmische Tragödie,
pp. 377-404, and Ernst von Plener, Erinnerungen, 3 vols. (Stuttgart, 1911-1921), 2:232-34. Most of the leading German-Austrian
politicians of the later nineteenth century endorsed this program issued in August 1882 at Linz, including not only such
leading liberals as Herbst, Plener, and Wurmbrand, but the founders of the German People's party (Deutsche Volkspartei), Heinrich
Friedjung and Adolf Fischhof; the Pan-German leader Georg von
Schönerer; and the future German Social Democrats Viktor Adler
and Engelbert Pernerstorfer (1850-1918). On the Whitsun program,
see chap. 9 below.

14. On the development of German parties during the eighties, see Charmatz, Deutsch-österreichische Politik, pp. 171-78,
and Plener, Erinnerungen, 2:290-98. The People's party was
founded in 1882. German representation in the Reichsrat after
the elections of 1885 was as follows: German Liberals (German-
Austrian club), 87; the more radical German club, successors to
the Volkspartei, 24; the Liechtenstein club, 19; the German-
Nationalist Union (Steinwender), 18; the Coronini club, 11; and
the Union of German Nationalists (Schönerer), 6. In the clerical Hohenwart club there were 34. On the short-lived People's
party, founded in the summer of 1882, see Plener, Erinnerungen,
2:230-31. Under pressure of the Russian war scare and the continuing Slavic resurgence in Cisleithania, and with the support
of the Imperial German embassy in Vienna, the German Liberals
and the German club constituted themselves on November 6, 1888,
as the "United German Left," with a total of 112 delegates, of
whom 88 adhered to the former party. See Plener, Erinnerungen,
2:362-67, and Charmatz, Deutsch-österreichische Politik, pp.
176-78.

15. See Srb, Politické dějiny, 1:677-81; Tobolka, Politické
dějiny, vol. 3, pt. 1, pp. 126-28; and Plener, Erinnerungen,
2:321-23, for the German Liberal reaction. Text in Národní
listy, September 24, 1886.

16. On Plener's presentation of the German Liberal proposal
of December 22, 1886, see the text in Plener, Reden, pp. 364-82.
After this proposal was rejected, the Germans walked out of the
diet and did not return until the spring of 1890. See the discussion in Srb, Politické dějiny, 1:682-87, with excerpts from
some of the debates. Similar proposals were advanced by Herbst
and Plener to the Bohemian Diet on September 16, 1884, and December 15, 1885, respectively. The text of the latter appears in

Plener, Reden, pp. 325-53. The growing Czech apprehension at
German demands for the division of Bohemia and at governmental
confiscation of Czech newspapers and harassment of the Czech minority in predominantly German districts of Bohemia is best illustrated in the well-documented memorandum from Alois Pravoslav
Trojan to Minister Pražák, dated September 15, 1886. The text
appears in Pražák-Kameníček, Paměti, 1:235-45.

17. Bismarck's viewing Czech advances in politics with alarm
is indicated by his dispatch of May 6, 1888, from Berlin, to Ambassador Reuss in Vienna, and by Bismarck's article of October 26,
1888, in the Kolnische Zeitung, critical of the "Slavicization
of Bohemia." The latter is cited in Národní listy, supplement
to October 27, 1888. The former appears as dispatch no. 335
(Berlin), UC-1x, reel 215, frames 619-21. On the war scare of
February 1888, see the Národní listy, supplement to February 9,
1888, February 11, 1888, on "the war scare," and February 24,
1888, on Bismarck's article in the Norddeutsche Allgemeine Zeitung. On the visit of Kaiser Wilhelm II to Vienna, see Národní
listy for October 2, 3, and 4, 1888. For a discussion of the
visit with citations from pertinent diplomatic reports see Jenks,
Iron Ring, pp. 226-27. Many articles by the Národní listy pertaining to imperial foreign policy during 1888 were confiscated
by the authorities. Among them were the article of October 1,
"On the Prussian Atmosphere," and that of October 13, on "The
German-Austrian Alliance and the Hungarians." See the official
announcements in Národní listy, supplements to October 1 and
October 21, 1888, respectively.

18. Pražák retained his post as Minister without Portfolio
for Czech Affairs. See Národní listy, supplement to October 14,
1888, for Young Czech criticism of the dismissal. To be sure,
the Germans denounced "the Czech Schönborn," and the Neue Freie
Presse of October 13, 1888, declared Schönborn to be "a friend
of [Bohemian] state rights." The Young Czechs attributed to
Schönborn not only clerical proclivities long documented (Národní listy, October 28, 1888, supplement) but pro-German views as
yet unrevealed. On the latter, see chap. 6 below.

19. Národní listy, May 12, 1887. Rieger's daughter, Marie
Červinková, noted in her diary on November 1, 1881, a similar
comment made by Rieger to his wife; Rieger-Heidler, Príspěvky,
2:158.

20. On the "crumbs" incident, see Národní listy, May 14
through 22, 1887; E. Grégr, Denník, 2:114-19, diary entries for
May 1887; and Rieger-Heidler, Príspěvky, 2:306, diary entry for
late May 1887 (no. 702), which concurs with E. Grégr's appraisal
of the situation. No evidence has come to light which contra-
dicts Grégr's word on this matter. On the newly reorganized

Young Czech party and its separate parliamentary club, see the
special report on the development of the party written in the
fall of 1889 by Alois Prazák, either for newspaper publication
or for Minister-President Taaffe, in Pražák-Kameníček, Paměti,
1:245-53. On Engel's action catching most Old Czechs by surprise, see the letters of Rieger to Marie Červinková, dated
May 22, 1887, and May 24, 1887, Rieger-Heidler, Příspěvky, 2:306-
07. The quotation is from the second letter. In the first,
Rieger commented on Engel's having "conspired" with Eim and the
Národní listy and on Engel's perhaps wanting "to play at being
Cato."

21. See Národní listy for January 27 and 28, 1888, for statements and commentary. This step was taken after Engel had ex-
plored the possibilities for rejoining the Czech club contingent
upon its reorganization and reform. The Old Czechs rejected any
compromise, and the Grégrs had not favored Engel's overture in
the first place. On this development see E. Grégr, Denník,
2:122, entry for January 26, 1888.

22. E. Grégr, Denník, 2:55. On the agricultural crisis and
the Young Czechs, see Krízek, "Krise cukrovarnictví."

23. For the electoral returns, see table 17 in the appendix.
The text of the state rights address to the crown and the Bohe-
mian Diet on October 10, 1889, by the Grégr brothers appears in
Srb, Politické dějiny, 1:749-59. On the contemporary develop-
ment of the party see the special report by Alois Pražák in
Pražák-Kameníček, Paměti, 1:245-53, dating from the fall of 1889.

24. Unless otherwise indicated, biographical data and character sketches of the Young Czechs discussed below have been drawn
from the following sources. The Ottův slovník naučný and the
Masarykův slovník naučný contain short biographical notices.
The political biographies in the latter encyclopedia, written
almost exclusively by Zdeněk V. Tobolka, are especially good.
For party lawyers, Michal Navrátil, Almanach českých právníků
(Prague, 1904) contains excellent biographical essays. For delegates to the diet and Reichsrat, see Navrátil's Sněm 1895 and
Nový sněm. Antal Stašek's Vzpomínky contains salient sketches
o the leading Young Czechs, whom he knew well. Tobolka, Politické dějiny, and Neruda, Podobizny, also from personal acquaintance, comprehensively portray some of the more important party
figures. Masaryk in his conversations with Karel Čapek, Hovory
s T. G. Masarykem (Prague, 1969), very briefly and sympatheti-
cally discusses the personalities of several former political
colleagues. Personal correspondence usually reveals much about
a person's character and ideas. For example, the letters in
Kaizl, Z mého života, and in LANM, Kramář papers, are basic to
understanding Kaizl and Kramář. Emanuel Engel is best seen in

his letters to Gustav Eim, PNP, Eim papers. Ervín Špindler is
likewise revealed in his letters to Julius Grégr, LANM, Julius
Grégr papers. LANM, Rieger papers and Rieger-Heidler, Přispěvky,
make critical and generally fair comments about Young Czech
leaders.

25. SÚA, PM 1860-70, 8/5/22/8, no. 36, 36a 70/1869; 8/1/15/29,
no. 3854/1870; 8/5/17/6, no. 915/1869 and no. 941/1869.

26. LANM, Julius Grégr papers, Špindler to Grégr, letters
nos. 5-12, 14-23, 25, 27-28, 31, and 33-36.

27. This cooperation is well revealed by correspondence relating to electoral campaigns during 1889, 1890, and 1891, in
the Buquoy papers, SA Trebon. See also František Vodňanský, Náš
zápas o III. sbor (České Budějovice, 1906), for an account of
the successful Czech takeover of the communal governing board
(obecní zastupitelstvo) of České Budějovice on November 6 to 11,
1906, and on Zátka and Czech politics generally at the turn of
the century.

28. Kratochvíl, 1820-93; Špindler, 1843-1918.

29. Ervín Špindler translated the poetry of Heine, Meissner,
and Wilbrandt into Czech and published his Básně (1866), Bělo-
horští mučedníci, historický román (1867), and Historické povídky
(1874-75) as contributions to Czech literature.

30. Čapek, Hovory s T. G. Masarykem, p. 93.

31. Stašek, Vzpomínky, pp. 532-33. Václav Janda, 1835-1902.

32. Counterparts to the middle-class leaders of the Podřipsko
canton in other areas included František Schwarz and Karel Adámek,
who built up strong party cadres in Plzeňsko and Hlinsko respectively. Other leading representatives among the twenty-three
party delegates to the Bohemian Diet from intensive agricultural
areas included the farmers Václav Krumbholz, long-time trustee
from Malé Čečovice, Jan Jaroš from Čáslavky u Černozic, Jindřich
Doležal from Starý Bydžov, Josef Horák, editor of the liberal
weekly Čáslavské listy (Čáslav news), and Václav Jindřich from
Citoliby, chairman of the farmers' sugar refining corporation in
Louny and a director of the Provincial Bank.

33. See the article on "Liběchov" in Čas, vol. 10, no. 37
(September 12, 1896):579-80.

34. This is confirmed by an examination of the electoral returns; see Navrátil, Almanach sněmu (1895-1901), pp. 59-79, for

the results of the 1889 diet elections. On the returns of 1891
see below, the last 3 pp. of chap. 5.

35. Nožička, Prokůpek. Prokůpek, 1832-1915.

36. The agrarian crisis affected all farmers of Austria-
Hungary beginning in the 1880s, as they could not compete with
grain and beef from the large mechanized farms of the Americas.
Prices for agricultural produce fell on European markets, the
price of wheat reaching an all-time low in 1891 before recovering. Czech agriculture was further hurt by the raising of tariffs against agricultural goods in the principal European countries, occasioned by falling agricultural prices. Especially
harmful were the increased tariffs in France, Germany, and Italy
between 1885 and 1887 on sugar beets. The use of new farming
methods, technology, and mechanized food processing by Czech
farmers in the Labe valley districts enabled them to weather the
crisis better than the small peasant farmers of South Bohemia
who relied on traditional farming methods. The great landowners
could always convert more cropland to forest and use their influence to gain government subsidies, an option not available to
the politically disfranchised small peasant. As a result, most
Czechs in rural areas, especially small and middling farmers,
were in an increasingly angry mood by the end of the eighties
and took out their frustrations on the great landowners and the
banks which held mortgages on their land and products. The de-
leterious effects of the agricultural tariff were recognized by
the nineties, when countries entered into reciprocal agreements
on exchange of agricultural produce, which, along with the more
widespread adoption of improved agricultural techniques, helped
ease the crisis. See Handwörterbuch der Staatswissenshaften,
vol. 1, "Agrarpolitik" and "Agrarstatistik" by J. Conrad, pp.
120-25 and 128-31. See also Křížek, "Krise cukrovarnictví," and
Pascu, Giurescu, Kovács, and Vajda, "La question agraire."

37. Frankenberger and Kubíček, Švehla, pp. 47ff., and Obrtel,
Moravští sedláci, pp. 246ff. See also Pozor, February 13, 1882,
for the "Programatický projev zemědělců na Hané." Tobolka, Politické dějiny, vol. 3, pt. 1, pp. 269ff.

38. The Old Czech leadership quickly and accurately perceived
the threat to their party from agrarian political organization
and ambitions. On June 12, 1883, Pražák wrote to Rieger that
"in recent times, our people, especially here in Moravia, are
most pleased to nominate only farmers for office in rural districts and to exclude the intelligentsia." See Rieger-Heidler,
Příspěvky, 1:190-91. On August 20, 1884, Rieger wrote to Karel
Mattus that he was very much troubled by the fact that in Bohemia as well as in Moravia "the notion is beginning to prevail

that only a farmer can adequately represent another farmer" in
politics. See Rieger-Heidler, Príspevky, 1:227-28.

39. See Chundela, Kubr: Sedlák a politik, pp. 41-43.
Stanislav Kubr, 1862-1908; Václav Krumbholz, 1846-1923. Krumbholz served as a Young Czech delegate to the diet from 1889 to
1901 and as a delegate to the Reichsrat beginning in 1891. On
Kubr's part in founding the Agrarian party, see chaps. 8 and 9
below.

40. Alfons Št'astný, O doplnění našeho národního programu:
Podává na krajanům svým na uváženou, 2d ed. (Prague, 1872). The
best source on Št'astný's political activity is the annotated
selection from his correspondence, Hugo Traub, ed., Ze života
Alfonse Št'astného (Prague, 1928). Especially valuable are the
letters exchanged with Edvard Grégr. Josef Vychodil, 1845-1913,
Jan Rataj, 1855-1915; Jan Rudolf Demel, 1833-1905; Josef Jeronym
Tvrdík, 1846-95. Tvrdík, the secretary of the association, was
a professor in the secondary school (reálka) at Prostějov and
the author of several works on history and archeology. He was
one of the few intellectuals associated with the Agrarian movement.

41. Št'astný expressed these opinions in letters to Edvard
Grégr of May 12, 1887, "dnes je jádro otázky sociální otázka
agrární," and of December 18, 1888, "šlechta je rakovinou na těle
státním." See Traub, Ze života Št'astného, pp. 269 and 313. See
also pp. 296-97 for Št'astný's letter of April 12, 1888, to Edvard Grégr in which he discussed conflict between conservative
great landowners and Czech peasants, noting how the former simply
could not comprehend the latter's efforts to become self-reliant.

42. Blažek, 1842-1910; Kaftan, 1841-1909; Tilšer, 1825-1913;
Dvořák, 1849-1916; Edvard Grégr, 1827-1907; Engel, 1844-1907;
Šamánek, 1846-1916; and Šíl, 1850-1933. Tilšer and Edvard Grégr
are discussed at length in chap. 3 above.

43. Kramář, "Za vedení národní strany svobodomyslné," in
Česká politika, 3:528; Čapek, Hovory s T. G. Masarykem, p. 93;
Stašek, Vzpomínky, pp. 520-21; and Penižek, Z mých pameti,
3:61-62, among others.

44. This is particularly evident in his extensive correspondence with Eim, noted in chap. 4 above, and in the Eim papers,
PNP. Eim's letters to Engel, in PNP, Engel papers, are less revealing, in large part because of Eim's habit of not dating most
of his letters. The long friendship between Eim and Engel,
dating back to the mid-eighties, is in itself extraordinary because of Eim's reputation as a difficult man to get along with.
Engel, as noted above, served as Eim's personal physician as

well as his friend and colleague. In a number of ways their
very different personalities were complementary.

45. J. S. Machar, Boží bojovníci, p. 8.

46. On Engel's literary career, see chap. 3 above. Engel's
decision to enter politics and public service is reported to his
friend V. Červinka, in letters of June 6, 1871, and July 19-21,
1871, in PNP, Engel papers, 6 R 78, nos. 16 and 17.

47. See the entry in the diary of Marie Červinková-Riegrová
(1854-95) for November 6, 1886, which records her long conversation with Engel in a railway coach where they chanced to meet.
Engel's opinion of the shortcomings of Old Czech party policy
and tactics are also quite candidly expressed, especially his
view that that party could not simultaneously try to be a party
supporting the government *and* a popular (populární) party. He
also thought that Rieger's commendable honesty and magnanimity
may not always have helped him in politics: "A good politician
must occasionally be a scoundrel." Rieger-Heidler, Příspěvký,
1:291-93.

48. On Jan Dvořák, 1849-1916, see Kramář, Paměti, p. 287,
and Stašek, Vzpomínky, p. 513.

49. Václav Šamánek, 1846-1916. Josef Šíl, a leading radical,
served in the diet from 1889 to 1901 and in the Reichsrat from
1891 to November 1896. Šíl's speech on Hus at the 1889 post-
Christmas meeting in Velím of the Young Czech club for the Kolín,
Kouřim, and Poděbrady districts is reported in Národní listy, November 29, 1889, supplement. Šamánek served as a Young Czech in
the diet from 1895 to 1908 and in the Reichsrat from 1893 to 1897.
A typical speech, which includes an introductory biographical
sketch, is Václav Šamánek's Veřejná schůze lidu na Žofíně dne 7.
května 1892 (Prague, 1892).

50. Chap. 3 above discusses Edvard Grégr's work in science
and medicine, his association with J. E. Purkyně, and his political activities up to 1874. Julius Grégr's political career and
editorship of the Národní listy are discussed in chap. 4 above.
The phrase "theatrical radicalism" is Špindler's. The relationship between the Grégr brothers is clearly revealed in their voluminous but intermittent correspondence in PNP, Edvard Grégr
papers, and LANM, Julius Grégr papers.

51. This was attested to by two of his principal opponents,
Gustav Eim and T. G. Masaryk, who agreed on little else.

52. Navrátil, Eim, p. 168.

53. Other lawyer founders were: Antonín Čížek, Arnošt Hnizdo, Jan Kratochvíl, Jan Strakatý, and Vincenc Vávra. See V. Škarda, Program 1897, pp. 139-41.

54. On Grégr and Sladkovský see above, chaps. 3 and 4 respectively. Kaizl (1854-1901), Kramář (1860-1937), and Rašín (1867-1923) will be discussed below. Čelakovský, 1846-1914; Fořt, 1850-1929; Stránský, 1855-1931.

55. Brzorád, born 1857; Slavík, 1846-1910; Tuček, 1845-1900; Pippich, 1849-1921; Podlipný, 1848-1914, see chap. 4 above; Pinkas (born 1863), first elected to the diet in 1895; Václav Škarda, see chap. 7 below covering the period when he entered party life; Podlipský, 1859-1900, son of Josef and Sofie Podlipský and brother-in-law of the poet Jaroslav Vrchlický, elected to the diet as a Young Czech in 1895; Dyk, 1852-1907, delegate to the diet 1889-1901 and delegate to the Reichsrat 1891-1907.

56. Karel Adámek, Z mých styků s dr. Aloisem Pravosl. Trojanem v letech 1879 až 1893 (Chrudim, 1910).

57. Neruda, Podobizny, 2:11. Ernst Plener considered Trojan to be a "jovial old Czech." See Plener, Erinnerungen, 2:306. On Trojan's joining the Young Czech party after his defeat as a National party candidate in the fourth-curial elections of July 1889 and after the Vienna Agreement of 1890, see Adámek, Z mých styků, pp. 74-86.

58. Sbírka zákonů rakouských, 3 vols. (Prague, 1863-64). On the importance of Škarda in the early sixties and his legacy see the two fine articles by Valentin Urfus, "Český státoprávní program na rozhraní let 1860-1861 a jeho ideové složky," Právněhistorické studie 8 (1962):127-72, and "Český státoprávní program a české dělnické hnutí v období vzniku první dělnické strany v Čechách," Právněhistorické studie 9 (1963):97-112. I wish to thank Professor Urfus for first calling the importance of Škarda to my attention.

59. Kučera, 1838-95.

60. Stašek, Vzpomínky, p. 521. Pacák, 1846-1914; Herold, 1850-1908.

61. Vašatý, 1836-98; Kounic, 1848-1913; Scharf, 1857-1922; and Březnovský, 1843-1918.

62. Formánek, born 1845; Hájek, born 1835; Wohanka, 1842-1931. Engel's statement to an interviewer from the St. Petersburg Viedomosti was later published and criticized in Samostatnost, August 29, 1903. This statement is also cited in Winters, "Hegemony," p. 312.

63. On the Realists and the social question, see Masaryk, Otázka sociální, and Kramář, "Sociální tradice našeho socialismu," pp. 30-31, in Hlas, který nebyl umlčen: soubor úvah a projevů, ed. Vladimír Sís (Prague, 1939). Masaryk, 1850-1937; Stašek (Zeman), 1843-1931; Drtina, 1861-1925; Rezek, 1853-1909.

64. Principal sources on the Realists include Jan Herben, Kniha vzpomínek (Prague, 1935), and Antal Stašek, Vzpomínky, both detailed and favorable though critical in evaluating events and personalities. Four works are critical in retrospect in light of Kramář's subsequent political career: Kramář, Paměti; Tobolka, Politické dějiny, vol. 3, pt. 1; Vladimír Sís, Karel Kramář: Život a dílo (Prague, 1930), and idem, Karel Kramář: Vůdce národa (Prague, 1936). Křížek, Masaryk a česká politika, is critical from a 1950s Marxist perspective and seldom credits the Realists with altruistic intentions. See also the Realist periodical Čas, a fortnightly from 1886 to 1889, a weekly from 1889 to 1901, and thereafter a daily; the monthly Atheneum, from 1884 through 1893; Naše doba, from 1893 to 1914 under Masaryk's editorship; the series of articles on Masaryk and the Realists in Edvard Beneš et al., eds., T. G. Masarykovi k šedesátým narozeninám (Prague, 1910); and Jan Muk et al., Památník Ministra Prof. Dr. A. Rezka (Jindřichův Hradec, 1936). See also Kaizl, Z mého života, 3 vols.

65. See the October 12, 1889, state rights manifesto in Srb, Politické dějiny, 2:745.

66. The extensive literature on the Progressive movement is discussed in chap. 6 below. The problems in defining the movement and in assessing its nature and contributions to Czech politics generally and to Young Czech politics specifically are also taken up in that chapter. Students called themselves "Progressives" as early as 1889 but did not talk about a "Progressive movement" until 1891.

67. Data on the social origins of student Progressives is presented by Karen Freeze, "The Young Progressives: The Czech Student Movement, 1887-1897," (Ph.D. diss., Columbia University, 1974), pp. 38-39. During the late eighties and early nineties, 85 percent of the students came from outside of Prague. The author of this book was one of four readers of Ms. Freeze's dissertation, which is the most thorough account of the student Progressives in English and the most analytical in any language. Her appendixes 6 through 10 present information on curriculum in Czech gymnasia and secondary schools (reálky), on enrollment at the Czech and German universities and at the Czech and German technical colleges, and the distribution of Czech students according to course of study, pp. 396-400.

68. On the history of the Academic Reading Society, see Wolf,

České studentstvo 1882-1912, pp. 8-44. On Slavia's becoming the
center of student activities after the disbanding of the society,
see pp. 47-56. On Young Czech support of the Progressives in
Slavia, see pp. 56-63. The AČS had as members between one-third
and one-half of all students enrolled in Prague at any one time.
It maintained a student library of more than 20,000 volumes and
hundreds of periodicals and sponsored extracurricular sporting
events and cultural activities.

69. See the inaugural issue of the Časopis českého studentstva (ČcSt), vol. 1, no. 1 (May 3, 1889), especially the article
"Studentstvo a veřejnost u nás," by Antonín Hajn, which was approved by the journal's editorial board. This article is reprinted in Antonín Hajn, Výbor prací, 1:13-21. Čížek, 1865-97;
Antonín Hajn, 1868-1949; and K. S. Sokol, 1867-1922.

70. T. G. Masaryk, "Několik myšlenek o úkolech českého studentstva," ČcSt, vol. 1, no. 2 (June 1889):39-46. This article
was reprinted as the last of five chapters in Masaryk's Naše
nynější krise (Prague, 1895).

71. The development of the Progressive movement after March
1891 is discussed in chap. 6 below.

72. On the governor's disbanding the society see the articles
by Antonín Hajn, "Naše situace" and "Další osudy rozpuštěného
Akademického cestářského spolku," ČcSt, vol. 1, no. 5 (November
1889), reprinted in his Výbor prací, 1:38-46 and 46-53. On January 16, 1890, imperial courts upheld the governor's action, thus
ending student and Young Czech efforts at appeal.

73. R. Wolf, České studentstvo, pp. 56-60ff.

74. "Program českého studentstva," ČcSt, vol. 2, no. 8 (May
15, 1890):139-42, reprinted in Antonín Hajn, Výbor prací, 1:103-
12. See also Jaroslav Werstadt, "Politické proudy ve studentstvu," Časopis pokrokového studentstva, vol. 13, no. 3 (December
1909):51-56. On student poverty and associated problems, see
Freeze, "The Young Progressives," pp. 146-55.

75. This program, titled "Co budeme dělat o prazdninách?"
appears in ČcSt, vol. 2, no. 12 (July 17, 1890):215-17. It is
reprinted in Antonín Hajn, Výbor prací, 1:117-21.

76. Sokol, Rašín, Čížek, and Hajn, who became editor-in-
chief in October 1890, had meanwhile been joined on the editorial board by Josef Škába and Václav J. Klofáč (1868-1942), a student journalist in the Barák tradition.

77. Národní listy and Hlas národu cover this bill and the

ensuing controversy during the last week of May 1887. Edvard
Grégr's diary entry for May 30, 1887, also comments on this and
related events from a Young Czech perspective. See Denník,
2:119.

78. On the Progressive students and the Hus controversy of
November and December 1889, see the article by Antonín Hajn,
"Mistr Jan Hus opětně souzen na českém sněmě!" in ČčSt, I (December 1889), reprinted in his Výbor prací, 1:56-68. The Hus monument is discussed earlier in this chapter.

79. R. Wolf, České studentstvo, p. 56.

80. This program, titled "Co očekáváme od strany svobodomyslné," appeared in ČčSt, vol. 3, no. 4 (February 19, 1891):55-58.

81. See table 17 in the Appendix for electoral returns in the
second, third, and fourth curias and for comparison to the 1883
diet elections. For quote by Franz Joseph: Čas 3 (1889):80.
Karl Tschuppik, Franz Joseph I: Der Untergang eines Reiches
(Dresden, 1928), pp. 400-06ff.

82. On Governor Franz Thun (1847-1916) the most complete
source is the collection of Franz Thun papers at RA Děčín, a
very rich set of letters and memoranda on Czech politics from
the late eighties until the end of 1915. On the Young Czechs
and Thun, see also Čapek, Hovory s T. G. Masarykem, p. 94, and
Antal Stašek, Vzpomínky, pp. 525-29, a very fine character
sketch. The former is the source on Thun's statement that "Čech
bud' je hulvát, nebo že líbá ruku."

83. On the Young Czechs extending fiscal as well as political support to the Moravian Peasant Union and to the Moravian
liberals of the People's party, see chap. 6 below.

84. The Czech text of the Agreement of 1890 may be found in
Srb, Politické dějiny, 2:772-77. The German text appears in
Gustav Kolmer, Parlament und Verfassung in Österreich, 8 vols.
(Vienna, 1902-14), 4:399-426. For the negative Young Czech reaction see LANM, Julius Grégr papers, file Vyrovnání; Karel
Adámek, Původ vídeňských úmluv o navrácení se Němcův do sněmu
království Českého (Chrudim, 1890); Karel Adámek, Vídeňské punktace o školách menšin (Chrudim, 1890); and [Karel Tůma], Pravda
o vyrovnání: Věnováno všem poctivým Čechům (Prague, 1890).
Young Czech sources generally exaggerate the extent to which the
Agreement of 1890 threatened Czech interests but offer criticisms of a specific and practical nature. Rieger had proposed
such a conference of Old Czechs, German Liberals, and conservative and constitutional great landowners as early as 1883, and
Jiří z Lobkowic had made an almost identical proposal in 1887;

but at neither date did the German Liberals accept the invitation. Thus all parties, but especially the German Liberals, did
not seek to make their compromise until each had sustained severe reverses at the polls. One can, in any event, talk about a
"compromise" Agreement in 1890 only if one considers solely the
interests of the parties involved. This approach, of course,
ignores the interests of other interested but uninvited parties.

85. On the Agreement of 1890 generally, see Skedl and Weiss,
Nachlass Taaffe, pp. 419ff; Karel Kazbunda, "Krise české politiky
a vídeňské jednání o t. zv. punktace roku 1890," ČČH 40 (1934):
80-108, 310-46, 491-528, and 41 (1935):41-82, 294-320, 514-54;
Karel Kramář in Půl století Národních listů, pp. 49-53; Václav
Vaníček in Masarykův sborník, 3:50-72, 122-45, 303-29; and Antonín Otakar Zeithammer, Zur Geschichte d. böhm. Ausgleichsver-
suche (Prague, 1912-13). Works like Jenks's Iron Ring, pp. 239-
74, May's Hapsburg Monarchy, and Kann's Multinational Empire
which base discussion of the Agreement of 1890 solely on German
sources reflect the German Liberal argument that this Agreement
constituted a true compromise. Works in English which give a
more balanced picture of the Agreement like Skilling's "Czech
Eighties" and Winters's "Kramář" also do not indicate the extent
to which it was designed to perpetuate the hegemony of privileged classes and interests.

86. LANM, Julius Grégr papers, Vyrovnání file; and dispatches
of Eim to Národní listy, January and February 1890.

87. Kaizl, Z mého života, 2:577-80, letter of Kaizl to Kramář of January 27, 1890, and again on February 15, 1890.

88. Pippich in Národní listy, January 30, 1890, and Trojan
in Národní listy, February 1, 1890.

89. Tobolka, Politické dějiny, vol. 3, pt. 1, pp. 203-14,
and Kolmer, Parlament, 4:423-24.

90. Skedl and Weiss, Nachlass Taaffe, pp. 477-78.

91. See Edvard Grégr's speech in the Reichsrat on April 16,
1890, and Rieger's reply of the following day: Národní listy,
April 18, 1890.

92. Čas 4 (1890):437-38.

93. LANM, Kramář papers, ANM 23, 1342-3, František Drtina to
Kramář from Paris, February 14, 1890. I thank Roland Hoffmann
for first calling this letter to my attention. Kramář to Kaizl
from Vasiljevskoj, June 23 and 29, 1890, in Kaizl, Z mého života,
2:590, 593-94.

94. Čas 4 (December 20, 1890):801. LANM, Julius Grégr papers, letters from Kramář dated December 9 and 16, 1890, and letter from Kaizl dated December 18, 1890. See also citations from n. 84, ch. 3. For a detailed account of Kramář's part in the negotiation based principally upon Kramář, Paměti, pp. 260ff., see Stanley, Winters, "Karel Kramář," pp. 177-233. The agreement signed by Tilšer, Grégr, Kaizl, Kramář, and Masaryk on December 13, 1890, is in Kaizl, 2:625. Křížek, Masaryk a česká politika, pp. 71-154, using a wider range of sources than Vaníček, "K počátkům realismu," emphasizes the opportunism of Masaryk, Kaizl, and Kramář in concluding the agreement with the Young Czechs, while Vaníček, like Herben in Deset let, emphasizes their having made an agreement mostly in conformity with their political principles. Křížek criticizes Herben's account but does not appear to have used the Vaníček article.

95. Karel Adámek, Z mých styků s Trojanem, p. 87.

96. In Bohemia, in the second, third, and fourth curias the Old Czech electoral totals were as follows: second, one seat, 27 votes or 40.9 percent; third, one seat, 16,608 votes or 42.7 percent; fourth, no seats, 3,767 electoral votes or 41.8 percent. All figures above are from Křížek, Masaryk a česká politika, p. 176, which used the data in Statistische Monatshefte, 1891, pp. 393ff.

97. The unrepresentative character of the second, third, and fourth curias is clearly indicated by tables 20A through 20D in the appendix.

98. The electoral platforms of the Young Czech party for 1889 and 1891 will be found in Václav Škarda, Národní strana svobodomyslná a její program, pp. 25-36 and 77-88 respectively.

Chapter 6

1. "Mladočeská osnova adressy," in Srb, Politické dějiny, 1:832-39. Important party speeches advocating state rights and civil liberties included those in the Reichsrat by Jan Slavík and Jan Vašatý on June 13 and June 22, 1891, respectively, and Edvard Brzorád's address on June 7, 1891, to the Liberal Political Association for Německý Brod and vicinity (Svobodomyslný spolek pro Německý Brod a okolí) that led to the endorsement of a state rights resolution. See Národní listy, June 14 and June 24 for the text of the first two speeches and June 11, 1891, for a summary and long extracts from the third. Young Czech critical evaluation of imperial foreign policy, especially reliance on the Triple Alliance, was well expressed by Karel Kramář in his speech of August 30, 1891, in Jičín, in which he pointed out how the peace was endangered by continuing Austro-Hungarian

and German expansion in the Balkans. The text of this speech is in Národní listy, September 2, 1891, "Poslanec dr. Kramář o zahraniční politice a trojspolku."

2. SA Třeboň, Buquoy papers, especially his exchange of letters with Albín Bráf and Karel of Schwarzenberg; SA Litoměřice, branch in Žitenice, Lobkowicz papers, correspondence of Karel of Schwarzenberg and Governor Franz Thun. On the Old Czechs, see Rieger-Heidler, Příspěvky, 2:471-83. The conservative great landowners continued to endorse state rights and equality between nationalities but would not support Young Czech efforts to make Czech an internal official language in Bohemia and Moravia. At their meeting of May 20, 1891, the conservatives had agreed that such an extension of the use of Czech might in the long run prove detrimental to a higher good than state rights--the unity of the empire. See the report in Národní listy, May 21, 1891, on this meeting, chaired by Karel of Schwarzenberg.

3. This is evident from the correspondence between Minister-President Taaffe and Governor Thun, published in Skedl and Weiss, Nachlass Taaffe, pp. 479-578, "Der Ausgleichslandtag."

4. On the exposition, see Výstavní Katalog Kralovského hlavního města Prahy (Prague, 1891), and the special daily newspaper Praha, denní list výstavní, published during the exhibition by Josef R. Vilímek and Jan Herben. See also the daily reports titled "Zemská jubilejní výstava" in the Národní listy. Many American Czechs returned to Prague to attend the exposition and to renew old ties. Young Czech Jaromír Čelakovský addressed one large reception for visiting Americans, along with two American Czechs, Mr. Kysela and Miss Kličkova. See Národní listy, June 26, 1891, "Přátelský večer na počest amerických našich krajanův."

5. See Thun's exchange of letters with Taaffe as the former helped persuade the emperor to come to Prague and then made preparations for his arrival, in Skedl and Weiss, Nachlass Taaffe, pp. 578-652, "Die Kaiserreise nach Prag und Reichenberg im Jahre 1891," supplemented by materials in the Franz Thun papers, RA Děčín, file on "Výstava 1891." In a dispatch to Taaffe (pp. 579-80), dated May 28, 1891, Thun recommended that the emperor not visit Liberec (Reichenberg) on the same trip, first because the Czechs would find such action insulting and second, because of the danger of demonstrations by the strong Social Democratic movement in that area.

6. The four districts were Králíky, Lanškroun, Police, and Ústí nad Orlicí. SZSČ, I. sezení III. výročního zasedání Českého sněmu z rok 1889, pp. 62-63, for the introduction of the bill on March 8, and pp. 137-38, for its first reading on March 14. Debate followed. The overwhelming Bohemian popular feeling against

the Agreement of 1890 is best illustrated by the 394 petitions
to the diet from self-governmental or private institutions among
the Czech minority in areas of Bohemia marked for German predominance by the Agreement, These appear grouped on various days
after March 14, in ibid., pp. 132-767. See the index, pp. 35-39,
for individual governmental bodies or organizations, "Rejstřík
1891-92." Among the numerous protests against the redrawing of
judicial districts in accordance with the Agreement of 1890 is
that of July 19, 1891, endorsed by nine communes in the Litoměřice district and twelve in the Třebenice district affected by
proposed redrawing of judicial districts. See Národní listy,
August 6, 1891, "Protest proti punktačnímu ohraničení," for the
text and argument. LANM, Julius Grégr papers, also contains many
letters and petitions from individuals or organizations not noted
by the diet. Many of these are in the file titled "Vyrovnání."
Others accompany letters from private correspondents and are filed
with papers of the appropriate individual. Rieger's assessment
of the events of March is clearly indicated by his letter of
April 20, 1892, to Karel Mattuš, on the problems of the Old Czech
party and its relationship to the Taaffe government. See Rieger-
Heidler, Příspěvky, 2:486-87.

7. František Tilšer et al., Návrh na obžalobu Jeho Excell. hr.
Bedřicha Schönborna, c.k. ministra spravedlnosti a jednání o
návrhu tom v říšské radě dne 4. a 5. května 1892 (Prague, 1892),
on indicting Schönborn. Further justification of the indictment
is Edvard Grégr's Řeč na schůzi voličské v Roudnici dne 22. května 1892 (Prague, 1892). Law no. 161 of July 25, 1867, which reserved powers to redraw administrative districts to the diets,
allowed the Reichsrat to prosecute officials for failure to live
up to state law, in this case, law no. 59 of June 11, 1868. Some
of the most comprehensive and critical evaluations of Schönborn's
actions will be found in several Young Czech speeches or articles,
including Pacák, "České obce hajte své právo!"
Two Old Czech delegates who had supported the government on
this issue, A. O. Zeithammer and Leopold Pollak, were raked over
the coals by the České Budějovice Chamber of Commerce at its
meeting of May 20, 1892, with Chairman Effmert presiding. Almost all persons in attendance spoke critically of Old Czech policy. See the long report on the meeting, including much of the
proceedings, in Národní listy, May 22, 1892.

8. Summaries of the above events appear in Charmatz, Innere
Geschichte, 2:104-08; Srb, Politické dějiny, 1:854-61; and Tobolka, Politické dějiny, vol. 3, pt. 2, pp. 29-47.

9. LANM, Bráf papers, Pražák to Bráf, no. 17, August 1, 1892.
Národní listy, August 5 and 6, 1892. Pražák-Kameníček, Paměti,
vol. 2, nos. 272 and 276, pp. 410-12, and on pp. 414-16, letters
of F. L. Rieger to Pražák, August 3 and September 7, 1892.

Subsequently Pražák took the title of baron and sat in the upper
house of the Recihsrat, where he continued to advise the Old
Czechs of political developments in Vienna.

10. On the transformation of the Moravian People's party and
the growth of the Lidové noviny, see R. Fischer, Pokroková Morava, 1:22ff. On the transformation wrought within one Moravian
city by these events, see Metoděj Zemek et al., Uherský Brod:
minulost i současnost slováckého města (Brno, 1972), p. 203.

11. At the June 29, 1892, congress of the People's party in
Brno, Tuček was elected party chairman and Stránský and Vychodil
vice-chairmen. See the report in Lidové noviny, June 30, 1892.
Old Czech support of the Agreement of 1890 in the Bohemian Diet
was not without its adverse effects upon the Old Czechs in Moravia. This Stránský and his associates, with the help of Young
Czechs from Bohemia, turned to advantage. Two articles from the
Olomouc Pozor very well describe growing disenchantment with the
Old Czechs in Moravia and criticize Pražák's policy of standing
by the Taaffe government in the expectation that by remaining
part of a parliamentary majority the Czechs could best advance
their interests in the long run, despite short-term setbacks like
enactment of the Agreement of 1890. The two long articles, "Vůd-
cové národa ve vládním světle" and "Smír v Čechách?" were reprinted by the Národní listy on June 7 and August 15, 1891, respectively.

12. Obrtel, Moravští sedláci, pp. 261-63 and chap. 12, pp.
264ff. V. Odraz, Morava do opposice (Prague, 1892), passim, describes the movement by that name, "Moravia takes up opposition"
(to the Taaffe government), that included the Peasant Union for
Moravia and the Political Association for Northern Moravia in addition to the People's party. On the organization of the Political Association for Northern Moravia on February 13, 1892, see
Rostislav Bartocha, Dr. Jan Oštádal: kulturní a národohospodár-
ský budovatel moravský, 1864-1927 (Olomouc, 1937), pp. 22-33.
Among the founders were Julius Ambros, Jan Oštádal, Josef Vychodil, and František Pokorný, the latter two secretary and chairman
respectively. The association included the seven northernmost
districts of Moravia. On Moravian enthusiasm for the Young Czech
victory and for the Prague Exposition during 1891 and some of the
political consequences, see Ambros, Vzpomínky, pp. 364-84.
"Eighteen ninety-one, an extraordinarily famous year! Can any
Czech ever forget it?" Ibid., p. 364. Among the several district political associations organized to support the People's
party was the Political club for the Velké Meziříčí district,
founded at Brno on December 14, 1891. Pacák and Stránský gave
short speeches. See Národní listy, December 16, 1891.

13. František Derka and František Vahalík, Česká universita

na Moravě: Časové otázky (Prague, 1891). On the development of
the language issue, see chap. 8 below. On the importance of both
moral and fiscal support from Czechs in Bohemia and Moravia to
those in Silesia, see "Čeho se nám ve Slezsku nedostává," Národní
listy, July 2, 1892, supplement. On the continuing demand among
Czechs in Silesia for a gymnasium in Opava, see the Reichsrat
speech by Young Czech delegate František Sláma on July 2, 1891,
"Řeč posl. dra. Slámy, pronesená ve včerejší schůzi snemovny po-
slancův," Czech text in Národní listy, July 3, 1891. Sláma
(1850-1917), a lawyer, by that time had served nearly ten years
as a judicial secretary and official in Silesia, where he often
represented Czech minority interests. The voters of the Hradec
Králové district elected him to the Reichsrat in March 1891. He
was noted for his literary as well as political writings.

14. Kramář's Reichsrat speech of July 5, 1892, is reprinted
in Kramář, Paměti, pp. 331-34. On Pacák's part, see Pacák, Boj
za immunitu, the introduction.

15. Edvard Grégr, Řeč přednesená v rozpočtové generální debatě na radě říšské dne 16. prosinec 1891 (Prague, 1891), pp. 24,
50. Similar sentiments were expressed in the diet by Julius
Grégr, Řeč přednesená v rozpočtové debatě na snemu král. českého
dne 5. dubna 1892 (Prague, 1892), and by Josef Herold, Řeč přednesená v rozpočtové generální debatě na zemském snemu království
Českého dne 7. dubna 1892 (Prague, 1892). Grégr's speech created
quite a stir and received much favorable attention in France and
Russia. See Národní listy, December 16, 1891, "Zahraničné hlasy
o řeči dra Ed. Grégra."

16. Herben's Kniha vzpomínek, pp. 436-43, gives the text of
the Realist program of 1890.

17. Březnovský, Vašatý, and Kounic remained the radical mavericks. The earlier division, with differences of opinion cordially argued, may best be seen in Špindler's voluminous correspondence with Julius Grégr in LANM, Julius Grégr papers, Špindler
letters from the 1880s.

18. This is especially evident in the exchange of letters between Engel and Eim during 1892, 1893, and 1894. PNP, Engel
papers, and PNP, Eim papers.

19. Kramář, Paměti, p. 286.

20. Čapek, Hovory s T. G. Masarykem, p. 92.

21. Kaizl, Z mého života, 3:96, on Masaryk's Strakonice speech.

22. Steed, Monarchy, pp. 138-44. Kaizl's speech in the

Reichsrat on July 14, 1892, appears in Kaizl, Z mého života,
3:172-85.

23. Accounts of this cooperation will be found in Jiří Kořalka, Vznik socialistického dělnického hnutí na Liberecku (Liberec,
1956), and Zdeněk Šolle, Ke vzniku první dělnické strany v naši
zemi (Prague, 1953). On the economic insecurity and physical
hardships endured by most workers see Jaroslav Purš, "The Working
Class Movement in the Czech Lands in the Expansive Phase of the
Industrial Revolution," Historica 10 (1965):67-157. On the relationship between the North Bohemian workers' movement of the late
sixties and early seventies and Eisenach Social Democracy in Imperial Germany, see Jiří Kořalka, "Die deutsch-österreichische
nationale Frage in den Anfängen der sozialdemokratischen Partei,"
Historica 3 (1961):109-58, and idem, "Vznik eisenašské sociální
demokracie roku 1869 a otázka Rakouska," ČsČH, vol. 7, no. 3
(1959):436-63.

24. Cach's Otázky výchovy thoroughly documents the interest
of workers in improving education for themselves and their children during the second half of the nineteenth century.

25. See Zdeněk Šolle, Internacionála a Rakousko (Prague, 1966),
pp. 11-63, and Cyrill Horáček, Počátky českého hnutí dělnického
(Prague, 1896).

26. The pioneer Czech Social Democrat Lev J. Palda expressed
these views quite forcefully at the New York congress of the International in November 1870. Zdeněk Šolle, "Die ersten Anhänger
der Internationalen Arbeiter-Association in Böhmen," Historica 7
(1963):183-84.

27. Ibid., pp. 145-84. See also Arnošt Klíma, Počátky českého dělnického hnutí (Prague, 1950), on the middle to late
seventies, and R. Maršan, Českoslovanská sociální demokracie, on
the period 1878 to 1884.

28. On the organization of this unified Austrian party in
accordance with aims of the First International see Zdeněk Šolle,
Internacionála a Rakousko, pp. 111-51.

29. Miloslav Volf, Naše dělnické hnutí v minulosti (Prague,
1947), pp. 65-70. Šolle, Socialistické dělnické hnutí, pp. 15-18.

30. K. Malý, Perzekuce dělnické třídy, and Gustav Habrman,
Z mého života: Vzpomínky (Prague, 1924). See also chap. 5 above
on Taaffe's policies.

31. Zdeněk Šolle, Dělnické hnutí v českých zemích koncem
minulého století (Prague, 1954), pp. 95-108, commentary, and

pp. 251-58, resolution adopted at Hainfeld, December 30, 1888, to January 2, 1889. On the development of Czech Social Democracy, see also the collection of essays in Adolf Mokrý, ed., Osmdesát let československé sociální demokracie, 1878-1958 (London, 1958).

32. PNP, Engel papers, 6585, letter dated January 1, 1892, from Vávra and Sedmidubský to the Young Czech parliamentary club of delegates, requesting subsidies for Naše obrana. Engel's notes show that the party executive committee gave 100 gulden and the club gave 200 gulden. The program of the Naše obrana group of May 16, 1890, is enclosed: "Českoslovanská nár. strana sociálně-demokratické." The later successful development of the Czech National Socialist party in relation to the Young Czechs and to Social Democracy will be discussed in chaps. 9 and 10.

33. A petition of February 14, 1893, by the Workers' Political Club in Prague summed up this view quite well; see Jan Havránek, Boj za všeobecné, přímé a rovné hlasovací právo roku 1893 (Prague, 1964), p. 31. So did the December 1887 and December 1893 resolutions noted below.

34. The Czech text of the "organizational order" adopted at České Budějovice appears in Šolle, Dělnické hnutí, pp. 261-62. The original appears in SÚA, PM 1891-1900:8/1317/134/1894 in German. The program and resolution adopted in Brno in December 1887, "Protokol sjezdu dělnictva českoslovanského odbývaného dne 25. a 26. prosinec 1887 v sále lužánském v Brně. Sestaven dle jednatelských zápisků od J.K.S. v Brně" (Brno, 1888), is reprinted in Šolle, Dělnické hnutí, pp. 247-50.

35. Jaroslav Vozka, Josef Steiner: Typ dělnického vůdce (Prague, 1932), pp. 53-54. Šolle, Dělnické hnutí, pp. 181-87 on the congress in České Budějovice and pp. 261-62 for the text of its resolution. Šolle's many books and articles, with the exception of a few published in the very early 1950s, comprise the most complete and balanced account by a single author of the Czech workers' movement in the later nineteenth century. Vozka's biography of Steiner is the most comprehensive published study of any single later nineteenth-century Czech Social Democratic leader. An informed and perceptive work, based in part on personal participation and observation, is Edvard Beneš's Stručný nástin vývoje moderního socialismu (Brandýs nad Labem, 1910 and 1911). Miloslav Volf's Naše dělnické hnutí v minulosti (Prague, 1947) remains a useful secondary account. Pages 151-61 discuss the Naše obrana group and pp. 161-70 the achievement of autonomy by Czech Social Democrats. Naše doba 1 (1894):532, reports on the March 1894 Vienna congress.

36. On Engels and Czech Social Democracy, see Vozka, pp. 51-52; Šolle, Dělnické hnutí, pp. 136-42; and Šolle, "Die Sozialdemokratie," pp. 351-54.

Notes to Pages 166-170

37. On the increasing number of strikes see the statistical
study by Zdeněk Šolle, Dělnické stávky v Čechách v druhé polo-
viné XIX. století (Prague, 1960). On the miners' strike in
northern Bohemian coal fields, see Jan Havránek, Hornická stávka
roku 1900 v severočeském uhelném revíru (Prague, 1953).

38. Young Czech programs of 1873, 1889 and 1891 on the working class. Also note Tuma, J. Grégr, p. 253ff.

39. Soukup, Revoluce práce, 1:452-53; and Roubík, Časopisect-
vo, 1863-95, pp. 21-22, 48-49. Barák edited the paper from January 1872 until his ouster in August 1874 by Social Democrats who
thought his views too nationalistic. Pecka and other Social
Democrats in June 1875 founded Budoucnost (The Future) to compete
with Dělnické listy and ran it successfully till its suppression
by Taaffe in 1882.

40. Verwaltungsarchiv, box 823, no. 3774, July 14, 1882; and
SÚA, PM 1881-90; 8/1/17/5282/1887.

41. SPHA, X, 2, 881-85, July 5, 1886.

42. E. Grégr, Denník, 2:100-01, entry for June 5, 1886.

43. SPHA, X, 10, 400-01, December 19, 1888; Rieger-Heidler,
Příspěvky, letter no. 961, Rieger to Karel Mattuš, February 26,
1890, pp. 436-38. Pražák-Kameníček, Paměti, vol. 2, nos. 212
and 213, letters of Rieger to Pražák dated June 25, 1887, and
August 24, 1888.

44. The cooperation between workers and students is discussed
below in the section on "the Young Czechs and the Progressive
movement." The literature on the Progressive movement is discussed in n. 55.

45. On the manuscripts controversy of the eighties, see
chap. 5 above.

46. J. S. Kvapil, ed., Sládek-Zeyer: Vzajemná korespondence
(Prague, 1957), no. 203, pp. 178-79.

47. On Čech's and Vrchlický's greeting the younger generation,
see Otakar Odložilík, Tři stati o české otázce (London, 1944-45),
pp. 4-6. On literary criticism, see V. Bitnar, J. B. Čapek, et al.
O českou literární kritiku, vudcí zjevy kritiky let devadesátých
(Prague, 1940), chapters on Šalda, 1867-1937, Krejčí, 1867-1941,
and Vodák, 1867-1940. Vrchlický, 1853-1912; Čech, 1846-1908.

48. Beginning in the nineties, Czechs sought to break away
from historical styles and developed new forms of expression in

music and the arts as well as in scholarship and literature.
Leos Janáček, Vítěslav Novák, and Otakar Ostrčil extended the
depth and range of Czech musical composition while building upon
the great heritage of Smetana and Dvořák. Antonín Slavíček and
Antonín Hudeček became the most famous Czech artists to paint in
the manner of impressionism. Jan Preisler and Bohumil Kubišta
pioneered in the painting of distinctively Czech works in the
styles of expressionism and cubism respectively. In Paris, Alfons Mucha became an internationally recognized leader in the
creation of art nouveau; and Frantisek Kupka of the left-wing
journal l'Assiette au beurre drew powerful and expressionistic
social caricature. After the turn of the century, the architects
Jan Kotěra, Pavel Janák, and others of the Secession group produced designs which ranked among the best in art nouveau and cu-
bist architecture. Jaroslav Smolka, Česká hudba naseho století
(Prague, 1961), pp. 21-33; F. X. Šalda, "Mladá hudební generace
v Čechach," in his Kritické projevy (Prague, 1950), 3:230-36;
Jan Tomeš, Antonín Slavíček (Prague, 1966). On Hudeček, Mucha,
and Preisler and their contemporaries, see Jaromír Neumann, Die
neue tschechische Malerei und ihre klassische Tradition (Prague,
1958). On Kubišta, see Luboš Hlaváček, Životní drama Bohumila
Kubišty (Prague, 1968). On Kupka, see Adolf Hoffmeister, Sto let
české karikatury, pp. 240-67. On architecture, see O. Dostál,
J. Pechar, and V. Procházka, Moderní architektura v československu (Prague, 1967), pp. 14-54. On the modernist and avant-garde
trends generally in European culture at the turn of the century,
see Maurice Rheims, The Flowering of Art Nouveau (New York, ca.
1968), and Jean Cassou, Emile Langui, and Nikolaus Pevsner, Les
sources du vingtième siècle (Paris, 1961). A general work on the
art nouveau or Secession style in fine and applied arts, with emphasis upon the Czech contribution, is Bojumír Mráz and Marcela
Mrázová's Secese (Prague, 1971). A thorough and critical study
of "developmental tendencies in Czech poetry at the end of the
eighties and the beginning of the nineties" is Jiří Brabec's Poezie na předělu doby: Vývojové tendence české poezie koncem let
osmdesátých a na počátku let devadesátých XIX. století (Prague,
1964).

49. T. G. Masaryk's Der Selbstmord als sociale Massenerscheinung der modernen Civilisation (Vienna, 1881) first appeared
in Czech as Sebevrazda: Hromadným jevem společenským moderní osvěty (Prague, 1904), and has recently been translated into English as Suicide and the Meaning of Civilization by R. G. Batson
and W. B. Weist (Chicago, 1970). See also F. V. Krejčí, "Několik
myšlenek o úpadku naší civilisace," Rozhledy, vol. 1, no. 1
(1895/96):260ff.

50. J. S. Machar, Boží bojovníci (Prague, 1895-96 and 1911);
Petr Bezruč, Slezské písně (Prague, 1903; Brno, 1920; Prague,
1946, 1956).

51. J. Vilém Mrštík, Santa Lucia (Prague, 1893); Mrštík,
1863-1912. Viktor Dyk, Prosinec (Prague, 1906), and Konec Hack-
enschmidův (Prague, 1904, 1928); Antonín Sova, Ivův román
(Prague, 1902).

52. "Česká moderna" ("Manifesto of the Czech Modernists"),
Rozhledy, vol. 1, no. 1 (1895/96):3. "We therefore condemn the
brutality which is perpetrated under nationalistic slogans by the
German parties as we would condemn it were it to be perpetrated
by our own." T. G. Masaryk, Organisujme se ku práci (Prague,
1903), p. 61, "I have often said and I shall emphasize again that
a program which is merely slogans will not suffice . . ."; Masaryk quoted in Čapek, Hovory s T. G. Masarykem, p. 103, "We have
liberated ourselves from our despotic masters, but we still have
to free ourselves from the despotism of words."

53. "Česká moderna," pp. 1-4. The twelve signators were Ota-
kar Březina, Václav Choc, Dr. K. Koerner, F. V. Krejčí, J. S.
Machar, J. Vilém Mrštík, Josef Pelcl, F. X. Šalda, J. K. Slejhar,
Antonín Sova, František Soukup, and Dr. Jan Třebický.

54. One should try to distinguish between three broad and
overlapping groups of young reform-minded intellectuals active
during the early and middle 1890s. Of those most concerned with
literature and the arts, some endorsed the "Modernist" manifesto;
of these, a majority, including those most politically active,
associated themselves at one time or another with the Progressive
movement. Working-class radical youth constituted a majority
and Progressives a minority of the young men arrested by the authorities in the fall of 1893 and convicted on the basis of false
testimony and fabricated evidence of participating in an Omladina
(Youth) conspiracy against the government. A number of accounts
understandably confuse the three groups--Modernists, Progressives,
and Omladináři--because so many young intellectuals were associated with at least two of the three. The following account (in
chap. 6) endeavors whenever possible to distinguish between the
groups. "Modernists" is used solely to describe those who signed
the Modernist Manifesto or who approved its publication in Rozhledy. "Progressives" is used to describe those active in the
Progressive movement in any of its phases after March 1891 as
well as those student activists associated with the Časopis českého studentstva or the progressive majority in "Slavia" before
that date. "Omladináři" or "Omladina members" is used to describe
only those young men either indicted or convicted in the Omladina
trials. As noted above, that group included a number of Progressives. "Omladináři" should be used in a restricted sense, because many friends and casual associates of the imprisoned heroes
later called themselves by that name, especially after the First
World War, during which some of the original Omladináři had participated in the struggle for Czechoslovak independence. A

number of the more important Progressives were directly involved
as either Modernists or as Omladináři but in no way was any one
person involved in all three groups. For example, Antonín Hajn,
K. Stanislav Sokol, Alois Rašín, Josef Škába, and A. Pravoslav
Veselý figured very prominently both as Progressives and as Omladináři, while six of the twelve Modernists participated at one
time or another actively in the Progressive movement--Václav
Choc, J. S. Machar, J. Vilém Mrštík, Josef Pelcl, František Soukup, and Jan Třebický. In all cases, the Progressive movement,
as the larger and more inclusive group, serves as the common de-
nominator.

55. On the Austrian and especially Viennese experience, see
Carl E. Schorske, "The Transformation of the Garden: Ideal and
Society in Austrian Literature," American Historical Review,
vol. 72, no. 4 (July 1967):1283-1320. The contrast between the
Czech and Austrian experience is discussed by Garver, "The Re-
orientation of Czech Politics," pp. 56-59.

56. Archival sources on the Progressive movement include
PNP, Antonín Hajn papers, and PNP, papers of the Klub omladinářů,
a disappointingly meager source, including mostly memorabilia
and articles published after 1919. Several comprehensive accounts of the Progressive movement have been written by participants. These include R. Wolf, České studentstvo, 1882-1912
(Prague, 1912), the most comprehensive history of student organizations and student university politics during the pre-war decades. Wolf witnessed only the later events and wrote about
developments in the eighties and nineties objectively and on the
basis of printed and oral testimony. A more complete account of
the Progressive movement in national politics is A. Pravoslav
Veselý's Omladina a pokrokové hnutí: Troch historie a trochu
vzpomínek (Prague, 1902). Veselý participated as a leader in
all important events after 1891 and offers critical commentary
on personalities and events as well as partisan enthusiasm. His
account still holds up well in all areas where he had access to
pertinent data. Josef Soukup, Omladináři: Bojovníci a mučedníci
za československou samostatnost: Okénka do slavných a památných
let devadesátých, 2d ed. (Prague, 1935), covers the same ground
as do Wolf and Veselý but less graphically and in less detail.
Soukup's effort to portray the Progressives and precursors of
Czechoslovak independence is at times tendentious, and he is often more adept at celebrating than at evaluating Progressive
achievements. His is nonetheless a useful work written from the
perspective of a partisan of the First Czechoslovak Republic.
Veselý in 1902 and Wolf in 1912 regarded the Progressive movement as a force which would help bring about the impending regeneration and reform of Czech society. Writing almost a generation later, Soukup and many of his contemporaries looked upon
the movement as a harbinger of Czechoslovak independence. His

work, like that of Josef Veselý, Z bojů za svobodu: Omladináři
v národním odboji a za Republiky (Prague, 1923), often emphasizes the contributions that those convicted in the Omladina
trials made more than two decades later to the achievement of
Czechoslovak independence. To a large extent, the linking of
the Progressive movement with the national revolution of 1918 is
justified. Both aimed, for example, at similar goals—national
autonomy, social reform, and extended civil rights. And a number of Progressives, including Rašín, Hajn, Sokol, and Škába,
played an important part in building the new Czechoslovak state.
But Progressives constituted only a minority among the makers of
Czechoslovak independence; and the leading architect of that independence, T. G. Masaryk, had been during the nineties an older
and sympathetic critic of the Progressive movement and its successor parties. Omladina convicts and Progressives Bořivoj Weigert and Jan Ziegloser edited a collection of forty-seven essays,
memoir accounts, and eulogies by associates titled Omladina 25
let po procesu: Vzpomínky (Prague, 1919). Though sometimes
self-serving and superficial, these short pieces illustrate important aspects of the Progressive movement. On the history of
Czech student activities and politics during the period from
1848 to the early seventies, see František August Slavík, Dějiny
českého studentstva (Prague, 1874).

Secondary scholarly accounts of the Progressive movement include Freeze, "The Young Progressives," and two useful surveys
by František Červinka, Boje a směry českého studentstva na sklonku minulého a na počátku našeho století (Prague, 1962), which
concentrates primarily on the Progressives after 1897, and his
more general survey of the Czech national movement, Český nacionalismus v XIX. století (Prague, 1965). Červinka's works, particularly the first, are tendentious to the extent of claiming
without adequate evidence that the Progressives deliberately
tried to deceive or mislead the working class. One should note
that Progressives offered several alternative programs for political and social reform and that electoral returns indicated
that none of these programs appealed to workers so well as those
of the Czechoslavonic Social Democratic party. Červinka takes
little interest in workers or trade union officials and shows
most enthusiasm for intellectual ideologues. Two articles by
Jan Havránek critically examine the early development of the
Progressive movement, the first, "Počátky a kořeny pokrokového
hnutí studentského na počátku devadesátých let 19. století,"
Acta Universitatis Carolinae: Historia Universitatis Carolinae
Pragensis 2 (1961), fasc. 1, pp. 5-33, emphasizing Progressive
youth at Charles-Ferdinand University. The second article discusses the cooperation of university and working-class youth
during the demonstrations for civil rights and universal suffrage
during 1893 and is titled "Protirakouské hnutí dělnické mládeže
a studentů a události roku 1893," ibid., fasc. 2, pp. 21-81.
Jan Galandauer picks up the story of the Progressives after 1897

in Politické dědictví Omladiny a pokrokového hnutí po roce
1897," ČsČH 12 (1964):797-818. On the academic background to
student politics see Karel Kazbunda, Stolice dějin.

The best collection of source materials on the Progressive
movement aside from the many student and Progressive journals is
Antonín Hajn's Výbor prací, 3 vols. (Prague, 1912-13). Also
valuable are the prison letters of Karel Stanislav Sokol, Vězenská korespondence Karla Stanislava Sokola z let 1893-1895, ed.
Bohuslava Sokolová (Prague, 1929). The most complete published
account of the Omladina trial is Proces s tak zvanou "Omladinou,"
ed. Antonín Čížek and Alois Hajn (September 1894; reprint,
Prague, 1900). Rich sources include the large collection of the
articles and papers of A. Pravoslav Veselý, Životopis a literární
pozůstalost spolu s výborem prací již otištěných, ed. Julius Myslík (Prague, 1905); the collected articles of Antonín Čížek, Výbor prací Antonína Čížka, edited by the editors of Samostatnost
(Prague, 1897); and, more valuable for the period after 1897, the
collected articles and programs of the Radical Progressive successors to the Progressive movement, R. Broz et al., eds., Směr
radikalně pokrokový ve studentstvu (1898-1908) (Prague, 1912),
incorporating an earlier published work edited by Jaromír Malý
and titled Snahy generace (Prague, 1908).

On the Progressive movement generally and on Moravian student
ties to the movement, see the memoirs of Richard Fischer, Cesta
mého života, vol. 2: Praha (Olomouc, 1934), pp. 28-77 on general
events and pp. 78-159 on the Moravská beseda in Prague.

57. Post-election Progressive expectations of the Young
Czechs are best summed up by the article and editorial "Klubu
neodvislých poslanců českých na radě říšské," ČcSt, vol. 3,
no. 17 (October 23, 1891), pp. 273-77.

58. Krásnohorská (1847-1926), a noted poet and writer of the
Ruch school, helped found the Ženské listy (The ladies' newspaper) in 1873 and edited it from 1874 to 1911. She supported the
Young Czech cause against the Old during the eighties and nineties. Her article appeared in ČcSt, vol. 1, no. 2 (1889/90),
pp. 37-39, and no. 3, pp. 84-86. Alois Hajn's Ženská otázka
v letech 1900-1920 (Prague, 1939), a collection of contemporary
articles, remains an excellent source on the emancipation of women as well as on Progressive efforts to promote it.

59. Antonín Hajn discusses this issue in "Nové pokroky v
ženské otázce v Čechách," Neodvislost, vol. 1, no. 3 (December 26,
1892). This article is reprinted in his Výbor prací, 1:327-37.

60. Progressive views on the relationship of Social Democracy
to Czech national emancipation are best presented by Antonín Hajn
in an article which appeared in ČcSt between January and June
1892 entitled "Otázka národnosti a mezinárodnosti v našem

dělnictvu." This article is reprinted in his Výbor prací, 1:249-
78. Hajn asked that the Young Czechs help workers make concrete
economic and political gains. Otherwise they could expect little
working-class support for national emancipation through Bohemian
state rights.

61. On the events in Kraków, see the eyewitness report and
commentary by Antonín Hajn, "Slavnost Mickiewiczova v Krakově,"
in ČcSt, vol. 2, nos. 12-14 (July 17, August 7, and September 24,
1890), reprinted in his Výbor prací, 1:121-38. This article is
the fullest account of the growing Polish and Ukrainian influence
on the Czech Progressive students. Hajn idealizes the Poles and
Ukrainians somewhat and exaggerates their achievements, perhaps
as one means of criticizing Czech shortcomings. Hajn, Rasín, and
Klofač were the Czech delegates.

62. On this and other congresses, see Otakar Odložilík, "Congresses of Slavic Youth, 1890-1892," The Annals of the Ukrainian
Academy, vol. 6, no. 3/4 (1958):21-36.

63. A. P. Veselý, 1873-1904. Antonín Hajn, Výbor prací,
1:285-311, for text of the congress resolution. A. P. Veselý,
Omladina, pp. 69-72

64. See Národní listy, May 18 and 19, 1891, and May 25, 1891,
for Young Czech criticism of the First Congress and Národní listy,
June 8-14, 1892, for Young Czech criticism of the Second. The
Progressives as a result came increasingly to view the Young
Czechs as unwarrantedly pro-Russian and too preoccupied with the
problems of domestic Czech politics. See the Progressive reply,
"Po sjezde, I," ČcSt, vol. 3, no. 12 (1892):196-200.

65. Text is in Antonín Hajn, Výbor prací, 1:178-79, 180-85,
"Sjezd pokrokového studentstva z Rakousko-Uherska v Praze ve
dnech 17., 18., a 19. května r. 1891," and the appended resolution of the Czech section, "Resoluce sekce české," pp. 185-97.
The line quoted above reflected the views of the congress but was
technically not part of the program.

66. The development of the successor parties to the Progressive movement is outlined in chaps. 9 and 10.

67. The divisions within the Progressive movement noted here
became pronounced only in the years after 1896. Červinka, Boje
a směry, exaggerates the differences during the years 1891
through 1893 by observing them in light of later developments.
More balanced appraisals will be found in Wolf, České studentstvo;
Freeze, "The Young Progressives," and Werstadt, "Politické proudy
ve studentstvu."

68. As chap. 8 indicates, members of this group, including Klofáč, formed the Czech National Socialist party in 1898. On František Vahalík, see R. Fischer, Cesta mého života, 2:121-25.

69. The ČčSt appeared in four volumes, the first from May 1889 through January 1890, the second from February to December 1890, and the last two for the calendar years 1891 and 1892. Nové proudy came out fortnightly for thirteen issues from February 1 through August 24, 1893, a total of 272 pages, with a circulation varying from 1,000 to 500 and averaging about 600. Neodvislost began publication on December 12, 1892, and ceased after its fortieth issue under governmental edict on September 11, 1893. The imperial authorities also refused to authorize publication of its successor Nezávislost, announced in Kolín on September 27, 1893. The Neodvislost Cooperative under Rašín's management had published the Young Czech biweekly Polaban in Kolín as well as the Neodvislost in Prague. As a successor to the former paper, the cooperative in October 1893 brought out the Nezávislé listy, edited by Rašín, which ran for fifteen issues until stopped by the authorities on January 21, 1894. Its successor, the biweekly Radikální listy, also owned by the Neodvislost Cooperative, began publication in Kolín on February 27, 1894, and continued in Brno before appearing in Prague in January 1896. Beginning in February 1893, the Časopis pokrokového studentstva ran intermittently through three volumes. J. Krajc and Albert Dutka edited the five issues that constituted the first volume from February through June 1893. It resumed publication in May 1894 for nine issues in a second volume under editor Antonín Klouda in Nový Bydžov and Hořice. It reappeared for a third year in Prague as a fortnightly under editor František Tomášek from November 1895 to July 1896. It came out for the fourth time in October 1900 under the same name and new management and ran from a fourth year (1900/01) through a seventeenth (1913/14). Data on publications is from Roubík, Bibliographie časopisectva . . . 1863-95. See also A. P. Veselý, Omladina, on Neodvislost, pp. 113-24, on Rozhledy, pp. 125-32, and on Nové proudy, pp. 133-42.

70. "What was the difference between the Old-Čechs and the Young-Čechs? . . . The distinction can easily be demonstrated by the following metaphor: 'Here is a corner,' and he turned up the white tablecloth from the edge of the table,--tne Old Čech comes, --tries it, pulls it, twists it, but the corner does not budge. That corner, notice, is Vienna's good will. The Old-Čech sits down peacefully, and with his nails scratches off a few splinters, and is quiet. The Young-Čech comes, takes a look at it,--the corner is immovable,--so he bangs at it with his fist, until the corner falls into his lap. That is the distinction." J. S. Machar, Magdalen, trans. Leo Wiener (New York, 1916), pp. 204-05.

71. See Josef Škába, "Nové proudy v českém socialismu," and

K. Stanislav Sokol, "Historické či přirozené?" Nové proudy 1
(1893):50-52 and 157-62. The latter copy of Nové proudy was confiscated. My copy of Nové proudy, vol. 1, has the article as it
was first published. Nové proudy at the library of Charles University has the number as issued after censorship.

72. Neodvislost, vol. 1, no. 1 (December 12, 1892). See also
"Co očekáváme od strany svobodomyslné?" Časopis českého studentstva, vol. 3, no. 4 (February 19, 1891).

73. A. P. Veselý, Omladina, p. 117, and Wolf, České studentstvo, p. 80, note that Neodvislost could take no stand against the
Young Czechs so long as they subsidized and sponsored it.

74. Josef Pelcl (1861-1916), who was born in Pardubice,
helped found and served as first editor of Rozhledy in Chrudím in
January 1892. The monthly review remained associated under
Pelcl's editorship with Progressive politics until 1905 and continued publication as a predominantly literary review until 1909.

75. Neumann (1875-1947) became a leading Czech Communist
writer after 1921. His memoirs, Vzpomínky (Prague, 1931; 2d ed.,
1948) contain several interesting vignettes on Progressive politics from the nineties to the First World War. His papers are in
PNP, Prague. A collection of his polemical and scholarly articles may be found in his recently reissued Stati a projevy, 2
vols. (Prague, 1964). Vorel (1869-1925) and Choc (1860-193?) are
discussed in subsequent chapters. The Choc papers, a valuable
source on Progressive and National Socialist politics before the
First World War, may be found in LANM. Noteworthy is the series
of articles by Krejčí on "the influence of the social movement on
literature" in Rozhledy, vol. 1, no. 2, pp. 35-38, and no. 3,
pp. 88-93, "Vliv sociálního hnutí na literaturu." See also the
article by Vorel, "O reálních potřebách české literatury," Rozhledy, vol. 1, no. 10, pp. 293-95.

76. The program advocated by Rozhledy in 1892 is best expressed by the editorial "Co chceme?" ("What do we want?") in
Rozhledy, vol. 1, no. 2, pp. 33-34, and by the series of articles
by Antonín Hajn, "O nás pro nás: kapitoly ze současného našeho
života," Rozhledy, vol. 1, no. 1, pp. 1-6; no. 2, pp. 49-50;
no. 3, pp. 86-88; no. 11, pp. 343-47; and no. 12, pp. 375-84.

77. On Antonín Hajn, see the sketch by his brother Alois in
"Dr. Antonín Hajn--šedesátníkem," in Alois Hajn, Život novinářuv,
1894-1930 (Prague, 1930), pp. 55-58. See also the commentaries
by Tobolka, Politické dějiny, vol. 3, pt. 2, pp. 48-49; and R.
Wolf, České studentstvo, pp. 76-77. Hajn's articles are collected
in his three-volume Výbor prací, an invaluable source on pre-war
Czech politics. Principal pre-war writings not there included

are Nebezpečí reakce ve školství (Prague, 1899), and "Státoprávní politika." While I was in Prague in 1967 and 1973, the Hajn papers in LANM were being arranged and were not available. Hašek's caricature of Hajn appears in his Kniha karikatury (Prague, 1964).

78. Antonín Hajn, Výbor prací, 1:391-429, reprints this series of articles. See also chap. 7 below.

79. The best source on Alois Hajn is his Život novinářuv. His articles on natural state rights appeared in Rozhledy, vol. 2, no. 5 (May 1893), and in Osvěta lidu, no. 507 (November 28, 1900).

80. Only Čížek was older by two years. Sokol was older by one month.

81. See the first article against capital punishment, "Trest smrti," Nové proudy, vol. 1, nos. 1 and 3, pp. 7-11 and 69-73. The Rašín papers, in PNP, are very fragmentary and small and contain little of political interest.

82. Rašín's principal scholarly works on economics are listed in the bibliography. His memoirs, incomplete at his death, Paměti Dra. Aloise Rašína, ed. Ladislav Rašín, 2d ed. (Prague, 1929), cover parts of his career during the pre-war era. On Rašín's life and political career the most complete work is Karel Hoch, Alois Rašín: Jeho život, dílo, a doba (Prague, 1934). Also useful is the memorial edition of eulogies and reminiscences, František Fousek, Josef Penízek, and Antonín Pimper, eds., Rašínuv památník (Prague, 1927).

83. Rašín would also long be remembered for having in 1918 flung back at the Bohemian German separatists the same tactless statement which General Windischgrätz made to the rebellious Czechs of Prague in June 1848: "We don't traffic with traitors."

84. Čížek's principal articles on politics and culture are collected in the memorial edition edited by the editorial board of Samostatnost and titled Výbor prací Antonína Čížka (Prague, 1897).

85. The authorities banned this translation of Tolstoy, among other works. Kronika presented a decidedly State Rights Radical and later State Rights Progressive viewpoint. For its summary of important political events as well as for editorial opinion it remains a valuable historical reference work. Sokol's Vězenská korespondence is among the best sources on the years in Bory prison and on the Progressive movement generally.

86. Prokop Grégr's relationship to the Národní listy is

discussed in the book, Národní listy, 1861-1941, p. 71. Prokop
Grégr, 1868-1926.

87. Klofáč (1868-1942) returned after 1896 to a successful
political career which is described in chaps. 9 and 10.

88. Škába, 1870-1933. On the North Bohemian National Union,
see chap. 4. After 1918, Škába published many articles and collections of essays on the Omladina affair and the Progressives
including Pamětní lístek K. St. Sokola (Prague, 1924), and
others listed in the bibliography. The story of how the Polish
song, "The Red Flag" ("Czerwony sztandar"), came to be translated
into Czech and adopted as the favorite song of the Omladina Progressives is told by Škába, "Pryč s tyrany" in Weigert and Ziegloser, Omladina 25 let, pp. 47-53. Škába suggested its adoption
and persuaded Běla Krapková to make the Czech translation. This
song, which began with the provocative words "Precz z tyranami,
precz z zrajcami" ("Down with tyrants, down with traitors"), became a favorite of Czech workers as well as of Progressive youth.

89. An important early policy statement of the Independent
party appears in Studentský sborník, vol. 1, no. 1, pp. 1-2.
Anti-Semitic views may be found typically in "O otázce židovské,"
vol. 1, nos. 3 and 4, pp. 41-43, and in the regularly featured
section "Hlidka antisemitická."

90. A. P. Veselý, Omladina, pp. 98-113. The fortnightly
journal Omladina appeared from October 1891 until its suppression
by the imperial authorities in October 1893. Successor publications of the same name continued in Most through 1894 and in
Ústi nad Labem beginning in November 1895. Another Progressive
workers' paper, Pokrokové listy, came out three times in 1893
and again for a short while in 1896.

91. Havránek's "Počátky a kořeny" and "Protirakouské hnutí
dělnické mládeže" emphasize this point.

92. A. P. Veselý, Omladina, p. 99.

93. František Modráček, "Anarchistický komunism v hnutí omla-
dinovém," in Weigert and Ziegloser, Omladina 25 let, p. 14. Myslík edited A. P. Veselý's unpublished correspondence and selections from his political writings in Antonín Pravoslav Veselý:
Životopis a literární pozůstalost spolu s výborem prací již otiš-
těnych (Prague, 1905).

94. See biographical sketch by J. Myslík in Veselý-Myslík,
Životopis a pozůstalost, pp. 5-77, and the poetic eulogy by
J. S. Machar, "Památce A. Pravoslava Veselého," ibid., pp. 1-2.
Another fine biographical study is by his brother Josef Veselý,

A. Pravoslav Veselý: Jeho životopis a ideály a ideály (Kladno, 1919), vol. 1. Vol. 2 (1920) contains the letters written by the brothers Veselý while imprisoned at Bory in 1894.

95. A. P. Veselý, Omladina, pp. 89-98, 143-48; and Masaryk, Naše nynější krise, pp. 4-5. On relations between workers and students, see also R. Fischer, Cesta mého života, 2:188-95. On the social background of Czech students, see above, chap. 5, and Freeze, "Young Progressives," pp. 38-39.

96. Antonín Sova, "Na okraj starší a novější sociální poezie," Literární rozhledy (1924), cited in Pozdrav bouřlivé noci (Prague, 1964), p. 59.

97. A. P. Veselý, Omladina, p. 92. The student wreath said, "From the students to a great fighter for truth." That from the workers read, "To a free thinker from the Czech Socialists."

98. Ibid., pp. 174-79. See also Národní listy, November 9, 1892, and June 2, 1893.

99. The most complete published sources are the thorough, carefully documented study, Havránek's Boj, and Slavík and Muk, Bojovník za právo, including a large selection from Slavík's correspondence.

100. Slavík and Muk, Bojovník za právo, no. 14, Eim to Slavík, August 11, 1892, p. 41, and discussion of Slavík's work in the party preceding its acceptance of the proposal for universal suffrage, pp. 14-15.

101. All Slavs except the Poles, who stood to lose ground to the Ukrainians. PNP, Engel papers, 6 s 83, notebook 7, executive committee meetings of February 18, 1893, where Engel led those in favor of Slavík's proposal, and of March 18, 1893. LANM, 6 T 90, parliamentary club minutes, III, no. 30, March 2, 1893. Adámek and Schwarz leading the minority opposed to universal suffrage and proposing to exclude illiterates, with Kaizl neutral and Engel and Slavík pressing for approval, no. 33, March 8, and no. 34, March 14, 1893. Final debates where approval given, no. 35, March 16, 1893.

102. See Ervín Špindler's speech at Lysá nad Labem, Národní listy, August 28, 1893, and Josef Herold's speech at Chrudim, Národní listy, July 17, 1893.

103. Rovnost, October 28, 1891.

104. The text of the Slavík bill appears in Havránek, Boj, app. 2, pp. 74-76 and is based on that published in Národní listy, March 18, 1893.

105. Kolmer, Parlament, 5:340-56; Plener, Erinnerungen, 3:86-90.

106. On the Belgian example, see the bibliography and discussion in Havránek, Boj, pp. 41-42.

107. Ibid., chap. 5. SÚA, PM, PŘ Prague, and SA Brno, PŘ Brno, contain voluminous police reports on demonstrations and party meetings throughout the spring and summer of 1893.

108. A. P. Veselý, Omladina, pp. 177-78, on the events of May 15, 1893. Governor Thun prohibited publication of news about the insult to the late Emperor Francis, but stories about the incident spread rapidly by word of mouth. Nepomuk's statue, as a symbol of clericalism and Habsburg oppression, was an ideal target. On May 15, see also Havránek, "Protirakouské hnutí dělnické mládeže," pp. 36-39.

109. Národní listy, May 17, 1893, afternoon edition, revised after confiscation, on "Bouřlivá schůze sněmovní," with both text and commentary on disturbances in the diet. See also Thun's thorough report, dated May 18, 1893, to Taaffe on the proceedings, Skedl and Weiss, Nachlass Taaffe, pp. 573-77. Other documents pertaining to stormy sessions in the diet and Thun's and Taaffe's decision to close it may be found on pp. 567-73 and 577-78.

110. The tearing down of street signs followed Governor Thun's decision of August 7, 1893, overruling the city council which had voted to replace the dual-language signs with signs only in Czech. The city fathers bore no direct responsibility for the demonstrations. See A. P. Veselý, Omladina, pp. 188-89.

111. Letter from Taaffe to Thun, September 1893, cited by Havránek, "Protirakouské hnutí dělnické mládeže," p. 74, and in which Franz Joseph's desire for a return to order is indicated.

112. On the events of August 17, 1893, see Národní listy, August 18 and 19, 1893; A. P. Veselý, Omladina, pp. 189-91; Josef Soukup, Omladináři, pp. 126-28; Havránek, "Protirakouské hnutí dělnické mládeže," pp. 66-74; and Freeze, "Young Progressives," pp. 225-28. All accounts stress the spontaneous nature of the demonstrations.

113. A. P. Veselý, Omladina, pp. 194-99, 213-20; Národní listy, September 10, 1893.

114. Proces s t. zv. Omladinou, p. 126; Národní listy, September 4, 1893.

115.   On the events of September 12, 1893, see Josef Soukup, Omladináři, pp. 129-31; A. P. Veselý, Omladina, pp. 221-29; Havránek, "Protirakouské hnutí dělnické mládeže," pp. 79-80; and Freeze, "Young Progressives," pp. 229-30.

116.   Václav Štěpánek, "12 září 1893 u Choděrů," in Weigert and Ziegloser, Omladina 25 let, pp. 68-77, describes events of the evening of September 12, with special reference to how he smashed the busts after none of the troublemakers in the restaurant made good on their threats to do the deed. Štěpánek proclaimed his innocence at the trial but was convicted for this act, among others.

117.   Národní listy, September 14, 1893, reprints the Czech text of Thun's proclamation dated September 12, 1893. Arbes, Thun, 2:240 and 257ff., documents all measures taken by Thun when he declared a state of emergency.

118.   Mrva's fabricated charges are in A. P. Veselý, Omladina, pp. 229-35.

119.   SPHA, vol. 11, no. 11, pp. 358-88ff. Histories of the Habsburg Monarchy in Western languages, including those by Arthur May, Robert Kann, and A. J. P. Taylor, do not take Slavík's bill or the extent of Socialist and Progressive agitation into consideration when discussing Taaffe's proposal for universal suffrage and therefore do not see the event in perspective. This is another example of their relying uncritically on biased Viennese sources. The extent to which Taaffe's bill was "watered down" is also not noted.

120.   See Reichsrat debates in SPHA, vol. 11, no. 11, pp. 356-65. Plener, Erinnerungen, 3:88-90.

121.   Národní listy, December 13, 1893.

122.   Josef Soukup, Omladináři, p. 27.

123.   The others arrested were Otakar Doležal, an eighteen-year-old machinist; František Dragoun, a seventeen-year-old factory worker; Josef Kříž, a twenty-eight-year-old glovemaker; Anna, his twenty-four-year-old wife; and Jindřich Vojtěch, a twenty-eight-year-old porter. See the proceedings of the trial with some commentary in Hajn and Čížek, Proces s t. zv. "Omladinou," passim, Antonín Hajn, Výbor prací, 1:342-69, a long article originally appearing in Rozhledy, vol. 3, and titled "List z nejnovější historie vnitřního našeho politického života," and Josef Soukup, Omladináři, pp. 143-51, give the most complete accounts of the Mrva affair, aside from A. P. Veselý, Omladina, pp. 261-68, 305-11. Kaizl's January 3, 1894, letter to Kramář describes the

consternation within the Young Czech party caused by this affair, Z mého života, 3:307-08.

124. Josef Soukup, Omladináři, pp. 19-20, 154; Hajn and Čížek, Proces s t. zv. "Omladinou," pp. 14-17, list the sentences
given to the defendants. For those persons cited above, they
were Ziegloser, eight years; Weigert, five years; Sokol, two and
one-half years; Rašín and Škába, two years each; Antonín Hajn and
Modráček, eighteen months each; and A. P. Veselý, seven months.

125. Josef Veselý, Z bojů za svobodu, pp. 16-17; Antonín
Hajn, Výbor prací, 1:342-75.

126. The complete censored text, "manifest poslanců o vými-
nečném stavu r. 1893," appears in Škarda, Program 1897, pp. 98-104.

127. PNP, Engel papers, 6 s 83, notebook 8, on minutes of the
Pardubice meeting and executive committee meetings, November 11,
1893 (no. 6), and January 8, 1894 (no. 12).

128. LANM, Pacák papers, Eim to Pacák, no. 12, January ?,
1894; no. 15, February ?, 1894, and no. 42, January 9, 1894.

129. Čas, vol. 8, no. 13 (March 30, 1894), pp. 204-
Čas, vol. 8, no. 14 (April 7, 1894), p. 211.

130. Masaryk's break with the Young Czech party had been pre-
cipitated by the Šromota affair, in which František Šromota, editor of the Old Czech Moravské orlice (Moravian Eagle), reported
in the July 5, 1893, issue how Governor Thun had in August 1891
intimidated Julius Grégr by threatening him with fines or imprisonment for publishing Národní listy articles critical of imperial foreign policy. Šromota gave as his source a letter from "a
certain prominent Czech politician." The Grégrs suspected Masaryk to have been that politician, but he denied taking part in
the affair. Three weeks later, the Grégrs believed their suspi-
cions confirmed when Čas published an article which scolded
Julius Grégr for having toadied to Governor Thun. Masaryk denied having written or approved publication of the article but
refused to identify the author. His association with Julius
Grégr, never cordial, came to an end; and many Young Czechs
questioned his ability to continue serving the party effectively.
Only in 1911, with the publication of the Kaizl papers, did it
transpire that Kaizl had written the offending article. Kaizl,
Z mého života, 3:252-58. LANM, Kramář papers contain newspaper
clippings pertinent to the affair. Masaryk's account is "Můj
poměr k Jul. Grégrovi," Čas, December 16, 1911, reprinted in
Jaromír Doležal, Masarykova cesta životem (Prague, 1921) 2:26-35.

Chapter 7

1. All information on Nymburk is drawn from F. Kulhánek and F. Mikolášek, Královské město Nymburk v přítomnosti a minulosti (Nymburk, 1911).

2. Nožička, Prokupek, pp. 77ff., 103-08.

3. After F. L. Rieger's death in 1903, the Nymburk District Board renamed the large central town square "Riegerovo náměsti" in his honor.

4. The Nymburk and Poděbrady districts in 1910 had according to Umgangssprache 82,466 inhabitants, of whom 81,299 were Czechs and 167 Germans, Statistisches Handbuch des Königreiches Böhmen (1913), pp. 19-21. In the Reichsrat, Nymburk was represented on the Prague Chamber of Commerce in the second curia, was with Kolín in the third, with Mladá Boleslav in the fourth, and after 1896 with Jičín in the fifth. In the diet, it went with the Prague Chamber of Commerce in the second, Mladá Boleslav in the third, and Benátky in the fourth.

5. Kaizl, Z mého života, 3:262-66. In his diary, Kaizl recorded debates of the executive committee on October 6, 1893, and of the trustees at Pardubice on October 8, 1893. For preliminary discussions see PNP, Engel papers, 6 R 80, debates of party executive committee, August 26, 1893.

6. Kaizl, Z mého života, 3:323-26, diary entry for July 14, 1894, reporting on the Prague meeting of that date. See also the report in Naše doba, vol. 1, no. 11 (August 1894):857-59, critical of the "Prague proposal."

7. On the initially unfavorable reaction of the moderates to these speeches see PNP, Engel papers, 6 s 83, notebook 3, fourteenth meeting of the party parliamentary commission, April 11, 1894, 3 pp., and K. Stanislav Sokol, Vězenská korespondence, pp. 68-70, letter of Josef Sokol to K. Stanislav Sokol dated April 13, 1894.

8. Correspondence among the leading architects of compromise during the spring and summer indicates that they lined up an overwhelming majority of party trustees to support their program at Nymburk. For example, PNP, Eim papers, 3a G 31, Engel to Eim, July 26 and August 26, 1894. LANM, Pacák papers, Adolf Stránský to Pacák, June 1, 1894.

9. PNP, Eim papers, 3a G 31, letters from Engel to Eim dated September 26, 1893, and March 24, 1894, on Julius Grégr.

10. PNP, Engel papers 6 s 83, notebook 7, twelfth session of the party executive committee, January 8, 1894. PNP, Eim papers, 3a G 31, Engel to Eim, January 19, 1894; Karel Adámek to Eim, January 2, 1894. PNP, Engel papers, 6 s 85-86, clipping "Rozhovor s G. Eimem," Moravská Orlice, vol. 32, no. 87, April 17, 1894. LANM, Young Czech parliamentary club minutes, twenty-sixth meeting, April 17, 1894, and thirty-first meeting, May 21, 1894. On April 8, 1894, at Sadská, Engel spoke publicly in support of the moderates' program of reaffirming anticlerical and civil libertarian views and continuing opposition to the Windischgratz government, Čas, vol. 8, no. 15 (April 14, 1894), p. 231.

11. Kaizl, Z mého života, 3:306-07, letter to Karel Kramář, December 26, 1893, pp. 320-21, diary entry, April 12, 1894, and pp. 324-25; Karel Kramář, Poznámky o české politice (Prague, 1906), pp. 11-12; Masaryk, Politická situace, pp. 29-33.

12. V. Škarda, "Politika etapová," pp. 544-49; idem, "O české politice: Řeč promluvená . . . 12. června 1904," in Výbor řečí, pp. 119-22.

13. Biographical data on the two Škardas from Michal Navrátil, ed., Almanach českých právníků, pp. 150-51; Michal Navrátil, Nový český sněm, pp. 330-32, and Masarykův slovník naučný, 7:42. The most interesting items from the correspondence of Václav Škarda are his forty-three letters to Bedřich Pacák in LANM, Pacák papers, from June 3, 1897, to August 13, 1901. Vladímir Škarda, 1863-1930.

14. Karel Kramář, "Za vedení Národní strany svobodomyslné," pp. 550-51, 559-64. Kramář misdates the Nymburk meeting or confuses it with the July 14 meeting of the clubs of delegates, typical of his carelessness with facts. The article is of value for his views of the events of 1894 after long reflection. Kaizl, Z mého života, 3:320-21, draft of a letter never sent to the executive committee, April 12, 1894. LANM, Pacák papers, Eim's letters to Pacák, nos. 12 and 13, January and April 1894.

15. Edvard Grégr, Otevřený list; PNP, Eim papers, 3a G 31, Edvard Grégr to Eim, January 25, 1894, argued that the time had come to turn problems raised by radical and progressive youth to the advantage of the party; and Engel's letter to Eim of January 28, 1894, in which Engel, speaking of Grégr's Otevřený list, stated that "the open letter to Dr. Rieger is tobacco which is a bit too strong but not at all bad."

16. Gustav Eim: "The Grégrs are a disaster for the Czech nation"--Eim's reaction to Edvard Grégr's speech of January 27, 1884, in Michal Navrátil, Gustav Eim: Geniální publicista a vynikající politik (Prague, 1923), p. 164.

17. Tobolka, Politické dějiny, vol. 3, pt. 2, p. 83.

18. Václav Škarda, Národní strana svobodomyslná, p. 11.

19. These fears were not groundless. K. Stanislav Sokol, Vězeňská korespondence, shows how well the Progressives imprisoned at Bory kept in touch with party politics through the exchange of correspondence between K. Stanislav Sokol and his father and friends. See especially pp. 98-100, secret letter from Antonín Čížek to K. Stanislav Sokol, September 9, 1894, reporting in detail on interparty alignments before the Nymburk meeting; pp. 104-10, secret letter from K. Stanislav Sokol to home and friends, dated September 17, 1894.

20. Čas, vol. 8, no. 16 (April 21, 1894):241-43.

21. Čas, vol. 8, no. 14 (April 7, 1894):211-12 on the debate between Kramář and Stránský, Kramář urging a firm policy against the radicals, Stránský holding to Engel's view that the party should restrain the radicals and go easy on the Národní listy, still the most influential national journal and nominal ally of the party. Čas, vol. 8, no. 12 (March 24, 1894):186-87, on Engel's position.

22. Radikální listy, vol. 1, no. 2 (March 10, 1894):3-4, articles on "The Nobility and the Young Czechs" and "From the Czech East," clippings from PNP, Engel papers, 6 s 85 and 6 s 86.

23. This is evident from correspondence between several of the leading conservative great landowners during 1894 and 1895. These letters may be found in the Lobkowicz papers in SA, Litoměřice and Žitenice, and in the Schwarzenberg and the Buquoy papers at SA, Třebon. One looks in vain in the published speeches and private correspondence of Plener and other German Liberal leaders to discover a comparable understanding of the policies and internal disputes of the Young Czech party. The imperial police in Prague and Vienna kept well-informed about party plans and problems. But their reports appear not to have been taken into account by German journalists and to have been largely forgotten in the memoirs of imperial statesmen.

24. On the September 28, 1897, meetings of the trustees seen in context, see Srb, Politické dějiny, 2:288. On the eighth party congress, see V. Škarda, Program 1912.

25. All translations and commentary are from the complete text of the Nymburk Resolution, which is to be found in Václav Škarda, Národní strana svobodomyslná, pp. 104-10. Text compared with that in Národní listy, July 15, 1894, and that in Srb, Politické dějiny, 1:907-10.

26. For the sources of all quotations and information just given, see n. 25 above.

27. The resolution of the sixth party congress and subsequent discussion may be found in Srb, Politické dějiny, 2:130-31.

28. LANM, Julius Grégr papers, letter of Edvard Grégr to J. Grégr, dated October 31, 1889, and letter from Gustav Eim, a friendly critic of the radicals, to Julius Grégr dated April 4, 1885. Tůma, J. Grégr, frequently makes this point.

29. Čas, vol. 8, no. 39 (September 29, 1894):609-10, 618. Naše doba, vol. 2, no. 1 (October 1894):54-55. PNP, Engel papers, 6 S 84, Plzeňský obzor (February 7, 1894), "Interview s Antonínem Hajnem."

30. LANM, 6 T 90, minutes, Young Czech club of delegates, vol. 4, no. 1, October 10, 1893: the club followed the September Pardubice instructions of the trustees in a course of "fundamental opposition." Good statements of the party's case for opposition are Gustav Eim's Proti koalici: Řeč proslovená v poslanecké sněmovně říšské rady při rozpravě o zatímním rozpočtu 15. března 1894 (Prague, 1894), and his Proč bojujeme proti vládě? Řeč poslance Gustava Eima pronesená v poslanecké sněmovně v rozpravě o zatímném rozpočtu dne 27. března 1895 (Pilsen, 1895).

31. Charmatz, Österreichs innere Geschichte, 2:116-28, gives a concise and witty but opinionated account. The issues and problems facing the Windischgrätz government are dealt with only very cursorily by the principal single-volume histories of the Dual Monarchy. Nothing appears to warrant a full-scale study of this rather ineffectual government or of its Minister-President. Kolmer, Parlament, 8 vols., gives a digest of the more important events in parliamentary politics. For Czech politics, see Srb, Politické dějiny, 1:892-929, and Josef Penízek, Česká aktivita v letech 1878-1918 (Prague, 1931), 2:245-76.

32. Other cabinet members were Marquis Olivier de Becquehem, Minister of the Interior; Count Julius Falkenhayn, Minister of Agriculture; Dr. Stanisław Madeyski, Minister of Worship and Public Instruction; Count Zeno Welserheimb, Minister of Defense; and Dr. Apollinaire Jaworski, Minister without Portfolio for Galician Affairs.

33. Charmatz, Österreichs innere Geschichte, 2:116.

34. F. L. Rieger gave the speech in the Bohemian Diet on that date which announced an end to all attempts to implement the Agreement of 1890. Řeč poslance Fr. L. Riegra na sněmu království českého v rozpočtové debatě dne 13. unora 1894 (Prague, 1894).

35. LANM, 6 T 90, minutes, Young Czech club of delegates, vol. 4, nos. 8 and 9, November 23 and 24, 1893, reporting on successful negotiations with delegate Klaič of the Southern Slavic club and delegate Romančuk of the Ruthenian (Ukrainian) club.

36. PNP, Eim papers, 3a G 31, letter of Kramář to Eim, dated November 17, 1893. The same statement is quoted without any footnote reference by Tobolka, Politické dějiny, vol. 3, pt. 1, p. 68.

37. LANM, 6 T 90, minutes, Young Czech club of delegates, vol. 5, no. 31, March 19, 1895; no. 33, March 22, 1895; and nos. 45 and 46, May 9 and 13, 1895. See also Kaizl, Z mého života, 3:353-55, diary entries from May 21 through May 31, 1895.

38. On the proposal in the Bohemian Diet, see Čas (January 19, 1895):43, and Národní listy, January 12 and 13, 1895. On the proposal in the Moravian Diet, see Lidové noviny, February 1 and 2, 1895. At a January 9, 1895, meeting of Czech delegates to the Moravian Diet, the vote went thirteen to six against Stránský's proposal to propose universal suffrage to the diet instead of merely reducing tax qualifications, enlarging the rural fourth curia, and making several other minor adjustments. See the report of this meeting in Čas (January 12, 1895):28. On events in both diets, see the general summary of events in Srb, Politické dějiny, 1:919-23.

39. Bedřich Pacák, ed., Boj za immunitu poslaneckých řečí vůbec a českých řečí zvláště (Prague, 1896), gives the most complete account of this Young Czech campaign and contains many contemporary sources, including pertinent laws and Reichsrat debates. Pacák published all speeches and decrees cited in the paragraph below.

40. SPHA, XI, 14, 518-20, May 23, 1894, speech by Josef Herold.

41. SPHA, XI, 15, 923-34, November 28, 1894, and XI, 16, 311-17, December 12, 1894, and Pacák, Boj za immunitu, pp. 183ff., 222-24.

42. Gustav Eim, "Řeč v poslanecké sněmovně o změně zákonův o časopisectvu 28. května 1894," in his Politické úvahy, pp. 440-62. This effort is discussed in detail in chap. 2 above. See also the commentary in Čas (June 2, 1894);8, favorable to the bill.

43. This came at Kramář's initiative, LANM, 6 T 90, minutes, Young Czech club of delegates, vol. 5, no. 6, November 6, 1894. Kramář's speech of November 12, 1894, is in SPHA, XI, 15, 514.

44. LANM, Engel papers, 6 s 82, folder containing correspondence between American and Czech-American newspapers and the Young Czech party. For example, see the letter of Jan Rosický, chairman of the Bohemian National Committee, to Engel, October 18, 1893. On general relations with the Czech-American press, see Tomáš Čapek, Naše Amerika (Prague, 1926), pp. 251-361.

45. Notable is the article by Gustav Eim, "Le peuple tchèque et la question tchèque," La Nation Tchèque 1 (1895):22-45.

46. See chap. 4 above on the Sokol movement.

47. The events in the diet during January and early February are summarized and critically evaluated in Čas (1895), January 5, pp. 9-10; January 12, pp. 27-28; January 19, pp. 43-44; January 26, pp. 57-58; and February 2, p. 73. Two editorials criticized Young Czech shortcomings in the diet, one contending that the party behaved "like a ram" (February 2, pp. 65-66) and the other evaluating the work of the diet after its last day in session (Febraury 16, pp. 97-99, "Poslední dni sněmovní"). The quotation of Thun is from Arbes, Thun, 2:176.

48. The decrees and commentary and excerpts from Czech protests are published in Arbes, Thun, 1:212-56, the decree texts on pp. 218-22.

49. Stašek, Vzpomínky, p. 527.

50. Srb, Politické dějiny, 1:924-25. Any "urgent proposal" requested that the standing order of business be set aside to deal with "urgent" matters at hand.

51. Kaizl, Z mého života, 3:352-74.

52. Sutter, Sprachenverordnungen, 1:264ff., correctly notes Czech efforts in leading the obstruction but does not offer a good case for German obstruction having derived primarily from the Czech example.

53. Volkszählung 1890 (Vienna, 1890). Celje itself had 4,000 inhabitants according to this census.

54. On railway acquisitions, see laws and discussion in Hermann Strach, ed., Geschichte der Eisenbahnen der oesterrichisch-ungarischen Monarchie, vol. 1, pt. 2 (Vienna, Děčín, and Leipzig, 1898), pp. 394, 407-09, 497-99.

55. Kolmer, Parlament, 5:513ff., reprints or summarizes the principal debates. Sutter, Sprachenverordnungen, 1:112-27, discusses the Celje dispute uncritically and using only German

sources. On the continuing importance of Celje during the later
nineties from a Czech Catholic perspective, see Karel Vondruška,
ed., "Celje a jiné příjemnosti," in Alétheia 3 (1899):189-93.

56. Plener, Erinnerungen, 3:288.

57. On Czech views and expectations after Kielmansegg's resignation and before Badeni's appointment, see Čas, vol. 9,
no. 38 (September 21, 1895):593-94. On the events and problems
during the late summer of 1895, see Peniżek, Česká aktivita,
2:260-66, and Tobolka, Politické dějiny, vol. 3, pt. 2, pp. 74-78.

58. V. Škarda, Program 1897, pp. 14-15. These views are more
thoroughly reviewed in PNP, Eim papers, letters from Engel to Eim
dated July 29, October 4, and October 14, 1895.

59. The three works by T. G. Masaryk are Česká otázka, the
collected essays comprising Naše nynější krise, and "K šestému
červenci: Naše obrození a naše reformace," Naše doba, vol. 2,
nos. 11 and 12 (September 20 and September 27, 1895):961-73,
1056-71, republished as Jan Hus with the same subtitle and minor
revisions (Prague, 1896).

60. I am indebted to Roland J. Hoffman of the University of
Tübingen for suggesting in 1967 that T. G. Masaryk might be considered the ideologist of the Czech question. Mr. Hoffmann is
now completing a doctoral dissertation on that subject.

61. Masaryk, "K šestému červenci," pp. 1062-63.

62. On Masaryk's intellectual development, see the brilliant
essay by Jaroslav Werstadt, Od "České otázky" k "Nové Evropě:"
Linie politického vývoje Masarykova (Prague, 1920).

63. Masaryk, Česká otázka, pp. 213-14. All notes refer to
the first edition of 1895.

64. Three chapters were revisions of previously published
articles, "On the Tasks of Czech Students," "The Development of
the Progressive Movement," and "The First Progressive Literary
Journal." in the fourth chapter, titled "Reformation or Revolution," Masaryk attacked Antonín Hajn for having endorsed radicalism and denigrated the "ideal of humanity." The first, originally "O úkolech českého studentstva," appeared in Časopis českého
studentstva 1 (June 2, 1889). The second came from Čas, vol. 4,
no. 15 (April 15, 1893). And the last was translated from an
article in Zeit (Vienna, November 17 and December 1, 1894). Kaizl
and other critics of "Our Present Crisis" accurately pointed out
its having been hastily assembled from three disparate articles
and a polemical attack on the Young Czech party.

65. In his fifty-nine-page introduction to the four essays on the Progressive movement, in his Naše Nynější krise, pp. vi-lxiv, and in his Politická situace, pp. 35-40.

66. Masaryk and the Škardas agreed; see V. Škarda, "Politika etapová," and Masaryk, Desorganisace mladočeské strany, pp. 9-30.

67. Although the task of critically responding to Masaryk's ideology of the Czech question fell largely to Josef Kaizl, two other Young Czechs, Ladislav Dvořák and Karel Kramář, published essays on Bohemian state rights designed to give the imperial government better historical grounds for accepting them. These works were Ladislav Dvořák's Podstata a význam českého státního práva (Prague, 1897) and Karel Kramář's České státní právo (Prague, 1896), the latter a Czech translation of the German original which appeared in Zeit in 1895. Kramář's competent but undistinguished essay offered two new historical interpretations. The first and most superficial contended that the centralization begun in 1749 by Maria Theresa rather than the Renewed Land Ordinance of 1627 constituted the greatest deviation from the still valid principles of Bohemian state rights. The second claimed that the Habsburgs, while ruling Bohemia without regard for its diet, had maintained in theory if not in fact the sovereignty of the Bohemian crown. This interpretation challenged but did not replace the traditional view that state rights had been preserved by the diet. Kramář argued in effect that the revival of Czech autonomy might justifiably occur under imperial auspices rather than through the diet. Except for catering to unrealistic hopes that the Habsburgs might restore Czech autonomy, Kramář's treatise, originally written for a German audience, contributed little of importance to contemporary Czech political debate.

68. The circumstances of the Šromota affair are described in chap. 6 above. It also indicates that the dispute between Professors Kaizl and Masaryk was based on political opinion and principles, not on any personal quarrel. Privately Kaizl suspected that Masaryk's criticism of the Young Czechs was motivated by personal reasons, but publicly he did not express this view.

69. Kaizl, České myšlénky, pp. 20-26, 33-35, 72.

70. Ibid., pp. 47-74.

71. Masaryk, Česká otázka, pp. 96-105; idem, Naše nynější krise, pp. vii-xv.

72. Kaizl, České myšlénky, pp. 77-101, 109-10.

73. Masaryk, Naše nynější krise, pp. xxiv-xxvi.

74. Kaizl, České myšlénky, p. 139.

75. Ibid., pp. 129-35, 145-46.

76. Masaryk, Česká otázka, pp. 232-33; idem, Naše nynější krise, pp. lix-lx.

77. Kaizl, České myšlénky, pp. 142-48, 156-57.

78. See the general discussion of the Masaryk and Kaizl debate in Zdeněk Šolle and Alena Gajanová, Po stopě dějin: Češi a Slováci v letech 1848-1938 (Prague, 1969), pp. 128-38.

79. Josef Pelcl, "Ke kritice Naší nynější krise," Rozhledy, vol. 5, nos. 1 and 2 (1895/96):10-15, 95-100.

80. Jan Herben, Masarykova sekta a Gollova škola (Prague, 1912); and Jan Slavík, Pekař contra Masaryk: Ke sporu o smysl českých dějin (Prague, 1929). On Masaryk's criticism of Goll, Rezek, and Kalousek in 1895, see his candid letter to Jindřich Vančura, Setpember 26, 1895, in ÚDKSČ, Masaryk archive.

81. Otakar Odložilík, "Modern Czech Historiography," SEER 30 (1951/52):376-92; and S. Harrison Thomson, "T. G. Masaryk and Czech Historiography," JCEA, vol. 10, no. 1 (1950):37-52, positively evaluate Masaryk's contribution to Czechoslovak historical literature up to 1950.

82. Secret letter No. 18, April 1894, pp. 49-57, in vol. 2 of Josef Veselý, ed., A. Pravoslav Veselý: Jeho život, zápasy a ideály, 2 vols. (Kladno, 1919-20). Passage quoted appears on p. 55.

83. From "The Czech Modernist Manifesto," (Česká moderná) in Rozhledy, vol. 5, no. 1 (1895/96), pp. 1-4, quotations from p. 3. The twelve who signed were Otakar Březina, Václav Choc, Dr. K. Koerner, F. V. Krejči, J. S. Machar, J. V. Mrštík, Josef Pelcl, F. X. Šalda, J. K. Slejhar, Antonín Sova, František Soukup, and Dr. Jan Třebický. Their relation to the Progressive movement is discussed in chap. 6, n. 53. On the relation of literature to politics in the Manifesto see above, chap. 6.

84. Boží bojovníci (Prague, 1896); I have read the third edition (1911) with a revised preface, as well as the first installments in Rozhledy 5 (1895/96).

85. In style and opinions, Č. Folklor was modeled upon Dr. Čenek Zíbrt, a pioneer scholar in Czech folklore. Generally Folklor's criticism of the "Vinohrady Manuscript" resembled the lavish praise once bestowed by many Czech critics on the bogus

Green Mountain and Queen's Court manuscripts. Sybilla was the
soothsayer of Czech legend and advisor to Queen Libuše. "Neplaval," which in Czech means "he didn't swim," corresponds roughly
to the German "Badenicht," which in turn resembles "Badeni."

86. "Bratr Anděl . . . muž, feldvébl-manipulant táboru," Boží
bojovníci, p. 34.

87. Ibid., pp. 6-12.

88. Building on this theme in Česká otázka were Masaryk's later works: Palackého idea národa českého (Prague, 1912); Karel
Havlíček: Snahy a tužby politického probuzení, 2d ed. (Prague,
1904); V čem je význam Karla Havlíčka? (Prague, 1906); Právo pri-
rozené a historické (Prague, 1900).

89. On Dyk, see František Červinka, Český nacionalismus v XIX
století, pp. 207-08, 222-23. See below, chaps. 9 and 10 on Dyk's
novels and work in politics.

90. On this development to the end of the war, see Werstadt,
Od "Ceské otázky" k "Nové Evropě," and Josef Král, Masaryk: Filo-
sof humanity a demokracie (Prague, 1947), pp. 7-32. Roland Hoffmann of the Univeristy of Tübingen has prepared a dissertation
on Masaryk as the ideologist of the Czech question.

91. T. G. Masaryk, Otázka sociální: Základy marxismu sociologické a filosofické (Prague, 1898). A recently published English translation and abridgement of this work is Erazim Kohák,
ed. and trans., Masaryk on Marx (Lewisburg, Pa., 1972).

92. T. G. Masaryk, Ideály humanitní: Několik kapitol (Prague,
1934); and T. G. Masaryk, Jak pracovat? (Prague, 1926). Both
available in English translation, T. G. Masaryk, The Ideals of
Humanity and How to Work, trans. W. Preston Warren, Marie J. Kohn-
Holoček, and H. E. Kennedy (London, 1938).

93. See the article by W. M. Kozłowski, "Český humanitism a
polský mesianism," in Masarykův sborník 6 (Prague, 1930/31):297-
350.

94. These events will be discussed in subsequent chapters.

Chapter 8

1. On May 15, 1895, the emperor had appointed another Pole,
Count Agenor Gołuchowski, Jr., as Austro-Hungarian foreign minister to replace Count Gustav Kálnoky. Agenor Gołuchowski, Sr.,
had as Austrian State Minister been responsible for issuing the
October Diploma of 1860.

2. Documentary surveys with commentary on the Badeni government include Kolmer, Parlament, 6:1-340, and Srb, Politické dějiny, 2:1-328.

3. One of the best sources on Badeni's ministry are the memoirs and selected papers of his finance minister, Leon Biliński, Wspomnienia i dokumenty, 1846-1919 (Warsaw, 1924), pp. 86-123. See also Tobolka, Politické dějiny, vol. 3, pt. 2, pp. 87-180. On autonomous Galicia and Badeni's service there, see Piotr Wandycz, The Lands of Partitioned Poland, 1795-1918 (Seattle, 1974), pp. 220-28. On the Poles of Galicia and on Badeni's rule as Minister-President see ibid., pp. 277-81. On the Czechs and Badeni in the perspective of Czech and Polish relations generally, see Václav Žáček, ed., Češi a Poláci v minulosti, 2:334-57, "Marné pokusy o politickou spolupráci."

4. Examples are Redlich, Franz Joseph, pp. 389-92; Hantsch, Die Geschichte Österreichs, vol. 2, and Gestalter; Richard Charmatz, Deutsch-österreichische Politik, pp. 81-84; Erich Zöllner, Geschichte Österreichs; and Viktor Bibl, Der Zerfall Österreichs, vol. 2: Von Revolution zu Revolution (Vienna, 1924), pp. 380-83.

5. On Kathrein's opinions, see Paul Molisch, ed., Briefe zur deutschen Politik in Österreich von 1848 bis 1918 (Vienna, 1934), pp. 342-44ff. For Young Czech views, see Penížek, Česká aktivita, 2:268-76, and Gustav Eim, "Z řečí promluvené na schůzi voličské ve Skutzi dne 19. dubna 1896," in his Politické úvahy, pp. 543-53. Národní listy maintained a very critical stance toward Badeni till April 1897.

6. SA Klášterec nad Ohří, letters from Oswald Thun-Salm to Badeni, 1896-97.

7. Halban was also a literary critic of note and wrote a number of works in German on contemporary Polish arts and letters.

8. Penížek, Z mých pamětí, 3:84-86.

9. On Gautsch, Koerber, Beck, Bienerth, and Stürgkh, see below, chap. 10.

10. Bráf, Život a dílo, vol. 1: Paměti, pp. 61-70. P. 62, Bráf reported that Badeni, when introduced to a German parliamentary delegate from the important north Bohemian town of Varnsdorf (Warnsdorf), had to ask where it was.

11. Kaizl's Reichsrat speech of October 28, 1895 (Czech text in Kaizl, Z mého života, 3:438-48) thus discussed Badeni's proposed reforms. For a more critical response, see also Národní listy, October 23 and 24, 1895, and Čas, October 26, 1895, pp.

673-74, and November 2, 1895, pp. 689-90. Kaizl, Z mého života, 3:438, has diary entries for October 22 and 23, 1895, on the need for an electoral victory before the party could deal with Badeni to advantage.

12. Many of the exhibits at the Ethnographic Exhibition came to constitute the nucleus of the fine collections of Prague's present Ethnographic Museum; 2,065,285 persons attended. On the exhibition, see the article "Řada volných úvah a kritických poznámek," by Jan Herben in Čas, October 26, 1895, pp. 677-78; December 21, 1895, pp. 808-09; and December 28, 1895, pp. 829-32; Jan Jakubec, "Národopisná výstava českoslovanská," Naše doba 2 (1894/95):813-21, 914-17, 999-1017, and 1110-15, and 3 (1895/96): 45-54, 212-19, 326-34, 415-22, 512-27, and 590-603; and Antonín Čížek, "Po národopisné výstavě," Radikální listy, vol. 2, no. 30 (1895), reprinted in Čížek, Výbor prací, pp. 135-37. On the Society for National Economy, see the article by Jan Kolouše, "Národohospodářský sjezd a česká národohospodářská společnost," Naše doba 3 (1895/96):816-21 and 885-91; his article in Čas, October 19, 1895, pp. 657-58; and Národní listy, October 14 and 15, 1895.

13. PNP, Eim papers, Engel to Eim, February 3, 1895, on predicting that Old Czechs could carry no more than ten seats and the Agrarians and Progressives no more than two each. Also Engel to Eim, May 13, 1895, after Engel's trip to South Bohemia.

14. Electoral proclamation adopted by the sixth Young Czech party congress, September 29, 1895, published in Národní listy, November 7, 1895, "Provolání k volbám do sněmu království českého roku 1895 schválené na VI. valném sjezdu strany dne 29. září 1895." See V. Škarda, Program 1897, pp. 111-24. A critical report on the congress, "Politics without politics," appears in Čas, October 5, 1895, pp. 625-30. For a summary of both critical and favorable reaction to the congress in regional newspapers, see Čas, October 12, 1895, pp. 642-45, "Krajinské listy o sjezdu mladočeské strany." Also critical was an editorial by Antonín Čížek, speaking for Progressives in the Radikální listy, vol. 2, no. 26 (1895), "Ke sjezdu národní strany svobodomyslné," reprinted in Čížek, Výbor prací, pp. 131-34.

15. SA Brno, Alois Pražak papers, G 60, letters from F. L. Rieger to Pražák, April 13, 1895, on Rieger's electoral proposal, and September 18, 1895, giving growing success of Hungarians and growing Imperial German influence in Vienna as further grounds for Old Czech passivity.

16. Karel Mattuš, Paměti (Prague, 1921), p. 158, on the Old Czech congress.

17. M. Vondrovic in Domažlice and Nová Kdyně ran a close race and forced the Young Czech victor, Antonín Černý, into a run-off with Old Czech Antonín Steidl. Jan Erhart ran third in Budějovice and vicinity. Čas in an editorial of November 9, 1895, "Před sněmovními volbami," strongly criticized the Young Czech party for adhering to Old Czech ways and for refusing to broaden its base, especially decrying its refusal to grant several mandates to Social Democratic representatives in the absence of universal manhood suffrage.

18. Navrátil, Almanach sněmu 1895-1901, gives the complete electoral returns on pp. 59-106, including electoral programs of the various parties and candidates. See also the complete returns in "Statistik der böhmischen Landtagswahlen im Herbst 1895," pp. xxxvii-lxix and 1-49, the latter pages including tables and an index, in Mittheilungen des Statistischen Landesamtes des Königreiches Böhmen, vol. 1, pt. 1 (Prague, 1899).

19. On the agrarian crisis, see K. Harmach, Obecní hospodářství, jeho vady a reforma (Prague, 1908), Čeněk Hevera, Obrana celní na ochranu českého rolnictví a průmyslu (Kolín, 1885), and Cyrill Horáček, Příspěvek k otázce agrární (Prague, 1894).

20. Frankenberger and Kubíček, Švehla, p. 62, give the complete text and commentary.

21. See table 17 in the appendix. The total decreased again to eighty-nine in October 1896 when the party expelled Jan Vašatý, who held the fourth-curial mandate from Sušice and Horažd'ovice. For the circumstances, see below, this chapter. The Young Czechs took great pride in their electoral victory. Karel Kramář, among others, declared that the party was no longer a mere political party but one truly representing the whole Czech nation. See Národní listy, November 24, 1895.

22. Other totals for German parties were: German Nationalists, eleven seats; German Christian Socialists, two; and German anti-Semites, one. This gave the Germans a total of sixty-eight seats. The conservative great landowners won seventy seats. The ex-officio representatives totalled six.

23. Karl Dědic, prominent Social Democratic senator during the First Czechoslovak Republic, and Josef Steiner, a leading Czech Social Democrat until his death in 1912.

24. In a close race from the third curia of Kolín, Sadská, Kouřím, and Poděbrady. The vote was 473 for Baxa to 442 for Young Czech J. V. Kalaš. Kolín made the difference. Baxa carried it 256 to 90.

25. Navrátil, Almanach sněmu 1895, p. 90. T. G. Masaryk, who was not a candidate, won 8 of 713 votes in the district including Slaný, Louny, Rakovník, and Velvary. On the dispute between Progressives concerning their relationship to the Young Czech party in November and December, 1895, see Antonín Hajn, Výbor prací, p. 441; A. P. Veselý, Omladina, pp. 386-89; and Rozhledy 5 (1895/96):261-62, the latter on the meeting of December 21, 1895, in Prague.

26. In the first election Šťastný won 117 votes to Lang's 116 out of 237 cast. In the second round the results were 120 and 109 out of 232.

27. PNP, Engel papers, 6 R 80, folder "Agrární sdružení," letter of October 27, 1896, and press clippings. Also PNP, Eim papers, Engel to Eim, February 3, October 14, and December 29, 1895.

28. Engel represented the urban third curia of Benešov, a city dependent on agriculture for its prosperity.

29. PNP, Engel papers, 6 R 80, folder "Agrární sdružení," Central Bohemian Peasant League to Engel, October 27, 1896.

30. Frankenberger and Kubíček, Švehla, pp. 63-68, and Chundela, Stanislav Kubr, pp. 74-76. Emanuel Engel represented the Young Czech party at the meeting. The Association held its first congress on December 27, 1897, at which it adopted a program of ten points for the political and economic advancement of Czech agriculturalists.

31. On full electoral results, see below and table 19 in the appendix.

32. Figures from Čas, vol. 10, no. 45 (November 7, 1896): 705-08, and Richard Fischer, Pokroková Morava, 1:48-49. The Germans controlled all seats elected by the Moravian chambers of commerce. The congress of the People's party in Moravia which convened in Brno on July 12, 1896, not only sanctioned the electoral agreement with the National party, but also approved an organizational statute for the party based on that of the Young Czech party. The party trustees had met on June 27, 1896, to prepare the congress agenda. For a critical review of the agreement and statute, see Čas, vol. 10, no. 28 (July 11, 1896):433-34, and no. 29 (July 18, 1896):458-59.

33. The development of Catholic parties in the Czech lands, of greater importance after 1900, is discussed in chap. 10 below.

34. Count Karl Coudenhove (1855-1913) remained governor until

1911, when he was succeeded by Francis Thun. Thun gave way in 1915 to Max Coudenhove, who presided over the surrender of imperial authority to the Czechoslovak National Council in October 1918.

35. Bráf, Život a dílo, vol. 1: Paměti, pp. 61-69, on the relationship between Badeni and Thun.

36. PNP, Eim papers, 3a G 31, letter from Josef Herold, January 9, 1896.

37. Národní listy, December 7, 1895. PNP, Eim papers, 3a G 31, E. Grégr to Eim, January 16, 1896.

38. PNP, Eim papers, letters from Engel to Eim, dated October 14 and December 29, 1895, and Tobolka, Politické dějiny, vol. 3, pt. 2, pp. 90-91.

39. LANM, 6 T 90, parliamentary club minutes, ses. 6, nos. 18, 24, and 25, March 3, 24, and 26, 1896.

40. Národní listy, February 22 and 23, 1896; Čas, vol. 10, no. 8 (February 22, 1896):113, 124-25; Slavík-Muk, Bojovník za právo, no. 27, p. 45, Jan Slavík to his wife, October 22, 1895.

41. Národní listy, October 4 and 5, 1895. Kaizl spoke to the meeting of the Board of Trustees of the Young Czech party in Prague on September 29, 1895, stating his fears that the Young Czech party was falling too much into Old Czech ways. See Kaizl, Z mého života, 3:433-35, diary entry on the meeting and the text of Kaizl's speech. Engel's account of this meeting is the manuscript "Sjezd důverníku . . . v Praze, 29 září 1895," PNP, Engel papers 6 S 82, envelope marked "První demise Badeního a následky."

42. Kaizl opened the attack on February 11. The attack is described and praised in Národní listy, February 12 and 13, 1896, and is critically reviewed in Naše doba, vol. 3, no. 5 (February 20, 1896):441-44. The text of Kaizl's opening speech is in Kaizl, Z mého života, 3:488-97.

43. This view is well expressed in Josef Herold, O státoprávní adrese (Prague, 1896), pp. 38-42ff.; in Kaizl's and Pacák's speeches to the diet on December 13, 1895, Řeči poslanců dr. B. Pacáka a dr. J. Kaizla z prosince roku 1895 (Prague, 1896); and in Karel Kramář's Reichsrat speech of December 10, 1895 (SPHA, XI, session 21, 961, 966) and diet speech of February 11, 1896. A more extreme speech with antidynastic overtones was Edvard Grégr's on February 11, 1896; Národní listy, February 12, 1896.

44. Česká politika, 3:578-80, and Srb, Politické dějiny, 2:81-86, print the text with commentary. See also table 18 in the appendix.

45. Srb, Politické dějiny, 2:86-103. Note especially Brzorád's speech of February 20, 1896. See Národní listy, February 21, 1896.

46. LANM, 6 T 90, parliamentary club minutes, ses. 6, no. 25,
March 26, 1896, and no. 29, April 20, 1896. See also Kaizl, Z
mého života, 3:500-02, diary entries for March 20 and 27, 1896.
This debate had begun with Badeni's presenting the voting reform
to the Reichsrat on February 20, 1896. Národní listy, February 22, 1896, had conditionally endorsed the proposal after
choosing to regard it as a first step toward the much more desirable universal manhood suffrage. In other words, if one could
not obtain the latter, passage of Badeni's proposal would be better than nothing at all. Later editorials, notably those of
March 28 and 31 and April 1, 1896, took much the same position,
alternately pointing out the incomplete and illogical form of
Badeni's proposed reform on the one hand while contending on the
other that partial reform would be better than no reform at all.
The delegates of the People's party in Moravia, led by Stránský,
had taken a more principled stand in favor of universal manhood
suffrage, even to the extent of threatening to vote against Badeni's proposal in any event. This view Stránský presented in
his speech at Přerov on March 29, 1896, which is reported extensively in Lidové noviny, March 30, 1896. But Stránský and the
Moravians soon agreed to abide by Young Czech policy on this
question.

47. Debates on this issue are summarized, with extensive quotations, by Kolmer, Parlament, 6:161-74, and Srb, Politické dějiny, 2:104-10. See also Čas, April 25, 1896, pp. 263-64. On
April 24, 1896, with only 235 of 350 delegates present, the
lower house rejected Slavík's proposal by a vote of 171 to 61.

48. Čas, vol. 10, no. 20 (May 16, 1896):305-07. On electoral
reform, the best case for the majority Young Czech policy will
be found in Gustav Eim's speech of April 18, 1896, in Chotěboř,
"Z řeči proslovené na schůzi voličské v Chotěboři," and speech
of April 19, 1896, in Hlinska, "Řeč před voliči v Hlinsku," especially the latter. See Eim, Politické úvahy, pp. 519-33 and
534-42 respectively. On general parliamentary problems in
April, see his speech to the voters in Skuteč on April 19, 1896,
ibid., pp. 543-53. The latter speech is especially critical of
the Moravian Old Czechs for opposing voting reform.

49. R. Fischer, Pokroková Morava, 1:48, and Lidové noviny,
October 4 and 5, 1896.

50. LANM, Julius Grégr papers; letters of sympathy sent to
Prokop Grégr upon the death of his father came from almost all
prominent Czech figures, including, for example, Alois Jirásek.

October 5, 1896. See also the memorial edition of the Národní listy, October 5, 1896, and the sympathetic but critical evaluations of Grégr's contribution to Czech politics by Jan Herben in Čas, October 10, 1896, pp. 642-45; by Rozhledy, vol. 6, no. 2 (1895/96):49-52; and by Naše doba, vol. 4, no. 1 (October 10, 1896):58-59. On the mood of unity in the party, see Čas, October, 1896, pp. 679-81, comparing the situation to that obtaining after Palacký's death twenty years before.

51. Rieger-Heidler, Príspěvky, vol. 2, no. 1196, p. 529, letter from F. L. Rieger to V. Červinka, October 6, 1896.

52. Karel Tůma, "Padesát let boje a práce," in Josef Anýž et al., Půl století Národních listů, pp. 28-34; Jaroslav Preiss et al., Osmdesát let Národních listů, pp. 69-76.

53. Kaizl, Z mého života, 3:545, 552, diary entries for October 28 and November 27, 1896, and for the January 19, 1897, negotiations. Josef Herold's November 28 speech in Chrudim as reported by Čas, vol. 10, no. 50 (December 12, 1896):793-94. SA Brno, Alois Pražák papers, Bedřich Prince Schwarzenberg to Pražák, April 18 and July 21, 1896, on Bohemian nobility's seeking understanding with Czechs and Germans.

54. The first phrase is Herold's from his speech of April 12, 1896, in Liben; the second and third phrases come from Eim's speech in Litoměřice on September 16, 1896. On the former see the text in six columns in the Národní listy, April 17, 1896; on the latter see the text in Eim, Politické úvahy, pp. 499-518, and critical commentary in Národní listy, September 17, 1896, and Čas, September 26, 1896, pp. 615-16.
On Vašatý's expulsion, see LANM, 6 T 90, parliamentary club minutes, vol. 7, no. 8, October 28, 1896; Srb, Politické dějiny, 2:148-49; and Čas, October 31, 1896, p. 689.
On the communal elections of October 1896 in Bohemia, see Čas, October 31, 1896, p. 689. On the diet elections of October 26, 1896, in Moravia, see Rozhledy, vol. 6, no. 2 (October 15, 1896): 85-88, on the eve of the elections, and no. 3 (November 15, 1896): 188-89 for commentary on electoral returns highly critical of People's party policies. Equally critical was Naše doba, vol. 4, no. 2 (November 10, 1896):157-58, "Kompromisy a volby moravské;" it was also alarmed about growing clerical influence, especially in the fourth curia, where, although the combined National and People's party slate won all but five mandates, its electoral vote of 1472 against 1215 for the clericals was alarmingly close. (These are the votes of electors, since indirect voting obtained in the fourth curia.) The People's party won seventeen of the thirty mandates.

55. Kaizl, Z mého života, 3:546, on the December 16, 1896,

476   Notes to Pages 229-232

meeting. Badeni met with great landowners on the nineteenth and
with German representatives on the twenty-first. Principal in-
traparty debates are those of LANM, 6 T 90, parliamentary club
minutes, vol. 7, no. 2, October 1, 1896, no. 8, October 28, 1896;
vol. 8, nos. 1 and 2, March 1897.

56. Navrátil, Eim, pp. 156ff., 167-68.

57. Penížek's tribute to Eim is the introduction to Eim,
Politické úvahy.

58. LANM, 6 T 90, parliamentary club minutes, ses. 7, nos.
2-8, October 1 to 28, 1896. Národní listy, December 2, 3, 5,
and 7, 1896.

59. LANM, Pacák papers, Engel to Pacák, April 10, 1896; Eim
to Pacák, September 25, 1896.

60. Rieger's speech reported with excerpts in Čas, vol. 9,
no. 3 (January 16, 1897):31-32. Národní listy, January 11, 1897.

61. Čas, vol. 11, no. 3 (January 16, 1897):31-34. Masaryk
also expressed such views in personal letters.

62. The development of the various Progressive parties after
1897 is discussed in chap. 9 below. On the general development
after 1900, see chap. 10 below and the discussion in Viktor Dyk
and Antonín Hajn, Státoprávně a pokrokově (Prague, 1913).

63. Contemporary accounts of the events of February 1897 are
Antonín Hajn, Výbor prací, 1:441-61, "Rozdvojení roku 1897;"
A. Pravoslav Veselý, Omladina, pp. 388-430; and the critical
article, "the End of Misunderstanding," in Rozhledy, vol. 6,
no. 12 (March 15, 1897), "Konec nedorozumění," pp. 529-37. Secondary accounts include R. Fischer, Pokroková Morava, p. 68;
Freeze, "Young Progressives," pp. 326-34; Hoch, Rašín, pp. 57-60;
and Tobolka, Politické dějiny, vol. 3, pt. 2, pp. 121-24.

64. On the Progressive Socialists, see A. P. Veselý, Omladina, pp. 431-41. On Modráček's views of Marxism, see František
Modráček, Marxův názor na dějiny a socialism (Prague, 1900), especially pp. 123-60ff. and 180ff. On Modráček's life and ideas
generally, see Otto Urban, "František Modráček," Revue dějin socialismu, no. 4 (1969):581-93. On Social Democratic views of
the divisions in the Progressive movement, see the two articles
by Josef Steiner, cited with quotations by Veselý, Omladina,
pp. 385-88: "Príznej'te barvu!" ("Show your colors!") and "Socialistické směry v Čechách," both first published by Sociální
demokrat.

65. Antonín Hajn, "Naše dělnictvo a české státní právo," in his Výbor prací, 3:48-69, especially pp. 48-52; Hoch, Rašín, pp. 49-50; Národní listy, March 1 and 2, 1897; Radikální listy, vol. 4, no. 22 (May 29, 1897):175-78.

66. Fischer, Pokroková Morava, 1:82-84.

67. On Čížek (1865-97), see the memorial edition of his selected writings, Výbor prací Antonína Čížka (Prague, 1897), edited by the editors of Samostatnost. See also the obituary by Antonín Hajn in Samostatnost, vol. 1, no. 10 (June 5, 1897), reprinted in Výbor prací, 1:461-65.

68. Fischer, Pokroková Morava, 1:49-59.

69. Pozor (The Examiner), published in Olomouc, criticized this very point on September 19, 1896.

70. Text is cited by Fischer, Pokroková Morava, 1:54-55.

71. The ten-point program is printed in ibid., pp. 61-62. See also Rozhledy, vol. 6, no. 7 (January 1, 1897):331-32; Čas, vol. 11, no. 1 (January 2, 1897), commented favorably that "Young Moravia has decided to establish itself as an independent party apart from all existing political parties in Moravia. We endorse that decision."

72. Fischer, Pokroková Morava, 1:75-76.

73. Národní listy, February 20, 1897; texts also in Srb, Politické dějiny, 2:185-87, and V. Škarda, Národní strana svobodomyslná, pp. 132-37.

74. Čas, vol. 11, no. 11 (March 13, 1897):6.

75. Ibid.

76. See table 19 in the appendix.

77. In the first election: Březnovský, 16,126; Dědic, 15,130; P. Josef Šimon, Christian Socialist candidate, 3,142; and independent František Saller, 109. In the run-off: Březnovský, 22,142; Dědic, 14,310. The predominantly Jewish district of Josefov went for Dědic 866 to 351 in the first and 799 to 433 in the second election. Čas, vol. 11, no. 12 (March 20, 1897) on German voting for Dědic. Figures from Jaromír Váňa, Volby do říšské rady v království Českém roku 1897 (Prague, 1897), pp. 14-15.

78. Refer to table 19 in the appendix.

478

79. On changes in the programs and development of the German parties from 1895 to 1906, see Charmatz, Deutsch-österreichische Politik, pp. 174-92.

80. Kaizl, Z mého života, 3:568-70, diary entries for March 23, 24, and 28, 1897.

81. LANM, 6 T 90, parliamentary club minutes. ses. 8, no. 3, April 2, 1897.

82. March 31 demands, a rehash of the 1897 program, are in Tobolka, Politické dějiny, vol. 3, pt. 2, pp. 147-49, and in Česká politika, 3:603. Kaizl, Z mého života, 3:576, diary entry for April 1, 1897, comments upon how he and Kramář assisted Engel in discussing the demands with Badeni. Kramář, Poznámky, pp. 17-18, in 1906 attributed the demands to "fears of radicalism." Contemporary documents indicate that the party simply wished to honor its electoral promises of March and its responsibilities to the electorate. If anyone was afraid of radicalism, it must have been Kramář himself.

83. The complete text with notes is in Srb, Politické dějiny, 2:221-26. All citations to the laws in the paragraph below refer to this text. Note the informed discussion of the text and its negotiation by Národní listy's Vienna correspondent, Josef Penízek, in Česká aktivita, 2:348-60.

84. Čas, vol. 11, no. 15 (April 10, 1897), pp. 226-29. See also Kaizl's Reichsrat speech of May 8, 1897, defending the ordinances in part by citing various historical precedents. The Czech text is in Kaizl, Z mého života, 3:601-11.

85. The two constitutional great landowners who advised Badeni throughout the negotiations, Count Oswald Thun-Salm and Joseph Maria Baernreither, questioned only the requirement that all officials learn both languages.

86. William L. Langer, The Diplomacy of Imperialism, 1890-1902, 2d ed. (New York, 1951), pp. 373-75. Alfred Francis Pribram, ed., Die politischen Geheimverträge Österreich-Ungarns, 1879-1914, nach den Akten des Wiener Staatsarchivs (Vienna and Leipzig, 1920), 1:78-82.

87. The text of the manifesto is in Srb, Politické dějiny, 2:215. It was signed on March 27 and read to the Reichsrat on March 30, 1897. Negotiations preceding the manifesto are discussed in Ibid., pp. 211-15; even Národní listy, March 29 and 30, 1897, favored the new majority.

88. SPHA, vol. 12, nos. 15-16 (1897) for the German text. The

Czech text appears in Šolle, Dělnické hnutí, p. 263, and Srb, Politické dějiny, 2:216.

89. Národní listy, April 1 and 2, 1897. By this date the Radikální listy also reflected Young Czech views on most questions relating to social democracy.

90. Neue Freie Presse, April 1, 1897. The Social Democratic Arbeiter-Zeitung, April 1, 1897, as expected backed their Czech colleagues.

91. The text is given in Srb, Politické dějiny, 2:217-18.

92. Neue Freie Presse, April 16, 1897. Jaromír Doležal, Osmdesát let T. G. Masaryka (Prague, 1929), p. 99. Masaryk's role in this is still debated.

93. Čas, vol. 1, no. 14 (April 3, 1897):209-10; and E. Grégr, Otevřený list. Alfons Šťastný, among others, had always found himself in agreement with Edvard Grégr on this issue. See Traub, Ze života Šťastného, pp. 144-46, letter of October 26, 1876.

94. LANM, Václav Škarda papers, letter from Josef Kaizl, dated April 2, 1897. Kaizl, Z mého života, 3:577-78, diary entry for April 3, 1897.

95. LANM, 6 T 90, parliamentary club minutes, ses. 8, no. 3, April 2, 1897. Kaizl, Z mého života, 3:578, diary entry for April 4, 1897. PNP, Engel papers, 6 s 82, parliamentary commission minutes, March 28, April 4, and April 8, 1897.

96. Kaizl, Z mého života, 3:579, letter to his wife, April 4, 1897.

97. LANM, 6 T 90, ses. 8, no. 4, April 6, 1897, the club of delegates approved Engel's motion that he join negotiations with parties of the right.

98. Radikální listy, May 29, 1897. For an earlier statement of this view see Radikální listy, January 12, 1894, article titled "Šlechta a Mladočeši," clipping in LANM, Engel papers, 6 s 85, "noviny."

99. Tobolka, Politické dějiny, vol. 3, pt. 2, pp. 151-52; Kaizl, Z mého života, 3:406; Penížek, Česká aktivita, 2:352-53.

100. For the text of article 19, see chap. 2 above.

101. Národní listy, April 23 and 24, 1897.

102. Kaizl, Z mého života, 3:590-91, diary entry of April 26,
1897, reported on the executive committee meeting.

Chapter 9

1. The most comprehensive account of German parties in later
nineteenth-century Cisleithania remains Charmatz, Deutsch-
österreichische Politik. Sutter's Sprachenverordnungen is invaluable on the Christian Socialist movement during the later nineties. A good general survey in English is Whiteside's "Germans
as Integrative Force," despite its exaggerating the influence of
Schönerer and accepting uncritically German statements about the
Czechs and Czech intentions. General histories of the Habsburg
Monarchy usually do not make distinctions between the views of
different German political parties in 1897, just as they generally ignore the differences between Czech parties or within the
Young Czech party.

For this section of chapter 9, I have relied primarily on Kolmer, Parlament, 6:218-331; Srb, Politické dějiny, 2:231-328;
Charmatz, Deutsch-österreichische Politik; Sutter, Sprachenverordnungen, 1:203ff., and Jiří Kořalka, "La montée du pangermanisme et l'Autriche-Hongrie, Historica 10 (1965):213-53, and Všeněmecký svaz a česka otázka koncem 19. století, Rozpravy, vol.
73, no. 14 (Prague, 1963), in addition to parliamentary debates,
diplomatic reports, newspaper accounts, police reports, and contemporary memoirs and letters cited below.

Sutter's Sprachenverordnungen, a competent and exhaustive account of German public opinion, goes astray when dealing with
the Czechs primarily because it uses no Czech sources and takes
its information second hand. There is no evidence whatsoever in
any Czech newspapers, party programs, or private correspondence
to indicate that the Czechs aimed to do in 1897 what they did
under international agreement and under vastly different circumstances in 1945--expel most of the German inhabitants from Bohemia, Moravia, and Silesia. Sutter's view of history is colored,
like the views of Redlich, Franz Joseph, Sieghart, Die letzten
Jahrzehnte, and Bibl, Zerfall, by a distaste and lack of understanding for popular political parties and parliamentary government. Like all general histories of the monarchy in Western
languages, except Macartney, Habsburg Empire, and Jászi, Dissolution, these works use no Slavic- or Hungarian-language sources
and therefore willy-nilly reflect very partisan German and imperial points of view. In these works there are also the unexamined, and I think untenable, assumptions that the Czechs should
have been satisfied with second-class citizenship and some material progress and that officials in Vienna best understood the
needs and aspirations of the non-German majority in Austria-
Hungary. There is also the view that if all parties had only
deferred to the higher wisdom of the emperor and his advisors
then no crisis or violence need have occurred. Why the parties

did not and could not obey the emperor is never objectively or carefully considered.

2. Tobolka, Politické dějiny, vol. 3, pt. 2, p. 156, and Srb, Politické dějiny, 2:227-28, 232-35, on the voting. The German Christian Socialists, Falkenhayn's German conservatives, the conservative great landowners, and all Slavs voted down the German proposals.

3. This was the view also of Heinrich von Srbik. See Andreas A. Posch, Heinrich von Srbik (Graz, 1948), p. 188.

4. This was the argument of the 1882 Linz program. The 1899 Whitsun demands modified the former by allowing for some Czech autonomy within the predominantly Czech districts of Bohemia.

5. Sutter, Sprachenverordnungen, 1:212ff, thoroughly explains how Germans in the Alpine lands through editorials and demonstrations forced the Christian Socialist movement there to abandon its initial posture of supporting the Badeni government as it had earlier supported the Windischgrätz and Taaffe governments.

6. See Hans Mommsen's informed discussion of this point, Die Sozial Demokratie, 1:275ff.

7. The complete text of Pacák's proposal is in Kaizl, Z mého života, 3:633-39. This proposal accompanied Pacák's letter to Kaizl dated July 28, 1897, and is discussed by Kaizl in his reply dated August 3, 1897, ibid., 3:633-40.

8. The violent German reaction, to be discussed in more detail below, is amply documented by police reports in SÚA, Prague, and in HHSA and VA, Vienna, in newspaper accounts, in the protocols of the Reichsrat, and in the reports of the French ambassador in Vienna and consul in Prague. See, for example, HHSA, Informations Bureau, Min. des Aussern (IB), Year 1897, 475/14 /2706, editorials from various Leipzig papers; 475/3336, "Der bayerische Schutzwall gegen das Czechenthum," Munich, November 7, 1897, and 475/3546, "Alldeutscher Burschenschaftertag."

9. The growing interest of the Imperial German public in Cisleithanian affairs and in the conflict between Czechs and Germans in Bohemia during the years 1897 and 1898 is comprehensively discussed in Klaus Szameitat, Die inneren Verhältnisse Österreich-Ungarns während des Jahres 1897 im Spiegel der reichsdeutschen öffentlichen Meinung (Würzburg, 1938).

10. Kořalka, "La montée," p. 239, citing Alldeutsche Blätter, vol. 7, no. 26 (June 27, 1897), An die Deutschen in der Ostmark und im Reiche.

11. Its predecessor the Allgemeiner deutscher Verband was founded in that year. The later name was adopted in 1894. Principal studies of the Pan-German League are Koralka, Všeněmecký svaz; Alfred Kruck, Geschichte des Alldeutschen Verbandes, 1890-1939 (Wiesbaden, 1954); and Mildred Wertheimer, The Pan-German League, 1890-1914 (New York, 1924).

12. Koralka, Všeněmecký svaz, p. 37, citing original Pan-German sources.

13. Ibid., pp. 36 and 56ff., citing Pan-German literature.

14. Pacák, Několik slov. This and other contemporary speeches and pamphlets by Young Czechs reveal intransigence on the issue of greater use of Czech in the civil service but willingness to make small concessions to German sensibilities and recognize the privileged status of German as defined by the Badeni ordinances. Czechs consistently defended parliamentary government and rarely used inflammatory rhetoric. See also Kaizl, Z mého života, 3:592-601, "Německo-český jázykový spor," and pp. 601-11, speech in the Reichsrat of May 8, 1897, against the attempt to impeach Badeni.

15. The Imperial German intervention of 1899 is discussed below.

16. Šolle, Socialistické dělnické hnutí, pp. 19-30.

17. Šolle, Dělnické hnutí, pp. 214-15.

18. In his letter to Karl Kautsky dated July 21, 1897, Viktor Adler admitted that the Austrian Social Democratic party had no "positive program" regarding the nationality question and proposed that the party take no part in what he regarded as an affair of middle-class parties. Adler's letter to Kautsky of August 2, 1897, expressed similar opinions. Both letters are in Viktor Adler, Briefwechsel mit Bebel und Kautsky, pp. 233 and 235. Friedrich Stampfer's article, "Für das böhmische Staatsrecht," published in Die Neue Zeit, vol. 17, no. 1 (Stuttgart, 1899):275-78. Kautsky's critical reply published in ibid., pp. 293-301. A discussion of the above is in Šolle, "Die Sozialdemokratie," pp. 359-68.

19. Šolle, "Die Sozialdemokratie," pp. 343-47, citing Kautsky's article, "Die moderne Nationalität," in Die Neue Zeit 5 (1887):393-405, 442-51. Viktor Adler had along with Georg von Schönerer and Heinrich Friedjung drawn up the Linz program of 1882 for German national aims within Austria.

20. Adler and Kautsky underestimated the popular appeal of modern nationalism, believing nationalism to be essentially a

product and tool of the bourgeoisie and expecting nationality
conflict to become a thing of the past. See Kautsky's letter to
Viktor Adler dated August 5, 1897, in which Kautsky asserted
quite mistakenly that national movements among the Slavs were
merely the work of "Rubels auf Reisen." Kautsky also agreed with
Adler that "Ebensowenig wie Ihr, weiss ich ein Programm für den
österreichischen Sprachenkampf." Letter in Viktor Adler, Briefwechsel, p. 236, cited in Šolle, "Die Sozialdemokratie," pp. 359-
60. Kautsky in the same letter asserted that Austrian Social
Democracy had taken a "neutral" stand during the 1897 crisis and
stood to profit from it.

On the German character of the Austrian Social Democratic party, see Mommsen, Die Sozial Demokratie, 1:155-57. Mommsen also
noted that the Austrian party was the only "German party" which
did not immediately participate in the obstruction of Parliament
against the Badeni decrees; ibid., p. 275.

21. Kaizl, Z mého života, 3:631-33 and 646, letters from
Kaizl to Kramář, July 27, 1897, and August 23, 1897. It has been
claimed in Kramář's defense that as First Vice-Speaker of Parliament, he was immature and inexperienced and had been insulted by
German delegates bent on having their own way against the parliamentary majority and all rules of procedure. Nonetheless, the
prevalence of less excitable and less ruthless men among Young
Czech delegates indicates that Kramář unjustifiably overreacted
and thereby helped exacerbate an already serious situation not of
his or the Czechs' making.

22. LANM, 6 T 90, parliamentary club minutes, ses. 8, no. 13
(May 10, 1897) and no. 15 (May 18, 1897), and ses. 12, nos. 19
and 20 (June 2, 1897).

23. Primarily from police reports to the Ministry of the Interior (for example, SÚA, PMV/R 1888-90, year 1897: 2/1-
3/1967/MI, 16/2/9299/MI). And reports to the Ministry of Foreign
Affairs and to its Information Bureau (for examples, HHSA, Min.
des Aussern, IB, year 1897: 475/1441/1544, 2706, 2787, 2813-34,
3168-69, 3259, and 3426). See also SÚA, PM, year 1897, 8564,
2366, 14498, 17027, and 1733.

24. LANM, 6 T 90, parliamentary club minutes, ses. 9, nos.
3, 4, and 7, September 25 and October 4 and 14, 1897. Kaizl, Z
mého života, 3:640-41, diary entry for August 7, 1897, a long
report on his conference with Badeni on August 5, 1897.

25. This was published in the various Czech and German dailies on that date. Koŕalka, Všenĕmecký svaz, p. 48.

26. Neue Freie Presse, October 31, 1897.

484 Notes to Pages 252-255

27. Národní listy, November 2, 1897.

28. Čas, vol. 11, no. 45 (November 6, 1897):713.

29. Antonín Sova, "Theodoru Mommsenovi," in his Pozdrav bouřlivé noci (Prague, 1964), pp. 80-81.

30. Josef Pekař, "Die Böhmen als die Apostel der Barbarisierung: Theodor Mommsen gewidmet," Politik, vol. 36, nos. 339, 342, and 345 (December 8, 11, and 14, 1897).

31. Václav Škarda, "Myšlenky o česko-německém smíru," in his Výbor statí, pp. 47-52, originally in Národní listy, June 20, 1897; and Edvard Grégr, "Speech in Behalf of the Czech Language," for examples.

32. Národní listy, December 14, 1897.

33. František Tilšer, Kdo hlásá pravdu: Kant či Lamarck a Monge? (Prague, 1901).

34. T. G. Masaryk, Ideály humanitní and Jak pracovat?

35. Pfersche was the delegate from the predominantly German Ústí nad Labem (Aussig) district in Bohemia.

36. Kaizl, Z mého života, 3:663-64, Kramář to Kaizl, November 20, 1897; Kaizl to Pacák, November 23, 1897.

37. Penížek, Česká aktivita, 2:383-88.

38. Národní listy, November 26, 1897; Lidové noviny, November 26 and 27, 1897.

39. Kolmer, Parlament, 5:318-19, including text of the Lex Falkenhayn. Tobolka, Politické dějiny, vol. 3, pt. 2, pp. 174-78. Kramář's account of these events appears in Česká politika, 3:607-17.

40. Národní listy, November 27 and 28, 1897. LANM, 6 T 90, parliamentary club minutes, ses. 9, no. 17, November 27, 1897.

41. Penížek, Česká aktivita, 2:418.

42. Slightly more than 6 percent of the Žatec population was Czech.

43. Events are described in the uncensored contemporary Czech reports published in France. L. Schmidt-Beauchez, La lutte de la Bohême contre le pangermanisme and "V. M.," La

vérité sur les événements de Prague. Mémorandum publié par les deux sociétés tchèques de Paris, la Beseda et le Sokol (Paris, 1898). See also Národní listy, November 28 through December 4, 1897, and reports of the Prague chief of police in SÚA. Archives diplomatiques, Volume NS Autriche-Hongrie 12, Report of French consul in Prague, M. Valois, dated December 1, 1897: "Les Allemands ont pris une attitude extrêmement provocante et se livrent dans différentes localités à des actes de sauvagerie. À Prague troubles sérieux depuis le 28. Déjà environ 200 blessés. . . . L'union des Tchèques est parfaite. Ils sont plus que jamais décidés à défendre énergiquement leurs droits et ne doutent pas du succès de leur cause. . . ."

44. Čas, vol. 11, no. 49 (December 4, 1897).

45. Archives diplomatiques, NS 12, October 9, 1899, Valois reporting on Thun's dismissal and the calm reaction on this and other occasions. "Les Tchèques sont de timides émeutiers."

46. Viktor Dyk, Prosinec (Prague, 1906), pp. 124-25, 366-74.

47. Viktor Dyk, Vzpomínky a komentáře, 1893-1918 (Prague, 1927), 1:77, 79. Dyk's romanticized view of these events was not typical of his contemporaries nor of the Young Czechs, whose more sober appraisal and more pessimistic outlook is discussed below. Dyk especially criticized Czech Social Democrats for having acted contrary to Czech national interests in 1897.

48. Redlich, Franz Joseph, p. 393, "Von diesem Augenblicke an war das Reich der Habsburger dem Untergange geweiht," and Šolle, Dělnické hnutí, pp. 240-41.

49. Emanuel Engel and Josef Herold, Dvě řeči o rakousko-uherském narovnání přednesené ve schůzi Klubu národní strany svobodomyslné dne 10. listopadu r. 1898 (Prague, 1898). Adolf Stránský, Řeč pronesená ve středu 25. řijna 1899 ve 4 schůzi poslanecké sněmovny v debatě o vládním prohlášení (Brno, 1899).

50. Česká politika, 3:609, 617-18; Kramář, Poznámky, pp. 21, 23-25.

51. Čas, vol. 11, no. 47 (November 20, 1897):738.

52. Čas, October 2, 1897, pp. 625-26, article "Souboj Badeniho a mladočeská politika."

53. Molisch, ed., Briefe zur deutschen Politik, p. 361.

54. LANM, Škarda papers, Kaizl to Škarda, February 23, 1899; also Kaizl, Z mého života, 3:877-80.

486   Notes to Pages 258-261

55. Srb, Politické dějiny, 2:417-22 on the cabinet.

56. Ottův slovník naučný, 18:209.

57. Srb, Politické dějiny, 2:450-57, 474-84, 539ff.

58. For the German text, see Kolmer, Parlament, 7:297ff. For the complete Czech text and critical and informed commentary, see Svatodušní program německý z roku 1899: Rozbor kritický (Prague, 1899). Also see Charmatz, Deutsch-österreichische Politik, pp. 187-88.

59. Appeals from the German ambassador in Vienna, Count Philipp Eulenburg, to Emperor Franz Joseph, in A. Mendelssohn-Bartholdy, I. Lepsius, and F. Thimme, eds., Die grosse Politik der europäischen Kabinette, 40 vols. in 54 (Berlin, 1922-26), vol. 13, nos. 3480 and 3486. Archives diplomatiques, NS Autriche-Hongrie 12, dispatch from Valois, French consul in Prague, dated December 1, 1897, claimed that Eulenburg also helped secure Badeni's dismissal.

60. Eulenburg, "Wendung zum Deutschtum," in a dispatch to Imperial German Foreign Minister Hohenlohe, on November 21, 1899 in A. Mendelssohn-Bartholdy, J. Lepsius, and F. Thimme, eds., Die Grosse Politik, vol. 13, no. 3513.

61. Archives diplomatiques, NS 12 (1897-1914), report of consul Valois dated October 18, 1899. On rioting in Vsetín, Moravia, see Matouš Václavek, Dějiny města Vsetína a okresu Vsackého (Vsetín, 1901), pp. 314-17; Národní listy, October 3, 5, 10, and 17, 1899.

62. This excludes the two-and-one-half-month rule by Count Manfred Clary-Aldringen, caretaker Minister-President from October 2, 1899, to December 21, 1899. See Kramář's account in Česká politika, 3:651-56. Also Tobolka, Politické dějiny, vol. 3, pt. 2, pp. 234-41.

63. On Antonín Rezek (1853-1909), ministr krajan in the Koerber government (1900-03), active Young Czech (1899-1903), professor of Austrian history at Charles University, and a founder of ČČH, see PNP, Rezek papers, which contain letters on Czech politics 1899-1905, and Jan Muk, et al., Památník ministra Prof. Dr. A. Rezka (Jindřichův Hradec, 1936), which includes a bibliography of Rezek's publications.

64. The apt words are those of Ervín Špindler. LANM, Pacák papers, no. 14, Špindler to Pacák, September 22, 1913.

65. LANM, Julius Grégr papers, Edvard Grégr to J. Grégr,

November 19, 1879 (letter no. 4), and January 28, 1884 (letter no. 11).

66. Slavík and Muk, Bojovník za právo, Slavík's letter of resignation to the executive committee, no. 45, May 23, 1898; also no. 47, reply further explaining his grounds, July 20, 1898, to no. 46, executive committee's query of July 18, 1898, pp. 53-55.

67. LANM, Pacák papers, Tilšer to Pacák, January 19, 1898.

68. Slavík and Muk, Bojovník za právo, no. 49, Šíl to Slavík, October 5, 1898, p. 55; no. 48, Václav Šamánek to Slavík, October 5, 1898, p. 55.

69. On Engel, see the appreciation by Kaizl in his letter to Václav Škarda, March 2, 1899, Z mého života, 3:881-83; see also Čapek, Hovory s T. G. Masarykem, p. 93; and Machar, Boží bojovníci, pp. 8-9.

70. Archives diplomatiques, NS Autriche-Hongrie 12 (1897-1914), dispatch from Valois to Paris, October 9, 1899. "Seul M. Engel, président du club Tchèque, a eu la franchise d'exposer la situation dans toute sa réalité et de dire, avec les ménagements d'usage, qu'il n'y a rien a espérer d'un souverain incapable de résister à la pression exercée par l'Allemagne. Après avoir émis des doubts sur le maintien de la majorité au Reichsrath, il a signalé l'impossibilité, pour les Tchèques, de se lancer dans une obstruction parlamentaire qui les exposerait aux brutalités de la populace de Vienne."

71. Two Aehrenthal papers from the Thun period, a letter to Foreign Minister Gołuchowski of January 15, 1898, and a "memorandum on language relationships in Bohemia," are published with commentary by Solomon Wank, "Zwei Dokumente Aehrenthals aus den Jahren 1898-99 zur Lösung der inneren Krise in Österreich-Ungarn," Mitteilungen des Österreichischen Staatsarchivs 19 (1966):339-62.

72. See chap. 10 below on the growth of the new Czech parties.

73. The Archduke Franz Ferdinand was no friend of any Czech political parties or of the conservative great landowners; see his letter of March 4, 1901, to Minister-President Koerber, in Sieghart, Die letzten Jahrzehnte, pp. 462-63.

74. Masaryk Archives, část 26, roku 1899, copy of Masaryk's letter to Kramář, dated January 9, 1899.

75. Archives diplomatiques, NS Autriche-Hongrie 4, dispatches of June 9 and June 19, 1898, from Budapest.

76. On late nineteenth-and early twentieth-century Czech-Polish relations the best general account is Žáček, ed., Češi a Poláci v minulosti, vol. 2, chaps. 7, 8, 9, and 10, pp. 246-375.

77. Srb, Politické dějiny, 2:344-45.

78. Stanislaus (Stanisław) Smolka, Polen, Böhmen und Deutsche (Vienna and Leipzig, 1898).

79. Žáček, ed., Češi a Poláci v minulosti, 2:339ff.

80. On later nineteenth-century Slovak history, see Holotík and Mésáros, eds., Dejiny Slovenska, vol. 2, and František Bokes, ed., Dokumenty k slovenskému národnému hnutiu v rokoch 1848-1914, 3 vols. (Bratislava, 1962-72). On Czech and Slovak relations in the decade before the First World War, see Josef Rotnágl, Češi a Slováci: Vzpomínky a úvahy nad dopisy a zápisky z let 1907-1918 (Prague, 1945); Albert Pražák et al., eds., Rotnágluv sborník (Prague, 1935); and L'udovít Holotík, ed., O vzájomných vzt'ahoch Čechov a Slovákov (Bratislava, 1956), articles on pp. 177-263.

81. František Bublávek and Martin Bartoň, Slovenský spolok "Detvan" v Prahe 1882-1913 (Prague, 1914); Vavro Šrobár, Z môjho života (Prague, 1946), pp. 261-66 and 296ff.

82. Jarmila Tkadlečková, "Slovakofilské hnutí v českých zemích koncem 19. století," in L. Holotík, ed., O vzájomných vzt'ahoch Čechov a Slovákov, pp. 218-29, especially 226-27.

83. On aid by Czech Social Democrats, especially Vlastimil Tusar, editor of Rovnost in Brno, and Antonín Němec, chief editor of Právo lidu in Prague, see Tobolka, Politické dějiny, vol. 3, pt. 2, pp. 371-73. On the Progressive Realists, see Holotík and Mésáros, Dejiny Slovenska, 2:511-14. On the Congress of Slavic Youth and the Slovaks, see Odložilík, "Congresses," pp. 1350-52.

84. Vavro Šrobár, Z môjho života, pp. 351-66 and 400-05. Albert Pražák, "Vliv T. G. Masaryka na Slovenské hlasisty," and Vavro Šrobár, "T. G. Masaryk a Slováci," in Slovensko Masarykovi, ed. Josef Rudinský (Bratislava and Prague, 1930), pp. 87-104. On intimidation and corruption in the 1906 Hungarian parliamentary elections see R. W. Seton-Watson, Corruption and Reform in Hungary: A Study of Electoral Practice (London, 1911). On earlier repression see Editors of Politik, Die Unterdrückung der Slovaken durch die Magyaren (Prague, 1903).

85. On this paragraph, see the memoirs by František Hlaváček, "Jihoslovanská pokroková generace z konce minulého a počátku tohoto století a její vztahy k československému kulturnímu a

politickému životu," offprint from Přehled 4 (1965/66), especially pp. 21-25.

86. On cooperation between Czechs, Slovaks, and Yugoslavs leading up to the First World War see Milada Paulová, Jihoslovanský odboj a česká maffie (Prague, 1928), 1:ix-x; Milada Paulová, Balkánské války, 1912-1913, a český lid (Prague, 1963); and Milada Paulová, Dějiny maffie (Prague, 1937), 1:11-69. The most comprehensive study to date of Czech-Yugoslav relations is Václav Žáček, Miroslav Tejchman et al., Češi a Jihoslované v minulosti: Od nejstarších dob do roku 1918 (Prague, 1975).

87. On Slavism and Neo-Slavism and on problems of the Slavic peoples, see Jaroslav Bidlo et al., Slovanstvo: Obraz jeho minulosti a přitomnosti (Prague, 1912), and chap. 1 above. On the second congress, see Čas, vol. 24, no. 187 (July 9, 1910).

88. On Czech-Russian relations from 1867 to 1914 the standard accounts are Josef Jirásek, Rusko a my, vol. 3: Dějiny vztahů československo-ruských od roku 1867 do roku 1894, 2d rev. ed. (Prague, 1945), and vol. 4: Dějiny vztahů československo-ruských od roku 1894 do roku 1914, 2d rev. ed. (Prague, 1945); Václav Čejchan, ed., Dějiny česko-ruských vztahů, 1770-1917 (Prague, 1967); and Theodor Syllaba, ed., K československo-ruským vztahům v oblasti ideologie na přelomu XIX. a XX. století (Prague, 1964).

89. Růžena Hávránková, "Zájem o balkánské Slovany jako složka českého slovanství v 19. století," Slovanské historické studie 7 (1968):196-217, and idem., "Česká veřejnost na pomoc protitureckým povstáním jižních Slovanů 1875-1877," Slovanské historické studie 6 (1966):5-53. On reports in American Czech newspapers, see Thomas Čapek, The Čechs (Bohemians) in America (Boston, 1920), p. 175. On the annexation of Bosnia-Hercegovina, see chap. 10 below.

90. See the informed discussion of Czech reactions to the Balkan wars in Paulová, Balkánské války 1912-1913 a český lid, especially pp. 46-74 and 84-91.

91. Antonín Hajn, "Krise národa českého," Pokroková Revue, vol. 1, no. 1 (January 1905), reprinted in his Výbor prací, 3:167-70.

92. For a general discussion of Austro-Hungarian foreign policy, see Hajo Holborn, "The Final Disintegration of the Habsburg Monarchy," Austrian History Yearbook, vol. 3, pt. 3 (1967): 189-205; and Wank, "Foreign Policy." The background for French diplomacy and the Austrian Slavs during the nineties is Jan Opočenský, "Francie a Rakoustí Slované v letech devadesátých," Slovanský Přehled 34 (1932):3-45 in reprint. A detailed study of

Russian foreign policy with regard to the Dual Monarchy from
1897 to 1900 will be found in chap. 4 of N. D. Ratner, Očerki po
istorii pangermanizma (Moscow, 1970). For German policy, the
most complete collection is J. Lepsius et al., eds., Die Grosse
Politik.

93. Archives diplomatiques, Autriche-Hongrie NS 12, dispatch
from Valois, French consul in Prague, dated December 1, 1897,
first paragraph. Cited also in Pavla Horská, "Česká otázka v
Rakousko-Uhersku 1898-1914," p. 451. Jiří Kořalka, "Diplomacie
Německé říše na konci 19. století o české svébytnosti a stát-
nosti," ČČH, vol. 15, no. 1 (1967):121-32, citing on p. 129 excerpts from Eulenburg's dispatch of February 10, 1899, from Po-
litisches Archiv des Auswärtigen Amtes, Osterreich 70, vol. 34,
1689/1899.

94. On the Palacký centennial and its repercussions, see SÚA,
PM, 8/1/15/1/1295 and 3372 (of the year 1898); and also Archives
diplomatiques, Autriche-Hongrie NS 12, dispatch dated June 23,
1898.

95. Kaizl's letter to V. Škarda of June 24, 1898, comparing
Komarov's "tactless" remarks to the "vulgar" remarks of Mommsen.
Kaizl, Z mého života, 3:795-96.

96. Langer, Diplomacy of Imperialism, pp. 373-76.

97. On 1868-71, see Odložilík, "Russia and Czech National
Aspirations," p. 439.

98. Kořalka, "Diplomacie Německé říše," p. 131, dispatch of
Eulenburg, February 10, 1899, to Wilhelm II, reporting on his
conversation with the Russian ambassador in Vienna.

99. See above, chap. 1.

100. No organization comparable to the Pan-German League
ever propagated Pan-Slavism. The Austrian and Hungarian police
indiscriminately labeled undesirable political activities by any
Slavic people as "Pan-Slavistic." German deputies in the Reichsrat did likewise when they charged that Czech attempts to establish a Czech gymnasium in Opava with funds provided in part by
the St. Petersberg Slavic Benevolent Society was part of a Pan-
Slav conspiracy.

101. Kořalka, "Diplomacie Německé říše," p. 131.

102. See the discussion by Langer, Diplomacy of Imperialism,
pp. 596-99, and Eurof Walters, "Franco-Russian Discussions on
the Partition of Austria-Hungary in 1899," SEER, vol. 28, no. 70
(1949):184-97.

103. On the Prague consulate and Austrian domestic and foreign policies see Pavla Horská, "Česká otázka," pp. 449-60. On the consulate's economic interests, J. F. N. Bradley, "Czech Nationalism in the Light of French Diplomatic Reports," SEER 42 (1963/64):38-53. On the French consulate and Czech domestic politics, see Pavla Horská, "Podíl české politiky z přelomu 19. a 20. století ve vztazích rakousko-francouzských," ČsČH, vol. 17, no. 5 (1969):760-62.

104. Archives diplomatiques, Autriche-Hongrie, NS 26, Valois's dispatch of July 18, 1901; text is reprinted in full in Horská, "Podíl," pp. 770-72.

105. Archives diplomatiques, NS 27, Autriche-Hongrie, Valois's dispatch dated October 29, 1902.

106. André Chéradame, L'Europe et la Question d'Autriche au seuil du XXe siècle (Paris, 1901), and L'Allemagne, la France et la question d'Autriche (Paris, 1902), informed works which exaggerated slightly the danger of the monarchy's collapse. René Henry, Questions d'Autriche-Hongrie et Question d'Orient (Paris, 1903).

107. "L'Europe sans l'Autriche," Revue des Deux Mondes, November 15, 1899.

108. See above, chap. 4.

109. On French commercial interests in Prague, see Rélation officielle du voyage et des réceptions du bureau du Conseil municipal de Paris à Prague, septembre 1908 (Paris, 1909).

110. Steed's Habsburg Monarchy and R. W. Seton-Watson's Southern Slav Question, Racial Problems, and Corruption and Reform are among their most noted works. Albert Henry Wratislaw (1821-89) published among many works a biography of Jan Hus in 1882 and a translation of the Queen's Court manuscript and other Czech poems in 1849. Count Francis Lützow (1849-1916) also published such works as Lectures on the Historians of Bohemia (London, 1905), The Story of Prague (London, 1902), and Life and Times of Master John Hus (London, 1909) as well as many articles and public lectures. Bohemia: A Historical Sketch (London, 1896) went through several revised editions and A History of Bohemian Literature (London, 1899; 2d ed., 1928) went through two. The most thorough study of Lützow's life and works is A. Sum, Hrabě Lutzöw: Památce českého vlastence (Prague, 1925).

111. See also Karel Kramář, Poznámky o české politice (Prague, 1906), pp. 54-60, on the redirection of Austrian foreign policy, and the article by Kramář, "Rakouská zahraniční

politika v XIX. století," in Česká politika, 1:49-180, especially pp. 155ff.

112. See Čapek, The Čechs in America, pp. 119-54, on Czech free-thinkers, radicals, and socialists in America, and pp. 164ff. on ties between Czech journalists in America and in the Czech lands. On Czech socialists in America establishing a Czech section of the First International in the United States, see Zdenĕk Šolle, "Die tschechischen Sektionen der I. Internationale in den Vereinigten Staaten von Amerika," Historica 8 (1964):101-34. On participation of Czech Americans in establishing an independent Czechoslovakia, see the two works by Vojta Benes, Vojáci zapomenuté fronty (Prague-Vršovice, 1923) and Československá Amerika v odboji, vol. 1: Od června 1914 do srpna 1915 (Prague, 1931).

113. František Soukup, Amerika: Řada obrazů amerického života (Prague, 1912); Gustav Habrman, Z mého života: Vzpomínky, 2d ed. (Prague, 1924), pp. 244-304.

114. Quotation from Masaryk's letter to the Národní listy, dated September 9, 1901, copy in Masaryk Archive, část 18, "Česka otázka." There is a similarly expressed opinion in a letter of January 10, 1901, to Národní listy, copy in Masaryk Archive, část 18. The Velím speech set forth a similar program of action with regard to the Czech relationship to Germany and the monarchy. Naše politická situace, řeč prof. T. G. Masaryka ve Velími 23 června 1901 (Prague, 1901).

Chapter 10

1. On Koerber, see Sieghart, Die letzten Jahrzehnte, pp. 44ff.; and Tobolka, Politické dějiny, vol. 3, pt. 2, pp. 300-56. The Beck government (February 1906 to November 1908) tried for a time to revert to a more parliamentary system, but the Bienerth and Stürgkh governments returned to Koerber's practices.

2. All ministers listed below are Young Czechs unless otherwise noted. Antonín Rezek, Minister without Portfolio for Czech Affairs in the Koerber government, January 1900 to July 1903; Antonín Randa, Old Czech, holding the same office for Koerber, October 1904 to January 1905, and in the Gautsche government, January 1905 to January 1906; Josef Fořt, Minister of Commerce in the Beck government, February 1906 to May 1907; František Fiedler, Minister of Public Works and succeeding Fořt in the Beck government, May 1907 to November 1908; Bedrich Pacák, Minister without Portfolio for Czech Affairs, February 1906 to May 1907 in the Beck government; Karel Prásek, Agrarian, same office, May 1907 to November 1908; Albín Bráf, Old Czech, Minister of Railways in the Beinerth government, November 1908 to January 1909; and Jan Žáček, Moravian Old Czech, Minister without

Portfolio for Czech Affairs, November 1908 to January 1909.

3. On influence of the Russian revolution of 1905 in helping
the campaign for universal manhood suffrage, see Oldriška Kodedová et al., eds., Prameny k revolučnímu hnutí a ohlasu první
ruské revoluce v českých zemích v letech 1905-1907, Rok 1905
(Prague, 1959), and Leta 1906-1907 (Prague, 1962).

4. Münch, Böhmische Tragödie, pp. 531-33, 721-26; Tobolka,
Politické dějiny, vol. 3, pt. 2, pp. 324-37 (1900), 515-22 (1904),
541-54 (1910), 573-79 (1912).

5. Tobolka, Politické dějiny, vol. 3, pt. 2, p. 390.

6. Cited in Macartney, Habsburg Empire, p. 797.

7. On the reform bill of February 14, 1914, in Galicia, not
effected before the war, see Ivan L. Rudnytsky, "The Ukrainians
in Galicia under Austrian Rule," Austrian History Yearbook, vol.
3, pt. 2 (1967):394-429. On the law of May 26, 1910, see Bernatzik, Verfassungsgesetze, pp. 938-72.

8. Česká politika, vol. 2, pt. 1, pp. 909-10; Josef Kolejka,
"'Moravský pakt' z roku 1905," CsČH, vol. 4, no. 4 (1956):590-615;
Bernatzik, Verfassungsgesetze, pp. 893ff.; R. Fischer, Pokroková
Morava, 1:186ff.; Tobolka, Politické dějiny, vol. 3, pt. 2, pp.
394-415, figures on 404. These sources also pertain to table 24
in the appendix, "Representation in the Moravian Diet before and
after 1905."

9. Časopis pokrokového studentstva, vol. 9, nos. 3-4 (1905/06):
85; Lidové noviny, November 17 and 18, 1905.

10. On the Progressive Bloc, see R. Fischer, Pokroková Morava,
2:313ff.

11. Šolle, Dělnické hnutí, pp. 214-15; Volf, Naše dělnické
hnutí, pp. 170-73; Akademie 5 (1901):4-9, 52-58.

12. On interpretations of the Brno program, see Bauer, Die
Nationalitätenfrage, pp. 528ff.; Hans Mommsen, Die Sozial Demokratie, pp. 336ff.; Zdeněk Šolle, in Oldřich Říha, ed., Přehled
československých dejin, vol. 2, pt. 1: 1848-1918 (Prague, 1960),
pp. 714-15; and Volf, Naše dělnické hnutí, pp. 186-89.

13. See the discussion in E. Beneš, Stručný nástin, 4:200-14;
František Modráček, "Národnostní otázka v sociální demokracii--
Lidový parlament v ohledu národnostnim," Akademie 13 (1909):295-
301; Šolle, Socialistické dělnické hnutí, chaps. 4 and 6; Lev
Winter, "Otázka národnostní v sociální demokracii," Akademie 12
(1908):151-65.

14. By the turn of the century, German Social Democrats showed no signs of continuing Friedrich Engel's policy of encouraging Czech Socialism, witness August Bebel's refusal to grant subsidies to Czech Social Democrats who wished to establish a daily in 1897. See Zdeněk Šolle, "Bebelovy dopisy o počátcích 'Práva lidu'," ČsČH, vol. 15, no. 3 (1967):439-48.

15. Soukup, Revoluce práce, 1:631ff. on the 1901 elections. See table 21 in the appendix. Akademie 5 (1901):114-19, 361-69.

16. On the German Workers' party and pre-war Austrian national socialist movements, see Whiteside, Austrian National Socialism, chap. 5, pp. 87ff.

17. On universal suffrage in 1907, see Kodedová, Prameny, and laws nos. 15, 16, and 17 of January 26, 1907, in Bernatzik, Verfassungsgesetze, pp. 756-807, and in Zákonník říšský (1907):57-107.

18. Šolle, Socialistické dělnické hnutí, pp. 31-40, and Akademie 15 (1911):5-13, 49-56, 319-25, 458-63, discuss these events.

19. Soukup, Revoluce práce, 1:769-71; R. Fischer, Pokroková Morava, 2:318-19, 362ff; Akademie 15 (1911):353-59, 374-91.

20. Šmeral had in 1904 set up the Circle of Marxist Students (Kroužek marxistických studentů) in opposition to Socialist veterans of the Omladina and most trade union leaders. This Circle has been regarded as a direct predecessor of the Czechoslovak Communist party, which Šmeral established in 1921. Subsequently Šmeral came to accept the Czechoslovak Republic and as party chairman became the leading proponent of a specifically Czechoslovak way to socialism until his removal at Stalin's behest after the Fifth Comintern Congress of 1925. The most complete account of Šmeral's student years will be found in F. Červinka, Boje a směry českého studentstva, especially pp. 115-17, 162-70.

21. Šolle, Socialistické dělnické hnutí, pp. 44ff.

22. Balbín's contribution was posthumous; his Defense of the Czech Language, written in 1670-77, was published in 1775.

23. On the Czech modernist movement, see Miloslav Kaňák, Z dějin reformního úsilí českého duchovenstva (Prague, 1951), pp. 73-100. On the modernist movement in general see Alec R. Vidler, The Modernist Movement in the Roman Church (Cambridge, Eng., 1934)

24. Notable was the debate between Masaryk and Dlouhý-Pokorný on whether the Austrian Catholic Church could respond to reform. Masaryk believed that it could not. On the atheism prevalent among early Czech Social Democrats, see Jiří Koralka, "Ateismis

průkopníků socialismu v Čechách," in Církve v našich dějinách, ed. Bohumil Černý (Prague, 1960), pp. 22-43.

25. By the encyclical Pascendi Dominici gregis. On the Unity of Catholic Clergy, see Kaňák, Z dějin úsilí, pp. 86-87.

26. On the founding of the Czechoslovak Church, see Miloslav Kaňák, Dr. Karel Farský (Prague, 1951), Stanislav Lahodný, Farský a naše dny (Prague, 1953), and Matthew Spinka, "The Religious Situation in Czechoslovakia," in Czechoslovakia, ed. Robert J. Kerner (Berkeley, 1949), chap. 15.

27. The condemnation of modernism and Svozil's withdrawal from the Church are discussed in Josef Svozil, "Z historie Katolické Moderny České," Česká Demokracie 3 (1911):138-43, 173-77, 191-98. Svozil left the party in 1925.

28. On Czech Catholics and the founding of the Czechoslovak Republic, see Josef Doležal, Politická cesta českého katolicismu, 1918-1928 (Prague, 1928), pp. 14ff., 45-54; and Ferdinand Peroutka, Budování státu: Československá politika v letech poprevratových (Prague, 1934), vol. 2, pt. 1, pp. 618-34.

29. On Loskot, see the informed biography by his wife Anežka Loskotova, Dr. František Loskot (Vsetín, 1933). Another example of the dilemma faced by Catholics, besides Svozil cited above, is Alois Hajn, "Proč jsem vystoupil z církve?," Osvěta lidu, no. 3 (January 8, 1907), reprinted in Alois Hajn, Život novinářův, 1894-1930 (Prague, 1930), pp. 82-83.

30. F. Loskot, Jste Čechové! Několik upřimných slov k Čechům Krkonosským (Jablonec nad Jizerou, 1897). On the Jablonec nad Jizerou area, see J. Z. K---l, "Jablonec n. Jiz. a česká veřejnost," Naše doba, vol. 9, no. 1 (1902):11-17, 90-97, and 184-90.

31. Figures for 1890, from Ottův slovník naučný, 6:187 and 17:667, indicate Protestant numbers as follows: Reformed (Calvinist) Church, predominantly Czech, 71,195 in Bohemia and 43,669 in Moravia and Silesia; Lutheran Church, predominantly German, 56,625 in Bohemia and 115,073 in Moravia and Silesia. Figures for Protestants of all denominations in 1910 listed in Statistisches Handbuch des Königreiches Böhmen (1913), p. 23: Bohemia, 177,832; Moravia, 74,513; and Silesia, 102,767.

32. František Bednář, The Transfer of Germans from Czechoslovakia from the Ideological and Ecclesiastical Standpoint (Prague, 1948), pp. 38-44. Some sections of this book are more polemical than scholarly.

33. Ferdinand Hrejsa, Dějiny české evangelické církve v Praze

a ve středních Čechách v posledních 250 letech (Prague, 1927), pp. 385-86. Luděk Brož, ed., Gestern und Heute: Ein Überblick über den tschechoslowakischen Protestantismus (Prague, 1955), pp. 35-37.

34. Wolf was a practicing Protestant; Schönerer was not. About 100,000 Germans in Cisleithania converted to Lutheranism in the three decades before 1900, but only a part of these were directly persuaded by Los von Rom. Erich Zöllner, Geschichte Österreichs, 3d ed. (Vienna, 1964), pp. 432ff., estimates 70,000.

35. I am indebted to the late Professor J. L. Hromádka for our conversation in October 1967, In Vinohrady, concerning this point.

36. A critical evaluation of Masaryk's Protestantism and moralistic outlook is Zdeněk Nejedlý, T. G. Masaryk, vol. 3: Na pražské universitě, 1882-1886 (Prague, 1935), pp. 292-308.

37. R. Fischer, Pokroková Morava, 2:243, 318.

38. SÚA, Český klub, no. 49, "1891 volby," letter to the Old Czech club of delegates from Father Václav Uhliř concerning the March 2, 1891, elections, and Český klub, no. 51, letters from Father Tykal, October 17, 1893, and from Father Vaneček, October 19, 1893.

39. J. Doležal, Politická cesta českého katolicismu, p. 7.

40. Navrátil, Nový český sněm, pp. 131-32 and 163; and Heidler, České strany, pp. 47-50.

41. Tobolka, Politické dějiny, vol. 3, pt. 2, pp. 103-11; and Heidler, České strany, p. 59. Hruban's memoirs, Moric Hruban, Paměti (Prague, 196) have recently been published and are a valuable source on the development of Catholic parties in particular and of Moravian politics generally.

42. In Bohemia the Orel numbered only 1,800 men and 800 women by 1914 and did not exceed 125 chapters in Moravia. Heidler, České strany, pp. 51 and 59.

43. See discussion below under section on Moravian People's Progressive party.

44. On German clerical movements, see Charmatz, Deutsch-österreichische Politik, pp. 243-57. On the Slovene clericals and their association with the Croatian Party of Rights, see Zwitter, "Slovenes."

45. On Jan Šrámek and the Catholic parties, see M. Hruban, K 60. narozeniná Jana Šrámka (Prague, 1930).

a 46. Obrana zemědělců, vol. 2, no. 41 (October 14, 1898), gives a report on the congress of the Association and its grour..s for severing ties to the Young Czech party. Pertinent pages of this issue saved by party chairman Engel, PNP, Engel papers, 6 R 80, in folder "Agrárni sdružení."

47. Membership up from 2,000 at the time of its founding. Frankenberger and Kubíček, Švehla, p. 84. This book is still the most complete published source on Agrarian party history and contains important programs and documents with comments upon them. See too E. Reich, ed., Památce Kuneše Sonntaga (Prague, 1932).

48. Kučera and Kučerová, O agrárnický stát, p. 17. This Marxist survey is generally critical and informative but occasionally polemical from a Stalinist perspective.

49. On social and economic background, see chap. 1 above; Česká politika, 4:33-51; and Franěk, Některé problémy. On the Union and Association, see Frankenberger and Kubíček, Švehla, pp. 49-57; and Kučera and Kučerová, O agrárnický stát, pp. 15-16.

50. Navrátil, Nový sněm, pp. 260-61.

51. Antonín Švehla, Sr. (1837-1900), father of Antonín Švehla, Jr. (1873-1933), and farmer in Hostivař near Prague, had served as vice-president of the Association of Czech Agriculturalists from its founding until his death in March 1900. Stanislav Kubr (1862-1908) and Emanuel Hrubý (1865-1933) served respectively as the first vice-president and secretary of both Association and party, and Karel Prášek (1868-1932) and Jan Antonín Prokůpek (1832-1915), among others, on its board of trustees.

52. Frankenberger and Kubíček, Švehla, pp. 81-94, 107-18; Kučera and Kučerová, O agrárnický stát, pp. 18-20ff. Tobolka, Politické dějiny, vol. 3, pt. 2, pp. 269-82, gives a comparatively short account of the Agrarian party which reflects partisan Young Czech views. Chundela, Stanislav Kubr, more thoroughly covers the same ground, especially pp. 42-87.

53. Obrtel, Moravští, pp. 235-62, on the Association, and pp. 263ff. on the Union.

54. See documents in František Roubík, ed., Petice venkovského lidu z Čech k Národnímu Výboru z roku 1848 (Prague, 1954), and Jiří Radimský and Milada Wurmová, eds., Petice moravského lidu k sněmu z roku 1848 (Prague, 1955). Klimeš, Česká vesnice, and František August Brauner, Böhmische Bauernzustände im Interesse

der Landeskultur und des Nationalwohlstandes besprochen (Vienna, 1847).

55. On the conflict and background, see Nožička, Prokůpek, pp. 78-79ff., 113-14.

56. On the predominance of estate owners in the Association, see the figures in Kučera and Kučerová, O agrárnický stát, pp. 16-17.

57. The Agrarian politician and estate owner Jan Dvořák should not be confused with Jan Dvořák, M.D., Young Czech stalwart (1849-1916). The latter was defeated in his bid for reelection in 1901 to the Reichsrat by the farmer and Agrarian candidate Jan Jareš.

58. Frankenberger and Kubíček, Švehla, pp. 105ff.; and Gustav Habrman and Alfred Meissner, Sociální demokracie a venkov: Referát soudruhů poslance G. Habrmana a dra. A. Meissnera na IX. sjezdu československ. sociálně democratické strany dělnické (Prague, 1909).

59. Jaroslav Marcha, ed., František Staněk: Politik, tribun, národohospodář, družstevník a buditel lidu venkovského: Memoary a dokumenty (Brno, 1927), pp. 48-50, 80-81, 197.

60. "Venkov je jedná rodina." Jaroslav César and Bohumil Černý, "O ideologii československého agrarismu," ČsČH 7 (1959): 271-72.

61. Heidler, České strany, pp. 27-29.

62. See table 17 in the appendix on the diet election of 1908.

63. See tables 19 and 22 in the appendix.

64. Marcha, Staněk, p. 49.

65. Frankenberger and Kubíček, Švehla, pp. 298-300; Kučera and Kučerová, O agrárnický stát, pp. 40-41. Prášek's program is in Právo venkova: týdenník politicko-hospodářský, vol. 1, no. 1 (December 22, 1911).

66. Josef Rotnágl, Češi a Slováci: Vzpomínky, pp. 40ff., 140ff., 193-200.

67. In 1918, Švehla, still party chairman, and Staněk and Udržal, chairmen respectively of the Czech Alliance (Český svaz) and the Slavic Union (Slovanská jednota) in the Austrian Parliament, after having long played the politics of watchful waiting,

gave their support to Masaryk and helped establish an independent Czechoslovakia. The Agrarian party, renamed the Republican
Party of Farmers and Peasants (Republikanská strana zemědělského
a malorolnického lidu), would rely heavily upon its organizational and electoral work of the pre-war years in establishing itself
as the leading party of the First Czechoslovak Republic. On
Švehla after 1918, see R. H. Bruce Lockhart, Retreat from Glory
(London, 1934), pp. 79-80, and Anthony Palecek, "Antonín Švehla:
Czech peasant Statesman," Slavic Review, vol. 21, no. 4 (1962):
699-708.

68. Discussion of the party's work in banking and credit may
be found in Frankenberger and Kubíček, Švehla, pp. 265-71, 360-61;
Chundela, Stanislav Kubr, pp. 220-21; Kučera and Kučerová, O
agrárnický stát, pp. 22-27; and especially in František Obrtel,
Zemědělské družstevnictví v Československu (Prague, 1928), with
emphasis on cooperatives and savings and loan societies.

69. Frankenberger and Kubíček, Švehla, pp. 276-77.

70. See table 10 in the appendix; Pimper, Banky, pp. 11, 39;
and J. Preiss, "O české banky," in his Několik úvah (Prague, 1929).

71. Figures from Kučera and Kučerová, O agrárnický stát, p. 25.

72. Program a zásady československé strany národně socialistické (Prague, 1933), pp. 241-46, a survey of party history; pp.
7ff., a theoretical discussion of party principles with occasional
reference to the past. Hanuš Sýkora and Karel Vokáč, eds., In
Memoriam Aloise Simonidesa (Prague, 1929), on founding and preparation to the founding, the most complete printed documentary
source, containing minutes of executive committee meetings in addition to selections from Simonides's own speeches and articles.
A collection of essays on party history and programs is Bohuslav
Šantrůček, ed., Buřiči a tvůrci: Vzpomínky, úvahy, kus historie,
životopisy, 1897-1947 (Prague, 1947). A lucid essay on party
principles is Karel Moudrý, Národní socialism (Prague, 1930).

73. Srb, Politické dějiny, 2:465-67, quoting from the text of
the 1898 party program. The 1901 program for the diet elections
is almost identical. See Navrátil, Nový sněm, pp. 132-33.

74. Sýkora and Vokáč, In Memoriam Aloise Simonidesa,
pp. 53-204, "Zápisky," the minutes of almost all early party assemblies and executive committee meetings.

75. See table 21 in the appendix.

76. Program a zásady, pp. 243-46.

77. "Rovnost národů, a rovnost v národě," F. S. Frabša, ed., Čtyřicet let československé strany národně socialistické v Liberci, 1906-1946 (Liberec, 1946), p. 32.

78. Though uncritical, Bohuslav Šantrůček's Václav Klofáč (1868-1928): Pohledy do života a díla (Prague, 1928) is still the standard and best biography of Klofáč. There is a good character sketch in Tobolka, Politické dějiny, vol. 3, pt. 2, pp. 128-30. See also Šantrůček, Buřiči, pp. 37-39; and Bohuslav Šantrůček and František Klátil, In Memoriam Václava J. Klofáče (Prague, 1945).

79. The complete account is Emil Špatný's Český antimilitarism: Kus historie a trochu vzpomínek (Prague, 1922).

80. Česká demokracie 3 (1911), no. 3, pp. 70-71, and no. 4, pp. 81-82.

81. On proposals to reform and extend communal social services, see the party study by Jan Vorel, Sociální politika obcí (Prague, 1904).

82. See tables 22A and 22B in the appendix.

83. Heidler, Strany, p. 37.

84. It will be remembered that Adolf Stránský, founder and editor of the Brno daily Lidové noviny, had with Young Czech subsidies pioneered the establishment of liberal and anticlerical Czech politics in Moravia. In 1891 he had founded the People's party (Lidová strana) and in alliance with Josef Vychodil of the Peasant Union for Moravia made the first liberal and democratic challenge to Old Czech and clerical preponderance in Moravia. That same year his party became the autonomous Moravian arm of the Young Czech party and sent three representatives to its executive committee in Prague. Stránský's close ties to the Czech Progressive movement dated back to January 1894, when he served as one of two defense attorneys for the Omladina "conspirators." The post-Nymburk rapprochement between Stránský and the more liberally minded Moravian Old Czechs led other Old Czechs to found the Catholic National party in Moravia in 1896 and led the progressive youth of Moravia to form their own autonomous organization, Young Moravia, in 1897.

85. The best source on Czech politics in Moravia after 1896 is R. Fischer, Pokroková Morava, 1:99-230 and 2:315ff., from which this account is largely drawn. See also Heidler, Strany, pp. 54-57. On Czech economic goals and activities in Moravia during the same years, see Moravskoslezská Revue 10 (1913/14), F. Kovářík, "Cíle českého průmyslu na Moravě a v Čechách,"

pp. 11-13, and F. Hodáč, "Zemské hospodářství," pp. 149-56, 237-40, and 285-89.

86. Artuš Drtil's "Separatism špatně pochopený," in his Výbor z prací, ed. František Šelepa (Prague, 1913), pp. 38-45, is a thoughtful essay on the different courses of Moravian and Bohemian politics since 1848.

87. For Stránský's speech against Young Czech language policies, see R. Fischer, Pokroková Morava, 1:142, December 28, 1902, to the Young Czech executive committee; 2:344-49 on debate with Kramář in 1911; and Adolf Stránský, Řeč pronesená ve středu 25. října 1899 ve 4. schůzi poslanecké sněmovny v debatě o vládním prohlášení (Brno, 1899), first signaling split.

88. A Progressive Moravian criticism of Young Czech policy is Artuš Drtil's "Naše stanovisko k reformě volebního řádu do zemského sněmu," in his Výbor z prací, pp. 60-63, and originally published in Jihočeské listy, August 17, 1907.

89. On Juda, see anon., Judův případ (Prostějov, 1906), and anon., Lutinov contra Juda (Prostějov, 1906). Church pressure forced Juda's transfer from the gymnasium in Prostějov to the reálka (Realschule) in Příbor. This case alerted all liberal and anticlerical groups in Moravia to the need for greater vigilance and concerted action.

90. Reporting on the merger of January 17, 1909, is "Splynutí strany lidové a mor. strany pokrokové," Přehled, vol. 7, no. 18 (January 22, 1909):324-26.

91. On the program of the latter, see R. Fischer, Pokroková Morava, 1:141-43.

92. See tables 17, 22A, and 22B in the appendix.

93. On the formation of these parties, see chaps. 6 and 7. On the program of the Radical Progressive party and advocacy of state rights based on "natural rights" rather than "historical rights," see Antonín Hajn, "Státoprávní politika." Brief histories of the progressive parties and the April 7, 1912, program of the State Rights Progressive party are contained in Hajn and Dyk, Státoprávně a pokrokově.

94. See table 22A in the appendix.

95. Hajn and Dyk, Státoprávně a pokrokově, p. 9 for quote; pp. 5-9 discuss the 1908 program and pp. 16-59 the April 7, 1912, program. See also Heidler, Strany, pp. 43-47.

96. Hajn and Dyk, Státoprávně a pokrokové, pp. 54-59.

97. A critical study of the relationship of T. G. Masaryk to the Progressive movement after 1900 is F. Vodsed'álek's Pro nové cesty české pokrokové politiky (Prague, 1914).

98. Typical of Progressive articles are Antonín Hajn, "K charakteristice ženského hnutí u nás" and "Několik slov o práci žen," in his Výbor prací, 3:37-45, 79-98. See also the collected articles by Alois Hajn, Ženská otázka v letech 1900-1920 (Prague, 1939).

99. Tereza Nováková, Ze ženského hnutí (Prague, ca. 1908), collects her articles on women's rights from the years 1893-1907. The first volume of the two-volume collection of essays and reminiscences, Albína Honzáková, ed., Kniha života F. F. Plamínkové: Sborník k 60. narozeninám (Prague, 1935), pertains in part to the pre-war years.

100. In 1910, Jews numbered 85,826, or 1.27 percent of the population, in Bohemia, and 41,158, or 1.57 percent, in Moravia. In Bohemia most were concentrated in larger cities, such as Prague with 18,041, or 8.06 percent. Statistisches Handbuch des Königreiches Böhmen (1913), pp. 22-23.

101. SÚA, PM 8/1/15/1, 1897, nos. 8564, 2366, 14498, 17027.

102. On "Svůj k svému" see Antonín Hajn, "Svůj k svému a-- české noviny," Samostatnost, vol. 9, no. 100 (December 16, 1905); and F. Hodáč, "Výklad hesla svůj k svému," Moravskoslezská Revue 10 (1913/14), pp. 131-32, citing Josef Kaizl's contention that the slogan required Czechs "not to buy anything that is Czech just because it is Czech, but, price and quality being equal, to give precedence to Czech products."

103. Vrba's principal anti-Semitic work was Národní sebeochrana: Úvahy o hmotném a mravním úpadku národa Českého (Prague, 1898). Anti-Semitic attacks on Social Democratic leadership follow p. 278. In the Studentský sborník strany neodvislé, see "O otázce židovské," in nos. 3 and 4 (1894):41-43, and "Hlícka anti-semitická," nos. 6 and 7 (1894):103-06. This student journal rejected anti-Semitism in 1896 under its new editors, Zdeněk Tobolka and Zdeněk Nejedlý.

104. Other electoral returns demonstrate the popularity of anti-Semitism among Bohemian Germans and its lack of appeal to Czechs. In the third- and fourth-curial elections in Bohemia in 1897, German anti-Semitic candidates carried 9.5 percent of the votes and four of fourteen seats in predominantly German districts. In contrast, Czech anti-Semitic candidates received only

0.8 percent of the vote in the same curias in predominantly
Czech areas. No Czech anti-Semitic candidates ran in the fourth
curia, but German anti-Semites received 15.5 percent of the vote
and three of thirteen seats. See Vaňa, Volby, p. 49. On similarities in 1901, see Akademie 5 (1901):145-52.

105. Národní listy, January 1, 1861.

106. Navrátil, Sněm 1895, s. v. "Scharf, Jakub." Scharf was
one of the founders of three Czech Jewish organizations: the
Czech Jewish National Union, the Society of Czech Academic Jews,
and the Ortomid Association.

107. Havránek, "Social Classes," pp. 200-02.

108. See Šípy for examples: Vol. 16, no. 45 (October 17,
1903); vol. 16, no. 50 (November 21, 1903); vol. 17, no. 35
(August 6, 1904).

109. The Národní listy after 1898 backed the anti-Dreyfusards
in France and equated support of Dreyfus's innocence with knuck-
ling under to Germany. Národní listy, July 8, 1900. Archives
diplomatiques, Autriche-Hongrie NS 26, dispatch from consul
Valois of July 18, 1901. Quoted in parts by Horská-Vrbová, "Podíl ceská politiky," pp. 770-72.

110. Alois Hajn, "Za svobodu přesvědčení," Osvěta lidu
(1899), no. 47, reprinted in Alois Hajn, Život novinářuv, pp.
199-202, defends Hilsner. Antonín Hajn's "Barnumovština anti-
semitská," Samostatnost, vol. 1, no. 57 (December 11, 1897), is
an attack on the anti-Semitism of Národní obrana and Nové listy
and the demagogic Young Czech attacks on the Jewish leadership
of Social Democracy in Národní listy.

111. Masaryk's defense of Hilsner and attack on anti-Semitism
was published as Význam processu polenského pro pověru rituelní
(Berlin, 1900) and in German translation (Berlin, 1900), and in
an article for Die Zeit, vol. 9, no. 3 (1899), "Die Nothwendig-
keit der Revision des Polnaer Processes." An analytical history
of the Hilsner affair is Bohumil Černý's Vražda v Polné (Prague,
1968). See also the pertinent essays in Benjamin R. Epstein,
ed., Thomas G. Masaryk and the Jews (New York, 1941).

112. Works by Frankenberger, Štern, and Plamínková are cited
in the bibliography.

113. On anti-Semitism in Austria, see Pulzer, Rise of Political Anti-Semitism, especially pp. 127-88 and 199-218, 247ff.
Karl Lueger, the notoriously and demagogically anti-Semitic
mayor of Vienna and an inspiration for Adolf Hitler, helped

504 Notes to Pages 303-306

establish the Austrian Christian Socialist party and encouraged it to make demagogic anti-Semitic pronouncements.

114. Masaryk, Naše nynější krise, p. lxiii, and idem, Česká otázka, pp. 229-34.

115. Masaryk, Desorganisace, pp. 46-52; idem, Naše situace: Řeč ve Velími, pp. 21-22; and idem, Politická situace, pp. 35-40.

116. Party history and programs are contained in Program české strany pokroková (Prague, 1912). On party history to 1906, see also J. J. Langner, "O českých stranách politických" (Pardubice, 1906), pp. 13-19, a reprint of an article appearing in Swiat Słowianski 2 (1906).

117. On self-government see Program české strany pokroková, pp. 168-69; and HHUSA, Plener papers, Seit 875, letter of Masaryk to Plener, July 3, 1899.

118. R. Fischer, Pokroková Morava, 2:242-43. See also the comprehensive study of Masaryk's successful candidacy from that district, Stanislav Jandík, Masaryk na Valašsku: Jeho boj o poslanecký mandát (Prague, 1936), especially pp. 142-52, 159-62, on the 1907 election. On Masaryk's service to the district as a deputy, see also Jaroslav Dorazil et al., Hrst vzpomínek na dobu poslanecké činnosti T. G. Masaryka na Valašsku (Valašské Meziříčí, 1935).

119. See above, chap. 9, "The Great Powers and the Czech Question." Also Vavro Šrobár, Z môjho života, pp. 351-66 and 400-05. Albert Pražak, "Vliv T. G. Masaryka na Slovenské hlasisty," and Vavro Šrobár, "T. G. Masaryk a Slováci," in Slovensko Masarykovi, ed. Josef Rudinský (Bratislava, 1930), pp. 87-104.

120. Masaryk, Otázka sociální; Kohák, Masaryk on Marx.

121. Karel Pichlík, Zahraniční odboj 1914/1918 bez legend (Prague, 1968), pp. 27-28.

122. T. G. Masaryk, Rusko a Evropa, 2 vols. (Prague, 1919-21); The Spirit of Russia, trans. Eden and Cedar Paul, 2 vols. (London, 1919-21). See also the recently published vol. 3 on Dostoevsky, trans. Robert Bass (New York, 1967).

123. Polemical attacks of the 1950s on Masaryk's political philosophy and political motives are Křížek, T. G. Masaryk a česká politika, a study of Masaryk and the Realist movement, and Václav Král, O Masarykově a Benešově kontrarevoluční politice (Prague, 1953). The first is tendentious in places and the latter primarily a propaganda piece. A recent critical study of

Masaryk's philosophy is Olga Louzilová, Masarykova filosofie člo-
věka (Prague, 1967). Milan Machovec provides a critical preface,
introduction, and notes to the most recently published selection
of Masaryk's writings, Tomáš G. Masaryk, 2d ed. (Prague, 1968).
Other useful studies include Lubomír Nový, Filosofie T. G. Masaryka (Prague, 1962), and the more comprehensive Miloslav Trapl,
Vědecké základy Masarykovy politiky (Brno, 1946).

124. Thoughtful recent interpretations are Zdeněk Šolle, "O
smyslu novodobého českého politického programu," ČsČH, vol. 18,
no. 1 (1970):1-22, and Otto Urban, "Masarykovo pojetí české
otázky," ČsČH, vol. 17, no. 2 (1969):527-52.

Chapter 11

1. See table 22A in the appendix. In the Reichsrat, the
Young Czechs lost one seat to the Radical Progressives, two each
to the National Socialists and the State Rights Radicals and five
to the Agrarians. In the Bohemian Diet, they lost five to the
Agrarians and three to the Old Czechs. On the Agrarian gains see
Frankenberger and Kubíček, Švehla, pp. 91-93.

2. Fořt and Edvard Grégr, along with the latter's nephew Prokop Grégr and others, led the radical minority who wanted the
party to oppose Koerber by obstruction in the Reichsrat until
concessions on language and civil rights would be forthcoming.
See PNP, Edvard Grégr papers, 179/44, manuscript Denník z řísské
rady od 28. ledna 1901 do 25. října 1901, pp. 155/1-155/6. See
also editorials in the Národní listy in 1901 and 1902 supporting
the radical position, including for example that of December 2,
1902, "Napřed nám vrat'te, co jste nám vzali!" PNP, Prokop Grégr
papers, 616/25/63, Vojtech Černý, Mladočeská politika ve Vídni,
manuscript article from 1903 against the policies of Kramář,
V. Škarda, and Stránský. Kaizl justified opportunistic cooperation with Koerber in lieu of principled obstruction in his letters to V. Škarda of August 27 and November 14, 1900, in Kaizl
Z mého života, 3:1085-86, 1093-94. Kramář did likewise in his
Poznámky, pp. 26-37. The limited extent of Young Czech cooperation with Koerber is illustrated by the fact, noted in chap. 9,
that party leaders authorized Antonín Rezek's becoming ministr
krajan on the understanding that in office he would not speak
for or represent the party.

3. The German parties gave Clary no help because, as their
Whitsun program demonstrated, they would settle for nothing less
than repeal of the Stremayr language ordinances of 1880 in whole
or in part, a concession that Clary would not grant. On Whitsun,
see anon., Svatodušní program německý. On Clary, see chap. 9,
n. 62.

4. On V. Škarda's arranging the pact with the Old Czechs for
the September 1901 diet elections, see LANM, Pacák papers, letters from V. Škarda dated March 13 and 24 and August 13, 1901;
Kaizl, Z mého života, 3:1082-83, letter of Kaizl to Škarda of
August 23, 1900. The Young Czechs had tried repeatedly during
that summer to make on their own terms an electoral agreement
with the Agrarian party in 1900 in the fourth curia but had been
rebuffed. See Kaizl's letter of May 9, 1901, to V. Škarda and
letters of July 31 and August 11, 1901 to B. Pacák in Kaizl, Z
mého života, 3:1153, 1177-80. The Agrarians had first proposed
agreement on terms less favorable to the Young Czechs.

5. National Socialist and Agrarian support for national and
state rights issues is noted in chap. 10 and well demonstrated
by the National Socialist party program of September 1902, the
"zde" campaign of 1903, and the alliance with Old and Young
Czechs in an electoral "cartel" in June 1911 before the Reichsrat
elections. In the case of the Agrarians, comparable evidence includes party platforms after December 1905 and association on
November 30, 1907, with Young and Old Czech and National Catholic
delegates in a Czech National Club (Národní klub český) in the
Reichsrat. The greater interest of both parties as opposed to
the Young Czechs in advancing social welfare measures is noted
in chap. 10 above and for the National Socialists is especially
evident in Jan Vorel, Sociální politika obcí.

6. On Young Czech support for the founding of the Czech National Council on June 17, 1900, see Fořt, Ven z přítmí!, pp.
191-95, and paragraph 8 of the party's platform for the Bohemian
diet elections of 1901 in M. Navrátil, Nový český sněm, p. 112.
The policy of the Council on the language issue resembled closely
that of the Young Czech party since 1897. See the most complete
policy statement on this issue, Národní Rada česká, ed., Posudek
Národní Rady české o vladní osnově Bienerthově . . . schváleny
dne 4. července 1909 (Prague, 1909), or the German edition titled
Gutachen des böhmischen Nationalrathes . . . (Prague, 1910).

7. See tables 22A and 22B in the appendix for the electoral
returns. In 1907, the Young Czechs ranked fourth in votes received after the Social Democrats, Agrarians, and clerical parties, and third in delegates elected after the Agrarians and the
Social Democrats. In 1911, the party fell to sixth in votes received following the Social Democrats, Agrarians, National Catholics, National Socialists, and Christian Socialists. It tied
for third in delegates elected with the National Socialists following the Agrarians and Social Democrats.

8. See chap. 10, n. 2 above, on Young and Old Czech ministers. Czech ministers in the Bienerth government were the Old
Czechs Albín Bráf and Jan Žáček. The best account of Bráf's

service in the two successive Bienerth ministries is in Josef
Gruber, "Životopis Albína Bráfa," in Gruber and Horáček, eds.,
Albín Bráf: Život a dílo, 5:312-65.

9. On the Young Czech, and especially Kramář's, role in encouraging Neo-Slavism and the holding of the Prague Neo-Slav Congress, see Karel Herman and Zdeněk Sládek, Slovanská politika
Karla Kramára (Prague, 1971). On the Congress, see the official
proceedings and commentary, Bohdan Pavlů, ed., Jednání I. přípravného Slovanského Sjezdu v Praze 1908 (Prague, 1910). On the
Czech role in Slavic economic development, see also Jaroslav
Preiss, "Slovanské vztahy hospodářské," pp. 85-106 in his Několik
úvah z let 1905-1907 (Prague, 1929).

10. Fiedler, 1858-1925; Tobolka, 1874-1951. Fiedler, Vyrovnání, on the decennial negotiations.

11. On Rašín's early political career, see above, chaps. 6
and 8. On his career as a Young Czech after 1905, see Hoch,
Rašín, pp. 85-132; and Fr. Fousek et al., eds., Rašínův památnik,
pp. 115-18.

12. PNP, Tobolka papers, especially correspondence with Karel
Kramář, indicates the great extent to which Kramář became Tobol-
ka's patron after 1909 and the extent to which Tobolka's editing
Kaizl's Z mého života received party support.

13. A good example of this is Kramář, "Za vedení národní
strany svobodomyslné." More partisan but nonetheless informative
on Young Czech policy in the Koerber era is Kramář, Poznámky.
The best critical evaluation of this work in its account of party
history up to 1901 is Masaryk, Politická situace. Well-documented
and precise by contrast to the above examples is Kramář, Paměti,
on the early nineties.

14. Kramář's influence and importance in the Young Czech party before 1906 is much exaggerated by most of the accounts published while he was titular head of that party (1908-18) and its
successor National Democracy (1918-39). Such accounts include
the works by Zdeněk Tobolka noted above, including Politické dějiny, and those by Vladimír Sís, including Karel Kramář: Život a
dílo and Karel Kramář: Vůdce národa. Because Kramář remained a
lively and controversial politician until well into the 1930s,
the public took much greater interest in his politics past and
present than in those of any deceased Young Czechs like Engel,
Pacák, or Škarda. This may account in large part for much of
the inadvertent exaggeration after 1912 of Kramář's political
importance during the years 1890 to 1906.

15. On the latter view, see Friedrich Wichtl, Dr. Karl

Kramarsch: Der Anstifter des Weltkrieges (Munich, 1918). Kramář's own views on the relation of the Czechs to Vienna are perhaps best expressed in his Poznámky, pp. 49-51. On Kramář's indictment and trial during the First World War, see Zdeněk Tobolka, ed., Proces Dra. Kramáře a jeho přátel, 2 vols. (Prague, 1918).

16. Prokop Grégr's opposition to Kramář's "positive" politics is explained in Prokop Grégr, Na obhájení stanoviska "Národních listů" (Prague, 1907). See also LANM, V. Škarda papers, letter from Prokop Grégr of January 4, 1906. Masaryk's critical evaluation will best be seen in Masaryk, Desorganisace mladočeské strany; idem, Politická situace; and idem, Naše situace: Řeč ve Velími.

17. These letters are in SA Děčín, Franz Thun papers, correspondence to Thun from Josef Kaizl, Bedřich Pacák, and Václav Škarda, among others. Some letters are cited individually in chap. 9.

Bibliography

Archival Sources

Prague, Czechoslovakia.

Literární archiv Národního musea (Literary Archive of the National Museum).

Private papers of Young Czechs:
Julius Grégr papers (Pozůstalost Julia Grégra). The second largest
source of materials on the Young Czech party is also the main source for
the 1870s and '80s and contains the best collection of letters by Edvard
Grégr and Ervín Špindler.
Karel Kramář papers (Pozůstalost Karla Kramáře). This extensive collection is of greatest importance to an understanding of Kramář's later
political career and his relationship to Kaizl and Masaryk during the
1890s.
Bedřich Pacák papers (Pozůstalost Bedřicha Pacáka). Pacák maintained
a wide-ranging political correspondence with all leading party figures,
including Eim, Engel, Julius Grégr, Václav Škarda, and Adolf Stránský.
Václav Škarda papers (Pozůstalost Václava Škardy). This invaluable
collection of letters, petitions, and statements best reveals party policy toward the Thun, Koerber, and Beck governments, and the operation of
the party executive committee.

Private papers of other Czech politicians:
Albín Bráf papers (Pozůstalost Albína Bráfa). Bráf's large collection
of letters is the most important source on Old Czech party history after
1900 and is indispensable to any study of the conservative great landowners.
Václav Choc papers (Pozůstalost Václava Choce). Here one finds revealing letters and documents on the formative years of the Czech National Socialist and Moravian Progressive parties as well as an interesting correspondence concerning Masaryk's politics after 1899. There
is little information specifically on the Young Czechs.
Bedřich Hlaváč papers (Pozůstalost Bedřicha Hlaváče). As the Vienna
correspondent for Čas after 1898, Hlaváč talked and corresponded with
many leading Czech politicians as well as imperial officials. Hlaváč's
papers are a better source on Masaryk and the Realists than on the Young
Czechs and include his unpublished "Vienna memoirs" (Vídeňské vzpomínky).

Památník národního písemnictví na Strahově (PNP)--Literary Archive of the
Memorial of National Literature.

Private papers of Young Czechs:
Emanuel Engel papers (Pozůstalost Emanuela Engla). These include the
extant archives of the Young Czech party from 1888 to 1901. Together
with the minutes of the party club of delegates to the Reichsrat, the

509

Engel papers comprise the most extensive and valuable source on party
history. It is still not entirely catalogued.

Gustav Eim papers (Pozůstalost Gustava Eima). This large collection
of letters from party leaders includes the best and largest number of
extant Engel letters.

Edvard Grégr papers (Pozůstalost Edvarda Grégra). These include a
small collection of letters from party associates and the Grégr diary
(denník) from 1848 to 1906 in manuscript. The largest part of this diary
through the year 1889 was edited and published by Zdeněk Tobolka in two
volumes, the first in 1908 and the second in 1914.

Prokop Grégr papers (Pozůstalost Prokopa Grégra). This rich and voluminous correspondence deals primarily with Czech politics and journalism
from 1901 to 1914. The exchange of letters between Prokop and his uncle
Edvard reflects as well as any correspondence the declining radical influence in the Young Czech party after the death of Julius Grégr in 1896.
Other interesting letters include those from Prokop Grégr's contacts
among journalists and scholars in France and elsewhere abroad.

Servác Heller papers (Pozůstalost Serváce Hellra). This small collection of letters on party affairs contains few letters that are dated.
It is of value principally in understanding Heller and his literary work.

Antonín Rezek papers (Pozůstalost Antonína Rezka). These papers contain a few letters, notably by Kaizl and Václav Škarda, pertaining primarily to Rezek's service as a minister in the Koerber government.

Alois Pravoslav Trojan papers (Pozůstalost Aloise Pravoslava Trojana).
These contain a small number of letters to and from prominent Young and
Old Czechs, primarily during the 1880s.

Private papers of other Czech politicians:

Jan Herben papers (Pozůstalost Jana Herbena). The Herben papers are
essential to any understanding of the Realists (People's party, later
Progressive party) and of Masaryk's politics. Little directly concerns
the Young Czechs apart from some critical and partisan evaluation.

Antonín Otakar Zeithammer papers (Pozůstalost Antonína Otakara Zeit-
hemmra). Together with the papers of Rieger, Pražák, and Bráf, this
collection is indispensable to any understanding of the Old Czech party
and of its relationship to the conservative great landowners. Many letters concern the Agreement of 1890.

The private papers of the following Czech writers contain a number of
letters concerning later nineteenth-century Czech politics. The Young
Czechs best represented are the Grégr brothers, Karel Kramář, and Václav Škarda.

J. S. Machar papers (Pozůstalost J. S. Machara).
E. Krásnohorská papers (Pozůstalost E. Krásnohorské).
Jaroslav Vlček papers (Pozůstalost Jaroslava Vlčka).
Václav Vlček papers (Pozůstalost Václava Vlčka).
Petr Bezruč (Vladimír Vašek) papers (Pozůstalost Petra Bezruče).

Státní ústřední archiv v Praze (SÚA)--The State Central Archive in Prague.

Papers of clubs of delegates to the Reichsrat or Bohemian Diet:
Český klub--1872-1917. Correspondence of the Czech club of delegates
was consulted only for the years 1889-98.

Klub poslanců strany národní, (1887-1894-95). Minutes of the Club of
delegates of the National (Old Czech) party in the Bohemian Diet are an
excellent source on internal party as well as parliamentary history.

Indispensable on relationship of the Old Czechs to the conservative
great landowners.

Český klub na říšské radě, 1881-90. Minutes of the Czech Club in
the Reichsrat cover the years from 1881 to 1888 when Young Czechs and Old
Czechs worked together in it. It served the Old Czechs alone after 1888
and ceased to function after their defeat in 1891. This is an important
source on Young Czechs as well as Old Czechs during the eighties.

Police reports.

Presidium místodržitelství tajné (PMT), 1874-1902. Reports of the Bohemian governor's secret police, including reports on the activities of
all political parties in Bohemia.

Presidium místodržitelství (PM), 1891-98. Reports of the Bohemian
provincial police.

Presidium ministerstva vnitra/R (PMV/R), 1888-1900. Reports of the
Imperial Ministry of the Interior (Vienna) on political activity in Bohemia.

Archiv ústavu dějin KSČ--Archive of the Institute for the History of the
Czechoslovak Communist Party.

Archiv TGM

All private correspondence and papers of T. B. Masaryk from the years
1889 through 1901 were consulted.

Státní museum československé tělesné výchovy a sportu v Praze, oddělení
archivní dokumentace--Archive of the State Museum of Physical Education and
Sport.

The archives of the Prague Sokol organization from 1862 to 1914 include
this valuable collection, indispensable to any study of the Sokol and its
influence on Czech politics and society.

Jan Podlipný papers (Pozůstalost Jana Podlipného). These papers of
the popular Sokol leader and Young Czech mayor of Prague better illumi-
nate the history of the Sokol than the Young Czech party.

Tomáš Černý papers (Pozůstalost Tomáše Černého). The correspondence
of Old Czech Tomáš Černý sheds more light on the first decade of the
Sokol in Prague and Bohemia.

Brno, Czechoslovakia.

Státní archiv v Brně (SA Brno)--State Archive in Brno.

Alois Pražák papers (Pozůstalost Aloise Pražáka). Pražák was the
chairman of the Old Czech party in Moravia and cabinet minister in two
posts in the Taaffe government. His private correspondence reveals many
aspects of Czech and Viennese politics from the 1860s to 1902.

Moravské místodržitelství Presidium (B 13). Reports of the Moravian
provincial police.

Policejní ředitelství (B 26). Reports of the Brno district police.
Such police reports serve historians in at least two ways. One can observe the relationship between the authoritarian monarchy and political
parties and can obtain information on party activities not readily
available elsewhere.

Litoměřice, Děčín, Libochovice, and Žitenice, Czechoslovakia.

Státní archiv v Litoměřicích--State Archive in Litoměřice.

Pobočky v Děčíně a Teplicích (SA Děčín and SA Teplice)--Branches in Děčín and Teplice.
     Papers of Count Francis Thun. These thoroughly cover Thun's service as Governor of Bohemia, first from 1889-95 and again from 1911-15; and as Minister-President of Cisleithania, 1898-
     source on the Young Czech relationship to Thun and his administrations.
     Papers of Count Manfred Clary-Aldringen. Minister-President of Cisleithania (1899-1900), he abolished the Badeni language ordinances.

Pobočka v Libochovicích (SA Libochovice)--Branch in Libochovice.
     Papers of the family Lexa von Aehrenthal. Especially interesting is the correspondence of Count Alois Lexa von Aehrenthal.

Pobočka v Žitenicích (SA Žitenice)--Branch in Žitenice.
     Papers of the Lobkowicz family. Especially valuable is the correspondence of George Kristián, Prince of Lobkowicz, Grand Marshall of Bohemia and Chairman of the Provincial Executive Council (Zemský výbor), 1883-1907. Included is material on the Agreement of 1890, operation of the Provincial Executive Council, and correspondence with Young and Old Czechs.

Pilsen (Plzeň), Czechoslovakia.

Státní archiv v Plzni (Pobočka v Kláštereci nad Ohří)--State Archive in Pilsen, Branch in Klášterec nad Ohří.

Private papers of Oswald Thun-Salm. Those that best discuss politics are his exchange of letters with Count Kazimierz Badeni from 1896 through 1898.

Městský archiv v Plzni--The Municipal Archive in Pilsen.

František Schwarz papers (Pozůstalost Františka Schwarza). This small collection of letters and testimonials sheds some light upon the activities of the leading Young Czech in Pilsen and the Pilsen region.

Třeboň, Czechoslovakia.

Státní archiv v Třeboni (SA Třeboň)--State archive in Třeboň.

Private papers of Charles Buquoy. This conservative great landowner was an associate of the Old Czechs in South Bohemia and a critic of Young Czech policies.

Vienna, Austria.

Haus-, Hof-, u. Staatsarchiv--The Dynastic, Court, and State Archive.

Papers of Ernst von Plener (Nachlass Plener). The German Liberal party chairman's private views of Czech politics did not differ from his public position. His papers nicely complement his publications.

Information Bureau, Ministry of Foreign Affairs--Police reports were
examined on Czech political activity, particularly on the Young Czech
party, 1890-99, and on the Badeni riots.

Allgemeines Verwaltungsarchiv--The General Administrative Archive.

The Presidium of the Ministry of the Interior contains correspondence
and police reports on Young Czech politics during the 1880s and '90s.

Paris, France.

Ministère des Affaires étrangères, Archives diplomatiques--The Diplomatic
Archives of the Ministry of Foreign Affairs.

Autriche-Hongrie, NS 4 from "the Hungarian Question," NS 4 through 11.
Autriche-Hongrie, NS 12, "the Czech Question."
Autriche-Hongrie, NS 26 and 27 from the series on "Austrian Foreign Po-
licy," NS 23 through 37.
Allemagne, NS 73, Reports concerning the activities of the Pan-German
League in Bohemia.

Government Publications

Hlavní věcni ukazovatel k stenografickým zprávám a jednacím protokolům sněmu
    království Českého za léta 1861 do 1882. Prague, 1882.
Statistický lexikon obcí v Čechách. Prague, 1923.
Statistisches Handbuch des Königreiches Böhmen, 2d edition, ed., Statistische
    Landesbureau des Kgr. Böhmen. Prague, 1913.
Stenografické zprávy sněmu Českého [Stenografische Berichte des böhmischen
    Landtages], Sessions II through XIX, 1883 to 1902.
Stenographische Protokolle über die Sitzungen des Hauses der Abgeordneten
    des österreichischen Reichsrathes, Sessions IX through XII, 1879 to 1901.
Vorläufige Ergebnisse der Volkszählung vom 31. December 1890 in den Reichs-
    rathe vertretenen Königreichen und Ländern, ed. K. K. Statistische
    Central-Commission. Vienna, 1891.
Zákonník říšský pro království země v radě říšské zastoupené, Rok 1870 do
    roku 1914, 45 volumes. Vienna, 1870-1914.
Zprávy Zemského statistického úřadu království Českého, 20 volumes. Prague,
    1899-1914.

Newspapers and Periodicals from the Period 1860 to 1914

These are still among the most complete and informative sources on Czech
politics during the late nineteenth and early twentieth centuries.

Akademie (The Academy). Beginning in 1897, the Czechoslavonic Social Demo-
    cratic party published this monthly in Prague with emphasis upon econom-
    ic and social developments and the theory and practice of politics.
Alétheia (The Greek word for truth). This monthly journal, published in
    Prague after October 1897, sought to attract readers among the Czech in-
    telligentsia and critically discussed politics and the arts and letters
    from a Roman Catholic perspective.
Athenaeum: listy pro literaturu a kritiku vedeckou (Athenaeum: a journal
    devoted to literature and scientific criticism). Published in Prague
    from 1883 to 1893, this scholarly Czech monthly had among its editors
    Josef Kaizl and T. G. Masaryk.

Čas (Time). Founded in Prague in 1886 as a fortnightly journal, Čas ex-
    panded to a weekly newspaper from 1889 to 1901 and thereafter to a daily.
    Under editor Jan Herben, it supported the "realists" of the early nine-
    ties and after 1900 upheld Masaryk's People's, later Progressive, party.
Časopis českého studentstva (The journal of Czech students). Published in
    Prague from May 1889 to December 1892, it was the fortnightly spokesman
    for "progressive Czech youth" and later the Progressive movement.
Časopis pokrokového studentstva (The journal of Progressive students). Like
    its predecessor of the same name published in Prague from 1893 to 1896,
    this monthly journal, established in October 1897, considered itself to
    be the heir and successor to the Časopis českého studentstva.
Čechische Revue (The Czech Review). Through this scholarly German-language
    monthly founded in 1907 and edited by Professor Arnošt Kraus, Czech
    scholars and writers sought to advance an understanding of their politics,
    culture, and society among German and West European intellectuals.
Cep: Agrární týdenník pro venkovský lid (The flail: an agrarian weekly for
    rural folk) was published in Prague beginning in January 1907.
Česká democracie (Czech democracy). This National Socialist monthly journal,
    established in Prague in 1909, devoted itself primarily to political
    questions.
České slovo (The Czech word). The daily newspaper of the National Socialist
    party was published in Prague beginning in 1908.
Česká revue (The Czech review). The Young Czech party began publication of
    this monthly journal in Prague in October 1897 in order to woo the in-
    telligentsia and compete with Naše doba, Akademie, and Alétheia.
Hlas národa (Voice of the nation). From its inception in March 1886, this
    daily served as the leading organ of the National, or Old Czech, party.
Hlasy od Blaníka (Voices from Blaník). This fortnightly paper, founded in
    January 1885 and after 1890 published by Emanuel Engel, served as the
    voice of the Young Czech party in south central Bohemia, emphasizing re-
    gional and agricultural concerns.
Jihočeský kraj: Revue věnovaná studiu a řešení jihočeské otázky (The south
    Bohemian region: a review dedicated to the study and solution of the
    southern Bohemian question). This monthly, published in Tábor beginning
    in 1910, stressed the social and economic problems of the region and the
    cultural achievements and political aspirations of its Czech inhabitants.
Der Kampf: sozialdemokratische Monatsschrift (The struggle: a Social Demo-
    cratic monthly). Published in Vienna from 1908 onward, it included
    thoughtful articles on the theory and practice of Social Democratic poli-
    tics in Austria-Hungary.
Kronika (The Chronicle). This monthly founded, edited, and published by K.
    Stanislav Sokol in Prague beginning in 1901, chronicled and commented
    upon the main events of every year, strongly emphasizing the political.
Labské proudy: list statopravní (Labe currents: a state rights newspaper).
    Published in Kolín from 1896 onward, this newspaper of State Rights
    Radical persuasion discussed topics of national as well as regional im-
    portance.
Lidové noviny (People's news). Founded in 1893 and edited by Adolf Stránsky,
    this daily of the Moravian people's party, initially an affiliate of the
    Young Czechs, became the leading Moravian daily and paper of record. Un-
    til firmly established, it received subsidies from the Young Czech party.
    Next to the Národní listy, it is the most important published source of
    information on the Young Czech party.
Melničan (The citizen of Mělník). This fortnightly, established in Mělník
    in May 1873, became after 1890 the spokesman for Young Czech interests
    in north central Bohemia. Like the Podřipan, the Pardubické noviny, and

the Plzeňský obzor, it is typical of the strong regional newspapers associated with the Young Czech party during the 1890s.

Menšinová revue (Minorities review). This monthly journal, published in Líny u Plzně, Bohemia, beginning in November 1911, emphasized problems and achievements of Czech minorities living in the predominately German-speaking areas of Bohemia, Moravia, and Silesia.

Moravsko-slezská revue (Moravian-Silesian review). Founded in 1906 in Moravská Ostrava, this monthly considered all questions affecting the Czechs of central and northern Moravia and Silesia.

Národní listy (National news). Established in Prague in January 1861, this newspaper became under the Grégr brothers the leading Czech daily and paper of record and the foremost voice of the Young Czech party.

Naše doba (Our era). This intellectual monthly was established in October 1893 by the Laichter family and T. G. Masaryk and edited by Masaryk until December 1914. Josef Kaizl served for the first year as an editor along with Masaryk. This periodical is of enduring interest because of its objective scholarly articles as well as because of its partisan editorial stand on domestic political issues.

La nation Tchèque (The Czech nation). Founded in 1895 in Prague and edited from its inception by Karel (Charles) Hipman, this annual magazine sought to reveal and interpret Czech problems, aims, and accomplishments to a French-speaking audience.

Neodvislost (Independence). This radical political weekly was published in Prague by Alois Rašín and edited by Antonín Hajn from its inception in December 1892 until its closure by the imperial authorities in November 1893. As an organ of the Progressive movement, it received for a time support from the Young Czech party.

Neue Freie Presse (The new free press). Founded in Vienna in 1864, this spokesman for German liberalism, the interests of Viennese capital, and the Ballplatz became the leading daily and paper of record in Austria-Hungary after 1867. Its coverage of Czech politics tended to be highly selective, critical, and partisan.

Neue Zeit (The new era). This, the leading German Social Democratic journal of political theory and praxis, was founded in 1882, edited in Berlin, and published in Stuttgart.

Nové proudy (New currents). K. Stanislav Sokol published this fortnightly journal of the Progressive movement from its first issue in February 1893 until its suppression by Governor Francis Thun in August 1893 after the thirteenth issue.

Nový život: mesíčník pro umění, vzdělání a zábavu (The new life: a monthly for art, education, and amusement). This Catholic Modernist journal aimed at an intellectual audience and was published in Moravia from 1896 to 1907, first in Prostějov and later in Nový Jičín.

Obecní listy: politický týdenník (Community news: a political weekly) was published in Prague, beginning in 1861.

Osvěta: listy pro rozhled v umění, vědě a politice (Enlightenment: a journal for the survey of developments in the arts, science, and politics). This leading intellectual monthly, initiated in Prague in March 1871, spoke more often for established trends than for innovation in politics or the arts and letters.

Podřipan (The citizen of Podřipsko). This, the principal Young Czech voice in Podřipsko, appeared weekly in Roudnice nad Labem beginning in August 1870. Ervín Špindler served as its editor-in-chief from 1874 to 1884 and from 1887 to 1890.

Pokroková revue (Progressive review). This monthly appealed to an intellectual audience and from its founding in 1904 to 1908 spoke editorially for the Radical Progressives. From 1908 until the war, it usually supported the objectives of the State Rights Progressive party formed by the merger in that year of the Radical Progressives with the State Rights Radicals.

Pravník: časopis věnovaný vědě právní i státní (The lawyer: a journal devoted to studying political science and the theory and practice of law) began publication in Prague in 1861 and included the following Young Czechs among the members of its editorial board: Edvard Grégr, Jan Kučera, Jiří Pražák, Jakub Škarda, and Rudolf of Thurn-Taxis.

Právo lidu (The rights of the people). This newspaper, founded as fortnightly in April 1893, became a daily in Prague in October 1897 and was the leading voice of Czechoslavonic Social Democracy.

Přehled: týdenník věnovaný veřejným otázkám (Survey: a weekly devoted to public questions). This progressive and reform-minded journal was published in Prague from September 1902 through 1914.

Radikální listy (Radical news). Established in Kolín in February 1894 as a fortnightly voice of the Progressive movement, this newspaper moved to Prague by 1896. From 1898 onward it usually spoke for the State Rights Radicals.

Rašple: humoristicko-satirický list dělného lidu (Punch: the magazine of humor and satire for working-class people). This Czech Social Democratic fortnightly paper of political cartoons and commentary was published in Brno beginning in 1890.

Rovnost (Equality). The principal Czech Social Democratic newspaper in Moravia appeared in Brno fortnightly from 1885 to 1894, weekly to 1898, twice a week to 1903 and thereafter weekly.

Rozhledy národohospodářské, sociální, politické a literární (Outlooks nomic, social, political, and literary). Progressive and reform-minded Czech intellectuals, including signatories of the Modernist manifesto, and editor Josef Pelcl put out this intellectual journal monthly in Chrudim from January 1892 through 1895 and thereafter fortnightly in Prague.

Samosprávný obzor: časopis věnovaný správě politické a zvláště samosprávě (The self-governmental review: a journal dedicated to political administration and especially to self-government). The Association of Self-Governmental Officials (Jednota samosprávných úředníků) published this in Prague as their official organ beginning in February 1879. František Schwarz served as editor from 1890 till his death, and Jakub Škarda served on the editorial committee during the eighties and nineties.

Samostatnost (Independence). This Radical Progressive journal was founded in 1897 and edited from its inception by Antonín Hajn. After 1908, it served as the "main State Rights Progressive newspaper."

Selské noviny: politicko-hospodářský týdenník Selské jednoty pro království České (Peasant news: the political and economic weekly of the Peasant Union for the kingdom of Bohemia). Alfons Šťastný founded this newspaper in 1889 in Tábor and published it in Padařov, Bohemia, and elsewhere after 1890.

Šípy (Barbs). Established in 1887, this satirical weekly spoke for Young Czech interests, often crudely, starting in 1890.

Snaha: měsíčník mladé generace svobodomyslné (Endeavor: monthly of the younger generation of Young Czechs) was published in Prague by the party's parliamentary club of delegates beginning in 1912.

Sociální reforma (Social reform). Established in Prague in 1909 and edited by Alois Simonides, this National Socialist monthly primarily featured topics on public health and social welfare.

Studentský sborník strany neodvislé (Student journal of the independent

party) began publication in Prague in May 1894 as an avowed opponent of
progressive student politics.
Venkov (The countryside). This most influential voice of the Czech Agrarian
party was published daily in Prague beginning in 1906.

Publications by Young Czechs

Leading Young Czechs published many books, articles, and pamphlets on
contemporary political, social, and economic problems. These works constitute the single most important source on party history and may be used effectively if evaluated critically in light of archival materials and of the
discrepancies between Young Czech goals and achievements. These works, the
product of reflection and deliberation, were designed to influence not only
the electorate but political opponents and potential political allies.

Short essays or speeches on timely issues in pamphlet form predominated
among Young Czech publications. These pamphlets complemented the press in
appealing to and in informing the electorate and often included the Czech
text of party speeches delivered in the diets or the Reichsrat. Some were
polemical tracts directed against the policies or opinions of political opponents. Still others sought to discuss and justify such cardinal tenets of
every party program as freedom of the press, Bohemian state rights, or universal suffrage.

Most leading Young Czechs wrote and published regularly throughout their
political careers. This was a remarkable feat for men like Adámek, Schwarz,
and Špindler who achieved distinction as writers and publicists while simultaneously pursuing careers in parliamentary politics, district self-
government, and business enterprise. Adámek published scores of works on
economic and cultural developments, several of them valuable reference works
to this day. František Schwarz was long recognized as the leading Young
Czech writer on the problems of self-government. Ervín Špindler continued
his literary career while extensively involved in business and in politics.
The Grégr brothers, Gustav Eim, Josef Penížek, Karel Tůma, and Servác Heller
produced many political works in addition to their prodigious journalistic
labor for the Národní listy. Josef Kaizl and Alois Rašín were successively
the leading party intellectuals and specialists in economic and political
theory. The practicing doctors in party politics wrote comparatively little,
producing an occasional pamphlet or published speech. Jan Dvořák was the
exception, publishing extensively on the politics of medicine and on problems of public health. Almost all peasant politicans in the party, including the Jandas, Purghart, and Kubr, wrote very little apart from speeches
and local newspaper articles, devoting most of their time instead to farming
and to frequent meetings with their constituents. Alfons Šťastný and Emanuel Hrubý were the exceptions to this rule.

The publications by Young Czechs listed below constitute only a part of
all publications. This list does not aim at being complete but does provide
a representative sample as well as listing some works by one prominent politician, T. G. Masaryk, who served the party less than three years and who
wrote critically of it and its policies after his resignation in 1893. Works
by Šťastný and on Kubr are listed in the next section of the bibliography.

Adámek, Karel. Karel Havlíček a ultramontáni: Příspěvek k dějinám politiky
    české. [Karel Havlíček and the Ultramontanists: A Contribution to
    Czech Political History], Roudnice nad Labem, 1877.
    This is typical of Adámek's several anticlerical works.
_____. "Na úsvitě nové aery Taaffeovy, 1879-1880," ["At the Dawn of the
    New Taaffe Era, 1879-1880,"], Česká revue, vol. 7 (1907-08), pp. 705-23.

This article sheds light on the Old Czechs and Young Czechs coming together in a single Czech club and on their negotiating an agreement with Taaffe.

Adámek, Karel. Našemu řemeslnictvu [To our artisans]. Prague, 1895.

_____. O reformě živnostenského řádu [On the reform of trade regulations]. Prague, 1897.

_____. Organisování zastupování zájmův rolnictva: Úvahy o III. članku vídeňských punktací [Organizing the representation of peasant interests: Considerations on the third article of the Vienna Agreement of 1890]. Chrudim, 1890.

_____. Památce Dr. Aloise Pravoslava Trojana [In memory of Dr. Alois Pravoslav Trojan]. Chrudim, 1910.

_____. "Paměti z doby Badeniovy," ["Reminiscences from the Badeni era"], Česká Revue, vol. 9 (1909-10), pp. 257-74, 339-55, 426-41.

These detailed memoirs, sympathetic to Badeni, include excerpts from private correspondence between party figures as well as report on important party meetings.

_____, et al. Památka čtyřicetileté činnosti okresního zastupitelstva Hlineckého: 1865-1905 [Memorial volume commemorating forty years of activity by the Hlinsko District Board of Representatives during the years 1865-1905]. Chotěbor, 1905.

One of the most comprehensive studies of a Czech district board in the later nineteenth century, this work is an indispensable source for any understanding of local self-government in Bohemia under the Dual Monarchy. This board enjoyed Adámek's mayoralty through forty years. A comprehensive bibliography of Adámek's works may be gleaned from the footnotes.

_____. Původ vídeňských úmluv o navrácení se Němcův do sněmu království Českého [The origin of the Vienna Agreement of 1890 and the return of the Germans to the Bohemian Diet]. Chrudim, 1890.

_____. Řeči Karla Adámka, poslance na Radě říšské: zasedání říšské Rady 1. 1879-1880 [The speeches of Karel Adámek during the first session of the Reichsrat, 1879-1880]. Prague, 1880.

_____. Vídeňské punktace o školách menšin [How the Vienna Agreement of 1890 concerns minority schools]. Chrudim, 1890.

_____. Vývoj živnostenské politiky na sněmu království Českého [The development of trade politics in the Diet of the Kingdom of Bohemia]. Prague, 1896.

_____. Z dějin osvobození rolnictva: Na 50 letou památku zrušení roboty [On the history of the emancipation of the peasantry: in commemoration of the 50th anniversary of the abolition of the robot]. Chrudim, 1899.

_____. Z mezinárodního bojiště hospodářského: úvahy o politice tržební [From the international economic battlefield: reflections on the politics of the market]. Chrudim, 1891.

_____. Z mých styků s dr. Aloisem Pravoslavem Trojanem v letech 1879 až 1893 [My relations with Dr. Alois Pravoslav Trojan during the years 1879 to 1893]. Chrudim, 1910.

This invaluable memoir includes long excerpts from private correspondence and is an excellent source on Trojan and on Czech politics during the Taaffe era.

_____. "Z mých styků s Gustavem Eimem," ["My relations with Gustav Eim"], Česka revue, vol. 9 (1909-10), pp. 92-113, 145-64.

This valuable source on Eim and on the arrangement of the party's agreement with Badeni includes excerpts from Eim's letters to Adámek.

_____. Z naší doby [Of our times]. 4 vols. Velké meziříčí, 1886-1890.

This thorough and comprehensive study of Czech economic and cultural

development during the first thirty years of constitutional rule is
still a useful reference work. The principal topics of each volume include: Vol. I: The development of industry and agriculture
         Vol. II: Schools, scientific societies, literature, and theater
         Vol. III: The fine arts, and social welfare services
         Vol. IV: Politics, recent economic and cultural developments
Adámek, Karel. Základy vývoje Maďarův, kulturně-historické rozhledy [The
basic principles of Hungarian development: Cultural-historical pros-
pects]. Prague, 1879.
_____. Živnostensko-politická činnost sněmu království Českého v letech
1898-1900 [The economic and political activity of the Bohemian Diet
during the years 1898-1900]. Prague, 1900.
Barák, Josef. Přednášky Josefa Baráka [Letters of Josef Barák], ed. Jan Podlipný and Václav Řezníček. Prague, 1884-85.
    The most complete collection of Barák's writings is interesting more
for its style than for its content. The tone is usually polemical.
Dvořák, Jan. Úkoly samosprávy na poli hygieny vůbec a sociální hygieny
zvlášt' [The tasks of self-government in the fields of hygiene in general
and in social hygiene in particular]. Litomyšl, ca. 1901-05.
    This is a typical publication of Jan Dvořák. He afterward published
regularly on the politics of medicine and sanitation in the Česká Revue.
Dvořák, Ladislav. Podstata a význam českého státního práva [The essence and
importance of Bohemian state rights]. Prague, 1897.
    A competent survey emphasizing historical rights and providing justi-
fication for Badeni's policies is part of this treatise.
Eim, Gustav. Politické úvahy [Political essays], ed. Josef Penížek.
Prague, 1898.
    The kernel of Eim's journalism, political essays, and parliamentary
speeches edited by his colleague and successor Josef Penížek is an indispensable source on later nineteenth-century Austro-Hungarian politics.
Includes the famous 1885 series of articles, "About us, for us," justifying active and responsible Czech parliamentary policies.
_____. Proč bojujeme proti vládě? Řeč poslance Gustava Eima pronesená
v poslanecké sněmovně v rozpravě o zatímném rozpočtu dne 27. března 1895
[Why are we struggling against the government? A speech by delegate
Gustav Eim delivered to the Chamber of Deputies of the Reichsrat during
the debate on the interim budget, March 27, 1895].
_____. Proti koalici: Řeč Gustava Eima proslovená v poslanecké sněmovně
říšské rady při rozpravě o zatímním rozpočtu 15. března 1894 [Against
the coalition: A speech by Gustav Eim delivered to the Chamber of Deputies of the Reichsrat during the debate on the interim budget, March 15,
1894]. Prague, 1894.
_____. Proti trojspolku: Řeč delegata Gustava Eima v rakouské delegaci
v pondělí, dne 17. října 1892 v Pešti. S dodatkem: Řeč téhož delegata
ve schůzi výboru delegačního 3. října 1892 [Against the Triple Alliance:
Speech of delegate Gustav Eim in the Austrian delegation on Monday, October 17, 1892, in Pest. Including a supplement: Speech of the same delegate in the delegation committee meeting of October 3, 1892]. Králové
Vinohrady, 1892.
    These two addresses taken together constitute an important Young Czech
statement, one of the few on foreign policy. As a member of the Delega-
tionen (see chap. 2), Eim could freely discuss foreign affairs as he
could not do in the Diet, Reichsrat, or the press. He argued in favor of
the monarchy's allying with its "natural" ally, France, and its "historical" ally, Russia.
_____(subj). Michal Navrátil. Gustav Eim: Geniální publicista a

vynikající politik [Gustav Eim: Publicist of genius and outstanding
Politician]. Prague, 1923.
    This, the most complete study to date on Eim, is organized topically
and includes bibliographical data and reminiscences. Navrátil admires
his former colleague Eim but writes objectively and takes into account
public criticism of Eim's policies. Eim is one of the few Young Czechs
about whom a definitive biography should be written.
Engel, Emanuel, and Josef Herold. Dvě řeči o rakousko-uherském narovnání
přednesené ve schůzi Klubu národní strany svobodomyslné dne 10. listopadu
r. 1898 [Two speeches on the Austro-Hungarian decennial compromise delivered at the meeting of the parliamentary club of the Young Czech party
on November 10, 1898]. Prague, 1898.
Fiedler, František. Rakousko-Uherská vyrovnání po roce 1878 [The Austro-
Hungarian decennial compromise after the year 1878]. Prague, 1903.
    This thorough scholarly study reflects Young Czech views on the
decennial agreements but discusses other standpoints.
Fořt, Josef. Jádro otázky nastávajícího rakousko-uherského vyrovnání [The
essence of the question of the forthcoming Austro-Hungarian compromise].
Prague, 1897.
    Because of his competence in dealing with tariffs and commercial ques-
tions, Fořt usually accompanied Czech delegates to the Delagationen.
_____. Příští Praha--město přístavní: Výňatek z přednášky [The future
Prague--a port city: Selections from a lecture]. Prague, 1910.
    This lecture discusses work done to date on projects initiated in 1884
to complete the canalization of the lower Vltava river from Prague-
Smíchov to its junction with the Labe (Elbe) at Mělník. By 1914, plans
called for direct waterborne commerce between Prague and Hamburg, a distance of 780 kilometers. Both Young and Old Czechs backed this project,
expecting, as did the Prague Chamber of Commerce and other sponsors, that
it would increase the prosperity and accelerate the growth of Prague.
_____. Ven z přítmí! Českých snah pohnutky, cíle a cesty [Out of the
Twilight: The motives, goals and ways and means of Czech endeavors].
Prague, 1905.
    This solid study of Czech positive policies in historical perspective
argues that these policies for the moment offer Czech parties the best
means of handling difficult problems in trying times.
Grégr, Edvard. Denník [Diary]. 2 vols. Vol. I: 1848-1870, Vol. II:
1874-1889, ed. Zdeněk V. Tobolka. Prague, 1908, 1914.
    This, the most revealing source on Edvard Grégr, shows him to be more
introspective and more appreciative of different viewpoints than his
speeches might indicate. It also reveals that he did not play the demagogue in defending civil liberties although he did at times give precedence to nationality issues. His comments on political events and decisions are factual and objective and reveal no arrogance or vindictiveness.
Examination of the original diaries in PNP, Edvard Grégr papers, enables
one to ascertain that Tobolka edited the published diary, as he edited
the Kaizl papers, with the aim of upholding Young Czech positive policies.
_____. K objasnění našich domácích sporů [Toward an explanation of our
domestic conflicts]. Prague, 1874.
    This was the first comprehensive treatise to advocate establishment of
an independent Young Czech party. This classic work also endorsed a
multi-party system and likened the proper relationship between Young and
Old Czechs to that between mainspring and escapement in a fine timepiece.
[_____.] Má-li se jíti na sněm? [Should we go to the Diet?]. Prague,
1873.
    This work advocates a Young Czech return to the Bohemian Diet in 1874

and introduces themes more fully discussed in K objasnění above.

Grégr, Edvard. Naše politika: Otevřený list panu dru. Fr. L. Riegrovi [Our politics: An open letter to Dr. F. L. Rieger]. 2d ed. Prague, 1876.
    This is the justification of the independent policies of the newly independent Young Czech party.

_____. Politické rozjímání před volbami do říšské rady [Political observations before the elections to the Reichsrat]. Prague, 1879.

_____. Řeč Dra. Edvarda Grégra na schůzi voličské v Roudnici dne 22. května 1892 [Speech by Dr. Edvard Grégr at the meeting of voters in Roudnice on May 22, 1892]. Prague, 1892.
    Grégr favored opposition to the Taaffe government and firmly endorsed the Young Czech indictment of Minister Schönborn.

_____. Řeč kterou měl dne 19. listopadu 1865 Dr. Edvard Grégr nad hrobem Jindřicha Fügnera, starosty pražského "Sokola" [Speech delivered on November 19, 1865, by Dr. Edvard Grégr at the grave of Jindřich Fügner, chairman of the Prague "Sokol"]. Prague, 1865.

_____. Řeč Dra. Edvarda Grégra přednesená v rozpočtové generální debatě na radě říšské dne 16 prosince 1891 [Speech of Dr. Edvard Grégr delivered during the budget debate in the Reichsrat on December 16, 1891]. 2d ed. Prague, 1891.
    Grégr's severe denunciation of Imperial policies toward the Czech nation occurred during the heyday of Young Czech radicalism.

_____. Slovo osudné: Časová úvaha o jazykových poměrech našich od Dra. Edvarda Grégra [A fateful word: Timely reflections on our linguistic relationships by Dr. Edvard Grégr]. Prague, 1883
    Together with "Speech in Behalf" below, this statement best defines the Young Czech position toward the language question during the eighties. This work is primarily a polemical tract against the Old Czechs directed to a Czech audience. "Speech in Behalf" is an attack upon the Wurmbrand bill and German Liberal policy on the language question.

_____. "Speech in Behalf of the Czech Language," 1884, in Europe in the Nineteenth Century: A Documentary Analysis of Change and Conflict, Vol. II: 1870-1914, ed. Eugene N. Anderson, Stanley J. Pincetl, Jr., and Donald J. Ziegler. Indianapolis, 1961.
    This 1884 Reichsrat speech is the only published translation in English of a speech by any Young Czech.

_____. (subj.) Langner, J. J. Dr. Eduard Grégr: Listek k osmdesátým narozeninám českého politika [Dr. Eduard Grégr: A leaflet commemorating the eightieth birthday of a Czech politician]. Pardubice, 1907.
    This brochure is a short appreciation with a representative selection of excerpts from important pamphlets and speeches.

Grégr, Julius; Špindler, Ervín; Švagrovský, August; and Šádek, František. Čtyři řeči pronesené na III. sjezdu národní strany svobodomyslné [Four speeches given during the Third Party Congress of the National Liberal Party]. Prague, 1879.
    This invaluable document in party history reflects a decision to rejoin the Old Czechs in a common club. Julius Grégr appealed for patriotism tempered by genuine liberalism and criticized German liberals for not living up to their liberal credo. Špindler defined now discredited passive opposition as naive and counterproductive. Švagrovský commended the continuance of "practical" politics, elaborating on several themes in Špindler's speech. Šádek, a Protestant minister, made an impassioned plea for maintaining liberal ideals in practice and seeking greater guarantees for civil rights, including full freedom of conscience in law.

Grégr, Julius. Na obranu rukopisu královédvorského a zelenohorského [In defense of the Queen's Court and Green Mountain Manuscripts]. 2d ed.

522 Bibliography

Prague, 1886.
An obdurate defense of the bogus manuscripts, recently exposed by Jan
Gebauer and other scholars, is made in this work.
_____, and herold, Josef. Reč poslance JUDr. Julia Grégra, pronesená na
sněmu král. Českého dne 5. května 1893 . . . a reč poslance JUDr. Jos.
herolda, promluvená při generální debatě rozpočtové na sněmu král. Českého dne 8. května 1893 [The Speech of deputy Dr. Julius Grégr delivered in
the Bohemian Diet on May 5, 1893 . . . and the speech of deputy Dr. Josef
herold given during the general budgetary debate in the Bohemian Diet on
May 8, 1893]. Prague, 1893.
Grégr, Julius (subj.] Tiskový soud Dra. Julia Grégra redaktora Národních
listů v měsíci červnu r. 1862 [The press trial of Dr. Julius Grégr, editor of the Národní listy, in the month of June 1862]. Prague, 1862.
The complete protocols of Julius Grégr's first trial by imperial judicial officials are a valuable document on imperial censorship and prosecution of the press.
_____(subj.) Holeček, Josef. Tragedie Julia Grégra [The tragedy of
Julius Grégr]. Prague, 1914.
This is a sympathetic biographical study and contemporary memoir by a
friend and associate.
_____(subj.) Tůma, Karel. Život Dra. Julia Grégra, slavného obrance svobody české [The life of Dr. Julius Grégr, renowned defender of Czech
freedom]. Prague, 1896.
This biography, largely uncritical and partisan toward Young Czech
radicalism, is by Karel Tůma, the associate of Julius Grégr and lead
writer for the Národní listy. The biography contains selections from
important party documents, Národní listy editorials, and private correspondence, making it a useful reference work and contemporary memoir.
Grégr, Prokop. Na obhájemí stanoviska "Narodních listů" [In defense of the
standpoint of the Národní listy]. Prague, 1907.
This essay is critical of Young Czech "positive policies."
heller, Servác. Z minulé doby našeho života národního, kulturního a politického: Vzpomínky a zápisky [From the past era of our national, cultural and political life]. 5 vols. Prague, 1916-25.
Herold, Josef. O české řeči úřední [On Czech official language]. Prague,
1909.
_____. O králi Jiřím Poděbradském, řeč Dra. Herolda proslovená při slavnosti odhalení pomníku krále Jiřího Poděbradského v Poděbradech, den 15.
srpna 1896 [On King George of Podebrady, speech given during the celebrations honoring the unveiling of the monument to King George of Poděbrady in Poděbrady]. Prague, 1896.
_____. "O národní autonomii," ["On national autonomy"], Česká Revue,
vol. 7 (1907-08), pp. 2-6.
_____. O státoprávní adrese, řeč proslovená na sněmu král. Českého dne
11. ledna 1896 [On state rights address, a speech given in the Bohemian
Diet on January 11, 1896]. Prague, 1896.
_____. Reč JUDra. Josefa Herolda přednesená v rozpočtové generální debatě na zemském sněmu království Českého dne 7. dubna 1892 [Speech of
Dr. Josef Herold given during general budgetary debate in the Bohemian
Diet on April 7, 1892]. Prague, 1892.
_____. "Reforma zemského zřízení," ["Reform of the provincial constitution"], Česká Revue, vol. 7 (1907-08), pp. 257-62, 339-45, 428-32,
468-73.
This article on provincial laws and institutions to 1907 and proposals
for their reform is a short survey of self-government.
Kaizl, Josef. České myslénky [Czech thoughts]. Prague, 1896.

Kaizl's famous polemic with Masaryk is discussed in chap. 8 above.
Kaizl, Josef. Finanční věda [Financial science]. 2 vols. Prague, 1892.
This work became the standard text of its day on the subject.
_____. Náprava rakouské měny [Reform of the Austrian currency]. Prague, 1890.
These proposals led to the 1892 currency reform by the Reichsrat.
_____. Národní hospodářství: pro studium akademické i soukromé v systematickém pořadu [The national economy: For academic and private study in a systematic manner]. Prague, 1883.
This was the finest textbook on national economy in its day in Czech.
_____. "Rovnoprávnost jazyková: Myšlénky Němcův," ["Linguistic equality of rights: Thoughts of the Germans"], Česká Revue, vol. 1 (1897-98), pp. 514-21.
_____. "Rovnoprávnost jazyková: Myšlénky Čechův," ["Linguistic equality of rights: Thoughts of the Czechs"], Česká Revue, vol. 1 (1897-98), pp. 697-707.
This and the work immediately above it are short lucid discussions of the language issue advocating a compromise.
_____. Vyrovnání s Uhry r. 1867 a 1877 [Compromise with Hungary in 1867 and 1877]. Prague, 1886.
_____. Z mého života [Of my life]. 3 vols. in 4, ed. Zdeněk V. Tobolka. Prague, 1911.
This massive work is the most complete printed source on Young Czech politics. It includes the Kaizl diary, the complete texts of all Kaizl's political speeches, and a large selection of correspondence from Kaizl to other leading party figures, including some letters to be found in collections like the Kramář papers, Václav Škarda papers, and Pacák papers. The Kaizl papers are still in private hands. Tobolka edited this work with a view to showing the "positive policies" of Kramář and the Young Czechs to best advantage. Despite this bias, Tobolka's scholarly work is an essential point for anyone studying later nineteenth-century Czech politics.
Kramář, Karel. České státní právo [Bohemian state rights]. Prague, 1896. The German edition is Das Böhmische Staatsrecht. Vienna, 1896.
This work is discussed in chap. 7.
_____. "České státní právo a česká strana lidová," ["Bohemian state rights and the Czech People's party"], Česká Revue, vol. 3 (1899-1900), pp. 1092-1105.
A defense of Bohemian State Rights against Masaryk's criticism and a critical evaluation of Masaryk's newly formed People's party.
_____. "Dějiny české politiky od vstupu Čechů na říšskou radu až do pádu strany staročeské," ["The history of Czech politics from the entry of the Czechs into Parliament up to the fall of the Old Czech party"] and "Za vedení národní strany svobodomyslné" ["Under the leadership of the National Liberal party"] in Česká politika, ed. Zdeněk V. Tobolka. Prague, 1906-13. Vol. 3, pp. 448-524 and pp. 525-795.
Together these essays superficially survey Czech politics from 1879 to 1912. Sometimes self-serving, the essays generally neglect the mass parties and seldom rise above summarizing parliamentary debates and Czech negotiations with imperial officials. The essays are of interest mainly for what they reveal about Kramář.
_____. "Evropa a česká otázka," ["Europe and the Czech question"], Česká Revue, vol. 6 (1902-03), pp. 1-8, 103-14.
The Czech text of his National Review article.
_____. O české politice [On Czech politics]. Prague, 1909.
Kramář gave this speech to a meeting of the student organization of the

Young Czech party on November 21, 1909.

Kramář, Karel. O úkolech svobodomyslného studentstva [Concerning the tasks
of liberal students]. Prague, 1908.

_____. Odpověd českoslovanským sociálním Demokratům: Řeč Dra. Kramáře
v Libni 21. května 1911 [Reply to the Czechoslavonic Social Democrats: A
speech by Dr. Kramář in Liben on May 21, 1911]. Prague, 1911.
K. K. upheld positive policies and the Young Czech record in social
welfare legislation, denying Social Democratic charges that he and his
party exclusively represented the interests of the upper middle classes.

_____. Offenes Schreiben an den Herrn Geheimrat Prof. Dr. Adolf Wagner
in Berlin. Prague, 1909. Reprint from journal Union.
Kramář wrote to deny his former professor's assertions that the Germans were responsible for almost all higher culture and progress in
Austria-Hungary.

_____. Paměti [Memoirs]. 2d ed. Prague, ca. 1939.
These memoirs cover Kramář's youth, his entry into politics as a Realist, and his career as a Young Czech from December 1890 to September
1893. The Memoirs are the most factual and objective of Kramář's writings, but in attempting to present a complete account and a favorable
impression of his own activities, Kramář sometimes lost sight of larger
forces and events and therefore did not always see his early career in
proper perspective.

_____. "Po sjezdu důverníků," ["After the meeting of the trustees"],
Česká revue, vol. 1 (1897-98), pp. 1-8.
Kramář discussed problems at the height of the Badeni crisis, October
1897.

_____. Poznámky o české politice [Notes on Czech Politics]. Prague,
1906.
In defending positive policies, K. was very concerned with justifying
Young Czech policy toward the Koerber government. His account of Czech
politics from Nymburk to the fall of Badeni exaggerated the intensity
of the conflict between radicals and moderates in the Young Czech party
in attempting to make a better case for the positive policies which followed the debacle of 1897 to 1899. See Masaryk's pointed criticisms of
this work below, Poznámky k poznamkách.

_____. "Rakouská zahraniční politika v XIX. století" ["Austrian foreign
policy in the nineteenth century"], in Česká politika, ed. Zdeněk V. Tobolka, Prague, 1906-13. Vol. I, pp. 49-183.
This survey of Austrian foreign policy seldom considers it in relation to domestic policy and says little that would upset the Habsburgs.

_____. "Svobodomyslné mládeži," ["Liberal youth"], Snaha [Endeavor],
vol. 1, nos. 2-3 (September 8, 1912), pp. 1-3.
Speaking before the public meeting of the first congress of Liberal
Youth in Turnov on July 21, 1912, Karel Kramář urged all to be loyal to
and constructively critical of the party.

_____. "Vstup realistů do strany mladočeské," ["Entry of the Realists
into the Young Czech party"] in Půl století "Národních listů" Almanach,
1860-1910. Prague, ca. 1910, pp. 49-53.
This item was designed to show Kramář to have played an important role
in the events described.

_____. "Z pathologie moderního hospodářství," ["Of the pathology of the
modern economy"], Athenaeum, vol. 6, no. 5 (February 15, 1889), pp.
129-34.
This article on economics reflected Kramář's studies in Germany with
the "socialists of the chair."

_____. "Za doktorem Riegrem," ["In memory of Dr. Rieger"], Česká revue, vol. 6 (1902-03), pp. 481-89.

This sympathetic portrait shows Kramář's respect and admiration for Rieger.

_____(subj.) Sís, Vladimír, ed. Dr. Karel Kramář: Život, dílo, práce: Vudce národa [Dr. Karel Kramář: Life, writings, work: leader of the nation]. Prague, 1936.

_____(subj.) Sís, Vladimír, ed. Odkaz a pravda Dr. Karla Kramáře [The legacy and truth of Dr. Karel Kramář]. Prague, 1939.

The two above works, both volumes of essays, are among the best works on Kramář.

_____(subj.) Němec, B., Pimper, A., and Holeček, V., eds. Sborník Dra. Karla Kramáře k jeho 70. narozeninám [A memorial volume for Dr. Karel Kramář on his seventieth birthday]. Prague, 1930.

This is the most comprehensive and most informative of the many memorial works on Kramář. A valuable reference article by Michal Navrátil, pp. 347-72, summarizes important biographical data in chronological order and lists all Kramář's important Reichsrat and Diet speeches.

Masaryk, Tomáš Garrigue. Česká otázka: Snahy a tužby národního obrození [The Czech question: Struggles and aspirations of the National Revival]. Prague, 1895.

_____. Demokratism v politice [Democracy in politics]. Prague, 1912.

_____. Hus českému studentstvu [Hus to the Czech students]. Prague, 1899.

_____. The Ideals of Humanity and How to Work. London, 1938.

_____. Jan Hus: Naše obrození a naše reformace [Jan Hus: Our revival and our reformation]. Prague, 1896.

_____. Karel Havlíček: Snahy a tužby politického probuzení [Karel Havlíček: Struggles and aspirations of political awakening]. 2d ed. Prague, 1904.

_____. Masaryk on Marx: An Abridged Edition of the Social Question: Philosophical and Sociological Foundations of Marxism. Ed. and trans. by Erazim V. Kohák. Lewisburg, Pa., 1972.

_____. Mnohoženství a jednoženství [Polygamy and Monogamy]. Prague, 1899.

_____. "Moravo, Moravičko milá!" ["Moravia, dear little Moravia!"], Čas, vol. 2, no. 2 (January 5, 1888). Reprinted, Břeclav, 1935.

_____. Naše nynější krise: Pád strany staročeské a počátkové směrů nových [Our present crisis: The fall of the Old Czech party and the beginning of new trends]. Prague, 1895.

_____. Nesnáze demokracie: dve úvahy [The difficulties of democracy: Two essays]. Prague, 1913.

_____. Nynejší krise a desorganisace mladočeské strany: Organisujme se ku práci [The present crisis and the disorganization of the Young Czech party: Let us organize ourselves for work]. Prague, 1903.

_____. O ethice a alkoholismu [On Ethics and Alcoholism]. Prague, 1912.

_____. Otázka sociální: Základy marxismu sociologické a filosofické [The social question: the sociological and philosophical foundations of Marxism]. Prague, 1898.

_____. Palackého idea národa českého [Palacký's idea of the Czech nation]. Prague, 1912. German edition in 1899.

_____. Politická situace: Poznámky ku poznámkám [The political situation: Notes on notes]. Prague, 1906.

This is Masaryk's reply to Kramář's Poznámky o české politice.

_____. Právo přirozené a historické [Rights natural and historical]. Prague, 1900.

_____. Rakouská zahraniční politika a diplomacie [Austrian foreign policy and diplomacy]. Prague, 1911.

Masaryk, Tomáš Garrigue. Řeč posl. T. G. Masaryka v debatě o zatinmím rozpočtu dne 20. července 1907 v poslanecké snemovně [Speech of delegate T. G. Masaryk during the debate on the interim budget on July 20, 1907, in the Chamber of Deputies]. Prague, 1907.

_____. Sebevražda hromadným jevem společenským moderní osvěty [Suicide as a mass phenomenon of modern civilization]. Prague, 1904. The German edition appeared in 1881 and an English edition in Chicago in 1970.

_____. Student a politika [The student and politics]. Prague, 1909.

_____. Tak zvaný velezrádný proces v Záhřebe [The so-called treason trial in Zagreb]. Prague, 1909.

_____. V čem je význam Karla Havlíčka? [In what is to be found the importance of Karel Havlíček?]. Prague, 1906.

_____. Vasič-Forgách-Aehrenthal: Einiges Material zur Charakteristik unserer Diplomatie. Prague, 1911.

_____. Význam processu polenského pro pověru rituelní [The importance of the Polná trial for ritual superstition]. Berlin, 1900.

_____. Základové konkretné logiky: Třídení a soustava věd [The fundamentals of concrete logic: The classification and organization of sciences]. Prague, 1885.

_____ (subj.) Beneš, Edvard, Drtina, František, et al., (eds.) T. G. Masarykovi k šedesátým narozeninám [To T. G. Masaryk in commemoration of his sixtieth birthday]. Prague, 1910.

_____ (subj.) Čapek, Karel. Hovory s T. G. Masarykem [Conversations with T. G. Masaryk]. Prague, 1969. English edition: President Masaryk Tells his Story. London, 1942.

_____ (subj.) Rádl, Emmanuel. La philosophie de T. G. Masaryk. Prague, 1938.

_____ (subj.) Rudinský, Josef (ed.). Slovensko Masarykovi [Slovakia to Masaryk]. Prague, 1930.

_____ (subj.) Šolle, Zdeněk. "O smyslu novodobého Českého politického programu," ["On the meaning of the modern Czech political program"], Český časopis historický, vol. 18, no. 1 (1970), pp. 1-22.

_____ (subj.) Vodsed'álek, F. Pro nové cesty české pokrokové politiky: Poznámky k Masarykovým vůdcím zásadám pokrokové politiky a navrhy reformy českého politického stranictví [For a new course for Czech progressive politics: Notes on Masaryk's guiding principles of progressive politics and proposals for the reform of the Czech political party system]. Prague, 1914.

_____ (subj.) Warren, W. Preston. Masaryk's Democracy: A Philosophy of Scientific and Moral Culture. London, 1941.

_____ (subj.) Wellek, René. "Masaryk's Philosophy," Essays on Czech Literature. The Hague, 1963.

_____ (subj.) Werstadt, Jaroslav. Od "České otázky" k "Nové Evrope:" Linie politického vývoje Masarykova [From the "Czech Question" to "The New Europe:" The course of Masaryk's political development]. Prague, 1920.

Only works by Masaryk relating directly to pre-World War Czech politics are included above. The interested reader may find an almost complete listing of Masaryk's pre-war works in the bibliographies compiled by Jaromír Doležal, Masarykova cesta životem [Masaryk's journey through life]. 2 vols. Prague, 1920-21, vol. II, pp. 218ff.; and in Jaromír Doležal, T. G. Masaryk v cizích jazycích [T. G. Masaryk in foreign languages]. Prague, 1938, which lists translations of Masaryk's works and works about Masaryk. The catalogue of the Masaryk-Beneš Collection at the University of California at Berkeley lists the works in the most complete collection of Masaryk materials in the United States.

Pacák, Bedřich. Boj za immunitu poslaneckých řečí vůbec a českých řečí
zvláště [The struggle to achieve the immunity of Reichsrat speeches in
general and Czech speeches in particular]. Prague, 1896.
    See comments in chap. 7.

_____. Několik slov pravdy k jazykovému nařízení [A few words of truth
concerning the language ordinances]. Prague, 1897.
    Pacák's defense of the Badeni language ordinances responded to misun-
derstanding and false charges by the German press and gave his story of
how the ordinances came to be issued.

Peníźek, Josef. Česká aktivita v letech 1878-1918 [Czech activity during
the years 1878-1918]. Vol. I: 1878-1887. Vol. II: 1887-1897. Prague,
1931.
    A history of later nineteenth-century Czech politics by Eim's succes-
sor as Vienna correspondent for the Národní listy, the work emphasizes
parliamentary politics with occasional memoirs by the observant Peníźek.

_____. Z mých pamětí z let 1878-1918 [My memoirs from the years 1878 to
1918]. 3 vols., in 1. Prague, 1922-28.
    These graphic reminiscences complement Czech Activity above and in-
clude an invaluable discussion of disputes in the Národní listy and between or about political personalities.

Rašín, Alois. Finanční a hospodářská politika československá do konce r.
1921 [The finanical and economic policy of Czechoslovakia up to the end
of the year 1921]. Prague, 1922. A revised edition appeared in the
series Economic and Social History of the World War edited by James T.
Shotwell as Financial Policy of Czechoslovakia during the First Year of
its History. Oxford, Eng., 1923.
    This is a lucid and solid work.

_____. Listy z vězení [Letters from prison], ed. Ladislav Rašín. Prague,
1937.
    These letters written during the First World War imprisonment contain
some reflections on the course and nature of pre-war Czech politics but
are of value principally for a study of wartime Czech politics and Rašín
himself.

_____. Národní hospodářství [National Economy]. 3d ed. Prague, 1922.
    Rašín's principal work on economics and finance is useful as a source
on Austro-Hungarian fiscal policy and on early Czechoslovak economic
policy.

_____. Paměti [Memoirs], ed. Ladislav Rašín. 2d ed. Prague, 1929.
    Incomplete at the time of Rašín's assassination in 1923, these memoirs
cover his childhood and youth, the formative years of the Progressive
movement, the Omladina trial, imprisonment at Bory, and his incarceration by the Habsburgs during World War I.

_____(subj.) Fousek, František, Peníźek, Josef, and Pimper, Antonín
(eds.). Rašínův památník [The Rašín Memorial Volume]. Prague, 1927.
    Of these articles and reminiscences in memory of Alois Rašín, more
concern his work in the Progressive movement and his politics from
1914 to 1923 than as a Young Czech deputy from 1907 to 1914.

_____(subj.) Hoch, Karel. Alois Rašín: Jeho život, dílo a doba [Alois
Rašín: His life, works, and times]. Prague, 1934.
    This thorough and solid work, although seldom critical, is still the
best biography of Rašín.

Rezek, Antonín (subj.). Muk, Jan, et al. Památník ministra Prof. Dr. A.
Rezka [Testimonial to minister and professor Dr. A. Rezek]. Jindřichův
Hradec, 1936.
    This work, the best on Rezek, contains a complete bibliography of

his scholarly as well as political writings.

Šamánek, Václav, et al. Veřejná schůze lidu na Žofíně dne 7. května 1892.
(Úplný obsah všech řečí na schůzi té promluvených.) S podobiznou a
stručným životopisem MUDra. Václava Šamánka, neohroženého zastance českého lidu a jeho práv v Liberci [Public meeting of the people on the
Žofín Island on May 7, 1892 (the complete contents of all speeches
given at that meeting.) With a portrait and a concise biography of
medical doctor Václav Šamánek, fearless advocate of the Czech people
and their rights in Liberec]. Prague, 1892.
     The title of this best single work on Šamánek is self-explanatory.
The meeting helped make Czechs in Prague aware of the dangers threatening the Czech minorities to the north if plans to implement the Agreement of 1890 were to be carried out.

Scharf, Jakub, et al. O politické situaci: Rokování "Josefovského občan-
ského klubu" v Praze ve schůzi konané dne 2. května 1892 [On the political situation: Debates by "the Josefov club" in Prague at a meeting
held on May 2, 1892]. Prague, 1892.

Schwarz, František. Jubilejní spis: Čtyřicet roků činnosti okresního zastupitelstva plzeňského, 1865-1905 [An anniversary volume: Forty years activity by the District Board of Representatives for Pilsen]. Plzeň
(Pilsen), 1905.
     This and the following works on self-government are discussed in
chap. 4.

_____. Listy o zřízení obecném [Letters concerning communal self-
governmental institutions]. Pilsen, 1869.

_____. Působení Václava Dobrovského jako okresního starosty [The work of
Václav Dobrovský as district mayor]. Prague, 1890.

_____. Starosta Václav Dobrovský, reformátor obce Nezdarovské [Mayor
Václav Dobrovský, reformer of the Nezdarov commune]. Prague, 1890.

_____. Výklad zákona obecního pro království České ze dne 16. dubna 1864
[Commentary on the communal law for the Kingdom of Bohemia of April 16,
1864). Prague, 1877.
     This is the best commentary on self-governmental laws for communes of
its time.

Škarda, Jakub (ed.) Sbírka zákonů rakouských [A collection of Austrian
laws]. 3 vols. Prague, 1863-64.
     This excellent selection with informed commentary is still a classic
work.

Škarda, Václav. Česká politika: řeč promluvená na krajském sjezdu Národní
strany svobodomyslné v Ml. Boleslavi 12. června 1904 [Czech politics:
speech delivered at the regional congress of the Young Czech party in
Mladá Boleslav on June 12, 1904]. Prague, 1904.
     This spirited defense of positive politics offers the best definition
of early twentieth-century Young Czech policy toward the Germans and on
the social question.

_____ (ed.) Národní strana svobodomyslná a její program [The Young Czech
party and its program]. Prague, 1897.
     This is the best and most comprehensive collection of Young Czech
party programs up to 1897 and includes an intelligent introductory essay
by the editor.

_____. "Politika etapová a základní názor strany svobodomyslné na českou
politiku" ["Politics by stages and the basic idea of the Liberal party
in Czech politics"], Česká revue, vol. 2, no. 2 (1898), pp. 536-51.
     This brilliant essay argues that the "politics by stages" followed by
the Young Czech party at the turn of the century continued the basic
policies established by the Young Czechs of the seventies. Despite

radical talk and demands for an ultimate state rights settlement, the
party had always favored an active and pragmatic politics. Škarda
slightly overstates his case for polemical purposes in trying to refute
radical Young Czech and Radical Progressive critics.

Škarda, Václav, et al. (eds.) Program národní strany svobodomyslné [The
program of the Young Czech party]. Prague, 1912.

This fine source partially summarizes the contents of the work Národní
strana svobodomyslné but also includes party programs from 1901 to 1912.

_____. Výbor statí a recí Dr. Václava Škardy [A collection of essays and
speeches by Dr. Václav Škarda], ed. Miloslava Sísová. Prague, 1912.

This best and most complete collection of Škarda's writings includes
"Politika etapová" among other speeches and articles.

_____ and Kramář, Karel. XXXVIII. valná schůze klubu Národní strany
svobodomyslné: Řeci Dra. V. Škardy a Dra. K. Kramáře [XXXVIII plenary
meeting of the club of the Young Czech party: Speeches by Dr. Václav
Škarda and Dr. K. Kramář]. Prague, 1912.

An excellent speech by Škarda, summing up the Young Czech position
toward the other Czech parties after the 1911 elections to the Reichsrat,
is given together with a long address by Kramář on the Young Czech relationship to the Bienerth and Gautsch governments and a short report by
Robert Maršan on 1911.

Sladkovský, Karel. Výbor z politických řecí a úvah Dra. Karla Sladkovského
[A selection from the political speeches and essays of Dr. Karel Slad-
kovský], ed. Servác Heller. Prague, 1899.

This is a fine representative selection and still the best edition.

_____. Výklad voleb zástupců dle práva a spravedlnosti [A treatise on
the election of representatives according to justice and fairness].
Prague, 1875.

_____(subj.) Matoušek, Josef. Karel Sladkovský a český radikalism za
revoluce a reakce [Karel Sladkovský and Czech radicalism in the time of
revolution and reaction]. Prague, 1929.

The best study of young Sladkovský and his abandoning revolutionary
radicalism for a democratic liberalism, this work contains a large selection of theretofore unpublished police reports on Sladkovský and political speeches and essays not printed in the Heller edition above.

Slavík, Jan. Nová dráha české politiky: Časová úvaha o dvou větách z
ústavy [The new course of Czech politics: A timely essay on two sections from the constitution]. Prague, 1899.

This work considers two sections of the Cisleithanian constitution in
the light of recent events concerning the demise of the Badeni government and Minister-President Thun's rule by decree. The first section
concerns "the law-making power of the provincial diets and the Reichsrat,"
and the second concerns the executive power. The work argued that the
recent breakdown of the Reichsrat could only be overcome by granting
greater autonomy to the provinces where solutions suitable to each different national and ethnic group might be found. Slavík had resigned
from the party in opposition to its cooperation with the Thun government.

_____. O rakousko-uherském narovnání [On the Austro-Hungarian decennial
compromise]. Prague, 1897.

_____. Řeč poslance dra Slavíka, pronesená ve včerejším sezení poslanécké
snemovny [Speech of deputy Dr. Slavík delivered during the evening session of the Chamber of Deputies]. Prague, Národní listy, June 14, 1891.

_____(subj.) Muk, Jan, ed. Dr. Jan Slavík, bojovník za všeobecné
hlasovací právo a práva národa: K 40. výrocí zavedení všeobecného
hlasovacího práva [Dr. Jan Slavík, fighter for universal suffrage and
the rights of the nation: In commemoration of the 40th anniversary of

the adoption of universal manhood suffrage]. Jindřichův Hradec, 1947.
    This account of Slavík's life and his long struggle for universal suf-
frage together with a selection from his private correspondence is an
important source for Czech and Cisleithanian politics.
Sokol, Josef. O podmínkách národní naší existence. Řeč poslance říšského
    Jos. Sokola na sjezdu Národní Jednoty Severočeské ve Dvoře Králové [On
    the bases of our national existence: A speech by Reichsrat delegate
    Josef Sokol given at the Congress of the North Bohemian National Union
    in Dvůr Králové nad Labem]. Prague, 1896.
    This short patriotic speech, fiery and undistinguished, is typical of
speeches given by Sokol and other Young Czechs at public gatherings.
Stránský, Adolf. Řeč poslance Dra. A. Stránského pronesená ve středu 25.
    října 1899 ve 4. schůzi poslanecké sněmovny v debatě o vládním pro-
    hlášení [Speech by delegate Adolf Stránský given on Wednesday, October
    25, 1899, in the 4th session of the Cahmber of Deputies of the Reichsrat
    during the debate on the government declaration]. Prague, 1899.
    This typically cogent speech by Adolf Stránský spearheaded the Young
Czech attack on the Clary government for having repealed the Badeni ordinances as amended by Gautsch.
Tilšer, František. Kdo hlása pravdu: Kant či Lamarck a Monge? [Who speaks
    the truth: Kant or Lamarck and Monge?] Prague, 1901.
    This is one of Tilšer's several attacks upon Kant and the idealist
tradition in German philosophy. These attacks should be understood in
the context of the Czech reaction to the Mommsen letter of October 1897,
and the German riots against the Badeni language ordinances.
_____, et al. Návrh na obžalobu Jeho Excell. hr. Bedřicha Schönborna a
    jednání a návrhu tom v říšské radě dne 4. a 5. května 1892 [Proposal for
    the indictment of His Excellency Count Friedrich Schönborn and the dis-
    cussion of this proposal in the Reichsrat on May 4 and 5, 1892].
    Prague, 1892.
_____. Ve službě panstva: Příspěvek k historii české politiky za doby
    převahy zástupců slechty konservativní nad národními poslanci v Českém
    klubu na radě říšské [In the service of the nobility: A contribution to
    the history of Czech politics during the time of the predominance of the
    representatives of the conservative nobility over the (Czech) national
    delegates in the Czech Club in the Reichsrat]. Český Brod, 1885.
    The principal Young Czech attack upon the alliance between the Old
Czech party and the conservative great landowners under Count Jindřich
Clam-Martinic, this essay defined the radical liberal Young Czech position on that alliance from 1887 to the Nymburk Congress in 1894. It
argued that Rieger gave the conservative nobles far more than he received and far more than was necessary and that the alliance principally
served the interests of the nobility by blunting the national and liberal aspirations of the Czech people. This classic work did not clearly
propose an alternative policy in any detail.
_____ et al. Pravda o vyrovnání: Věnaváno všem poctivým Čechům [The
    truth about the compromise: Dedicated to all honest Czechs]. Prague,
    1890.
    The principal Young Czech statement on the Vienna Agreement of 1890,
this work contains the Board of Trustees statement of January 3, 1890,
the Club of Delegates' statement of January 25, the text of the agreement, and the discussion of that agreement by the Club of Delegates according to the complete protocols. Most remarks and introductory comments are by Tilšer, then chairman of the club, and speeches by the
Grégr brothers, Herold, H. Janda, Scharf, and Vašatý are included.
Tobolka, Zdeněk V. (ed.) Česká politika [Czech politics], 5 vols. in 6.

Prague, 1906-13.

An encyclopaedia of Czech politics and social sciences that serves as a standard reference work on all aspects of later nineteenth- and early twentieth-century Czech society, this contains articles by Karel Kadlec, Karel Kramář, František Fiedler, T. G. Masaryk, and Zdeněk Tobolka.

Tobolka, Zdeněk V. Politické dějiny československého národa od r. 1848 až do dnešní doby [Political history of the Czechoslovak nation from the year 1848 up to the present time], 4 vols in 5. Vol. I: 1848-1859; Vol. II: 1860-1879; Vol. III, Part 1: 1879-1891; Vol. III, part 2: 1891-1914; Vol. IV: 1914-1918. Prague, 1932, 1933, 1932, 1936, 1937.

To date the most comprehensive political history of the Czechs and Slovaks from 1848 to 1918, its text is in many parts based on archival sources though no footnotes or bibliography are provided in any volume. As a thorough record of parliamentary politics, it rivals the documentary works by Adolf Srb. It suffers primarily from a loose, sometimes amorphous organization, an excessively narrow concentration on parliamentary and party history--the relationships between politics, the economy, and cultural life are never clearly revealed--and a pronounced bias in favor of the "positive policies" of the Young Czechs. The work is greatly enhanced by Tobolka's portraits of leading politicians drawn from memory as well as from documents and by other accounts in the form of memoirs. The omission of some political opponents like Dyk, Machar, Pelcl, and Borský is striking. Despite all its faults, the work remains a starting point for all studies of nineteenth-century Czech history.

Trojan, Alois Pravoslav. Dr. Trojan ke svým voličům a krajanům i všem Čechům . . . [Dr. Trojan to his voters, countrymen and all Czechs]. Prague, 1888.

Tůma, Karel. Potlačený národ: Obraz osudův lidu irského pod cizovládou britskou [Suppressed nation: A portrait of the fate of the Irish people under foreign British rule]. Kutná Hora, 1882.

This book is typical of Tůma's many works on foreign national and liberal movements, ten of which are listed above, p. 414, n. 58.

Vasatý, Jan. "Řeč posl. dra. Vasatého pronesená v poslanecké sněmovně dne 22 června 1891." [Speech of deputy Dr. Vasatý delivered in the Chamber of Deputies in the Reichsrat on June 22, 1891]. Prague, Národní listy, June 24, 1891.

Published Documents, Letters, Memoirs, Political Party Programs,
Speeches, and Contemporary Political Treatises
Pertaining to the Period 1860-1914

Contemporary Pamphlets

Political pamphlets, newspapers, books, and periodicals were, along with speeches and rallies, the principal means of communication between political parties and the electorate. Timely, cogent, and as a rule partisan, the pamphlet usually presented a more comprehensive and thoughtful account of problems than the more hastily written newspaper articles. A study of political pamphlets is therefore indispensable to an understanding of later nineteenth- and early twentieth-century Czech politics. Pamphlets in the bibliography below are indicated by (P).

Ambros, Julius. Z malých kořenů: Vzpomínky a úvahy z vývoje národního života v Olomouci. Olomouc, 1912.

Anon. Der böhmische Streit: Nachklänge aus dem böhmischen Landtage. Vienna, 1898. (P)

Anon. Pryč s volební opravou Badeniho! Prague, 1896. (P)

Anon. Svatodušní program německý z roku 1899: Rozbor kritický. Prague, 1899. (P)

Arbes, Jakub. J. Ex. hrabě František Thun z Hohensteina, c. k. místodržící v království Českém: Kritika úřadní činnosti Jeho Excellence. 3 vols. in 1. Smíchov, 1895.

_____. Pláč koruny České neboli Persekuce lidu českého v letech 1868-1873. 2d ed. Prague, 1894.

_____. Persekuce lidu českého v letech 1869-1873. Prague, 1896.

_____. Z ovzduší politiky: K. V. Šembera contra J. S. Skrejšovský: z pathologie politického života českého and Jan Rapp: Příspěvek k dějinám rakouské judikatury, ed. Josef Moravec. Prague, 1957.

"Astyanax." Čeho nám třeba! Několik slov k úkolům doby. Prague, 1903. (P)

Bačkovský, František. Národní obětiny, jejích vznik, rozvoj, význam a úspěchy. Prague, 1889.

Bauer, Otto. Die Nationalitäten Frage und die Sozialdemokratie. 2d ed. Vienna, 1924.

Baxa, Bohumil. Sněm království Českého. Prague, 1913 or 1914.

Beneš, Edvard. Stručný nástin vývoje moderního socialismu. Brandys nad Labem, 1910.

Bernatzik, Edmund. Die österreichischen Verfassungsgesetze mit erläuterungen. 2d, rev. ed. Vienna, 1911.

Berner, Arnošt. Socialistický katechismus nebo-li Červená abeceda. Prague, 1897.

Biliński, Leon. Wspomnienia i dokumenty, 1846-1914. Warsaw, 1924.

Boháč, Antonín. Boj o české menšiny v zemích českých v posledních dvou letech. Prague, 1909. (P)

_____. O české otázce menšinové. Olomouc, 1910. (P)

Borský, Lev. Před válkou o válce: Úvahy o zahraniční politice s předmluvou Jana Heidlera. Prague, 1920.

Bráf, Albín. Kterak pokracuje myšlénka povinného pojišt'ování dělnického: V "Pražském klubu" přednesl dne 20. března 1896. Prague, 1896.

_____. O některých starších a novějších projektech rakouských v příčině samosprávy. Prague, 1897.

_____. Spisy Dra. Albína Bráfa. 3 vols. Prague, 1913-1915.

_____. Život a dílo, ed. Josef Gruber and Cyril Horáček. 5 vols. Prague--Karlín, 1922-1924.

Brandl, V. Kritická úvaha o pojednání Alfonsa Št'astného "Ježíš a jeho poměr ku křest'anství." Brno, 1873. (P)

Brož, Rudolf. Česká škola politická. Prague, 1911. (P)

_____ et al. Mladá inteligenci: Z cyklu přednášek pro arbiturienty, klubu radikálně pokrokového studentstva Antonín Čížek. Prague, 1901.

Černý, A. B., and Vojtíšek, Václav. Jan Herain: Obraz života, působení a vzpomínky. Prague, 1915.

Černý, Jan M. (ed.) Boj za právo: Sborník aktů politických u věcech a národa českého od roku 1848, s výklady historickými. Prague, 1893.

Chalupný, Emanuel. Drobné spisy E. Chalupného. Vol. I: Úvahy politické; vol. III: Feuilletony. Prague, 1911, 1913.

_____. Vznik české strany pokrokové: Historické vzpomínky. Tábor, 1911.

Charmatz, Richard. Deutsch-österreichische Politik. Leipzig, 1907.

Chéradame, André. L'Allemagne, la France, et la question d'Autriche. Paris, 1902.

_____. L'Europe et la question d'Autriche au seuil du XXe siècle. Paris, 1901.

Choc, Václav. Vojenské úkoly české politiky. Prague, 1904.

Chundela, Václav. Stanislav Kubr, zakladatel české strany agrární, sedlák a politik: Příspěvek k dějinám zemědělského hnutí. Prague, 1933.

Čížek, Karel. Otázka jatečni v Praze a v předměstích: Druhá zpráva podana obecnímu výboru karlínskému dne 12. července 1893 . . . Prague, 1893. (P)
Derka, František and Vahalík, František. Česká universita na Moravě. Prague, 1891. (P)
Diviš, Jan V. Vzpomínky cukrovarníka, 1866-1874. Prague, 1923.
Dlasek, Josef. Paměti sedláka Josefa Dlaska, ed. Fr. Kutnar. Prague, 1941.
Dlask, J. Žaloba 23.000 českých dítek z Podkrušnohoří: Vydáno ve prospěch boje za českou školu v Bohosudově u Teplic. Most, 1909. (P)
Drozd, Jan. Cesty veřejného mínění: Jindy a nyní, sociální politické úvahy. Prague, 1901. (P)
Drtil, Artuš. Výbor z prací. Prague, 1913.
Fischer, Richard. Cesta mého života. Vol. II: Praha. Olomouc, 1934.
_____. Pokroková Morava, 1893-1918. 2 vols. Prague, 1937.
Frič, Josef Václav. Paměti do třiceti let. 4 vols. Prague, 1886-1887.
_____. Spisy. Vol. I: Politické články z let 1847-1864, ed. Otto Šimáček and Božena Šimáčkova. Prague, 1956.
Fügner, Jindřich (subj.) Brunner, V. H., Renata Tyršová, et al. Jindřich Fügner, 1822-1922, k stým narozeninám prvého starosty pražské Telocvičné Jednoty Sokol. Prague, 1922.
Fučík, Milan. Sokolstvo a naše doba. Prague, 1897. (P)
Gargas, Sigismund. Zur Regelund des Auswanderungswesens in Österreich. Vienna, 1913.
Gay, Ernest, and Weiss, René (eds.) Relation officielle du voyage et des réceptions du bureau du conseil municipal de Paris à Prague, septembre 1908. Paris, 1909.
Gioja, Flavio. Schwarz-gelb als politischer Leitfaden. Kremsier (Kroměříž), 1895. (P)
Graf, Josef. Die Wahrheit über den deutsch-böhmischen Ausgleich. Vienna, 1890. (P)
Gruber, Josef. Obchodní a živnostenská komora v Praze v prvním půlstoletí svého trvání, 1850-1900. Prague, 1900.
Gumplowicz, Ludwig. Das oesterreichische Staatsrecht. 2d ed. Vienna, 1902.
Günther, Franz. Der oesterreichische Grossgrundbesitzer: Ein Handbuch für den Grossgrundbesitzer und Domainebeamten. Vienna, 1883.
Habrman, G., and Meissner, A. Sociální demokracie a venkov. Prague, n.d., ca. 1908.
Habrman, Gustav. Z mého života: Vzpomínky. Prague, 1924.
Hajn, Alois. Život novinářův, 1894-1930: Výběr clanků, feuilletonů, řečí a projevů. Vol. I. Prague, 1930.
_____. Ženská otázka v letech 1900-1920: Retrospektiva a kulturně historický dokument. Prague, 1939.
Hajn, Antonín. Nebezpečí reakce ve školství. Prague, 1899.
_____. Výbor prací. 3 vols. Prague, 1912-1913.
_____ et al. Památce Gustava Čadka. Prague, 1913.
_____, and Dyk, Viktor (eds.) Státoprávne a pokrokové: Program strany státoprávne pokrokové. Prague, 1913.
Harmach, K. Obecní hospodářství, jeho vady a reforma. Prague, 1908. (P)
Heidler, Jan. České strany politické v Čechách, na Moravě a ve Slezsku. Prague, 1914.
_____. Počátky ústavního života v Rakousku od r. 1848--1870: Přednáska . . . ve Volné Lidové Škole 15. XI. 1910. Plzeň (Pilsen), 1910.(P)
Hejret, Jan. K programu realistův. Prague, 1900. (P)
_____. Pangermanismus a slovanstvo. Prague, 1909. (P)
Herben, Jan. Kniha vzpomínek. Prague, 1935.
Hevera, Čeněk. Obrana celní na ochranu českého rolnictví a průmyslu: Na hospadářském sjezdu v Chotěboři dne 8. září 1885. Kolín, 1885. (P)

Hodač, Václav (ed.) Činnost hospodářského okresního odboru Slanského za
    jeho tříletého trvání. Slany, 1864.
Horáček, Cyrill. Otázka dělnických bytů a pokusy o její řešení u nás.
    Prague, 1903. (P)
_____. Počátky českého hnutí dělnického. Prague, 1896.
_____. Příspěvek k otázce agrární. Prague, 1894. (P)
Horálek, František. Pryč se smiřovačkama! Příspěvek ku správnému rozřešení
    jazykové i národnostní otázky v Rakousku. Vinohrady--Prague, 1904. (P)
Hořica, Ignát. Pamatujte na Slezsko! Úvahy a feuilletony. Prague, 1895.
    (P)
_____. Poslední řeč poslance Ignáte Hořice, proslovená v poslanecké
    sněmovně dne 12. března 1902. Prague, 1902. (P)
hořínek, Vojtěch. Palackého pasivní oposice. Prague, 1898. (P)
Hubka, Antonín. Čechové v Dolních Rakousích: Studie z cest. Prague,
    1901. (P)
_____. Menšinová práce: K jubileu dvacetiletého trvání Národní Jednoty
    Pošumavské. Prague, 1904.
_____. Soukromé sčítání lidu r. 1900 a Gautschovy volební předlohy,
    sestavil vzhledem k Jihočeským okresům. Prague, 1906.
_____ and Joklík, František. Vládní předlohy jazykové: Vládní předloha
    o krajských vládách. Prague, 1900.
Hýbeš, Josef. Výbor z článků a projevů, ed. Otakar Franěk. Prague, 1956.
_____. Zajímavé vzpomínky na činnost soudruhův a organisací od vzniku
    hnutí až do konce let sedmdesátých. Brno, 1900. (P)
Hýsek, Miroslav. Literární Morava v letech 1849-1885. Prague, 1911.
Jechová, Květa and Klusáčková, Soňa (eds.) Dokumenty k počátkům dělnického
    hnutí v Čechách, 1864-1874. Prague, 1961.
Jelínek, Jan. Odstraňte kolek novinářský! Uvolněte tisk! Několik ukázek
    z rakouské svobody tiskové jež "strážcům" veřejného mínění. Prague,
    1899. (P)
Ještědský, V. T. Spravedlnost základem státu. Zaveďte pořádek! Horní
    Růžodol, 1913. (P)
Jiroušek, T. J. Sabinismus, barákovství, pokrokářství a "národní" dělnictvo.
    Prague, 1897. (P)
Joachim, Václav. Úkoly české samosprávy . . . Prague, 1913. (P)
Joklík, František. Kritika programu realismu. Prague, 1900.
Jozífek, O. Dvě generace Zeithammrů. Prague, 1901. (P)
Juda (subj.) Anon. Judův případ. Prostějov, 1906. (P)
Juda (subj.) Anon. Lutinov contra Juda. Prostějov, 1906. (P)
Kalina, Antonín Pravoslav. Úvahy a výzvy. Prague--Smíchov, 1912.
Kampelík, František Cyrill. Stav Rakouska a jeho budoucnost. Hradec
    Králové, 1860.
"Kein Bezirkshauptmann." Zur Revision der Böhm. Gemeinde-Ordnung.: Eine
    Erwiderung auf die Brochure des Hrn. k. k. Bezirkshauptmannes Müller
    in Böhm. Leipa. Prague, 1879. (P)
Klofáč, Václav et al. Slovanský jih: Články. Prague, 1911.
Koerner, E. (ed.) Nový zákon o živnostenských soudech a soudnictví ve
    sporech z živnostenského poměru pracovního, učebního z námezdního ze den
    27. listopadu 1896 č. 218 ř. z. Prague, 1897.
Kolmer, Gustav. Parlament und Verfassung in Oesterreich. 8 vols. Vienna,
    1902-14.
Kosík, K. (ed.) Čeští radikální demokraté (výbor politických statí).
    Prague, 1953.
Kotík, Antonín. Pláč koruny České: Některé dokumenty jako příspěvek k
    dějinám Prusko-Rakouské Války roku 1866. Prague, 1919. (P)
Kudela, Josef. O Slezsku. Prague, 1909. (P)

Kunětická, B. Viková. O ženském mandátu do sněmu král. Českého (Předneseno 22. února 1913 na veřejné schůzi v Praze]. Prague, 1913. (P)

Langner, J. J. O českých stranách politických, originally published in the monthly journal Swiat Słowianski in Krakow, vol. 2 (February—March 1906). Pardubice, 1906. (P)

Lenz, Fr. Tvrdé srdce: Leopold hrabě Kolovrat Krakovský, gentleman a oźebračený pachtýř. Prague, 1909. (P)

Lobkowicz, Frederick Prince of. Generální sněmy koruny České v době habsburské. Prague, 1903. (P)

Lobkowicz, George Prince of (subj.) Anon. Jiří kníže z Lobkowicz a samospráva v království českém: K slavnosti sedmdesátých narozenin svého dlouholetého předsedy vydal Zemský Výbor království Českého. Prague, 1905.

Lichtner, Rudolf (ed.) Památník zpěváckého spolku Hlaholu v Praze, vydaný na oslavu 50tileté činnosti, 1861-1911. Prague, 1911.

Lorenz, Max. Marxovská sociální demokracie, se svolením spisovatele, trans. Jaroslav Preiss and Alois Rašín. Kladno, n.d. (P)

Lukášek, Josef. Dr. Augustin Smetana: Vzpomínka k 100 letému výročí jeho narození. Prague, 1914. (P)

Lukavský, František. Menšinové školství na Plzeňsku. Plzeň (Pilsen), 1913. (P)

Lützow, Francis. Bohemia: A Historical Sketch. London, 1910.

_____ and Srb, Vladimír (eds.) Bohemian Section at the Austrian Exhibition, Earl's Court, London, 1906: Guide to the Bohemian Section and to the Kingdom of Bohemia. Prague, 1906.

Machač, Ladislav, Hajn, Antonín, Hubka, Antonín, et al. Státoprávní politika. Prague, 1903.

Marcha, Jaroslav (ed.) František Staněk, 1867-1927, politik, tribun, národohospodář, družstevník, buditel lidu venkovského: Memoary a dokumenty. Brno, 1927.

Mattus, Karel. Několik myšlének o českém státu. Prague, 1870.

_____. Paměti. Prague, 1921.

Maysl, A. (ed.) Okres Slanský na národopisné výstavě českoslovanské v Praze roku 1895. Prague, 1895. (P)

Modráček, František. Otázka národní v sociální demokracii Rakouska. Prague, 1908.

_____. Samospráva práce. Prague, 1918.

_____, et al. Zásady směru radikálně socialistického v českoslovanské sociální demokracii. 2d ed. Prague, 1917. (P)

Mokrý, L. České menšinové školy: Kulturním skandálem dvacátého století. Most, ca. 1907. (P)

Molisch, Paul (ed.) Briefe zur deutschen Politik in Österreich von 1848 bis 1918. Vienna, 1934.

Müller, Karel. Druhé zasedání sněmu království Českého v měsíci dubnu 1867 a naše šlechta. Prague, 1867.

_____. Pamětní zasedání sněmu království Českého v měsíci únoru r. 1867 a jeho rozpuštění: Dle stenografických zápisku podává. Prague, 1867.

Murko, Matyáš. Paměti. Prague, 1921.

Myslík, Julius. Epistola o zrádcích lidu českého! Prague, 1897. (P)

Národní Jednota Pošumavská (ed.) Jazyková předloha vládní. Prague, 1909. (P)

Národní Rada Česká. Posudek Národní Rady České o vládní osnově Beinerthově. Prague, 1909.

National Socialist Party, Czechoslovak. Program a zásady československé strany národně-socialistické. Prague, 1933.

Navrátil, Michal (ed.) Almanach českých právníků k prvnímu sjezdu českých právníků v Praze roku 1904. Prague, 1904.

Navrátil, Michal (ed.) Almanach sněmu království Českého, 1895-1901.
    Prague, 1896.
_____(ed.) Kalendář politický a kulturních událostí v roce 1893.
    Louny, 1893.
_____(ed.) Nový český sněm, 1901-1907. Tábor, 1902.
Neklan, Alexander. Neklanuv politický program (Česká otázka). Prague, 1897.
Neumann, Stanislav K. Vzpomínky. Prague, 1948.
Nováková, Teréza. Ze ženského hnutí. Prague, 1912.
Nožička, Josef. Jan Antonín Prokůpek: Apoštol hospodářského pokroku a
    národní svornosti. Prague, 1939.
Obrtel, František. Moravští sedláci v druhé polovici 19. století. Prague,
    1919.
_____. Od redakčního stolku. Prague--Karlín, 1912.
_____. Zemědělské družstevnictví v Československu. Prague, 1928.
Odraz, V. Morava do opposice. Prague, 1892. (P)
Palacký, František. Spisy drobné. Vol. I: Spisy a řeči z oboru politiky,
    ed. Bohuš Rieger. Prague, 1898.
Parish, Oskar Baron. Vzpomínky z doby Badeního. Prague, 1906.
Pauly, Jan. Populární úvod do sociální otázky. Prague, 1899. (P)
Pavlů, Bohdan (ed.) Jednání I. přípravného Slovanského sjezdu v Praze 1908.
    Prague, 1910.
Pilník, K. Vědecké pojednání o malém průmyslu a malých živnostnících
    vzhledem na nynější pokročilý stav kultury. Olomouc, 1890. (P)
Plener, Ernst. Erinnerungen. 3 vols. Stuttgart, 1911-1921.
_____. Reden. Stuttgart, 1911.
Pražák, Albert. Alois Vojtěch Šmilovský: Životopis, doprovozený vyňatky
    jeho korrespondence. Prague, 1911.
Pražák, Alois. Paměti a listář Dra. Aloise Pražáka, ed. František Kameníček.
    2 vols. Prague, 1926-1927.
Pražák, Jiří (ed.) Zákony z oboru ústavy obecní a zemské které k potřebě
    studujících vysokých škol a praktiků. 2nd ed. Prague, 1904.
Příkryl, Ondřej. Volební oprava na sněm zemský v moravských smírovačkách.
    Brno, 1904. (P)
Progressive party, Czech (Realists). Rámcový program české strany lidové
    (realistické). Prague, 1900.
_____. Program české strany pokrokové schválen třetím valným sjezdem
    strany, konaným v Praze 6. a 7. ledna 1912. Prague, 1912.
Reich, Edvard (ed.) Památce Kuneše Sonntaga: Soubor příspěvků jeho přátel
    a spolupracovníků. Prague, 1932.
Rieger, Bohuš. Drobné spisy Bohuše svobodného pána Riegra. 2 vols.
    Prague, 1914-1915.
_____. O rakousko-uherském vyrovnání r. 1867 s přehledem vývoje do r.
    1899. Prague, 1903.
Rieger, František Ladislav, et al. Čechy, země i národ: Obraz statisticko-
    historický, jejž s pomocí jiných spisovatelů vzdělal Dr. Fr. L. Rieger.
    Prague, 1863.
_____ et al. Manifest mladočeský o úmluvách vídeňských: Rozpravy v
    "Českém klubu" konaná dne 23. února 1890: K druhému vydání připojen
    zároveň List Dra. Fr. L. Riegra k předsedovi poslanců mladočeských
    prof. Tilšerovi. Prague, 1890.
_____ and Palacká, Marie. Milostné dopisy Frant. Lad. Riegra a Marie
    Palacké, ed. Karel Stloukal. Prague, 1932.
_____. Příspěvky k listáři dra. Františka Ladislava Riegra, ed. Jan
    Heidler. 2 vols. Prague, 1924-1926.
_____. Řeč poslance dra. Fr. L. Riegra na sněmu království Českého v
    rozpočtové debatě dne 13. února 1894. Prague, 1894.

Bibliography 537

Rieger, František Ladislav. Řeči dra. Frant. Lad. Riegra a jeho jednání v zákonodárných sborech, 1848-1867, ed. J. Kalousek. 4 vols. Prague, 1883-1888.

_____(subj.) Jahn, Jiljí V. František Ladislav Rieger: Obraz životopisný. Prague, 1889.

_____(subj.) Kalfus, A., Karel Mašek et al. Od kolébky Riegrovy. Prague, 1908.

Rolíček, Rudolf. Agrární politika. Prague, 1912.

S., P. Audiatur et Altera Pars! Ein Beitrag zur deutsch-böhmischen Streitfrage. Prague, 1898. (P)

S. P. Slovanská slavnost a slovanská krev. Kladno, 1898. (P)

Šafr, Václav. Národní očista. Prague, 1898. (P)

Scheiner, Josef E. Dějiny sokolstva v prvém jeho pětadvacetiletí. Prague, 1887.

Schmidt-Beauchez. L. La lutte de la Bohême contre le pangermanisme. *And* V. M. La vérité sur les événements de Prague: Mémorandum publié par les deux sociétés tchèques de Paris, la Beseda et le Sokol. Paris, 1898.

Sedláček, August. Paměti z mého života. Prague, 1924.

Sieghart, Rudolf. Die letzten Jahrzehnte einer Grossmacht: Menschen, Völker, Probleme des Habsburger-Reiches. Berlin, 1932.

Šimek, Josef. Moje paměti a vzpomínky. Prague, 1927.

Sjezd českých měst v království Českém. Sjezd českých měst království Českého v Kolíně: Stenografický protokol jednání sjezdového, v Kolíně, dne 27. října 1907. Kolín, 1907.

_____. Druhý sjezd českých měst v Praze 26-28. září 1908: Stenografické protokoly o jednání sjezdu. Prague, 1908.

_____. Tretí sjezd českých měst z království Českého v král. městě Klatovech ve dnech 21.-23. srpna 1909: Stenografický protokol o jednání sjezdovém. Prague, 1910.

_____. Čtvrtý sjezd českých měst z království Českého v královském hlav. městě Praze ve dnech 15.-17. října 1911: Zápis o jednání sjezdovém. Prague, 1911.

Škaba, Josef, and Weigert, Bořivoj (eds.) Na paměť K. Stan. Sokola k 10. výročí jeho smrti. Prague, 1932.

Skedl, Arthur and Weiss, Egon (eds.) Der politische Nachlass des Grafen Eduard Taaffe. Vienna, 1922.

Skrbek, Jaroslav (ed.) Zápisky vysockého omladináře, politického vezně F. M. Hájka ze svatováclavské trestnice v Praze. Železný Brod, 1936.

Skrejšovský, Jan Stanislav (subj.) Anon. Skrejšovský a družstvo "Politik." Prague, 1878. (P)

Šmeral, Bohumír. Historické práce, 1908-1940, eds. Ružena Kříženecká a Eva Mysková. Prague, 1961.

Smolka, Stanislaus. Polen, Böhmen und Deutsche. Vienna, 1898.

Sněm království Českého. Jednací řád pro český sněm zemský. Prague, 1889.

_____. Seznam komisí, pořadatelů a verifidátorů: II. výr. zasedání sněmu království Českého z roku 1901. Prague, 1907. (P)

Sociálně demokratická strana dělnická, československá. Protokol sjezdu dělnictva československého, odbývaného dne 25. a 26. prosince 1887 v sále lužánském v Brně: Sestaven dle jednatelských zápisků. Brno, 1888.

_____. Protokol III. řádného sjezdu českoslovanské sociálně-demokratické strany v Rakousku, konaného dne 10., 11. a 12. dubna 1898 v Brně v Dělnickém domě. Prague, 1898.

_____. Zpráva výkonného výboru ku III. řádnému sjezdu českoslovanské sociálně-demokratické strany v Rakousku. Vienna, 1898.

_____. Protokol čtvrtého řádného sjezdu Českoslovanské strany sociálně demokratické konaného ve dnech 8., 9., a 10. září v Českých Budějovicích zároveň s programem a všemi . . . řády strany. Prague, 1900.

Sociálně demokratická strana dělnická, českoslovanská. Zpráva zastupitelstva
    českoslovanské sociálně-demokratické strany v Rakousku ku IV. řádnému
    sjezdu v Českých Budějovicích. Vienna, 1900.
_____. Protokol VI. sjezdu českoslovanské sociálně demokratické strany
    dělnické dne 30., 31. října a 1. listopadu 1904 v Prostějově. Prague,
    1904.
Sociálně demokratická strana dělnická v Rakousku (Sozialdemokratische Arbeit-
    erpartei in Oesterreich). Protokol sjezdu sociální demokracie v Rakousku
    konaného ve dnech 24. až 29. září 1899 v Brně. Prague, 1899.
_____. Protokol společného sjezdu sociálně demokratické strany dělnické v
    Rakousku konaném ve Vídni 2. - 6. listopadu 1901. Prague, 1901.
Sokol, Karel Stanislav. Vězeňská korespondence Karla Stanislava Sokola z let
    1893-1895, ed. Bohuslava Sokolová. Prague, 1929.
Šolc, Jindřich. Zápas o právo jazyka českého v úřadech a soudech: Z usnesení
    výkonného výboru důverníků strany národní. Prague, 1897. (P)
Šolle, Zdeněk (ed.) Průkopníci socialismu u nás. Prague, 1954.
Soukup, František. Druhé volby v páté kurii a sociální demokracie. Prague,
    1901. (P)
_____. Odzbrojení--nebo revoluce: Řeč poslance soudruha dra. Františka
    Soukupa v rakouské delegaci 22. a 23. února 1911. Prague, 1911. (P)
_____. Proč se bojeme za všeobecné, rovné, přímé a tajné právo hlasovací?
    Prague, 1904. (P)
_____. Řeč k svědomí Evropy: Sociální demokracie na ochranu uherských
    Slováků: Řeč . . . ve schůzi říšské rady den 11. prosince 1907.
    Prague, 1908. (P)
_____. Revoluce práce: Dějinný vývoj socialismu a československé
    sociálně demokratické strany dělnické. 2 vols. Prague, 1938.
Soukup, Josef. Omladináři: Bojovníci a mučedníci za Československou samo-
    statnost. Okénka do slavných a památných let devadesátých. 2nd ed.
    Prague, 1935.
Špatný, Emil. Český antimilitarism: Kus historie a trochu vzpomínek.
    Prague, 1922.
Srb, Adolf. František Šimáček: Jeho život a působení. Prague, 1910.
_____. Politické dějiny národa českého od roku 1861. Vol. I: Až do
    nastoupení ministerstva Badeniova r. 1895. Vol. II: Od nastoupení
    Badeniova do odstoupení Thunova. Prague, 1895-1901.
_____. Politické dějiny národa českého od počátku doby konstituční do
    r. 1918. 2 vols. Prague, 1926. (An abridged revision of the above work)
_____. Sněm Český na základě císařského diplomu z r. 1860 a císařského
    patentu z r. 1861, pak volební řád pro sněm a jednací řád snemovní.
    Prague, 1883.
_____. Z půl století: Vzpomínky Adolfa Srba. 2 vols. Prague, 1913-1916.
Srb, Edvard. Vylidňování venkova: Jeho příčiny, důsledky a kterak jemu
    čeliti. Prague, 1908. (P)
Stašek, Antal. [pseudonym for Zeman, Antonín]. Vzpomínky. Prague, 1925.
Šťastný, Alfons. O doplnění našeho národního programu: Podává na krajanům
    svým na uváženou. 2d ed. Prague, 1872. (P)
_____. Ze života Alfonse Šťastného, ed. Hugo Traub. Prague, 1928.
Stejný, Tomáš, and St., Fr. Rozpravy sociálně politické. Prague, 1894. (P)
Sum, Antonín (ed.) Hrabě Lützow: Památce českého vlastence: Hrst vzpomínek
    Prague, 1925.
Svoboda, J. [pseudonym for Arbes, Jakub]. Z bojův o vykořenění lidské bídy:
    Několik kapitol a většina spisů od J. Svobody. Prague, 1892. (P)
Sýkora, Hanuš. Čeho je nám ve Vídni třeba? Prague, 1911. (P)
_____. Dobyvatelé. Prague, 1927.
_____, and Vokáč, Karel (eds.) In memoriam Aloise Simonidesa. Prague,
    1929.

Tomek, W. W. Paměti z mého žiwota. 2 vols. Prague, 1904-1905.

Topolský, Josef. Útok prof. Masaryka na církev katolickou. Hradec Králové, 1907. (P)

Trakala, Josef. Česká státoprávní a národnosti otázka (zvláštní otisk z Osvěty Ročn. 1889). Prague, 1889. (P)

Tučný, František. Přes realism. Prague, 1913. (P)

Tyrš, Miroslav. Náš úkol, směr a cíl. Prague, 1871.

_____. Úvahy a řeči Dra. Miroslava Tyrše, ed. Josef Scheiner. 4 vols. Prague, 1901-1920.

Vacek, Václav. Atentát na 26 milionů státních občanů: K boji proti daňovému plánu finančního ministra Bilinského. Prague, 1908. (P)

_____. Prvé období lidového parlamentu: Činnost poslanců sociálně demokratických a měšťáckých stran českých na radě říšské v období 1908-1911. Prague, 1911.

_____. Rok lidového parlamentu: Činnost poslanců sociálně demokratických a měšťáckých stran českých na radě říšské v obdobi 1907-1908. Prague, 1908.

Váňa, Jaromír (ed.) Volby do říšské rady v království Českém roku 1897. Prague, 1897.

Váša, Pavel. Pod Řípem: Kniha dětství. 3d ed. Prague, 1941.

Vašica, Jaroslav, et al. Pametní list k jubileu 20letého trvání Národní jednoty pro jihozápadní Moravu. Brno, 1906.

Veselý, Antonín Pravoslav. Omladina a pokrokové hnutí: Trochu historie a trochu vzpomínek. Prague, 1902.

_____. Životopis a literární pozůstalost spolu z výborem prací již otištěných, ed. Julius Myslík. Prague, 1905.

Veselý, Josef (ed.) A. Pravoslav Veselý: Jeho život, zápasy a ideály. 2 vols. Kladno, 1919-1920.

_____. Z bojů za svobodu: Omladináři v národním odboji a za republiky. Prague, 1923.

Vodsed'álek, František. Pro nové cesty české pokrokové politiky. Prague, 1914.

_____ [under pseud. J. Kalivoda]. Volní myslitelé v Čechách. Prague, 1907.

Vorel, Jan. Sociální politika obcí. Prague, 1904.

Vrba, Rudolf. Boj proti klerikalismu: Drobná perspektiva moderní společnosti. Prague, 1895.

_____. Der Nationalitäten und Verfassungsconflict in Oesterreich. Prague, 1900.

_____. Otázka zemědělská: Úvahy o zachování stavu rolnického. Prague, 1896.

_____. Stávky: Několik úvah z bojiště práce kapitálem. Prague, 1900.

Weigert, Bořivoj and Ziegloser, Jan (eds.) Omladina 25 let po procesu: Vzpomínky. Prague, 1919.

Winter, Lev. Kartely: Studie národohospodářská. Prague, 1902.

Wolf, R. České studentstvo v době prvního tricetiletí české university (1882-1912). Prague, 1912.

Zápotocký, Ladislav. K srdci lidu: Úvahy a vzpomínky, ed. L. Fikar and J. Kristek. Prague, 1949.

Selected Secondary Sources

This list of selected monographs, articles, and bibliographical guides emphasizes political and social history and excludes all works of literature and encyclopedias and most books on local history that are cited above in the footnotes.

Anderle, Josef. "Major Contributions of Czechs and Slovaks to Austrian and
    Hungarian History, 1918-1945," AHY, vol. 6-7 (1970/71), pp. 169-220.
Anderson, Eugene N. and Pauline R. Anderson. Political Institutions and So-
    cial Change in Continental Europe in the Nineteenth Century. Berkeley,
    1967.
Bachmann, Harald. "Sozialstruktur und Parteientwicklung im nordwestböhmisch-
    en Kohlenrevier vor dem zusammenbruch der Monarchie," Bohemia: Jahrbuch
    des Collegium Carolinum, vol. 10 (1969), pp. 270-86.
Benedikt, Heinrich. Die wirtschaftliche Entwicklung in der Franz Joseph
    Zeit. Vienna, 1958.
Beneš, Edvard. Úvahy o Slovanství: Hlavní problémy slovanské politiky.
    Prague, 1947.
Beránek, Jan. Rakouský militarismus a boj proti němu v Čechách. Prague,
    1955.
Beránková, Milena. Český buržoasní tisk v druhé polovině 19. století.
    Prague, 1964.
Berchtold, Klaus (ed.) Österreichische Parteiprogramme, 1868-1966. Munich,
    1967.
Bianchi, Leonard and Ladislav Hubenák (eds.) Dejiny štátu a práva na území
    československa v období kapitalizmu. 2 vols. Bratislava, 1973.
Bibl, Viktor. Der Zerfall Österreichs. Vol. 2: Von Revolution zu Revolu-
    tion 1848-1918. Vienna, 1924.
Boháč, Antonín. "Narodní rozhraničení v Čechách ve světle statistiky," Naše
    doba, vol. 15 (1908), pp. 368-73 and 439-48.
Bösl, Karl (ed.) Handbuch der Geschichte der böhmischen Länder. 4 vols.
    Stuttgart, 1966-70.
Bradley, J. F. N. "Czech Nationalism in the Light of French Diplomatic Re-
    ports, 1867-1914," SEER, vol. 42, no. 98 (December 1963), pp. 38-53.
_____. "Czech Nationalism and Socialism in 1905," American Slavic and
    East European Review, vol. 19, no. 1 (1960), pp. 74-84.
_____. "Czech Pan-Slavism before the First World War," SEER, vol. 40,
    no. 94 (December 1961), pp. 184-205.
Brock, Peter and H. Gordon Skilling (eds.) The Czech Renascence of the
    Nineteenth Century: Essays presented to Otakar Odložilík in Honour of
    his Seventieth Birthday. Toronto, 1970.
Brügel, Johann Wolfgang. Tschechen und Deutsche: 1918-1938. Munich, 1967.
Brügel, Ludwig. Geschichte der österreichischen Sozialdemokratie. 5 vols.
    Vienna, 1922-25.
_____. Soziale Gesetzgebung in Österreich von 1848 bis 1918. Vienna,
    1919.
Burešová, Zdenka. "Úloha sociální demokracie a Rovnosti na Moravě v boji
    o organizaci v letech 1890-1893," Časopis Matice moravské, vol. 74,
    no. 1-2 (1955), pp. 130-38.
Čejchan, Václav. Dejiny cesko-ruských vztahů, 1770-1917. Prague, 1967.
Čepelák, Václav (ed.) Dejiny Plzně od roku 1788 do roku 1918. Pilsen, 1967.
Červinka, František. Boje a směry českého studentstva na sklonku minulého
    a na počátku našeho století. Prague, 1962.
_____. Český nacionalismus v XIX. století. Prague, 1965.
_____. "Polemika o poměru tsv. akademické inteligence k dělnické třídě
    na konci minulého a počátkem našeho století," Historia Universitatis
    Carolinae Pragensis, vol. 2, no. 2 (1961), pp. 3-20.
Chalupa, Aleš. Zemský výbor v Čechách: Inventar. 4 vols. in 2 parts.
    Part 1: 1791-1873. Part 2: 1874-1928. Prague, 1959.
Charmatz, Richard. Österreichs innere Geschichte von 1848 bis 1907. 3d ed.
    Berlin, 1918.
_____. Wegweiser durch die Literatur der österreichischen Geschichte.
    Stuttgart, 1912.

Chodounský, K. Jan Evangelista Purkyně: Pùsobení jeho pro rozvoj české kultury. Prague, 1927.

Daicoviciu, C. and Miron Constantinescu (eds.) La désagrégation de la Monarchie Austro-Hongroise 1900--1918. Bucharest, 1965.

Denis, Ernest. La Bohême depuis la montagne-blanche. 2 vols. Paris, 1903.

Deutsch, Julius. Geschichte der österreichischen Gewerkschaftbewegungen. Vienna, 1908.

Droz, Jacques. L'Europe central: Evolution historique de l'idée de "Mit-tleeuropa." Paris, 1960.

Eisenmann, Louis. Le compromis austro-hongrois de 1867. Paris, 1904.

Engel-Janosi, Friedrich. Österreich und der Vatikan, 1846-1918. 2 vols. Graz, 1958, 1960.

Fellner, Fritz. Der Dreibund. Vienna, 1960.

_____. "Kaiser Franz Joseph und das Parlament," Mitteilungen des öster-reichischen Staatsarchivs, vol. 9 (1956), pp. 310-19.

Fischel, Alfred. Der Panslawismus bis zum Weltkrieg. Stuttgart, 1919.

Fischer, Eric. "The Negotiations for a National Ausgleich in Austria in 1871," JCEA, vol. 2, no. 2 (1942), pp. 134-45.

Franek, Otakar. "Dělnické hnutí na Moravě v devadesátých letech 19. stole-tí," Časopis Matice moravské, vol. 74, no. 1-2 (1955), pp. 7-23.

Franek, Rudolf. Některé problémy sociálního postavení rolnictva v Čechách na konci 19. a počatkem 20. století. Rozpravy, vol. 77, no. 6. Prague, 1967.

Freeze, Karen Johnson. "The Young Progressives: The Czech Student Movement, 1887-1897." Ph.D. dissertation, Columbia University, 1974.

Freudenberger, Herman. "Three Mercantilistic Proto-Factories," The Business History Review, vol. 40, no. 2 (1966), pp. 167-89.

Galandauer, Jan. "Politické dědictví Omladiny a pokrokového hnutí po roce 1897," ČsČH, vol. 12, no. 6 (1964), pp. 979-818.

Garver, Bruce M. "The Reorientation of Czech Politics during the 1890s: A Step toward an Independent Czechoslovakia?" Communications: Conférence internationale du 50e anniversaire de la République tchécoslovaque," vol. 2, pp. 45-113. Prague, 1968.

Grobelný, Andělín. "Dělnické hnutí ve Slezsku a na Ostravsku v letech 1868-1871," Slezský sborník, vol. 60, no. 1 (1962), pp. 1-28.

_____. Slezsko v období národních táborů v letech 1868-1871. Ostrava, 1962.

Gruber, Josef. "Živnostenská společenstva a spolky," Obchodní sborník, no. 9, part 3 (1899), pp. 3-25.

Guth, Otakar (ed.) Vzpomínky a úvahy, 1876-1926: Vydáno k jubileu padesáti-letého trvání Akademického spolku "Kapper" v Praze. Prague, 1926.

Hájek, Jiří. Václav Šolc, pěvec probuzení českého pracujících lidu. Prague, 1950.

Hantsch, Hugo. Die Geschichte Österreichs. Vol. 2. 2d ed. Graz, 1953.

_____. (ed.) Gestalter der Geschicke Österreichs. Innsbruck and Vienna, 1962.

_____. Leopold Graf Berchtold, Grandseigneur und Staatsmann. 2 vols. Graz, 1963.

_____. Die Nationalitäten Frage in alten Oesterreich: Das Problem der konstruktiven Reichsgestaltung. Vienna, 1953.

Hanus, Josef. Národní Museum a naše obrozeni. 2 vols. Prague, 1921-23.

Havel, Vladimír. "Rozdělní pozemkové držby v obvodu obchodní Komory Česko-Budějovice," Jihočeský kraj: Revue venovaná studiu a řešení jihočeské otázky, vol. 2, nos. 8, 9, 10 (1911), pp. 296-302, 332-43.

Havránek, Jan. Boj za všeobecné, přímé a rovné hlasovací právo roku 1893. Rozpravy, vol. 74, no. 2 (Prague, 1964).

Havránek, Jan. "The Development of Czech Nationalism," AHY, vol. 3, pt. 2 (1967), pp. 223-60.

_____. "Die ökonomische und politische Lage der Bauernshaft in den böhmischen Ländern in den letzten Jahrzehnten des 19. Jahrhunderts," Jahrbuch für Wirtschaftsgeschichte (1966), pt. 2, pp. 96-136.

_____. Hornická stávka roku 1900 v severočeském hnědouhelném revíru, Rozpravy, vol. 63, no. 2 (Prague, 1953).

_____. "Počátky a kořeny pokrokového hnutí studentského na počátku devadesátých let 19. století," Historia Universitatis Carolinae Pragensis, vol. 2, no. 1 (1961), pp. 5-33.

_____. "Protirakouské hnutí dělnické mládeže a studentů a události roku 1893," Historica Universitatis Carolinae Pragensis, vol. 2, no. 2 (1961), pp. 21-85.

_____. "Social Classes, Nationality Ratios and Demographic Trends in Prague, 1880-1910," trans. R. F. Samsour, Historica, vol. 13 (1968), pp. 171-208.

Hávránková, Růžena. "Zájem o balkánské Slovany jako složka českého slovanství v 19. století," Slovanské historické studie, vol. 7 (1968), pp. 195-217.

Hipman, Karel (ed.) Les tchèques au XIXème siècle. Prague, 1902.

Hlaváč, Bedřich. František Josef I: Život, povaha, doba. Prague, 1933.

Holborn, Hajo. "The Final Disintegration of the Habsburg Monarchy," AHY, vol. 3, pt. 3 (1967), pp. 189-205.

Holeček, Josef. Česká šlechta: Výklady časové i historické. Prague, 1918.

Honzáková, Albína (ed.) Kniha života F. F. Plamínkové: Práce a osobnost sborník k 60. narozeninám. 2 vols. Prague--Smíchov, 1935.

Horecký, Paul L. (ed.) East Central Europe: A Guide to Basic Publications. Chicago, 1970.

_____. and David H. Kraus (eds.) East Central and Southeast Europe: A Handbook of Library and Archival Resources in North America. Santa Barbara, 1976.

Horská, Pavla. "Česká otázka v Rakousko-Uhersku 1897-1914 ve světle zpráv francouzských zastupitelských úřadů," ČsČH, vol. 15, no. 3 (1967), pp. 449-60.

_____. Český průmysl a tzv. druhá průmyslová revoluce, Rozpravy, vol. 75, no. 3 (Prague, 1965).

_____. Hlavní otázky vzniku a vývoje českého strojírenství do roku 1918. Prague, 1959.

_____. Počátky elektrisace v českých zemích, Rozpravy, vol. 71, no. 13 (Prague, 1961).

_____. "Podíl České politiky z přelomu 19. a 20. století ve vztazích rakousko-francouzských," ČsČH, vol. 17, no. 5 (1969), pp. 760-72.

Houser, Jaroslav. Dětská práce a její právní úprava v našich zemích za kapitalismu, Rozpravy, vol. 72, no. 6 (Prague, 1962).

Hříbek, Jan. "Rozvoj železnic a územní rozsah ostravské průmyslové oblasti do první světové války," Slezský sborník, vol. 66, no. 2 (1968), pp. 164-181.

Hrubý, Emanuel, et al. Náš vývoj v severních Čechách pod ochranou Národní jednoty severočeské. Prague, 1936.

Hugelmann, Karl Gottfried (ed.) Das Nationalitätenrecht des alten Österreich. Vienna, 1934.

Janák, Jan. "Pokus buržoazie o rozkol brněnského dělnického hnutí roku 1871," Brno v minulosti a dnes, vol. 3 (1961), pp. 52-62.

_____. "K předhistorii vzniku mladočeského směru v táboru moravské buržoazie," Sborník prací filosofické fakulty brněnské university, Ser. C, vol. 9 (1962), pp. 109-128.

Janák, Jan. "Táborové hnutí na Moravě v letech 1868-1874," Časopis Matice moravské, vol. 77 (1958), pp. 290-324.
_____. Vývoj spravy v českých zemích v epoše kapitalismu. Vol. 1: Obdobi 1848-1918. Prague, 1965.
Janáček, Josef (ed) Dějiny Prahy. Prague, 1964.
Jászi, Oscar. The Dissolution of the Habsburg Monarchy. Chicago, 1929.
Jelavich, Barbara. The Habsburg Empire in European Affairs, 1814-1918. Chicago, 1969.
Jenks, William A. Austria Under the Iron Ring, 1879-1893. Charlottesville, Va., 1965.
_____. The Austrian Electoral Reform of 1907. New York, 1950.
Jindra, Zdeněk. "K rozvoji českého bankovního kapitálu před první světovou válkou," CsČH, vol. 5, no. 3 (1957), pp. 506-26.
_____. "Prumyslové monopoly v Rakousku-Uhersku," CsČH, vol. 4, no. 2 (1956), pp. 231-70.
Jirásek, Josef. Rusko a my: Studie vztahu československo-ruských od nejstarsích dob do roku 1914. 2d rev. ed. 4 vols. Prague and Brno, 1945-1946.
Jordan, František. "Brněnský program rakouské sociální demokracie z roku 1882 a jeho význam v českém delnickém hnutí," Sborník prací filosofické fakulty brněnské university, Ser. C, vol. 4 (1955), pp. 55-71.
_____. "Radikální delnické hnutí na Moravě v osmdesátých letech minulého století," Sborník Matice moravské, vol. 79 (1960), pp. 5-44.
Kann, Robert A. The Habsburg Monarchy: A Study in Integration and Disintegration. New York, 1957.
_____. The Multinational Empire: Nationalism and National Reform in the Habsburg Monarchy, 1848-1918. 2 vols. New York, 1950.
Kapras, Jan. Češi a nemci v českém státě, přehled historický. Mladá Boleslav, ca. 1926.
_____. Právní dějiny zemí koruny České. 3 vols. Prague, 1913-37.
Kárníková, Ludmila. Vývoj obyvatelstva v českých zemích, 1754-1914. Prague, 1965.
_____. Vývoj uhelného prumyslu v českých zemích do r. 1880. Prague, 1960.
Kazbunda, Karel. "Česká politika na počátku éry Belcrediho," ČČH, vol. 39, no. 1 (1933), pp. 102-19.
_____. "Ke zmaru českého vyrovnání," ČČH, vol. 37 (1931), pp. 512-73.
_____. "Kolem dubnového snemu českého z r. 1867," ČČH, vol. 38 (1932), pp. 285-346.
_____. "Krise české politiky a vídeňská jednání o t. zv. punktace roku 1890," ČČH, vol. 40 (1934), pp. 80-108, 310-346, 491-528, and vol. 41 (1935), pp. 41-82, 294-320, 514-554.
_____. "Národní program český r 1860 a zápas o politický list," ČČH, vol. 33 (1927), pp. 473-547.
_____. "Otázka české korunovace r 1861," ČČH, vol. 33 (1927), pp. 60-116.
Kimball, Stanley Buchholz. Czech Nationalism: A Study of the National Theatre Movement, 1845-83. Urbana, Ill., 1964.
Kočí, Josef and J. Koralka. "The History of the Habsburg Monarchy (1526-1918) in Czechoslovak Historiography since 1945," AHY, vol. 2 (1966), pp. 198-223.
Kodedová, Oldřiška. "Národnostní otázka v letech 1905-1907 (Situace v Čechách)," CsČH, vol. 3, no. 2 (1955), pp. 192-222.
_____. "Organizační predpoklady vzniku novodobé masové delnické strany v Rakousku na počátku 90. let 19 století," CsČH, vol. 9, no. 5 (1963), pp. 671-92.

Kodedová, Oldřiška. Postavení zemědělského proletariátu v Čechách koncem
    19. století: Zemědělský proletariát na fürstenberském panství v letech
    1880-1900, Rozpravy, vol. 77, no. 7 (Prague, 1967).
_____. "Vývoj organizační struktury sociální demokracie v českých zemích
    v 90 letech 19. století," Sborník historický, vol. 7 (1964), pp. 79-127.
Kohn, Hans. Pan-Slavism: Its History and Ideology. 2d ed., rev. New York,
    1960.
Kolejka, Josef. "'Moravský pakt' z roku 1905," ČsČH, vol. 4, no. 4 (1956),
    pp. 590-615.
Konirsh, Suzanne G. "Constitutional Aspects of the Struggle between Germans
    and Czechs in the Austro-Hungarian Monarchy," The Journal of Modern His-
    tory, vol. 27 (March-December 1955), pp. 231-61.
Koralka, Jiří. "Die deutsch-österreichische nationale Frage in den Anfängen
    der sozialdemokratischen Partei," Historica, vol. 3 (1961), pp. 109-58.
_____. "La montée du pangermanisme et l'Autriche-Hongrie," Historica,
    vol. 10 (1965), pp. 213-53.
_____. "Some Remarks on the Concepts of Nationalism and International-
    ism," trans. R. F. Samsour, Historica, vol. 8 (1966), pp. 209-16.
_____. Všeněmecký svaz a česká otázka koncem 19. století, Rozpravy,
    vol. 73, no. 12 (Prague, 1963).
_____. "Vznik eisenasské sociální demokracie roku 1869 a otázka Rakous-
    ka," ČsČH, vol. 7, no. 3 (1959), pp. 436-63.
_____. Vznik socialistického dělnického hnutí na Jihlavsku. Liberec,
    1956.
_____. "Zur internationalen Rolle der Entstehung der tschechischen Ar-
    beiterbewegung im alten Österreich," Österreichische Osthefte, vol. 7,
    no. 4 (1965), pp. 275-85.
Kratochvíl, Milos. O vývoji městské správy pražské od roku 1848. Prague,
    1936.
Krčmář, Jan (ed.) Randův jubilejní památník: K stému výročí narození Anto-
    nína Randy. Prague, 1934.
Křížek, Jurij, "Annexion de la Bosnie et Herzégovine," Historica, vol. 9
    (1964), pp. 135-203.
_____. "Česká buržoasní politika a 'česká otázka' v letech 1900-1914,"
    ČsČH, vol. 4, no. 4 (1958), pp. 621-61.
_____. "La crise du dualisme et le dernier Compromis austro-hongrois
    (1897-1907), Historica, vol. 12 (1966), pp. 71-145.
_____. "Krise cukrovarnictví v českých zemích v osmdesátých letech
    minulého století a její význam pro vzrůst rolnického hnutí," ČsČH,
    vol. 4 (1956), no. 2, pp. 270-98, no. 3, pp. 417-47; vol. 5 (1957),
    no. 3, pp. 473-506; vol. 6 (1958), no. 1, pp. 46-59.
_____. T. G. Masaryk a česká politika: Politické vystoupení českých
    "realistů" v letech 1887-1893. Prague, 1959.
_____. Die wirtschaftlichen Grundzüge des österreichisch-ungarischen
    Imperialismus in der Vorkriegszeit (1900-1914), Rozpravy, vol. 73, no.
    14 (Prague, 1963).
Krofta, Kamil. Byli jsme za Rakouska . . . Úvahy historické a politické
    Prague, 1936.
_____. Dějiny československé. Prague, 1946.
_____. Přehled dějin selského stavu v Čechách a na Moravě. Prague, 1919.
Kubricht, Andrew Paul. "The Czech Agrarian Party, 1899-1914: A Study of
    National and Political Agitation in the Habsburg Monarchy." Ph.D. dis-
    sertation, Ohio State University, 1974.
Kucera, Eduard and Zdenka Kucerová. O agrárnický stát. Prague, 1955.
Kutnar, Frantisek. Počátky hromadného vystěhovalectví z Čech v období Bach-
    ova absolutismu, Rozpravy, vol. 74, no. 15 (Prague, 1964).

Leger, Louis, La renaissance tchèque au XIX siècle. Paris, 1911.

Lepa, Jindrich (ed.) Šedesát let telocvične jednoty Sokol I. na Smíchové. Prague--Smíchov, 1928.

Lepsík, Josef. Stavy obležení v Čechách v letech 1848-1953, Rozpravy, vol. 70, no. 12 (Prague, 1960).

Leser, Norbert. Zwischen Reformismus und Bolschewismus: Der Austromarxismus als Theorie und Praxis. Vienna, 1968.

Linek, Josef. "Podstata Švihovy aféry," Novinářský sborník, vol. 9, no. 4 (1964), pp. 431-36.

Macartney, C. A. The Habsburg Empire, 1790-1914. New York, 1969.

Macek, Josef (ed.) 25 ans d'historiographie tchécoslovaque 1936-1960. Prague, 1960.

Malická, Libuše. Delnický noviná̌r, Antonín Macek. Prague, 1956.

Malý, Jaromír. Antonín Žalud Vysokomýtský, český spisovatel a redaktor, 1815--1873. Písek, 1924.

Malý, Karel. Policejní a soudní perzekuce delnické třídy v druhé polovine 19. století v Čechách. Prague, 1967.

Maška, Edvard. "Václav Klement: prukopník českého automobilismu," České postavy, vol. 2 (1940), pp. 215-35.

Mastálko, Josef (ed.) České mensiny kraje českolipského: sepsali menšinoví pracovnici. Bela pod Bezdezem, 1921.

Matejcek, Antonín. Národní divadlo a jeho výtvarníci. Prague, 1934.

May, Arthur J. The Hapsburg Monarchy, 1867-1914. Cambridge, Mass., 1951.

――――. Vienna in the Age of Franz Joseph. Norman, Okla., 1966.

Míka, Zdenek. "Alfons Šťastný a rolnické hnutí v I. polovine devadesátých let minulého století," Jihocěský sborník historický, vol. 37 (1968).

Mokrý, Adolf (ed.) Osmdesát let československé sociální demokracie, 1878-1958. London, 1958.

Molisch, Paul. Geschichte der deutschnationalen Bewegung in Oesterreich an ihren Anfängen bis zur Zerfall der Monarchie. Jena, 1926.

Moravec, F. V. "Úkoly samosprávy v našem programu kulturním," Škola našeho venkova, vol. 8 (1904), 94-97, 172-76, 216-21, 256-60, 301-06, 350-55, and 395-400.

Münch, Hermann. Böhmische Tragödie: Das Schicksal Mitteleuropas im Lichte des Tschechischen Frage. Berlin, 1949.

Navrátil, Michal. JUDr. Karel Mattus, vynikající státník a kulturní prácovník. Prague, 1929.

Nejedlý, Zdenek. T. G. Masaryk. 4 vols in 5. Prague, 1930-37.

Nozicka, Josef. Naše první okresní zalozna hospodárska: 75 let OZH v Roudnici nad Labem. Prague, 1940.

Odlozilík, Otakar. "Congresses of Slavic Youth, 1890-1892," The Annals of the Ukrainian Academy, vol. 6, nos. 3, 4 (1958), pp. 1327-57.

――――. "Enter Masaryk: A Prelude to his Political Career," JCEA, vol. 10, no. 1 (April 1950), pp. 21-36.

――――. "Na predelu dob," Zítrek, vol. 2 (1943), pp. 20-38.

――――. Nástin československých dějin. 3d ed. London, 1943.

――――. "Russia and Czech National Aspirations," JCEA, vol. 22, no. 4 (January 1963), pp. 407-39.

――――. "The Czechs on the Eve of the 1848 Revolution," Harvard Slavic Studies, vol. 1 (1953), pp. 179-217.

――――. "The Slavic Congress of 1848," The Polish Review, vol. 4 (1959), pp. 3-15.

――――. Tri stati o české otázce. London, 1944-45.

Opocenský, Jan. "Francie a Rakouští slovane v letech devadesátých," Slovanský Prehled, vol. 34 (1932), pp. 3-45 in reprint.

Palecek, Anthony. "Antonín Švehla: Czech Peasant Statesman," SR, vol. 21, no. 4 (1962), pp. 699-708.
_____. "The Rise and Fall of the Czech Agrarian Party," East European Quarterly, vol. 5 (June 1971), pp. 177-201.
Papousek, Jaroslav. "T. G. Masaryk a československé dějepisectví," ČČH, vol. 44 (1938), pp. 1-29.
Paulová, Milada. Balkánské války 1912-1913 a český lid, Rozpravy, vol. 73, no. 4 (Prague, 1963).
Pavlík, Frantisek (ed.) Památník města Královských Vinohradů. Prague, 1929.
Pech, Stanley Z. The Czech Revolution of 1848. Chapel Hill, 1969.
_____. "F. L. Rieger: The Road from Liberalism to Conservatism," JCEA, vol. 17, no. 1 (April 1957), pp. 3-23.
_____. "Passive Resistance of the Czechs, 1863-1879," SEER, vol. 36, no. 87 (June 1958), pp. 434-52.
Pfaff, Ivan. Jan Neruda a české demokratické hnutí v letech šedesátých, Rozpravy, vol. 73, no. 8 (Prague, 1963).
Plaschka, Richard Georg. Von Palacký bis Pekař. Graz, 1955.
Prelog, Milan. Pouť Slovanů do Moskvy roku 1867, trans. Milada Paulova. Prague, 1931.
Pribram, Alfred F. The Secret Treaties of Austria-Hungary, 1879-1914. 2 vols. Cambridge, Eng., 1920-22.
Prinz, Friedrich. "Nation und Gesellschaft in den böhmischen Ländern im 19. und 20. Jahrhundert," pp. 333-49 in F. Prinz, F. Schmale, and F. Seibt (eds.), Geschichte und Gesellschaft: Festschrift für Karl Bösl zum 65. Geburtstag. Stuttgart, 1974.
Purš, Jaroslav. "The Industrial Revolution in the Czech Lands," Historica, vol. 2 (1960), pp. 183-272.
_____. "Jan Neruda a Bratři červeného praporu," ČsČH, vol. 10, no. 4 (1962), pp. 469-95.
_____. K případu Karla Sabiny, Rozpravy, vol. 69, no. 8 (Prague, 1959).
_____. "The Situation of the Working Class in the Czech Lands in the Phase of the Expansion and Completion of the Industrial Revolution (1849-1873)," Historica, vol. 6 (1963), pp. 145-238.
_____. "Tábory v českých zemích v letech 1868-1871," ČsČH, vol. 6 (1958), no. 2, pp. 234-66; no. 3, pp. 446-70; and no. 4, pp. 661-90.
_____. "The Working Class Movement in the Czech Lands in the Expansive Phase of Industrial Revolution," Historica, vol. 10 (1965), pp. 67-158.
Rádl, Emanuel. Válka Čechů s Němci. Prague, 1928.
Rapant, Daniel. Slovenské povstanie roku 1848-49. 5 vols. Bratislava, 1937-72.
Rechcigl, Miroslav, Jr. (ed.) The Czechoslovak Contribution to World Culture. The Hague, 1964.
Redlich, Joseph. Kaiser Franz Joseph von Österreich. Berlin, 1929.
_____. Das oesterreichische Staats- und Reichsproblem; geschichtliche Darstellung der inneren Politik der habsburgischen Monarchie von 1848 bis zum Untergang des Reiches. 2 vols. Leipzig, 1920, 1926.
Říha, Oldřich and Julius Mésáros (eds.) Přehled československých dějin. Vol. 2: 1848-1918. Prague, 1960.
Rosenberg, Hans. "Political and Social Consequences of the Great Depression of 1873-1896 in Central Europe," Economic History Review, vol. 13, no. 1 (1943), pp. 58-73.
Roubík, Frantisek. Bibliografie časopisectva v Čechách z let 1863-1895. Prague, 1936.
Rudnytsky, Ivan L. "The Ukrainians in Galicia under Austrian Rule," AHY, vol. 3, pt. 2 (1967), pp. 394-429.

Šafránek, Jan. Školy české: Obraz jejich vývoje a osudů. 2 vols. Prague, 1913, 1919.

Šantrůček, Bohuslav (ed.) Buřiči a tvůrci: Vzpomínky, úvahy, kus historie, životopisy, 1897-1947. Prague, 1947.

_____. Václav Klofáč (1868-1928): Pohledy do života a díla. Prague, 1928.

Schorske, Carl. "Politics in a New Key: An Austrian Triptych," Journal of Modern History, vol. 39, no. 4 (December 1967).

_____. "The Transformation of the Garden: Ideal and Society in Austrian Literature," American Historical Review, vol. 72, no. 4 (July 1967), pp. 1283-1320.

Šesták, Miroslav. Revoluční spolupráce Evžena Kvaternika s J. F. Fričem v letech 1863-1864, Rozpravy, vol. 75, no. 1 (Prague, 1965).

Seton-Watson, Robert W. A History of the Czechs and Slovaks. London, 1943.

_____. Corruption and Reform in Hungary. London, 1911.

_____. Racial Problems in Hungary. London, 1908.

_____. The Southern Slav Question and the Habsburg Monarchy. London, 1911.

Skácelík, František (ed.) Sedmdesát let Umělecké besedy, 1863-1933. Prague, 1933.

Skilling, H. Gordon. "The Partition of the University in Prague," SEER, vol. 27, no. 69 (1949), pp. 430-49.

_____. "The Politics of the Czech Eighties," The Czech Renascence of the Nineteenth Century, ed. P. Brock and H. G. Skilling (Toronto, 1970), pp. 254-81.

Šmejkal, Edvard. Tyrš v politickém zápase českého národa. Brno, 1932.

Šmerda, Milan. "Východní Evropa v evropských dějinách (úvahy a náměty)," Slovanské historické studie, vol. 7 (1968), pp. 69-92.

Šolle, Zdeněk. "Bebelovy dopisy o počátcích 'Práva lidu'," ČsČH, vol. 15, no. 3 (1967), pp. 439-48.

_____. Dělnické hnutí v českých zemích koncem minulého století (1887-1897). 2d ed. Prague, 1954.

_____. Dělnické stávky v Čechách v druhé polovině XIX. století. Prague, 1960.

_____. "Die ersten Anhänger der Internationalen Arbeiter-Assoziation in Böhmen," Historica, vol. 7 (1963), pp. 145-84.

_____. "Die I. Internationale und Österreich," Historica, vol. 10 (1965), pp. 255-300.

_____. Internacionála a Rakousko. Prague, 1966.

_____. "Kontinuität und Wandel in der sozialen Entwicklung der böhmischen Länder, 1872 bis 1930," Aktuelle Forschungsprobleme um die Erste Tschechoslowakische Republik, ed. Karl Bösl (Munich, 1969), pp. 23-47.

_____. "K počátkům dělnického hnutí v Praze," ČsČH, vol. 5, no. 4 (1957), pp. 664-87; vol. 6, no. 2 (1958), pp. 266-310; vol. 7, no. 1 (1959), pp. 49-70.

_____. "Masarykova idea československého státu," Dějiny a součastnost, vol. 10, no. 6 (1968), pp. 14-21.

_____. Průkopníci: J. B. Pecka, L. Zápotocký, J. Hybeš. Prague, 1974.

_____. "První internacionala a vznik sociálně demokratické strany na neudörfelském sjezdu 1874," ČsČH, vol. 7, no. 5 (1964), pp. 668-86.

_____. "Die Sozialdemokratie in der Habsburger Monarchie und die tschechische Frage," Archiv für Sozialgeschichte, vol. 6/7 (1966/67), pp. 315-90.

_____. "Vliv masarykismu na české dělnické hnutí koncem minulého století," Nová mysl, no. 3 (1954), pp. 286-301.

Součkova, Milada. The Parnassian Jaroslav Vrchlický. The Hague, 1964.

Stampfer, Friedrich. "Für das böhmische Staatsrecht," Die Neue Zeit, vol.
     17, no. 1 (1899), pp. 275-78.

Šťastný, Vladislav. "Polemika v Času roku 1891 o polsko-ruské otázce,"
     Slovanské historické studie, vol. 5 (1963), pp. 85-125.

_____(ed.) Slovanství v národním životě Čechů a Slováků. Prague, 1968.

Steed, Henry Wickham. The Hapsburg Monarchy. 3d ed. London, 1914.

Steiner, Josef. Utrpení sociální demokracie československé a postup strany
     v Rakousku. Prague, 1902.

Stern, Fritz. "The Political Consequences of the Unpolitical German,"
     History: A Meridian Periodical, vol. 3 (September 1960), pp. 109-34.

Stompfe, Alois. Devadesát let Besedy Měšťanské v Praze. Prague, 1936.

Stránský, Josef B. (ed.) Z vývoje české technické tvorby: Sborník vydaný
     k 75. výročí založení Spolku českých inženýrů v Praze. Prague, 1940.

Strejček, Ferdinand. Lumírovci a jejich boje kolem roku 1880. Prague, 1915.

_____. O Svatopluku Čechovi. Prague, 1908.

Sturm, Rudolf. Czechoslovakia: A Bibliographic Guide. Washington, D.C.,
     1967.

Šujan, František. Dějepis Brna. 2d ed. Brno, 1928.

Sutter, Berthold. Die Badenischen Sprachenverordnungen von 1897. 2 vols.
     Graz, 1960, 1966.

Svoboda, Jan Fr. Jihočeské menšiny: Vývoj kulturní, národnostní a školský.
     České Budějovice, 1925.

Taborský, František (ed.) Paní Renáta Tyršová: Památník na počest jejich
     sedmdesátých narozenin. Prague, 1926.

Tapié, Victor, Monarchie et peuples du Danube. Paris, 1969.

Taylor, A. J. P. The Habsburg Monarchy, 1809-1918. London, 1948.

Thomson, S. Harrison, "A Century of a Phantom: Panslavism and the Western
     Slavs," JCEA, vol. 11, no. 1 (April 1951), pp. 57-77.

_____. Czechoslovakia in European History. 2d ed. Princeton, 1953.

_____. "The Czechs as Integrating and Disintegrating Factors in the
     Habsburg Empire," AHY, vol. 3, pt. 2 (1967), pp. 203-22.

_____. T. G. Masaryk and Czech Historiography," JCEA, vol. 10, no. 1
     (April 1950), pp. 37-52.

_____. "Thomas Garrigue Masaryk--Philosopher in Action," University of
     Toronto Quarterly, vol. 18, no. 4 (1949), pp. 328-39.

Tieftrunk, Karel. Dějiny matice české. Prague, 1881.

Tomsa, Bohuš. Masarykův zápas a právo přirozené. Bratislava, 1928.

Traub, H. Naše politické dějiny v 19. století. Prague, 1926.

Urban, Otto. "Die Gesellschaftlich Stellung und Funktion der tschechischen
     Arbeiterschaft und Intelligenz vor dem ersten Weltkrieg," Acta Univer-
     sitatis Carolinae--Philosophica et Historica, vol. 4 (1969), pp. 53-76.

_____."Karl Kautsky a utváření Marxismu jako politické ideologie masové
     socialistické strany na sklonku 19. století," ČsČH, vol. 17, no. 1
     (1969), pp. 1-18.

_____. "Masarykovo pojetí české otázky," ČsČH, vol. 17, no. 4 (1969),
     pp. 527-52.

Urfus, Valentin. "České úsilí o změnu volebního řádu pro zemský sněm v
     šedesátých a počátkem sedmdesátých let minulého století," Sborník his-
     torický, vol. 19 (1972), pp. 49-91.

_____. "Český státoprávní program a české dělnické hnutí v období vzniku
     první dělnické strany v Čechách," Právněhistorické studie, vol. 9 (1963),
     pp. 97-112.

_____. "Český státoprávní program na rozhraní let 1860-1861 a jeho
     ideové složky," Právněhistorické studie, vol. 8 (1962), pp. 127-72.

Vaníček, Václav. "K počátkům realismu," Masarykův sborník, vol. 2 (1926/27), pp. 289-300; vol. 3 (1928-/29), pp. 50-72, 122-45, 210-21, and 303-29.

Vávra, Zdeněk. Tendence v dlouhodobém vývoji reprodukce obyvatelstva českých zemí z léta 1870-1944, Rozpravy, vol. 72, no. 9 (Prague, 1962).

Vlček, Karel. Tábory lidu ve Slezsku. Hrabyně, 1938.

Vozka, Jaroslav. Josef Steiner: Typ dělnického vůdce. Prague, 1932.

Vyhlídal, Jan. Naše Slezsko. Prague, 1900.

Wandycz, Piotr S. The Lands of Partitioned Poland, 1795-1918. Seattle, 1974.

_____. "The Poles in the Habsburg Monarchy," AHY, vol. 3, pt. 2 (1967), pp. 261-86.

Wank, Solomon. "Foreign Policy and the Nationality Problem in Austria-Hungary, 1867-1914," AHY, vol. 3, pt. 3 (1967), pp. 37-56.

_____. "Zwei Dokumente Aehrenthals aus den Jahren 1898-99 zur Lösung der inneren Krise in Österreich-Ungarn," Mitteilungen des Österreichischen Staatsarchivs, vol. 19 (1966), pp. 339-62.

Wellek, René. Essays on Czech Literature. The Hague, 1963.

Wenzl, František. Dějiny založen a družstevního podnikání na Moravě do roku 1885. Prague, 1937.

Whiteside, Andrew G. Austrian National Socialism before 1918. The Hague, 1962.

_____. "The Germans as an Integrative Force in Imperial Austria: the Dilemma of Dominance," AHY, vol. 3, pt. 1 (1967), pp. 157-200.

Winter, Eduard. Frühliberalismus in der Donaumonarchie. Religiouse, nationale, und wissenschaftliche Strömungen von 1790-1868. Berlin, 1968.

Winters, Stanley B. "Karel Kramář's Early Political Career." Ph.D. dissertation, Rutgers University, 1965.

_____. "The Young Czech Party (1874-1914): An Appraisal," SR, vol. 28, no. 3 (September 1969), pp. 426-44.

Wiskemann, Elizabeth. Czechs and Germans: A Study of the Struggle in the Historic Provinces of Bohemia and Moravia. 2d ed. London, 1967.

Wright, William E. Serf, Seigneur, and Sovereign: Agrarian Reform in Eighteenth-Century Bohemia. Minneapolis, 1966.

Wurmová, Milada. Soupis moravských novin a časopisů z let 1848--1918. Brno, 1955.

Zacek, Joseph F. "Nationalism in Czechoslovakia," Nationalism in Eastern Europe, ed. Peter F. Sugar and Ivo J. Lederer (Seattle, 1969), pp. 166-206.

_____. "Palacký and his History of the Czech Nation," JCEA, vol. 23, no. 4 (January 1964), pp. 412-23.

_____. Palacký: The Historian as Scholar and Nationalist. The Hague, 1970.

Žáček, Václav. "Češi a Poláci v době lednového povstání polského r. 1863," ČsČH, vol. 9, no. 6 (1963), pp. 717-41.

_____. (ed.) Češi a Poláci v minulosti. Vol. 2: období kapitalismu a imperialismu. Prague, 1967.

_____, Miroslav Tejchman, et al. Češi a jihoslované v minulosti: Od nejstarších dob do roku 1918. Prague, 1975.

_____. "K dějinám austro-slavismu rakouských Slovanů," Slovanské historické studie, vol. 7 (1968), pp. 129-80.

_____. Ohlas polského povstání r. 1863 v Čechách. Prague, 1935.

Zöllner, Erich. Geschichte Österreichs von den Anfängen bis zur Gegenwart. 3d ed. Munich, 1966.

Zwitter, Fran. "The Slovenes and the Habsburg Monarchy," AHY, vol. 3, pt. 2 (1967), pp. 159-88.

JN
2210
.G37   27,963

CAMROSE LUTHERAN COLLEGE
LIBRARY

27,963

JN   Garver, Bruce M.
2210
.G37   The Young Czech
          party, 1874-1901,
          and the emergence
          of a multi-party
          system

DATE			
FEB 11 81			

CAMROSE LUTHERAN COLLEGE
LIBRARY

Ⓢ THE BAKER & TAYLOR CO